The Android™ Tablet Developer's Cookbook

The Android™ Tablet Developer's Cookbook

B.M. Harwani

✦ Addison-Wesley

Upper Saddle River, NJ • Boston • Indianapolis • San Francisco
New York • Toronto • Montreal • London • Munich • Paris • Madrid
Cape Town • Sydney • Tokyo • Singapore • Mexico City

The publisher offers excellent discounts on this book when ordered in quantity for bulk purchases or special sales, which may include electronic versions and/or custom covers and content particular to your business, training goals, marketing focus, and branding interests. For more information, please contact:

U.S. Corporate and Government Sales
(800) 382-3419
corpsales@pearsontechgroup.com

For sales outside the United States, please contact:

International Sales
international@pearsoned.com

Visit us on the Web: informit.com/aw

Library of Congress Cataloging-in-Publication Data is on file.

Copyright © 2013 Pearson Education, Inc.

ISBN-13: 978-0-321-88530-2
ISBN-10: 0-321-88530-9

Text printed in the United States on recycled paper at RR Donnelley in Crawfordsville, Indiana.

First printing: May 2013

Editor-in-Chief
Mark L. Taub

Executive Editor
Laura Lewin

Development Editor
Songlin Qiu

Managing Editor
Kristy Hart

Project Editor
Betsy Gratner

Copy Editor
Gill Editorial Services

Indexer
Tim Wright

Proofreader
Debbie Williams

Technical Reviewers
James Becwar
Romin Irani
Prashant Thakkar

Editorial Assistant
Olivia Basegio

Cover Designer
Chuti Prasertsith

Senior Compositor
Gloria Schurick

❖

*Dedicated to my mother, Mrs. Nita Harwani,
and Dr. Martin Cooper.*

*Mom, you are a great teacher. When I look at you, I feel the
heights of love, patience, sacrifice, hard work, and emotions.*

*Dr. Martin Cooper, the inventor of the modern cell phone, has
revolutionized communication technology. His amazing and
dedicated research led to the development of cell phones that
interconnect the world even while moving. Today we can't
think of life without cell phones. Can we?*

❖

Contents at a Glance

Acknowledgments

I am grateful to Laura Lewin, executive editor, for believing in me and giving me an opportunity to create this work.

My gratitude to Songlin Qiu who, as a development editor, offered significant feedback that shaped these chapters. She played a vital role in improving the structure and the quality of information.

I must thank James Becwar, Romin Irani, and Prashant Thakkar (Pandhi), the technical reviewers, for their excellent, detailed review of the work and the many helpful comments and suggestions they made.

Special thanks to Karen Gill, the copy editor, for first-class structural and language editing. I appreciate her efforts in enhancing the contents of the book and making it sound polished.

Big and ongoing thanks to Olivia Basegio, editorial assistant, for doing a great job, and sincere thanks to the whole team for getting the book published on time.

A great big thank-you to the editorial and production staff and the entire team at Pearson Technology Group who worked tirelessly to produce this book. I really enjoyed working with each of you.

I am also thankful to my family, who is my small world: Anushka, my wife, and my wonderful children, Chirag and Naman, for inspiring and motivating me and above all for forgiving me for spending so much time on my computer.

I must mention my dear students who have been a good teacher for me. Their interesting problems and queries have helped me understand reader expectations and inspired me to write books with a practical approach.

About the Author

B.M. Harwani is founder and owner of Microchip Computer Education (MCE), based in Ajmer, India, which provides computer education in all programming and Web developing platforms. He graduated with a BE in computer engineering from the University of Pune, and has a C Level (Master's Diploma in Computer Technology) from DOEACC, Government of India. Being involved in the teaching field for more than 19 years, he has developed the art of explaining even the most complicated topics in a straightforward and easily understandable fashion. He wrote *Android Programming Unleashed* (Sams Publishing), among other books, and has taught programming courses for 17 years. To know more, visit Harwani's blog at http://bmharwani.com/blog.

Introduction

Android is Google's open source and free Java-based platform for mobile development. Tablets are getting more popular every day. They are gadgets that fall between smartphones and personal computers. They have faster processors than smartphones but much less processing power than computers. They are handy and lightweight. From a tablet, you can watch videos, listen to music, surf the Web, make calls over Wi-Fi networks, read electronic documents, play games, and launch apps.

An Android tablet is a touch-screen, mobile device that runs the Android operating system. Google fueled the development of Android tablets with the release of Android 3.0 SDK. Actually, Android 3.0 SDK was designed with tablets in mind (that is, larger screen devices). The launch of Android 3.0 SDK compelled manufacturers around the world to produce Android tablets. As the market becomes flooded with Android tablets, developers are attracted to developing apps for the growing Android tablet market. Looking at the huge demand of developing applications for Android tablet inspired me to write this book.

Who Should Read This Book

Like any good book, this book provides easy-to-reuse code designed to solve real-world problems for intermediate to advanced users. The book covers the range from basic to complex problems that developers usually come across. The book will be beneficial for developers and instructors who want to learn or teach Android tablet programming. In short, it is a useful reference for anyone who wants to understand all key aspects of Android tablet programming and wants to find quick answers to different critical problems that appear while developing Android applications.

Key Topics That This Book Covers

This book is comprehensive and covers each topic in deep detail. Key topics covered include the following:

- Activities and Android activity life cycle
- Starting activity using intent and passing data from one activity to another
- Displaying and using `ListFragment`, `DialogFragment`, and `PreferenceFragment`
- Creating tabbed and drop-down list ActionBar
- Creating custom content providers
- Using frame-by-frame and tweening animation
- Using accelerometer, proximity, and gyroscope sensors
- Using JSON for managing data exchange formats
- Enabling and disabling Wi-Fi and using Wi-Fi Direct
- Using `RemoteViews` and creating and updating home screen widgets
- Creating and rendering graphics using OpenGL
- Cutting, copying, and pasting text using the system clipboard
- Reading and writing into NFC tags
- Transferring data using Android Beam
- Applying smooth coloring, rotating, scaling, and translating graphics
- Capturing image, audio, and video using built-in intent as well as Java code
- Using EasyTracker Library and GoogleAnalytics Singleton for tracking Android applications

The book is completely up to date with the latest Jelly Bean 4.2.

Key Benefits That This Book Provides

By the time you finish this book, you will be well versed with the following concepts:

- Adding and removing fragments with device orientation
- Implementing communication between fragments
- Displaying action items, action views, and the submenu in the ActionBar
- Creating a stack of images using `StackView`
- Displaying a list of options using `ListPopupWindow` and `PopupMenu`
- Dragging and dropping text and images
- Creating and using notifications
- Creating and using pending intent to start an activity
- Using loaders for accessing information

- Using `ValueAnimator` and `ObjectAnimator` to animate views
- Implementing multiple animations using `AnimatorSet`
- Applying layout animation
- Applying hardware acceleration for improving graphic system performance
- Using view layers and `SurfaceView` to improve graphics application performance
- Applying transformations using `TextureView`
- Transferring files through Bluetooth
- Using threads and multiple threads
- Using `WebView`, `WebViewClient` class, and `WebViewFragment` for displaying Web pages
- Supporting different platform versions
- Supporting older Android versions
- Adapting to screen orientations
- How Android tablet apps are different from Phone apps
- Porting apps between small-screen phones and tablets

How This Book Is Organized

This book is structured in six parts:

- **Part I: User Interface Techniques**

  In Chapter 1, "Overview of Android Tablet Applications," you will learn about the sizes
  and features of various Android tablets. You will also learn to create Android virtual
  devices and discover the directory structure of Android projects. In addition, you will
  learn about activities and different phases in the Android activity life cycle. You will
  learn how an activity is started using intent and how data is passed from one activity to
  another.

  Chapter 2, "Fragments," focuses on understanding the concept of fragments. You will
  learn the life cycle of a fragment and the procedure to create foreground fragments. You
  will also come to know the difference between foreground and background fragments
  and discover how to add and remove fragments with device orientation. You will learn
  how `FragmentManager` and `FragmentTransaction` handle fragments. In addition, you
  will learn to create fragments dynamically at runtime and implement communication
  between fragments. Finally, you will study the procedure to display options through
  `ListFragment`, display dialogs through `DialogFragment`, and set user preferences using
  `PreferenceFragment`.

  Chapter 3, "ActionBars in Action," focuses on understanding the usage of ActionBars in
  Android applications. You will learn the difference between the menu and the ActionBar.
  You will discover how to toggle the ActionBar's visibility, understand its different

components, and walk through the procedure to display action items in the ActionBar. You will learn to display action views and submenus in an ActionBar. Finally, you will learn to create a tabbed and a drop-down list in an ActionBar.

Chapter 4, "New Widgets," focuses on the working of new widgets. You will learn to display the Calendar in the Android application, display and select numbers through `NumberPicker`, and create a stack of images using `StackView`. You will also learn to display a list of options using `ListPopupWindow` and `PopupMenu`.

- **Part II: Managing Content**

In Chapter 5, "System Clipboard and Drag and Drop," you will learn how to drag and drop text and images. Also, you will learn to cut, copy, and paste text using the system clipboard.

In Chapter 6, "Notifications and Pending Intents," you will learn about pending intents and how intents are broadcasted. You will also come to understand the Android notification system. You will learn to create notifications, use `Notification.Builder`, and obtain a `NotificationManager`. Finally, you will create notifications and use pending intent to start an activity.

Chapter 7, "Loaders," focuses on understanding the concept of loaders. You will also learn about content providers and how to use `CursorLoader` to access information from a contact's content provider. Finally, you will learn to create your own custom content providers.

- **Part III: Multimedia Techniques**

In Chapter 8, "Animation," you will learn about different types of animations. You will learn to use `ValueAnimator` and `ObjectAnimator` in animating views. You will learn to implement multiple animations using `AnimatorSet`. Also, you will study frame-by-frame animation and tweening animation. You will learn to apply layout animation and the procedure to collect and sequence animations using `AnimationSet`.

In Chapter 9, "Hardware Accelerated 2D," you will learn to use hardware acceleration. You will learn to use view layers and improve performance of graphics-based applications using `SurfaceView`. Finally, you will learn to apply transformations using `TextureView`.

Chapter 10, "Creating and Rendering Graphics," explains different APIs that are required for displaying graphics. You will learn to create and render a rectangle using OpenGL. Also, you will come to understand the difference between coloring a vertex and lighting. In addition to this, you will learn to apply smooth coloring and rotate, scale, and translate graphics.

Chapter 11, "Recording Audio, Video, and Images," explains the technique of capturing an image using built-in intent and Java code. You will learn to record audio and video using built-in intent and through Java code, understand `CamcorderProfile`, `MediaRecorder`, and their methods.

- **Part IV: Networking and Hardware Interface**

  Chapter 12, "Wireless Connectivity," focuses on how connections between devices are established wirelessly. You will learn to pair two Bluetooth-enabled devices, manually transfer files from one device to another using Bluetooth and the procedure, and pair a Bluetooth device with a Windows PC. You will also learn to enable a local Bluetooth device, display the list of paired devices, and transfer files through Bluetooth. Finally, you will learn the concept of Wi-Fi, discover how to enable and disable Wi-Fi, and understand the usage of Wi-Fi Direct.

  In Chapter 13, "Cores and Threads," you will learn the utility of multicore processor architectures. You will understand the utility of Garbage Collection (GC). You will also learn about threads and multiple threads. Finally, you will learn about the `AsyncTask` class.

  In Chapter 14, "Keyboards and Sensors," you will learn how to change Android keyboards and input methods. You will learn about sensors and display the list of sensors supported by a device. Finally, you will learn to use Accelerometer, Proximity, and Gyroscope sensors.

- **Part V: Exploring the Web**

  In Chapter 15, "JSON," you will learn the concept of JSON. You will learn to use `JSONObject`, nest `JSONObjects`, and use `JSONArray` to keep information. Also, you will learn to use JsonReader and JsonWriter.

  In Chapter 16, "WebViews," you will learn to display Web pages using `WebView`. Also, you will learn to use the `WebViewClient` class and the `WebViewFragment`.

- **Part VI: Advanced Android Techniques**

  In Chapter 17, "Adding Support for the Small Screen," you will learn about factors for supporting various screens and densities. You will learn how different platform versions are supported in Android applications and how Android Support Library is used to support older Android versions. You will learn to adapt to screen orientation by anchoring controls. Also, you will learn to define alternate layouts to handle screen orientation.

  In Chapter 18, "Home Screen Widgets," you will learn about `RemoteViews`, app widgets, and home screen widgets. You will come to understand the app widget life cycle methods. In addition, you will learn to create a home screen widget and update it through a Button control. Finally, you will learn to update a home screen widget using `AlarmManager`.

  In Chapter 19, "Android Beam," you will learn about Near Field Communication (NFC) and the role of NFC tags. Also, you will learn about the structures used in exchanging information with NFC Tags, read and write into NFC tags. Finally, you will come to understand Android beam and how data is transferred using it.

  In Chapter 20, "Application Analytics and Tracking," you will learn the concept of application analytics and tracking. You will learn to use EasyTracker Library and GoogleAnalytics Singleton to track Android applications.

Code Examples for This Book

All the Android recipes discussed in this book are available to download from the publisher's Web site at www.informit.com/title/9780321885302. Download the code bundle provided at the site and unzip it. Follow these steps to use the provided code:

1. Launch Eclipse.

2. Select File, Import. From the Import dialog that opens, select Existing Projects into Workspace and then click Next.

3. In the following dialog, click the Browse button to locate and select the folder where you unzipped the code bundle.

4. After you select the code bundle, all the Android projects enclosed in it will appear in the Projects box. By default, all the projects will be found checked. You can uncheck project(s) that you don't want to import and then click Finish. That's it. The projects will be imported into Eclipse and are ready to run.

Assumptions

The following three things are assumed in all the recipes developed in this book:

- Until specified, the `android:minSdkVersion` and `android:targetSdkVersion` attributes of all the apps in this book are assumed to be 11 and 17, respectively. API Level 11 and 17 refer to the Android 3.0 (Honeycomb) and Android 4.2 (Jelly Bean) respectively. It also means that the applications developed in this book require a minimum of API Level 11 to run. Also, the applications are compiled and designed to run on API Level 17.

- An XML file, `dimens.xml`, is assumed to be created in the `res/values` folder with the code as shown here:

```xml
<?xml version="1.0" encoding="utf-8"?>
<resources>
    <dimen name="text_size">14sp</dimen>
</resources>
```

- Two folders, `values-sw600dp` and `values-sw720dp`, are assumed to be created in the `res` folder. Also, the `dimens.xml` file from the `res/values` folder is assumed to be copied into these two folders. To match the 7-inch and 10-inch tablet screens, the dimension resource `text_size` in the `dimens.xml` file in the `values-sw600dp` and `values-sw720dp` folders is assumed to be modified to `24sp` and `32sp`, respectively. For more information, refer to the recipe "Converting an Android Phone Application into an Android Tablet Application" in Chapter 1.

1

Overview of Android Tablet Applications

The Android 3.0 SDK was designed and released with tablets in mind. This SDK introduced several new features to support widescreen devices, including a new user interface optimized for tablets, multicore processor support, enhanced multitasking, and enhanced web browser features.

This chapter covers the features of Android tablets, differences between Android phones and tablets, and the procedure to make phone applications compatible with Android tablets. You will come to understand the directory structure of an Android project. In addition, you will perform activities and learn about the Android activity life cycle. Finally, you will learn how to start an activity using intent and how to pass data from one activity to another.

Recipe: Introducing Android Tablets

Tablet sizes typically start at 7 inches and go up to 12, measured diagonally. There are so many tablets available on the market, including Google Nexus 7, Google Nexus 10, Samsung Galaxy Note 10.1, Toshiba AT300, Amazon Kindle Fire HD, Asus Transformer Pad 300, and Samsung Galaxy Tab 8.9. Here the discussion will focus on tablets made by Google: Google Nexus 7 and Google Nexus 10.

Google Nexus 7 is a tablet launched by Google (see Figure 1.1 [left]). Google made it in collaboration with Asus, a budget computer producer. It is a 7-inch tablet that has a phone-like user interface. The tablet uses a new layout designed for 7-inch tablets. Here are a few of its features:

- Its dimensions are 198.5 × 120 × 10.5mm.
- It has a high resolution of 800 × 1280 pixels.
- Its display type is multitouch, and it is protected by Corning Glass.
- It operates on Android 4.1 Jelly Bean, which is efficient and reliable.

- Its price ranges from $200 to $250 depending on the chosen model, making it an affordable device.

- The screen density is tvdpi, so it provides the expected user interface (UI) size at a proper distance. Also, the bitmaps can be scaled easily without noticing. The tvdpi represents a pixel density that is built for TVs and enables Android apps to be viewed on a TV without blurriness. Apps look better on screens with tvdpi density than those found on other 7-inch tablets that have mdpi density.

- It has a powerful quad-core Tegra processor that delivers great gaming visuals.

- It supports 2G and 3G networks and provides Wi-Fi 802.11 b/g/n, Bluetooth, and NFC connectivity.

- It is available in 8GB and 16GB storage capacities.

The Google Nexus 10 is made by Google in collaboration with Samsung (see Figure 1.1 [right]). This tablet, as its name suggests, has a 10-inch display. Here are a few of its features:

- It has a dual-core chip that makes it a high-performance tablet.

- It has a high resolution and an aspect ratio of 16:9.

- It has the latest 4.2 version of the operating system (OS) on board.

- It supports Wi-Fi and comes in 16GB and 32GB models.

- It costs $399 for the 16GB model and $499 for the 32GB one.

To learn more about Google Nexus, visit www.google.com/nexus/#/features.

Figure 1.1   Google Nexus 7 (left) and Google Nexus 10 (right)

Recipe: Knowing Differences Between Android Phones and Android Tablets

The first difference between Android phones and Android tablets is in screen size. Most of the phone screens measure between 3 and 5 inches, whereas most tablet screens measure between 7 and 12 inches.

The second difference is in the pixel resolution of the screen. *Pixel resolution* is the total number of pixels a screen displays. Here are the pixel resolutions of phones and tablets:

- Phones usually have a resolution of 800 × 480.
- 7-inch tablets usually have a resolution of 1,024 × 600.
- 10.1-inch tablets usually have a resolution of 1,280 × 800.

Density, or the number of pixels in a fixed area of the display, is a third difference between tablets and phones. Size remains the same when pixel and density are increased together. As an example, screen1 has a size of 100 × 100px. It is considered equal to the screen2 size of 150 × 150px if the density of screen2 is 1.5 times that of screen1. Also, a graphic displayed on a device will appear half its size on a device of double density.

The devices can be of low, medium, high, or extra high densities. A medium-density (mdpi) device has 160 pixels per inch. Similarly, a high-density (hdpi) and extra-high-density (xhdpi) device has 240 pixels per inch and 320 pixels per inch, respectively. To standardize the screen size, Android treats mdpi as the base density. That is, for mdpi devices, 1 dp = 1 pixel, where dp stands for device-independent pixel. The density of all other devices is converted to mdpi for uniformity. The following examples will make it clearer:

- The screen size of an Android phone (mdpi) of 320 × 480px is 320dp × 480dp (because for mdpi devices, 1 pixel is equal to 1 dp).
- The screen size of an Android phone (hdpi) of 480 × 800px is (480 × 160 / 240) × (800 × 160 / 240), or 320dp × 533dp.
- The screen size of an Android tablet (xdpi) of 1600 × 2560px is (1600 × 160 / 320) × (2560 × 160 / 320), or 800dp × 1280dp.

The formula for converting actual physical pixels (px) into a device-independent (dp) unit is given here:

dp = px × (density / 160)

Android categorizes the screens in small, normal, large, and extra large sizes. The sizes of these screens follow:

- Extra large screens are at least 960dp × 720dp.
- Large screens are at least 640dp × 480dp.
- Normal screens are at least 470dp × 320dp.
- Small screens are at least 426dp × 320dp.

The screen sizes of a phone, a 7-inch tablet, and a 10-inch tablet are considered normal, large, and extra large screens, respectively. When developing applications, the width of the screen is considered while placing the UI controls. Usual screen widths of phones and tablets are given here:

- The screen width of a phone is 320dp.
- The screen width of a 7-inch tablet is 600dp.
- The screen width of a 10-inch tablet is 720dp.

Recipe: Making an Application Compatible for the Android Phone and the Android Tablet

Android makes it easy to develop an application that runs well on a range of devices of different screen sizes. It enables development of a single application that can be distributed widely to all the desired targeted devices. All that is required is to optimize the layouts and other UI components for each targeted screen configuration. While developing applications to be run on Android phones as well as on Android tablets, take care of the following things:

- The UI controls should not look stretched unnecessarily to fill up the blank space. Pad the controls to reduce their width.
- Use multipane layouts to make best use of the wider screen. Use fragments wherever necessary.
- Define separate layouts for normal, large, and extra large screens.
- Modify the font size and other dimensions of the UI controls as per the layouts.
- The graphics, icons, and other bitmaps used in the application must match the densities of the phone and tablet screens.
- Use `wrap_content`, `match_parent`, or `dp` units when specifying dimensions in XML layout files. Do not specify fixed sizes for the UI controls.
- Declare a `<supports-screens>` element with appropriate attributes in the `AndroidManifest.xml` file, as needed.

Recipe: Creating Android Virtual Devices

An Android Virtual Device (AVD) represents a device configuration. Different Android devices have different configurations. To test whether the Android application is compatible with a set of Android devices, you create AVDs that represent their configuration and test your application on them. You will create three AVDs: for an Android phone, for a 7-inch tablet, and for a 10-inch tablet. To create an AVD for the phone and tablets in Eclipse, select the Window, AVD Manager option. An Android Virtual Device Manager dialog opens, as shown in Figure 1.2. The dialog box displays a list of existing AVDs, letting you create new AVDs and manage existing AVDs. Assuming no AVD is yet defined, an empty list is displayed.

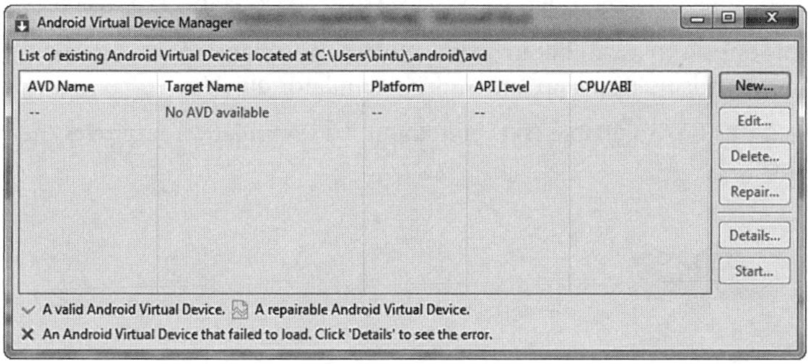

Figure 1.2   The AVD Manager window

Select the New button to define a new AVD. A Create New Android Virtual Device (AVD) dialog box appears (see Figure 1.3). The fields are listed here:

- **AVD Name**—Specifies the name of the AVD. Enter the name as PhoneAVD. You will first create an AVD for an Android phone, followed by one for an Android tablet.

- **Device**—Specifies the device for which the application has to be tested. Select the device as Nexus S (4.0", 480 × 800:hdpi).

- **Target**—Specifies the target API level. Your application will be tested against the specified API level. Set the target to the latest API: Android 4.2.2 - API Level 17.

- **CPU/ABI**—Determines the processor that you want to emulate on your device. Select the ARM (armeabi-v7a) option.

- **Keyboard**—To use the physical keyboard on the computer along with the one displayed on the emulator screen, check the Hardware Keyboard Present check box.

- **Skin**—On checking the Display a Skin with Hardware Controls check box, the emulator will be displayed, along with physical device buttons on the right side. The controls include Basic controls (speaker, on/off buttons), Home, Menu, Back, and Search buttons.

- **Front Camera/Back Camera**—If you have a webcam attached to your computer and want to use it in your application, select the Webcam0 option from the drop-down menu. Choose the Emulated option if you don't have a webcam. Leave the option on the default, None, if the application does not require a camera.

- **Memory Options**—Define the device RAM and VM Heap. Leave the values to their default values.

- **Internal Storage**—Defines the internal storage of the device. Again, leave it to its default value of 200MiB.

- **SD Card**—Extends the storage capacity of the device. Large data files such as audio and video, for which the built-in flash memory is insufficient, are stored on the SD card. Set the size of SD card to 128MiB. The larger the allocated SD card space, the longer it will take to create the AVD. Unless it is required, keep the SD card space as low as possible.

- **Snapshot**—Enable this option to avoid booting the emulator and start it from the last saved snapshot. This option is used to start the Android emulator quickly.

- **Use Host GPU**—Check this box to enable GPU emulation. GPU emulation improves the emulator's performance.

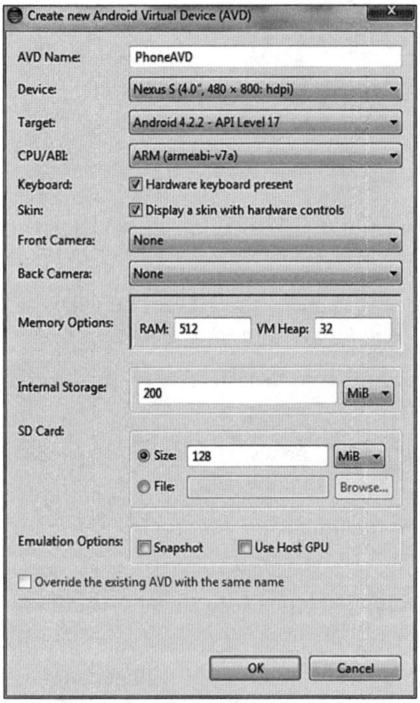

Figure 1.3   Specifications of new AVD, PhoneAVD

The new AVD, PhoneAVD, will be created. Similarly, create the AVDs for 7-inch and 10-inch tablets using the names Tablet7AVD and Tablet10AVD. While defining Tablet10AVD, select the option 10.1" WXGA (Tablet) (1280 × 800:mdpi) for specifying the target device (see Figure 1.4 [top]) because it matches the screen size of most of the 10-inch tablets. For Tablet7AVD, select the 7.0" WSVGA (Tablet) (1024 × 600:mdpi) option for the target device. All three AVDs will be displayed in the list of existing AVDs, as shown in Figure 1.4 (bottom). Select the Refresh button if the newly created AVDs don't appear in the list.

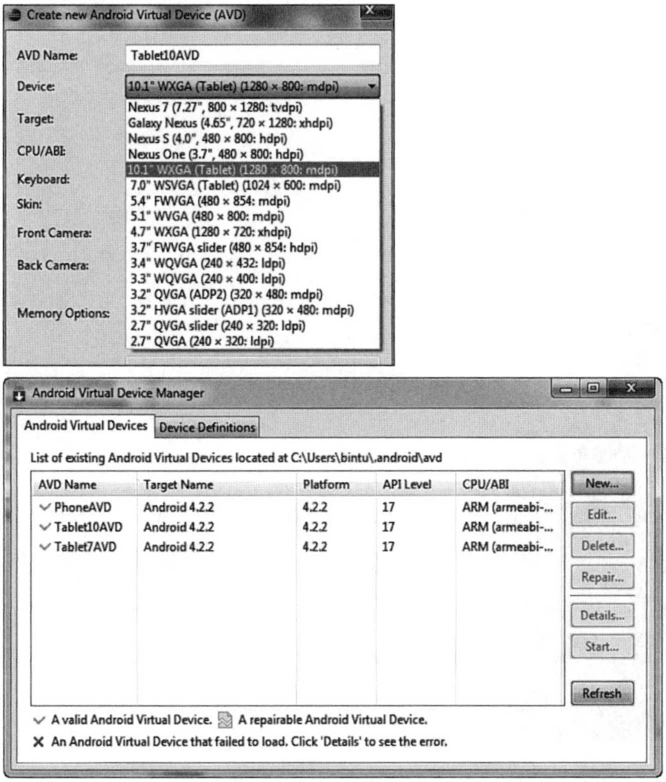

Figure 1.4   Options displayed in the Device drop-down list (top) and the newly created AVDs listed in the AVD Manager (bottom)

To launch your newly created AVDs, select them in the AVD Manager window and then select the Start button. The AVD emulator will be launched and will appear as shown in Figure 1.5. The Android phone emulator in portrait and landscape orientation will appear as shown in Figure 1.5 (top). You can compare the sizes of the 7-inch tablet emulator (see Figure 1.5 [middle]) and the 10-inch tablet emulator (see Figure 1.5 [bottom]).

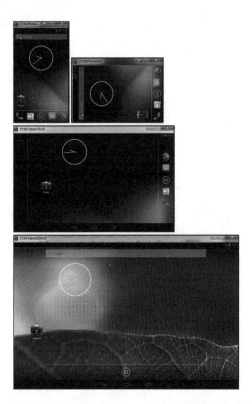

Figure 1.5   The phone emulator in portrait and landscape orientation (top), 7-inch tablet emulator (middle), and 10-inch tablet emulator (bottom)

Recipe: Understanding the Directory Structure of an Android Project

Now you'll create a new Android project to understand different files and directories that are automatically created for you by the Android Developer Tools (ADT) plug-in.

Launch Eclipse and choose File, New, Android Application Project, or click the Android Project Creator icon on the Eclipse toolbar. You will see a dialog box, as shown in Figure 1.6 (top). In the Application Name box, enter the name of the Android Tablet project as `FirstAndroidTabletApp`. The Project Name is automatically assigned, which is the same as the application name by default. Because it is a unique identifier, enter the package name as `com.androidtablet.firstandroidtabletapp`.

Select API 11: Android 3.0 (Honeycomb) from the Minimum Required SDK drop-down to indicate that the application will require at least API level 11 to run. Select Android 4.2 (API 17) as the Target SDK, because it is expected to be the version that your target audience will use. Also, select the Android 4.2 (API 17) option for Compile With to compile the application with this SDK. Select the desired theme for the application from the Theme drop-down. By default, the Holo Light with Dark Action Bar theme is selected for the new application.

Because this is a new project, select the Create Project in Workspace check box to create the project files at the Workspace location that was specified when you opened Eclipse for the first time. The Create Custom Launcher Icon check box is selected by default; it enables you to define the icon of your application. Similarly, the Create Activity check box is checked by default to create an activity file for your application automatically. Click the Next button to move to the next dialog box: Configure Launcher Icon. It is meant for configuring the icon for the application. Because you want to have a default icon for your application, keeping the default options selected in the dialog box, click Next to move further. The next dialog prompts you to select whether you want to create an activity. Also, it prompts for the type of activity. Because you want to create a blank activity, select the Create Activity check box and the Blank Activity option. Then click Next.

The next dialog (see Figure 1.6 [bottom]) asks you to enter information for the newly created activity. Name the activity `FirstAndroidTabletAppActivity`. The layout filename and title name automatically change to reflect the newly assigned activity name. The layout name will become `activity_first_android_tablet_app`, and the title of the application will be changed to `FirstAndroidTabletAppActivity`. You can always change the auto-assigned layout filename and application title. Because you don't want navigation (tab or drop-down) in this application, keep the default None for the Navigation Type option. Keeping the auto-assigned layout filename and the title unchanged, click the Finish button after supplying the required information.

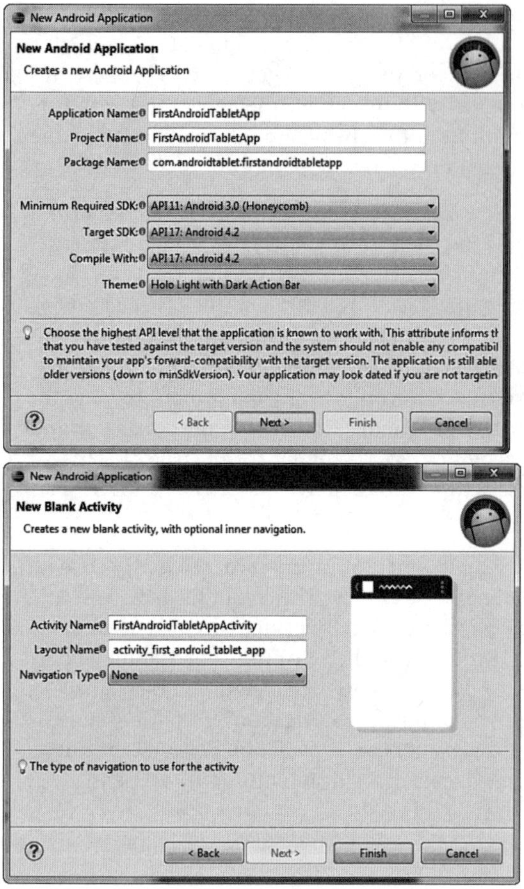

Figure 1.6   Dialog for entering information of new application (top) and dialog to enter information of the application's default activity (bottom)

ADT will create the application and all the necessary files. Figure 1.7 shows the directory structure of the files and directories that are automatically created for your new Android project.

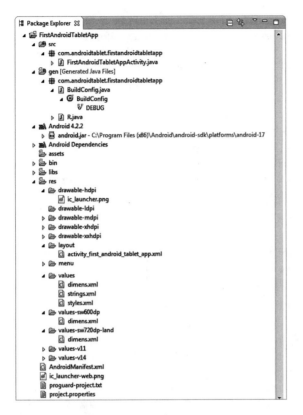

Figure 1.7   The directory structure of the `FirstAndroidTabletApp` project

An overview of the files and directories shown in Figure 1.7 is discussed here:

- **/src folder**—Contains the entire Java source file of the application. The folder contains a directory structure corresponding to the package name supplied in the application. The folder contains the project's default package: `com.androidtablet.firstandroid` `tabletapp`. On expanding the package, you'll find the activity of the application, the `FirstAndroidTabletAppActivity.java` file, within it.

- **/src/com.androidtablet.firstandroidtabletapp**—Refers to the package name of the application. To avoid collision among the class names, variable names, and so on with those of other Android applications, each application has to be packaged in a unique container.

- **/src/com.androidtablet.firstandroidtabletapp/ FirstAndroidTabletAppActivity.java**—The default activity file of the application. Each application has at least one activity that acts as the main entry point to the application. The activity file is automatically defined as the default launch activity in the Android Manifest file.

- **/gen folder**—Contains Java files generated by ADT after compiling the application. That is, the gen folder comes into existence after compiling the application for the first time. The folder contains an R.java file that contains references for all the resources that are defined in the /res directory. It also contains a BuildConfig.java file that runs code only in debug mode. Finally, it contains a DEBUG constant that helps in running debug-only functions.

- **/gen/com.androidtablet.firstandroidtabletapp/R.java**—All the layout and other resource information that is coded in the XML files is converted into Java source code and placed in the R.java file. Therefore, the file contains the ID of all the application resources. The R.java file is compiled into the Java byte code files and then converted into .dex format. You should never edit this file by hand, because it is automatically overwritten when you add or edit resources.

- **Android4.2.2/android.jar**—The Android SDK .jar file for the target platform.

- **/assets folder**—Empty by default. It stores raw asset files that may be required in the application. It may contain fonts, external .jar files, and so on to be used in the application. The assets folder is like a resource folder where uncompiled resources of the project are kept. No IDs are generated for the resources kept here.

- **/bin folder**—Stores the compiled version of the application.

- **/res folder**—All application resources (images, layout files, and string files) are kept here. Instead of hard-coding an image or string in an application, a better approach is to create a respective resource in the /res folder and include its reference in the application. This way, you can change the image or string or any other resource anytime without disturbing the code. Each resource is assigned a unique resource ID, which automatically appears in the R.java file and thus in the R class after compilation, enabling you to refer to the resource in the code. To categorize and arrange the resources, four subdirectories are created by default: drawable, layout, menu, and values.

- **/res/drawable-xxhdpi, /res/drawable-xhdpi, /res/drawable-hdpi, /res/drawable-mdpi, /res/drawable-ldpi**—The application's icon and graphic resources are kept in these folders. Because devices have screens of different densities, the graphics of different resolutions are kept in these folders. Usually, graphics of 480dpi, 320dpi, 240dpi, 160dpi, and 120dpi are used in Android applications. The graphics with 480dpi, 320dpi, 240dpi, 160dpi, and 120dpi are stored in the res/drawable-xxhdpi, res/drawable-xhdpi, res/drawable-hdpi/, res/drawable-mdpi, and res/drawable-ldpi folders, respectively. The application will pick up the graphic from the correct folder after determining the density of the current device.

- **/res/layout**—Stores the layout file(s) in XML format.

- **/res/layout/activity_first_android_tablet_app.xml**—The layout file used by FirstAndroidTabletAppActivity to draw views on the screen. The views or controls are arranged in the specified layout.

- **/res/menu**—The menu folder that stores the menu XML file.

- **/res/values**—Stores all the values resources. The values resources include many types, including string resource, dimension resource, and color resource.

- **/res/values/strings.xml**—Contains the string resources. String resources contain the text matter to be assigned to different controls of the applications. This file also defines string arrays.

- **/res/values/dimens.xml**—Contains the dimension resources. To make an Android project compatible to screens of phones and tablets, the dimension resources are defined in the dimens.xml file.

- **/res/values-sw600dp, /res/values-sw720dp-land**—Contains the dimension resources for 7-inch and 10-inch tablets respectively; i.e., for large and extra large screens.

- **/res/values-v11, /res/values-v14**—Contains the themes for API level 11 and 14 respectively.

- **AndroidManifest.xml**—The central configuration file for the application.

- **Proguard-project.txt**—Defines how ProGuard optimizes the application's code. ProGuard is a tool that removes unused code from the Android application and optimizes it, thereby increasing performance. It also obfuscates the code to help protect it from decompilation.

- **project.properties**—A build file that Eclipse and the Android ADT plug-ins use. It contains project settings such as the build target. You can use this file to change various project properties. If required, the file should not be edited directly but through editors available in Eclipse.

Recipe: Converting an Android Phone Application into an Android Tablet Application

Because of the difference in screen sizes of Android phones and tablets, separate layouts should be defined for tablets. While defining the tablet layouts, consider the following two important points:

- Increase the font size of the UI controls.

- Fill up the blank space that is available on the right side due to the wider screen.

Prior to Android 3.2, layouts for tablets were put in the directories with the large and extra large configuration qualifiers. For example, the res/layout-large/ and res/layout-xlarge/ directories were used for storing layout resources of large and extra large screens. Recall that 7-inch and 10-inch tablets are considered large and extra large screen devices. From Android 3.2 and higher levels, the qualifiers for the layout directories are based on the amount of space required by the layout. For example, if the layout requires the minimum screen space of 600dp, the layout resources will be kept in the res/layout-sw600dp/ directory. If the screen width of the device is at least 600dp, only the resources in the res/layout-sw600dp/ directory will be used.

> **Note**
>
> The `sw` term used in the resources directories refers to the smallest width. The smallest width qualifier, `sw<N>dp`, represents the smaller of the screen's two sides, regardless of the device's current orientation.

Similarly, if 720dp is the smallest available width supported by your tablet layout, you can define its layout resources in the `res/layout-sw720dp/` directory.

To support the screens for Android phones and 7-inch and 10-inch tablets, you need to provide layouts in the following three directories:

- `res/layout/activity_layout.xml`   # For phones
- `res/layout-sw600dp/activity_layout.xml` # For 7-inch tablets
- `res/layout-sw720dp/activity_layout.xml` # For 10-inch tablets

The usual orientation of a tablet is landscape. So you put the landscape-oriented layout files of the 7-inch and 10-inch tablets in the `res/layout-sw600dp` and `res/layout-sw720dp` folders, respectively. Also, create `res/layout-sw600dp-port` and `res/layout-sw720dp-port` folders for keeping portrait-oriented layout files for the tablets if required.

To practically understand the procedure of converting an Android phone application into a tablet application, open the Android project, `FirstAndroidTabletApp`, that you created in the previous recipe. The default code in the activity layout file `activity_first_android_tablet_app.xml` is shown in Listing 1.1.

Listing 1.1   **Default Code in the Activity Layout File** `activity_first_android_tablet_app.xml`

```xml
<RelativeLayout xmlns:android="http://schemas.android.com/apk/res/android"
    xmlns:tools="http://schemas.android.com/tools"
    android:layout_width="match_parent"
    android:layout_height="match_parent"
    android:paddingBottom="@dimen/activity_vertical_margin"
    android:paddingLeft="@dimen/activity_horizontal_margin"
    android:paddingRight="@dimen/activity_horizontal_margin"
    android:paddingTop="@dimen/activity_vertical_margin"
    tools:context=".FirstAndroidTabletAppActivity" >
    <TextView
        android:layout_width="wrap_content"
        android:layout_height="wrap_content"
        android:text="@string/hello_world" />
</RelativeLayout>
```

You can see that the default code in the layout file will print the text `Hello world!` at the top left corner of the screen, as shown in Figure 1.8. The text will appear at the standard margin space from the borders of the screen.

Figure 1.8   Output of the `FirstAndroidTabletApp` on the phone emulator

The size of the text `Hello world!` appears fine on the phone, but on the 10-inch tablet, the text appears so small that it is almost invisible (see Figure 1.9).

Figure 1.9   Output of the `FirstAndroidTabletApp` on the 10-inch tablet emulator

The first step to make the application compatible for phones as well as for tablets is to adjust the size of the UI controls. Because the current application comprises a `TextView` control, add the `android:textSize` attribute to its layout file for adjusting the font size of the text being displayed. Also, remove the default margin attributes from the `RelativeLayout` container. After adding the attribute, the activity layout file will appear as shown in Listing 1.2. Only the code in bold is newly added.

Listing 1.2   **Code in the Activity Layout File** `activity_first_android_tablet_app.xml`

```
<RelativeLayout xmlns:android="http://schemas.android.com/apk/res/android"
    xmlns:tools="http://schemas.android.com/tools"
    android:layout_width="match_parent"
    android:layout_height="match_parent"
    tools:context=".FirstAndroidTabletAppActivity" >
    <TextView
        android:layout_width="wrap_content"
        android:layout_height="wrap_content"
        android:text="@string/hello_world"
        android:textSize="@dimen/text_size" />
</RelativeLayout>
```

You can see that the dimension resource `text_size` assigns the font size to the text displayed through the `TextView` control. To define the dimension resource, add an XML file called `dimens.xml` to the `res/values` folder of your application. Define the `text_size` dimension resource by writing the following code in the `dimens.xml` file:

```
<?xml version="1.0" encoding="utf-8"?>
<resources>
    <dimen name="text_size">14sp</dimen>
</resources>
```

> **Note**
>
> Android 4.2.2 automatically creates the `dimens.xml` file in the `res/values` folder.

The preceding code will assign the 14sp size to the text that is displayed in Android phones and tablets. The 14sp size is fine for the Android phone but is quite small for the Android tablets. To define separate dimension resource for the 7-inch and 10-inch tablets, create two folders named `values-sw600dp` and `values-sw720dp` in the `res` folder of your application.

> **Note**
>
> Android 4.2.2 automatically creates two folders, `values-sw600dp` and `values-sw720dp-land`, with the `dimens.xml` file.

Copy the `dimens.xml` file from the `res/values` folder to the newly created folders `values-sw600dp` and `values-sw720dp`. To define the text size for the 7-inch tablet, open the `dimens.xml` file in the `values-sw600dp` folder and increase the value of the `text_size` resource to 24sp, as shown in the next code:

```
<?xml version="1.0" encoding="utf-8"?>
<resources>
    <dimen name="text_size">24sp</dimen>
</resources>
```

Similarly, for the 10-inch tablet, open the `dimens.xml` file in the `values-sw720dp` folder and set the `text_size` resource to 32sp, as shown in the code:

```
<?xml version="1.0" encoding="utf-8"?>
<resources>
    <dimen name="text_size">32sp</dimen>
</resources>
```

The dimension resource `text_size` is set to display the text on the Android phone, 7-inch, and 10-inch tablets in 14sp, 24sp, and 32sp font sizes, respectively. After adding the `dimens.xml` file to the `values` folder and creating the `values-sw600dp` and `values-sw720dp` folders in the `res` folder, the application will appear in Package Explorer as shown in Figure 1.10 (left).

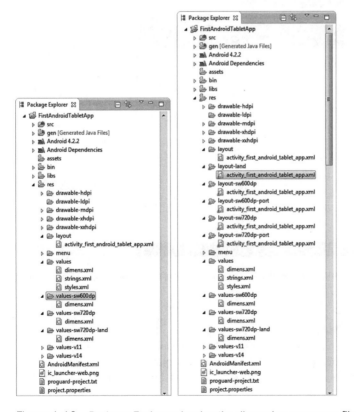

Figure 1.10   Package Explorer showing the dimension resources files and folders (left) and the Package Explorer showing the folders storing the layout resources of the 7-inch and 10-inch tablets (right)

When 24sp and 32sp font size are applied to the text that is displayed through 7-inch and 10-inch tablets, the text will appear more readable and brighter than 14sp font size. Figure 1.11 (top) shows the output of the application on a 7-inch tablet emulator, and Figure 1.11 (bottom) shows the output of the application on a 10-inch tablet emulator.

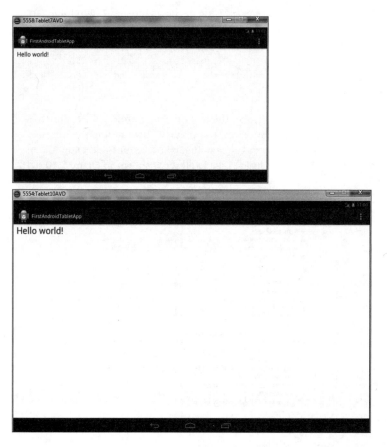

Figure 1.11   Hello world! text message displayed in a 7-inch tablet emulator (top) and a 10-inch tablet emulator (bottom)

You have used the same layout file for the phone and tablets up to this point. Because the normal orientation of a tablet is landscape and because it has a wider screen, there is always a lot of blank space to the right side of the screen. So you might require a separate layout for the tablets to arrange the UI controls and to use the extra space. To define a separate layout for the tablets, create two folders named `layout-sw600dp` and `layout-sw720dp` in the `res` folder, where `layout-sw600dp` will be used to define the layout resources for the 7-inch tablets, and `layout-sw720dp` will keep layout resources for the 10-inch tablets. Copy the activity layout file `activity_first_android_tablet_app.xml` from the `/res/layout` folder to the newly created `layout-sw600dp` and `layout-sw720dp` folders. The `res/layout` folder will now be used for keeping the layout resources for phones only.

Define the layout for the 7-inch tablet by modifying the layout file `activity_first_android_tablet_app.xml` (in the `res/layout-sw600dp` folder) to appear as shown in Listing 1.3.

Listing 1.3   **Code in the Activity Layout File** `activity_first_android_tablet_app.xml` **for a 7-Inch Tablet**

```
<LinearLayout xmlns:android="http://schemas.android.com/apk/res/android"
    android:orientation="vertical"
    android:layout_width="match_parent"
    android:layout_height="match_parent">
    <TextView
        android:layout_width="wrap_content"
        android:layout_height="wrap_content"
        android:text="7 inch Tablet in landscape orientation"
        android:textSize="@dimen/text_size"
        android:textStyle="bold"  />
</LinearLayout>
```

You can see that a `TextView` control contained in the `LinearLayout` container is set to display the text message `7 inch Tablet in landscape orientation`. The text will appear in bold and in the font size that is defined in the `text_size` dimension resource. Similarly, for the 10-inch tablet, modify the layout file `activity_first_android_tablet_app.xml` found in the `layout-sw720dp` folder. In this layout file, write the code as shown in Listing 1.3 with a small difference. Modify the text message to appear as shown in the next statement:

```
android:text="10 inch Tablet in landscape orientation"
```

After running the application, the phone emulator will still display the same old `Hello world!` message, but the 7-inch and 10-inch tablet emulators will display the messages `7 inch Tablet in landscape orientation` and `10 inch Tablet in landscape orientation`, respectively. Figure 1.12 shows the text message in the 10-inch tablet emulator when in landscape orientation.

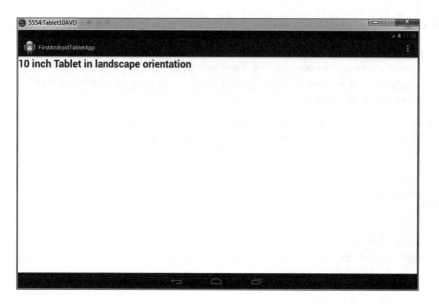

Figure 1.12   Text message displayed on 10-inch tablet emulator in landscape orientation

The text message displayed by the 7-inch and 10-inch tablet emulators will be the same whether it is in landscape or portrait orientation. What if you want to change the layout for the tablets when users switch to portrait orientation?

To define the separate layout for the tablets when users switch to portrait orientation, you need to create two folders named `layout-sw600dp-port` and `layout-sw720dp-port` in the res folder of your application. Again, copy the activity layout file `activity_first_android_tablet_app.xml` from the `/res/layout` folder to the newly created `layout-sw600dp-port` and `layout-sw720dp-port` folders. To define the layout for the 7-inch tablet when in portrait orientation, modify the layout file `activity_first_android_tablet_app.xml` in the `layout-sw600dp-port` folder to appear as shown in Listing 1.4.

Listing 1.4   **Code in the Activity Layout File** `activity_first_android_tablet_app.xml` **for 7-Inch Tablet in Portrait Orientation**

```
<LinearLayout xmlns:android="http://schemas.android.com/apk/res/android"
    android:orientation="vertical"
    android:layout_width="match_parent"
    android:layout_height="match_parent">
    <TextView
        android:layout_width="wrap_content"
        android:layout_height="wrap_content"
        android:text="7 inch Tablet in portrait orientation"
        android:textSize="@dimen/text_size"
        android:textStyle="bold" />
</LinearLayout>
```

You can see that the `TextView` control is set to display the text message `7 inch Tablet in portrait orientation`. The text will appear in bold and in the font size that is defined in the `text_size` dimension resource. For the 10-inch tablet, modify the layout file `activity_first_android_tablet_app.xml` found in the `layout-sw720dp-port` folder to appear as shown in Listing 1.4 with a small difference in the text message. Use the following statement for the text message in the layout file for a 10-inch tablet:

```
android:text="10 inch Tablet in portrait orientation"
```

After running the application, the 7-inch and 10-inch tablet emulators in portrait orientation display the messages `7 inch Tablet in portrait orientation` and `10 inch Tablet in portrait orientation`, respectively. Figure 1.13 shows the text message in a 10-inch tablet emulator when in portrait orientation.

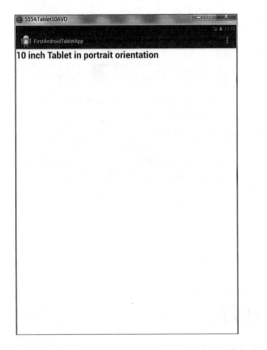

Figure 1.13   Text message displayed on 10-inch tablet emulator in portrait orientation

You have heard enough about the tablet layouts in the portrait and landscape orientation. The only thing left to make this application completely compatible for Android phones and tablets is to define the layout for the phone in landscape orientation. At the moment, the same layout that is defined in the `res/layout` folder will be used for portrait and landscape orientation. That is, as you saw in portrait orientation, the phone in landscape mode will display the same `Hello world!` message (see Figure 1.14 [left]). To define a separate phone layout for landscape orientation, you need to create a new folder named `layout-land`. So create the `layout-land` folder in the `res` folder of your application and copy the layout file `activity_first_android_tablet_app.xml` from the `res/layout` folder to the `layout-land` folder. To define the layout for the phone in landscape orientation, modify the layout file `activity_first_android_tablet_app.xml` to appear as shown in Listing 1.5.

Listing 1.5   **Code in the Activity Layout File** `activity_first_android_tablet_app.xml` **for Android Phone in Landscape Orientation**

```
<RelativeLayout xmlns:android="http://schemas.android.com/apk/res/android"
    xmlns:tools="http://schemas.android.com/tools"
    android:layout_width="match_parent"
    android:layout_height="match_parent"
    tools:context=".FirstAndroidTabletAppActivity" >
    <TextView
        android:layout_width="wrap_content"
        android:layout_height="wrap_content"
        android:text="Phone in landscape orientation"
        android:textSize="@dimen/text_size"
        android:textStyle="bold" />
</RelativeLayout>
```

The `TextView` is set to display the text `Phone in landscape orientation`. The text will appear in bold at the center of the screen and in the size defined by the `text_size` dimension resource. After creating all the files and folders as discussed in this recipe, the application will appear as shown in Figure 1.10 (right) in the Package Explorer. Now, on running the application, instead of the `Hello world!` message that is displayed in portrait orientation, the phone when switched to landscape orientation will display the text `Phone in landscape orientation` at the center of the screen (see Figure 1.14 [right]).

Figure 1.14   The `Hello world!` text message displayed in phone in landscape orientation (left) and the modified text `Phone in landscape orientation` displayed in phone in landscape orientation (right)

To summarize, the following are the steps to make an Android application compatible to run on Android phones as well as on the tablets:

1. Create an XML file `dimens.xml` in the `res/values` folder with the code as shown here:

```
<?xml version="1.0" encoding="utf-8"?>
<resources>
        <dimen name="text_size">14sp</dimen>
</resources>
```

2. Create two folders named `values-sw600dp` and `values-sw720dp` in the `res` folder. Copy the file `dimens.xml` from the `res/values` folder to these two folders. Open the `dimens.xml` file in the two folders, and change the text size in the `text_size` dimension resource to 24sp and 32sp, respectively.

3. Modify the activity layout file, and assign dimension resources to the `size` attribute of all the UI controls, as shown in this statement:

```
android:textSize="@dimen/text_size"
```

4. If the layout of the UI controls in tablets is different from the phone layout, create two folders named `layout-sw600dp` and `layout-sw720dp` in the `res` folder. Then copy the activity layout file from the `res/layout` folder into these two folders. Organize the UI controls in the copied layout file in these folders to utilize the extra blank space on the right.

5. If you want separate layout when the tablet(s) is oriented to portrait mode, create two folders named `layout-sw600dp-port` and `layout-sw720dp-port`. Copy the activity layout file from the `res/layout` folder in these two folders. Arrange the UI controls in the copied layout file to suit the portrait orientation of the tablet(s).

6. On the phone, if the layout for the portrait and landscape orientation is different, create the `layout-land` folder in the `res` folder, and copy the activity layout file from the `res/layout` folder in the `layout-land` folder. In the `layout-land` folder, organize the UI controls in the layout file to suit the landscape orientation of the phone.

Recipe: Forcing an Application to Run Only on Tablets

To make an application to target only the tablets, you need to specify the following two things:

- Ensure the device is running Android 3.0 (Honeycomb) or higher.
- Ensure the device has a large or extra large screen (that is, the screen is at least seven inches).

To make an application to run only on large and extra large screen devices, irrespective of the Android version installed on the device, modify the `Android Manifest.xml` file to appear as shown here:

```
<manifest ... >
    <supports-screens android:smallScreens="false"
        android:normalScreens="false"
        android:largeScreens="true"
        android:xlargeScreens="true" />
</manifest>
```

You can also use the `requiresSmallestWidthDp` attribute of the `<supports-screens>` element to specify the minimum width of the device on which your application can run. `android:requiresSmallestWidthDp` can define the minimum dimension of the screen space (in dp units) that is required by your application UI to run. The device that has the width equal to or greater than the specified value mentioned in the `requiresSmallestWidthDp` attribute will be able to run the application. The following statement will make the application run only on devices that are at least 600dp wide:

```
<manifest ... >
    <supports-screens android:requiresSmallestWidthDp="600" />
    ...
</manifest>
```

Recipe: Understanding Activities

A screen of an application comprising the controls that the user interacts with is displayed through an activity. Each screen is represented by an activity. A simple application may consist of just one activity, whereas large applications contain several activities. Each activity of an application operates independently of the others. A stack of activities is maintained while running an application, and the activity at the top of the stack is the one that is currently being displayed. When you press the Back button, the activity is popped from the stack, making the previous activity the current activity, which displays the previous screen. The transition from one activity to another is accomplished through the use of asynchronous messages called *intents*. Intents can pass data from one activity to another. All the activities in the application must be defined in the application's manifest file. Each activity in an Android application is either a direct subclass of the activity base class or a subclass of an activity subclass.

Recipe: Understanding the Android Activity Life Cycle

The Android activity life cycle defines the states or events that an activity goes through from its creation until its end. The activity monitors and reacts to these events by executing methods that override the activity class methods for each event. The list of methods executed during different events of an Android activity life cycle is shown in Table 1.1.

Table 1.1   **List of Methods Instantiated During Different Events of an Android Activity Life Cycle**

Methods	Description
onCreate()	The method called when the activity is created. It initializes the activity and is used to create views of the application, open persistent data files required by the activity, and so on.
onStart()	The method called just before the activity becomes visible on the screen. An activity can be in either a foreground state or a background state. When an activity switches to a background state, the onStop() method is executed; when it switches to the foreground state, the onResume() method is invoked.
onResume()	The method called whenever the activity becomes the foreground activity, whether it is right after the execution of the onStart() method or when some other foreground activity exits and the activity appears at the top of the activity stack, making it a foreground activity. A foreground activity interacts with the user, receives keyboard and touch inputs, and accordingly generates the response.
onPause()	The method called when the activity is stopped and no longer visible in the foreground and some other activity is switched to the foreground. Because the activity is not visible, this method contains commands to minimize consumption of resources and to store the activity state, which will be used when the activity resumes to the foreground. You can use this method to suspend any action that consumes CPU cycles or battery.
onStop()	The method called when the activity is no longer visible, either because another activity is switched to the foreground or because the activity is being destroyed.
onDestroy()	The method used when the activity is completed and is about to be destroyed. The method may or may not be called (that is, the system may simply terminate the process). You can use this method to release the resources consumed by the activity.

Following is the summary of the activity life cycle (see Figure 1.15):

- When an activity starts, the onCreate(), onStart(), and onResume() methods are invoked leading activity to the running state.
- When the Back button is pressed, the onPause(), onStop(), and onDestroy() methods are invoked and the activity ends.
- When the Home button is pressed, the activity is paused or interrupted, resulting in invoking the onPause() and onStop() methods.
- When an activity is run in a paused state, it is restored to the running state by invoking the onRestart(), onStart(), and onResume() methods.

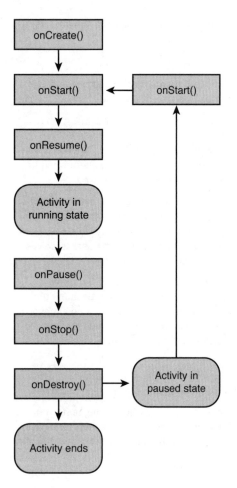

Figure 1.15   Life cycle of an activity

To understand the sequence of the methods that are invoked during an activity life cycle, create an Android project called `ActivityLifecycleApp`. In the Java activity file, `ActivityLifecycleAppActivity.java`, write the code shown in Listing 1.6.

Listing 1.6   **Code Written in the Java Activity File** `ActivityLifecycleAppActivity.java`

```
package com.androidtablet.activitylifecycleapp;


import android.os.Bundle;
import android.app.Activity;
import android.util.Log;
```

```java
public class ActivityLifecycleAppActivity extends Activity {
    private static final String tag = "State: ";
    @Override
    public void onCreate(Bundle savedInstanceState) {
        super.onCreate(savedInstanceState);
        setContentView(R.layout.activity_activity_lifecycle
            _app);
        Log.d(tag,"onCreate");
    }

    @Override
    protected void onStart() {
        super.onStart();
        Log.d(tag,"onStart");
    }

    @Override
    protected void onRestart() {
        super.onRestart();
        Log.d(tag,"onRestart");
    }

    @Override
    protected void onResume() {
        super.onResume();
        Log.d(tag,"onResume");
    };

    @Override
    protected void onPause() {
        super.onPause();
        Log.d(tag,"onPause");
    }
    @Override
    protected void onStop() {
        super.onStop();
        Log.d(tag,"onStop");
    };
    @Override
    protected void onDestroy() {
        super.onDestroy();
        Log.d(tag,"onDestroy");
    };
}
```

After running the application, you can see the log messages in the LogCat window (see Figure 1.16). If you don't find the LogCat window on the screen, select Windows, Show View, Other. From the Show View dialog box that pops up, select the LogCat option and then the OK button. The LogCat window will appear at the bottom. The application will display three messages: onCreate, onStart, and onResume. This confirms that the activity is now in a running state.

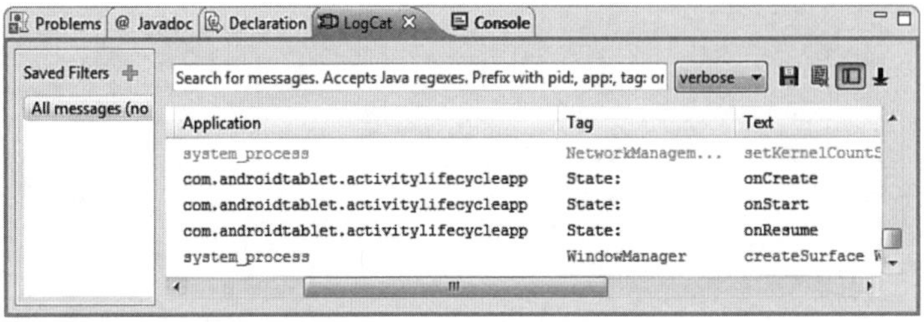

Figure 1.16   LogCat window displaying log messages representing activity life cycle methods

If you press the Home button, the activity pauses but does not end. The messages onPause and onStop but not onDestroy that appear in the LogCat window confirm that the activity is in a paused state (see Figure 1.17 [bottom]). If the application is run when the activity is in a paused state, it will not be reloaded and is simply restored to its running state. Restoring an activity to its running state is confirmed by the messages onRestart, onStart, and onResume, which appear in the LogCat window. On selecting the Back key, the activity ends, which is confirmed by the display of three messages, onPause, onStop, and onDestroy, in the LogCat window.

In the LogCat window, all messages that occur while executing the application are displayed. To see only the log messages related to the methods invoked in your application, add a LogCat filter. Click on the green plus in the top left of the LogCat window. In the Logcat Message Filter Settings window that opens, assign the Filter Name as Lifecycle (see Figure 1.17 [top]). In the By Log Tag field, enter the tag State: so that only the log messages containing this tag are filtered out for you. After selecting the OK button, only the log messages related to the State tag will be displayed, as shown in Figure 1.17 (bottom).

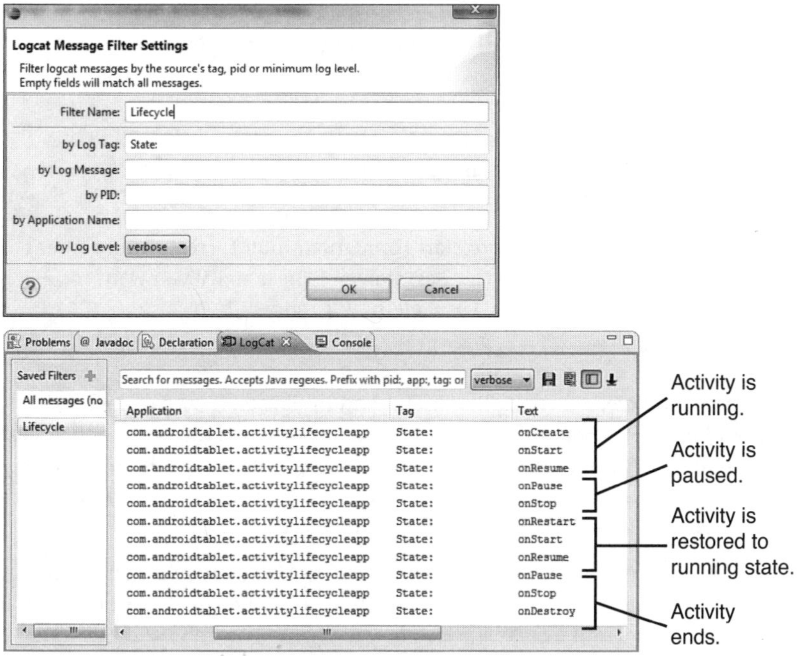

Logcat Message Filter Settings

Filter logcat messages by the source's tag, pid or minimum log level.
Empty fields will match all messages.

Filter Name:	Lifecycle
by Log Tag:	State:
by Log Message:	
by PID:	
by Application Name:	
by Log Level:	verbose ▼

OK   Cancel

Problems | @ Javadoc | Declaration | LogCat ✕ | Console

Saved Filters	Search for messages. Accepts Java regexes. Prefix with pid;, app;, tag: or verbose ▼		
All messages (no	**Application**	**Tag**	**Text**
Lifecycle	com.androidtablet.activitylifecycleapp	State:	onCreate
	com.androidtablet.activitylifecycleapp	State:	onStart
	com.androidtablet.activitylifecycleapp	State:	onResume
	com.androidtablet.activitylifecycleapp	State:	onPause
	com.androidtablet.activitylifecycleapp	State:	onStop
	com.androidtablet.activitylifecycleapp	State:	onRestart
	com.androidtablet.activitylifecycleapp	State:	onStart
	com.androidtablet.activitylifecycleapp	State:	onResume
	com.androidtablet.activitylifecycleapp	State:	onPause
	com.androidtablet.activitylifecycleapp	State:	onStop
	com.androidtablet.activitylifecycleapp	State:	onDestroy

Activity is
running.

Activity is
paused.

Activity is
restored to
running state.

Activity
ends.

Figure 1.17   Dialog for creating LogCat filter (top) and Log messages representing activity life cycle (bottom)

Recipe: Starting Activity Using Intent

The structure that is used to start, stop, and transition between activities within an application is called an *intent*. An intent is a data structure that describes operations to perform in an Android application. It consists of action that the application needs to perform, data to operate on, and other information helpful in executing the operation. Intent can be explicit or implicit as follows:

- **Explicit intent**—In an explicit intent, you specify the activity required to respond to the intent; that is, you explicitly designate the target component. Because the developers of other applications have no idea of the component names in your application, explicit intent is limited to use within an application, such as transferring internal messages.

- **Implicit intent**—In an implicit intent, you just declare intent and leave it to the platform to find an activity that can respond to the intent. That is, you don't specify the target component that should respond to the intent. This type of intent is used for activating components of other applications. It is the job of the Android platform to search for the most suitable component to handle the implicit intent.

The method used to start an activity is `startActivity()`. First create an implicit or explicit intent object and pass it to the `startActivity()` method in the format shown here:

```
startActivity(my_intent);
```

Here, `my_intent` refers to the intent that is passed to the method as a parameter. The `startActivity()` method finds and starts the single activity that best matches the given intent.

To explicitly specify the activity that you want to start through an intent, create a new intent specifying the current application context and the class name of the activity you want to launch and pass this intent to the `startActivity()` method, as shown here:

```
startActivity(new Intent(this, WelcomeActivity.class));
```

In the preceding statement, you created an explicit intent and initialized it by passing the activity context `this` and the `WelcomeActivity`'s class instance, which is the activity that you want to launch. The intent object is passed to the `startActivity()` method, which launches the activity described by `WelcomeActivity.class`. If `startActivity()` is unable to find the specified activity, an `android.content.ActivityNotFoundException` is thrown.

Now you will explore the concept of creating and starting your own activity using an example. You will create an application that displays a `Button` control, which when clicked starts a new activity. The activity that will start will display a welcome message to the user. So create a new Android Project called `IntentApp`.

To display a `Button` control, write the code as shown in Listing 1.7 in the activity layout file `activity_intent_app.xml`.

Listing 1.7   Code Written in the Activity Layout File `activity_intent_app.xml`

```
<LinearLayout xmlns:android="http://schemas.android.com/apk/res/android"
    android:orientation="vertical"
    android:layout_width="match_parent"
    android:layout_height="match_parent">
    <Button
        android:layout_width="match_parent"
        android:layout_height="wrap_content"
        android:id="@+id/start_button"
        android:text="Start Activity"
        android:textSize="@dimen/text_size" />
</LinearLayout>
```

You can see that a `Button` control with ID `start_button` is defined with the caption `Start Activity`. You want to start an activity when the Start Activity button is clicked. Call the new activity `WelcomeActivity`. Because the `WelcomeActivity` needs to display a welcome message to the user, create a new layout file for your `WelcomeActivity`. So, from the Package Explorer window, right-click the `res/layout` folder and select the New, Android XML File option. A dialog box appears asking for information about the new Android XML file. In the File text box, enter the filename as `welcome` (no need to add an `.xml` extension). Select the LinearLayout option from the Root Element, which denotes that you want to create a linear layout file. Finally, select the Finish button. The layout file `welcome.xml` will be created in the `res/layout` folder.

To display a welcome message, you need to define a `TextView` control in the layout file. After defining the `TextView` control, the layout file `welcome.xml` will appear as shown in Listing 1.8.

Listing 1.8   Code Written in the `welcome.xml` File

```xml
<?xml version="1.0" encoding="utf-8"?>
<LinearLayout xmlns:android="http://schemas.android.com/apk/res/android"
    android:orientation="vertical"
    android:layout_width="match_parent"
    android:layout_height="match_parent">
    <TextView
        android:layout_width="match_parent"
        android:layout_height="wrap_content"
        android:text=" Welcome to the New Activity "
        android:textSize="@dimen/text_size"
        android:textStyle="bold" />
</LinearLayout>
```

After the layout file is completed, it's time to create your new activity, `WelcomeActivity`, in the package `com.androidtablet.intentapp` that's inside the `src` folder of the application. So, right-click the package `com.androidtablet.intentapp` and select the New, Class option. A New Java Class dialog box appears, requesting that you enter the name of the Java file. In the Name text box, enter the name of the activity file: `WelcomeActivity` (no need to add `.java` extension). Keeping all the default options selected, select the Finish button to create the Java file.

The activity `WelcomeActivity.java` will be added to the package. The `WelcomeActivity` is supposed to display a welcome message to the user through the `TextView` control defined in the layout file `welcome.xml`. To load the UI defined in the layout file `welcome.xml`, write code as shown in Listing 1.9 in the `WelcomeActivity.java` file.

Listing 1.9   Code Written in the `WelcomeActivity.java` File

```java
package com.androidtablet.intentapp;

import android.app.Activity;
import android.os.Bundle;

public class WelcomeActivity extends Activity {
```

```
@Override
protected void onCreate(Bundle savedInstanceState) {
    super.onCreate(savedInstanceState);
    setContentView(R.layout.welcome);
}
```
}

Only the components that are declared in the application's manifest file, `AndroidManifest.xml`, are visible to Android and hence can be used to run the application. This means that the new activity, `WelcomeActivity.java`, must be declared in the `AndroidManifest.xml` file to make it visible to Android and start it. The `AndroidManifest.xml` file is shown in Listing 1.10. The statement in bold is added to register the newly created activity, `WelcomeActivity.java`.

Listing 1.10   Code in the `AndroidManifest.xml` File

```
<manifest xmlns:android="http://schemas.android.com/apk/res/android"
    package="com.androidtablet.intentapp"
    android:versionCode="1"
    android:versionName="1.0" >
    <uses-sdk
        android:minSdkVersion="11"
        android:targetSdkVersion="17" />
    <application
        android:allowBackup="true"
        android:icon="@drawable/ic_launcher"
        android:label="@string/app_name"
        android:theme="@style/AppTheme" >
        <activity
            android:name=
            "com.androidtablet.intentapp.IntentAppActivity"
            android:label="@string/app_name">
            <intent-filter>
                <action android:name= "android.intent.
                    action.MAIN" />
                <category android:name="android.intent.
                    category.LAUNCHER" />
            </intent-filter>
        </activity>
        <activity android:name=".WelcomeActivity" android:label=
            "@string/app_name" />
    </application>
</manifest>
```

After registering the activity, `WelcomeActivity.java`, in the `AndroidManifest.xml` file, you can now start it by using the `startActivity()` method that was discussed at the beginning of the recipe. Because the new activity will be started from the default activity file of the application, IntentAppActivity.java, the startActivity() method needs to be added to the same file. The code in the default activity file, intentAppActivity.java, after adding the startActivity() method, will appear as shown in Listing 1.11.

Listing 1.11   **Code Written in the** IntentAppActivity.java **File**

```
package com.androidtablet.intentapp;

import android.os.Bundle;
import android.app.Activity;
import android.widget.Button;
import android.view.View;
import android.content.Intent;

public class IntentAppActivity extends Activity {

    @Override
    public void onCreate(Bundle savedInstanceState) {
        super.onCreate(savedInstanceState);
        setContentView(R.layout.activity_intent_app);
        Button startButton = (Button)this.findViewById(
            R.id.start_button);
        startButton.setOnClickListener(new Button.
            OnClickListener(){
            public void onClick(View v)  {
                startActivity(new Intent(getBaseContext(),
                    WelcomeActivity.class));
            }
        });
    }
}
```

The Button control is accessed from the layout file through its ID, start_button, and is mapped to the Button object startButton. When startButton is clicked, the startActivity() method is invoked. The startActivity() method creates an explicit intent, which explicitly specifies that the activity file, WelcomeActivity.java, is to be run when Button is clicked. The getBaseContext() method used in the preceding code returns an instance of the Context class. The instance of the Context class refers to the application.

After running the application, you get a Button, Start Activity on the screen, as shown in Figure 1.18 (top). On clicking the Start Activity button, the new activity, WelcomeActivity, will start displaying the welcome message on the screen (see Figure 1.18 [bottom]).

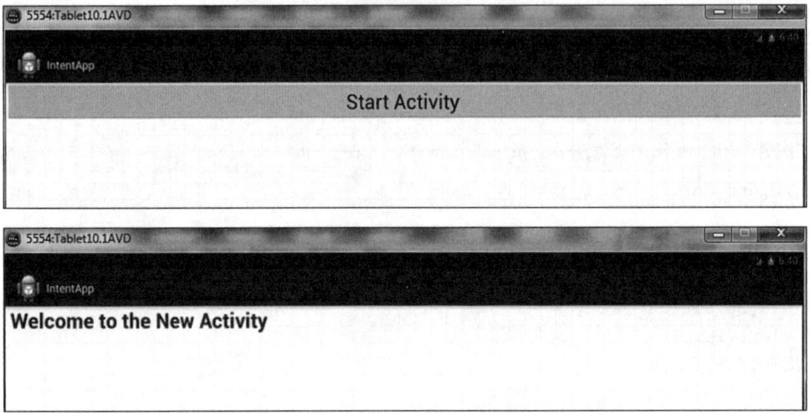

Figure 1.18   Start Activity button displayed on application startup (top) and the new activity, `WelcomeActivity`, starts displaying welcome message (bottom)

Recipe: Passing Data from One Activity to Another

In this recipe, you will learn to pass data from one activity to another. To do this, you make use of the Bundle object. That is, you create a `Bundle` object and insert a value of type String, Short, Float, and so on into it using a key. The key is used in retrieving the data from the `Bundle` object later. The following code inserts a string into a `Bundle` object using the key username:

```
Bundle dataBundle = new Bundle();
dataBundle.putString("username", "Kelly");
Intent welcomeIntent = new Intent(getBaseContext(),
    WelcomeActivity.class);
welcomeIntent.putExtras(dataBundle);
startActivityForResult(welcomeIntent,
    WELCOME_REQUEST_CODE);
```

In this code, you see that a `Bundle` object by the name `dataBundle` is created. In the `dataBundle` object, a name, `Kelly`, is stored under the key `username`. An intent called `welcomeIntent` is created specifying the current application context and the class name of the subactivity `WelcomeActivity`—the activity that you want to launch. The `dataBundle` object containing the data to be passed to the subactivity is added to the `welcomeIntent` using the `putExtras()` method. Finally, the intent is passed to the `startActivityForResult()` method. The `startActivityForResult()` will launch the specified subactivity and will deliver the result when it is finished. That is, when the launched subactivity exits, the `onActivityResult()` method will be called with the given request code. You can analyze the value of the request code to determine whether the subactivity was successfully executed.

In the subactivity, you can retrieve the data passed through the `Bundle` object. The given code that follows shows how it is done:

```
Bundle extras = getIntent().getExtras();
if(extras !=null) {
    String userName=extras.getString("username");
}
```

You can see that a `Bundle` object, `extras`, is created. The `getExtras()` method is called to retrieve the extended data from the intent. That is, the `dataBundle` sent through the `welcomeIntent` is retrieved and assigned to the `Bundle` object `extras`. Using the `getString()` method, the string stored in the `Bundle` object under the key `username` is accessed and assigned to `userName` for further processing.

It will be easier to understand the previously discussed concept through a running example. Create a new Android project called `CommunicateDataApp`. In this application, you will send a name entered by the user to a subactivity where a welcome message is displayed along with the sent name. On clicking a `Button` control from the subactivity, the user will be navigated back to the main activity.

Because you want the user to enter a name and click a `Button` control to send the entered name to the subactivity, you need to define `EditText`, `Button`, and `TextView` controls in the activity layout file `activity_communicate_data_app.xml`. After defining the three controls, the activity layout file `activity_communicate_data_app.xml` will appear, as shown in Listing 1.12.

Listing 1.12   **Code Written in the Activity Layout File** `activity_communicate_data_app.xml`

```
<LinearLayout xmlns:android="http://schemas.android.com/apk/res/android"
    android:orientation="vertical"
    android:layout_width="match_parent"
    android:layout_height="match_parent">
    <EditText
        android:layout_width="match_parent"
        android:layout_height="wrap_content"
        android:hint="Enter your name"
        android:textSize="@dimen/text_size"
        android:id="@+id/user_name"/>
    <Button
        android:id="@+id/start_button"
        android:layout_width="match_parent"
        android:layout_height="wrap_content"
        android:text="Start Activity"
        android:textSize="@dimen/text_size" />
    <TextView
        android:layout_width="match_parent"
        android:layout_height="wrap_content"
```

```
                    android:id="@+id/response"
                    android:textSize="@dimen/text_size"
                    android:textStyle="bold" />
</LinearLayout>
```

You can see that the EditText, Button, and TextView controls are defined with IDs, user_ name, start_button, and response. In the EditText control, the name will be entered, and the Button control will be used to launch the subactivity—the one to send the entered name and use the TextView control to display a text message when you navigate back to the main activity from the subactivity.

Next, you need to write code in the main Java activity file to do the following tasks:

- Fetch the name entered in the EditText control.
- Create a Bundle object.
- Put the name in the Bundle object.
- Create an intent to specify the subactivity that you want to launch.
- Add the Bundle object to the intent.
- Launch the subactivity with a request code.
- Analyze the request code to learn about execution of the subactivity.

To do all the preceding tasks, the code shown in Listing 1.13 is written in the main Java activity file: CommunicateDataAppActivity.java.

Listing 1.13   **Code Written in the Java Activity File** CommunicateDataAppActivity.java

```
package com.androidtablet.communicatedataapp;

import android.os.Bundle;
import android.app.Activity;
import android.widget.EditText;
import android.widget.Button;
import android.widget.TextView;
import android.view.View;
import android.content.Intent;
import android.widget.Toast;

public class CommunicateDataAppActivity extends Activity {
    private static final int WELCOME_REQUEST_CODE = 0;
    TextView response;
    @Override
    public void onCreate(Bundle savedInstanceState) {
        super.onCreate(savedInstanceState);
        setContentView(R.layout.activity_communicate_data_app);
```

```
        Button startButton = (Button)this.findViewById(
            R.id.start_button);
        final EditText userName=(EditText)findViewById(
            R.id.user_name);
        response=(TextView)findViewById(R.id.response);
        startButton.setOnClickListener(new Button.OnClickListener(){
            public void onClick(View v)  {
            if(userName.getText().length() >0) {
                Bundle dataBundle = new Bundle();
                dataBundle.putString("username", userName.
                    getText().toString());
                Intent welcomeIntent = new Intent(
                    getBaseContext(), WelcomeActivity.class);
                welcomeIntent.putExtras(dataBundle);
                startActivityForResult(welcomeIntent,
                    WELCOME_REQUEST_CODE);
            }
            else
                Toast.makeText(CommunicateDataAppActivity.this,
                    "Please Enter Name", Toast.LENGTH_SHORT).
                    show();
            }
        });
    }


    @Override
    protected void onActivityResult(int requestCode, int
        resultCode, Intent data) {
        super.onActivityResult(requestCode, resultCode, data);
        if (requestCode ==WELCOME_REQUEST_CODE) {
            if (resultCode == RESULT_OK) {
                response.setText("Back from the
                    WelcomeActivity");
            }
        }
    }
}
```

The subactivity that you want to launch is WelcomeActivity. In this subactivity, you want to display the name sent by the main activity, along with a welcome message. Also, you want to display a Button control, which when clicked will take you back to the main activity. Therefore, you need to define a layout for the subactivity. Right-click the res/layout folder and add an XML file called welcome.xml. Define the TextView and Button control in the layout file welcome.xml, as shown in Listing 1.14.

Listing 1.14   **Code Written in the Layout File** `welcome.xml`

```xml
<?xml version="1.0" encoding="utf-8"?>
<LinearLayout xmlns:android="http://schemas.android.com/apk/res/android"
    android:layout_width="match_parent"
    android:layout_height="match_parent"
    android:orientation="vertical" >
    <TextView
        android:layout_width="match_parent"
        android:layout_height="wrap_content"
        android:id="@+id/welcomemsg"
        android:text="This is WelcomeActivity"
        android:textSize="@dimen/text_size"
        android:textStyle="bold"  />
    <Button
        android:id="@+id/goback_button"
        android:layout_width="match_parent"
        android:layout_height="wrap_content"
        android:textSize="@dimen/text_size"
        android:text="Go Back"/>
</LinearLayout>
```

You can see that the `TextView` and `Button` controls are defined with IDs `welcomemsg` and `goback_button`, respectively. The `TextView` is initialized to display the text `This is WelcomeActivity`, and the `Button` control is set to display the caption `Go Back`.

Now it's time to add a Java class file to the application for your subactivity. Right-click the package `com.androidtablet.communicatedataapp` in the Package Explorer window and add a Java class file called `WelcomeActivity.java`. The subactivity `WelcomeActivity.java` is supposed to do the following tasks:

- Access the `Bundle` object containing the data sent by the main activity.
- Access the name stored in the `Bundle` object and display it through the `TextView` control with a welcome message.
- Terminate the subactivity, set the value of the request code, and return to the main activity when the `Button` control is clicked.

To do these tasks, the code shown in Listing 1.15 is written into the subactivity `WelcomeActivity.java` file.

Listing 1.15   **Code Written into the Subactivity** `WelcomeActivity.java` **File**

```java
package com.androidtablet.communicatedataapp;

import android.app.Activity;
import android.os.Bundle;
```

```
import android.widget.TextView;
import android.widget.Button;
import android.view.View;

public class WelcomeActivity extends Activity {
    @Override
    protected void onCreate(Bundle savedInstanceState) {
        super.onCreate(savedInstanceState);
        setContentView(R.layout.welcome);
        final TextView welcomeMsg=(TextView)findViewById(
            R.id.welcomemsg);
        Bundle extras = getIntent().getExtras();
        if(extras !=null) {
            String userName=extras.getString("username");
            welcomeMsg.setText("Welcome "+userName+" !");
        }
        Button gobackButton = (Button)this.findViewById(
            R.id.goback_button);
        gobackButton.setOnClickListener(new Button.
            OnClickListener(){
            public void onClick(View v) {
                setResult(RESULT_OK, null);
                finish();
            }
        });
    }
}
```

To inform the Android project about your subactivity `WelcomeActivity` in the
`AndroidManifest.xml` file, add the following statement in the `<application>` element:

```
<activity android:name=".WelcomeActivity" android:label=
    "@string/app_name" />
```

Now your application is ready to run. On running the application, the main activity prompts
the user to enter a name in the `EditText` control (see Figure 1.19 [top]). After the user enters a
name and selects the Start Activity button, the subactivity `WelcomeActivity` will be launched
displaying welcome message and the name entered in the main activity (see Figure 1.19
[middle]). After selecting the Go Back button from the subactivity, you will be navigated back
to the main activity. The `TextView` control confirms the navigation from the subactivity to
the main activity by displaying the message `Back` from the `WelcomeActivity` (see Figure 1.19
[bottom]).

Figure 1.19   Username entered in the first activity (top), welcome message displayed in the second activity along with the passed name from the first activity (middle), and navigating back to the first activity (bottom)

Summary

In this chapter, you learned about Google Nexus 7 and 10 features, differences between Android phones and tablets, and the procedure to make an Android phone application compatible for Android tablets. You saw how to create and run AVD for Android phones and tablets. You discovered the usage of different files and directories created in an Android project. Also, you learned about activities and the Android activity life cycle. Finally, you went through the steps to start an activity using intent and pass data from one activity to another.

In the next chapter, you will learn about the use of fragments, what their life cycle is like, and how they are practically applied in Android applications. You will also see how fragments can be dynamically added to an application through Java code. In addition, you will see how data is communicated among two fragments. Finally, you will learn how to create the specialized fragments ListFragment, DialogFragment, and PreferenceFragment.

2

Fragments

This chapter is focused on understanding fragments. So that Android applications are more manageable, they are often divided into fragments. Having their own independent user interface, fragments can be easily added or removed from an application, making it suitable to different screen sizes. In this chapter, you will learn about the use of fragments, their life cycle, and how they are practically applied in Android applications. You will also see how fragments can be added dynamically to an application through Java code. In addition to this, you will learn how data is communicated among two fragments. The chapter will explain using the specialized fragments `ListFragment`, `DialogFragment`, and `PreferenceFragment`. You will learn to display options through the `ListFragment` display dialog with `DialogFragment` and set user preferences with `PreferenceFragment`.

To support phones, 7-inch tablets, and 10-inch tablets, it is assumed that you will follow these three steps in all the applications in this book:

1. Create an XML file named `dimens.xml` in the `res/values` folder with the following given code:

```xml
<?xml version="1.0" encoding="utf-8"?>
<resources>
    <dimen name="text_size">14sp</dimen>
</resources>
```

2. Create two folders named `values-sw600dp` and `values-sw720dp` in the `res` folder, and copy the `dimens.xml` file from the `res/values` folder into these two folders.

3. Set the value of the dimension resource `text_size` in the `dimens.xml` file found in the `values-sw600dp` and `values-sw720dp` folders to `24sp` and `32sp`, respectively.

Refer to the recipe "Converting an Android Phone Application into an Android Tablet Application" in Chapter 1, "Overview of Android Tablet Applications," for more information.

Recipe: Introducing Fragments

Fragments enable you to fragment or divide your activities into encapsulated reusable modules, each with its own user interface, making your application suitable to different screen sizes. That is, depending on the available screen size, you can add or remove fragments in your activities.

The width and height of the screen changes when a device is oriented from portrait to landscape mode. In landscape mode, the screen becomes wider and shows empty space on the right. The height becomes smaller and hides the controls on the bottom of the display. There is a difference in screen sizes between the Android tablets, too.

When developing an application, you need to arrange views in such a way that the user can view everything in both landscape and portrait mode. If you don't organize the views with this in mind, problems will arise if the user switches modes while running an application. Fragments enable you to arrange views that suit both landscape and portrait mode.

A *fragment* is a combination of an activity and a layout and contains a set of views that make up an independent and atomic user interface. For example, one or more fragments can be embedded in the activity to fill up the blank space that appears on the right when switching from portrait to landscape mode. Similarly, the fragment(s) can be dynamically removed if the screen size is unable to accommodate the views. That is, the fragments make it possible for you to manage the views depending on the target device and configuration.

For example, assume that you have two fragments, `Fragment1` and `Fragment2`, each having its own set of views. If the device is in portrait mode, you can create two activities, each having a single fragment, and display one activity at a time. If the device screen is able to accommodate views of both `Fragment1` and `Fragment2`, these can be embedded into a single activity to fill up the screen.

A fragment is like a subactivity with its own life cycle and view hierarchy. You can add or remove fragments while the activity is running. The fragments exist within the context of an activity and cannot be used without one.

Recipe: Understanding the Life Cycle of a Fragment

To create a fragment, you need to extend the `Fragment` class and implement several life cycle callback methods. The life cycle of a fragment(s) is affected by the activity's life cycle in which it is embedded. That is, when the activity is paused, all the fragments in it are paused. Similarly, if an activity is destroyed, all its fragments are destroyed as well. The life cycle of a fragment includes several callback methods (see Figure 2.1), as listed here:

- **onAttach()**—Called when the fragment is attached to the activity.

- **onCreate()**—Called when creating the fragment. The method is used to initialize the items of the fragment that you want to retain when the fragment is resumed after it is paused or stopped.

- **onCreateView()**—Called to create the view for the fragment.

- **onActivityCreated()**—Called when the activity's onCreate() method is returned.

- **onStart()**—Called when the fragment is visible to the user. This method is associated with the activity's onStart().

- **onResume()**—Called when the fragment is visible and is running. The method is associated with the activity's onResume().

- **onPause()**—Called when the fragment is visible but does not have focus. The method is attached to the activity's onPause().

- **onStop()**—Called when the fragment is not visible. The method is associated with the activity's onStop().

- **onDestroyView()**—Called when the fragment is supposed to be saved or destroyed. The view hierarchy is removed from the fragment.

- **onDestroy()**—Called when the fragment is no longer in use. No view hierarchy is associated with the fragment, but the fragment is still attached to the activity.

- **onDetach()**—Called when the fragment is detached from the activity and resources allocated to the fragment are released.

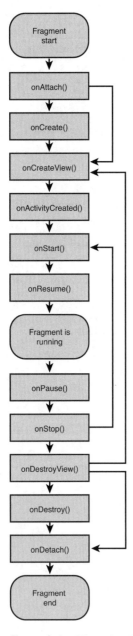

Figure 2.1   Life cycle of a fragment

Recipe: Creating Foreground Fragments, and Knowing the Difference Between Foreground and Background Fragments

The *foreground fragments* are those that interact with the user, take input, and process and display the desired result. Foreground fragments contain a set of views, making them visible on the screen. The background fragments, on the other hand, are those that don't interface with the users but perform the assigned tasks within the activity in the background. Because these fragments don't contain any user interface (UI) controls, the onCreateView() method is not called while defining background fragments.

To understand the concept of foreground fragments, create an Android project called ForegroundFragmentApp. In this application, you are going to create two fragments: Fragment1 and Fragment2. Fragment1 will contain a selection widget, ListView, that displays a couple of products to choose from. Fragment2 will contain a TextView control to display the product that was selected from the ListView of Fragment1. The fragments use individual XML layout files to define their views, so for the two fragments, add two XML files called fragment1.xml and fragment2.xml to the res/layout folder.

To define a ListView control in the first fragment, write the code shown in Listing 2.1 into the XML file fragment1.xml.

Listing 2.1   **Code Written into the XML File** fragment1.xml

```xml
<?xml version="1.0" encoding="utf-8"?>
<LinearLayout xmlns:android="http://schemas.android.com/apk/res/android"
    android:layout_width="match_parent"
    android:layout_height="match_parent"
    android:orientation="vertical"
    android:background="#0000FF" >
    <ListView
        android:id="@+id/products_list"
        android:layout_width="match_parent"
        android:layout_height="match_parent"
        android:drawSelectorOnTop="false" />
</LinearLayout>
```

You can see here that a ListView selection widget is defined with the ID products_list. For distinguishing the two fragments, the background of this fragment is set to blue. To define a TextView control for the second fragment, the code shown in Listing 2.2 is written into the XML file, fragment2.xml.

Listing 2.2   **Code Written into the XML File** `fragment2.xml`

```
<?xml version="1.0" encoding="utf-8"?>
<LinearLayout xmlns:android="http://schemas.android.com/apk/res/android"
    android:layout_width="match_parent"
    android:layout_height="match_parent"
    android:orientation="vertical" >
    <TextView
        android:id="@+id/selectedopt"
        android:layout_width="match_parent"
        android:layout_height="wrap_content"
        android:text=" Please select a product "
        android:textSize="@dimen/text_size"
        android:textStyle="bold"  />
</LinearLayout>
```

You can see that a `selectedopt` `TextView` control is defined and set to display `Please select a product`. The text displayed through the `TextView` control will appear in bold and in a size specified in the `text_size` dimension resource.

> **Note**
>
> The `text_size` dimension resource is assumed to be already defined in the `dimens.xml` file in `values`, `values-sw600dp` and `values-sw720dp` folders of your application

The default size of the list items displayed in `ListView` are suitable for phones but are quite smaller for tablets. To resize the list items of the `ListView` as per the device screen size, add one more XML file named `list_item.xml` to the `res/layout` folder. Write the following code in the `list_item.xml` file:

```
<?xml version="1.0" encoding="utf-8"?>
<TextView xmlns:android="http://schemas.android.com/apk/res/android"
    android:layout_width="match_parent"
    android:layout_height="match_parent"
    android:padding="6dp"
    android:textSize="@dimen/text_size"
    android:textStyle="bold" />
```

According to the preceding code, the list items of the `ListView` will be padded by 6dp spaces and will appear in bold and in the size defined in the dimension resource `text_size`.

Each fragment has a Java class that loads its UI from the XML file, so for the two fragments, you need to add two Java classes to your application. Add `Fragment1Activity.java` and `Fragment2Activity.java` to the `com.androidtablet.foregroundfragmentsapp` package of the application. The code shown in Listing 2.3 is written into the Java class file of the first fragment, `Fragment1Activity.java`.

Listing 2.3   **Code Written into the Java Class File** `Fragment1Activity.java`

```java
package com.androidtablet.foregroundfragmentapp;

import android.app.Fragment;
import android.os.Bundle;
import android.view.ViewGroup;
import android.view.View;
import android.view.LayoutInflater;
import android.widget.ListView;
import android.widget.ArrayAdapter;
import android.content.Context;
import android.widget.AdapterView;
import android.widget.AdapterView.OnItemClickListener;
import android.widget.TextView;
import android.app.Activity;

public class Fragment1Activity extends Fragment {
    OnOptionSelectedListener  myListener;

    @Override
    public View onCreateView(LayoutInflater inflater, ViewGroup
        container, Bundle savedInstanceState) {
        Context c = getActivity().getApplicationContext();
        View vw = inflater.inflate(R.layout.fragment1,
            container, false);
        String[] products={"Camera", "Laptop", "Watch",
            "Smartphone", "Television"};
        ListView productsList = (ListView) vw.findViewById(
            R.id.products_list);
        ArrayAdapter<String> arrayAdpt= new ArrayAdapter<String>
            (c, R.layout.list_item, products);
        productsList.setAdapter(arrayAdpt);
        productsList.setOnItemClickListener(new
            OnItemClickListener(){
            @Override
            public void onItemClick(AdapterView<?> parent, View
                v, int position, long id){
                myListener.onOptionSelected(((TextView)
                    v).getText().toString());
            }
        });
        return vw;
    }
    public interface OnOptionSelectedListener {
        public void onOptionSelected(String message);
    }
```

```
@Override
public void onAttach(Activity activity) {
    super.onAttach(activity);
    try {
        myListener = (OnOptionSelectedListener) activity;
    } catch (ClassCastException e) {
        throw new ClassCastException(activity.toString() + "
        must implement OnItemClickListener");
    }
}
}
```

You can see that the Java class for the fragment extends the Fragment base class. To access and draw the UI for the fragment, the onCreateView() method is overridden. In the onCreateView() method, a LayoutInflater object is used to inflate the UI—the ListView control you defined in the fragment1.xml file. The ListView and TextView controls are accessed from the layout files and mapped to the objects productsList and selectedOpt, respectively. The arrayAdpt array adapter containing the elements of the array, products in TextView form, is assigned to the ListView control for displaying choices to the user. The OnItemClickListener interface is implemented via an anonymous class that implements a callback method, onItemClick(). The reference to the anonymous class is passed to the ListView, productsList, to invoke the callback method onItemClick() when any of the items in ListView is clicked.

You see that an interface OnOptionSelectedListener is defined and that it has a single method: onOptionSelected(). This means that the activity associated with this fragment needs to implement the OnOptionSelectedListener interface and define the body of the onOptionSelected() method. When any item from the ListView is selected, the onOptionSelected() method in the implementing activity will be called, passing the selected item name as a parameter to it.

To load the UI of the second fragment from the XML file fragment2.xml, write the code shown in Listing 2.4 into the Java class file of the second fragment, Fragment2Activity. java.

Listing 2.4   **Code Written into the Java Class File** Fragment2Activity.java

```
package com.androidtablet.foregroundfragmentapp;

import android.app.Fragment;
import android.os.Bundle;
import android.view.ViewGroup;
import android.view.View;
import android.view.LayoutInflater;
import android.widget.TextView;
```

```
public class Fragment2Activity extends Fragment {
    @Override
    public View onCreateView(LayoutInflater inflater, ViewGroup
        container, Bundle savedInstanceState) {
        return inflater.inflate(R.layout.fragment2, container,
            false);
    }

    public void dispOption(String msg){
        TextView selectedOpt = (TextView) getActivity().
            findViewById(R.id.selectedopt);
        selectedOpt.setText("You have selected "+msg);
    }
}
```

Like the Java class of the first fragment, this class extends the `Fragment` base class. The
`onCreateView()` method is overridden, where a `LayoutInflater` object is used to inflate
the `TextView` control you defined in the `fragment2.xml` file. The `dispOption()` method is
defined, where the `TextView` control with ID `selectedopt` is accessed and set to display the
product name passed to it as the parameter.

> **Note**
>
> The `getActivity()` method used in the preceding code returns the activity with which the cur-
> rent fragment is associated. This method enables activity and fragment interaction.

To accommodate both the fragments in the application, the code shown in Listing 2.5 is
written into the layout file `activity_foreground_fragment_app.xml`.

Listing 2.5 **The Layout File** `activity_foreground_fragment_app.xml` **After Adding the
Two Fragments**

```
<LinearLayout xmlns:android="http://schemas.android.com/apk/res/android"
    xmlns:tools="http://schemas.android.com/tools"
    android:layout_width="match_parent"
    android:layout_height="match_parent"
    android:orientation="horizontal" >
    <fragment
        android:name="com.androidtablet.foregroundfragmentapp.
            Fragment1Activity"
        android:id="@+id/fragment1"
        android:layout_weight="1"
        android:layout_width="wrap_content"
        android:layout_height="match_parent" />
    <fragment
        android:name="com.androidtablet.foregroundfragmentapp.
```

```
            Fragment2Activity"
        android:id="@+id/fragment2"
        android:layout_weight="0"
        android:layout_width="wrap_content"
        android:layout_height="match_parent" />
</LinearLayout>
```

Here you can see that the two fragments are added to the activity through the <fragment>
elements. The fragments are assigned the IDs fragment1 and fragment2, respectively. The
fragments are set to refer to their respective Java class through the android:name attribute.
The first fragment refers to its Java class file Fragment1Activity, which was placed in the
com.androidtablet.foregroundfragmentapp package. The orientation of the container,
LinearLayout, was set to Horizontal, so the fragments will appear beside each other.

The Java activity file needs to implement the OnOptionSelectedListener interface and hence define its onOptionSelected() method. Recall that you defined an
OnOptionSelectedListener interface in the Fragment1Activity.java file. The code written
in the Java activity file, ForegroundFragmentAppActivity.java, is shown in Listing 2.6.

Listing 2.6   **Code Written into the Java Activity File** ForegroundFragmentAppActivity.java

```
package com.androidtablet.foregroundfragmentapp;

import android.app.Activity;
import android.os.Bundle;
import com.androidtablet.foregroundfragmentapp.
    Fragment1Activity.OnOptionSelectedListener;

public class ForegroundFragmentAppActivity extends Activity
    implements OnOptionSelectedListener {
    @Override
    public void onCreate(Bundle savedInstanceState) {
        super.onCreate(savedInstanceState);
        setContentView(R.layout.activity_foreground_
            fragment_app);
    }
    public void onOptionSelected(String msg) {
        Fragment2Activity frag2 = (Fragment2Activity)
            getFragmentManager().findFragmentById(
            R.id.fragment2);
        frag2.dispOption(msg);
    }
}
```

The onOptionSelected() method will be invoked when any item from the ListView is selected. To the onOptionSelected() method, the item name selected from the ListView is passed as a parameter. The item name is displayed on the screen by calling the dispOption() method of fragment2. That is, using FragmentManager, fragment2 is accessed and the dispOption() method defined in its activity, Fragment2Activity, is invoked.

After you run the application on the tablets, the two UIs defined in Fragment1 and Fragment2 will appear side by side. The ListView of Fragment1 displays the list of items, and Fragment2 displays the TextView asking users to Please select a product, as shown in Figure 2.2 (top). After a product has been selected from the ListView, its name will be displayed through the TextView, as shown in Figure 2.2 (bottom).

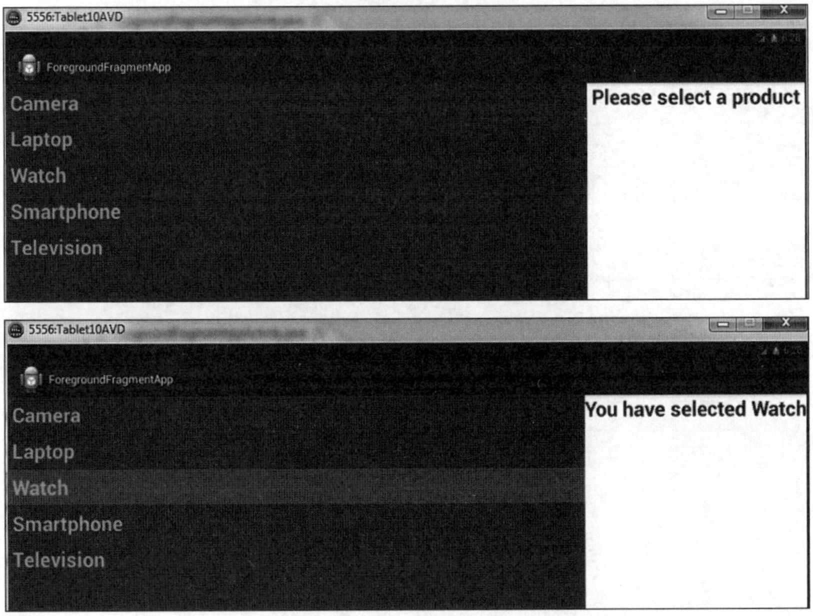

Figure 2.2   ListView and TextView controls displayed in the tablet via two fragments (top) and the TextView of the second fragment showing the item selected from the ListView of the first fragment (bottom)

When an application is run on the Android phone in landscape orientation, as expected, the contents of the two fragments, Fragment1 and Fragment2, will appear side by side. The ListView of Fragment1 will display the list of items, and Fragment2 will display a TextView prompting the user to select a product, as shown in Figure 2.3 (top). The name of the selected product from the ListView is displayed through the TextView, as shown in Figure 2.3 (bottom).

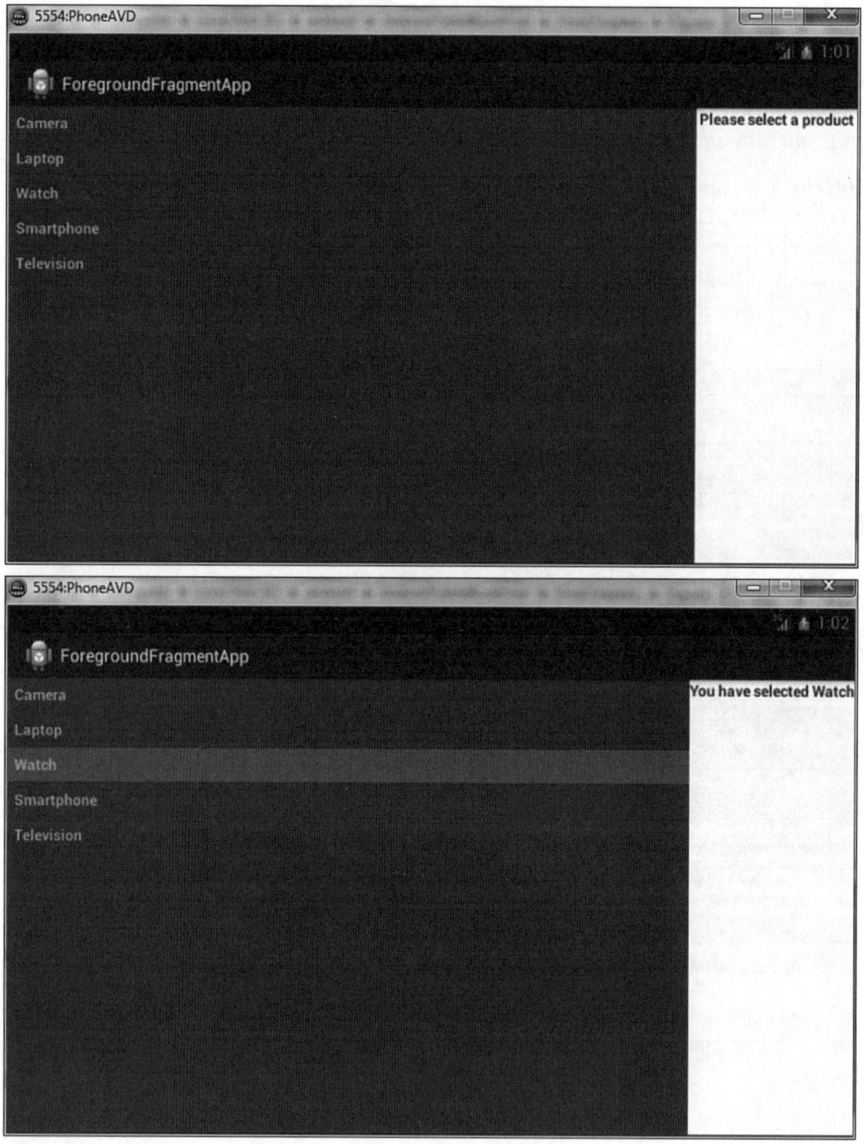

Figure 2.3   `ListView` and `TextView` displayed in the phone in landscape orientation (top) and the `TextView` of the second fragment showing the item selected from the `ListView` (bottom)

Because in landscape orientation the Android phone has enough width, there is no space issue with displaying the contents of the fragments side by side. The actual problem with this application is that the two fragments' content will appear side by side even when the phone is in portrait orientation (see Figure 2.4 [left] and [right]). In portrait orientation, the width of the phone is not sufficient to display the content of two fragments simultaneously. As a result, the content of the two fragments shrinks.

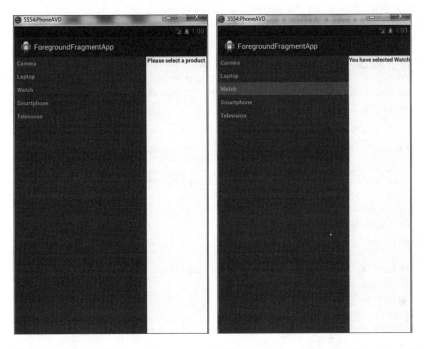

Figure 2.4 `ListView` and `TextView` displayed side by side in the phone in portrait orientation (left) and the `TextView` showing the name of the item selected from the `ListView` (right)

What is expected is that when the phone is in portrait orientation, only the content of one fragment is displayed on the screen. That is, only the `ListView` must appear displaying the list of products. When any product is selected from the `ListView`, the name of the selected product should appear on another screen. You will learn to do so in the next recipe.

Recipe: Adding and Removing Fragments with Device Orientation

The main benefit of using fragments is the freedom to add fragments to the activity when a device is switched to landscape mode or when it has empty space on the right. It's also easier to remove fragments when the device switches to portrait mode. Modify your

ForegroundFragmentApp application in such a way that when the device is an Android phone and it is in portrait mode, only one fragment is made visible; when the device is any tablet or a phone in landscape mode, two fragments are made visible side by side to fill up the empty space on the right.

In other words, you want only the ListView control to appear when the phone is in portrait mode. When an item is selected from the ListView, the TextView should appear on the next screen in another activity. Also when the phone is in landscape mode or when the device is any tablet, both controls, the ListView and TextView, should appear beside each other because there will be enough space on the right.

The layout file activity_foreground_fragment_app.xml is set to display the views when the device is in portrait mode. Because you want only Fragment1 to be visible when the phone is in portrait mode, the layout file activity_foreground_fragment_app.xml is modified to appear as shown in Listing 2.7.

Listing 2.7 **The Layout File** activity_foreground_fragment_app.xml **with a Single Fragment**

```
<LinearLayout xmlns:android="http://schemas.android.com/apk/res/android"
    xmlns:tools="http://schemas.android.com/tools"
    android:layout_width="match_parent"
    android:layout_height="match_parent"
    android:orientation="horizontal" >
    <fragment
        android:name="com.androidtablet.foregroundfragmentapp.
            Fragment1Activity"
        android:id="@+id/fragment1"
        android:layout_weight="1"
        android:layout_width="wrap_content"
        android:layout_height="match_parent" />
</LinearLayout>
```

You can see that Fragment1 with the ID fragment1 is added to the layout file. This means that only the ListView control of Fragment1 will be displayed when the phone is in portrait mode. Because you want the UI of Fragment1 and Fragment2 to appear when the phone is in landscape mode, create a folder called layout-land in the res folder and copy the XML file activity_foreground_fragment_app.xml from the res/layout folder to the res/layout-land folder.

Remember: When a phone switches to landscape mode, the layout file from the res/layout-land folder is used to display views on the screen. When the phone switches to portrait mode, the layout file from the res/layout folder is used for displaying views on the screen.

To the activity_foreground_fragment_app.xml file in the res/layout-land folder, add the two fragments Fragment1 and Fragment2. After adding these two fragments, the file will appear as shown in Listing 2.8.

Listing 2.8   **The Layout File** `activity_foreground_fragment_app.xml` **with Two Fragments**

```
<LinearLayout xmlns:android="http://schemas.android.com/apk/res/android"
    xmlns:tools="http://schemas.android.com/tools"
    android:layout_width="match_parent"
    android:layout_height="match_parent"
    android:orientation="horizontal" >
    <fragment
        android:name="com.androidtablet.foregroundfragmentapp.
            Fragment1Activity"
        android:id="@+id/fragment1"
        android:layout_weight="1"
        android:layout_width="wrap_content"
        android:layout_height="match_parent" />
    <fragment
        android:name="com.androidtablet.foregroundfragmentapp.
            Fragment2Activity"
        android:id="@+id/fragment2"
        android:layout_weight="0"
        android:layout_width="wrap_content"
        android:layout_height="match_parent" />
</LinearLayout>
```

You can see that `Fragment1` and `Fragment2` were added to the layout file.

Next, you need to modify the Java class of `Fragment1`, `Fragment1Activity`, to appear as shown in Listing 2.9. Only the code in bold is newly added; the rest is the same as you saw in Listing 2.3.

Listing 2.9   **Code Written into the Java Class** `Fragment1Activity.java`

```
package com.androidtablet.foregroundfragmentapp;

import android.app.Fragment;
import android.os.Bundle;
import android.view.ViewGroup;
import android.view.View;
import android.view.LayoutInflater;
import android.widget.ListView;
import android.widget.ArrayAdapter;
import android.content.Context;
import android.widget.AdapterView;
import android.widget.AdapterView.OnItemClickListener;
import android.widget.TextView;
import android.app.Activity;
import android.content.res.Configuration;
import android.content.Intent;
```

```
public class Fragment1Activity extends Fragment {
    OnOptionSelectedListener  myListener;
    boolean large, xlarge;

    @Override
    public View onCreateView(LayoutInflater inflater, ViewGroup
        container, Bundle savedInstanceState) {
        Context c = getActivity().getApplicationContext();
        View vw = inflater.inflate(R.layout.fragment1,
            container, false);
        String[] products={"Camera", "Laptop", "Watch",
            "Smartphone", "Television"};
        large = ((getResources().getConfiguration().screenLayout
            & Configuration.SCREENLAYOUT_SIZE_MASK) ==
            Configuration.SCREENLAYOUT_SIZE_LARGE);
        xlarge =((getResources().getConfiguration().screenLayout
            & Configuration.SCREENLAYOUT_SIZE_MASK) ==
            Configuration.SCREENLAYOUT_SIZE_XLARGE);
        ListView productsList = (ListView) vw.findViewById(
            R.id.products_list);
        ArrayAdapter<String> arrayAdpt= new ArrayAdapter<String>
            (c, R.layout.list_item, products);
        productsList.setAdapter(arrayAdpt);
        productsList.setOnItemClickListener(new
            OnItemClickListener(){
            @Override
            public void onItemClick(AdapterView<?> parent, View
                v, int position, long id){
                if (getResources().getConfiguration().orientation
                    == Configuration.ORIENTATION_LANDSCAPE ||
                    large || xlarge){
                    myListener.onOptionSelected(((TextView)
                        v).getText().toString());
                } else {
                    Intent intent = new Intent(getActivity().
                    getApplicationContext(),
                    DisplayItemActivity.class);
                    intent.putExtra("item", ((TextView)
                        v).getText().toString());
                    startActivity(intent);
                }
            }
        });
        return vw;
    }
    public interface OnOptionSelectedListener {
        public void onOptionSelected(String message);
```

```
    }

    @Override
    public void onAttach(Activity activity) {
        super.onAttach(activity);
        try {
            myListener = (OnOptionSelectedListener) activity;
        } catch (ClassCastException e) {
            throw new ClassCastException(activity.toString() + "
            must implement OnItemClickListener");
        }
    }
}
```

Take a look at the onItemClick() method that is called when any item in the ListView shown through Fragment1 is selected. In the method, you first check to see if the device is of large screen or extra large screen (tablet) or if it is in landscape mode. You know that Fragment2 will be available when the device is in landscape mode or has a large or extra large screen. So if the device has a large screen or is in landscape mode, the onOptionSelected() method in the implementing activity will be called, passing the selected item name as parameter to it so that is displayed on the screen via TextView control of Fragment2.

If the device is of normal screen (phone) and is in portrait mode, Fragment2 will not be available, so the item name selected from the ListView will be displayed in another screen. Displaying another screen requires another activity. To start an activity, you first need to create a new intent specifying the current application context and the class name of the activity that you want to launch. Then you need to pass this intent to the startActivity() method. While creating a new intent, specify the class name of the new activity as DisplayItemActivity. Because you want to display the item that is selected from the ListView in the new activity, you put the selected item in the intent under the item key. In the DisplayItemActivity, you will retrieve the selected item using this key.

Add a Java class called DisplayItemActivity.java to your project and write the content as shown in Listing 2.10.

Listing 2.10 Code Written into the Activity File for the Second Fragment
DisplayItemActivity.java

```
package com.androidtablet.foregroundfragmentapp;

import android.app.Activity;
import android.content.res.Configuration;
import android.os.Bundle;
import android.widget.TextView;

public class DisplayItemActivity extends Activity{
    @Override
```

```
protected void onCreate(Bundle savedInstanceState) {
    super.onCreate(savedInstanceState);
    if (getResources().getConfiguration().orientation ==
        Configuration.ORIENTATION_LANDSCAPE) {
        finish();
        return;
    }
    setContentView(R.layout.fragment2);
    Bundle extras = getIntent().getExtras();
    if (extras != null) {
        String selectedItem = extras.getString("item");
        TextView selectedOpt = (TextView) findViewById(R.id.selectedopt);
        selectedOpt.setText("You have selected "+selectedItem);
    }
}
}
}
```

Here you check to see if the device is in landscape mode. If it is, you finish the activity (termi-nate the screen). It is not required because the views of both the fragments can be accom-modated in a single screen. If the device is an Android phone and it is in portrait mode, the getExtras() method is called to see if anything is passed to it. If any Bundle is passed to the intent, the value stored in it under the item key is accessed. The TextView from the fragment2.xml is accessed and mapped to a TextView object, selectedOpt, and the value passed to the intent (the name of the item selected from the ListView) is displayed via the TextView control.

Recall that only the components that are declared in the application's manifest file, AndroidManifest.xml, are visible to Android. Hence, the newly added activity, DisplayItemActivity.java, must be declared in AndroidManifest.xml to make it visible to Android through the following statement:

```
<activity android:name=".DisplayItemActivity" android:label="@string/app_name" />
```

In this application, you want the application to behave the same when the device is a phone and is in landscape orientation and when the device is a tablet in either orientation. So copy the layout resources of the phone in landscape mode (that is, the content in the layout-land folder) into the resource folders of the tablets. You have not yet created the resource folders for the tablets. So create two folders named layout-sw600dp and layout-sw720dp in the res folder, and copy the activity layout file activity_foreground_fragment_app.xml from the res/layout-land folder to both of these folders.

After running the application, if the device is an Android phone (of normal screen) and is in portrait mode, only the UI of Fragment1 will be visible, as shown in Figure 2.5 (left). When an item from the ListView is selected, the selected item name is displayed via TextView on the new screen or activity, as shown in Figure 2.5 (right).

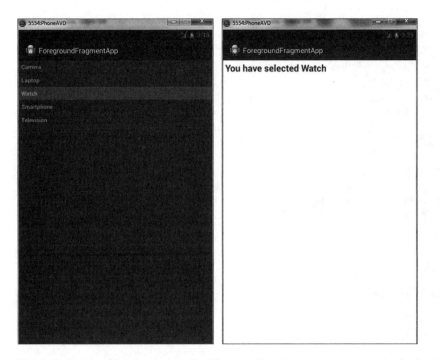

Figure 2.5   In portrait mode, only the UI of the first fragment, ListView, is displayed (left), and the item selected from the ListView is displayed via another activity (right).

When the device is switched to landscape mode or has a large or extra large screen (tablet), the UI of both the fragments, ListView and TextView, will be visible side by side, as shown in Figure 2.6 (top). The selected item from the ListView is shown via the TextView on the same screen, as you see in Figure 2.6 (bottom).

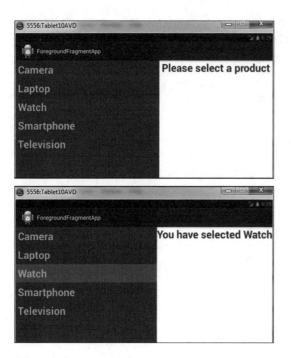

Figure 2.6   A phone in landscape orientation or a tablet in either orientation will display the UI of both the fragments, ListView and TextView, side by side (top), and the item selected from the ListView will be displayed via the TextView of the second fragment on the same screen (bottom).

Recipe: Understanding the Role of FragmentManager and FragmentTransaction in Handling Fragments

As the name suggests, the FragmentManager is used to manage fragments in an activity. It provides the methods to access the fragments that are available in the activity and enables you to perform the FragmentTransaction required to add, remove, and replace fragments. To access the FragmentManager, use the getFragmentManager() method, as shown here:

```
FragmentManager fragmentManager = getFragmentManager();
```

To perform fragment transactions, you use the instance of the FragmentTransaction as shown here:

```
FragmentTransaction fragmentTransaction = fragmentManager.beginTransaction();
```

A new FragmentTransaction is created using the beginTransaction() method of the FragmentManager. The following code shows how to add a fragment:

```
private static final String TAG1 = "1";
FragmentManager fragmentManager = getFragmentManager()
   FragmentTransaction fragmentTransaction = fragmentManager.beginTransaction();
Fragment1Activity fragment = new Fragment1Activity();
fragmentTransaction.add(R.id.fragment_container, fragment, TAG1);
fragmentTransaction.commit();
```

Here, the `Fragment1Activity` is the Java class of the fragment, which is also used to load the UI of the fragment from its XML file. You assume that the `fragment_container` is the ID of the container that exists in the layout file where you want to put your fragment. Usually, `LinearLayout` or `FrameLayout` is used as the `fragment_container`. `TAG1` refers to the unique ID to identify and access the fragment. You use the `commit()` method to apply the changes. The commit does not happen immediately and might happen later, when the thread is ready. Because there might be a delay in the `commit()` method, don't try to get reference to the fragment that you just created.

> **Note**
> To add fragments dynamically, a container view must exist in the layout in which the views of the fragment will be displayed.

Before adding a fragment, it is wise to check whether one already exists by modifying the code as shown here:

```
private static final String TAG1 = "1";
FragmentManager fragmentManager = getFragmentManager();
FragmentTransaction fragmentTransaction =
    fragmentManager.beginTransaction();
if(null==fragmentManager.findFragmentByTag(TAG1)){
    Fragment1Activity fragment = new Fragment1Activity();
    fragmentTransaction.add(R.id.fragment_container,
        fragment, TAG1);
}
fragmentTransaction.commit();
```

You can see that the `findFragmentByTag()` method of the `FragmentManager` checks to see if any fragment with the given tag exists. One more method that can be used to identify a fragment is `findFragmentById()`. The `findFragmentById()` method identifies the fragment that is added to the activity layout; otherwise, the `findFragmentByTag()` method is preferred. The `Fragment1Activity` in the preceding code is a Java class meant for loading the views defined in the fragment's layout file.

To replace the fragment or content that is being displayed in the `fragment_container` with the `View(s)` from another fragment, use the `replace()` method of the `FragmentTransaction`, as shown here:

```
private static final String TAG2 = "2";
fragmentTransact.replace(R.id.fragment_container, fragment2, TAG2);
```

In this statement, the view(s) of `fragment2` will replace the content being displayed in the `fragment_container` of the activity layout. To remove a fragment, you identify it either through the `findFragmentById()` or `findFragmentByTag()` methods and then use the `remove()` method of `FragmentTransaction`. The code that follows identifies the fragment via the `findFragmentById()` method and then removes it:

```
FragmentTransaction fragmentTransaction =
    fragmentManager.beginTransaction();
Fragment fragment =  fragmentManager.findFragmentById(
    R.id.fragment);
fragmentTransaction.remove(fragment);
fragmentTransaction.commit();
```

Here you assume that a fragment with the `fragment` ID exists in the activity. To identify the fragment through the `findFragmentByTag()` method, the statement can be replaced by the following:

```
Fragment fragment = fragmentManager.findFragmentByTag(TAG1);
```

Recipe: Creating Fragments Dynamically at Runtime

Besides defining fragments statically by using <fragment> elements in the layout file of the application, you can define them through code at runtime. For creating, adding, and replacing fragments to an activity dynamically, you use the `FragmentManager`.

You will better understand the concept of defining a fragment dynamically through a running example. Create an Android project called `FragmentsByCodeApp`. In this application, you will be creating two fragments dynamically: `Fragment1` and `Fragment2`. `Fragment1` will contain a selection widget, `ListView`, that displays a couple of products to choose from. `Fragment2` will contain a `TextView` control to display the product that was selected from the `ListView` of `Fragment1`.

To accommodate the two fragments in the application, you need to define their respective containers. You will define two `FrameLayouts` as containers for the two fragments in the layout file `activity_fragments_by_code_app.xml`, as shown in Listing 2.11.

Listing 2.11   **Code Written into the Layout File** `activity_fragments_by_code_app.xml`

```
<LinearLayout xmlns:android="http://schemas.android.com/apk/res/android"
    xmlns:tools="http://schemas.android.com/tools"
    android:layout_width="match_parent"
    android:layout_height="match_parent"
    android:orientation="horizontal" >
    <LinearLayout
        android:id="@+id/frag1_container"
        android:layout_width="wrap_content"
        android:layout_height="match_parent"
        android:layout_weight="1" />
```

```
    <LinearLayout
        android:id="@+id/frag2_container"
        android:layout_width="wrap_content"
        android:layout_height="match_parent"
        android:layout_weight="0" />
</LinearLayout>
```

Here you can see that the two `LinearLayout` containers are added to the activity with IDs `frag1_container` and `frag2_container`, respectively. Through Java code, you will be defining two fragments dynamically and will store them in these two containers. The orientation of the outermost container, `LinearLayout`, is set to horizontal, so the fragments will appear beside each other. Out of the two fragments that you want to define, the first fragment will display a selection widget, `ListView`, to show a few products, and the second fragment will display a `TextView` control to display the selected product from the `ListView`. To define views for the two fragments, you add two XML files called `fragment1.xml` and `fragment2.xml` to the `res/layout` folder of the project. To define `ListView` for the first fragment, you add the code as shown in Listing 2.12 to the XML file `fragment1.xml`.

Listing 2.12 **Code Written into the XML File** `fragment1.xml`

```
<?xml version="1.0" encoding="utf-8"?>
<LinearLayout xmlns:android="http://schemas.android.com/apk/res/android"
    android:layout_width="match_parent"
    android:layout_height="match_parent"
    android:orientation="vertical"
    android:background="#0000FF"  >
    <ListView
        android:id="@+id/products_list"
        android:layout_width="match_parent"
        android:layout_height="match_parent"
        android:drawSelectorOnTop="false" />
</LinearLayout>
```

You can see here that a `ListView` selection widget is defined with the ID `products_list`. For distinguishing the two fragments, the background of this fragment is set to blue. To define a `TextView` control for the second fragment, the code shown in Listing 2.13 is written into the XML file `fragment2.xml`.

Listing 2.13 **Code Written into the XML File** `fragment2.xml`

```
<?xml version="1.0" encoding="utf-8"?>
<LinearLayout xmlns:android="http://schemas.android.com/apk/res/android"
    android:layout_width="match_parent"
    android:layout_height="match_parent"
    android:orientation="vertical" >
    <TextView
```

```
            android:id="@+id/selectedopt"
            android:layout_width="match_parent"
            android:layout_height="wrap_content"
            android:text=" Please select a product "
            android:textSize="@dimen/text_size"
            android:textStyle="bold"  />
</LinearLayout>
```

You can see that a `selectedopt` `TextView` control is defined and set to display the message `Please select a product`. The text is set to appear in bold and in the size defined in the dimension resource, `text_size`.

To resize the list items of the `ListView` as per the device screen size, add an XML file named `list_item.xml` to the `res/layout` folder. Write the code as shown below in the `list_item.xml` file:

```
<?xml version="1.0" encoding="utf-8"?>
<TextView xmlns:android="http://schemas.android.com/apk/res/android"
    android:layout_width="match_parent"
    android:layout_height="match_parent"
    android:padding="6dp"
    android:textSize="@dimen/text_size"
    android:textStyle="bold" />
```

The preceding code will pad the list items of the `ListView` by 6dp spaces and will make them appear in bold and in the size defined in the dimension resource `text_size`.

To load UI from the respective XML files, `fragment1.xml` and `fragment2.xml`, you will add Java class for each of the two fragments. Two Java classes called `Fragment1Activity.java` and `Fragment2Activity.java` are added to the `com.androidtablet.fragmentsbycodeapp` package of the application. The code shown in Listing 2.14 is written into the Java class file of the first fragment, `Fragment1Activity.java`.

Listing 2.14   Code Written into the Java Class File `Fragment1Activity.java`

```
package com.androidtablet.fragmentsbycodeapp;

import android.app.Fragment;
import android.os.Bundle;
import android.view.ViewGroup;
import android.view.View;
import android.view.LayoutInflater;
import android.widget.ListView;
import android.widget.ArrayAdapter;
import android.content.Context;
import android.widget.AdapterView;
import android.widget.AdapterView.OnItemClickListener;
```

```
import android.widget.TextView;
import android.app.Activity;

public class Fragment1Activity extends Fragment {
    OnOptionSelectedListener  myListener;

    @Override
    public View onCreateView(LayoutInflater inflater,
        ViewGroup container, Bundle savedInstanceState) {
        Context c = getActivity().getApplicationContext();
        View vw = inflater.inflate(R.layout.fragment1,
            container, false);
        String[] products={"Camera", "Laptop",
            "Watch", "Smartphone", "Television"};
        ListView productsList = (ListView) vw.
            findViewById(R.id.products_list);
        ArrayAdapter<String> arrayAdpt= new ArrayAdapter
            <String>(c, R.layout.list_item, products);
        productsList.setAdapter(arrayAdpt);
        productsList.setOnItemClickListener(new
            OnItemClickListener(){
            @Override
            public void onItemClick(AdapterView<?> parent,
                View v, int position, long id){
                myListener.onOptionSelected(((TextView)
                    v).getText().toString());
            }
        });
        return vw;
    }
    public interface OnOptionSelectedListener {
        public void onOptionSelected(String message);
    }

    @Override
    public void onAttach(Activity activity) {
        super.onAttach(activity);
        try {
            myListener = (OnOptionSelectedListener)
                activity;
        } catch (ClassCastException e) {
            throw new ClassCastException(activity.toString() +
            " must implement OnItemClickListener");
        }
    }
}
```

You can see that the Java class `Fragment1Activity` extends the `Fragment` base class. In the `onCreateView()` method, a `LayoutInflater` object is used to inflate the `ListView` control defined in the `fragment1.xml` file. The `ListView` control is accessed from the layout file and is mapped to the object `productsList`. The `arrayAdpt` array adapter containing the elements of the array `products` is assigned to the `ListView` control to show different products on the screen. The `OnItemClickListener` interface is implemented via an anonymous class that implements a callback method, `onItemClick()`. The reference to the anonymous class is passed to the `ListView`, `productsList`, to invoke the callback method `onItemClick()` when any item in `ListView` is clicked.

An `OnOptionSelectedListener` interface is defined with a single method: `onOptionSelected()`. The activity associated with this fragment will implement the `OnOptionSelectedListener` interface and will define the body of the `onOptionSelected()` method. In the `onItemClick()` method, the `onOptionSelected()` method is accessed, passing the item name that is selected from the `ListView` to it.

Next, you need to write code in the Java class file `Fragment2Activity.java` to accomplish the following two tasks:

- Load the UI of the second fragment from the XML file, `fragment2.xml`.

- Define the `dispOption()` method that will display the product name selected by the user.

To complete these two tasks, the code shown in Listing 2.15 is written into the Java class file `Fragment2Activity.java`.

Listing 2.15   **Code Written into the Java Class File** `Fragment2.Activity.java`

```
package com.androidtablet.fragmentsbycodeapp;

import android.app.Fragment;
import android.os.Bundle;
import android.view.ViewGroup;
import android.view.View;
import android.view.LayoutInflater;
import android.widget.TextView;

public class Fragment2Activity extends Fragment {
    @Override
    public View onCreateView(LayoutInflater inflater,
        ViewGroup container, Bundle savedInstanceState) {
        return inflater.inflate(R.layout.fragment2,
            container, false);
    }

    public void dispOption(String msg){
        TextView selectedOpt = (TextView) getActivity().
```

```
            findViewById(R.id.selectedopt);
        selectedOpt.setText("You have selected "+msg);
    }
}
```

Again, to create the fragment, the Java class `Fragment2Activity` extends the `Fragment` base class. The `onCreateView()` method is overridden, whereby a `LayoutInflater` object is used to inflate the `TextView` control defined in the `fragment2.xml` file. The product name selected from the `ListView` is passed to the `dispOption()` method that displays it through the `TextView` control.

To create two fragments and add them to their respective containers, `frag1_container` and `frag2_container` defined in the activity layout file, you write the code shown in Listing 2.16 to the main Java activity file, `FragmentsByCodeAppActivity.java`.

Listing 2.16 **Code Written into the Java Activity File** `FragmentsByCodeAppActivity.java`

```
package com.androidtablet.fragmentsbycodeapp;

import android.os.Bundle;
import android.app.Activity;
import android.app.FragmentTransaction;
import android.app.FragmentManager;
import com.androidtablet.fragmentsbycodeapp.
    Fragment1Activity.OnOptionSelectedListener;

public class FragmentsByCodeAppActivity extends Activity implements
OnOptionSelectedListener {
    private static final String TAG1 = "1";
    private static final String TAG2 = "2";
    @Override
    public void onCreate(Bundle savedInstanceState) {
        super.onCreate(savedInstanceState);
        setContentView(R.layout.activity_fragments
            _by_code_app);
        FragmentManager fragmentManager =
            getFragmentManager();
        FragmentTransaction fragmentTransaction =
            fragmentManager.beginTransaction();
        if(null==fragmentManager.findFragmentByTag(TAG1)){
            Fragment1Activity fragment1 = new
                Fragment1Activity();
            fragmentTransaction.add(R.id.frag1_container,
                fragment1, TAG1);
        }
        if(null==fragmentManager.findFragmentByTag(TAG2)){
            Fragment2Activity fragment2 = new
```

```
            Fragment2Activity();
        fragmentTransaction.add(R.id.frag2_container,
            fragment2, TAG2);
    }
    fragmentTransaction.commit();
}

public void onOptionSelected(String msg){
    Fragment2Activity frag2 = (Fragment2Activity)
        getFragmentManager().findFragmentById(R.id.
        frag2_container);
    frag2.dispOption(msg);
}
}
```

You can see that in the preceding code, a `FragmentManager` object is defined to access the fragments. To perform a transaction related to fragments, such as adding, removing, or replacing fragments, a `FragmentTransaction` object named `fragmentTransaction` is defined. A new `FragmentTransaction` is created using the `beginTransaction()` method of the `FragmentManager`.

To the ID of the first fragment container, `frag1_container`, that exists in the layout file, you add your first fragment for display. Before adding the fragment, you check to see if it already exists. Using the `findFragmentByTag()` method of the `FragmentManager`, you check whether any fragment with the tag `TAG1` already exists. If the fragment does not exist, you define an object of `Fragment1Activity` named `fragment1` and add it to the `frag1_container`. `Fragment1Activity` is a Java class that is associated to `fragment1` and is meant to load the views defined in the fragment's layout file, `fragment1.xml`. Similarly, you add a second fragment, `fragment2`, to the second fragment container, `frag2_container`, defined in the layout file. Finally, the transaction process (addition of the fragments to their respective containers) is applied by calling the `commit()` method on the `FragmentTransaction` class.

The `onOptionSelected()` method will be invoked when any item from the `ListView` is selected. The item name selected from the `ListView` is passed to this method as a parameter. The item name is displayed on the screen by calling the `dispOption()` method of `fragment2`. After running the application, the first fragment displays the `ListView` showing a few products. Also, the second fragment displays a `TextView` initialized to display the directive text message `Please select a product` (see Figure 2.7 [top]). After selecting a product from the `ListView`, its name will be displayed through the `TextView` control defined in the second fragment, as shown in Figure 2.7 (bottom).

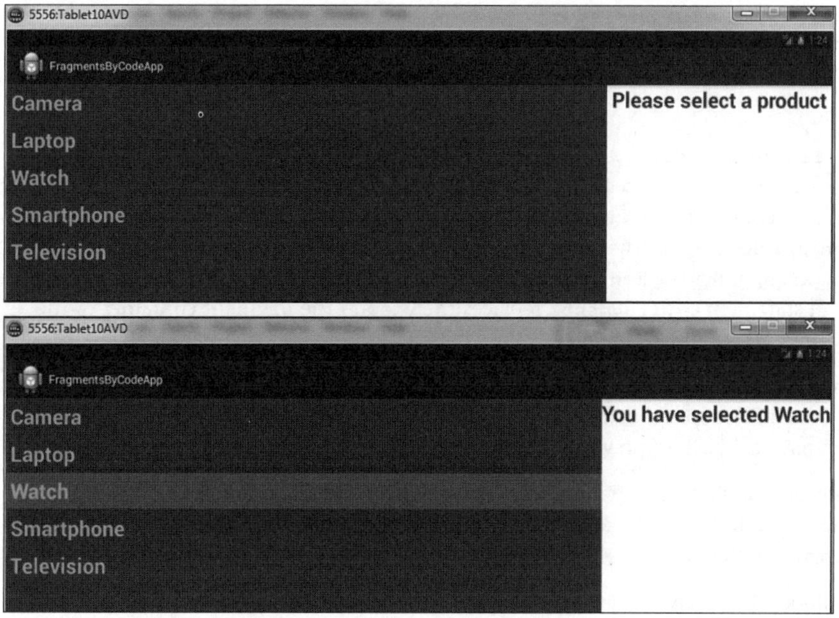

Figure 2.7   `ListView` and `TextView` controls displayed via two fragments (top) and the `TextView` of the second fragment showing the item selected from the `ListView` of the first fragment (bottom)

Recipe: Implementing Communication Between Fragments

To pass data among the fragments, two methods are provided by the `Fragment` class: `setArguments()` and `getArguments()`. The `setArguments()` method stores a `Bundle` in the fragment, whereas the `getArguments()` method retrieves the `Bundle` to fetch the passed information.

The following code passes information from `fragment1` to `fragment2`. You assume that `frag2_container` is the ID of the fragment container that exists in the layout file where you want to display `fragment2`.

```
Fragment2Activity fragment2 = new Fragment2Activity(); #1
Bundle args = new Bundle();                             #2
String message=" Message from Fragment 1";             #3
if(null==fragmentManager.findFragmentByTag(TAG2)){     #4
    args.putString("msg", message);                    #5
    fragment2.setArguments(args);                      #6
    fragmentTransaction.replace(R.id.frag2_container,
        fragment2);                                    #7
```

```
    String tag = null;                              #8
    fragmentTransaction.addToBackStack(tag);        #9
    fragmentTransaction.commit();
}
```

Statement #1, Fragment2Activity, represents the Java class of fragment2. A Java class instance called fragment2 is created. Statement #2 creates a Bundle object called args. A message string is defined in #3 that you want to pass to fragment2. Statement #4 checks to see if fragment2 doesn't already exist in the layout. The message variable is saved in the Bundle object, args, under the msg key in #5. The Bundle object, args, is stored in fragment2 in #6. Through statement #7, fragment2 replaces the View in the fragment container of the layout file. Statements #8 and #9 are meant for navigating to the previous fragment.

The activity stack keeps track of previous activities. When you press the Back button, the activities in the activity stack pop up, making their views visible. In other words, the activity stack enables you to navigate back to previous screens by using the Back button.

The same concept is applicable to fragments. To add the FragmentTransaction to the back stack, you need to call the addToBackStack() method of FragmentTransaction before calling the commit() method.

In the code snippet shown earlier, fragment2 replaces the fragment that was being displayed in the fragment container of the layout file. The previous fragment will be added to the back stack, making its views invisible. Pressing the Back button will then reverse the previous FragmentTransaction and return the view of the previous fragment.

You might wonder how the content passed through Bundle is retrieved in the receiving fragment. The answer is that you use the getArguments() method to access the content passed to the fragment via the Bundle that was saved through the setArguments() method. The code that follows accesses the Bundle object passed to the fragment. It also accesses the content passed under the msg key and assigns it to the messageReceived string:

```
String messageReceived ="";
@Override
public View onCreateView(LayoutInflater inflater,
    ViewGroup container, Bundle savedInstanceState) {
    Bundle bundle=getArguments();
    if(bundle !=null) {
        messageReceived = bundle.getString("msg");
    }
}
```

To understand communication among fragments, try sending the text message Message from Fragment 1 from fragment1 to fragment2 in the FragmentsByCodeApp application that you just created in the previous problem. Modify the code in the main Java activity file, FragmentsByCodeAppActivity.java, to appear as shown in Listing 2.17. Only the code in bold has been modified; the rest is the same as shown in Listing 2.16.

Listing 2.17   **Code Written into the Java Activity File** `FragmentsByCodeAppActivity.java`

```java
package com.androidtablet.fragmentsbycodeapp;

import android.os.Bundle;
import android.app.Activity;
import android.app.FragmentTransaction;
import android.app.FragmentManager;
import com.androidtablet.fragmentsbycodeapp.
    Fragment1Activity.OnOptionSelectedListener;

public class FragmentsByCodeAppActivity extends Activity
    implements OnOptionSelectedListener {
    private static final String TAG1 = "1";
    private static final String TAG2 = "2";

    @Override
    public void onCreate(Bundle savedInstanceState) {
        super.onCreate(savedInstanceState);
        setContentView(R.layout.activity_fragments_
            by_code_app);
        FragmentManager fragmentManager =
            getFragmentManager();
        FragmentTransaction fragmentTransaction =
            fragmentManager.beginTransaction();
        if(null==fragmentManager.findFragmentByTag(TAG1)){
            Fragment1Activity fragment1 = new
                Fragment1Activity();
            fragmentTransaction.add(R.id.frag1_container,
                fragment1, TAG1);
        }
        Bundle args = new Bundle();
        String message="Message from Fragment 1";
        if(null==fragmentManager.findFragmentByTag(TAG2)){
            Fragment2Activity fragment2 = new
                Fragment2Activity();
            args.putString("msg", message);
            fragment2.setArguments(args);
            fragmentTransaction.add(R.id.frag2_container,
                fragment2, TAG2);
        }
        fragmentTransaction.commit();
    }
    public void onOptionSelected(String msg){
        Fragment2Activity frag2 = (Fragment2Activity)
            getFragmentManager().findFragmentById(
            R.id.frag2_container);
```

```
                frag2.dispOption(msg);
        }
}
```

You can see that the `Bundle` instance `args` is created. To the `args` `Bundle`, the text message that you want to send to `fragment2`, `Message from Fragment 1`, is added under the `msg` key. It is through this key that the text message will be retrieved in the receiving fragment (that is, in `fragment2`). The `args` `Bundle` is attached to `fragment2` through the `setArguments()` method. After attaching the `Bundle`, `fragment2` is added to its container, `frag2_container`, defined in the activity layout.

To access the bundle sent by the first fragment, to access the data from the bundle, and to display it through the second fragment, you modify the Java class file of the second fragment, `Fragment2Activity.java`, to appear as shown in Listing 2.18. Only the code in bold is modified; the rest was shown earlier in Listing 2.15.

Listing 2.18   **Code Written into the Java Class File** `Fragment2Activity.java`

```
package com.androidtablet.fragmentsbycodeapp;

import android.app.Fragment;
import android.os.Bundle;
import android.view.ViewGroup;
import android.view.View;
import android.view.LayoutInflater;
import android.widget.TextView;

public class Fragment2Activity extends Fragment {
    TextView selectedOpt;
    String messageReceived="";

    @Override
    public View onCreateView(LayoutInflater inflater,
        ViewGroup container, Bundle savedInstanceState) {
        View vw= inflater.inflate(R.layout.fragment2,
            container, false);
        Bundle bundle=getArguments();
        if(bundle !=null) {
            messageReceived = bundle.getString("msg");
            selectedOpt = (TextView) vw.findViewById(
                R.id.selectedopt);
            selectedOpt.setText(messageReceived);
        }
        return vw;
    }
```

```
public void dispOption(String msg){
    selectedOpt = (TextView) getActivity().
        findViewById(R.id.selectedopt);
    selectedOpt.setText("You have selected "+msg);
}
}
```

You can see in the preceding code that the Bundle sent by fragment1 is retrieved in this fragment through the getArguments() method. From the Bundle, the text message that was sent is fetched using the msg key. The retrieved text message from the Bundle is displayed through the TextView control in the second fragment.

After running the application, the two fragments are displayed: fragment1 showing the list of products, and fragment2 showing the text message Message from Fragment 1 sent from fragment1 (see Figure 2.8 [top]). After selecting a product, its name will be displayed through the TextView control in fragment2 (see Figure 2.8 [bottom]).

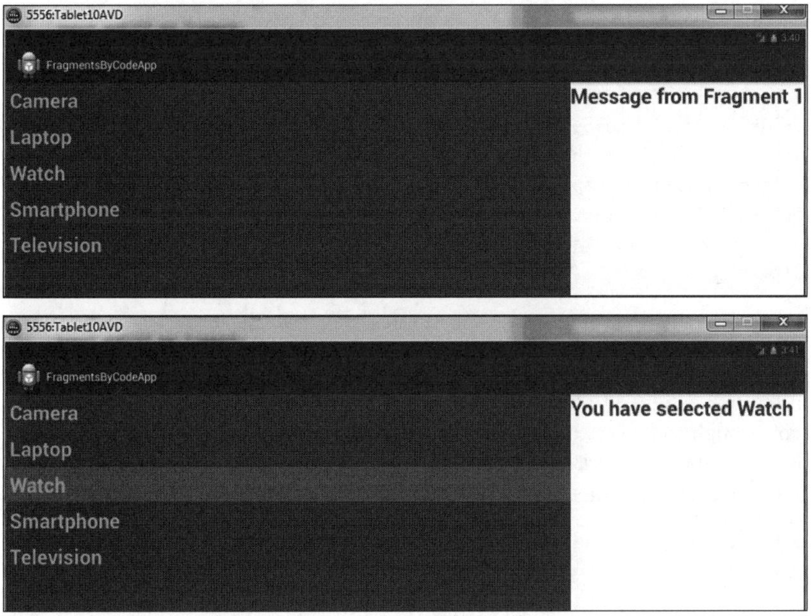

Figure 2.8   Text message sent by the first fragment displayed through TextView control in second fragment (top) and the TextView of the second fragment, showing the item selected from the ListView of the first fragment (bottom)

Besides the Fragment base class, a fragment can extend a few other subclasses of the Fragment class, such as DialogFragment, ListFragment, and PreferenceFragment.

Recipe: Displaying Options Using ListFragment

A ListFragment is a fragment that contains a built-in ListView that can be set to display items from a specified data source. The data source can be an array or a cursor. To understand ListFragments, create an application consisting of a ListView and a TextView. The ListView will display some items to choose from. The item selected from the ListView will be displayed through a TextView. In this application, the ListView will be displayed via a ListFragment, and the TextView will be displayed via a simple fragment. The item selected from the ListView in the ListFragment will be displayed through the TextView in the simple fragment. Name the new Android project ListFragmentApp. You will first create a fragment to hold the TextView control. Add an XML file called fragment2.xml to the res/layout folder of your project. Listing 2.19 shows how to define a TextView control in fragment2.xml.

Listing 2.19   **Code in the XML File** fragment2.xml

```
<?xml version="1.0" encoding="utf-8"?>
<LinearLayout xmlns:android="http://schemas.android.com/apk/res/android"
    android:layout_width="match_parent"
    android:layout_height="match_parent"
    android:orientation="vertical" >
    <TextView
        android:id="@+id/selectedopt"
        android:layout_width="match_parent"
        android:layout_height="wrap_content"
        android:text="Please select a product"
        android:textSize="@dimen/text_size"
        android:textStyle="bold"  />
 </LinearLayout>
```

You can see that a TextView control with the ID selectedopt is defined in a LinearLayout container. The initial text assigned to the TextView control is Please select a product. The text displayed through the TextView will appear in bold and in a size defined in the text_size dimension resource. This TextView control will be assigned text through Java code to indicate the item selected from the ListView.

To make the size of ListView items adjustable to the device screen size, add an XML file named list_item.xml to the res/layout folder. Write the code as shown in the list_item. xml file:

```
<?xml version="1.0" encoding="utf-8"?>
<TextView xmlns:android="http://schemas.android.com/apk/res/android"
    android:layout_width="match_parent"
    android:layout_height="match_parent"
    android:padding="6dp"
    android:textSize="@dimen/text_size"
    android:textStyle="bold" />
```

According to the preceding code, the list items of the `ListView` will be padded by 6dp space, will appear in bold, and will be the size defined in the dimension resource `text_size`.

To load the UI of the fragment from `fragment2.xml`, you need to create a Java class file. So add a Java class file called `Fragment2Activity.java` under the `com.androidtablet.listfragmentapp` package. Write the code shown in Listing 2.20 into the Java class file `Fragment2Activity.java`.

Listing 2.20 **Code Written into the Java Class File of the Second Fragment,** `Fragment2Activity`

```
package com.androidtablet.listfragmentapp;

import android.app.Fragment;
import android.os.Bundle;
import android.view.ViewGroup;
import android.view.View;
import android.view.LayoutInflater;
import android.widget.TextView;

public class Fragment2Activity extends Fragment {
    public View onCreateView(LayoutInflater inflater, ViewGroup
        container, Bundle savedInstanceState) {
        return inflater.inflate(R.layout.fragment2, container,
            false);
    }

    public void dispOption(String msg){
        TextView selectedOpt = (TextView) getActivity().
            findViewById(R.id.selectedopt);
        selectedOpt.setText("You have selected "+msg);
    }
}
```

You can see that the Java class extends the `Fragment` base class. The `onCreateView()` method is overridden when a `LayoutInflater` object is used to inflate the `TextView` control UI that you defined in the `fragment2.xml` file.

You will be using `ListFragment` to display the `ListView` control. As I said earlier, the `ListFragment` already contains a `ListView`, so you don't need to define a UI for this fragment. You can directly add a Java class file that extends the `ListFragment` class. In this Java class file, you will write code to define the items to be displayed through the `ListView` of the `ListFragment` and to display the item selected from the `ListView` through the `TextView` of `Fragment2`. So add a Java class called `Fragment1Activity.java` to the project, and write the code shown in Listing 2.21.

Listing 2.21   **Code Written into the Java Class for the First Fragment,** `Fragment1Activity.`
`java`

```
package com.androidtablet.listfragmentapp;

import android.app.ListFragment;
import android.os.Bundle;
import android.widget.ArrayAdapter;
import android.view.View;
import android.widget.ListView;
import android.widget.TextView;

public class Fragment1Activity extends ListFragment {
    String[] products={"Camera", "Laptop", "Watch",
        "Smartphone", "Television"};

    @Override
    public void onCreate(Bundle savedInstanceState) {
        super.onCreate(savedInstanceState);
        ArrayAdapter<String> arrayAdpt = new ArrayAdapter
            <String>(getActivity(),R.layout.list_item,
                products);
        setListAdapter(arrayAdpt);
    }

    @Override
    public void onListItemClick(ListView l, View v, int
        position, long id) {
        Fragment2Activity frag = (Fragment2Activity)
            getFragmentManager().findFragmentById(
            R.id.fragment2);
        frag.dispOption(((TextView) v).getText().toString());
    }
}
```

As expected, the Java class extends the `ListFragment` base class to create a `Fragment` with
`ListView`. To display content through the `ListView` of the `ListFragment`, an array called
products is defined, and product names are assigned to it. In the `onCreate()` method, an
`ArrayAdapter` object called `arrayAdpt` is defined to display the elements of the products
array in the `simple_list_item_1` mode. By using the `setListAdapter()` method, the
content in the `ArrayAdapter` object, `arrayAdpt`, is assigned to the `ListView` for display. As
expected, the `onListItemClick()` method will be invoked when any of the products displayed
through the `ListView` control is selected. In this method, you display the name of the selected
product through the `TextView` control that you defined in `fragment2.xml`.

To accommodate both the fragments in the application, code is written into `activity_list_`
`fragment_app.xml`, as shown in Listing 2.22.

Listing 2.22   **The `activity_list_fragment_app.xml` Layout File After Adding Two Fragments**

```
<LinearLayout xmlns:android="http://schemas.android.com/apk/res/android"
    android:layout_width="match_parent"
    android:layout_height="match_parent"
    android:orientation="horizontal" >
    <fragment
        android:name="com.androidtablet.listfragmentapp.
            Fragment1Activity"
        android:id="@+id/fragment1"
        android:layout_weight="1"
        android:layout_width="wrap_content"
        android:layout_height="match_parent" />
    <fragment
        android:name="com.androidtablet.listfragmentapp.
            Fragment2Activity"
        android:id="@+id/fragment2"
        android:layout_weight="0"
        android:layout_width="wrap_content"
        android:layout_height="match_parent" />
</LinearLayout>
```

You can see that `fragment1` and `fragment2` fragments are added to the activity through the `<fragment>` elements. The fragments are set to refer to their respective Java classes through the `android:name` attribute. You don't have to write code into the Java activity file of the application `ListFragmentAppActivity.java`. You leave the default code in the activity file unchanged, as shown in Listing 2.23.

Listing 2.23   **Default Code in the Java Activity File `ListFragmentAppActivity.java`**

```
package com.androidtablet.listfragmentapp;

import android.app.Activity;
import android.os.Bundle;

public class ListFragmentAppActivity extends Activity {
    @Override
    public void onCreate(Bundle savedInstanceState) {
        super.onCreate(savedInstanceState);
        setContentView(R.layout.activity_list_fragment_app);
    }
}
```

After running the application, you will see the two fragments side by side, as shown in Figure 2.9 (top). The `ListView` on the left side appears through the `ListFragment`. The content in the `ListView` is displayed via the Java class file of the `ListFragment`, `Fragment1Activity.java`. The item selected from the `ListView` is displayed through the `TextView` defined in `Fragment2`, as shown in Figure 2.9 (bottom).

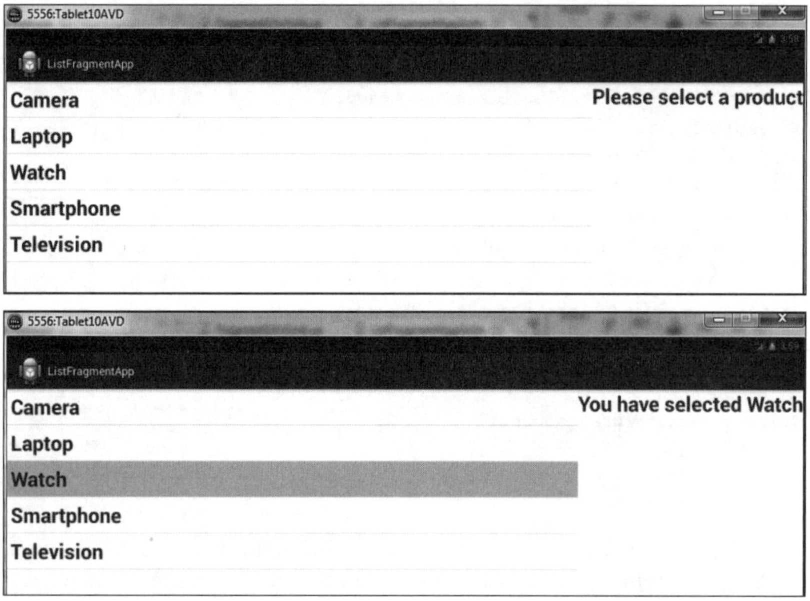

Figure 2.9   The `ListView` displayed via `ListFragment` (top) and the item selected from the `ListView` of `ListFragment`, displayed via the `TextView` of the second fragment (bottom)

Recipe: Displaying Dialog Through `DialogFragment`

In Android, dialogs are asynchronous. Synchronous dialogs are those in which the activity suspends its execution until a dialog is dismissed. While the user is interacting with the dialog, no further execution will take place. Asynchronous dialogs are those in which activity continues its normal execution while users can interact with the dialog. The activity accesses user interaction with the dialog by implementing callback methods. The dialogs in Android are modal in nature; while a dialog is open, users cannot access any other part of the application. The benefit of calling dialogs asynchronously is that it not only increases code efficiency but also provides you with the capability to dismiss the dialog through code.

You can display a `DialogFragment` by extending the `DialogFragment` base class, which in turn is derived from the `Fragment` class. To demonstrate `DialogFragment`, create a new Android project called `DialogFragmentApp`. In this project, you will use two fragments. One will show a `DialogFragment`, and the other will display a `TextView`. The user's interaction with the `DialogFragment` is conveyed through the `TextView` control in the second fragment.

The selected button in the `DialogFragment` is displayed via the `TextView` control in the second fragment.

Before beginning the creation of `DialogFragment`, define the UI of the simple fragment that consists of a `TextView`. To do so, add an XML file called `fragment2.xml` to the `res/layout` folder. Write the code shown in Listing 2.24 into the `fragment2.xml` file.

Listing 2.24   **Code Written into the XML File** `fragment2.xml`

```xml
<?xml version="1.0" encoding="utf-8"?>
<LinearLayout xmlns:android="http://schemas.android.com/apk/res/android"
    android:layout_width="match_parent"
    android:layout_height="match_parent"
    android:orientation="vertical" >
    <TextView
        android:id="@+id/selectedopt"
        android:layout_width="match_parent"
        android:layout_height="wrap_content"
        android:text="Select Open Dialog Button"
        android:textSize="@dimen/text_size"
        android:textStyle="bold" />
</LinearLayout>
```

You can see that a `TextView` control is defined inside a `LinearLayout` container. The `TextView` is assigned the `selectedopt` ID and initialized to display the text, `Select Open Dialog Button`. The text displayed through `TextView` will appear in bold and in the font size defined by the dimension resource `text_size`. This `TextView` will display the option selected by the user in the `DialogFragment`.

To load the UI of the fragment from `fragment2.xml`, a Java class file called `Fragment2Activity.java` is added to the project. Write the code shown in Listing 2.25 into the Java file `Fragment2Activity.java`.

Listing 2.25   **Code Written into the Java Class for the Second Fragment,** `Fragment2Activity.java`

```java
package com.androidtablet.dialogfragmentapp;

import android.app.Fragment;
import android.os.Bundle;
import android.view.ViewGroup;
import android.view.View;
import android.view.LayoutInflater;

public class Fragment2Activity extends Fragment {
    @Override
    public View onCreateView(LayoutInflater inflater, ViewGroup
```

```
        container, Bundle savedInstanceState) {
        return inflater.inflate(R.layout.fragment2, container,
            false);
    }
}
```

The Java class extends the `Fragment` base class. The `onCreateView()` method is overridden when a `LayoutInflater` object is used to inflate the `TextView` control UI that you defined in the `fragment2.xml` file.

To accommodate the fragment defined in `fragment2.xml`, you need to write code into the layout file, `activity_dialog_fragment_app.xml`, as shown in Listing 2.26.

Listing 2.26 **The Layout File** `activity_dialog_fragment_app.xml` **After Adding a Fragment and a Button**

```
<LinearLayout xmlns:android="http://schemas.android.com/apk/res/android"
    android:layout_width="match_parent"
    android:layout_height="match_parent"
    android:orientation="horizontal" >
    <fragment
        android:name="com.androidtablet.dialogfragmentapp.
            Fragment2Activity"
        android:id="@+id/fragment2"
        android:layout_weight="0"
        android:layout_width="wrap_content"
        android:layout_height="match_parent" />
    <Button
        android:id="@+id/dialog_button"
        android:layout_width="match_parent"
        android:layout_height="wrap_content"
        android:text="Open Dialog"
        android:textSize="@dimen/text_size" />
</LinearLayout>
```

A `Button` control is defined because you want the `DialogFragment` to appear only when a button is selected in the application. Both the `Fragment` and the `Button` controls are nested inside the `LinearLayout` container. The `Fragment` is assigned the ID `fragment2` and is set to refer to its Java class through the `android:name` attribute. The `Button` control is assigned the ID `dialog_button`, and the caption is assigned as `Open Dialog`. The caption in the `Button` control will appear in the font size defined in the dimension resource, `text_size`. `fragment2` is meant to display a `TextView` to show the option selected by the user in the `DialogFragment`.

Now it's time to write code to show a `DialogFragment`. As mentioned earlier, to show `DialogFragment`, a Java class needs to extend the `DialogFragment` class. Add a Java class

called `Fragment1Activity.java` under the package `com.androidtablet.`
`dialogfragmentapp`. To display a `DialogFragment`, write the code shown in Listing 2.27 into
the `Fragment1Activity.java` file.

Listing 2.27   **Code Written into the Java Class File of the First Fragment,**
`Fragment1Activity.java`

```java
package com.androidtablet.dialogfragmentapp;

import android.app.DialogFragment;
import android.os.Bundle;
import android.app.Dialog;
import android.app.AlertDialog;
import android.content.DialogInterface;

public class Fragment1Activity extends DialogFragment{
    static Fragment1Activity newInstance(String title) {
        Fragment1Activity fragment = new Fragment1Activity();
        Bundle args = new Bundle();
        args.putString("title", title);
        fragment.setArguments(args);
        return fragment;
    }


    @Override
    public Dialog onCreateDialog(Bundle savedInstanceState) {
        String title = getArguments().getString("title");
        Dialog diag = new AlertDialog.Builder(getActivity())
        .setIcon(R.drawable.ic_launcher)
        .setTitle(title)
        .setPositiveButton("OK", new DialogInterface.
            OnClickListener() {
            public void onClick(DialogInterface dialog, int
                whichButton) {
                ((DialogFragmentAppActivity) getActivity()).
                    PositiveButton();
            }
        })
        .setNegativeButton("Cancel", new DialogInterface.
            OnClickListener() {
            public void onClick(DialogInterface dialog, int
                whichButton) {
                ((DialogFragmentAppActivity) getActivity()).
                    NegativeButton();
            }
        }).create();
        return diag;
```

```
      }
}
```

To create the `DialogFragment`, the Java class extends the `DialogFragment` class. The `newInstance()` method creates a new instance of the fragment. The title of the `DialogFragment` is passed to this method as an argument, which in turn is stored in the `Bundle` object and associated with the fragment that is returned by this method.

To create the view hierarchy of the `DialogFragment`, the `onCreateDialog()` method of the `DialogFragment` class is overridden, and a `Bundle` object carrying the title of the fragment and other information, if any, is passed to it. In the `onCreateDialog()` method, an alert dialog builder is used to create a dialog object. In the `onCreateDialog()` method, an `AlertDialog` with two buttons, OK and Cancel, is created, and the title that has to be displayed in the fragment is obtained from the `title` argument saved in the `Bundle` object. An `onClickListener()` is associated with the two buttons, OK and Cancel, which results in invoking the respective `onClick()` method when the button is clicked. When OK is selected, the `PositiveButton()` method from the activity will be called. Similarly, when Cancel is selected, the `NegativeButton()` method from the activity is called. The method returns the created `AlertDialog`.

In the Java activity file, you need to write code to invoke the `DialogFragment`. The code must be written to take the necessary action when OK or Cancel is selected from the `DialogFragment`. The code written into the Java activity file `DialogFragmentAppActivity.java` is shown in Listing 2.28.

Listing 2.28   **Code Written into the Java Activity File** `DialogFragmentAppActivity.java`

```java
package com.androidtablet.dialogfragmentapp;

import android.app.Activity;
import android.os.Bundle;
import android.widget.Button;
import android.view.View;
import android.widget.TextView;

public class DialogFragmentAppActivity extends Activity {
    @Override
    public void onCreate(Bundle savedInstanceState) {
        super.onCreate(savedInstanceState);
        setContentView(R.layout.activity_dialog_fragment_app);
        Button dialogButton = (Button)findViewById(
            R.id.dialog_button);
        dialogButton.setOnClickListener(new Button.
            OnClickListener(){
            @Override
            public void onClick(View arg0) {
                Fragment1Activity dialogFragment =
```

```
                        Fragment1Activity.newInstance( "Continue
                        Processing?" );
                    dialogFragment.show(getFragmentManager(),
                        "Dialog Fragment Example");
                }
        });
    }

    public void PositiveButton() {
        TextView selectedOpt = (TextView)findViewById(
            R.id.selectedopt);
        selectedOpt.setText("You have selected OK button");
    }

    public void NegativeButton() {
        TextView selectedOpt = (TextView) findViewById(
            R.id.selectedopt);
        selectedOpt.setText("You have selected Cancel button");
    }
}
```

You want the `DialogFragment` to appear when the button is selected from the application. So you see that the `dialogButton Button` control is captured from the layout file and is mapped to the `Button` object, dialogButton. An `OnClickListener` is associated with the `Button` control, and the `onClick()` callback method is called if the `Button` control is selected from the application. In the `onClick()` method, the `DialogFragment` is formed by creating a dialogFragment instance of the `Fragment1Activity` Java class file. The title of the `DialogFragment` is passed to it as `Continue processing`.

The `DialogFragment` is made visible by calling its `show()` method. The `show()` method adds the fragment to the given `FragmentManager`. The code also defines the two methods, `PositiveButton()` and `NegativeButton()`, which will be invoked when OK and Cancel from the `DialogFragment` are selected. In both the `PositiveButton()` and `NegativeButton()` methods, the `selectedOpt TextView` control that you defined in `fragment2.xml` is accessed and is mapped to the `TextView` object, selectedOpt. When OK is selected, the message `You have selected OK button` appears in the `TextView` through the `selectedOpt` instance. Similarly, when Cancel from the `DialogFragment` is selected, the message `You have selected Cancel button` appears in the `TextView` of the second fragment.

When you run the application, a `TextView` and a `Button` control are displayed (see Figure 2.10 [first]). The `TextView` is displayed through `fragment2.xml`. The `TextView` displays an initial text, `Select Open Dialog Button`, directing the user to select the Open Dialog button. After you click the Open Dialog button, a dialog fragment titled `Continue Processing` opens. It shows two buttons, OK and Cancel, as shown in Figure 2.10 (second). After you click the OK button from the `DialogFragment`, the message `You have selected OK button` is shown through the `TextView` control, as shown in Figure 2.10 (third). Click the Open Dialog button again, and the `DialogFragment` opens up once more. This time, if you select Cancel from the `DialogFragment`, the `TextView` will display the message `You have selected Cancel` `button`, as shown in Figure 2.10 (fourth).

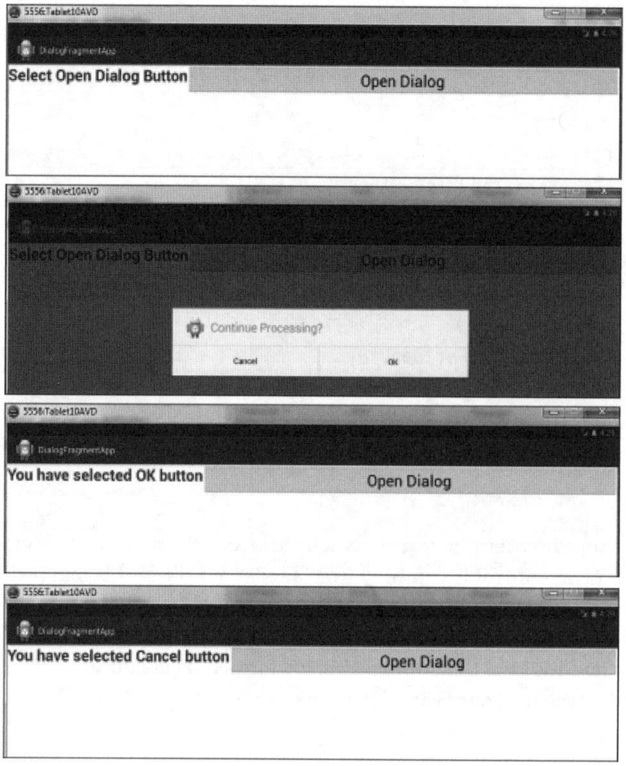

Figure 2.10   The `TextView` and `Button` displayed on application startup (first); the `DialogFragment` appears after clicking the button (second); the `TextView` showing that the `DialogFragment` OK button was clicked (third); and the `TextView` showing that the `DialogFragment` Cancel button was clicked (fourth).

A dialog fragment is displayed modally. Therefore, it is used in applications where you want to alert the user by displaying important messages or want the user's feedback before processing further.

Recipe: Setting User's Preferences with `PreferenceFragment`

`PreferenceFragment` is a fragment that enables users to configure and personalize an application. `PreferenceFragment` can contain several preference views that help in uniformly setting application preferences with minimum effort. The list of preference views that can be displayed via a `PreferenceFragment` is shown in Table 2.1. The preference views are modified by the

`SharedPreferences`. The `SharePreferences` class enables you to save and retrieve persistent key-value pairs that represent user preferences.

Table 2.1 **Preference Views That Can Be Displayed in** `PreferenceFragments`

Preference View	Description
`PreferenceScreen`	The root element of the XML used to define a preference screen
`CheckBoxPreference`	Displays a simple check box that returns `true` when checked; otherwise, returns false
`ListPreference`	Displays a list of radio buttons allowing the user to select one
`EditTextPreference`	Displays a dialog with an `EditText` control allowing the user to enter text
`RingtonePreference`	Displays radio buttons indicating the ringtones available for selection
`PreferenceCategory`	Used in grouping related preferences in categories
`Preference`	A custom preference that acts like a `Button` control

To understand how application preferences are set, create a new Android project called `PrefFragmentApp`. There are two ways of displaying preference views in a `PreferenceFragment`: through an XML file and through code. We prefer the XML approach, so you will first add a folder called `xml` into the `res` folder. Inside the `res/xml` folder, you will add an XML file called `preferences.xml`. This file will contain the preference views you want to display to the user to configure the application. The options selected by the user in preference views will persist in the application. The code written into the `preferences.xml` file is shown in Listing 2.29.

Listing 2.29 **Code Written into the XML File** `preferences.xml`

```xml
<?xml version="1.0" encoding="utf-8"?>
<PreferenceScreen xmlns:android="http://schemas.android.com/apk/res/android" >
    <PreferenceCategory android:title="Category 1">
        <CheckBoxPreference
            android:title="Newsletter"
            android:defaultValue="false"
            android:key="Newskey" />
        <EditTextPreference android:key="Namekey"
            android:title="Enter your name: "
            android:dialogTitle="Enter your name" >
        </EditTextPreference>
    </PreferenceCategory>
    <PreferenceCategory android:title="Category 2">
        <RingtonePreference android:showDefault="true"
            android:key="Audio" android:title="Select sound"
```

```
                android:ringtoneType="notification" >
        </RingtonePreference>
        <ListPreference android:title="Products List "
            android:key="products_list"
            android:entries="@array/products"
            android:entryValues="@array/prodselected"
            android:dialogTitle="Choose a product" >
        </ListPreference>
    </PreferenceCategory>
    <Preference
        android:title="Submit"
        android:key="submitPref" />
</PreferenceScreen>
```

You can see that the preference views are shown in two categories: Category 1 and Category 2. Category 1 includes two preference views: a CheckBoxPreference and an EditTextPreference. Category 2 includes the RingtonePreference and ListPreference. Every preference view needs to have an android:key value that identifies and accesses its value. The android:title attribute is used to assign initial text to the preference view, and the android:defaultValue attribute is used to assign a default value to the preference view.

The CheckBoxPreference displays a check box as its UI element, and it stores a value in Boolean form—either true or false. The value true is stored when the check box in CheckBoxPreference is selected and false when the check box is not selected. The default value false is assigned to the CheckBoxPreference using the android:defaultValue attribute.

The EditTextPreference is assigned the Namekey key, and the title Enter your name: will appear as the text of the preference view. When the EditTextPreference is selected, a dialog titled Enter Your Information will be displayed, asking the user to enter information. When the user clicks OK, the entered information is saved to the preference store.

The RingtonePreference will open a dialog box showing the list of ringtones and allow the user to select a default ringtone or silent mode. The key assigned to the RingtonePreference is Audio, and the dialog box is assigned the title Select Sound. The android:ringtoneType attribute helps in determining the list of ringtones to be displayed. Valid values for the android:ringtoneType attribute are ringtone, notification, alarm, and all.

The ListPreference shows a dialog box listing a set of preferences in the form of radio buttons, allowing the user to select one of them. The dialog box will be titled Choose a Product and is assigned the key products_list. The android:entries attribute assigns a string-array named products to the ListPreference to show the list of preferences. That is, the elements in the products array will display text for the radio buttons displayed via the ListPreference. The android:entryValues attribute defines another array, prodselected, to hold the values of the elements defined in the products array. The android:entryValues attribute represents an array that stores the values corresponding to the radio button selected by the user.

The <Preference> elements display a Submit button in the `PreferenceFragment` that users click after selecting the desired preferences from preference views to either store the preferences or perform another action. The Submit button is assigned the key `submitPref`, which will identify it in the Java code.

Next, you need to define two arrays in the `strings.xml` resource file: one to display text for the radio button in the `ListPreference`, and the second to store the values of the corresponding elements in the first array. After defining the two arrays, the `strings.xml` file will appear as shown in Listing 2.30.

Listing 2.30   **The Strings Resource File, `strings.xml`, After Defining the Two Arrays**

```xml
<?xml version="1.0" encoding="utf-8"?>
<resources>
    <string name="app_name">PrefFragmentApp</string>
    <string name="menu_settings">Settings</string>
    <string-array name="products">
        <item>Camera</item>
        <item>Laptop</item>
        <item>Watch</item>
        <item>Smartphone</item>
        <item>Television</item>
    </string-array>
    <string-array name="prodselected">
        <item>You have selected Camera</item>
        <item>You have selected Laptop</item>
        <item>You have selected Watch</item>
        <item>You have selected Smartphone</item>
        <item>You have selected Television</item>
    </string-array>
</resources>
```

The elements in the `products` array are used to display text for the radio buttons shown in the `ListPreference`, and the elements in the `prodselected` array show the values that will be returned if the corresponding element in the `products` array is selected.

To load the preference views defined in `preferences.xml`, a Java class file called `PrefFragActivity.java` is added to the project. Write the code shown in Listing 2.31 into the Java class file `PrefFragActivity.java`.

Listing 2.31   **Code Written into the Java Class File `PrefFragActivity.java`**

```java
package com.androidtablet.preffragmentapp;

import android.os.Bundle;
import android.app.Activity;
import android.preference.Preference;
```

```
import android.preference.Preference.OnPreferenceClickListener;
import android.preference.PreferenceFragment;

public class PrefFragActivity extends Activity {
    public void onCreate(Bundle savedInstanceState) {
        super.onCreate(savedInstanceState);
        getFragmentManager().beginTransaction().replace(
            android.R.id.content, new PrefsFragment()).commit();
    }

    public static class PrefsFragment extends PreferenceFragment
    {
        @Override
        public void onCreate(Bundle savedInstanceState) {
            super.onCreate(savedInstanceState);
            addPreferencesFromResource(R.xml.preferences);
            Preference submitPref = (Preference) findPreference(
                "submitPref");
            submitPref.setOnPreferenceClickListener(new
                OnPreferenceClickListener() {
                public boolean onPreferenceClick(Preference
                    preference) {
                    getActivity().finish();
                    return true;
                }
            });
        }
    }
}
```

To create the PreferenceFragment, a Java class called PrefsFragment is defined that extends the PreferenceFragment class. The addPreferencesFromResource() method is called to load the preference views in the PreferenceFragment from the XML file, preferences.xml. The Submit button defined in the preferences.xml file through the <Preference> element is accessed and mapped to the Preference object, submitPref. An OnPreferenceClickListener event handler is added to the submitPref object. Its callback method, onPreferenceClick(), is implemented and executes when the submitPref object is clicked. In the onPreferenceClick() method, you finish by closing the PreferenceFragment and returning to PreferenceFragActivity.java to take necessary action on the selected preferences. Through the Java activity file, PrefFragmentAppActivity.java, you will display the preferences selected by the user via TextView controls.

To display the options selected from the preference views shown in the PreferenceFragment, you need to define four TextView controls in the layout file, activity_pref_fragment.xml. After defining the four TextView controls, activity_pref_fragment_app.xml will appear, as shown in Listing 2.32.

Listing 2.32   **The Layout File** `activity_pref_fragment_app.xml` **After Adding the Four**
`TextView` **Controls**

```xml
<LinearLayout xmlns:android="http://schemas.android.com/apk/res/android"
    android:layout_width="match_parent"
    android:layout_height="match_parent"
    android:orientation="vertical" >
    <TextView
        android:layout_width="match_parent"
        android:layout_height="wrap_content"
        android:id="@+id/newsletter"
        android:textSize="@dimen/text_size"
        android:textStyle="bold" />
    <TextView
        android:layout_width="match_parent"
        android:layout_height="wrap_content"
        android:id="@+id/name"
        android:textSize="@dimen/text_size"
        android:textStyle="bold" />
    <TextView
        android:layout_width="match_parent"
        android:layout_height="wrap_content"
        android:id="@+id/ringtone"
        android:textSize="@dimen/text_size"
        android:textStyle="bold" />
    <TextView
        android:layout_width="match_parent"
        android:layout_height="wrap_content"
        android:id="@+id/product"
        android:textSize="@dimen/text_size"
        android:textStyle="bold" />
</LinearLayout>
```

You can see that the four `TextView` controls are assigned the IDs `newsletter`, `name`,
`ringtone`, and `product`. The `TextView` controls are vertically arranged inside the
`LinearLayout` container. The `newsletter` `TextView` will be used to indicate whether the user
has checked the check box in the `CheckBoxPreference`. The `name` `TextView` will be used to
display the name entered by the user in the `EditTextPreference`. The `ringtone` `TextView`
will be used to display the type of ringtone selected by the user in the `RingtonePreference`.
The `product` `TextView` will be used to display the product selected by the user in the
`ListPreference`. The text displayed through `TextView` will appear in bold and in the font size
defined in the dimension resource `text_size`.

To display the `PreferenceFragment` and show the preferences selected by the
user, you need to write the code shown in Listing 2.33 into the main activity file,
`PrefFragmentAppActivity.java`.

Listing 2.33   Code Written into the Main Activity File, `PrefFragmentAppActivity.java`

```java
package com.androidtablet.preffragmentapp;

import android.app.Activity;
import android.os.Bundle;
import android.content.Intent;
import android.preference.PreferenceManager;
import android.content.SharedPreferences;
import android.widget.TextView;

public class PrefFragmentAppActivity extends Activity {
    @Override
    public void onCreate(Bundle savedInstanceState) {
        super.onCreate(savedInstanceState);
        setContentView(R.layout.activity_pref_fragment_app);
        startActivity(new Intent(this, PrefFragActivity.class));
    }

    @Override
    public void onResume() {
        super.onResume();
        SharedPreferences prefs=PreferenceManager.
            getDefaultSharedPreferences(this);
        TextView newsletter=(TextView)findViewById(
            R.id.newsletter);
        TextView name=(TextView)findViewById(R.id.name);
        TextView ringtone=(TextView)findViewById(R.id.ringtone);
        TextView product=(TextView)findViewById(R.id.product);
        if(Boolean.valueOf(prefs.getBoolean("Newskey", false)))
            newsletter.setText("You have selected Newsletter");
        else
            newsletter.setText("");
        ringtone.setText("The ringtone selected is "+prefs.
            getString("Audio", "Silent"));
        name.setText("The name entered is "+prefs.getString(
            "Namekey",""));
        String selectedProduct = prefs.getString(
            "products_list", "Camera");
        product.setText(selectedProduct);
    }
}
```

To display the `PreferenceFragment`, its activity class, `PrefFragActivity.class`, is started. To show the preferences selected by the user in the `PreferenceFragment`, the `TextView` controls defined in the layout file, `activity_pref_fragment_app.xml`, are accessed and mapped to the `TextView` objects. The `newsletter`, `name`, `ringtone`, and `product` `TextView` controls are mapped to the `TextView` objects `newsletter`, `name`, `ringtone`, and `product`, respectively.

To find the options selected in the preference views, a `SharedPreferences` object called `prefs` is created. Remember, to retrieve values from the `SharedPreferences` object via the `getInt()`, `getString()`, or `getBoolean()` methods, you need to provide the key whose value you want and optionally a default value to return if the key is not present.

To read the value of `CheckBoxPreference`, you access the shared preferences and call the `getBoolean()` method, passing the key of the `CheckBoxPreference` to it. When the `CheckBoxPreference` `Newskey` key is passed to the `getBoolean()` method of the `SharedPreference` instance, it will return `true` or `false`, indicating whether the check box in `CheckBoxPreference` is checked.

Thereafter, `EditTextPreference` is accessed by passing its `Namekey` key to the `getString()` method of the `SharedPreference` instance. An empty string is considered the default if the user does not enter a name. Similarly, the `RingtonePreference` and `ListPreference` are accessed by passing their keys, `Audio` and `products_list`, to the `getString()` method of the `SharedPreference` instance. The preferences selected by the user in the preference views are displayed via `TextView` controls. You can see that the default ringtone, if not supplied by the user, is set to Silent, and the default selected product is set to Camera.

To make the newly added activity, `PrefFragActivity.java`, visible to Android, it is declared in `AndroidManifest.xml` by adding the following statement in it:

```
<activity android:name=".PrefFragActivity" android:label="@string/app_name" />
```

After running the application, you will see the preference views defined in `Category 1` and `Category 2`. The `CheckBoxPreference` check box is unchecked by default. When the check box is selected, it will be checked, as shown in Figure 2.11 (first). When the `EditTextPreference` with text `Enter your name:` is selected, a dialog box titled Enter Your Name pops up. You can enter a name or cancel the operation by selecting Cancel. Enter `Kelly`, as shown in Figure 2.11 (second), and then click OK to go back to the `PreferenceFragment`. When Select Sound is clicked, which represents `RingtonePreference`, a dialog box prompting the user to select a ringtone type is opened, as shown in Figure 2.11 (third). Select a default ringtone and then click the OK button to return to the `PreferenceFragment`. After selecting the `ListPreference` represented by the Products List, a dialog box titled Choose a Product opens up showing several products in the form of radio buttons, as you can see in Figure 2.11 (fourth). Select Watch.

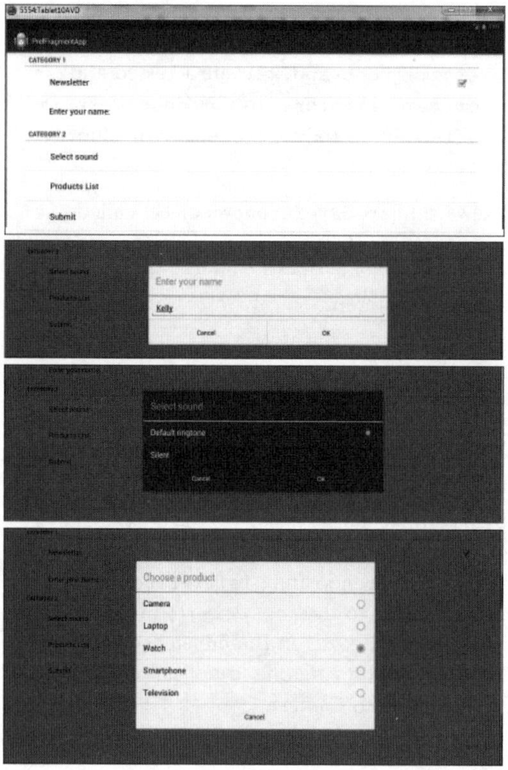

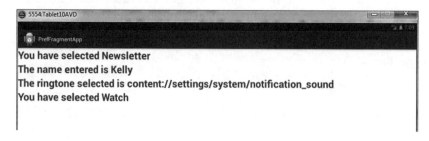

Figure 2.11   A PreferenceFragment showing different preference views (first); the EditTextPreference prompting for name (second); the RingtonePreference prompting to select a ringtone type (third); and the ListPreference showing selectable products in the form of radio buttons (fourth)

After selecting a product, you automatically return to the PreferenceFragment. Finally, you click the Submit button at the bottom of the PreferenceFragment to close the fragment and display the selected preferences. All the selected preferences are shown through the TextView controls, as you can see in Figure 2.12.

Figure 2.12   All the selected preferences displayed via TextView controls

Summary

In this chapter, you saw the usage of fragments and their practical implementation in making an application suitable to different screen sizes. You learned about the fragments life cycle and how to add them dynamically to Android applications at runtime. You discovered the way to pass data from one fragment to another. Finally, you learned the procedure to use specialized fragments (that is, display options through `ListFragment`), display dialog through `DialogFragment`, and set user's preferences through `PreferenceFragment`.

In the next chapter, you will learn to use ActionBar and discover its advantage over the menu. You will come to understand how ActionBar is enabled in an Android application and learn about its different components. You will learn to display action items in ActionBar, navigate to an application's home after selecting the application's icon, and display action views in ActionBar. Also, you will learn to display submenus in ActionBar and create a tabbed ActionBar and drop-down list ActionBar.

3

ActionBars in Action

Most commonly used key actions for an application are displayed through the ActionBar. The ActionBar displays an application's logo, action items, and action views. The ActionBar can be in the form of tabbed and drop-down lists as well. In this chapter, you will learn to use the ActionBar in an Android application and see how it differs from using the menu. You will discover how to enable the ActionBar and toggle its visibility and learn about different ActionBar components. You will also learn how to display an action item in the ActionBar and how an application's icon is used to navigate to an application's home. In addition, you will learn to display action views and submenus in the ActionBar. Finally, you will learn to create tabbed and drop-down list ActionBars.

Recipe: Understanding the Difference Between the Menu and the ActionBar

The ActionBar is a window feature that replaces the title bar at the top of an activity, displaying navigation and important application functionality. It provides a consistent user interface (UI) for an application. It helps in displaying the common key actions that you want to be visible on the screen while running the application.

Menus also help in invoking different application functionalities, but they have a drawback: Menus are displayed or invoked after pressing the Menu button on the AVD or device. Many Android devices no longer have a dedicated menu button, so ActionBars are the preferable substitute. The action items that appear in the ActionBar are instantly accessible without having to press the Menu button.

By default, the ActionBar includes the application logo on the left side, followed by the activity title and action items (if any) on the right side. Action items are equivalent to items that you see in application menus. The application's logo can be linked to the application's home page—that is, wherever you are in the application, if you tap the logo, you can be navigated to the home page.

The ActionBar is enabled if an application uses the default `Theme.Holo` theme and has a target (or minimum) SDK version of 11 or higher.

Example:

```
<uses-sdk android:targetSdkVersion="11" />
```

> **Note**
>
> To use ActionBar, the application's `minSdkVersion` needs to be 11 or greater; otherwise, it will give a compile time error.

Recipe: Toggling ActionBar Visibility

To toggle the visibility of the ActionBar at runtime, you can use its show and hide methods as shown here:

```
ActionBar actionBar = getActionBar();
actionBar.hide();   // It  hides the ActionBar
actionBar.show();   // It makes the ActionBar visible
```

Here, the `getActionBar()` method is called to get the ActionBar object. Its `hide()` and `show()` methods are for hiding and showing the ActionBar, respectively.

To hide the ActionBar in an activity, you can also apply a theme that doesn't support ActionBars. In the `AndroidManifest.xml` file, you can set the theme for the activity to `Theme.Holo.NoActionBar`, as shown here:

```
<activity android:label="@string/app_name"
android:name=".ActionBarApp"
android:theme="@android:style/Theme.Holo.NoActionBar">
```

Hiding and showing of the ActionBar leads to redrawing the layout. You can avoid this by using the `android:windowActionBarOverlay` attribute. Also, if you use the custom theme, set the `android:windowActionBar` attribute to `false` to remove the ActionBar.

The visibility of the icon or logo in the ActionBar is controlled by passing a Boolean value to the `setDisplayShowHomeEnabled()` method. Passing `false` to this method will hide the logo or icon in the ActionBar. Similarly, passing `true` to this method will make the logo or icon visible in the ActionBar, as shown here:

```
actionBar.setDisplayShowHomeEnabled(true);
```

You can control the visibility of the title in the ActionBar by passing a Boolean value to the `setDisplayShowTitleEnabled()` method. For example, following the statement shown next hides the title in the ActionBar:

```
actionBar.setDisplayShowTitleEnabled(false);
```

Recipe: Understanding the ActionBar Components

The ActionBar is composed of the following components:

- **Application's icon/logo**—Displayed at the upper left on the ActionBar.

- **Activity title**—Displays the title for the ActionBar.

- **Tabs**—Displays the tabs of the ActionBar if the navigation mode set is `tabs` (see Figure 3.1 [middle]).

- **Drop-down list**—Displays the action items in the form of a drop-down list if the navigation mode set is `list navigation` (see Figure 3.1 [bottom]).

- **Action items**—Displays different application functionalities. To invoke a module or perform a task, an appropriate action item is selected from the ActionBar. You can also collect a group of related action items into a submenu.

- **Action views**—Displays custom views in the ActionBar. Figure 3.1 (middle) shows an action view in the form of a search widget.

- **Overflow menu**—Displays action items that could not be accommodated in the ActionBar.

- **Overflow menu button**—Appears as three vertical dots (see Figure 3.1 [top]). After selecting it, the hidden action items are displayed in an Overflow menu.

- **Submenu**—Represents a collection of menu items related to a menu item. When a menu item is clicked, its submenu (if any) pops up.

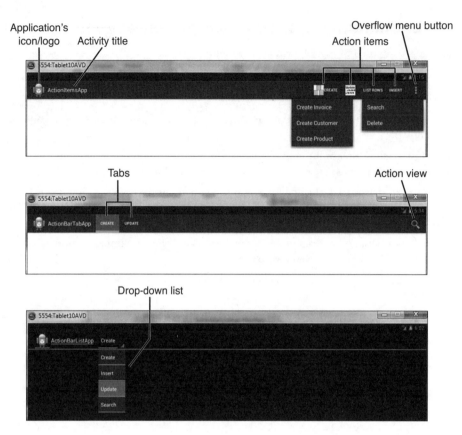

Figure 3.1   Screen showing ActionBar components (top); screen showing action tabs and action view (middle); and screen showing drop-down list (bottom)

Recipe: Displaying Action Items in the ActionBar

To display action items in the ActionBar, you need to add an `android:showAsAction` attribute to the menu items when defining them in the menu file. The `showAsAction` attribute determines how to display the action item. The value of the `showAsAction` attribute can be any one of the following:

- **`always`**—Makes the action item appear on the ActionBar.
- **`ifRoom`**—Makes the action item appear in the ActionBar, but only if there is room available on it. If there's not enough room, the item will appear in the Overflow menu.

- **never**—Makes the menu item always appear in the Overflow menu. To display the Overflow menu, press the Menu button on the AVD or the Overflow menu button on the physical device.

- **withText**—Displays the title of the action item along with the icon (if any). This attribute value can be set with other values by separating them with a pipe (|).

- **collapseActionView**—Makes the action view associated with the action item collapsible. That is, the action view collapses to a normal action item.

Now you'll explore the concept of the ActionBar with a running application. Create a new Android project called `ActionItemsApp`. Set values of `minSdkVersion` and `targetSdkVersion` attributes to 14 and 17, respectively. In this application, you will display two action items called Create and Update. The action items are the clickable items that appear in the ActionBar. You can define action items in the `activity_ action_items_app.xml` menu file (the filename depends on the name of the Android project) that is provided by default in the `res/menu` folder of your application. After defining the two action items, Create and Update, the `activity_action_items_app.xml` menu file will appear as shown in Listing 3.1.

Listing 3.1   **Code Written into the** `activity_action_items_app.xml` **Menu File**

```
<menu xmlns:android="http://schemas.android.com/apk/res/android" >
    <item android:id="@+id/create "
        android:title="Create"
        android:icon="@drawable/create"
        android:orderInCategory="0"
        android:showAsAction="ifRoom|withText" />
    <item android:id="@+id/update"
        android:title="Update"
        android:icon="@drawable/update"
        android:showAsAction="always"  />
</menu>
```

You can see that the Create action item is set to appear in the ActionBar if there is enough space. Also, the action item will appear with the title text `Create`. The Update action item is set to appear in the ActionBar. Because you want to represent the Create and Update action items with icons, the `create.png` and `update.png` image files need to be copied into the `res/ drawable` folders of the application.

Now your application is ready to run. There is no need to write any code in the `activity_ action_items_app.xml` layout file or the `ActionItemsAppActivity.java` Java activity file. After running the application, you see the two action items shown in Figure 3.2.

Figure 3.2   Two action items, Create and Update, displayed on the ActionBar

If the action item appears with only the icon and you long-press (click and hold) the item, the text assigned in the `android:title` attribute will appear as a tooltip.

When you increase the number of action items in the ActionBar, the ones that can accommodate in the ActionBar will appear there as action items, and the rest of them will be hidden. Whenever there are action items that are not visible, an Overflow menu button will appear on the right in the ActionBar. After selecting the Overflow menu button, the hidden action items will appear there. To see this happen, increase the number of action items in the `activity_action_items_app.xml` menu file, which will appear as shown in Listing 3.2.

Listing 3.2   **Code Written into the** `activity_action_items_app.xml` **Menu File**

```xml
<menu xmlns:android="http://schemas.android.com/apk/res/android">
    <item android:id="@+id/create"
        android:title="Create"
        android:icon="@drawable/create"
        android:orderInCategory="0"
        android:showAsAction="ifRoom|withText" />
    <item android:id="@+id/update"
        android:title="Update"
        android:icon="@drawable/update"
        android:showAsAction="always"  />
    <item android:id="@+id/list_rows"
        android:title="List Rows"
        android:showAsAction="ifRoom" />
    <item android:id="@+id/search_row"
        android:title="Search"
        android:showAsAction="ifRoom" />
    <item android:id="@+id/delete_row"
        android:title="Delete"
        android:showAsAction="never" />
    <item android:id="@+id/insert_row"
        android:title="Insert"
        android:showAsAction="always"  />
</menu>
```

You can see that four action items—List Rows, Search, Delete, and Insert—were added to the ActionBar. The List Row and Search are set to appear in the ActionBar if there is enough space; otherwise, they appear in the Overflow menu. The Delete action item will never appear in the ActionBar even if there is enough space, but it will always appear in the Overflow menu. The Insert action item is set to always appear in the ActionBar.

After running the application, you find that four action items out of six will appear in the ActionBar, along with an Overflow menu button on the right. The action items that are visible in the ActionBar are Create, Update, List Rows, and Insert (see Figure 3.3 [top]). After selecting the Overflow menu button, the hidden action items, Search and Delete, will appear in the Overflow menu (see Figure 3.3 [bottom]).

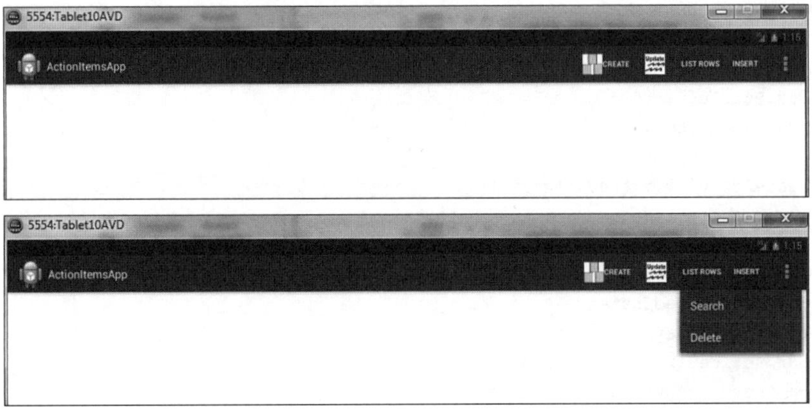

Figure 3.3   Visible action items and the Overflow menu button (top) and the hidden action items in the Overflow menu (bottom)

The `collapseActionView` value of the `showAsAction` attribute is explained in the recipe, "Displaying Action Views in the ActionBar."

Recipe: Navigating to the Application Home Page After Selecting the Application Icon

If the user clicks the ActionBar logo or icon, it navigates him to the home page of the application. The application home here means the application's main activity—that is, the root of your activity stack.

By default, the logo or icon displayed in the ActionBar is nonclickable. To make the logo or icon clickable, you must call the ActionBar's `setHomeButtonEnabled method()` and pass the Boolean value `true` to it, as shown here:

```
actionBar.setHomeButtonEnabled(true);
```

Clicking the logo or icon is considered a menu item click and is handled by the onOptionsItemSelected handler of your activity. When the logo or icon is clicked, it is as if a menu item with the android.R.id.home ID is clicked. In other words, after you click the logo or icon, the onOptionItemSelected() method is called, passing the android.R.id.home to it as a parameter. Assuming the current activity is CreateActivity and the home or root activity that you want to navigate to after clicking the icon is ActionItemsAppActivity, the code will appear as shown in Listing 3.3.

Listing 3.3   **Code Written into the** CreateActivity.java **Activity File**

```
package com.androidtablet.actionitemsapp;

import android.app.ActionBar;
import android.app.Activity;
import android.content.Intent;
import android.os.Bundle;
import android.view.MenuItem;

public class CreateActivity extends Activity {

    @Override
    protected void onCreate(Bundle savedInstanceState){
        super.onCreate(savedInstanceState);
        setContentView(R.layout.create);
        ActionBar actionBar = getActionBar();
        actionBar.setHomeButtonEnabled(true);
    }

    @Override
    public boolean onOptionsItemSelected(MenuItem item) {          #1
        switch (item.getItemId()) {
            case  (android.R.id.home) :
                Intent intent = new Intent(this,
                    ActionItemsAppActivity.class);
                intent.addFlags(Intent.FLAG_ACTIVITY_CLEAR_TOP);
                startActivity(intent);
                break;
            default:
                return super.onOptionsItemSelected(item);
        }
        return true;
    }
}
```

The preceding code assumes that a layout file named `create.xml` exists in the `res/layout` folder. To navigate to the home activity, you use an intent flag called `FLAG_ACTIVITY_CLEAR_TOP` that closes all activities begun since the start of the home activity. In the preceding code, you can see that the ActionBar object `actionBar` is accessed by calling the `getActionBar()` method, and the Boolean value `true` is passed to the `setHomeButtonEnabled()` method, which makes the application's logo clickable. Clicking the application's logo generates a click event on a menu item with the `android.R.id.home` ID. In the handler method, `onOptionsItemSelected()`, you check whether the menu item with the `android.R.id.home` ID is clicked—that is, whether the application's logo was clicked. If the application's logo was clicked, you navigate back to the main activity of the application, `ActionItemsAppActivity.class`, by clearing all the activities (if any) on the top of the stack.

In Android 4.1 and higher versions, the entire `onOptionsItemSelected` method represented by statement #1 in the preceding code can be removed. That is, you can navigate to the main activity by adding the following statement to the `AndroidManifest.xml` file:

```
<activity android:name=".CreateActivity" android:label="@string/app_name"
android:parentActivityName="ActionItemsAppActivity"/>
```

Recipe: Displaying Action Views in the ActionBar

Action views provide an embedded control for more immediate action behaviors. Basically, action views allow a custom view to be placed in the ActionBar. The most common action view used in Android applications is `SearchView`. `SearchView` provides a user interface to enter a search query and submit a request to a search provider. It also shows a list of query suggestions or results, if available, allowing a user to select from them. To check for the occurrence of an event in `SearchView`, the `setOnQueryTextListener` is set as a listener to respond to the text entered or changed by the user. `OnQueryTextListener` requires two methods: `onQueryTextChange` and `onQueryTextSubmit`. The `onQueryTextChange` method is called whenever a user makes changes in the search text, and `onQueryTextSubmit` is called when the user presses Enter or Search.

To understand how action view is used in an Android application, create an Android project called `ActionViewApp`. In the application, you will display `SearchView` as an action view, where a user can enter the text to search for. To display `SearchView`, write the code shown in Listing 3.4 into the `activity_action_view_app.xml` menu file, which is found in the `res/menu` folder.

Listing 3.4   **Code Written into the** `activity_ action_view_app.xml` **Menu File**

```
<menu xmlns:android="http://schemas.android.com/apk/res/android" >
    <item android:id="@+id/action_search"
        android:title="Search"
        android:showAsAction="ifRoom"
        android:actionViewClass="android.widget.SearchView"/>
</menu>
```

With this code, `SearchView` will appear in the form of an icon, as shown in Figure 3.4 (top). You can also make `SearchView` appear in the form of an action item by setting the `android:showAsAction` attribute as shown here:

```
android:showAsAction="ifRoom|collapseActionView"
```

Recall, the `collapseActionView` makes the action view associated with the action item collapsible; that is, it makes the action view collapse to a normal action item. Now, the `SearchView` will appear as an action item, as shown in Figure 3.4 (middle). After selecting the `SearchView` in either format (icon or action item), a search box will open, allowing the user to enter text to search for (see Figure 3.4 [bottom]).

Figure 3.4   `SearchView` appears in the form of an icon (top); `SearchView` appears in the form of an action item (middle); and search box appears after selecting the `SearchView` (bottom)

To understand how the `setOnQueryTextListener` event listener performs, you will display log messages showing the text the user entered or changed in the search box. You will also display the final text entered in the search box. To do all this, you write the code shown in Listing 3.5 into the `ActionViewAppActivity.java` Java activity file.

Listing 3.5   **Code Written into the** `ActionViewAppActivity.java` **Java Activity File**

```
package com.androidtablet.actionviewapp;

import android.os.Bundle;
import android.app.Activity;
import android.view.Menu;
import android.view.MenuInflater;
import android.widget.SearchView;
import android.widget.SearchView.OnQueryTextListener;
```

```java
import android.util.Log;

public class ActionViewAppActivity extends Activity {

    @Override
    public void onCreate(Bundle savedInstanceState) {
        super.onCreate(savedInstanceState);
        setContentView(R.layout.activity_action_view_app);
    }

    @Override
    public boolean onCreateOptionsMenu(Menu menu) {
        MenuInflater inflater = getMenuInflater();
        inflater.inflate(R.menu.activity_action_view_app, menu);
        SearchView searchView = (SearchView) menu.findItem(
            R.id.action_search).getActionView();
        searchView.setOnQueryTextListener(new
            OnQueryTextListener(){
            @Override
            public boolean onQueryTextChange(String newText) {
                Log.d("New Text:", newText);
                return false;
            }
            @Override
            public boolean onQueryTextSubmit(String query) {
                Log.d("Final Text:", query);
                return false;
            }
        });
        return true;
    }
}
```

Here, you can see that the SearchView widget with the action_search ID is accessed from the menu file and is assigned to the SearchView object, searchView. The setOnQueryTextListener is associated with the SearchView object, searchView, so that necessary actions can be taken when the user enters or submits text in the search box. When the user enters or changes any text in the search box, the onQueryTextChange() method is invoked. In the onQueryTextChange() method, you display the modified text in the search box using log messages. When the user finishes entering text in the search box by pressing Enter or the Search button, the onQueryTextSubmit() method is called, and you display the entire text entered in the search box with log messages.

After running the application, you see SearchView in the form of an icon in the ActionBar (see Figure 3.5 [top]). When the user selects the SearchView action view in the ActionBar, a search box appears, prompting for the text to search for (see Figure 3.5 [middle]). The text entered in the search box appears in the log messages, as shown in Figure 3.5 (bottom).

Figure 3.5   `SearchView` displayed on application startup (top); search box appears after selecting `SearchView` to enter text (middle); and log messages showing how text was entered or modified in the search box (bottom)

Recipe: Displaying a Submenu in the ActionBar

To display submenus in the ActionBar, you need to group the menu items of the submenu within a <menu> tag and nest it inside the action item with which you want to associate the submenu. Consider a situation in which you want to create two action items: Create and Update. When the user clicks the Create action item, a submenu pops up displaying three menu items: Create Invoice, Create Customer, and Create Product. To understand how a submenu is defined for an action item, create an Android project called `ActionBarSubmenu`. To create the Create and Update action items and a submenu within Create, write the code shown in Listing 3.6 into the `activity_action_bar_submenu.xml` menu file found in the /res/ menu folder.

Listing 3.6 **Code Written into the** `activity_action_bar_submenu.xml` **Menu File**

```xml
<menu
    xmlns:android="http://schemas.android.com/apk/res/android">
    <item android:id="@+id/create"
        android:title="Create"
        android:orderInCategory="0"
        android:showAsAction="ifRoom"  >
        <menu>
            <item android:id="@+id/create_invoice"
                android:title="Create Invoice"  />
            <item android:id="@+id/create_customer"
                android:title="Create Customer"  />
            <item android:id="@+id/create_product"
                android:title="Create Product" />
        </menu>
    </item>
        <item android:id="@+id/update"
        android:title="Update"
        android:showAsAction="always"  />
</menu>
```

You can see that this code includes the android:showAsAction attribute to display the menu items in the ActionBar if the space permits. The <menu> element defined inside the Create action item defines the submenu consisting of three menu items: Create Invoice, Create Customer, and Create Product.

To show the response when any action or menu item is selected, you need to define a TextView control in the layout file, called activity_action_bar_submenu.xml. The TextView will display the text indicating which action menu or action item is pressed. After you define the TextView control, the activity_action_bar_submenu.xml layout file will appear as shown in Listing 3.7.

Listing 3.7 **Code Written into the** `activity_action_bar_submenu.xml` **Layout File**

```xml
<LinearLayout
    xmlns:android="http://schemas.android.com/apk/res/android"
    android:layout_width="match_parent"
    android:layout_height="match_parent"
    android:orientation="vertical" >
    <TextView
        android:layout_width="match_parent"
        android:layout_height="wrap_content"
        android:id="@+id/selectedopt"
        android:textSize="@dimen/text_size"
        android:textStyle="bold" />
</LinearLayout>
```

To identify the `TextView` in Java code, it is assigned the `selectedopt` ID. The text displayed through the `TextView` control will appear in bold and in 18dp size. To display the response when any menu or action item is selected, modify `ActionBarSubmenuActivity.java` to appear as shown in Listing 3.8. The code will display the text indicating which menu or action item is selected.

Listing 3.8   Code Written into the `ActionBarSubmenuActivity.java` Java Activity File

```java
package com.androidtablet.actionbarsubmenu;

import android.os.Bundle;
import android.app.Activity;
import android.view.Menu;
import android.view.MenuInflater;
import android.view.MenuItem;
import android.widget.TextView;

public class ActionBarSubmenuActivity extends Activity {

    private TextView selectedOpt;
    @Override
    public void onCreate(Bundle savedInstanceState) {
        super.onCreate(savedInstanceState);
        setContentView(R.layout.activity_action_bar_submenu);
        selectedOpt=(TextView)findViewById(R.id.selectedopt);
    }
    @Override
    public boolean onCreateOptionsMenu(Menu menu) {
        MenuInflater inflater = getMenuInflater();
        inflater.inflate(R.menu.activity_action_bar_submenu,
            menu);
        return true;
    }
    @Override
    public boolean onOptionsItemSelected(MenuItem item) {
        switch (item.getItemId()) {
            case R.id.create:
                selectedOpt.setText("You have selected Create
                    option");
                break;
            case R.id.update:
                selectedOpt.setText("You have selected Update
                    option");
                break;
            case R.id.create_invoice:
                selectedOpt.setText("You have selected Create
                    Invoice option");
```

```
                break;
            case R.id.create_customer:
                selectedOpt.setText("You have selected Create
                    Customer option");
                break;
            case R.id.create_product:
                selectedOpt.setText("You have selected Create
                    Product option");
                break;
        }
        return true;
    }
}
```

To display the ActionBar, you inflate or merge the menu defined in the `activity_action_bar_submenu.xml` menu file. By doing so, you get the `MenuInflater` from the activity class. An object, `inflater`, is created from the `MenuInflater` class, and the `inflater's` inflate method is called to inflate, or merge, the menu defined in `activity_action_bar_submenu`. The `onCreateOptionsMenu()` method is set to return the Boolean value `true` to allow Android to display the menu.

All the menu or action items selected are handled through the `onOptionsItemSelected()` method. The selected menu or action item is passed to this method as the `MenuItem` parameter. You override this method in the activity by writing the code you want to execute when a menu or action item is selected. In the method, you extract the ID of the selected menu or action item to identify it and then take the respective action. The `getItemId()` method helps to discover the ID of the selected menu or action item. Thereafter, through the `switch` statement, you display the text message indicating which menu or action item is selected using the `TextView` object, `selectedOpt`.

After running the application, you see the Create and Update action items appear in the ActionBar (see Figure 3.6 [top]). After you select the Create action item, the `TextView` displays the message `You have selected Create option`. A submenu appears, as shown in Figure 3.6 (middle), after you select the Create action item. After you select any menu item from the submenu, the respective text message will appear via the `TextView`. For example, after you select the `Create Customer` menu item from the submenu, the text message `You have selected Create Customer option` appears, as shown in Figure 3.6 (bottom).

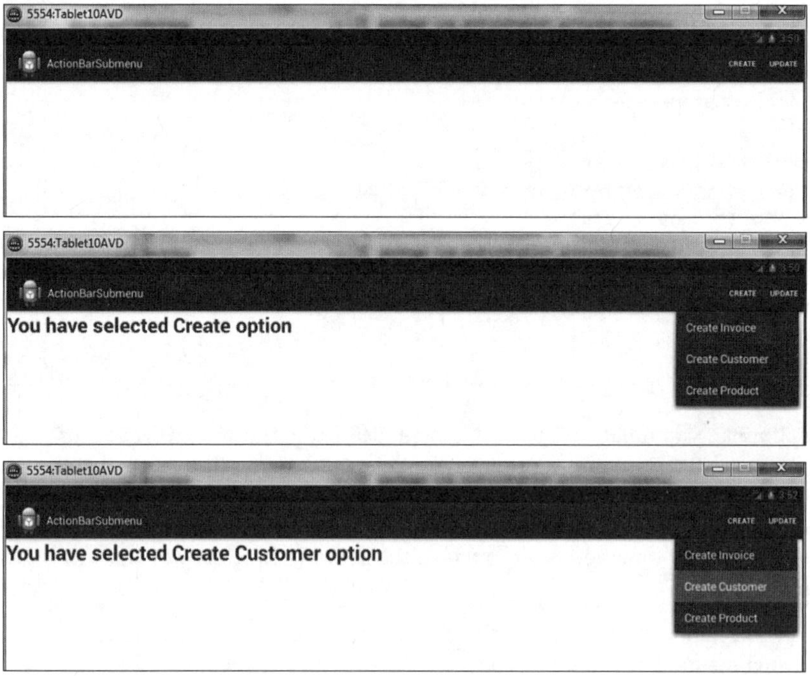

Figure 3.6   Two action items displayed on application startup (top); the submenu pops up after selecting the Create action item (middle); and the `TextView` control indicates which menu item from the submenu is selected (bottom).

Can you make a menu item checkable? Certainly.

To make any menu item checkable, you assign the Boolean value `true` to its `android:checkable` attribute. For example, to make the `Create Product` menu item shown in the submenu checkable (see Figure 3.6 [middle]), you write the code shown here:

```
<item android:id="@+id/create_product"
    android:title="Create Product"
    android:checkable="true" />
```

This code will make the Create Product menu item appear as a checkable menu item (see Figure 3.7 [top]).

You can also make menu items appear as radio buttons. That is, you can make the user select a single menu item in a group. If a menu item in a group is selected, any previously selected menu item will be automatically deselected.

To understand the concept of radio buttons, add a group of mutually exclusive menu items to the Update action item. The group shows the menu items Update Code, Update Name, and Update Price. These menu items will appear as radio buttons, so only one menu item can be selected in the group. When a menu item is selected, any previously selected menu item will be automatically deselected. To add a mutually exclusive group of menu items to the Update action item, the `activity_action_bar_submenu.xml` menu file is modified to appear as shown in Listing 3.9.

Listing 3.9 **Code Written into the** `activity_action_bar_submenu.xml` **Menu File**

```
<menu
    xmlns:android="http://schemas.android.com/apk/res/android">
    <item android:id="@+id/create"
        android:title="Create"
        android:orderInCategory="0"
        android:showAsAction="ifRoom|withText" >
        <menu>
            <item android:id="@+id/create_invoice"
                android:title="Create Invoice"  />
            <item android:id="@+id/create_customer"
                android:title="Create Customer"  />
            <item android:id="@+id/create_product"
                android:title="Create Product"
                android:checkable="true" />
        </menu>
    </item>
    <item android:id="@+id/update"
        android:title="Update"
        android:showAsAction="always" >
        <menu>
            <group android:checkableBehavior="single">
                <item android:id="@+id/update_code"
                    android:title="Update Code"
                    android:checked="true" />
                <item android:id="@+id/update_name"
                    android:title="Update Name"  />
                <item android:id="@+id/update_price"
                    android:title="Update Price" />
            </group>
        </menu>
    </item>
</menu>
```

You can see that menu items are nested in the `<group>` element and the `android:checkableBehavior=single` attribute is associated with the group to ensure that only a single menu item in the group is selected at a time. Hence, the Update Code, Update Name, and Update Price menu items will appear as radio buttons. To know which of the radio buttons is selected, you add the code as shown in Listing 3.10 in the `ActionBarSubmenuActivity.java` file. Only the code in bold is newly added; the rest is the same as in Listing 3.8.

Listing 3.10   Code in the `ActionBarSubmenuActivity.java` **Java Activity File**

```java
package com.androidtablet.actionbarsubmenu;

import android.os.Bundle;
import android.app.Activity;
import android.view.Menu;
import android.view.MenuInflater;
import android.view.MenuItem;
import android.widget.TextView;

public class ActionBarSubmenuActivity extends Activity {
    private TextView selectedOpt;
    @Override
    public void onCreate(Bundle savedInstanceState) {
        super.onCreate(savedInstanceState);
        setContentView(R.layout.activity_action_bar_submenu);
        selectedOpt=(TextView)findViewById(R.id.selectedopt);
    }
    @Override
    public boolean onCreateOptionsMenu(Menu menu) {
        MenuInflater inflater = getMenuInflater();
        inflater.inflate(R.menu.activity_action_bar_submenu,
            menu);
        return true;
    }


    @Override
    public boolean onOptionsItemSelected(MenuItem item) {
        switch (item.getItemId()) {
            case R.id.create:
                selectedOpt.setText("You have selected Create
                    option");
                break;
            case R.id.update:
                selectedOpt.setText("You have selected Update
                    option");
                break;
            case R.id.create_invoice:
                selectedOpt.setText("You have selected Create
                    Invoice option");
                break;
            case R.id.create_customer:
                selectedOpt.setText("You have selected Create
                    Customer option");
                break;
            case R.id.create_product:
                selectedOpt.setText("You have selected Create
```

```
                    Product option");
             break;
         case R.id.update_code:
             selectedOpt.setText("You have selected Update
                 Code option");
             break;
         case R.id.update_name:
             selectedOpt.setText("You have selected Update
                 Name option");
             break;
         case R.id.update_price:
             selectedOpt.setText("You have selected Update
                 Price option");
             break;
     }
     return true;
   }
}
```

After you run the application and select an Update action item, a submenu appears, displaying
the menu items Update Code, Update Name, and Update Price in the form of radio buttons.
When a menu item is selected, any previously selected menu item will be deselected and the
respective text message will appear via the `TextView`. For example, after you select the Update
Code menu item from the submenu, the text message `You have selected Update Code`
`option` appears, as shown in Figure 3.7 (bottom).

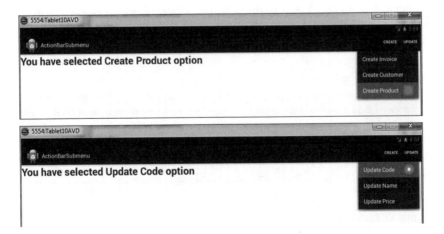

Figure 3.7   The Create Product menu item appearing as checkable (top), and menu items
appearing as radio buttons (bottom)

Recipe: Creating a Tabbed ActionBar

Tabbed ActionBars are like buttons with a custom handler that are designed to be used with the fragment manager. To display navigation tabs in the ActionBar, the `setNavigationMode()` method is called, passing the value `ActionBar.NAVIGATION_MODE_TABS` as a parameter, as shown here:

```
actionBar.setNavigationMode(ActionBar.NAVIGATION_MODE_TABS);
```

After determining the navigation mode, the tabs are added to the ActionBar by calling its `addTab()` method, as shown here:

```
actionBar.addTab(actionBar.newTab().setText("Create").
    setTabListener(this));
```

The code creates a new tab, sets its text to Create, attaches a `TabListener` to it, and finally adds the newly created tab to the ActionBar. For example, the `setText()` method used here sets the text of the tab. You can call the `setIcon()` method to define an image for the tab. You can also call the `setContentDescription()` method to supply more detailed tab information.

Example:

```
Tab tab1 = actionBar.newTab();
tabOne.setText("Create")
.setIcon(R.drawable.ic_launcher)
.setContentDescription("Creating the Invoice")
.setTabListener(this));
actionBar.addTab(tab1);
```

This code adds a tab with text called Create to the tabbed ActionBar. The icon assigned to the tab is the default icon, `ic_launcher`, and the detailed assigned description is `Creating the Invoice`. When you click a tab, the event is handled by the `TabListener` that performs the desired task.

Now you'll explore the concept of the tabbed ActionBar using an actual example. Create an Android project called `ActionBarTabApp`. In this application, you will create two tabs: Create and Update. When any tab is selected, the respective fragment will be invoked displaying a text message informing the fragment is active. The views of the two fragments will be displayed through the individual XML layout files. So add two XML files to the `res/layout` folder called `createfragment.xml` and `updatefragment.xml`, respectively.

In the `createfragment.xml`, write the code as shown in Listing 3.11.

Listing 3.11   **Code Written into the `createfragment.xml` File**

```
<?xml version="1.0" encoding="utf-8"?>
<LinearLayout xmlns:android="http://schemas.android.com/apk/res/android"
    android:layout_width="match_parent"
    android:layout_height="match_parent"
    android:orientation="vertical" >
```

```
    <TextView
        android:id="@+id/create_textview"
        android:layout_width="match_parent"
        android:layout_height="wrap_content"
        android:text=" This is Create Fragment "
        android:textSize="@dimen/text_size"
        android:textStyle="bold"   />
</LinearLayout>
```

You can see that a `TextView` is defined in the preceding layout file that is initialized to display the text `This is Create Fragment`. The message when displayed will indicate that the first fragment is invoked. Similarly, in the `updatefragment.xml`, write the code as shown in Listing 3.12.

Listing 3.12   **Code Written into the** `updatefragment.xml` **File**

```
<?xml version="1.0" encoding="utf-8"?>
<LinearLayout xmlns:android="http://schemas.android.com/apk/res/android"
    android:layout_width="match_parent"
    android:layout_height="match_parent"
    android:orientation="vertical" >
    <TextView
        android:id="@+id/update_textview"
        android:layout_width="match_parent"
        android:layout_height="wrap_content"
        android:text=" This is Update Fragment "
        android:textSize="@dimen/text_size"
        android:textStyle="bold"   />
</LinearLayout>
```

Again, a `TextView` control is defined in the layout file for the second fragment. The `TextView` is initialized to display the text `This is Update Fragment` to indicate that the second fragment is invoked.

To display the content of the desired fragment when an action tab is selected, you need to define a fragment container in the activity layout file. So, in the activity layout file `activity_action_bar_tab_app.xml`, write the code as shown in Listing 3.13.

Listing 3.13   **Code Written into the Activity Layout File** `activity_action_bar_tab_app.xml`

```
<LinearLayout
xmlns:android="http://schemas.android.com/apk/res/android"
    xmlns:tools="http://schemas.android.com/tools"
    android:layout_width="match_parent"
    android:layout_height="match_parent"
    android:orientation="horizontal" >
```

```
    <LinearLayout
        android:id="@+id/fragment_container"
        android:layout_width="wrap_content"
        android:layout_height="match_parent" />
</LinearLayout>
```

To load the views of the two fragments, add two Java class files called `CreateActivity.java` and `UpdateActivity.java` to the `com.androidtablet.actionbartabapp` package of your Android project.

To load the `View` defined in the layout file `createfragment.xml`, write the code as shown in Listing 3.14 into the `CreateActivity.java` file.

Listing 3.14   Code Written into the `CreateActivity.java` File

```
package com.androidtablet.actionbartabapp;

import android.app.Fragment;
import android.view.View;
import android.view.ViewGroup;
import android.view.LayoutInflater;
import android.os.Bundle;

public class CreateActivity extends Fragment {
    @Override
    public View onCreateView(LayoutInflater inflater, ViewGroup
        container, Bundle savedInstanceState) {
        return inflater.inflate(R.layout.createfragment,
            container, false);
    }
}
```

Again, to load the view defined in the layout file `updatefragment.xml`, write the code as shown in Listing 3.15 into the `UpdateActivity.java` file.

Listing 3.15   Code Written into the `UpdateActivity.java` File

```
package com.androidtablet.actionbartabapp;

import android.app.Fragment;
import android.view.View;
import android.view.ViewGroup;
import android.view.LayoutInflater;
import android.os.Bundle;
```

```
public class UpdateActivity extends Fragment {
    @Override
    public View onCreateView(LayoutInflater inflater, ViewGroup
        container, Bundle savedInstanceState) {
        return inflater.inflate(R.layout.updatefragment,
            container, false);
    }
}
```

Next, you need to write Java code in the main activity file, `ActionBarTabAppActivity.java`, to do the following tasks:

- Define two tabs—`Create` and `Update`—in the application
- Define and associate tab listeners to the two tabs
- Activate the Create and Update fragment when the respective tab is clicked.

To perform all the preceding tasks, write the code as shown in Listing 3.16 into the Java activity file `ActionBarTabAppActivity.java`.

Listing 3.16   **Code Written into the** `ActionBarTabAppActivity.java` **Java Activity File**

```
package com.androidtablet.actionbartabapp;

import android.os.Bundle;
import android.app.Activity;
import android.app.ActionBar;
import android.app.ActionBar.Tab;
import android.app.FragmentTransaction;
import android.util.Log;
import android.app.FragmentManager;
import android.app.Fragment;

public class ActionBarTabAppActivity extends Activity  {
    @Override
    public void onCreate(Bundle savedInstanceState) {
        super.onCreate(savedInstanceState);
        setContentView(R.layout.activity_action_bar_tab_app);
        Fragment createFragment = new CreateActivity();
        Fragment updateFragment = new UpdateActivity();
        ActionBar actionBar = getActionBar();
        actionBar.setNavigationMode(ActionBar.NAVIGATION_
            MODE_TABS);
        actionBar.setDisplayShowTitleEnabled(true);
        ActionBar.Tab CreateTab = actionBar.newTab().
            setText("Create");
```

```
        ActionBar.Tab UpdateTab = actionBar.newTab().
            setText("Update");
        CreateTab.setTabListener(new MyTabsListener(
            createFragment));
        UpdateTab.setTabListener(new MyTabsListener(
            updateFragment));
        actionBar.addTab(CreateTab);
        actionBar.addTab(UpdateTab);
    }
    protected class MyTabsListener implements ActionBar.
        TabListener {
        Fragment fragment;
        public MyTabsListener(Fragment fragment){
            this.fragment = fragment;
        }

        public void onTabSelected(Tab tab, FragmentTransaction
            ft) {
            ft.replace(R.id.fragment_container, fragment, null);
        }

        public void onTabUnselected(Tab tab, FragmentTransaction
            ft) {
            ft.remove(fragment);
            getFragmentManager().popBackStack(null,
                FragmentManager.POP_BACK_STACK_INCLUSIVE);
        }

        public void onTabReselected(Tab tab, FragmentTransaction
            ft) {
        Log.d("Tab", String.valueOf(tab.getPosition()) +
            " re-selected");
        }
    }
}
```

In the preceding code, you can see that the ActionBar object is created by calling the getActionBar() method. To make the ActionBar appear as tabs, set its navigation mode to ActionBar.NAVIGATION_MODE_TABS. You can make the activity title invisible by passing the Boolean value false to the setDisplayShowTitleEnabled() method. Thereafter, you create two tabs labeled Create and Update and add them to the ActionBar.

The TabListener event listener is associated with both the tabs. When either of the tabs is selected, the onTabSelected() method is invoked, and the desired fragment is invoked. The onTabSelected() method activates the respective fragment displaying the views defined in its layout file. When a tab is selected, the onTabUnselected() method is called, and the tab that is not selected is passed to it as the parameter. The fragment associated to the unselected tab is removed from the stack, making it invisible.

The onTabUnselected() method displays the position of the unselected tab. After running the application, you see the tabbed ActionBar showing two tabs: Create and Update. After you select the Create tab, the fragment associated to it is invoked displaying a message This is Create Fragment, as shown in Figure 3.8 (top). Similarly, after selecting the Update tab, the fragment associated to it is invoked displaying the text message This is Update Fragment, as shown in Figure 3.8 (bottom).

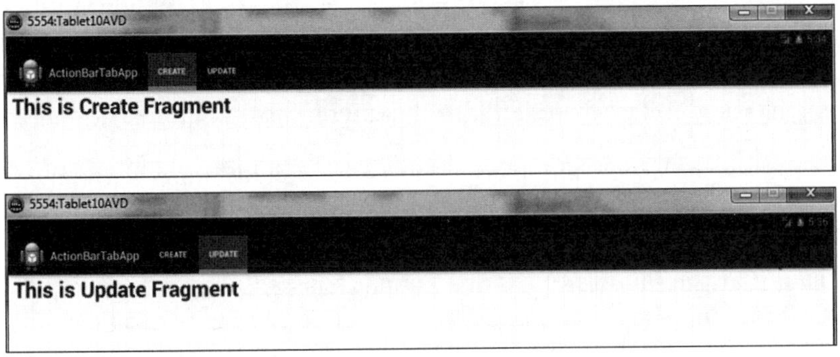

Figure 3.8   Screen showing two tabs in the tabbed ActionBar (top), and the log messages displayed after selecting the action tabs (bottom)

Recipe: Creating a Drop-Down List ActionBar

In a drop-down list ActionBar, the action items are displayed in the form of a drop-down list. To display a drop-down list in the ActionBar, you call its setNavigationMode() method, passing the ActionBar.NAVIGATION_MODE_LIST value to it as a parameter, as shown here:

```
actionBar.setNavigationMode(ActionBar.NAVIGATION_MODE_LIST);
```

The drop-down list appears as a spinner, displaying a list of available options, allowing the user to select one of them. To display action items in a drop-down list, you will use an adapter that implements the SpinnerAdapter interface; for example, you might use an ArrayAdapter, SimpleCursorAdapter, or any baseadapter. In the application that you are going to create, you will be using an ArrayAdapter, because it the simplest of the adapters that acts as the data source for the selection widgets. You will be following these steps to create the application:

1. Define a string array containing the strings that you want to be displayed in the drop-down list.

2. Create an `ArrayAdapter` that displays the elements of the array in the form of drop-down items. That is, you wrap or cast the elements of the array into the spinner drop-down items.

3. Assign the `ArrayAdapter` to the ActionBar to display the action items. To assign the `ArrayAdapter` to the ActionBar and attach an event listener to the drop-down items that will be displayed, call the `setListNavigationCallbacks()` method, passing the adapter and `OnNavigationListener` to it as parameters as shown here:

```
String[] items = new String[] { "Create", "Insert", "Update", "Search" };
ArrayAdapter<String> adapter = new ArrayAdapter<String>(this, android.R.layout.
simple_spinner_dropdown_item, items);
ActionBar actionBar = getActionBar();
actionBar.setNavigationMode(ActionBar.NAVIGATION_MODE_LIST);
actionBar.setListNavigationCallbacks(adapter, onNavigationItemSelected);
```

In the preceding code, a string array, `items`, is defined and consists of the strings you want to display in the drop-down list ActionBar. An `ArrayAdapter` called `adapter` is created to hold the string array items and cast the array elements into the spinner drop-down items.

The ActionBar object `actionBar` is created, and its navigation mode is set to `ActionBar.NAVIGATION_MODE_LIST`. The `setListNavigationCallbacks()` method is called on the `actionBar`, passing the `ArrayAdapter`, `adapter`, and `onNavigationSelected` listener to it as parameters. You assign the callbacks to handle drop-down selections. When a user selects an action item from the drop-down list, the `onNavigationItemSelected` handler is called, into which you can write the code to perform the desired action.

Try creating a drop-down list ActionBar. First create an Android project called `ActionBarListApp`. In this application, you will display a few action items in the form of a drop-down list. When any of the action items is selected, the respective log message is displayed. In the `ActionBarListAppActivity.java` Java activity file, write the code shown in Listing 3.17.

Listing 3.17   Code Written into the `ActionBarListAppActivity.java` Java Activity File

```
package com.androidtablet.actionbarlistapp;

import android.os.Bundle;
import android.app.Activity;
import android.app.ActionBar.OnNavigationListener;
import android.app.ActionBar;
import android.widget.ArrayAdapter;
import android.util.Log;

public class ActionBarListAppActivity extends Activity {

    @Override
    public void onCreate(Bundle savedInstanceState) {
```

```
    super.onCreate(savedInstanceState);
    String[] items = new String[] { "Create", "Insert",
        "Update", "Search" };
    ArrayAdapter<String> adapter = new ArrayAdapter<String>(
        this, android.R.layout.simple_spinner_dropdown_
        item, items);
    ActionBar actionBar = getActionBar();
    actionBar.setNavigationMode(ActionBar.NAVIGATION_
        MODE_LIST);
    actionBar.setListNavigationCallbacks(adapter,
        onNavigationItemSelected);
}
OnNavigationListener onNavigationItemSelected = new
    OnNavigationListener() {
    @Override
    public boolean onNavigationItemSelected(int
        itemPosition, long itemId) {
        Log.d("Option ", String.valueOf(itemId) +
            " is selected");
        return true;
    }
};
}
```

Here, you notice that when an action item from the drop-down list is selected, the
onNavigationItemSelected() method is called. The itemPosition and itemId
parameters in the onNavigationItemSelected() method contain the information about the
position and ID of the selected action item. A log message—the ID of the selected action
item—is displayed. The IDs are sequentially assigned to the action items in the drop-down list
beginning with 0. Don't forget to set the value of the android:minSdkVersion attribute to 11
or higher in the AndroidManifest.xml file to enable the ActionBar.

After running the application, you see a spinner, as shown in Figure 3.9 (first). The spinner
shows the first item of the drop-down list: Create. The default style shows the first item in a
dark color, which is almost invisible against the dark background color. Open the styles.
xml file from the res/values folder, and add a custom style called MyActionBar to it with the
following statement:

```
<style name="MyActionBar" parent="@android:style/Widget.Holo.Light.ActionBar" />
```

After you add the style, the styles.xml file will appear as shown in Listing 3.18.

Listing 3.18   **Code Written into the** styles.xml **File**

```
<resources >
<style name="AppBaseTheme" parent="android:Theme.Light" >
</style>
```

```
<style name="AppTheme" parent="AppBaseTheme">
</style>
<style name="MyActionBar" parent="@android:style/Widget.
    Holo.Light.ActionBar" />
</resources>
```

To implement this style in your application, open the `AndroidManifest.xml` file and set the value of the `android:theme` attribute, as shown here:

```
android:theme="@style/MyActionBar"
```

This statement applies the `MyActionBar` style to your application. The output will now appear as shown in Figure 3.9 (second).

After you select the spinner, the drop-down list opens showing all the available action items (see Figure 3.9 [third]). Select the Update action item, and it will appear as the spinner's header (as shown in Figure 3.9 [fourth]), telling the user that it was selected in the previous selection.

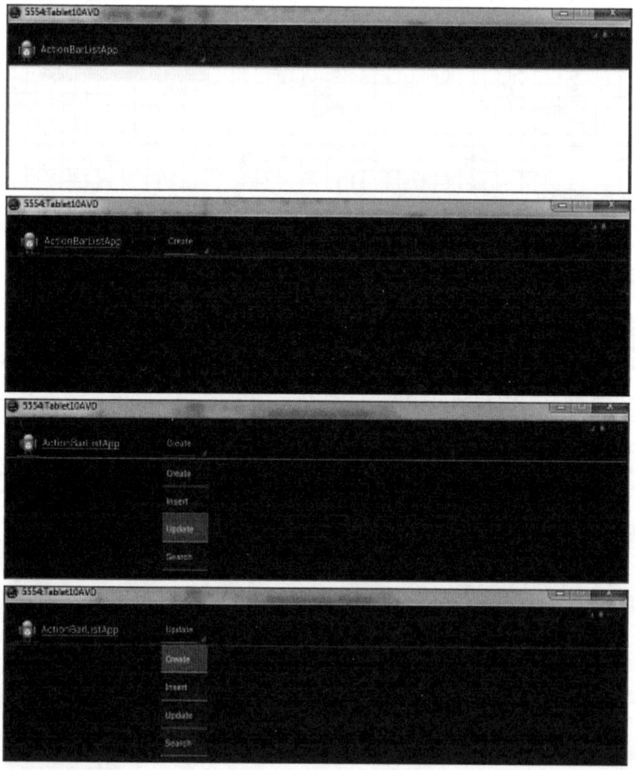

Figure 3.9   The first item of the spinner is almost invisible (first); the first item of the Spinner is visible (second); all actions are displayed after selecting the list (third); the selected list item displayed at the beginning of the list (fourth).

Figure 3.10 shows the log messages that are displayed after selecting the Update and Create action items from the drop-down list. The ID of the selected drop-down item is displayed using the `itemId` parameter in the `onNavigationItemSelected()` method.

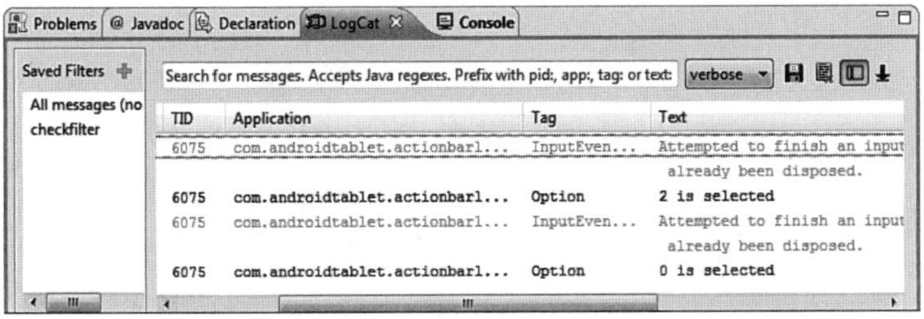

Figure 3.10   Log messages displayed after selecting the actions from the list ActionBar

Summary

In this chapter, you saw the usage of the ActionBar in displaying key actions of an application. You learned to toggle visibility of the ActionBar, saw how the different components worked, and discovered the procedure to display action items and action views in the ActionBar. You learned to display submenus in the ActionBar and how to create both tabbed and drop-down list ActionBars.

In the next chapter, you will learn about the new widgets that have become available since API 11 level. You will learn to display the calendar in the Android application through `CalendarView` and display a range of numbers through `NumberPicker`. You will also learn to display a stack of images using the `StackView` widget. Finally, you will learn to display a list of options using `ListPopupWindow` and display suggestions through `PopupMenu`.

New Widgets

In this chapter, you are going to discover the new widgets that have become available since API 11 level. You will learn to display the calendar in the Android application through `CalendarView` and display a range of numbers through `NumberPicker`. You will also learn to display a stack of images using the `StackView` widget. Finally, you will learn to display a list of options using `ListPopupWindow` and display suggestions through `PopupMenu`.

Recipe: Displaying the Calendar in an Android Application

To display the calendar in an Android application, you will use `CalendarView`. This is a configurable widget that displays and selects dates. By default, the calendar of the current month is displayed, but you can scroll through to the desired date. To select a date, just tap on it.

To view a calendar, create an Android project called `CalendarViewApp`. The application will display a calendar of the current month by default. The user can scroll through the calendar to display dates of a particular month. After selecting a date, it will be displayed through `Toast`. The application will also contain a `Button` control that, when clicked, will display `DatePickerDialog`, allowing the user to display the calendar of the desired month.

Because your application needs a button and a calendar, you must define both `Button` and `CalendarView` in the activity layout file. After you define the `Button` and `CalendarView`, the activity layout file `activity_calendar_view_app.xml` will appear as shown in Listing 4.1.

Listing 4.1   **Code Written in the Activity Layout File** `activity_calendar_view_app.xml`

```xml
<LinearLayout xmlns:android="http://schemas.android.com/apk/res/android"
    xmlns:tools="http://schemas.android.com/tools"
    android:orientation="vertical"
    android:layout_width="match_parent"
    android:layout_height="match_parent" >
    <Button android:id="@+id/date_picker_button"
        android:layout_width="match_parent"
        android:layout_height="wrap_content"
        android:text="Open Date Picker"
        android:textSize="@dimen/text_size" />
    <CalendarView
        android:id="@+id/calendar_view"
        android:layout_width="match_parent"
        android:layout_height="match_parent" />
</LinearLayout>
```

To access and identify Java code, the `Button` and `CalendarView` are assigned the ID, `date_picker_button` and `calendar_view`, respectively. Next, you need to write Java code to perform the following tasks:

- Display the `CalendarView` defined in the activity layout file.

- Associate an event listener, `setOnClickListener`, to the `Button` control to display `DatePickerDialog`.

- Associate `OnDateSetListener` to `DatePickerDialog` to display the calendar of the selected date through `CalendarView`.

- Associate an event listener to the `CalendarView` to display the selected date on the screen.

To accomplish the preceding tasks, you write code as shown in Listing 4.2 in the Java activity file `CalendarViewAppActivity.java`.

Listing 4.2   **Code Written in the Java Activity File** `CalendarViewAppActivity.java`

```java
package com.androidtablet.calendarviewapp;

import android.os.Bundle;
import android.app.Activity;
import android.widget.CalendarView;
import android.widget.CalendarView.OnDateChangeListener;
import android.widget.Toast;
import java.util.Calendar;
```

```
import android.app.DatePickerDialog;
import android.widget.DatePicker;
import android.widget.Button;
import android.view.View;
import android.view.View.OnClickListener;

public class CalendarViewAppActivity extends Activity {
    private CalendarView calendarView;
    private int yr, mon, dy;
    private Calendar selectedDate;

    @Override
    public void onCreate(Bundle savedInstanceState) {
        super.onCreate(savedInstanceState);
        setContentView(R.layout.activity_calendar_view_app);
        Calendar c = Calendar.getInstance();
        yr = c.get(Calendar.YEAR);
        mon = c.get(Calendar.MONTH);
        dy = c.get(Calendar.DAY_OF_MONTH);
        Button datePickerButton = (Button) findViewById(
            R.id.date_picker_button);
        calendarView = (CalendarView) findViewById(
            R.id.calendar_view);
        datePickerButton.setOnClickListener(new
            OnClickListener() {
            public void onClick(View v) {
                new DatePickerDialog(CalendarViewAppActivity.
                    this, dateListener, yr, mon, dy).show();
            }
        });
        calendarView.setOnDateChangeListener(new
            OnDateChangeListener() {
            @Override
            public void onSelectedDayChange(CalendarView view,
                int year, int month, int dayOfMonth) {
                Toast.makeText(getApplicationContext(),"Selected
                    date is "+(month+1)+"-"+dayOfMonth+"-"+
                    year, Toast.LENGTH_SHORT). show();
            }
        });
    }

    private DatePickerDialog.OnDateSetListener dateListener =
        new DatePickerDialog.OnDateSetListener() {
```

```
        public void onDateSet(DatePicker view, int year, int
            monthOfYear, int dayOfMonth){
            selectedDate=Calendar.getInstance();
            yr=year;
            mon=monthOfYear;
            dy=dayOfMonth;
            selectedDate.set(yr, mon, dy);
            calendarView.setDate(selectedDate.getTimeInMillis());
        }
    };
}
```

You can see in the preceding code that the CalendarView with ID calendar_view is accessed from the layout file and is mapped to the CalendarView object calendarView. Also, the Button control with ID date_picker_button is accessed from the layout file and is mapped to the Button object datePickerButton. setOnClickListener is associated to the Button control, and its callback method, onClick, executes when the Button is clicked. In the onClick callback method, DatePickerDialog is invoked to display the current date.

The OnDateSetListener is associated to the Date Picker dialog so that when any date is selected from the Date Picker dialog, the CalendarView is set to display the calendar of the selected month and year.

The setOnDateChangeListener is associated to the CalendarView. When any date is selected or changed in the CalendarView, the callback method onSelectedDayChange() is called. Using the onSelectedDayChange() method, you display the selected date through Toast. The thing to remember here is that the month is 0 based, so you must add 1 to it before displaying.

After running the application, you see the CalendarView displaying the calendar of the current month (see Figure 4.1 [top]). To see the calendar of the desired month, select the Open Date Picker button, which opens DatePickerDialog. From DatePickerDialog, you can select the date from the calendar (see Figure 4.1 [middle]). After selecting a date from DatePickerDialog and selecting Done, the calendar of the selected date will be displayed. Also, after you select a date from the CalendarView, it is displayed through Toast, as shown in Figure 4.1 (bottom).

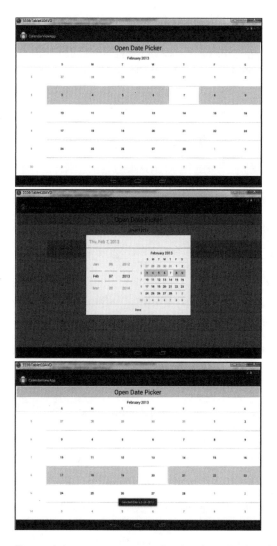

Figure 4.1 `CalendarView` showing the calendar of the current month (top); `DatePickerDialog` opens after selecting the Open Date Picker button (middle); `CalendarView` displays the calendar of the date selected from `DatePicker` (bottom).

Recipe: Displaying and Selecting Numbers Through `NumberPicker`

In this recipe, you will learn to display a `NumberPicker` that displays numbers in the specified range. The number that is selected from the `NumberPicker` is displayed through `TextView`. Create a new Android project called `NumberPickerApp`.

You just want to display `TextView` and `NumberPicker` in this application. The `NumberPicker` will display the numbers between the specified range, and the `TextView` will display the number selected from the `NumberPicker`. To define the `TextView` and `NumberPicker`, write the code shown in Listing 4.3 to the activity layout file `activity_number_picker_app.xml`.

Listing 4.3   **Code Written in the Activity Layout File** `activity_number_picker_app.xml`

```xml
<LinearLayout
    xmlns:android="http://schemas.android.com/apk/res/android"
    xmlns:tools="http://schemas.android.com/tools"
    android:layout_width="match_parent"
    android:layout_height="match_parent"
    android:orientation="vertical" >
    <TextView
        android:layout_width="wrap_content"
        android:layout_height="wrap_content"
        android:layout_centerHorizontal="true"
        android:text="Select a number from NumberPicker"
        android:id="@+id/numberview"
        android:textSize="@dimen/text_size"
        android:textStyle="bold"  />
    <NumberPicker android:id="@+id/numberpicker"
        android:layout_width="wrap_content"
        android:layout_height="wrap_content"  />
</LinearLayout>
```

You can see that the `TextView` control is assigned the ID `numberview` and is initialized to display the text `Select a number from NumberPicker`. The text displayed through `TextView` will appear in bold and in the size defined by the dimension resource `text_size`. To access and identify Java code, assign `NumberPicker` the ID `numberpicker`.

In the main Java activity file, you need to write the Java code to do the following tasks:

- Access the `TextView` and `NumberPicker` from the layout file, and map them to the respective objects.

- Set the maximum and minimum numerical values to be displayed through `NumberPicker`.

- Associate an event listener to the `NumberPicker` to listen if the current value in `NumberPicker` is changed.

- Display the number selected from the `NumberPicker` through `TextView`.

To perform all these tasks, write the code shown in Listing 4.4 to the Java activity file `NumberPickerAppActivity.java`.

Listing 4.4   **Code Written in the Java Activity File** `NumberPickerAppActivity.java`

```java
package com.androidtablet.numberpickerapp;

import android.os.Bundle;
import android.app.Activity;
import android.widget.NumberPicker;
import android.widget.TextView;

public class NumberPickerAppActivity extends Activity {
    TextView numberView;

    @Override
    public void onCreate(Bundle savedInstanceState) {
        super.onCreate(savedInstanceState);
        setContentView(R.layout.activity_number_picker_app);
        numberView = (TextView)findViewById(R.id.numberview);
        NumberPicker numberPicker = (NumberPicker) findViewById(R.id.numberpicker);
        numberPicker.setMaxValue(100);          #1
        numberPicker.setMinValue(0);            #2
        numberPicker.setWrapSelectorWheel(true);
        numberPicker.setOnValueChangedListener( new NumberPicker.
            OnValueChangeListener() {
            @Override
            public void onValueChange(NumberPicker picker, int
                oldVal, int newVal) {
                numberView.setText("Selected number is "+
                    newVal);
            }
        });
    }
}
```

You can see that the `TextView` control with ID `numberview` is accessed from the layout file and mapped to the `TextView` object `numberView`. Similarly, `NumberPicker` with ID `numberpicker` is accessed from the layout file and is mapped to the `NumberPicker` object `numberPicker`. The minimum and maximum values to be displayed through `NumberPicker` are set to 0 and 100, respectively.

The `setWrapSelectorWheel()` method is set to `true` to make the selector wheel wrap around the minimum and maximum values that are displayed through `NumberPicker`. When the range of values (that is, maximum value – minimum values) displayed through `NumberPicker` is more than the number of numerical shown in the selector wheel, wrapping is enabled by default. (The selector wheel wraps around the maximum and minimum values by default.)

The `setOnValueChangedListener` is associated with the `NumberPicker`. When the current value is changed in the `NumberPicker`, the callback method `onValueChange` is invoked. In the `onValueChange` method, the newly selected number in the `NumberPicker` is displayed through the `TextView` control.

After you run the application, the TextView will display a text message directing the user to Select a number from NumberPicker. The NumberPicker displays the assigned minimum value in editable form. The lesser value is shown above, and a greater value is shown below (see Figure 4.2 [top]). You can change the number by scrolling up or down and by tapping on the lesser or greater value shown above and below. When you tap a number, it is displayed through the TextView control, as shown in Figure 4.2 (bottom).

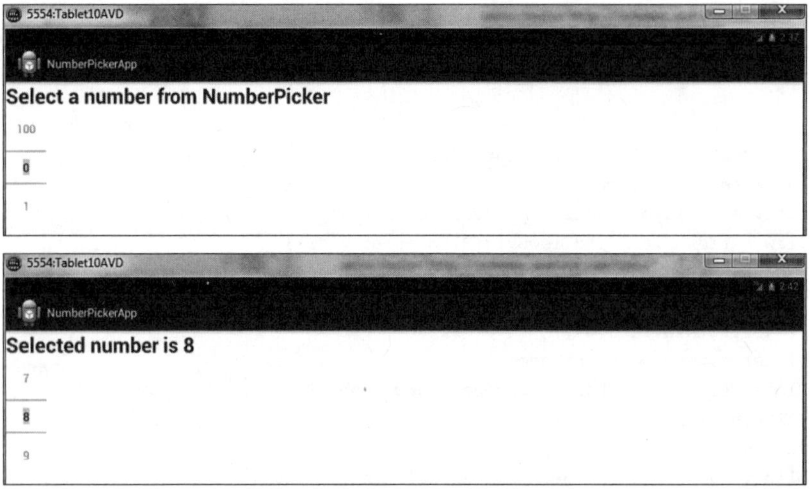

Figure 4.2 NumberPicker displaying the numbers beginning from the set minimum value (top) and the selected number displayed through TextView (bottom)

You can display any range of values through the NumberPicker. For example, to display odd values from 1 to 19, you can replace the statements #1 and #2 in Listing 4.4 with the following code:

```
String[] stringArray = new String[10];
int n=1;
for(int i=0; i<10; i++){
    stringArray[i] = Integer.toString(n);
    n+=2;
}
numberPicker.setMaxValue(stringArray.length-1);
numberPicker.setMinValue(0);
numberPicker.setDisplayedValues(stringArray);
```

You can see that a String array called stringArray is defined and values 1,3,5... 19 are stored in it. The min value of the NumberPicker is set to 0. The max value of NumberPicker is set equal to the length of stringArray -1 because you want to display all the elements of the array stringArray. Thereafter, through the setDisplayedValues() method, the values in the stringArray are displayed through NumberPicker.

Because the current theme in the Android application is derived from `Theme_Holo` or `Theme_Holo_Light`, the `NumberPicker` appears as shown in Figure 4.2 (that is, the current value as editable with lesser and greater value shown above and below the `NumberPicker`, respectively). If you change the theme of your application, you can change the appearance of the `NumberPicker`. For example, the following statements applied in the `AndroidManifest.xml` file will set the current theme of the application to be derived from `Theme`:

```
<application
        android:icon="@drawable/ic_launcher"
        android:label="@string/app_name"
        android:theme="@android:style/Theme.Black.NoTitleBar" >
```

The preceding statements will change the theme of the application to `Theme.Black.NoTitleBar` and hence the appearance of the `NumberPicker` widget. In other words, the `NumberPicker` will display the current value in editable form with an increment and decrement button displayed above and below, respectively (see Figure 4.3 [top]). After you change the current value, it will be displayed through `TextView`, as shown in Figure 4.3 (bottom).

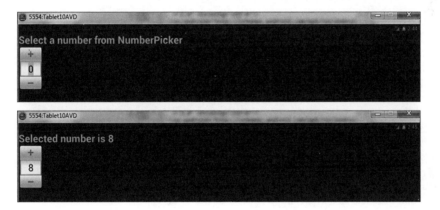

Figure 4.3   `NumberPicker` with black background, increment, and decrement buttons on changing the theme of the application (top), and the selected number displayed through `TextView` (bottom)

Recipe: Creating a Stack of Images Using `StackView`

`StackView` helps in arranging items in the form of stacked cards, where the front item can be flipped to bring the item behind it to the front. In addition to images, you can stack objects composed of text and other data, too.

In this recipe, you will learn to stack images in the `StackView`. So create a new Android project called `StackViewApp`. The only control that you need to define in the activity layout file is `StackView` widget. After defining the `StackView` widget, the activity layout file `activity_stack_view_app.xml` will appear, as shown in Listing 4.5.

Listing 4.5   **Code Written in the Activity Layout File** `activity_stack_view_app.xml`

```xml
<FrameLayout
    xmlns:android="http://schemas.android.com/apk/res/android"
    xmlns:tools="http://schemas.android.com/tools"
    android:layout_width="match_parent"
    android:layout_height="match_parent" >
    <StackView
        android:id="@+id/stackview"
        android:layout_width="match_parent"
        android:layout_height="match_parent"
        android:animateLayoutChanges="true">
    </StackView>
</FrameLayout>
```

To access and identify the `StackView` in Java code, assign the control the ID `stackview`. The value of the `android:animateLayoutChanges` attribute is set to `true` so that changes occurring in the layout will not mandate running `LayoutTransition`.

To represent the stack item that you want to stack in `StackView`, you need to define an XML file in the `res/layout` folder. Right-click the `res/layout` folder in the Package Explorer window, and add an XML file called `item.xml`. Because you want to stack only the images, only an `ImageView` control is defined in the `item.xml` file. After you define the `ImageView`, the `item.xml` file will appear, as shown in Listing 4.6.

Listing 4.6   **Code Written in the** `item.xml` **File**

```xml
<?xml version="1.0" encoding="utf-8"?>
<FrameLayout
    xmlns:android="http://schemas.android.com/apk/res/android"
    android:layout_width="match_parent"
    android:layout_height="match_parent" >
    <ImageView
        android:id="@+id/imageview"
        android:layout_width="match_parent"
        android:layout_height="match_parent"
        android:src="@drawable/ic_launcher"  />
</FrameLayout>
```

You can see that the `ImageView` control is assigned the ID `imageview` and is initialized to display the `ic_launcher.png` file. In all, you want to display five images through the `StackView` control. Assuming the five image filenames are `prod1.png`, `prod2.png`, `prod3.png`, `prod4.png`, and `prod5.png`, copy them to the `res/drawable` folders. It's time to write code in the Java activity file to perform the following tasks:

- Access the StackView from the layout file and map it to the StackView object.

- Define an array to contain the resource IDs of the images that you copied into res/ drawable folders. This array will act as a data source, providing the images that you want to display.

- Define a custom adapter called ImageAdapter that will extend the BaseAdapter abstract class to define the content to be displayed through the StackView control.

- Display the adapter's content (images) via StackView, and set ImageAdapter to the StackView object via the setAdapter() method.

To accomplish all the preceding tasks, write the code as shown in Listing 4.7 in the Java activity file StackViewAppActivity.java.

Listing 4.7   **Code Written in the Java Activity File** StackViewAppActivity.java

```java
package com.androidtablet.stackviewapp;

import android.os.Bundle;
import android.app.Activity;
import android.content.Context;
import android.view.LayoutInflater;
import android.view.View;
import android.view.ViewGroup;
import android.widget.ImageView;
import android.widget.StackView;
import android.widget.BaseAdapter;

public class StackViewAppActivity extends Activity {
    @Override
    public void onCreate(Bundle savedInstanceState) {
        super.onCreate(savedInstanceState);
        setContentView(R.layout.activity_stack_view_app);
        StackView stackView = (StackView)this.findViewById(
            R.id.stackview);
        stackView.setAdapter(new ImageAdapter(this));
    }

    public class ImageAdapter extends BaseAdapter {
        private Context contxt;
        Integer[] images = {
            R.drawable.prod1,
            R.drawable.prod2,
            R.drawable.prod3,
            R.drawable.prod4,
            R.drawable.prod5
        };
```

```
        public ImageAdapter(Context c) {
            contxt = c;
        }

        public int getCount() {
            return images.length;
        }

        public Object getItem(int position) {
            return position;
        }

        public long getItemId(int position) {
            return position;
        }

        public View getView(int position, View view, ViewGroup
            parent) {
            if (view == null) {
                LayoutInflater vi = (LayoutInflater)
                    getBaseContext().getSystemService(
                    Context.LAYOUT_INFLATER_SERVICE);
                view = vi.inflate(R.layout.item, null, false);
            }
            ImageView imageView = (ImageView) view.findViewById(
                R.id.imageview);
            imageView.setImageResource(images[position]);
            return view;
        }
    }
}
```

The ImageAdapter is set to the StackView control, so it can access the adapter methods to display content (images). The adapter's methods—getCount(), getItem(), and getItemId()—are used to determine the number of images to be displayed and the unique identifier of the specified image. The getView() method is used to retrieve the appropriate view or image at the specified position. The ImageView defined in the item.xml file is accessed and is used to display images through the StackView.

After running the application, you find the stack of items (images) (see Figure 4.4 [left]). When you flip the front image, the images in back are moved to the front, as shown in Figure 4.4 [right]).

Figure 4.4   StackView displaying images (left), and the hidden images displayed in the front after flipping the front images (right)

The size of the images when an application is run on a phone may appear fine. But on a tablet, the images appear very small. To scale the images according to the screen size of the device, you need to modify the item.xml file. Open the item.xml file in the res/layout folder, and modify it to appear as shown in Listing 4.8. Only the code in bold is the modified code; the rest is the same that you saw in Listing 4.6.

Listing 4.8   **Code Written in the** item.xml **File**

```xml
<?xml version="1.0" encoding="utf-8"?>
<FrameLayout
    xmlns:android="http://schemas.android.com/apk/res/android"
    android:layout_width="match_parent"
    android:layout_height="match_parent" >
    <ImageView
        android:id="@+id/imageview"
        android:layout_width="@dimen/image_width"
        android:layout_height="@dimen/image_height"
        android:src="@drawable/ic_launcher"  />
</FrameLayout>
```

The image(s) that will be displayed through StackView are assigned the width and height through the dimension resources image_width and image_height, respectively.

To define the dimension resources `image_width` and `image_height`, open the `dimens.xml` file from the `res/values` folder. You assume that the dimension file `dimens.xml` already exists in the `res/values` folder of the application. You also assume that two folders named `values-sw600dp` and `values-sw720dp` exist in the `res` folder, and both the folders contain a dimension file named `dimens.xml`.

To define the width and height for the images when an application runs on a phone, open the `dimens.xml` file in the `res/values` folder, and write the following code in it:

```xml
<?xml version="1.0" encoding="utf-8"?>
<resources>
    <dimen name="image_width">100dp</dimen>
    <dimen name="image_height">200dp</dimen>
</resources>
```

You can see that on the phone, the `StackView` will display the images of width and height 100dp and 200dp, respectively.

Again, to define the width and height for the images when an application is viewed on a 7-inch tablet, open the dimension file `dimens.xml` in the `res/values-sw600dp` folder, and write the following code in it:

```xml
<?xml version="1.0" encoding="utf-8"?>
<resources>
    <dimen name="image_width">200dp</dimen>
    <dimen name="image_height">300dp</dimen>
</resources>
```

The preceding code will assign 200dp width and 300dp height to the images displayed through `StackView` on a 7-inch tablet. For defining the image dimensions for a 10-inch tablet, open the dimension file `dimens.xml` found in the `res/values-sw720dp` folder, and write the following code in it:

```xml
<?xml version="1.0" encoding="utf-8"?>
<resources>
    <dimen name="image_width">300dp</dimen>
    <dimen name="image_height">400dp</dimen>
</resources>
```

The preceding code will make the images appear 300dp wide and 400dp high in `StackView` when an application runs on a 10-inch tablet.

After you run the application on a 10-inch tablet, the `StackView` will appear as shown on the phone in Figure 4.5 (left). Compared to Figure 4.4 (left), you can see that the images appear quite big and clear on a tablet. When you flip a front image, the images at the back move to the front, as shown in Figure 4.5 (right).

Figure 4.5 `StackView` displaying enlarged images (left); the images at the back appear in the front when you flip the front images (right).

Recipe: Displaying a List of Options Using `ListPopupWindow`

You can use `ListPopupWindow` to anchor to a host view and display a list of options. In this recipe, you will learn to anchor `ListPopupWindow` to an `EditText` control. When the user clicks in the `EditText` control, `ListPopupWindow` will appear displaying a list of options. After the user selects an option from `ListPopupWindow`, it will be assigned to the `EditText` control. Create a new Android project called `ListPopupWindowApp`.

You want to anchor `ListPopupWindow` to an `EditText` control, so define an `EditText` control in the layout file. After you define an `EditText` control, the activity layout file `activity_list_popup_window_app.xml` will appear as shown in Listing 4.9.

Listing 4.9 **Code Written in the Activity Layout File** `activity_list_popup_window_app.xml`

```
<LinearLayout
    xmlns:android="http://schemas.android.com/apk/res/android"
    android:orientation="vertical"
    android:layout_width="match_parent"
    android:layout_height="match_parent">
    <EditText
```

```
    android:layout_width="match_parent"
    android:layout_height="wrap_content"
    android:id="@+id/product_name"
    android:hint="Enter product name"
    android:textSize="@dimen/text_size" />
</LinearLayout>
```

You can see that the EditText control is assigned the ID product_name. In this application, you will prompt the user to enter a product name in the EditText control. The text Enter product name is displayed in the EditText control. The text entered into the EditText control will appear in the font size defined by the dimension resource text_size.

The default size of the list items displayed in a ListView is suitable for phones but is quite smaller for tablets. To resize the list items of the ListView as per the device screen size, add one more XML file named list_item.xml to the res/layout folder. Write the code as shown in Listing 4.10 to the list_item.xml file.

Listing 4.10 **Code Written in the** list_item.xml **File**

```
<?xml version="1.0" encoding="utf-8"?>
<TextView xmlns:android="http://schemas.android.com/apk/res/android"
    android:layout_width="match_parent"
    android:layout_height="match_parent"
    android:padding="6dp"
    android:textSize="@dimen/text_size"
    android:textStyle="bold" />
```

According to the preceding code, the list items of the ListView will be padded by 6dp spaces, will appear in bold, and will be the size defined in the dimension resource text_size.

Next, you need to write Java code to perform the following tasks:

- Access the EditText control from the layout file and map it to the EditText object.

- Define an object of ListPopupWindow.

- Define ArrayAdapter and set it to the list of products you want to display through ListPopupWindow.

- Set ArrayAdapter to ListPopupWindow to display the list of products defined in ArrayAdapter.

- Set the height and width of ListPopupWindow.

- Assign a modal nature to ListPopupWindow (that is, the control will not return to the caller until the ListPopupWindow is dismissed). ListPopupWindow will be dismissed either by selecting a product from ListPopupWindow or by clicking anywhere outside ListPopupWindow.

- Anchor `ListPopupWindow` to the `EditText` control.

- Associate `setOnItemClickListener` to the `EditText` control so that when the user clicks in the `EditText`, `ListPopupWindow` opens and shows the list of products.

- Set the activity class to implement `OnItemClickListener`. When an option is selected from `ListPopupWindow`, it is assigned to the `EditText` control.

To perform these listed tasks, write the code shown in Listing 4.11 to the main Java activity file, `ListPopupWindowAppActivity.java`.

Listing 4.11   **Code Written in the Java Activity File** `ListPopupWindowAppActivity.java`

```java
package com.androidtablet.listpopupwindowapp;

import android.os.Bundle;
import android.app.Activity;
import android.widget.ListPopupWindow;
import android.view.View;
import android.widget.ArrayAdapter;
import android.widget.EditText;
import android.widget.AdapterView.OnItemClickListener;
import android.widget.AdapterView;
import android.view.View.OnClickListener;

public class ListPopupWindowAppActivity extends Activity
    implements OnItemClickListener {
    EditText productName;
    ListPopupWindow listPopupWindow;
    String[] products={"Camera", "Laptop", "Watch","Smartphone",
        "Television"};

    @Override
    public void onCreate(Bundle savedInstanceState) {
        super.onCreate(savedInstanceState);
        setContentView(R.layout.activity_list_popup_window_app);
        productName = (EditText) findViewById(
            R.id.product_name);
        listPopupWindow = new ListPopupWindow(
            ListPopupWindowAppActivity.this);
        listPopupWindow.setAdapter(new ArrayAdapter(
            ListPopupWindowAppActivity.this,
            R.layout.list_item, products));
        listPopupWindow.setAnchorView(productName);
        listPopupWindow.setWidth(300);
        listPopupWindow.setHeight(400);
```

```
        listPopupWindow.setModal(true);
        listPopupWindow.setOnItemClickListener(
            ListPopupWindowAppActivity.this);
        productName.setOnClickListener(new OnClickListener() {
            public void onClick(View v) {
                listPopupWindow.show();
            }
        });
    }

    @Override
    public void onItemClick(AdapterView<?> parent, View view,
        int position, long id) {
        productName.setText(products[position]);
        listPopupWindow.dismiss();
    }
}
```

In the preceding code, you see the use of an `ArrayAdapter`, which acts as the data source for `ListPopupWindow`. An `ArrayAdapter` makes use of a `TextView` control to represent the child views in a view (that is, it displays the elements of the `products` array via a `TextView` control). The `ArrayAdapter` constructor used earlier consists of the following:

- **`ListPopupWindowAppActivity.this`**—The current context.

- **`R.layout.list_item`**—Points to the `TextView` that you defined in the `list_item.xml` file. The `TextView` will be used to display each item in `ListPopupWindow`. The elements of the `products` array are wrapped in a view before being assigned to the widget for display. Therefore, the `R.layout.list_item` simply turns the strings defined in the products array into a `TextView` for display in `ListPopupWindow`.

- **`products`**—Acts as a data source.

After running the application, you get an `EditText` control with the message `Enter product name` (see Figure 4.6 [(top)]). Click in the `EditText` control, and `ListPopupWindow` appears showing the list of products (see Figure 4.6 [middle]). After you select a product from `ListPopupWindow`, it will appear in the `EditText` control (see Figure 4.6 [bottom]).

Figure 4.6   `EditText` prompting to enter a product name (top); `ListPopupWindow` appears showing the options after clicking in the `EditText` control (middle); the selected product from `ListPopupWindow` appears in `EditText` (bottom).

Recipe: Suggesting Options Using `PopupMenu`

`PopupMenu` displays a menu in a modal pop-up window. You can anchor it to a view and make it display the desired menu items or options. In this recipe, you will anchor `PopupMenu` to an `EditText` control to display a list of suggestions while entering data in the `EditText` control. The difference between the previous recipe and this one is that the list of options is displayed through `PopupMenu` instead of `ListPopupWindow`.

Create a new Android project called `PopupMenuApp`. Because you want to anchor `PopupMenu` to the `EditText` control, it is defined in the layout file `activity_popup_menu_app.xml` using the code shown in Listing 4.12.

Listing 4.12   Code Written in the Activity Layout File `activity_popup_menu_app.xml`

```xml
<LinearLayout
    xmlns:android="http://schemas.android.com/apk/res/android"
    android:orientation="vertical"
    android:layout_width="match_parent"
    android:layout_height="match_parent">
    <EditText
        android:layout_width="match_parent"
        android:layout_height="wrap_content"
        android:id="@+id/product_name"
        android:hint="Enter product name"
        android:textSize="@dimen/text_size" />
</LinearLayout>
```

You can see that the `EditText` control is assigned the ID product_name and is set to display the message `Enter product name`.

You will define the menu items or options for `PopupMenu` through the XML file. In other words, you will inflate the menu through an XML file. To the `res/menu` folder, add an XML file called `popupmenu.xml`. You want to display product names in the form of suggestions in the `EditText` control, so define the menu items in the form of product names in the `popupmenu.xml` file. The menu items are defined as shown in Listing 4.13 in the `popupmenu.xml` file.

Listing 4.13   Code Written in the `popupmenu.xml` **File**

```xml
<?xml version="1.0" encoding="utf-8"?>
<menu xmlns:android="http://schemas.android.com/apk/res/android">
    <group android:id="@+id/group_popupmenu">
        <item android:id="@+id/camera"
            android:title="Camera"
            android:textSize="@dimen/text_size" />
        <item android:id="@+id/laptop"
            android:title="Laptop"
            android:textSize="@dimen/text_size" />
        <item android:id="@+id/watch"
            android:title="Watch"
            android:textSize="@dimen/text_size" />
        <item android:id="@+id/smartphone"
            android:title="Smartphone"
            android:textSize="@dimen/text_size" />
        <item android:id="@+id/television"
            android:title="Television"
            android:textSize="@dimen/text_size"   />
    </group>
</menu>
```

You can see that products, `Camera`, `Laptop`, `Watch`, `Smartphone`, and `Television` are defined as menu items in the `popupmenu.xml` file. Each product name is assigned a unique ID, too.

You need to write Java code to accomplish the following tasks:

- Access the `EditText` control defined in the layout file and map it to the `EditText` object.

- Define the `PopupMenu` object and inflate the menu items or product name defined in the `popupmenu.xml` file to be displayed through `PopupMenu`.

- Associate `setOnClickListener` to the `EditText` control to listen for an occurrence of the click event in the `EditText` control.

- Display the `PopupMenu` when the user clicks in the `EditText` control.

- Associate `setOnMenuItemClickListener` to `PopupMenu`.

- When any menu item (product) is selected from `PopupMenu`, it is assigned to the `EditText` control.

To perform the preceding tasks, write the code shown in Listing 4.14 into the main Java activity file, `PopupMenuAppActivity.java`.

Listing 4.14   **Code Written in the Java Activity File** `PopupMenuAppActivity.java`

```
package com.androidtablet.popupmenuapp;

import android.os.Bundle;
import android.app.Activity;
import android.widget.EditText;
import android.view.View.OnClickListener;
import android.view.View;
import android.widget.PopupMenu;
import android.view.MenuItem;

public class PopupMenuAppActivity extends Activity {
    EditText productName;
    PopupMenu popupMenu;

    @Override
    public void onCreate(Bundle savedInstanceState) {
        super.onCreate(savedInstanceState);
        setContentView(R.layout.activity_popup_menu_app);
        productName = (EditText) findViewById(
            R.id.product_name);
        popupMenu = new PopupMenu(PopupMenuAppActivity.this,
            productName);
```

```
        popupMenu.getMenuInflater().inflate( R.menu.popupmenu,
            popupMenu.getMenu());
    productName.setOnClickListener(new OnClickListener() {
        public void onClick(View v) {
            popupMenu.setOnMenuItemClickListener(new
                PopupMenu.OnMenuItemClickListener() {
                @Override
                public boolean onMenuItemClick(MenuItem
                    item) {
                    productName.setText(item.toString());
                    return true;
                }
            });
            popupMenu.show();
        }
    });
    }
}
```

After you run the application, the EditText appears on startup. The EditText control displays a message directing the user to enter a product name (see Figure 4.7 [top]). When the user clicks in the EditText control, the PopupMenu appears showing product names in the form of menu items (see Figure 4.7 [middle]). The user selects a product from the PopupMenu, and it is assigned to the EditText control (see Figure 4.7 [bottom]).

You see that PopupMenu appears below the anchor view (EditText control) because there is enough space below the EditText control. If there is not enough space, PopupMenu would have appeared above the anchor view.

Figure 4.7   `EditText` prompting to enter a product name (top); `PopupMenu` appears showing the options after clicking in the `EditText` control (middle); the selected product from `PopupMenu` appears in the `EditText` (bottom).

Summary

In this chapter, you learned to display the calendar in an Android application through `CalendarView` and saw how a date selected from the calendar is displayed. You also learned to display a range of numbers through `NumberPicker`. You walked through the procedure to display a stack of images using the `StackView` widget. Finally, you learned to display a list of options using `ListPopupWindow` and display suggestions through `PopupMenu`.

The next chapter is focused on understanding `ClipData` and `DragEvent`. You will learn about the system clipboard and the procedure to drag and drop text and images.

5

System Clipboard
and Drag and Drop

The drag and drop operation is common in almost all applications. Whether it is selecting an item to purchase while shopping online or arranging items in order of preference, drag and drop is used often. In this chapter, you will learn to drag and drop text as well as images. You will learn to listen to drag events, create a drag shadow, and add the dropped view to the target view. Also, you will learn to utilize the system clipboard to implement cut, copy, and paste operations in the Android applications.

Recipe: Understanding Drag and Drop Operation

Drag and drop operation refers to the procedure of clicking and moving one view to another in the current activity. The views can be in different layouts. To select the view to drag, you usually press the view. When you drag the view, a shadow is displayed to represent the view being dragged. The drag operation ends when the dragged shadow is released on the drop zones. The *drop zones* refer to the views that are supposed to accept the dragged view.

While dragging and dropping operations, a drag event is sent to the drag event listeners or callback methods of all the views in the current layout. So when you are implementing the drag and drop operation, you need to define the views for drop zones, or where you want to drop the dragged views. Also, you need to define drag event listener objects. When data is dropped over a `View` object, it is sent to the listener or callback method in the drag event.

> **Note**
>
> Each `View` object has an `onDragEvent()` callback method.

The following classes are used to perform drag and drop operations:

- **ClipData**—Object contains the view to be passed or dropped to the drop zone views.

- **DragEvent**—Object that is generated when the view is dragged.

- **DragShadowBuilder**—Displays the look and feel of the view being dragged. If this class is not implemented, the source view representation will appear by default.

When the drag operation begins, the startDrag() method is called. This method initiates the generation of drag events. The startDrag() method can be called for any view in the current layout. A view receives a drag event with either a drag event listener that implements View.OnDragListener or with its onDragEvent(DragEvent) callback method. The drag event is generated in the form of a DragEvent object. The object contains an action type that informs the listener about the specific action happening in the drag-drop process. The method used to learn the action type is getAction(). Six possible action types are defined by constants in the DragEvent class, as shown in Table 5.1.

Table 5.1   **Brief Description of the Constants in the DragEvent Class**

Action Type	Description
DragEvent.ACTION_DRAG_STARTED	Indicates that the drag event has started
DragEvent.ACTION_DRAG_ENTERED	Indicates that the drag shadow has entered the bounding box of the target view (view that is ready to accept the dragged view).
DragEvent.ACTION_DRAG_EXITED	Indicates that the drop shadow is dragged outside the bounding box of the target view.
DragEvent.ACTION_DRAG_LOCATION	Indicates that the drag operation is in process and the drop shadow is inside the bounding box of the target view.
DragEvent.ACTION_DROP	Indicates that the drag shadow is released or dropped within the bounding box of the target view.
DragEvent.ACTION_DRAG_ENDED	Indicates that the drop operation is complete and the drag shadow is released outside the bounding box of the target view.

Specifically, the following things happen during a drag and drop process:

- When a user begins the drag operation, the startDrag() method is called, which in turn generates a drag event. A drag event with action type ACTION_DRAG_STARTED is sent to the drag event listeners for all the View objects in the current layout. The drag event contains the data that is passed to the startDrag() method while starting the drag operation.

- Only the drag event listeners that return the Boolean value `true` are able to receive drag events. The drag event listener that returns `false` will not receive drag events for the current operation. That is, until the current drag and drop operation is finished, these drag event listeners will not be able to receive drag events. When the drag and drop operation is complete, the drag event with action type `ACTION_DRAG_ENDED` is generated.

- The drag event listener may alter its `View` object's appearance in response to the event. For example, when the drag shadow enters the bounding box of the target view, the drag event listener may highlight the target view to indicate that it is ready to accept the view being dragged. When the drag shadow enters the bounding box of the target view, the drag event with action type `ACTION_DRAG_ENTERED` is generated. When the drag shadow is released within the bounding box of a target view, a drag event with the action type `ACTION_DROP` is generated. If the drag shadow is released at some other location than the target view, no `ACTION_DROP` drag event is generated. After the drag event with action type `ACTION_DROP` is generated, the drag event with action type `ACTION_DRAG_ENDED` is generated to indicate that the drag and drop operation is complete.

When the drag event starts, you can create the representation of a view being dragged by extending the `DragShadowBuilder` class.

Recipe: Dragging and Dropping Text

In this recipe, you will learn to drag and drop text. You will create two `ListView` controls. One will display some item names, and the other will be empty. When you click and drag any item name displayed in the first `ListView` and drop it to the second `ListView`, the item name will be added to the second `ListView`. You can click and drag any number of text or item names from one `ListView` to another.

To understand the whole procedure practically, you will create an Android project called `DragDropListApp`. In this application, you require two `TextView` and two `ListView` controls. The `ListView` that contains some text to be dragged will be called `Source List`, and the one that is empty will be called `Target List`. Each `TextView` will be displayed above a `ListView` to indicate the type of `ListView` below it. To define two `TextView` and two `ListView` controls, the code as shown in Listing 5.1 is written in the activity layout file `activity_drag_drop_list_app.xml`.

The `TextView` and `ListView` pairs are contained within `LinearLayout` containers to align them. Two `LinearLayout` containers are defined with vertical orientation, where each contains the `TextView` and `ListView` displayed one below the other. The two `LinearLayout` containers are in turn nested inside an outer `LinearLayout` container with horizontal orientation to display the two `LinearLayout` containers one beside the other.

Listing 5.1   Code Written in the Activity Layout File `activity_drag_drop_list_app.xml`

```
<LinearLayout
    xmlns:android="http://schemas.android.com/apk/res/android"
    android:layout_width="match_parent"
```

```
        android:layout_height="match_parent"
        android:orientation="horizontal" >
        <LinearLayout
            android:layout_width="match_parent"
            android:layout_height="match_parent"
            android:orientation="vertical"
            android:layout_weight="1" >
            <TextView
                android:layout_width="match_parent"
                android:layout_height="wrap_content"
                android:text="Source List"
                android:textSize="@dimen/text_size"
            android:textStyle="bold"  />
            <ListView
                android:id="@+id/sourcelist"
                android:layout_width="match_parent"
                android:layout_height="wrap_content"/>
        </LinearLayout>
        <LinearLayout
            android:id="@+id/targetlayout"
            android:layout_width="match_parent"
            android:layout_height="match_parent"
            android:orientation="vertical"
            android:layout_weight="1"
            android:paddingLeft="10dp" >
            <TextView
                android:layout_width="match_parent"
                android:layout_height="wrap_content"
                android:text="Target List"
                android:textSize="@dimen/text_size"
                android:textStyle="bold"  />
            <ListView
                android:id="@+id/targetlist"
                android:layout_width="match_parent"
                android:layout_height="wrap_content"/>
        </LinearLayout>
</LinearLayout>
```

You can see that the two ListView controls are assigned the IDs sourcelist and targetlist. The two TextView controls shown above the ListView controls are initialized to display the text Source List and Target List, respectively to inform whether the ListView displayed below is the source ListView or target ListView. The text displayed through TextView controls will appear in the font size defined in the dimension resource text_size. The LinearLayout containing the target ListView is assigned the ID targetlayout.

The default size of the list items displayed in `ListView` is suitable for phones but quite small for tablets. To resize the list items of the `ListView` as per the device screen size, add one more XML file named `list_item.xml` to the `res/layout` folder. Write the following code into the `list_item.xml` file:

```xml
<?xml version="1.0" encoding="utf-8"?>
<TextView xmlns:android="http://schemas.android.com/apk/res/android"
    android:layout_width="match_parent"
    android:layout_height="match_parent"
    android:padding="6dp"
    android:textSize="@dimen/text_size"
    android:textStyle="bold" />
```

The preceding code will pad the list items of the `ListView` by 6dp spaces, will appear in bold, and will be sized according to the dimension resource `text_size`.

Next, you need to write Java code to perform the following tasks:

- Define an array and `ArrayAdapter` to show the items in the source `ListView`.
- Associate `setOnItemLongClickListener` to the source `ListView` to listen for the long clicks that occur while selecting items from it.
- Define a custom `DragEventListener` class that implements the `View.OnDragListener` interface to listen to the `DragEvent` and take necessary actions.
- Define a custom `ShadowBuilder` class that extends `View.DragShadowBuilder` to define the dimension of the drag shadow.
- Add the item to the target `ListView` when it is dropped over it.

To accomplish the preceding tasks, write the code as shown in Listing 5.2 to the main Java activity file, `DragDropListAppActivity.java`.

Listing 5.2   **Code Written in the Java Activity File** `DragDropListAppActivity.java`

```java
package com.androidtablet.dragdroplistapp;

import android.os.Bundle;
import android.app.Activity;
import java.util.ArrayList;
import java.util.List;
import android.content.ClipData;
import android.content.ClipDescription;
import android.graphics.Canvas;
import android.graphics.Color;
import android.graphics.Point;
import android.graphics.drawable.ColorDrawable;
import android.graphics.drawable.Drawable;
import android.view.DragEvent;
```

```java
import android.view.View;
import android.view.View.DragShadowBuilder;
import android.widget.AdapterView;
import android.widget.AdapterView.OnItemLongClickListener;
import android.widget.ArrayAdapter;
import android.widget.LinearLayout;
import android.widget.ListView;
import android.util.Log;

public class DragDropListAppActivity extends Activity {
    LinearLayout targetLayout;
    ListView sourceListView, targetListView;
    DragEventListener dragEventListener = new
        DragEventListener();
    String[] food ={"Pizza","Hot Dog","Chowmein","Burger",
        "Sandwich","Finger Fries","Cold Drink","Ice Cream" };
    List<String> targetArrayList;
    ArrayAdapter<String> targetAdapter;

    @Override
    public void onCreate(Bundle savedInstanceState) {
        super.onCreate(savedInstanceState);
        setContentView(R.layout.activity_drag_drop_list_app);
        sourceListView = (ListView)findViewById(
            R.id.sourcelist);                              #1
        targetListView = (ListView)findViewById(
            R.id.targetlist);                              #2
        targetLayout = (LinearLayout)findViewById(
            R.id.targetlayout);                            #3
        sourceListView.setTag("Source ListView");          #4
        targetListView.setTag("Target ListView");          #5
        targetLayout.setTag("Target Layout");              #6
        sourceListView.setAdapter(new ArrayAdapter<String>(
            this, R.layout.list_item, food));              #7
        sourceListView.setOnItemLongClickListener(
            sourceListItemLongClickListener);
        targetArrayList = new ArrayList<String>();         #8
        targetAdapter = new ArrayAdapter<String>(this,
            R.layout.list_item, targetArrayList);
        targetListView.setAdapter(targetAdapter);
        sourceListView.setOnDragListener(dragEventListener); #9
        targetLayout.setOnDragListener(dragEventListener);  #10
    }

    OnItemLongClickListener sourceListItemLongClickListener   =
        new OnItemLongClickListener(){
        @Override
```

```
    public boolean onItemLongClick(AdapterView<?> l, View v,
        int position, long id) {
        ClipData.Item foodItem = new ClipData.Item(
            food[position]);
        String[] clipDescription = {ClipDescription.
            MIMETYPE_TEXT_PLAIN};
        ClipData dragData = new ClipData((CharSequence)
            v.getTag(), clipDescription, foodItem);      #11
        DragShadowBuilder foodItemShadow = new
            ShadowBuilder(v);                            #12
        v.startDrag(dragData, foodItemShadow,
            food[position], 0);
        return true;
    }
};

private static class ShadowBuilder extends
    View.DragShadowBuilder {                             #13
    private static Drawable shadow;
    public ShadowBuilder(View v) {                       #14
        super(v);
        shadow = new ColorDrawable(Color.CYAN);
    }

    @Override
    public void onProvideShadowMetrics (Point size, Point
        touch){                                          #15
        int width = getView().getWidth();
        int height = getView().getHeight();
        shadow.setBounds(0, 0, width, height);
        size.set(width, height);
        touch.set(width / 2, height / 2);
    }

    @Override
    public void onDrawShadow(Canvas canvas) {       #16
        shadow.draw(canvas);
    }
}

protected class DragEventListener implements
    View.OnDragListener {                                #17
    @Override
    public boolean onDrag(View v, DragEvent event) { #18
        switch(event.getAction()) {                      #19
            case DragEvent.ACTION_DRAG_STARTED:
                if (event.getClipDescription().hasMimeType(
```

```
                            ClipDescription. MIMETYPE_TEXT_PLAIN)) {
                            Log.d((String) v.getTag(),
                                "ACTION_DRAG_STARTED accepted");
                            return true;
                        }
                        else{
                            Log.d((String) v.getTag(),
                                "ACTION_DRAG_STARTED rejected");
                            return false;
                        }
                    case DragEvent.ACTION_DRAG_ENTERED:
                        Log.d((String) v.getTag(),
                            "ACTION_DRAG_ENTERED");
                        return true;
                    case DragEvent.ACTION_DRAG_LOCATION:
                        Log.d((String) v.getTag(),
                            "ACTION_DRAG_LOCATION " + event.getX() +
                            " : " + event.getY());
                        return true;
                    case DragEvent.ACTION_DRAG_EXITED:
                        Log.d((String) v.getTag(),
                            "ACTION_DRAG_EXITED");
                        return true;
                    case DragEvent.ACTION_DROP:
                        ClipData.Item foodItem =
                            event.getClipData().getItemAt(0);
                        Log.d((String) v.getTag(), "ACTION_DROP");
                        if(v == targetLayout){
                            String droppedItem = foodItem.getText().
                                toString();
                            Log.d("Item dropped is ", droppedItem);
                            targetArrayList.add(droppedItem);
                            targetAdapter.notifyDataSetChanged();
                            return true;
                        }
                        else
                            return false;
                    case DragEvent.ACTION_DRAG_ENDED:
                        if (event.getResult())
                            Log.d((String) v.getTag(),
                                "ACTION_DRAG_ENDED successfully");
                        else
                            Log.d((String) v.getTag(), "Failure:
                                ACTION_DRAG_ENDED");
                            return true;
```

```
            default:
                Log.d((String) v.getTag(), "Not Known");
                return false;
        }
    }
  }
}
```

Here is how Listing 5.2 functions:

- Statements #1 and #2 access the `ListView` with IDs, a source list, and a target list from the activity layout file and map them to the `ListView` objects `sourceListView` and `targetListView`, respectively.

- Statement #3 accesses the target `LinearLayout` container carrying the target `ListView` from the layout file and maps it to the `LinearLayout` object `targetLayout`.

- Statements, #4, #5, and #6 associate the metadata in the form of tags to the two `ListViews` and the target `LinearLayout`. The tags help in displaying information about the views and containers involved in the drag and drop operation.

- Statement #7 defines an array followed by an `ArrayAdapter` and sets it to the source `ListView` to display the items through it. The items displayed through the source `ListView` are the ones that the user can drag and drop to the target `ListView`.

- Statement #8 associates `setOnItemLongClickListener` to the source `ListView`. When any item from the source `ListView` is long-clicked (clicked and held), the callback method `onItemLongClick` will be called.

- Statements #9 and #10 associate `setOnDragListener` to both the source and the target `ListView` controls.

- In the `onItemLongClick` method (#11) that is called when any item is long-clicked, you define a `ClipData` object named `dragData` to represent the item that is selected from the source `ListView`. To define a `ClipData` object, three things are required: tag or metadata of the view, MIME type describing the data, and text of the item being dragged. Therefore, a string array named `clipDescription` is defined where the MIME type describing the data in the clip is stored.

- Statement #12 defines the `DragShadowBuilder` object named `foodItemShadow` to display the drag shadow or image of the item while being dragged during drag and drop operation. By default, the drag shadow represents an image that resembles the item being dragged.

- To create a drag shadow, define a custom class `ShadowBuilder` (#13) that extends `View.DragShadowBuilder`.

- The constructor of the `ShadowBuilder` class (#14) constructs a shadow image of the item in CYAN color. By default, the dimension and appearance of the shadow will be the same as the dragged view and the touch point over the center of the view.

- The `onProvideShadowMetrics()` method (#15) is overridden to specify the metrics for the drag shadow. That is, you can specify the dimension of the drag shadow and the point that should be centered under the touch point while dragging through this method. In the method, you compute the width and height of the view being dragged and use the `setBounds()` method to set the size of the drag shadow. The size of the drag shadow is set equal to the width and height of the dragged view. Also, the touch point is set as the center of the view to center the shadow under the touch point. The dimension of the view computed in this method is used in constructing a `Canvas` object.

- Thereafter, the `onDrawShadow()` method (#16) is overridden to draw the shadow in the `Canvas` in the dimension or size determined through the `onProvideShadowMetrics()` method.

- A `DragEventListener` class is defined that implements the `View.OnDragListener` interface (#17).

- When an item or view is selected and dragged, `DragEvent` is generated and `onDrag()` is invoked (#18). The `onDrag()` method has two parameters: `View`, which receives the drag event, and `DragEvent`, which represents the event that is generated during drag and drop operation and contains information of the view being dragged and the information related to the drag operation. The `onDrag()` method returns the Boolean value `true` if the drag event is handled successfully; otherwise, it returns `false`. In the `onDrag()` method, the `getAction()` method is called on the `DragEvent` object (#19) to learn the action type that indicates the state of the drag and drop operation.

After running the application, you get two `ListView` controls: one shows the list of items, and the other is empty. Above each `ListView` control is displayed a `TextView` control. The two `TextView` controls are initialized to display the text `Source List` and `Target List`, respectively to indicate the purpose of the `ListView` shown below it (see Figure 5.1 [top]). After you click an item from the source `ListView` and drag it to the target `ListView`, a drag shadow moves along with the mouse pointer, as shown in Figure 5.1 (middle). After you drop the item on the target `ListView`, the dropped item is added to the target `ListView` (see Figure 5.1 [bottom]).

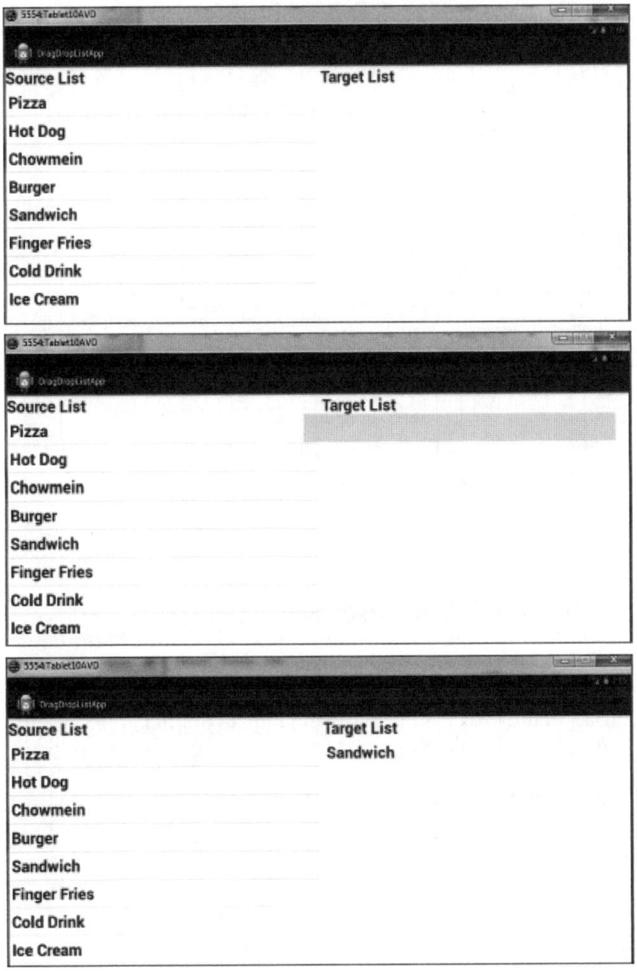

Figure 5.1   Source list and target list displayed on application startup (top); drag shadow appears after clicking and dragging item from the source ListView (middle); and dropped item appears in the target ListView (bottom).

Different actions take place on the source ListView and the target layout while drag and drop operations are displayed through the log messages in Figure 5.2. The figure not only indicates the beginning and the end of the drag operation, but displays the locations through which the drag shadow was moved.

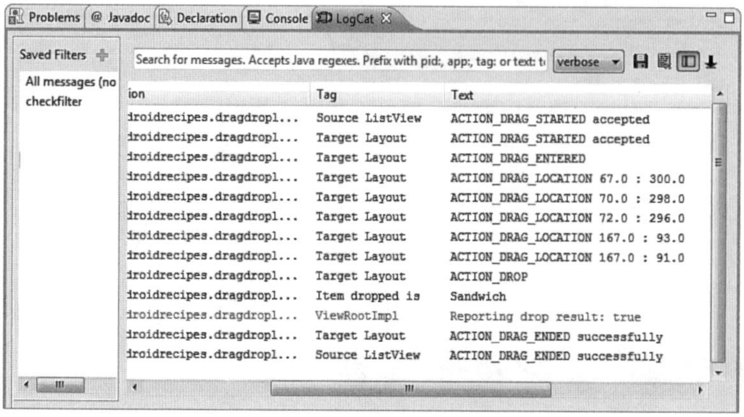

Figure 5.2   Log messages showing different actions performed during drag and drop operation performed on the source `ListView` and the target layout

Recipe: Dragging and Dropping Images

In this recipe, you will learn to drag and drop images. You will learn to display two `GridViews`: one containing a few images and the other initially empty. When any image is clicked and dragged from the first `GridView`, a drag shadow will move with the mouse pointer to represent the dragged image. When you drop the image to the second `GridView`, it will be added to it.

You will create a new Android project called `DragAndDropImage`. In this application, you want to display two `GridView` controls and two `TextView` controls. A `TextView` control will be displayed on top of each `GridView`. The two `TextView` controls will be initialized to display the text `Source Grid` and `Target Grid`, respectively, to indicate the purpose of the `GridView` shown below it. For alignment, the `TextView` and `GridView` are nested within `LinearLayout` containers. To display the `GridView` and `TextView` controls in the desired layout, the code as shown in Listing 5.3 is written in the activity layout file `activity_drag_and_drop_image.xml`.

Listing 5.3   **Code Written in the Activity Layout File** `activity_drag_and_drop_image.xml`

```
<LinearLayout
xmlns:android="http://schemas.android.com/apk/res/android"
    xmlns:tools="http://schemas.android.com/tools"
    android:layout_width="match_parent"
    android:layout_height="match_parent"
    android:orientation="vertical" >
    <LinearLayout
        android:layout_width="match_parent"
        android:layout_height="match_parent"
```

```
            android:orientation="vertical"
            android:layout_weight="1" >
        <TextView
            android:layout_width="match_parent"
            android:layout_height="wrap_content"
            android:text="Source Grid"
            android:textSize="@dimen/text_size"
            android:textStyle="bold"  />
        <GridView
            android:id="@+id/sourcegrid_view"
            android:layout_width="match_parent"
            android:layout_height="wrap_content"
            android:horizontalSpacing="10dip"
            android:numColumns="4"
            android:verticalSpacing="10dip"
            android:columnWidth="100dip"
            android:stretchMode="columnWidth"
            android:gravity="center"  />
    </LinearLayout>
    <LinearLayout
        android:layout_width="match_parent"
        android:layout_height="match_parent"
        android:orientation="vertical"
        android:layout_weight="1"
        android:paddingTop="40dp" >
        <TextView
            android:layout_width="match_parent"
            android:layout_height="wrap_content"
            android:text="Target Grid"
            android:textSize="@dimen/text_size"
            android:textStyle="bold"  />
        <GridView
            android:id="@+id/targetgrid_view"
            android:layout_width="match_parent"
            android:layout_height="match_parent"
            android:horizontalSpacing="10dip"
            android:numColumns="4"
            android:verticalSpacing="10dip"  />
    </LinearLayout>
</LinearLayout>
```

You can see that the two GridView controls are assigned the IDs sourcegrid_view and
targetgrid_view. The two TextView controls that are displayed above the two GridView
controls are initialized to display the text Source Grid and Target Grid, respectively. The
two TextView and GridView controls are arranged in the "vertical"-oriented LinearLayout
containers, which in turn are arranged in the "horizontal"-oriented outer LinearLayout
container.

After defining the layout, you need to copy the images to the `res/drawable` folders. You will be using seven images in this application. Assume that the image filenames are `image1.jpg`, `image2.jpg`, `image3.jpg`, `image4.jpg`, `image5.jpg`, `image6.jpg`, and `image7.jpg`. Copy these images to all four `res/drawable` folders.

Because this application is compatible to run on phones and tablets, you need to resize the `GridView` layout based on the screen size on which the application is run. By resizing the `GridView`, the images displayed through it will be resized automatically. More specifically, you want the images to appear comparatively smaller on phones than on tablets. You will do so by defining dimension resources.

Assuming the dimension file `dimens.xml` already exists in the `res/values` folder, you will add the dimensions to the file to resize the images as per the device's screen on which the application is run. Write the following code in the `dimens.xml` file:

```xml
<?xml version="1.0" encoding="utf-8"?>
<resources>
    <dimen name="text_size">14sp</dimen>
    <dimen name="layout_width">100dp</dimen>
    <dimen name="layout_height">120dp</dimen>
</resources>
```

The three dimension resources `text_size`, `layout_width`, and `layout_height` define the font size of the text, width, and height of the layout. These dimension resources are for normal screen devices (phones).

To define the dimension resources for a 7-inch tablet, open the `dimens.xml` file in the `res/values-sw600dp` folder and write the following code in it:

```xml
<?xml version="1.0" encoding="utf-8"?>
<resources>
    <dimen name="text_size">24sp</dimen>
    <dimen name="layout_width">140dp</dimen>
    <dimen name="layout_height">160dp</dimen>
</resources>
```

Finally, to define dimensions for extra-large screen devices (10-inch tablets), open the `dimens.xml` file in the `values-sw720dp` folder and write the following code in it:

```xml
<?xml version="1.0" encoding="utf-8"?>
<resources>
    <dimen name="text_size">32sp</dimen>
        <dimen name="layout_width">180dp</dimen>
    <dimen name="layout_height">200dp</dimen>
</resources>
```

By comparing the dimension resources of phones, 7-inch tablets, and 10-inch tablets, you can see that text and `GridView` layout is resized based on the device screen size.

Next, you need to write Java code to perform the following tasks:

- Access the source and target `GridView` from the layout file and map them to the respective `GridView` objects.

- Define `ArrayList` to store the information of the images to be displayed through the source `GridView`.

- Define an `ImageAdapter` class that extends `BaseAdapter`. The `ImageAdapter` is set to the source `GridView` to show the images defined in the `ArrayList`. Also, define a `TargetAdapter` to display the images that will be dropped to the target `GridView`.

- Associate `setOnItemLongClickListener` to the source `GridView` to listen for any image being long-clicked, and take necessary actions.

- Associate `setOnDragListener` to both the `GridView` controls to listen to `DragEvent`.

- Define `ClipData` to represent the image that is selected from the source `GridView`.

- Define the `ShadowBuilder` class that extends `View.DragShadowBuilder` to define the dimension of the drag shadow and to draw it.

- Define the `DragEventListener` class that implements the `View.OnDragListener` interface to listen to the generated `DragEvent` and different actions that take place while dragging and dropping.

- Add the image that is dropped on the target `GridView` to its `ImageAdapter` so that the dropped image appears in the target `GridView`.

To perform all the preceding actions, write the code as shown in Listing 5.4 to the Java activity file `DragAndDropImageActivity.java`.

Listing 5.4   **Code Written in the Java Activity File** `DragAndDropImageActivity.java`

```java
package com.androidtablet.draganddropimage;

import android.os.Bundle;
import android.app.Activity;
import java.util.ArrayList;
import android.widget.BaseAdapter;
import android.widget.ImageView;
import android.widget.GridView;
import android.widget.AdapterView.OnItemLongClickListener;
import android.view.DragEvent;
import android.view.View;
import android.content.ClipDescription;
import android.content.ClipData;
import android.widget.AdapterView;
import android.view.ViewGroup;
import android.view.View.DragShadowBuilder;
import android.graphics.Point;
import android.graphics.Canvas;
import android.util.Log;
```

```java
public class DragAndDropImageActivity extends Activity {
    GridView sourceGridView;
    GridView targetGridView;
    private ArrayList <Integer> drawables;
    private ArrayList <Integer>  targetdrawables = new ArrayList
        <Integer>();
    DragEventListener dragEventListener = new
        DragEventListener();
    TargetAdapter targetAdapter;

    @Override
    public void onCreate(Bundle savedInstanceState) {
        super.onCreate(savedInstanceState);
        setContentView(R.layout.activity_drag_and_drop_image);
        drawables = new ArrayList<Integer>();
        drawables.add(R.drawable.image1);
        drawables.add(R.drawable.image2);
        drawables.add(R.drawable.image3);
        drawables.add(R.drawable.image4);
        drawables.add(R.drawable.image5);
        drawables.add(R.drawable.image6);
        drawables.add(R.drawable.image7);
        sourceGridView = (GridView) findViewById(
            R.id.sourcegrid_view);
        targetGridView = (GridView) findViewById(
            R.id.targetgrid_view);
        sourceGridView.setAdapter(new ImageAdapter());
        sourceGridView.setOnItemLongClickListener(
            sourceGridLongClickListener);
        sourceGridView.setOnDragListener(dragEventListener);
        targetGridView.setOnDragListener(dragEventListener);
        targetAdapter=new TargetAdapter();
        targetGridView.setAdapter(targetAdapter);
        sourceGridView.setTag("Source GridView");
        targetGridView.setTag("Target GridView");
    }

    OnItemLongClickListener sourceGridLongClickListener    = new
        OnItemLongClickListener() {
        @Override
        public boolean onItemLongClick(AdapterView<?> l, View v,
            int position, long id) {
            ClipData.Item item = new ClipData.Item(drawables.
                get(position).toString());
            String[] clipDescription = {ClipDescription.
                MIMETYPE_TEXT_PLAIN};
            ClipData dragData = new ClipData((CharSequence)
                v.getTag(), clipDescription,item);
            DragShadowBuilder itemShadow = new ShadowBuilder(v);
```

```
            v.startDrag(dragData, itemShadow, drawables.
                get(position), 0);
            return true;
        }
    };

    private static class ShadowBuilder extends View.
        DragShadowBuilder {
        private static View view;
        public ShadowBuilder(View v) {
            super(v);
            view=v;
        }

        @Override
        public void onProvideShadowMetrics (Point size, Point
            touch){
            int width = getView().getWidth();
            int height = getView().getHeight();
            size.set(width, height);
            touch.set(width / 2, height / 2);
        }

        @Override
        public void onDrawShadow(Canvas canvas) {
            view.draw(canvas);
        }
    }

    protected class ImageAdapter extends BaseAdapter{
        @Override
        public View getView(int position, View convertView,
            ViewGroup gridView) {
            ImageView imageView = new ImageView(
                DragAndDropImageActivity.this);
            imageView.setImageResource((Integer) drawables.
                get(position));
            int layout_width = (int) getResources().
                getDimension(R.dimen.layout_width);
            int layout_height = (int) getResources().
                getDimension(R.dimen.layout_height);
            imageView.setLayoutParams(new GridView.LayoutParams(
                layout_width, layout_height));
            imageView.setLongClickable(true);
            imageView.setTag(String.valueOf(position));
            return imageView;
        }
```

```java
        @Override
        public long getItemId(int position) {
            return position;
        }

        @Override
        public Object getItem(int position) {
            return drawables.get(position);
        }

        @Override
        public int getCount() {
            return drawables.size();
        }
    }

    protected class TargetAdapter extends BaseAdapter{
        @Override
        public View getView(int position, View convertView,
            ViewGroup gridView) {
            ImageView imageView = new ImageView(
                DragAndDropImageActivity.this);
            imageView.setImageResource((Integer)
                targetdrawables.get(position));
            int layout_width = (int) getResources().
                getDimension(R.dimen.layout_width);
            int layout_height = (int) getResources().
                getDimension(R.dimen.layout_height);
            imageView.setLayoutParams(new GridView.LayoutParams(
                layout_width, layout_height));
            imageView.setLongClickable(true);
            imageView.setTag(String.valueOf(position));
            return imageView;
        }
        @Override
        public long getItemId(int position) {
            return position;
        }

        @Override
        public Object getItem(int position) {
            return targetdrawables.get(position);
        }

        @Override
        public int getCount() {
            return targetdrawables.size();
        }
    }
```

```
protected class DragEventListener implements View.
    OnDragListener {
    @Override
    public boolean onDrag(View v, DragEvent event) {
        switch (event.getAction()) {
            case DragEvent.ACTION_DRAG_STARTED:
                if (event.getClipDescription().hasMimeType(
                    ClipDescription.MIMETYPE_TEXT_PLAIN)) {
                    Log.d((String) v.getTag(), "ACTION_DRAG_
                        STARTED accepted");
                    return true;
                }else{
                    Log.d((String) v.getTag(), "ACTION_DRAG_
                        STARTED rejected");
                    return false;
                }
            case DragEvent.ACTION_DRAG_ENTERED:
                Log.d((String) v.getTag(), "ACTION_DRAG_
                    ENTERED");
                return true;
            case DragEvent.ACTION_DRAG_EXITED:
                Log.d((String) v.getTag(), "ACTION_DRAG_
                    EXITED");
                return true;
            case DragEvent.ACTION_DRAG_LOCATION:
                return true;
            case DragEvent.ACTION_DROP:
                if(v == targetGridView){
                    ClipData.Item item = event.
                        getClipData().getItemAt(0);
                    Log.d((String) v.getTag(), "ACTION_
                        DROP");
                    String droppedItem = item.getText().
                        toString();
                    targetdrawables.add(Integer.parseInt(
                        droppedItem));
                    targetAdapter.notifyDataSetChanged();
                    return true;
                }
                else
                    return false;
            case DragEvent.ACTION_DRAG_ENDED:
                if (event.getResult())
                    Log.d((String) v.getTag(), "ACTION_DRAG_
                        ENDED successfully");
                else
                    Log.d((String) v.getTag(), "Failure:
                        ACTION_DRAG_ENDED");
                return true;
```

```
                    default:
                        Log.d((String) v.getTag(), "Not Known");
                        return false;
                }
            }
        }
    }
}
```

After running the application, you will find two GridView controls on the screen. One GridView shows the images, and the other is empty. The two TextView controls display the text Source Grid and Target Grid to indicate the purpose of the GridView. Because of the limited space, the images in the second row of the Source Grid are partially visible (see Figure 5.3 [top]). When you slide the grid, the images in the second row of Source Grid will become visible (see Figure 5.3 [bottom]).

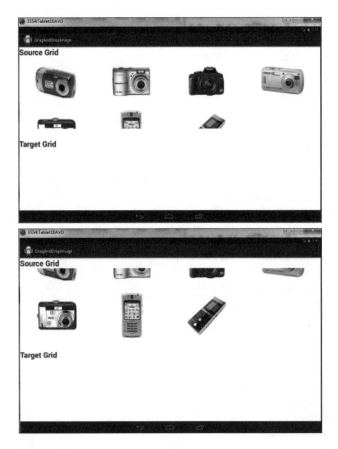

Figure 5.3   Source Grid and Target Grid appear on application startup (top), and hidden images appear in the Source Grid after flipping in the grid (bottom).

When any image is clicked in the source GridView and dragged, a drag shadow representing the image being dragged moves along with the mouse pointer (see Figure 5.4 [top]). After you drop the shadow of the image to the target GridView, the image is added to it (see Figure 5.4 [middle]). The target GridView might appear as shown in Figure 5.4 (bottom) when a few images are dragged and dropped over it.

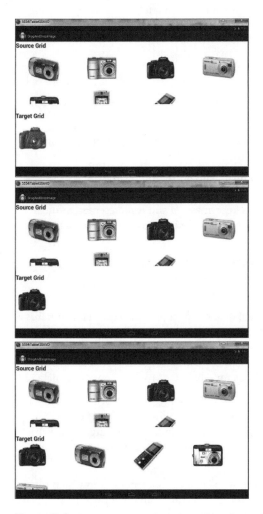

Figure 5.4   Drag shadow of the image appears while dragging an image from the Source Grid to the Target Grid (top); the dropped image appears in the Target Grid (middle); images appear in the Target Grid after a couple of drag and drop operations (bottom).

Recipe: Cutting, Copying, and Pasting Text Using the System Clipboard

To cut, copy, and paste content from one view to another in an Android application and even across applications, you use `ClipboardManager`. `ClipboardManager` is the class that represents the system clipboard. To use it, you do not instantiate it but get a reference to it by invoking the `getSystemService(CLIPBOARD_SERVICE)` method. For example, the following statement gets a reference to the `ClipboardManager` class:

```
ClipboardManager clipManager= (ClipboardManager)
getSystemService(CLIPBOARD_SERVICE);
```

Two methods of the `ClipboardManager` that are frequently used in cut, copy, and paste operations are given here:

- **`setPrimaryClip()`**—Sets the current primary clip on the clipboard. It is the primary clip that is used in cut, copy, and paste operations.

- **`getPrimaryClip()`**—Returns the current primary clip on the clipboard.

The data that is copied or cut into the clipboard is known as *clip* and is represented through `ClipData`. That is, to represent the data copied or cut into the clipboard, a `ClipData` object is created that comprises the following two objects:

- **`ClipDescription` object**—Contains a description (metadata) of the clip. It has an array of MIME types for the clip's data. These MIME types are examined before pasting the clip to ensure that the available MIME types can be handled.

- **`ClipData.Item` object**—Contains the actual data cut or copied into the clipboard. It is a `CharSequence` object that contains formatting. The object can store text, URI, or intent data.

The `ClipData` class provides the following methods for creating `ClipData` containing data of different types:

- **`newPlainText(label, text)`**—Creates a `ClipData` object in which the `ClipData.Item` object contains the supplied `text` argument. The supplied `label` argument will be assigned to the label of the `ClipDescription` object, and the MIME type is set to `MIMETYPE_TEXT_PLAIN`.

- **`newUri(content_resolver, label, URI)`**—Creates a `ClipData` object in which the `ClipData.Item` object contains the supplied URI. The `label` argument will be assigned to the label of the `ClipDescription` object, and the MIME type is set to `MIMETYPE_TEXT_URILIST`. To retrieve the information of the URI, use the content_ resolver.

- **`newIntent(label, intent)`**—Creates a `ClipData` object in which the `ClipData.Item` object contains the supplied intent. The supplied label argument will be assigned to the label of the `ClipDescription` object, and the MIME type is set to `MIMETYPE_TEXT_INTENT`.

> **Note**
>
> The clipboard can hold only one `ClipData` at a time. A `ClipData` contains a `ClipDescription` object and one or more `ClipData.Item` objects.

To see how text is cut, copied, and pasted, you will create a new Android project called `CopyPasteApp`. In the application, you will create two `EditText` controls and three `Button` controls. The three `Button` controls will be assigned the captions `Cut`, `Copy`, and `Paste`, respectively. The text matter is written in the first `EditText` control. After you click the Copy button, the text written in the first `EditText` control is copied into the system clipboard in the form of `ClipData`. That is, the text of the `EditText` control is assigned to the `ClipData.Item` object of the `ClipData`. When you click the Paste button, the plain text stored in the `ClipData.Item` of the `ClipData` object is assigned to the second `EditText` control.

Similarly, when you click the Cut button, the text in the first `EditText` control is assigned to the `ClipData.Item` of the `ClipData` object and is deleted from the `EditText` control. Again, after you click the Paste button, the text in the `ClipData.Item` object is assigned to the second `EditText` control.

After defining the two `EditText` and the three `Button` controls, the activity layout file `activity_copy_paste_app.xml` will appear as shown in Listing 5.5.

Listing 5.5   Code Written in the Activity Layout File `activity_copy_paste_app.xml`

```
<RelativeLayout
xmlns:android="http://schemas.android.com/apk/res/android"
    xmlns:tools="http://schemas.android.com/tools"
    android:layout_width="match_parent"
    android:layout_height="match_parent" >
    <EditText
        android:id="@+id/edittext1"
        android:layout_width="match_parent"
        android:layout_height="wrap_content"
        android:hint="Enter text in this box"
        android:minLines="5"
        android:layout_marginTop="15dip"
        android:layout_marginLeft="20dip"
        android:textSize="@dimen/text_size" />
    <Button
        android:id="@+id/cut_button"
        android:layout_width="wrap_content"
        android:layout_height="wrap_content"
        android:text="Cut"
        android:textSize="@dimen/text_size"
        android:layout_below="@id/edittext1"  />
    <Button
        android:id="@+id/copy_button"
```

```
            android:layout_width="wrap_content"
            android:layout_height="wrap_content"
            android:text="Copy"
            android:textSize="@dimen/text_size"
            android:layout_below="@id/edittext1"
            android:layout_toRightOf="@id/cut_button"/>
        <Button
            android:id="@+id/paste_button"
            android:layout_width="wrap_content"
            android:layout_height="wrap_content"
            android:text="Paste"
            android:textSize="@dimen/text_size"
            android:layout_below="@id/edittext1"
            android:layout_toRightOf="@id/copy_button" />
        <EditText
            android:id="@+id/edittext2"
            android:layout_width="match_parent"
            android:layout_height="wrap_content"
            android:minLines="5"
            android:textSize="@dimen/text_size"
            android:layout_marginTop="15dip"
            android:layout_marginLeft="20dip"
            android:layout_below="@id/copy_button" />
</RelativeLayout>
```

You can see that the height of the two EditText controls is set to display a minimum of five lines. To access and identify the two EditText controls, set the IDs edittext1 and edittext2 to them, respectively. The three Button controls are assigned the IDs cut_button, copy_button and paste_button, respectively. The text entered into the EditText controls and the caption of the Button controls will appear in the font size defined in the dimension resource text_size.

Now write Java code to accomplish the following tasks:

- Access the two EditText and three Button controls defined in the activity layout file and map them to the respective objects.

- Associate setOnClickListener to the three Button controls so that when any of the Button controls is clicked, the respective callback method onClick() is invoked.

- Define the ClipboardManager object to represent the system clipboard.

- Define the ClipData object to contain the text that is copied or cut.

- Set the primary clip on the clipboard to the ClipData object when the Cut or Copy button is clicked.

- Access the primary clip to retrieve the ClipData when the Paste button is clicked.

Access the `ClipData.Item` object from the `ClipData`. Fill the second `EditText` control with the plain text contained in the `ClipData.Item` object.

To perform the preceding tasks, write the code as shown in Listing 5.6 to the main Java activity file, `CopyPasteAppActivity.java`.

Listing 5.6   **Code Written in the Java Activity File** `CopyPasteAppActivity.java`

```java
package com.androidtablet.copypasteapp;

import android.os.Bundle;
import android.app.Activity;
import android.content.ClipboardManager;
import android.widget.EditText;
import android.widget.Button;
import android.view.View.OnClickListener;
import android.view.View;
import android.content.ClipData;

public class CopyPasteAppActivity extends Activity {
    EditText editText1, editText2;
    ClipboardManager clipManager;
    Button cutButton, copyButton, pasteButton;

    @Override
    public void onCreate(Bundle savedInstanceState) {
        super.onCreate(savedInstanceState);
        setContentView(R.layout.activity_copy_paste_app);
        editText1 = (EditText) findViewById(R.id.edittext1);
        editText2 = (EditText) findViewById(R.id.edittext2);
        clipManager= (ClipboardManager) getSystemService(
            CLIPBOARD_SERVICE);
        cutButton = (Button)this.findViewById(R.id.cut_button);
        cutButton.setOnClickListener(new OnClickListener(){
            public void onClick(View view) {
                ClipData clipData = ClipData.newPlainText(
                    "data", editText1.getText());
                clipManager.setPrimaryClip(clipData);
                editText1.setText("");
            }
        });
        copyButton = (Button)this.findViewById(R.id.copy_
            button);
        copyButton.setOnClickListener(new OnClickListener(){
            public void onClick(View view) {
                ClipData clipData = ClipData.newPlainText(
                    "data", editText1.getText());
```

```
                clipManager.setPrimaryClip(clipData);
            }
        });
        pasteButton = (Button)this.findViewById( R.id.paste_
            button);
        pasteButton.setOnClickListener(new OnClickListener(){
            public void onClick(View view) {
                if (clipManager.hasPrimaryClip()){
                    ClipData clipData = clipManager.
                        getPrimaryClip();
                    editText2.setText(clipData.getItemAt(0).
                        getText());
                }
            }
        });
    }
}
```

After running the application, you get two empty `EditText` controls and three `Button` controls on startup (see Figure 5.5 [top]). When you enter some text in the first `EditText` control and click the Copy button followed by the Paste button, the text in the first `EditText` control is copied and pasted into the second `EditText` control (see Figure 5.5 [middle]). When you select the Cut button, the text from the first `EditText` control is deleted and stored in the form of a `ClipData` object. When you select the Paste button, the text from the `ClipData` object is pasted in the second `EditText` control, as shown in Figure 5.5 (bottom).

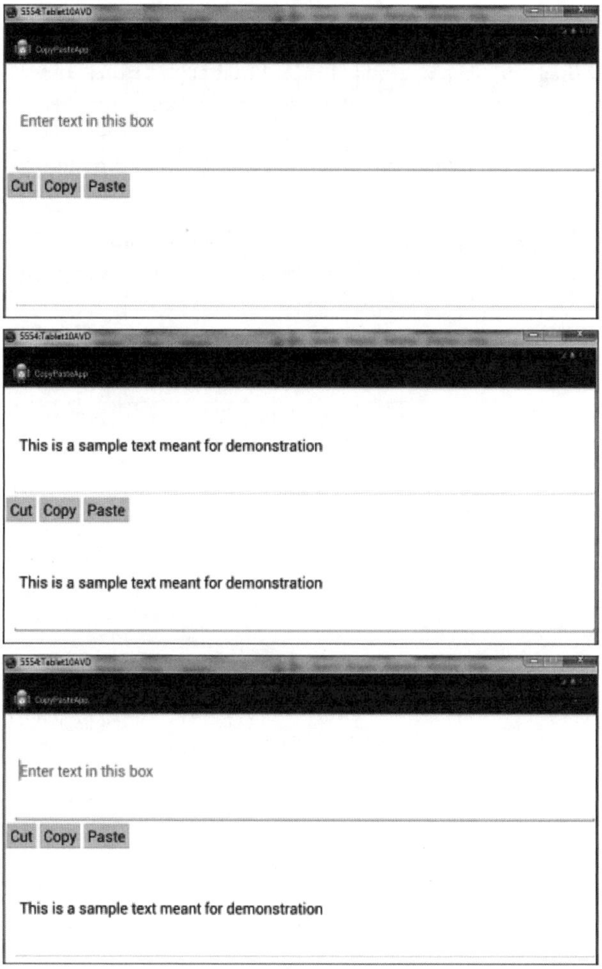

Figure 5.5   Two EditText controls and three Button controls appear on application startup (top); the text from the top EditText copied and pasted to the below EditText (middle); the text cut from the top EditText and pasted below EditText (bottom).

Summary

In this chapter, you learned to apply drag and drop operations in Android applications. You learned to listen to `DragEvent`, track different actions that occur during drag and drop, create a drag shadow, and add the view to the drop zone. You dragged and dropped text as well as images. You discovered how to access the system clipboard and apply cut, copy, and paste operations to the Android applications.

In the next chapter, you will learn to use pending intents to start an activity and broadcast an intent. You will also create broadcast receivers to listen to the broadcasted intent and learn about a system to notify users.

6

Notifications and Pending Intents

Notifications, as the name suggests, refer to the messages or events that require a user's attention. Notifications in Honeycomb and onward are displayed in the form of an icon in the notification area. Users can open the notification drawer to see the notification details. On tablets, the notification area is integrated with the system bar at the bottom of the screen. The notification drawer is opened by touching anywhere inside the notification area. On clicking the notification, the designated pending intent activity is called to perform the desired action. Therefore, notifications and pending intents are somewhat connected. In this chapter, you will come to understand pending intents in detail, learn to broadcast intent, and create broadcast receivers to listen to the broadcasted intent. You will also learn about the Android notification system and use pending intent to start an activity using the notification system.

Recipe: Understanding Pending Intents

A pending intent is a variation of a regular intent. Recall from Chapter 1, "Overview of Android Tablet Applications," that a regular intent is defined as a structure that is used to start, stop, and implement transition between activities within an application. A pending intent, as the name suggests, is an intent that is stored and kept pending to be invoked in the future. A pending intent is created through the `PendingIntent` class, and it wraps a regular intent that will be invoked in the future when a certain event occurs. Assuming the current activity (application context) is `PendingIntentAppActivity`, the code that follows creates a pending intent named `pendIntent`:

```
Intent intent = new Intent(PendingIntentAppActivity.this, TargetActivity.class);
PendingIntent pendIntent = PendingIntent.getActivity(PendingIntentAppActivity.this, 0,
intent, 0);
```

You create an intent object by supplying the current application context and the activity name, `TargetActivity.class`—the one that you want to launch. Thereafter, a `PendingIntent` object called `pendIntent` is created by supplying the following four parameters to the `getActivity()` method:

- The current application context in which the pending intent will start the activity.

- A request code for the sender. It is usually used to distinguish two pending intents. When a request code is not used, the 0 value is supplied for this parameter.

- The intent of the activity to be launched is passed for this parameter.

- Flags determine the action to take in certain conditions. For example, flags help determine the action to take if a pending intent already exists. You supply a value of 0 for this parameter to take default action. Listed next are the constants to be used for flags:

  - **FLAG_CANCEL_CURRENT**—It will cancel the current pending intent (if it exists) before creating a new one.

  - **FLAG_NO_CREATE**—It will return null if the pending intent does not already exist. It will not create a new one.

  - **FLAG_ONE_SHOT**—The created pending intent will be used once.

  - **FLAG_UPDATE_CURRENT**—It will replace the extra data of the existing pending intent with that of the new one.

Note
A pending intent can be invoked even if the calling process is killed.

A regular intent can start an activity, service, or broadcast receiver, as indicated by the following three methods:

- startActivity(intent)

- startService(intent)

- sendBroadcast(intent)

The respective methods for creating a pending intent for an activity, service, and broadcast receiver are as follows:

- PendingIntent.getActivity(context, 0, intent, flag)

- PendingIntent.getService(context, 0, intent, flag)

- PendingIntent.getBroadcast(context, 0, intent, flag)

Example:

Assuming the current activity is PendingIntentAppActivity (application context), the following statements create a pending intent to start an activity:

```
int requestCode = 0;
int flags = 0;
```

```
Intent activityIntent = new Intent(PendingIntentAppActivity.this,
TargetActivity.class);
PendingIntent.getActivity(PendingIntentAppActivity.this, requestCode, activityIntent,
flags);
```

Recipe: Broadcasting an Intent

Intents are capable of sending structured messages. You can use intents to send messages such as the arrival of new mail, a battery that is low, and the completion of a download. In other words, such messages can be broadcast as an intent object.

Note
Broadcast intents notify applications of system or application events.

To broadcast an intent, you create an intent object, assign a specific action to it, attach data or a message to the broadcast receiver, and then broadcast it. You can optionally put an extra message or data on the intent. Methods involved in broadcasting an intent are shown in Table 6.1.

Table 6.1   **Methods Involved in Broadcasting an Intent**

Method	Description
`putExtra()`	Used to add data or a message to the intent that you want to send to the broadcast receiver.
	Syntax:
	`putExtra(String name, String value)`
	Here, `name` is the key or name of the value that you want to pass along with the intent. `name` is used to identify the value.
`setAction()`	Used to set the action to perform on the data or message being sent with the intent.
	Syntax:
	`setAction(String action)`
	The Broadcast receiver uses the `getAction()` method to retrieve the action to be performed on the received data.
`sendBroadcast()`	Available on the `Context` class, this method sends the broadcast intent to all the registered intent receivers.
	Syntax:
	`void sendBroadcast(intent_to_broadcast)`
	Here, the `intent_to_broadcast` parameter represents the intent that you want to broadcast.

The following code broadcasts an intent:

```
public static String BROADCAST_STRING = "com.androidtablet.broadcastingintent";
Intent broadcastIntent = new Intent();
broadcastIntent.putExtra("message", "New Message arrived");
broadcastIntent.setAction(BROADCAST_STRING);
sendBroadcast(broadcastIntent);
```

You can see that an intent object called `broadcastIntent` is created. The data or message to be passed along with the intent is `New Message arrived`, and the name or key assigned to this message is `message`. The action string is made unique by using a namespace similar to a Java class. You can see that `com.androidtablet.broadcastingintent` is assigned as action to the intent. Finally, the `broadcastIntent` is sent or broadcasted and received by the broadcast receivers.

To listen and respond to the broadcasted intent, you implement broadcast receivers. A broadcast intent can invoke more than one broadcast receiver. A broadcast receiver is a class that extends the `BroadcastReceiver`. It also needs to be registered as a receiver in an Android application via the `AndroidManifest.xml` file or through code at runtime. If it is not registered in the manifest file, it won't run. The broadcast receiver class needs to implement the `onReceive()` method. The following is the sample code of an `onReceive()` method:

```
public void onReceive(Context context, Intent intent) {
    String actionName = intent.getAction();
    if(actionName != null && actionName.equals("com.androidtablet.
broadcastingintent")) {
        String msg = intent.getStringExtra("message");
        Log.d("Received Message: ",msg);
    }
}
```

These `getAction()` and `getStringExtra()` methods perform the following tasks:

- **getAction()**—Retrieves the action to be performed from the intent object. It is the action that indicates the task to be performed on the data passed along with the intent.

  Syntax:

  ```
  getAction()
  ```

- **getStringExtra()**—Retrieves the extended data from the intent.

  Syntax:

  ```
  getStringExtra(String name)
  ```

Here, `name` represents the key or the name that was assigned to the value while adding data to the intent through the `putExtra()` method.

In the `onReceive()` method, you access the intent object passed as a parameter. From the intent object, you retrieve the action that is supposed to be performed. If the action to be performed is not `null` and matches the one that is sent by the sender activity, the message or data that is passed along with the intent is extracted from the intent and is logged.

To better understand how an intent is broadcasted, create an Android project called `BroadcastingIntent`. In this application, a button will be displayed with the caption `Broadcast Intent`. After you click the button, an intent with a specific message will be broadcasted. The broadcasted intent is then received through a broadcast receiver, and the message sent with the intent is extracted and displayed. To define a `Button` control, write the code shown in Listing 6.1 into the `activity_broadcasting_intent.xml` layout file.

Listing 6.1 **Code Written into** `activity_broadcasting_intent.xml`

```xml
<LinearLayout xmlns:android="http://schemas.android.com/apk/res/android"
    android:layout_width="match_parent"
    android:layout_height="match_parent"
    android:orientation="vertical" >
    <Button
        android:id="@+id/broadcast_button"
        android:text="Broadcast Intent"
        android:layout_width="wrap_content"
        android:layout_height="wrap_content"
        android:layout_gravity="center"
        android:textSize="@dimen/text_size" />
</LinearLayout>
```

You can see that the `Button` control is assigned the `broadcast_button` ID, which will identify it in the Java code. The caption assigned to the `Button` control is `Broadcast Intent`. Next, you need to write code in the Java activity file to define an intent object, assign an action, add a specific message to it, and then broadcast it. To do so, write the code shown in Listing 6.2 into the Java activity file `BroadcastingIntentActivity.java`.

Listing 6.2 **Code Written into** `BroadcastingIntentActivity.java`

```java
package com.androidtablet.broadcastingintent;

import android.app.Activity;
import android.os.Bundle;
import android.content.Intent;
import android.widget.Button;
import android.view.View;

public class BroadcastingIntentActivity extends Activity {
    public static String BROADCAST_STRING =
        "com.androidtablet.broadcastintent";
    @Override
    public void onCreate(Bundle savedInstanceState) {
        super.onCreate(savedInstanceState);
        setContentView(R.layout.activity_broadcasting_intent);
        Button broadcastButton = (Button) this.findViewById(
            R.id.broadcast_button);
```

```
        broadcastButton.setOnClickListener(new Button.
            OnClickListener(){
            public void onClick(View v) {
                Intent broadcastIntent = new Intent();
                broadcastIntent.putExtra("message", "New Message
                    arrived");
                broadcastIntent.setAction(BROADCAST_STRING);
                sendBroadcast(broadcastIntent);
            }
        });
    }
}
```

Here you can see that the `Button` control with the `broadcast_button` ID is accessed from the layout file and is mapped to the `Button` object, `broadcastButton`. A `setOnClickListener` is associated with the `Button` control. When the `Button` control is clicked, the callback method `onClick()` is invoked. In the `onClick()` method, an intent object called `broadcastIntent` is defined. The message `New Message arrived` is added to the `broadcastIntent` object with the key `message`. With the help of a static string, `BROADCAST_STRING`, a unique action, `com.androidtablet.broadcastintent`, is assigned to the intent object `broadcastIntent`. Finally, the intent is broadcasted by calling the `sendBroadcast()` method.

The next step is defining an activity that will act as a broadcast receiver. So to the package `com.androidtablet.broadcastingintent` of your application, add a Java file named `ReceiveBroadcastActivity.java`. To respond to the broadcasted intent and to access the data or message passed along with it, write the code shown in Listing 6.3 in the Java file `ReceiveBroadcastActivity.java`.

Listing 6.3   **Code Written into** `ReceiveBroadcastActivity.java`

```
package com.androidtablet.broadcastingintent;

import android.content.BroadcastReceiver;
import android.content.Intent;
import android.content.Context;
import android.util.Log;

public class ReceiveBroadcastActivity extends BroadcastReceiver {
    @Override
    public void onReceive(Context context, Intent intent) {
        String actionName = intent.getAction();
        if(actionName != null && actionName.equals(
            "com.androidtablet.broadcastintent")) {
            String msg = intent.getStringExtra("message");
            Log.d("Text Received from Broadcast
                Intent: ", msg);
```

```
        }
    }
}
```

As mentioned earlier, to receive the broadcasted intent, the Java class needs to extend the `BroadcastReceiver` class. The class also overrides the `onReceive()` method. In the `onReceive()` method, you use the intent parameter, which represents the received intent object. From the intent object, you access the action to be performed on the data passed along with the intent. You check to see if the action is not null and match the action with the one that was supplied while broadcasting the intent. Thereafter, the data from the intent object is accessed and is displayed.

The `ReceiveBroadcastActivity.java` file, which is the broadcast receiver, has to be registered in the manifest file. The code for registering the activity follows:

```
<receiver android:name=".ReceiveBroadcastActivity">
    <intent-filter>
        <action android:name="com.androidtablet.
            broadcastintent"> </action>
    </intent-filter>
</receiver>
```

You can see that the `<receiver>` tag is used in the manifest file to register the broadcast receiver. The tag also designates the `ReceiveBroadcastActivity.class` as the recipient of the intent whose action is `com.androidtablet.broadcastintent`. Listing 6.4 shows the code in the `AndroidManifest.xml` file. Only the code in bold has been added; the rest is the default code that the Android SDK auto-generates.

Listing 6.4   **Code in the `AndroidManifest.xml` File**

```
<?xml version="1.0" encoding="utf-8"?>
<manifest xmlns:android="http://schemas.android.com/apk/res/android"
    package="com.androidtablet.broadcastintentapp"
    android:versionCode="1"
    android:versionName="1.0" >
    <uses-sdk android:minSdkVersion="11"
        android:targetSdkVersion="17" />
    <application
        android:icon="@drawable/ic_launcher"
        android:label="@string/app_name"
        android:theme="@style/AppTheme" >
        <activity
            android:name=".BroadcastIntentAppActivity"
            android:label="@string/title_activity_broadcast_
                intent_app" >
            <intent-filter>
                <action android:name="android.intent.action.
```

```
                    MAIN" />
            <category android:name="android.intent.category.
                LAUNCHER" />
        </intent-filter>
    </activity>
    <receiver android:name=".ReceiveBroadcastActivity">
        <intent-filter>
            <action android:name="com.androidtablet.
                broadcastintent"></action>
        </intent-filter>
    </receiver>
</application>
</manifest>
```

After running the application, you see a button with the caption `Broadcast Intent` displayed on the screen, as shown in Figure 6.1 (top). After you click the Broadcast Intent button, an intent with the message `New Message arrived` is broadcasted. The `ReceiveBroadcastActivity.class` receives the broadcasted intent, extracts the message `New Message arrived` from it, and logs it. The logged message appears in the LogCat window, as shown in Figure 6.1 (bottom).

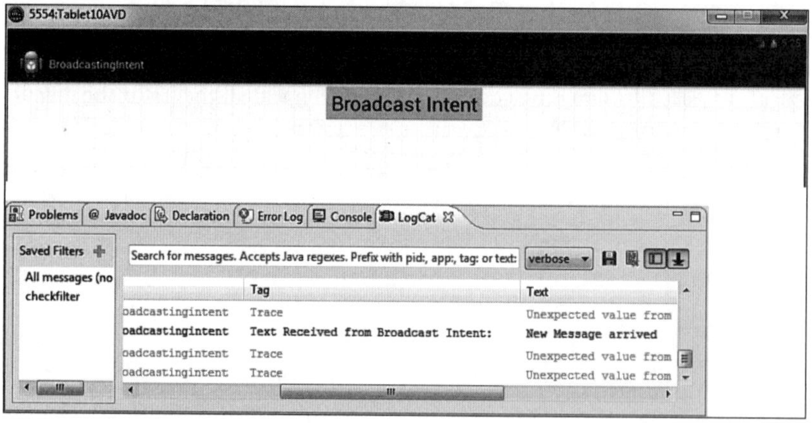

Figure 6.1   Application showing the Broadcast Intent button on startup (top) and logged messages displayed in the LogCat window (bottom)

Note

You can have more than one receiver receive the broadcasted intent.

You can even add a broadcast receiver dynamically. To do this, you add the code shown in Listing 6.5 to the Java activity file `BroadcastingIntentActivity.java`. Only the code in bold is newly added; the rest is the same as in Listing 6.2.

Listing 6.5   Code in the `BroadcastingIntentActivity.java` **File**

```java
package com.androidtablet.broadcastingintent;

import android.app.Activity;
import android.os.Bundle;
import android.content.Intent;
import android.widget.Button;
import android.view.View;
import android.content.BroadcastReceiver;
import android.content.IntentFilter;
import android.content.Context;
import android.util.Log;

public class BroadcastingIntentActivity extends Activity {
    public static String BROADCAST_STRING =
        "com.androidtablet.broadcastintent";
    @Override
    public void onCreate(Bundle savedInstanceState) {
        super.onCreate(savedInstanceState);
        setContentView(R.layout.activity_broadcasting_intent);
        Button broadcastButton = (Button) this.findViewById(
            R.id.broadcast_button);
        broadcastButton.setOnClickListener(new Button.
            OnClickListener(){
            public void onClick(View v) {
                Intent broadcastIntent = new Intent();
                broadcastIntent.putExtra("message", "New Message
                    arrived");
                broadcastIntent.setAction(BROADCAST_STRING);
                sendBroadcast(broadcastIntent);
            }
        });
    }

    private BroadcastReceiver myBroadcastReceiver =   new
        BroadcastReceiver() {
        @Override
        public void onReceive(Context context, Intent intent) {
            String actionName = intent.getAction();
            if(actionName != null && actionName.equals(
                "com.androidtablet.broadcastintent")) {
                String msg = intent.getStringExtra("message");
                Log.d("Text Received from Broadcast Intent: ",
                    msg);
            }
        }
```

```
    };

    public void onResume() {
        super.onResume();
        IntentFilter intentFilter = new IntentFilter();
        intentFilter.addAction("com.androidtablet.
            broadcastintent");
        registerReceiver(myBroadcastReceiver, intentFilter);
    }

    public void onPause() {
        super.onPause();
        unregisterReceiver(myBroadcastReceiver);
    }
}
```

In the preceding code, you see that an intent carrying the text message New Message arrived is broadcasted when the Button control is clicked. To respond to the broadcasted intent and to access the data passed along with it, a broadcast receiver called myBroadcastReceiver is defined. In the onReceive() method of the broadcast receiver, the intent parameter is used and represents the received intent object. From the intent object, the action is accessed and compared with the one that is supplied while broadcasting the intent. Thereafter, the data from the intent object is accessed and displayed. In the onResume() method of the activity, an intent filter is defined, and the dynamically added broadcast receiver called myBroadcastReceiver is registered to act as the recipient of the intent whose action is com.androidtablet.broadcastintent.

Recipe: Understanding Android Notification System

The Android notification system provides you with several ways of alerting users. For example, the user can be notified with text, a vibration, blinking lights, and sound indicators. Notification appears as an icon in the notification area. On tablets, the notification area is integrated with the system bar at the bottom of the screen. Users can open the notification drawer to see the details of the notification. The notification drawer is opened by touching anywhere inside the notification area. After tapping the notification, the users are navigated to the intent that is defined by the notification. The notification will never launch an activity automatically but will simply notify the user and launch the activity only when the notification is selected. Besides an icon and ticker text, the notification can have a title and body text that is displayed when the full notification is being displayed. Compared with Toast, the notifications are persistent in nature.

For creating notifications, the following two classes are used:

- **Notification**—The object that defines the information to be displayed, which can be text to display on the status/expanded status bar, an icon displayed with the text, the number of times the notification is triggered, and so on.

- **NotificationManager**—The base object with which notifications are handled. It displays the information encapsulated in the Notification object, which is displayed via the notify() method.

Recipe: Creating Notifications

The first step in creating notifications is to create a Notification object and configure it by defining notification properties. The following code shows how to do so:

```
Notification notification = new Notification();
notification.icon = R.drawable.glowingbulb;
notification.tickerText = "There is a new notification";
notification.when = System.currentTimeMillis();
notification.flags |= Notification.FLAG_AUTO_CANCEL;
```

Here, you see that a Notification object called notification is created, and its public members are used to configure it:

- **icon**—Assigns the notification icon.

- **tickerText**—Assigns the small notification text.

- **when**—Assigns the time when the notification occurred. You use the system time to specify the time that the notification occurred.

- **flag**—Assigns the constant that determines the subsequent action when the notification is selected from the notification window. You usually assign the FLAG_AUTO_CANCEL constant to this public variable, which specifies that the notification be cancelled automatically after it is selected from the notifications.

You can also assign a notification icon, ticker text, and time of occurrence through the Notification object constructor, as shown next:

```
Notification notification  = new Notification(R.drawable.glowingbulb, "There is a new
notification", System.currentTimeMillis());
```

After receiving the notification, you may choose to take a necessary action. You make use of the PendingIntent class to switch to the desired intent when the notification is tapped.

The PendingIntent class enables you to create intents that can be triggered by your application when an event occurs. Assuming that the current activity is named PendingIntentAppActivity, the code that follows creates a PendingIntent object called pendIntent:

```
Intent intent = new Intent(PendingIntentAppActivity.this, TargetActivity.class);
PendingIntent pendIntent = PendingIntent.getActivity(PendingIntentAppActivity.this, 0,
intent, 0);
```

To display text after expanding the notification and to specify the pending intent that you want to launch, use the Notification.Builder.

Recipe: Using `Notification.Builder`

`Notification.Builder` is the builder class for notification objects that provides several methods to configure notification. A few of the methods are given in Table 6.2.

Table 6.2   `Notification.Builder` **Class Methods**

Method	Description
setSmallIcon()	Used to supply the small icon resource that will be displayed to represent the notification in the status bar.
	Syntax:
	`setSmallIcon(int icon)`
	where the `icon` parameter represents the resource ID of the drawable to be used as the icon of the notification.
setAutoCancel()	Used to determine whether you want to make the notification invisible when it is tapped. The Boolean value `true` is supplied to this method to make the notification invisible.
	Syntax:
	`setAutoCancel(boolean autoCancel)`
setTicker()	Used to supply the ticker text that is displayed in the status bar when the notification arrives.
	Syntax:
	`setTicker(CharSequence textMessage)`
setWhen()	Used to supply the time of occurrence of the notification.
	Syntax:
	`setWhen(long timeOfOccurrence)`
setContentTitle()	Used to supply the title of the notification when the status bar is expanded.
	Syntax:
	`setContentTitle(CharSequence title)`
setContentText()	Used to supply the text of the notification.
	Syntax:
	`setContentText(CharSequence text)`
setContentIntent()	Used to supply a `PendingIntent` to be sent when the notification is tapped.
	Syntax:
	`setContentIntent(PendingIntent intent)`

Assuming the current activity is named `PendingIntentAppActivity`, the following code shows how to use the `Notification.Builder` methods shown in Table 6.2 to configure the notification:

```
Notification.Builder builder = new Notification.Builder(PendingIntentAppActivity.this)
.setSmallIcon(R.drawable.ic_launcher)
.setAutoCancel(true)
.setTicker("There is a new notification")
.setWhen(System.currentTimeMillis())
.setContentTitle("New E-mail")
.setContentText("You have one unread message.")
.setContentIntent(pendIntent);
notification = builder.build();
```

The preceding code configures a notification as shown here:

- Sets the `ic_launcher.png` image as the notification icon
- Makes the notification invisible when tapped
- Assigns the text `There is a new notification` as the ticker text of the notification
- Sets the current time as the time of occurrence of the notification
- Sets the title of the notification as `New E-mail`
- Sets the body text of the notification as `You have one unread message.`
- Fires the specified pending intent, `pendIntent`, when the notification is tapped

The configuration notification created through the `Notification.Builder` object is assigned to the `Notification` object called `notification`.

Recipe: Obtaining a `NotificationManager`

The `NotificationManager` class executes and manages all status notifications. To obtain a valid `NotificationManager`, you use the `getSystemService()` method:

```
NotificationManager notificationManager = (NotificationManager)
getSystemService(NOTIFICATION_SERVICE);
```

After obtaining the `NotificationManager` object, you can invoke its `notify()` method to notify users by displaying the notification.

Syntax:

```
notify(uniqueID, notficationObject)
```

where the `uniqueID` parameter represents the application unique identifier, and the `notificationObject` parameter represents the `Notification` object that you want to display. The `uniqueID` can be used for updating or removing the notification.

Example:

```
notificationManager.notify(0, notification);
```

Recipe: Creating Notification and Using Pending Intent to Start an Activity

In this recipe, you will learn to create a pending intent that launches an activity on occurrence of a notification. The recipe will display a `Button` control that creates a notification when it is clicked. A ticker text informing occurrence of a notification will appear in the system bar. When you expand the notification, its detailed information, including icon, title, and body text, will be displayed. When you tap the notification, the pending intent will launch the designated activity. The designated activity will display the message `WelcomeActivity` launched by the pending intent. The recipe will help you understand the Android notification system and its connection with the pending intent.

Create an Android project called `PendingIntentApp`. You will begin with defining the layout of the target activity that will be launched by the pending intent. Because the target activity will simply display a text message indicating that the activity is launched, you only need to define a `TextView` control in the target activity's layout file. So add an XML file to the `res/layout` folder, and name it `welcome.xml`. In the `welcome.xml` file, define the `TextView` control as shown in Listing 6.6.

Listing 6.6   **Code Written in the** `welcome.xml` **File**

```xml
<?xml version="1.0" encoding="utf-8"?>
<LinearLayout xmlns:android="http://schemas.android.com/apk/res/android"
    android:layout_width="match_parent"
    android:layout_height="match_parent"
    android:orientation="vertical" >
    <TextView
        android:layout_width="match_parent"
        android:layout_height="wrap_content"
        android:text=" WelcomeActivity launched by the pending
            Intent "
        android:textSize="@dimen/text_size"
        android:textStyle="bold" />
</LinearLayout>
```

You can see that the `TextView` is initialized to display the `WelcomeActivity` text launched by the pending intent. The text will appear in bold and in the size defined by the `text_size` dimension resource.

For the target activity that will be launched by the pending intent, add a Java file to the `com.androidtablet.pendingintentapp` package of your project. Assign the name `WelcomeActivity.java` to the newly added Java file. The new activity has nothing to do but display the `TextView` defined in its layout file, `welcome.xml`. The code written in the new activity `WelcomeActivity.java` is shown in Listing 6.7.

Listing 6.7   **Code Written in the Java File** `WelcomeActivity.java`

```
package com.androidtablet.pendingintentapp;

import android.app.Activity;
import android.os.Bundle;

public class WelcomeActivity extends Activity {
    @Override
    protected void onCreate(Bundle savedInstanceState) {
        super.onCreate(savedInstanceState);
        setContentView(R.layout.welcome);
    }
}
```

You can see that `welcome.xml` is set as the `ContentView` of the new activity `WelcomeActivity.java`.

Next, you need to define views for the activity layout file. Because notification in your application will be created after you click a `Button` control, you have to define a `Button` control in the layout file. After you define a `Button` control, the activity layout file `activity_pending_intent_app.xml` will appear, as shown in Listing 6.8.

Listing 6.8   **Code Written in the Activity Layout File** `activity_pending_intent_app.xml`

```
<LinearLayout xmlns:android="http://schemas.android.com/apk/res/android"
    android:layout_width="match_parent"
    android:layout_height="match_parent"
    android:orientation="vertical" >
    <Button
        android:id="@+id/createbutton"
        android:layout_width="wrap_content"
        android:layout_height="wrap_content"
        android:text="Create Notification"
        android:textSize="@dimen/text_size"
        android:layout_gravity="center" />
</LinearLayout>
```

You can see that the `Button` control is assigned the `createbutton` ID and a caption called `Create Notification`. The caption of the button is set to appear in the size defined in the dimension resource `text_size`. The ID of the `Button` control will identify it in the Java code.

To represent notification through an icon, copy the image file `glowingbulb.png` to the `res/drawable` folders.

Next, you need to write the code in the Java activity file `PendingIntentAppActivity.java` to perform the following tasks:

- Create a `Notification` object and configure it to display an icon, title, and text.

- Create a `PendingIntent` object to launch the activity when the notification is tapped.

- Create a `NotificationManager` object to display and manage the notification.

To perform these tasks, write the code shown in Listing 6.9 into the main activity `PendingIntentAppActivity.java` file.

Listing 6.9   **Code Written in the Java Activity File** `PendingIntentAppActivity.java`

```java
package com.androidtablet.pendingintentapp;

import android.os.Bundle;
import android.app.Activity;
import android.content.Intent;
import android.app.PendingIntent;
import android.app.NotificationManager;
import android.app.Notification;
import android.widget.Button;
import android.view.View.OnClickListener;
import android.view.View;

public class PendingIntentAppActivity extends Activity {
    @Override
    public void onCreate(Bundle savedInstanceState) {
        super.onCreate(savedInstanceState);
        setContentView(R.layout.activity_pending_intent_app);
        Button createButton = (Button) findViewById(
            R.id.createbutton);
        createButton.setOnClickListener(new OnClickListener() {
            @Override
            public void onClick(View v) {
                Intent intent = new Intent(
                    PendingIntentAppActivity. this,
                    WelcomeActivity.class);
                PendingIntent pendIntent = PendingIntent.
                    getActivity(PendingIntentAppActivity.this,0,
                    intent, 0);
                NotificationManager notificationManager =
                    (NotificationManager) getSystemService(
                    NOTIFICATION_SERVICE);
                Notification notification = new Notification();
                Notification.Builder builder = new Notification.
                    Builder(PendingIntentAppActivity.this)
                .setSmallIcon(R.drawable.glowingbulb)
                .setAutoCancel(true)
                .setTicker("Notification to launch Pending
```

```
                            Intent")
                        .setWhen(System.currentTimeMillis())
                        .setContentTitle("Message")
                        .setContentText("Let us launch the pending
                            Intent")
                        .setContentIntent(pendIntent);
                    notification = builder.build();
                    notificationManager.notify(0, notification);
            }
        });
    }
}
```

The Android application will never recognize the newly added activity until it is mentioned in the `AndroidManifest.xml` configuration file. So, in the `AndroidManifest.xml` file, add the following statement to inform the Android application about the newly added activity, `WelcomeActivity`:

```
<activity android:name=".WelcomeActivity" android:label="@string/app_name" />
```

The preceding statement has to be nested in the `<application>` element of the `AndroidManifest.xml` file.

Also, don't forget to set the value of the `android:minSdkVersion` attribute to value 16 because the `build()` method of the `Notification.Builder` class works only with API level 16. In earlier API levels, instead of using the `build()` method, the `getNotification()` method was used. The `getNotification()` method that was added in API level 11 is now deprecated.

The following statements when used in the `AndroidManifest.xml` file confirm that the minimum API level required to run this application is 16, and the preferred API level on which the application is designed to run is 17:

```
<uses-sdk
    android:minSdkVersion="16"
    android:targetSdkVersion="17" />
```

Now your application is ready to run. When you run the application, a `Button` control with the caption `Create Notification` will be displayed (see Figure 6.2 [first]). After clicking the Create Notification button, you see a notification and its ticker text `Notification to launch Pending Intent` displayed at the top of the screen in the status bar (Figure 6.2 [second]. After pulling down the status bar, you see the title of the notification, its icon, and its body text displayed, as shown in Figure 6.2 (third). The title of the notification is `Message`, and the text reads `Let us launch the pending Intent`. After you select the notification, a new activity will be launched by the pending intent and is confirmed by the message `WelcomeActivity launched by the pending Intent` via its `TextView` control (see Figure 6.2 [fourth]).

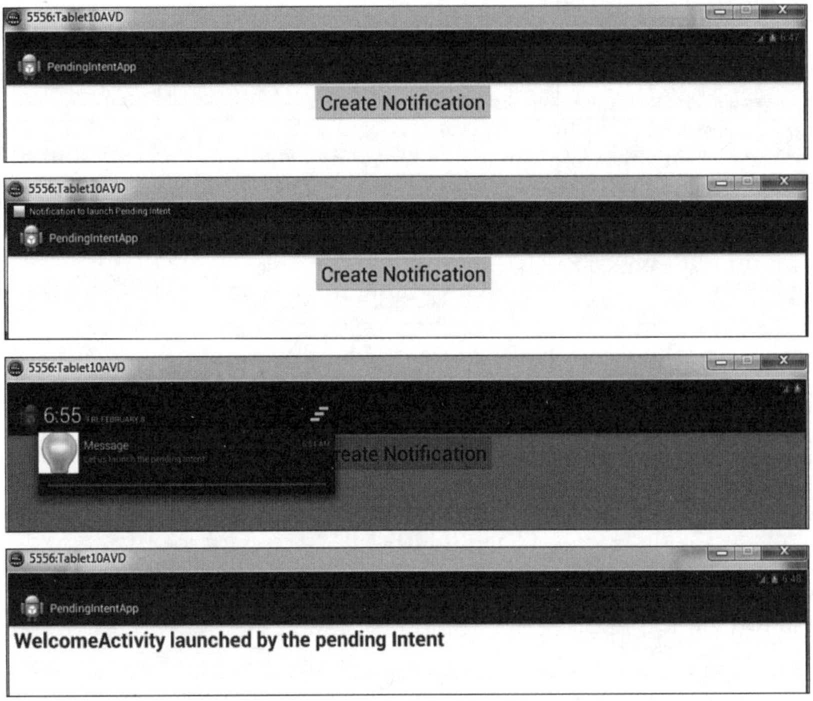

Figure 6.2   Application showing the `Button` control with the caption `Create Notification` (first); notification created and informed through the ticker text in the status bar (second); details of notification appear on expanding it (third); the `WelcomeActivity` launched by the pending intent on clicking the notification (fourth)

Summary

In this chapter, you learned about notifications and their role in alerting users about the occurrence of events. You saw how to create notifications and define their icon, title, ticker text, and body text. You also learned about pending intents and how to use them along with the Android notification system. Finally, you followed the procedure to broadcast an intent and create broadcast receivers to listen to the broadcasted intent.

In the next chapter, you will learn about the `Loader` class and its callback methods. Also, you will learn to use cursor loaders in accessing information from database tables. Finally, you will see the role of loaders in contefnt providers.

7

Loaders

Many of an Android application's tasks are not performed on the main thread, but asynchronously on a separate thread. This increases the application's user interface (UI) performance. Loaders, too, asynchronously load data and monitor the underlying data source for changes. In this chapter, you will learn about loaders—particularly, `CursorLoader`. You will use `CursorLoader` to access information in the `Contacts` content provider. Finally, you will learn to create your own custom content provider.

Recipe: Understanding Loaders

As the name suggests, loaders are used to load data asynchronously. They are accessible in an activity and a fragment through the `LoaderManager`. The `LoaderManager` handles the life cycle of loaders and the underlying queries and cursors. Loaders can load any kind of data source, but you will focus on cursor loading.

The `CursorLoader` class is used for managing cursors. It manages cursor life cycles, performs asynchronous queries against content providers, monitors changes in the included query, and so on. It also confirms if the cursor is closed when the activity is terminated.

To use a `CursorLoader`, you need to create a new `LoaderManager.LoaderCallbacks` implementation:

```
LoaderManager.LoaderCallbacks<Cursor> loaderCallback = new
LoaderManager.LoaderCallbacks<Cursor>()
```

You access the `LoaderManager` by calling the `getLoaderManager()` method. To initialize a new loader, you call the `LoaderManager's` `initLoader()` method. Here is the syntax for using the `initLoader()` method:

```
getLoaderManager().initLoader(loader_ID, bundle, loader_Callbacks);
```

- `loader_ID` represents the loader identifier.
- `bundle` represents the optional arguments bundle. You can pass a `null` value to this parameter if it isn't required.
- `loader_callbacks` is the reference to the loader callback implementation.

Example:

```
Bundle args = null;
getLoaderManager().initLoader(0, args,this);
```

Here, you have ID 0 as the loader identifier. If a loader corresponding to the specified identifier does not exist, it is created.

Whenever the `initLoader()` method is called, the existing loader is returned. To re-create a loader, call the `restartLoader()` method. Here is the syntax for using the method:

```
getLoaderManager().restartLoader(loader_ID, bundle, loader_Callbacks);
```

The loader callbacks consist of three handlers:

- **onCreateLoader()**—Called when the loader is initialized. It creates and returns a new `CursorLoader` object. The `CursorLoader` carries the columns that are specified in the projection `String` array.

- **onLoadFinished()**—When the `LoaderManager` has completed the asynchronous query, the `onLoadFinished` handler is called, with the data cursor passed in as a parameter.

- **onLoaderReset()**—When the `LoaderManager` resets the `CursorLoader`, `onLoaderReset` is called. This handler releases any references to data the query returns.

Remember, the `LoaderManager` closes the cursor automatically, so there is no need to explicitly close it.

The best way to understand the `CursorLoader` is to use it in accessing information from content providers.

Recipe: Understanding Content Provider

A content provider acts as a data store and provides an interface to access its contents. Unlike a database, where information can be accessed only by the package in which it was created, information in a content provider can be shared across packages. The following are a few of the characteristics of content providers:

- Like a database, you can query, add, edit, delete, and update data in content providers.

- Data can be stored in a database, files, and over a network.

- A content provider acts as a wrapper around the data store to make it resemble Web services. That is, the data in content providers is exposed as a service.

Android ships with several built-in content providers. The most common ones are shown in Table 7.1.

Table 7.1   **Built-In Content Providers**

Content Provider	Usage
Contacts	Stores contact details
Media Store	Stores media files such as audio, video, and images
Settings	Stores the device's settings and preferences
Browser	Stores data such as browser bookmarks and browser history
CallLog	Stores data such as missed calls and call details

To fetch data from a content provider, you specify the query string in the form of a uniform resource identifier (URI). The syntax of the query URI appears as follows:

```
<standard_prefix>://<authority><data_path>/<id>
```

The meanings of different tags used in a query URI are shown in Table 7.2.

Table 7.2   **Tags Used in Query URIs**

Tag	Meaning
Standard prefix	For content providers, the standard prefix is always `content://`.
Authority	Specifies the name of the content provider. It appears as a domain name for the content provider. The fully qualified name is not essential for accessing the Android built-in content providers. For third-party content providers, a fully qualified name is recommended. For example, the Android built-in content provider `contacts` is accessed as `com.google.android.contacts`. Third-party content providers are referenced via a fully qualified name such as `com.bmharwani.provider`.
Data path	Specifies the kind of data requested. For example, to access the Android tutorial from the `bmharwani` content provider, the URI would appear as `content://com.bmharwani.provider.AndroidTutorial`.
ID	Specifies the specific content that is requested. For example, to access the Android tutorial with the ID 2 from the `bmharwani` content provider, the URI would be `content://com.bmharwani.provider.AndroidTutorial/2`.

The following examples will make the concept of a content provider URI clearer.

- The URI to identify a directory or a collection of Android tutorials in the `bmharwani` database:

```
content://com.bmharwani.provider.AndroidTutorial
```

- The URI to identify a specific tutorial:

`content://com.bmharwani.provider.AndroidTutorial/#`

where # is the ID of a particular tutorial.

- Likewise, the URI to identify a collection of people in the `contacts` database:

`content://contacts/people/`

Because `contacts` is the built-in Android content provider, you do not need a fully qualified URI to identify a specific person. The URI for the person with an ID of 10 in the `contacts` database:

`content://contacts/people/10`

Recipe: Using `CursorLoader` to Access Information in the `Contacts` Content Provider

Before you learn to access the contacts information in the `Contacts` content provider, you must learn how to insert contact information with the device/emulator. The contacts are named as people in the emulator. To access the contact information, open the Apps list on the device/emulator and click the People icon (see Figure 7.1 [top]). A page is displayed informing you that no contact exists in the device emulator. Three buttons are displayed on the screen: Create a New Contact, Sign In to an Account, and Import Contacts, as shown in Figure 7.1 (bottom).

Figure 7.1   Icons in the device emulator representing different applications (top); screen showing different options after clicking the People icon (bottom)

After selecting Create a New Contact, a dialog appears informing you that new contacts will not be backed up. The dialog also asks whether you want to add an account that backs up contacts online. Two options will be displayed: Keep Local and Add Account. Select Keep Local. A blank form is displayed asking for information about the new contact, such as contact name, phone number, organization, designation, address, home address, and email address (see Figure 7.2 [top]). After entering the personal profile information, click Done at the top to save it. The contact will be created, showing the saved information with a left-pointing arrow at the top. After selecting the arrow, you jump to the screen that shows an alphabetized list of contacts. To add more contacts, click the People icon on the top right that has a plus sign below it.

After you add two contacts, the list of contacts might appear as shown in Figure 7.2 (bottom). You can set up the user's contact information by selecting the Set Up My Profile option. Once you have selected a contact from the list, the profile information will be displayed.

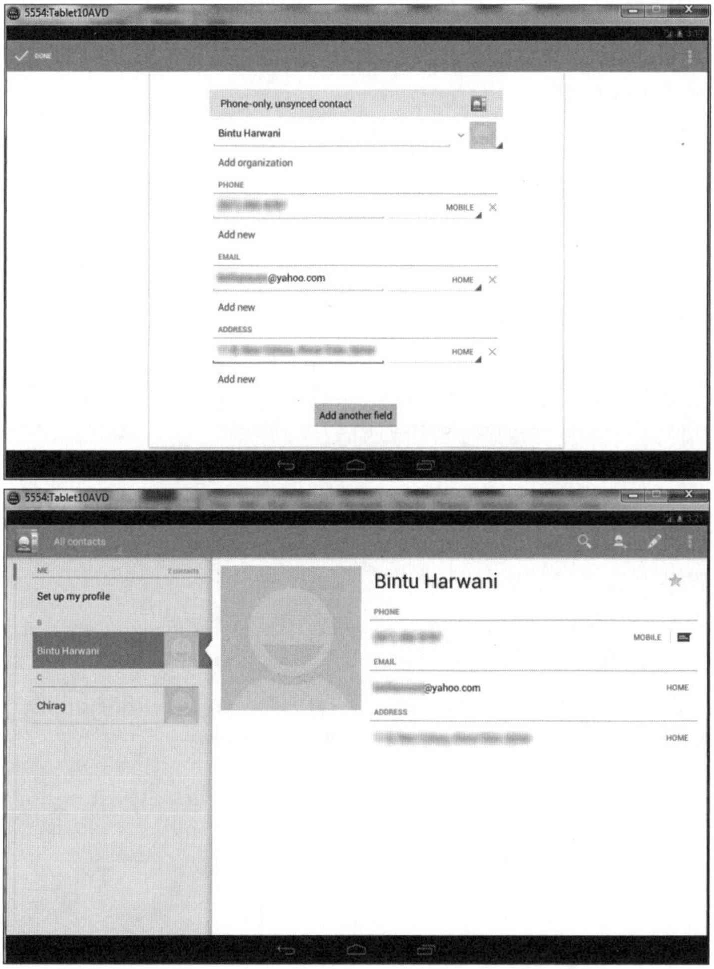

Figure 7.2   Form to enter information about the new contact (top), and the list of contacts displayed (bottom)

You can access the contact information on your device in an Android application. Create a new Android project called `AccessContactsApp`. This application will access the contact information and display it via `ListView`. To define a `ListView` control, add the code shown in Listing 7.1 into the `activity_access_contacts_app.xml` layout file.

Listing 7.1   Code Written into `activity_access_contacts_app.xml`

```
<LinearLayout xmlns:android="http://schemas.android.com/apk/res/android"
    android:layout_width="match_parent"
    android:layout_height="match_parent"
    android:orientation="vertical" >
    <ListView
        android:id="@+id/contactslist"
        android:layout_width="match_parent"
        android:layout_height="match_parent"
        android:drawSelectorOnTop="false"
        android:textFilterEnabled="true" />
</LinearLayout>
```

You can see that a `ListView` is defined with the ID `contactslist`. You will use the ID to access the `ListView` in the Java code.

The default size of the list items displayed in the `ListView` is suitable for phones but is quite smaller for tablets. To resize the list items of the `ListView` as per the device screen size, add one more XML file named `list_item.xml` to the `res/layout` folder. Write the following code in the `list_item.xml` file:

```
<?xml version="1.0" encoding="utf-8"?>
<TextView xmlns:android="http://schemas.android.com/apk/res/android"
    android:layout_width="match_parent"
    android:layout_height="match_parent"
    android:padding="6dp"
    android:textSize="@dimen/text_size"
    android:textStyle="bold" />
```

The preceding code will pad the list items of the `ListView` by 6dp spaces and will make them appear in bold and in the size defined in the dimension resource `text_size`.

To access the contacts information and to display it through `ListView`, write the code shown in Listing 7.2 into the Java activity file `AccessContactsAppActivity.java`.

Listing 7.2   Code Written into `AccessContactsAppActivity.java`

```
package com.androidtablet.accesscontactsapp;

import android.app.Activity;
import android.os.Bundle;
import android.net.Uri;
```

```java
import android.database.Cursor;
import android.content.CursorLoader;
import android.provider.ContactsContract;
import android.widget.ListView;
import java.util.ArrayList;
import android.widget.ArrayAdapter;

public class AccessContactsAppActivity extends Activity {
    ArrayList<String> contactRows=new ArrayList<String>();
    final String[] nocontact={"No Contacts on the Device"};

    @Override
    public void onCreate(Bundle savedInstanceState) {
        super.onCreate(savedInstanceState);
        setContentView(R.layout.activity_access_contacts_app);
        final ListView contactsList=(ListView) findViewById(
            R.id.contactslist);
        Uri contactsUri = Uri.parse("content:// contacts/
            people");
        String[] projection = new String[] {ContactsContract.
         Contacts._ID, ContactsContract.Contacts.DISPLAY_NAME };
        Cursor c;
        CursorLoader cursorLoader = new CursorLoader(this,
            contactsUri, projection, null, null , null);
        c = cursorLoader.loadInBackground();
        contactRows.clear();
        c.moveToFirst();
        while(c.isAfterLast()==false){
            String contactID = c.getString(c.getColumnIndex(
            ContactsContract.Contacts._ID));
            String contactDisplayName = c.getString(
                c.getColumnIndex(ContactsContract.Contacts
                .DISPLAY_NAME));
            contactRows.add(contactID+ " "+contactDisplayName);
            c.moveToNext();
        }
        if (c != null && !c.isClosed()) {
            c.close();
        }
        if(contactRows.isEmpty()) {
            ArrayAdapter<String> arrayAdpt=new  ArrayAdapter
                <String>(this, R.layout.list_item, nocontact);
            contactsList.setAdapter(arrayAdpt);
        }
        else {
            ArrayAdapter<String> arrayAdpt=new ArrayAdapter
                <String>(this, R.layout.list_item, contactRows);
            contactsList.setAdapter(arrayAdpt);
```

```
        }
    }
}
```

You define a `contactsUri` URI for the contacts provider. Thereafter, a `projection` string array is defined to specify the columns that you want to extract from the `contacts` database. With the help of a `CursorLoader`, you load rows from the contacts provider and assign them to the cursor, `c`. Thereafter, using a `while` loop, the information in the cursor is extracted. Because you want to display only the ID and the contact name, the information in the `ContactsContract.Contacts._ID` and `ContactsContract.Contacts.DISPLAY_NAME` columns is accessed and assigned to the `contactRows` `ArrayList`. If `contactRows` is not empty, an `ArrayAdapter` object called `arrayAdpt` is defined through it. Finally, a `ListView` control is filled with the information in the `arrayAdpt` `ArrayAdapter`.

To access information in the contacts provider in your app, you need to add the following permission to the `AndroidManifest.xml` file:

```
<uses-permission android:name="android.permission.READ_CONTACTS" />
```

Add the lines in bold to `AndroidManifest.xml`, as shown in Listing 7.3.

Listing 7.3   **Code in** `AndroidManifest.xml`

```xml
<manifest xmlns:android="http://schemas.android.com/apk/res/android"
    package="com.androidtablet.accesscontactsapp"
    android:versionCode="1"
    android:versionName="1.0" >
    <uses-sdk android:minSdkVersion="11"
        android:targetSdkVersion="17" />
    <uses-permission android:name="android.permission.
        READ_CONTACTS"/>
    <application
        android:icon="@drawable/ic_launcher"
        android:label="@string/app_name"
        android:theme="@style/AppTheme" >
        <activity
            android:name=".AccessContactsAppActivity"
            android:label="@string/title_activity_access_
                contacts_app" >
            <intent-filter>
                <action android:name="android.intent.action.
                    MAIN" />
                <category android:name="android.intent.category.
                    LAUNCHER" />
            </intent-filter>
        </activity>
    </application>
</manifest>
```

With the preceding lines, your application will be able to access the information in the `Contacts` content provider. Assuming there are two contacts on your device/emulator when you run the application, the contact information will be accessed and displayed through the `ListView` control, as shown in Figure 7.3.

Figure 7.3   The contact information accessed from the device/emulator and displayed via `ListView`

Recipe: Creating a Custom Content Provider

In this recipe and in the following two recipes, you will learn to create your own content provider that maintains information related to different products. In this content provider, you will be able to enter new product information, list products, update product information, and even delete products that are no longer required. More specifically, the application (the content provider) will allow users to enter their name and price of different products, display a scrollable list of stored products, and delete and update product information. To make the task of creating a custom content provider simple to understand, you will split it into the following three phases:

- Entering product information
- Listing product information
- Editing product information

In this recipe, you will focus on the first phase of entering product information. Create a new Android project called `CustomContentProviderApp`. You will be performing three steps to complete the first phase of your custom content provider:

- Create a form to enter information about different products.
- Create a Java class file to act as your custom content provider. In the class, you will define a database for your content provider, content URI, to fetch data from the content provider and define MIME types and other elements of a content provider.
- Write code in the main Java activity file to insert rows into the content provider.

As a first step, you will display a form that enables users to enter information about different products. The form will include EditText controls to allow users to enter the product name and its price. The form will display two Button controls: one to add product information, and the other to display the list of products that are already stored in the content provider. For displaying such a user interface, write the code shown in Listing 7.4 into the activity_custom_content_provider_app.xml layout file.

Listing 7.4   **Code Written into** activity_custom_content_provider_app.xml

```xml
<RelativeLayout xmlns:android="http://schemas.android.com/apk/res/android"
    android:layout_width="match_parent"
    android:layout_height="match_parent"  >
    <TextView
        android:id="@+id/productform"
        android:text = "Enter Products Information"
        android:layout_width="wrap_content"
        android:layout_height="wrap_content"
        android:textSize="@dimen/heading_size"
        android:textStyle="bold"
        android:padding="10dip"
        android:layout_centerHorizontal="true"/>
    <TextView
        android:id="@+id/product_view"
        android:layout_width="wrap_content"
        android:layout_height="wrap_content"
        android:text="Product Name"
        android:layout_below="@id/productform"
        android:textSize="@dimen/text_size"
        android:textStyle="bold" />
    <EditText
        android:id="@+id/product_name"
        android:layout_height="wrap_content"
        android:layout_width="@dimen/product_width"
        android:textSize="@dimen/text_size"
        android:layout_below="@id/productform"
        android:layout_toRightOf="@id/product_view" />
    <TextView
        android:id="@+id/price_view"
        android:layout_width="wrap_content"
        android:layout_height="wrap_content"
        android:text="Price"
        android:layout_below="@id/product_name"
        android:textSize="@dimen/text_size"
        android:textStyle="bold" />
    <EditText
        android:id="@+id/price"
        android:layout_height="wrap_content"
```

```
            android:layout_width="@dimen/price_width"
            android:textSize="@dimen/text_size"
            android:layout_marginLeft="20dip"
            android:layout_toRightOf="@id/price_view"
            android:layout_below="@id/product_name" />
    <Button
            android:text="Add Product Info"
            android:id="@+id/add_productinfo"
            android:layout_width="wrap_content"
            android:layout_height="wrap_content"
            android:textSize="@dimen/text_size"
            android:layout_below="@id/price"
            android:layout_marginLeft="20dip"  />
    <Button
            android:text="Show Product Info"
            android:id="@+id/list_productinfo"
            android:layout_width="wrap_content"
            android:layout_height="wrap_content"
            android:textSize="@dimen/text_size"
            android:layout_toRightOf="@id/add_productinfo"
            android:layout_below="@id/price"  />
</RelativeLayout>
```

Here you see that the three `TextView` controls are defined and assigned the text `Enter Products Information`, `Product Name`, and `Price`. The two `EditText` controls are assigned the IDs `product_name` and `price`. The two `Button` controls are assigned the IDs `add_productinfo` and `list_productinfo`. The captions assigned to the two `Button` controls are `Add Product Info` and `Show Product Info`. The IDs assigned to the controls allow you to access them in Java code.

You can see that the `TextView` that displays the header of the form is assigned the font size defined in the dimension resource `heading_size`. The font size of the rest of the `TextView` controls is defined through the dimension resource `text_size`. Similarly, the dimension resources `product_width` and `price_width` define the width of two `EditText` controls, respectively. Define the dimension resources for all three types of Android devices: phones, 7-inch tablets, and 10-inch tablets. The dimension resources for phones are defined in the `res/values` folder, and for tablets, the `res/values-sw600dp` and `res/values-sw720dp` folders are used.

For phones, open the dimension resource file `dimens.xml` in the `res/values` folder and define four resources—`heading_size`, `text_size`, `product_width`, and `price_width`—by writing the following code in it:

```
<?xml version="1.0" encoding="utf-8"?>
<resources>
    <dimen name="heading_size">18sp</dimen>
    <dimen name="text_size">14sp</dimen>
```

```
    <dimen name="product_width">250dp</dimen>
    <dimen name="price_width">100dp</dimen>
</resources>
```

To define dimension resources for 7-inch tablets, open the `dimens.xml` file in `res/values-sw600dp` and write the following code in it:

```
<?xml version="1.0" encoding="utf-8"?>
<resources>
    <dimen name="heading_size">28sp</dimen>
    <dimen name="text_size">24sp</dimen>
    <dimen name="product_width">400dp</dimen>
    <dimen name="price_width">150dp</dimen>
</resources>
```

Similarly, define the dimension resources for 10-inch tablets by opening the `dimens.xml` file in `res/values-sw720dp` and writing the following code in it:

```
<?xml version="1.0" encoding="utf-8"?>
<resources>
    <dimen name="heading_size">36sp</dimen>
    <dimen name="text_size">32sp</dimen>
        <dimen name="product_width">500dp</dimen>
    <dimen name="price_width">200dp</dimen>
</resources>
```

Next, add a Java class file to your project that will act as your custom content provider. Call the added class `ProductsProvider`. In this class, you will perform the following tasks:

- Define a database for your content provider. To store product names and their corresponding prices, you will create a database called `Products`. In the `Products` database, you will create a single table called `productinfo`. The `productinfo` table will consist of two columns, `product` and `price`, that store the product names and their respective prices.

- Define the content URI to fetch data from the content provider. A `UriMatcher` object will be defined and populated with the two URIs. The URI ending in `productinfo` will represent a request for all rows, and the one ending in `productinfo/#` will represent a request for a single row. Also, a content resolver will be defined; data is fetched using the content URI through a content resolver.

- Define MIME types for a single row and a collection of rows. A content provider returns the MIME type of the data it is returning.

- To make the content provider functional, implement the `getType()`, `query()`, `insert()`, `update()`, and `delete()` methods. To identify the data type of the content provider, define the `getType()` method. To enable users to query the content provider for the desired row(s), define the `query()` method. Create a `SQLiteQueryBuilder` object—a helper class that is required to create and execute SQL queries on a SQLite database instance. To insert a new row into the content provider, define the `insert()`

method. After inserting the row, call the `notifyChange()` method of the content
resolver to notify any registered observers about the insert operation. Define the
`update()` method to update the information in the content provider. Also, define the
`delete()` method to delete information in the content provider.

To perform all the preceding tasks, write the code shown in Listing 7.5 into the
`ProductsProvider.java` Java file.

Listing 7.5   **Code Written into** `ProductsProvider.java`

```
package com.androidtablet.customcontentproviderapp;

import android.content.ContentProvider;
import android.content.UriMatcher;
import android.net.Uri;
import android.database.sqlite.SQLiteOpenHelper;
import android.database.sqlite.SQLiteDatabase;
import android.content.Context;
import android.content.ContentValues;
import android.content.ContentUris;
import android.database.SQLException;
import android.database.Cursor;
import android.text.TextUtils;
import android.database.sqlite.SQLiteQueryBuilder;
import android.content.ContentResolver;

public class ProductsProvider extends ContentProvider {
    static final String DB_NAME = "Products.db";
    static final String DB_TABLE = "productinfo";
    static final int DB_VERSION = 1;
    static final String CREATE_TABLE ="CREATE TABLE " + DB_TABLE
        + " (_id INTEGER PRIMARY KEY AUTOINCREMENT, product TEXT
        not null, price TEXT not null);";
    static final String ID = "_id";
    static final String PRODUCT = "product";
    static final String PRICE = "price";
    static final String AUTHORITY="com.bmharwani.provider.
        Products";
    static final Uri CONTENT_URI =Uri.parse("content://"+
        AUTHORITY+"/productinfo");
    static final int ALLROWS = 1;
    static final int SINGLEROW = 2;
    private static final UriMatcher URIMATCHER;
    static{
        URIMATCHER = new UriMatcher(UriMatcher.NO_MATCH);
        URIMATCHER.addURI(AUTHORITY, "productinfo", ALLROWS);
```

```
        URIMATCHER.addURI(AUTHORITY, "productinfo/#",
        SINGLEROW);
    }
    SQLiteDatabase ProductsDB;
    public static final String CONTENT_ITEM_TYPE =
        ContentResolver.CURSOR_ITEM_BASE_TYPE+"/productinfo";

    @Override
    public boolean onCreate() {
        Context context = getContext();
        SQHelper helper = new SQHelper(context);
        ProductsDB = helper.getWritableDatabase();
        return (ProductsDB == null)? false:true;
    }

    @Override
    public String getType(Uri uri) {
        switch (URIMATCHER.match(uri)){
            case ALLROWS:
                return "vnd.android.cursor.dir/vnd.products.
                    productinfo";
            case SINGLEROW:
                return "vnd.android.cursor.item/vnd.products.
                    productinfo";
            default:
                throw new IllegalArgumentException("Unsupported
                    URI: " + uri);
        }
    }

    @Override
    public Cursor query(Uri uri, String[] projection, String
        criteria, String[] criteriaValues, String sortColumn) {
        SQLiteQueryBuilder queryBuilder = new
            SQLiteQueryBuilder();
        queryBuilder.setTables(DB_TABLE);
        if (URIMATCHER.match(uri) == SINGLEROW)
            queryBuilder.appendWhere(ID + " = " +
                uri.getPathSegments().get(1));
        if (sortColumn==null || sortColumn=="")
            sortColumn = "product";
        Cursor c = queryBuilder.query(ProductsDB,projection,
            criteria,criteriaValues,null,null,sortColumn);
        c.setNotificationUri(getContext().getContentResolver(),
            uri);
        return c;
    }
```

```java
@Override
public Uri insert(Uri uri, ContentValues contentValues) {
    long rowID = ProductsDB.insert(DB_TABLE,null,
        contentValues);
    if (rowID >0) {
        Uri _uri = ContentUris.withAppendedId(CONTENT_URI,
            rowID);
        getContext().getContentResolver().notifyChange(_uri,
            null);
        return _uri;
    }
    throw new SQLException("Error: New row could not be
        inserted ");
}


@Override
public int update(Uri uri, ContentValues contentValues,
    String criteria, String[] criteriaValues) {
    int count = 0;
    switch (URIMATCHER.match(uri)){
        case ALLROWS:
            count = ProductsDB.update(DB_TABLE,
                contentValues, criteria,criteriaValues);
            break;
        case SINGLEROW:
            count = ProductsDB.update(DB_TABLE,
                contentValues, ID + " = " + uri.
                getPathSegments().get(1) +(! TextUtils.
                isEmpty(criteria) ? " AND (" +criteria + ')':
                ""),criteriaValues);
            break;
        default: throw new IllegalArgumentException("URI not
            found: " + uri);
    }
    getContext().getContentResolver().notifyChange(uri,
        null);
    return count;
}


@Override
public int delete(Uri rowUri, String criteria, String[]
    criteriaValues) {
    int count=0;
    switch (URIMATCHER.match(rowUri)){
        case ALLROWS:
            count = ProductsDB.delete(DB_TABLE, criteria,
                criteriaValues);
```

```
                    break;
              case SINGLEROW:
                    String id = rowUri.getPathSegments().get(1);
                    count = ProductsDB.delete(DB_TABLE, ID + " = " +
                    id +(!TextUtils.isEmpty(criteria) ? " AND ("
                    +criteria + ')': ""),criteriaValues);
                    break;
              default: throw new IllegalArgumentException("URI not
                    found: " + rowUri);
        }
        getContext().getContentResolver().notifyChange(rowUri,
              null);
        return count;
    }

    private static class SQHelper extends SQLiteOpenHelper {
        SQHelper(Context context) {
              super(context, DB_NAME, null, DB_VERSION);
        }

        @Override
        public void onCreate(SQLiteDatabase db) {
              db.execSQL(CREATE_TABLE);
        }

        @Override
        public void onUpgrade(SQLiteDatabase db, int oldVersion,
              int newVersion) {
              db.execSQL("DROP TABLE IF EXISTS "+ DB_TABLE);
              onCreate(db);
        }
    }
}
```

You can see that the onCreate() method is overridden to initialize the data source to be accessed through the content provider. In the method, you define a SQHelper object and open the Products.db database in write mode.

To insert rows into the content provider and access its existing information, write the code shown in Listing 7.6 into the Java activity file CustomContentProviderAppActivity.java.

Listing 7.6   **Code Written into the Java Activity File** CustomContentProviderAppActivity.
java

```
package com.androidtablet.customcontentproviderapp;

import android.app.Activity;
import android.os.Bundle;
```

```java
import android.view.View;
import android.content.ContentValues;
import android.widget.Toast;
import android.widget.EditText;
import android.widget.Button;
import android.content.Intent;

public class CustomContentProviderAppActivity extends Activity {
    @Override
    public void onCreate(Bundle savedInstanceState) {
        super.onCreate(savedInstanceState);
        setContentView(R.layout.activity_custom_content_
            provider_app);
        Button addProductButton = (Button) this.findViewById(
            R.id.add_productinfo);
        addProductButton.setOnClickListener(new Button.
            OnClickListener(){
            @Override
            public void onClick(View v) {
                ContentValues contentValues = new
                    ContentValues();
                EditText productName = (EditText)
                    findViewById(R.id.product_name);
                EditText productPrice = (EditText)
                    findViewById(R.id.price);
                contentValues.put(ProductsProvider.PRODUCT,
                    productName.getText().toString());
                contentValues.put(ProductsProvider.PRICE,
                    productPrice.getText().toString());
                getContentResolver().insert(ProductsProvider.
                    CONTENT_URI, contentValues);
                Toast.makeText(CustomContentProviderAppActivity.
                    this, "Row inserted", Toast.LENGTH_SHORT).
                    show();
                productName.setText("");
                productPrice.setText("");
            }
        });

        Button listProductButton = (Button)this.findViewById(
            R.id.list_productinfo);
        listProductButton.setOnClickListener(new Button.
            OnClickListener(){
            public void onClick(View v) {
                startActivity(new Intent(
                    CustomContentProviderAppActivity.this,
                    ShowProductActivity.class));          #1
```

```
                }
            });
        }
    }
}
```

Statement #1 in the previous code listing is accessing the class that accesses and lists the content in your content provider. In this recipe, you are focusing only on entering content into the content provider, not listing it. You will be learning the procedure for accessing and listing content in the content provider in the next recipe. Temporarily, comment out the statement #1 in Listing 7.6.

You can see that the add_productinfo and list_productinfo Button controls are accessed from the layout file and mapped to the addProductButton and listProductButton Button objects. The addProductButton button performs the insert operation, and listProductButton shows the existing information in the content provider.

To insert a row into the content provider, you first collect it in the ContentValues object. ContentValues is a dictionary of key/value pairs where you can store the information of a single record. Thereafter, it is the job of the content resolver to insert that record into the content provider using a URI. The content resolver resolves the URI reference to the right provider and inserts the information held by the ContentValues object into the provider.

To add product information, you fetch the data the user entered into the two EditText controls. Thereafter, you create a new ContentValues object and populate it with the information entered into the EditText controls. Because your content provider is in the same package you are accessing, you use the ProductsProvider.PRODUCT and ProductsProvider.PRICE constants to refer to the product and price columns of the database table.

To enable the content resolver to discover your content provider, you must register it in the application manifest file. The <provider> tag and its android:name and android:authorities attributes are used to register the content provider. The android:name attribute is the provider's class name, and the android:authorities attribute defines the base URI of the provider's authority. In your application, the provider's class name is ProductsProvider. The format for defining a content provider's authority is given here:

com.<CompanyName>.provider.<ApplicationName>

Assuming the CompanyName is bmharwani and the ApplicationName is Products, the base URI of your provider's authority will be com.bmharwani.provider.Products.

Hence, the complete provider tag that will be used to register your content provider is

```
<provider android:name=".ProductsProvider"
android:authorities="com.bmharwani.provider.Products">
```

Open the AndroidManifest.xml file and register your content provider by writing the following code in the <application> element:

```
<provider android:name=".ProductsProvider"
android:authorities="com.bmharwani.provider.Products">
```

This finishes your first phase of creating a custom content provider. When you run the application, you get a blank form prompting for the name and the price of the product. Enter the product information and click the Add Product Info button, and the information will be stored in the content provider. The `Toast` message `Row inserted` appears on the screen to confirm the successful insertion of product information. See Figure 7.4.

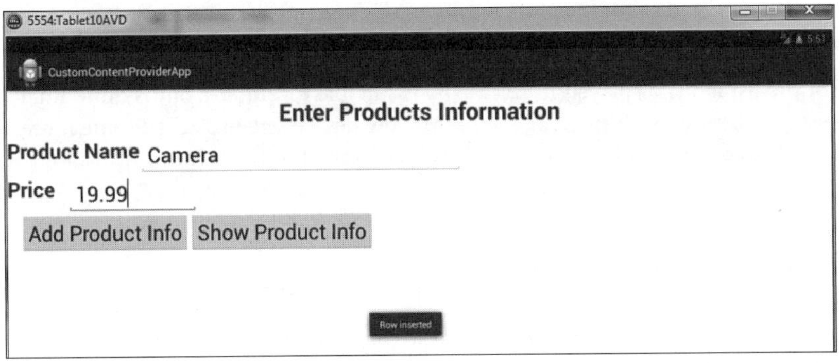

Figure 7.4   The `Toast` message `Row inserted` appears after you successfully add product information in the content provider

No action will take place after you click the Show Product Info button. To enable this button and to display information that is stored in your content provider, you must proceed to the second phase of creating a custom content provider: the listing phase.

Recipe: Listing Information in a Custom Content Provider

The Show Product Info button in Figure 7.4 is supposed to display the information of the products stored in your content provider. For doing so, you will create a new Java activity called `ShowProductActivity` that will access content from the content provider. The `ShowProductActivity` will be started or initiated when someone clicks the Show Product Info button. The information (rows accessed from the content provider) will be displayed through the `ListView` control.

To display information in the content provider through a `ListView`, add a layout file called `showproduct.xml` to the `res/layout` folder. To define a `ListView` control in the `showproduct.xml` file, add the code shown in Listing 7.7.

Listing 7.7   **Code Written into** `showproduct.xml` **File**

```
<?xml version="1.0" encoding="utf-8"?>
<LinearLayout xmlns:android="http://schemas.android.com/apk/res/android"
    android:layout_width="match_parent"
    android:layout_height="match_parent"
    android:orientation="vertical" >
```

```
<ListView
    android:id="@android:id/list"
    android:layout_width="match_parent"
    android:layout_height="match_parent"
    android:drawSelectorOnTop="false" />
</LinearLayout>
```

You can see that a `ListView` control with the ID `list` is defined in the layout file.

The default size of the list items displayed in `ListView` is suitable for phones but is quite small for tablets. To resize the list items of the `ListView` as per the device screen size, add one more XML file named `list_item.xml` to the `res/layout` folder. Write the code shown in Listing 7.8 to the `list_item.xml` file.

Listing 7.8   **Code Written in the `list_item.xml` File**

```
<?xml version="1.0" encoding="utf-8"?>
<LinearLayout xmlns:android="http://schemas.android.com/apk/res/android"
    android:layout_width="match_parent"
    android:layout_height="match_parent"
    android:orientation="vertical" >
<TextView
    android:id="@+id/product_name"
    android:layout_width="match_parent"
    android:layout_height="match_parent"
    android:padding="6dp"
    android:textSize="@dimen/text_size"
    android:textStyle="bold" />
</LinearLayout>
```

The preceding code will pad the list items of the `ListView` by 6dp spaces and make them appear in bold and in the size defined in the dimension resource `text_size`.

To load the `ListView` defined in the `showproduct.xml` file, add a Java class file called `ShowProductActivity.java` to the `com.androidtablet.customcontentproviderapp` package of the project.

To fetch all the rows from the content provider and to display them through the `ListView` control through `CursorLoaders`, write the code shown in Listing 7.9 into `ShowProductActivity.java`.

Listing 7.9   **Code Written into `ShowProductActivity.java`**

```
package com.androidtablet.customcontentproviderapp;

import android.app.ListActivity;
import android.os.Bundle;
```

```java
import android.widget.SimpleCursorAdapter;
import android.app.LoaderManager.LoaderCallbacks;
import android.content.CursorLoader;
import android.content.Loader;
import android.database.Cursor;
import android.widget.ListView;
import android.content.Intent;
import android.net.Uri;
import android.view.View;

public class ShowProductActivity extends ListActivity implements
LoaderCallbacks<Cursor> {
    private SimpleCursorAdapter adapter;

    @Override
    protected void onCreate(Bundle savedInstanceState) {
        super.onCreate(savedInstanceState);
        setContentView(R.layout.showproduct);
        String[] columns = new String[] { ProductsProvider.
            PRODUCT};
        int[] toIds = new int[] {R.id.product_name};
        getLoaderManager().initLoader(0, null,this);
        adapter = new SimpleCursorAdapter(this,
            R.layout.list_item, null, columns, toIds, 0);
        setListAdapter(adapter);
    }

    @Override
    public Loader<Cursor> onCreateLoader(int id, Bundle args) {
        String[] projection = new String[] {ProductsProvider.ID,
            ProductsProvider.PRODUCT, ProductsProvider.PRICE} ;
        CursorLoader cursorLoader = new CursorLoader(this,
            ProductsProvider.CONTENT_URI, projection, null,
            null, null);
        return cursorLoader;
    }

    @Override
    public void onLoadFinished(Loader<Cursor> loader, Cursor
        data) {
        adapter.swapCursor(data);
    }

    @Override
    public void onLoaderReset(Loader<Cursor> loader) {
        adapter.swapCursor(null);
    }
```

```
@Override                                             #1
protected void onListItemClick(ListView l, View v, int
    position, long id) {                              #2
    super.onListItemClick(l, v, position, id);        #3
    Intent intent = new Intent(this,
        MaintainProductActivity.class);               #4
    Uri uri = Uri.parse(ProductsProvider.CONTENT_URI + "/" +
        id);                                          #5
    intent.putExtra(ProductsProvider.CONTENT_ITEM_TYPE,
        uri);                                         #6
    startActivity(intent);                            #7
}                                                     #8
}
```

To use a `CursorLoader`, you need to create a new `LoaderManager.LoaderCallbacks` implementation:

```
public class ShowProductActivity extends ListActivity implements
LoaderCallbacks<Cursor>
```

You can see that the `LoaderManager` is accessed by calling the `getLoaderManager()` method. To initialize a new loader, the Loader Manager's `initLoader()` method is called. Through `SimpleCursorAdapter`, the data in the `ProductsProvider.PRODUCT` column of the content provider is accessed and displayed through the `ListView` control.

> **Note**
>
> Comment out the entire `onListItemClick()` method (statements #1 through #8) in Listing 7.9 because it will be used in the following recipe to maintain content in the content provider. Because the current recipe focuses only on listing the content in the content provider and not maintaining it, comment out the `onListItemClick()` method temporarily. Also, remove the comment from statement #1 in Listing 7.6 that you placed in the previous recipe to enable listing of information in the content provider.

To enable your application to identify the `ShowProductActivity` class that you added in this recipe, add the following statement in the `<application>` element of the `AndroidManifest.xml` file:

```
<activity android:name=".ShowProductActivity"
    android:label="@string/app_name" />
```

The second phase of your custom content provider (listing information in the content provider) is complete and ready to run. On running the application, you get a form to enter new product information. To do this, fill the boxes and click the Add Product Info button. To see the list of products stored in your content provider, click the Show Product Info button (see Figure 7.5 [top]). Figure 7.5 (bottom) shows the product information that is accessed from your content provider and is displayed via `ListView`.

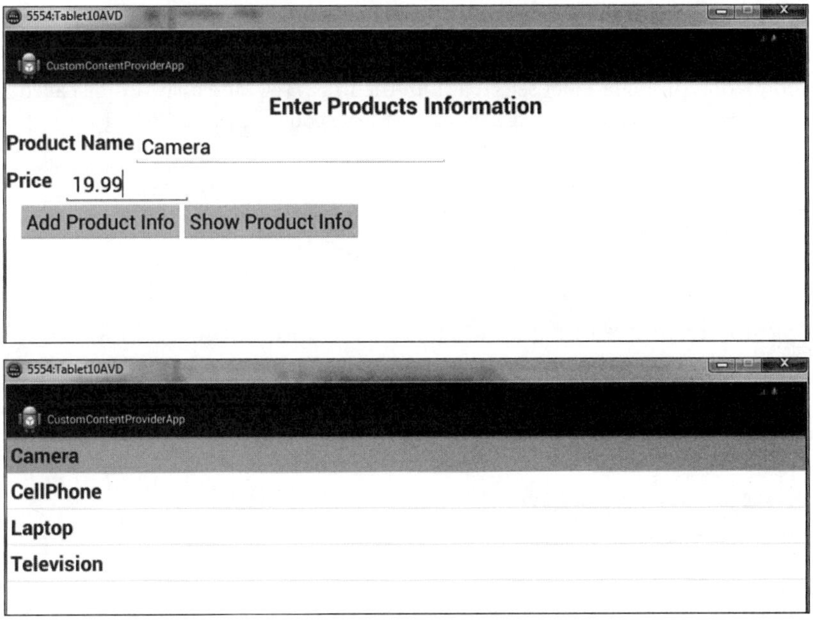

Figure 7.5   Two buttons to add and list content in the content provider (top), and the information accessed from the content provider displayed through ListView (bottom)

When you click any of the products in the ListView, nothing will happen as of now. In the following recipe, you will learn to edit and delete product information that is selected from the ListView.

Two phases—creating and listing phases of "creating custom content provider"—are complete. Now proceed to the maintenance phase: updating and deleting content in the content provider.

Recipe: Updating and Deleting Information in a Custom Content Provider

By maintaining the content provider, you want to enable users to delete and update content there. To maintain content in your custom content provider, you will add a Java class, MaintainProductActivity.class, to your project. To the MaintainProductActivity. class, you will pass the URI of the row—the product that is selected from the ListView.

In the MaintainProductActivity, you will delete and update content in the content provider. That is, you will display the selected product name and its price through EditText controls and provide two Button controls, Update and Delete, to the user. The user can modify the information in the content provider by updating the data displayed in the

`EditText` controls and clicking Update. The user can delete the row from the content provider by clicking Delete.

To display the information of the product selected from the `ListView`, add a layout file called `maintainproduct.xml` to the `res/layout` folder, and add the code shown in Listing 7.10.

Listing 7.10   **Code Written into** `maintainproduct.xml`

```xml
<?xml version="1.0" encoding="utf-8"?>
<RelativeLayout xmlns:android="http://schemas.android.com/apk/res/android"
    android:layout_width="match_parent"
    android:layout_height="match_parent" >
    <TextView
        android:id="@+id/product_view"
        android:layout_width="wrap_content"
        android:layout_height="wrap_content"
        android:text="Product Name"
        android:textSize="@dimen/text_size"
        android:textStyle="bold" />
    <EditText
        android:id="@+id/product_name"
        android:layout_height="wrap_content"
        android:layout_width="@dimen/product_width"
        android:textSize="@dimen/text_size"
        android:layout_toRightOf="@id/product_view" />
    <TextView
        android:id="@+id/price_view"
        android:layout_width="wrap_content"
        android:layout_height="wrap_content"
        android:text="Price"
        android:layout_below="@id/product_name"
        android:textSize="@dimen/text_size"
        android:textStyle="bold" />
    <EditText
        android:id="@+id/price"
        android:layout_height="wrap_content"
        android:layout_width="@dimen/price_width"
        android:textSize="@dimen/text_size"
        android:layout_marginLeft="20dip"
        android:layout_toRightOf="@id/price_view"
        android:layout_below="@id/product_name" />
    <Button
        android:text="Delete"
        android:id="@+id/delete_productinfo"
        android:layout_width="wrap_content"
        android:layout_height="wrap_content"
        android:textSize="@dimen/text_size"
```

```
            android:layout_below="@id/price"
            android:layout_marginLeft="70dip"   />
    <Button
            android:text="Update"
            android:id="@+id/update_productinfo"
            android:layout_width="wrap_content"
            android:layout_height="wrap_content"
            android:textSize="@dimen/text_size"
            android:layout_toRightOf="@id/delete_productinfo"
            android:layout_below="@id/price"
            android:layout_marginLeft="10dip"/>
</RelativeLayout>
```

You can see that the two EditText controls that will be used for displaying the product names and the price are assigned the IDs product_name and price. The two Button controls with the Delete and Update captions are assigned the IDs delete_productinfo and update_ productinfo. The IDs will identify and access these controls in the Java code.

To load the views defined in the preceding layout file, a Java class file called MaintainProductActivity.java is added to the com.androidtablet. customcontentproviderapp package of the project. To delete and update information in the content provider, write the code shown in Listing 7.11 into the MaintainProductActivity.java file.

Listing 7.11 **Code Written into** MaintainProductActivity.java

```
package com.androidtablet.customcontentproviderapp;

import android.os.Bundle;
import android.app.Activity;
import android.widget.EditText;
import android.widget.Button;
import android.net.Uri;
import android.content.ContentValues;
import android.database.Cursor;
import android.view.View;
import android.widget.Toast;

public class MaintainProductActivity extends Activity {
    EditText productName, price;
    Uri uri;
    @Override
    protected void onCreate(Bundle savedInstanceState) {
        super.onCreate(savedInstanceState);
        setContentView(R.layout.maintainproduct);
        productName  = (EditText) findViewById(R.id.
            product_name);
```

```
price = (EditText) findViewById(R.id.price);
Bundle extras = getIntent().getExtras();
uri = (extras == null) ? null: (Uri) extras.
    getParcelable(ProductsProvider.CONTENT_ITEM_TYPE);
if (extras != null) {
    uri = extras.getParcelable(ProductsProvider.CONTENT_
        ITEM_TYPE);
    String[] projection = new String[]
        {ProductsProvider.ID, ProductsProvider.PRODUCT,
        ProductsProvider.PRICE} ;
    Cursor cursor = getContentResolver().query(uri,
        projection, null, null, null);
    if (cursor != null) {
        cursor.moveToFirst();
        productName.setText(cursor.getString(cursor.
            getColumnIndexOrThrow (ProductsProvider.
            PRODUCT)));
        price.setText(cursor.getString(cursor.
            getColumnIndexOrThrow (ProductsProvider.
            PRICE)));
        cursor.close();
    }
}
Button deleteProductInfo  = (Button) findViewById(
    R.id.delete_productinfo);
Button updateProductInfo = (Button) findViewById(
    R.id.update_productinfo);
deleteProductInfo.setOnClickListener(new Button.
    OnClickListener(){
    @Override
    public void onClick(View v) {
        int count = getContentResolver().delete(uri,
            null, null);
        if(count >0)
            Toast.makeText(MaintainProductActivity.this,
                "Row deleted", Toast.LENGTH_SHORT).show();
    }
});
updateProductInfo.setOnClickListener(new Button.
    OnClickListener(){
    @Override
    public void onClick(View v) {
        ContentValues contentValues = new
            ContentValues();
        contentValues.put(ProductsProvider.PRODUCT,
            productName.getText().toString());
        contentValues.put(ProductsProvider.PRICE,
```

```
                    price.getText().toString());
              getContentResolver().update(uri, contentValues,
                  null,null);
              Toast.makeText(MaintainProductActivity.this,
                  "Row updated", Toast.LENGTH_SHORT).show();
          }
      });
   }
}
```

You access the `EditText` controls with the `product_name` and `price` IDs from the `maintainproduct.xml` layout file and map them to the `productName` and `price` `EditText` objects. You access the URI of the selected product name from the `ListView` that is passed through the `Bundle` object. Thereafter, you call the `query()` method to access the row from the content provider with the specified URI. The `query()` method is called to get the price of the selected product so that the product name and its price can be assigned and displayed through `EditText` controls.

To delete a row, call the `delete()` method of the content resolver. To the `delete()` method, you pass the content URI of the row to be deleted. To update a row, you call the `update()` method of the content resolver. To the `update()` method, you pass the URI of the row to be updated along with the `ContentValues` object that contains the updated or new content of the respective columns.

To enable your application to identify the `MaintainProductActivity` class that you added in this recipe, add the following statement in the `<application>` element of the `AndroidManifest.xml` file:

```
<activity android:name=".MaintainProductActivity"
    android:label="@string/app_name" />
```

After adding the preceding statement, the `AndroidManifest.xml` file will appear as shown in Listing 7.12. The code in bold is newly added; the rest is the default code. The added code registers your custom content provider and defines the `ShowProductActivity` and `MaintainProductActivity` activities that you added to your application so that your application can identify them.

Listing 7.12   **Code Written into** `AndroidManifest.xml`

```
<manifest xmlns:android="http://schemas.android.com/apk/res/android"
    package="com.androidtablet.customcontentproviderapp"
    android:versionCode="1"
    android:versionName="1.0" >
    <uses-sdk android:minSdkVersion="11"
        android:targetSdkVersion="17" />
    <application
        android:icon="@drawable/ic_launcher"
```

```
        android:label="@string/app_name"
        android:theme="@style/AppTheme" >
        <activity
            android:name=".CustomContentProviderAppActivity"
            android:label="@string/title_activity_custom_
                content_provider_app" >
            <intent-filter>
                <action android:name="android.intent.action.
                    MAIN" />
                <category android:name="android.intent.category.
                    LAUNCHER" />
            </intent-filter>
        </activity>
        <activity android:name=".ShowProductActivity"
            android:label="@string/app_name" />
        <activity android:name=".MaintainProductActivity"
            android:label="@string/app_name" />
        <provider android:name="ProductsProvider"
          android:authorities="com.bmharwani.provider.Products">
        </provider>
    </application>
</manifest>
```

The maintenance phase of your custom content provider is complete, so remove the comment from the onListItemClick() method in the ShowProductActivity class (see Listing 7.9). Recall that you commented out this method in the previous recipe.

Your custom content provider is complete and ready to run. After running the application, you get a screen to enter the product information. Enter the product name and its price, and click Add Product Info to save it in the content provider. The Toast message Row inserted appears after each successful insertion (see Figure 7.6 [top]). Once you insert rows in the content provider and click the Show Product Info button, you see all the products listed in the ListView (see Figure 7.6 [middle]). After selecting a product from the ListView, its details will be displayed. To modify the product name or price, simply update the content in the EditText controls and click the Update button. The information in the content provider will be updated. Figure 7.6 (bottom) shows the updated row. The Toast message Row updated appears when a row is successfully updated.

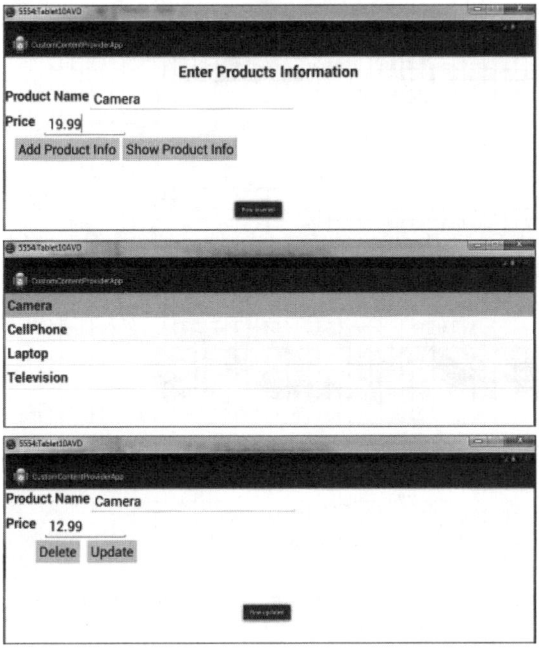

Figure 7.6   Entering the product name and price information (top); information from the content provider accessed and displayed (middle); updating information of the selected product (bottom)

After clicking the Delete button, the selected product and its price will be deleted from the content provider and the Toast message Row deleted appears on the screen, as shown in Figure 7.7 (top). Figure 7.7 (bottom) confirms that the selected row was deleted from the content provider; it is no longer shown in the ListView control.

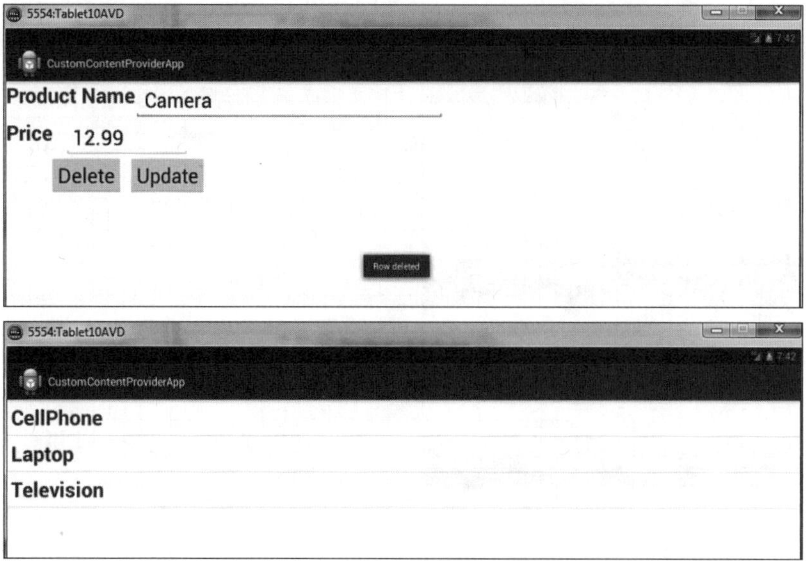

Figure 7.7   Deleting a selected product from the content provider (top); information of the existing products in the content provider is accessed and displayed (bottom).

Summary

In this chapter, you came to understand the role of loaders for loading data from the underlying data source asynchronously. You learned the usage of `CursorLoader` in fetching information from content providers. You also learned to use `CursorLoader` to access information in the `Contacts` content provider. Finally, you followed the procedure to create your own custom content provider.

The next chapter is focused on animations. You will learn about property animation and will see how `ValueAnimator` and `ObjectAnimator` are used in animating views and objects. You will also learn to implement multiple animations.

8

Animation

Animations make an application more attractive and dynamic. You can use animation in developing game applications, educational tutorials, and demonstrations. In this chapter, you learn the different types of animation that Android supports. You implement property animation by using `ValueAnimator` and `ObjectAnimator`. Also, you implement multiple animations using `AnimatorSet`. In addition, you use frame-by-frame animation, tweening animation, and layout animation. Finally, you learn to collect and sequence animations using `AnimationSet`.

Recipe: Understanding Types of Animations

Broadly, Android supports two types of animations: property and view animation:

- **Property animation**—This is a robust framework with which you can animate properties of any object. That is, you can define an animation to change any object property over a specified length of time. Property animation also allows you to reverse and repeat animation if required. Also, for smooth transition, interpolators can be used in property animation. The following are the two animators that you can use to animate the values of a property:

  `ValueAnimator`—The ValueAnimator keeps track of the current value of the property that it is animating and the time duration of animation. To work with `ValueAnimator`, you supply the starting and ending values for the property to animate along with the duration of the animation. Considering the supplied values and the duration, the `ValueAnimator` computes the animation values. Through the help of listeners, the updates in the values are fetched and applied to the properties of the desired objects.

  `ObjectAnimator`—This is a subclass of `ValueAnimator` that is popularly used to process and apply generated animation values on the desired objects. To use `ObjectAnimator`, you select an object, a property of the object to animate, and the set of values to apply to the object's property over the supplied time duration.

- **View animation**—The view animation framework enables you to animate `View` objects. There are three types of animations that you can do with this framework:

- **Frame-by-frame animation**—A series of images arranged in frames is displayed at regular intervals. Each image differs slightly from the previous image and is displayed for a short duration to imply motion.

- **Tweening animation**—This considers two key images: the beginning and ending states of the images. In-between images that show the gradual transformation of the image from the beginning state to the ending state are created automatically. Tweening animation can be applied to any graphic, text, or other view. Android provides tweening animation support for several common image transformations, including `alpha`, `rotate`, `scale`, and `translate`.

- **Layout animation**—As the name suggests, layout animation is used for applying animation to the layouts. Animation is applied to each child view in the layout while it is added or removed. There is no need to explicitly start the animation; it will automatically start when the layout is displayed.

A few of the methods and constants that are used while performing animation are briefly described in Table 8.1.

Table 8.1   Brief Description of the Methods and Constants Used in Animation

Method/Constant	Description
`setDuration(long length_of_animation)`	Determines the length of the animation. The `length_of_animation` is supplied in milliseconds. The default length of the animation is 300 milliseconds.
`setRepeatCount(int count)`	Determines the number of times to repeat the animation. If the count is 0, the animation doesn't repeat. The animation repeats if the count is positive or `INFINITE`. The default value of the count is 0.
`public void setRepeatMode(int value)`	Determines the action of the animation when it reaches the end. The value parameter can be either `RESTART` or `REVERSE`. The method works only when repeat count is either positive or `INFINITE`.
`INFINITE`	Used to repeat the animation indefinitely.
`RESTART`	Restarts the animation from the beginning when the animation reaches the end. The animation restarts only if the repeat count is either positive or `INFINITE`.

Method/Constant	Description
REVERSE	Reverses the direction of animation when the animation reaches its end (that is, the animation reverses its direction after every iteration). The animation reverses only if the repeat count is either positive or INFINITE.

Recipe: Using `ValueAnimator`

The procedure for animating the properties of any view through the `ValueAnimator` class is simple. You just need to supply the starting and ending values for the property to animate and the duration of the animation and then call the `start()` method to begin the animation. A few of the methods used with the `ValueAnimator` class are briefly described in Table 8.2.

Table 8.2   **Brief Description of the Methods Used with the** `ValueAnimator` **Class**

Method	Description
ofInt(int value1, value2...)	Creates and returns a `ValueAnimator` that animates between the given integer values.
ofFloat(float value1, value2...)	Creates and returns a `ValueAnimator` that animates between the given float values.
ofObject(Object target_object, String property, TypeEvaluator evaluator, Object value1, value2..)	Creates and returns a `ValueAnimator` that animates between the given object values. The `target_object` represents the object whose property is to be animated. The `property` represents the property name to be animated (see Table 8.3 for the list of property names). The `evaluator` represents the `TypeEvaluator` that will be called on each animation frame. The `value1, value2..` represent a set of values that the animation will animate over the given duration.
getAnimatedValue()	Returns the most recent value calculated by the `ValueAnimator`. The method is used when there is just one property being animated.
getAnimatedValue(property)	Returns the most recent value calculated by the `ValueAnimator` for the specified property.

> **Note**
>
> The `TypeEvaluator` provides the necessary interpolation between the object values to derive the animated value. That is, by interpolating the supplied object values, the `TypeEvaluator` returns a value that represents the proportion between the given object values.

Various properties of objects that can be animated are briefly described in Table 8.3.

Table 8.3   **Brief Description of the Property Names That Can Be Animated**

Property	Description
`translationX` and `translationY`	Determine the location of an object from the left and top coordinates of its layout container.
`rotation`, `rotationX`, and `rotationY`	Determine the rotation of an object around the specified pivot point.
`scaleX` and `scaleY`	Determine the direction of scaling of an object around its pivot point.
`pivotX` and `pivotY`	Determine the location of the pivot point around which the rotation and scaling transforms occur. By default, the pivot point is located at the center of the object.
`alpha`	Represents the alpha transparency on an object. This value is 1 (opaque) by default, with a value of 0 representing full transparency (not visible).

> **Note**
>
> After you animate or change the property of any object, it automatically calls the `invalidate()` method to refresh the screen.

This recipe is focused on understanding how `ValueAnimator` computes animation values between the supplied range over the specified time duration. The recipe will produce integer values from 10 to 20 over a period of 3000 milliseconds using the `ValueAnimator` class. Create a new Android project called `ValueAnimatorApp`. You want the application to produce the integer values on the click of a button, so define a `Button` control in the activity layout file. After you define a `Button` control, the activity layout file `activity_value_animator_app.xml` will appear as shown in Listing 8.1.

Listing 8.1   **Code Written into the Activity Layout File** `activity_value_animator_app.xml`

```
<LinearLayout xmlns:android="http://schemas.android.com/apk/res/android"
    android:layout_width="match_parent"
```

```
        android:layout_height="match_parent"
        android:orientation="vertical" >
        <Button
            android:id="@+id/value_anim_button"
            android:layout_width="wrap_content"
            android:layout_height="wrap_content"
            android:text="Start ValueAnimator"
            android:textSize="@dimen/text_size"
            android:layout_gravity="center"
            android:layout_marginTop="50dp" />
    </LinearLayout>
```

You can see that the `Button` control is assigned the ID `value_anim_button` and is set to display the caption `Start ValueAnimator`. The caption will appear in the font size defined in the dimension resource `text_size`. Also, the button is set to appear at the distance of 50dp from the top and be horizontally centered.

Next, you need to write Java code to do the following tasks:

- Access the `Button` control defined in the layout file and map it to the `Button` object.

- Associate `setOnClickListener` to the `Button` control to listen for the occurrence of the click event on the `Button` control.

- Define the `ValueAnimator` object and set its value range and the duration of animation.

- Associate `addUpdateListener` to the `ValueAnimator` object to listen for the update events that might occur during the animation.

- Display the animation values generated by the `ValueAnimator` in the form of log messages.

To perform these tasks, write the code shown in Listing 8.2 in the Java activity file `ValueAnimatorAppActivity.java`.

Listing 8.2   **Code Written into the Java Activity File** `ValueAnimatorAppActivity.java`

```
package com.androidtablet.valueanimatorapp;

import android.app.Activity;
import android.os.Bundle;
import android.view.View;
import android.view.View.OnClickListener;
import android.widget.Button;
import android.animation.ValueAnimator;
import android.util.Log;

public class ValueAnimatorAppActivity extends Activity {
    @Override
```

```
public void onCreate(Bundle savedInstanceState) {
    super.onCreate(savedInstanceState);
    setContentView(R.layout.activity_value_animator_app);
    Button valueAnimatorButton = (Button) findViewById(
      R.id.value_anim_button);
    valueAnimatorButton.setOnClickListener(new
      OnClickListener() {
        @Override
        public void onClick(View v) {
            ValueAnimator anim = ValueAnimator.ofInt(10, 20);
            anim.setDuration(3000);
            anim.addUpdateListener(new
            ValueAnimator.AnimatorUpdateListener(){
                public void onAnimationUpdate(
              ValueAnimator animation)  {
                    Integer value = Integer.parseInt(animation.
                  getAnimatedValue().toString());
                    Log.d("value: ",value.toString());
                }
            });
            anim.start();
        }
    });
  }
}
```

In the preceding code, you define a ValueAnimator object called anim that will generate an integer animation value from 10 to 20. The duration of animation is set to 3 seconds. By default, the duration of animation is 300ms. The addUpdateListener is associated to the ValueAnimator object anim to listen for update events that occur during the animation. By default, the callback onAnimationUpdate is called in every 10ms. Hence, the onAnimationUpdate method will be called many times for 3 seconds displaying the integer values between 10 and 20.

After running the application, you get a Button control with the caption Start ValueAnimator (see Figure 8.1 [top]). Select the Button control, and the ValueAnimator will generate the integer values between 10 and 20 over the duration of 3 seconds, as shown in Figure 8.1 (bottom).

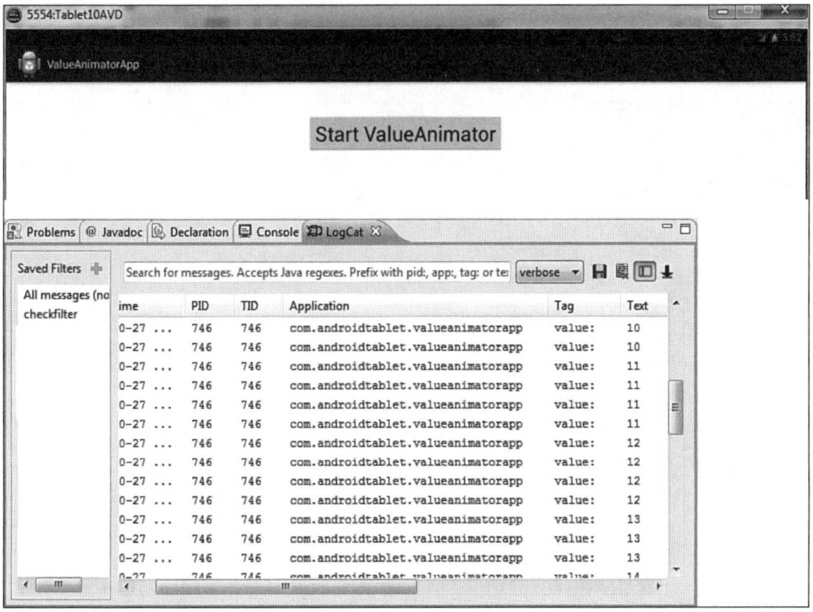

Figure 8.1   Button control with caption `Start ValueAnimator` displayed on application startup (top), and the log messages showing the integer values between `10` and `20` (bottom)

As mentioned earlier, by using `ValueAnimator`s, you can animate any object. To see how to use `ValueAnimator` for animating an object, modify your current Android application `ValueAnimatorApp`. In addition to a `Button` control, you will display a `TextView` control in the application. Click the button, and the `TextView` control will stretch and shrink infinitely. More specifically, the `TextView` will stretch horizontally to 3.5 times its original size and then shrink back to its original size. When it is shrunk back to its original size, the `TextView` control will again stretch horizontally. This way the animation will continue infinitely.

To add a `TextView` control, modify the code in the activity layout file `activity_value_animator_app.xml` to appear as shown in Listing 8.3. Only the code in bold is newly added; the rest is the same as in Listing 8.1.

Listing 8.3   **Code Written into the Activity Layout File** `activity_value_animator_app.xml`

```
<LinearLayout
    xmlns:android="http://schemas.android.com/apk/res/android"
    android:layout_width="match_parent"
    android:layout_height="match_parent"
    android:orientation="vertical" >
    <TextView
        android:layout_width="match_parent"
```

```
        android:layout_height="wrap_content"
        android:gravity="center"
        android:text="This is Sample Text"
        android:textSize="@dimen/text_size"
        android:id="@+id/textview"
        android:textStyle="bold"
        android:layout_marginTop="10dp" />
    <Button
        android:id="@+id/value_anim_button"
        android:layout_width="wrap_content"
        android:layout_height="wrap_content"
        android:text="Start ValueAnimator"
        android:textSize="@dimen/text_size"
        android:layout_gravity="center"
        android:layout_marginTop="50dp" />
</LinearLayout>
```

You can see that the `TextView` control is initialized to display the text `This is Sample Text` and is set to appear at the horizontal center of the screen. The control is assigned the ID `TextView` and is set to appear at the distance of 10dp from the top of the screen. Also, it is set to display the text in bold and in the font size defined in the dimension resource `text_size`. Next, you need to modify the Java activity file `ValueAnimatorAppActivity.java` to perform the following tasks:

- Access the `TextView` control from the layout file and map it to the `TextView` object.

- Because you want to stretch the `TextView` control to 3.5 times its original size, you need to set the `ValueAnimator` object to generate the float values in the range 1.0 and 3.5.

- Because you want the animation to reverse, or switch, when it reaches the end (in other words, you want the `TextView` to be resized to its original dimensions after it is stretched), you set the repeat mode of the animation to `REVERSE`.

- Because you want the animation to continue infinitely, you set the repeat count of the animation to `INFINITE`.

- In the `onAnimationUpdate` callback method, access the generated animation value and apply it to the `setTextScaleX` property of the `TextView` control to stretch and shrink it.

To accomplish all these tasks, modify the Java activity file `ValueAnimatorAppActivity.java` to appear as shown in Listing 8.4.

Listing 8.4 **Code Written into the Java Activity File** `ValueAnimatorAppActivity.java`

```
package com.androidtablet.valueanimatorapp;

import android.app.Activity;
import android.os.Bundle;
```

```
import android.view.View;
import android.view.View.OnClickListener;
import android.widget.Button;
import android.animation.ValueAnimator;
import android.widget.TextView;
import android.animation.ValueAnimator.AnimatorUpdateListener;

public class ValueAnimatorAppActivity extends Activity {
    @Override
    public void onCreate(Bundle savedInstanceState) {
        super.onCreate(savedInstanceState);
        setContentView(R.layout.activity_value_animator_app);
        final TextView textView = (TextView)this.findViewById(
         R.id.textview);
        Button valueAnimatorButton = (Button) findViewById(
         R.id.value_anim_button);
        valueAnimatorButton.setOnClickListener(new
         OnClickListener() {
            @Override
            public void onClick(View v) {
                ValueAnimator anim = ValueAnimator.ofFloat(1f, 3.5f);
                anim.setRepeatCount(ValueAnimator.INFINITE);
                anim.setRepeatMode(ValueAnimator.REVERSE);
                anim.setDuration(3000);
                anim.addUpdateListener(new AnimatorUpdateListener() {
                    @Override
                    public void onAnimationUpdate(ValueAnimator
                     animation) {
                        float value = (Float)animation.getAnimatedValue();
                        textView.setTextScaleX(value);
                    }
                });
                anim.start();
            }
        });
    }
}
```

In the preceding code, you see that the `setTextScaleX()` method specifies the scale value by which the `TextView` must be stretched horizontally. Through the `ofFloat()` method, float values between 1 and 3.5 will be generated; therefore, the `TextView` will be stretched horizontally from its original size to 3.5 times over a 3-second duration. Because the REVERSE constant is used on `ValueAnimator`, the `TextView` will reverse its animation after reaching the end. (In other words, when the `TextView` is scaled horizontally to 3.5 times its original size, it will start shrinking back to its original size.) The animation will continue infinitely because the INFINITE constant on `ValueAnimator` is used.

After running the application, you see a `TextView` and a `Button` control on startup. The `TextView` is initialized to display the text `This is Sample Text`, and the caption displayed on the `Button` control is `Start ValueAnimator` (see Figure 8.2 [top]). After you click the `Button` control, the `TextView` control will stretch horizontally to 3.5 times its original size in a 3-second duration (see Figure 8.2 [bottom]). Once stretched, the `TextView` will shrink back to its original size. When returned to its original size, again, the `TextView` will stretch and the process will continue infinitely.

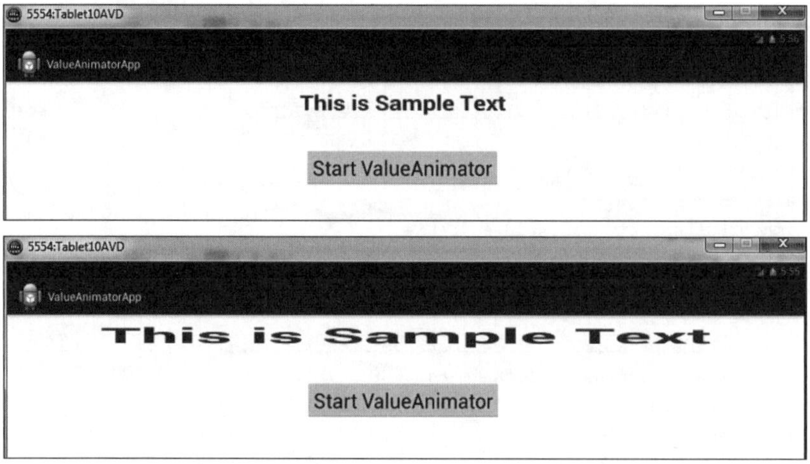

Figure 8.2   `TextView` and `Button` control displayed on application startup (top), and the `TextView` control stretched to 3.5 times its original size (bottom)

Recipe: Using `ObjectAnimator` to Animate Views

The simplest technique for creating property animations is using an `ObjectAnimator`. The `ObjectAnimator` class includes the `ofFloat`, `ofInt`, and `ofobject` static methods. These methods generate required values in the specified range that can be applied to the given property of the target object. That is, the `ObjectAnimator` class provides the methods that create animation by implementing a transition in the specified property of the target object between the provided values.

To understand how `ObjectAnimator` is used in animating objects, create a new Android project called `ObjectAnimatorApp`. In this application, you will define a `TextView` and a `ToggleButton` control. On every click of the `ToggleButton`, the `TextView` will fade out and fade in alternatively. To define `TextView` and `ToggleButton` controls, write the code shown in Listing 8.5 to the activity layout file `activity_object_animator_app.xml`.

Listing 8.5   **Code Written into the Activity Layout File** `activity_object_animator_app.xml`

```xml
<LinearLayout xmlns:android="http://schemas.android.com/apk/res/android"
    android:layout_width="match_parent"
    android:layout_height="match_parent"
    android:orientation="vertical" >
    <TextView
        android:id="@+id/textview"
        android:layout_width="match_parent"
        android:layout_height="wrap_content"
        android:gravity="center"
        android:text="ObjectAnimator Demo"
        android:textSize="@dimen/text_size"
        android:textStyle="bold"
        android:layout_marginTop="200dp"/>
    <ToggleButton
      android:id="@+id/toggle_button"
        android:layout_width="wrap_content"
        android:layout_height="wrap_content"
        android:textSize="@dimen/text_size"
        android:layout_gravity="center"
        android:layout_marginTop="200dp" />
</LinearLayout>
```

You can see that the `TextView` control is initialized to display the text `ObjectAnimator Demo` and is set to display at the horizontal center of the screen. The control is assigned the ID `TextView` and is set to appear at the distance of 200dp from the top. Also, it is set to display the text in bold and in the font size defined in the dimension resource `text_size`. Below the `TextView`, a `ToggleButton` control is defined that is assigned the ID `toggle_button`. The `ToggleButton` is set to appear at the distance of 200dp from the `TextView` displayed above it and be horizontally centered.

In the Java activity file, you need to write code to perform the following tasks:

- Access the `TextView` and `ToggleButton` control from the layout file and map them to the respective objects.
- Associate `setOnClickListener` to the `Button` control to listen for the occurrence of a click event on it.
- Define the `ObjectAnimator` named `fadeOut` that changes the alpha property of the `TextView` control from its current value to 0 (that is, it makes the `TextView` control transparent or invisible) over the duration of 5 seconds.
- Define another `ObjectAnimator` object named `fadeIn` that changes the alpha property of the `TextView` control from its current value to 1 (that is, it makes the `TextView` control opaque, or fully visible) over the duration of 5 seconds.
- Start the `ObjectAnimator` objects `fadeOut` and `fadeIn` alternatively with every click of the `ToggleButton` control. The `TextView` control will fade out when `ToggleButton` is clicked once and will fade in when `ToggleButton` is clicked again.

To perform all these tasks, write the code shown in Listing 8.6 to the Java activity file
`ObjectAnimatorAppActivity.java`.

Listing 8.6   Code Written into the Java Activity File `ObjectAnimatorAppActivity.java`

```java
package com.androidtablet.objectanimatorapp;

import android.os.Bundle;
import android.app.Activity;
import android.widget.ToggleButton;
import android.view.View.OnClickListener;
import android.widget.TextView;
import android.view.View;
import android.animation.ObjectAnimator;

public class ObjectAnimatorAppActivity extends Activity {
    @Override
    public void onCreate(Bundle savedInstanceState) {
        super.onCreate(savedInstanceState);
        setContentView(R.layout.activity_object_animator_app);
        final TextView textView = (TextView)this.findViewById(
         R.id.textview);
        final ToggleButton toggleButton = (ToggleButton)
         findViewById(R.id.toggle_button);
        toggleButton.setText("Fade Out");
        toggleButton.setOnClickListener(new OnClickListener() {
            public void onClick(View v) {
                if (toggleButton.isChecked()) {
                    toggleButton.setText("Fade In");
                    ObjectAnimator fadeOut =ObjectAnimator.ofFloat(
                  textView, "alpha", 0f);
                    fadeOut.setDuration(5000);
                    fadeOut.start();
                }
                else {
                    toggleButton.setText("Fade Out");
                    ObjectAnimator fadeIn =ObjectAnimator.ofFloat(
                  textView, "alpha", 1f);
                    fadeIn.setDuration(5000);
                    fadeIn.start();
                }
            }
        });
    }
}
```

The ofFloat method used in the preceding program needs a little explanation:

The ofFloat method creates and returns an ObjectAnimator that animates the specified property of the given object between the specified float values. The syntax for using the method follows:

```
public static ObjectAnimator.ofFloat(Object target_object, String property, float
value1, value2...)
```

- where target_object represents the object whose property is to be animated.
- property represents the name of the property to be animated. Table 8.3 shows the list of property names that you can animate.
- values represent a set of values in the range of which the animation will take place over the given duration. If a single value is supplied, it represents the ending value. Two values, if supplied, represent the starting and ending values—the range between which the animation will take place. If more than two values are supplied, they represent the starting value, the values to animate during animation, and the ending value.

You can see in the preceding code that the ofFloat() method is used to define the ObjectAnimator objects that change the alpha property of the TextView control, hence implementing fade-out and fade-in operations.

After running the application, you get the TextView and ToggleButton control on startup. The TextView is initialized to display the text ObjectAnimator Demo. The initial caption assigned to the ToggleButton control is Fade Out, as shown in Figure 8.3 (top). Select the ToggleButton, and the TextView control will begin fading out over the duration of 5 seconds. Also, the caption on the ToggleButton will change to Fade In, as shown in Figure 8.3 (bottom).

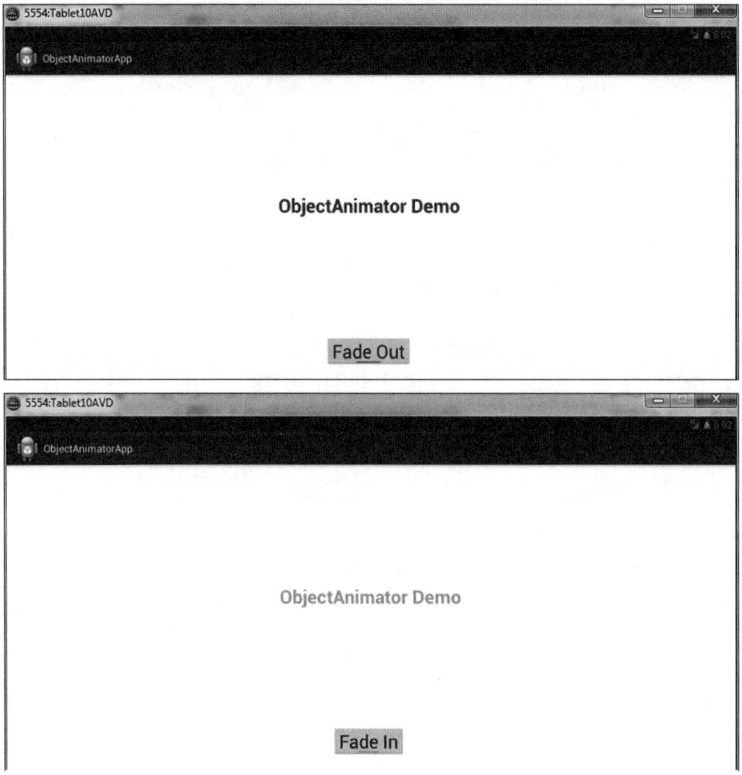

Figure 8.3   `TextView` and `ToggleButton` on application startup (top); `TextView` gradually fades out after clicking the `ToggleButton` once (bottom)

The `Fade In` caption on the `ToggleButton` indicates that if the `ToggleButton` is clicked again, the `TextView` control will gradually fade in, or gradually become visible again (see Figure 8.4 [top]). When the animation completes, the `TextView` becomes completely visible, and the caption on the `ToggleButton` changes to `Fade Out` (see Figure 8.4 [bottom]).

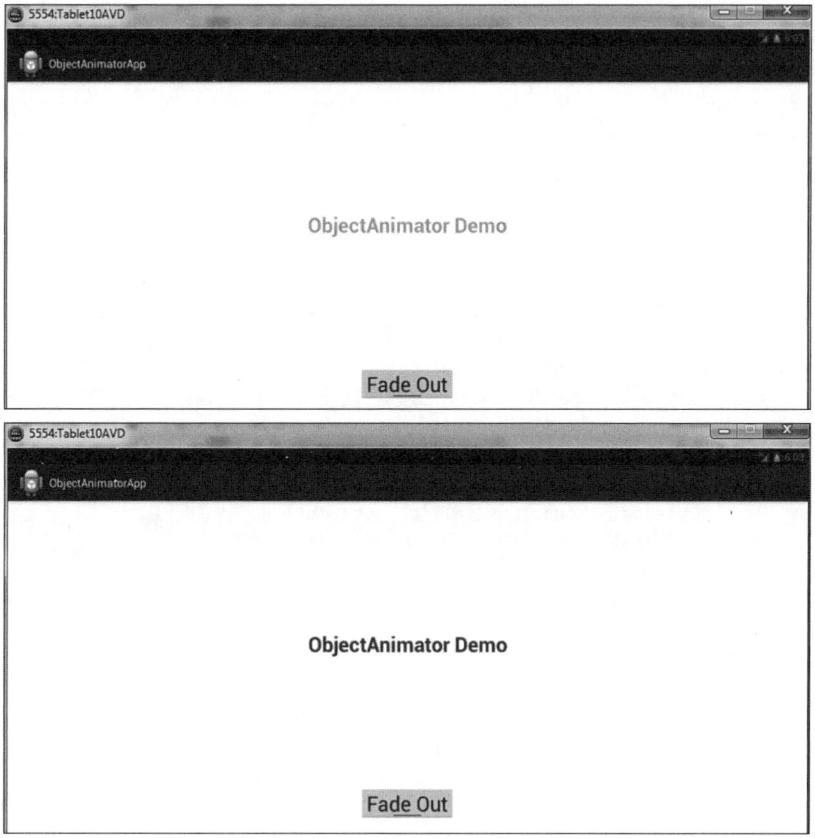

Figure 8.4   `TextView` gradually fades in after clicking the `ToggleButton` again (top); the `TextView` and `ToggleButton` when animation is over (bottom)

You can animate any property of the given object through `ObjectAnimator`. In the current Android application `ObjectAnimatorApp`, try animating the rotation property of the `TextView` control through `ObjectAnimator`. In other words, modify the application to rotate the `TextView` control in a clockwise and counterclockwise direction. To do so, you need to modify the Java activity file `ObjectAnimatorAppActivity.java` to appear as shown in Listing 8.7. Only the code in bold is modified; the rest is the same as in Listing 8.6.

Listing 8.7   **Code in the Java Activity File** `ObjectAnimatorAppActivity.java`

```
package com.androidtablet.objectanimatorapp;

import android.os.Bundle;
import android.app.Activity;
```

```
import android.widget.ToggleButton;
import android.view.View.OnClickListener;
import android.widget.TextView;
import android.view.View;
import android.animation.ObjectAnimator;

public class ObjectAnimatorAppActivity extends Activity {
    @Override
    public void onCreate(Bundle savedInstanceState) {
        super.onCreate(savedInstanceState);
        setContentView(R.layout.activity_object_animator_app);
        final TextView textView = (TextView)this.findViewById(R.id.textview);
        final ToggleButton toggleButton = (ToggleButton)
         findViewById(R.id.toggle_button);
        toggleButton.setText("Rotate Clockwise");
        final ObjectAnimator objAnim = ObjectAnimator.ofFloat(textView,
            "rotation", 0f, 360f).setDuration(5000);
        toggleButton.setOnClickListener(new OnClickListener() {
            public void onClick(View v) {
                if (toggleButton.isChecked()) {
                    toggleButton.setText("Rotate Clockwise followed by
                        Counterclockwise");
                    objAnim.setRepeatMode(ObjectAnimator.RESTART);
                }
                else  {
                    toggleButton.setText("Rotate Clockwise");
                    objAnim.setRepeatMode(ObjectAnimator.REVERSE);
                }
                objAnim.setRepeatCount(ObjectAnimator.INFINITE);
                objAnim.start();
            }
        });
    }
}
```

You can see that the ToggleButton control is initially set to display the caption Rotate Clockwise. An ObjectAnimator object named objAnim is defined. It changes the rotation property of the TextView control from 0 to 360 degrees over the duration of 5 seconds. Using the ofFloat() method, float values between 0 and 360 are generated through ObjectAnimator and are applied to the rotation property of the TextView control to rotate it in a clockwise direction.

To make the TextView control rotate in both directions (clockwise followed by counterclockwise), set the repeat mode of the ObjectAnimator to REVERSE in the onClick callback method of the ToggleButton. To make the TextView animate infinitely, the repeat count of the ObjectAnimator object is set to INFINITE.

After running the application, you get a `TextView` and a `ToggleButton` control on startup. The `TextView` displays the text `ObjectAnimator Demo`, and the initial caption assigned to the `ToggleButton` control is `Rotate Clockwise`, as shown in Figure 8.5 (top). Once you select the `ToggleButton`, the `TextView` control will begin rotating gradually in a clockwise direction over the duration of 5 seconds. Also, the caption on the `ToggleButton` changes to `Rotate Clockwise` followed by `Counterclockwise`, as shown in Figure 8.5 (middle). The caption `Rotate Clockwise` followed by `Counterclockwise` indicates that if the `ToggleButton` is clicked again, the `TextView` control will rotate in a clockwise direction followed by a counterclockwise direction (see Figure 8.5 [bottom]).

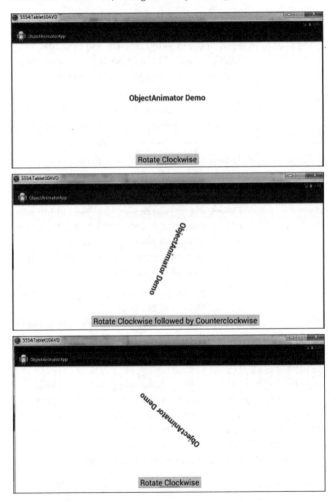

Figure 8.5 `TextView` and `ToggleButton` on application startup (top); `TextView` rotates in clockwise direction after clicking the `ToggleButton` once (middle); `TextView` rotates in clockwise direction followed by counterclockwise direction when `ToggleButton` is clicked again (bottom)

Recipe: Multiple Animations Using `AnimatorSet`

`AnimatorSet` is a class that can be used to play a set of animator objects in the specified order. Methods for adding animations to an `AnimatorSet` are given in Table 8.4.

Table 8.4   Brief Description of Methods Used for Adding Animations to the `AnimatorSet` Class

Method	Description
`play(Animator anim)`	The method creates a `Builder` object that constructs the `AnimatorSet` based on the specified dependencies. For example, the following statement will make the `AnimatorSet` play anim1 and anim2 simultaneously: `play(anim1).with(anim2)`
	Similarly, the following statement will make the `AnimatorSet` play anim1 followed by anim2: `play(anim1).before(anim2)`
	The following statement will make the `AnimatorSet` play anim1 after anim2: `play(anim1).after(anim2)`
`playSequentially(Animator anim1, anim2...)`	Makes the `AnimatorSet` play each of the supplied animations in sequential order, one after another. You can also pass `List<Animator>` anims as a parameter to this method to indicate the list of animations to play.
`playTogether(Animator anim1, anim2...)`	Makes the `AnimatorSet` play all the supplied animations simultaneously. You can also pass `Collection<Animator>` anims to this method to indicate the list of animations to play.

To see how two animations are set to play together in sequential order using `AnimatorSet`, create an Android project called `MultiAnimApp`. In this application, you will use a `TextView` and an `ImageView` control. You will apply two animations—scale and rotation—on the `ImageView`. (The `ImageView` will rotate and will simultaneously scale.) Also, you will modify the alpha property of the `TextView` consecutively. When `TextView` becomes completely invisible, it fades in gradually. The fade-out and fade-in animation will occur consecutively.

To define `TextView` and `ImageView` controls, write the code shown in Listing 8.8 to the activity layout file `activity_multi_anim_app.xml`.

Listing 8.8   Code Written into the Activity Layout File `activity_multi_anim_app.xml`

```xml
<RelativeLayout xmlns:android="http://schemas.android.com/apk/res/android"
    xmlns:tools="http://schemas.android.com/tools"
    android:layout_width="match_parent"
    android:layout_height="match_parent" >
    <ImageView
        android:id="@+id/imgview"
        android:src="@drawable/ic_launcher"
        android:layout_width="@dimen/image_width"
        android:layout_height="@dimen/image_height"
        android:layout_marginTop="50dip"
        android:layout_marginLeft="50dip" />
    <TextView
        android:layout_width="match_parent"
        android:layout_height="wrap_content"
        android:text="AnimatorSet Demo"
        android:id="@+id/textview"
        android:textSize="@dimen/text_size"
        android:textStyle="bold"
        android:layout_marginTop="50dp"
        android:layout_toRightOf="@id/imgview"
        android:layout_marginLeft="50dp" />
</RelativeLayout>
```

You can see that the `ImageView` control is defined and is assigned the ID `imgview` and is set to appear at the distance of 50dp from the top of the container and at the distance of 50dp from the left border of the screen. The `ImageView` control is initialized to display the `ic_launcer.png` image by default. The width and height of the image displayed through the `ImageView` control is determined by the dimension resources `image_width` and `image_height`, respectively. Below the `ImageView`, a `TextView` control is initialized to display the text `AnimatorSet Demo` and is set to appear at the center of the screen horizontally. The control is assigned the ID `TextView` and is set to appear at the distance of 50dp from the top of the screen and 50dp to the right of the `ImageView`. Also, it is set to display the text in bold and at the size defined in the dimension resource `text_size`.

Assuming the dimension file `dimens.xml` already exists in the `res/values` folder, add the dimensions to the file to resize the images as per the device's screen on which the application is run. Write the following code in the `dimens.xml` file:

```xml
<?xml version="1.0" encoding="utf-8"?>
<resources>
    <dimen name="text_size">14sp</dimen>
    <dimen name="image_width">100dp</dimen>
    <dimen name="image_height">120dp</dimen>
</resources>
```

The three dimension resources `text_size`, `image_width`, and `image_height` define the font size of the text and the width and height of the image. These dimension resources are for normal screen devices (phones).

To define the dimension resources for 7-inch tablets, open the `dimens.xml` file in the `res/values-sw600dp` folder and write the following code in it:

```
<?xml version="1.0" encoding="utf-8"?>
<resources>
    <dimen name="text_size">24sp</dimen>
    <dimen name="image_width">140dp</dimen>
    <dimen name="image_height">160dp</dimen>
</resources>
```

Finally, to define dimensions for extra-large screen devices (10-inch tablets), open the `dimens.xml` file in the `values-sw720dp` folder and write the following code in it:

```
<?xml version="1.0" encoding="utf-8"?>
<resources>
    <dimen name="text_size">32sp</dimen>
    <dimen name="image_width">180dp</dimen>
    <dimen name="image_height">200dp</dimen>
</resources>
```

By comparing the dimension resources of phones, 7-inch tablets, and 10-inch tablets, you can see that the text and images in the application are resized on the basis of the device screen size.

In the Java activity file, you need to write code to perform the following tasks:

- Access the `TextView` and `ImageView` controls defined in the layout file, and map them to the respective objects.

- Define an `AnimatorSet` object.

- Use the `playTogether()` method on the `AnimatorSet` object to perform the scale and rotation animation simultaneously on the `ImageView` control. Set the duration of the combined animation to 20 seconds. The `ImageView` will rotate 360 degrees in a clockwise direction and will simultaneously scale horizontally to twice its original size.

- Use the `playSequentially()` method on the `AnimatorSet` object to apply fade-out (alpha animation) followed by fade-in animation on the `TextView` control. The alpha property of the `TextView` control is changed to 0. (In other words, the `TextView` control is made invisible first.) When the `TextView` control becomes completely invisible, the alpha property is changed to 1. (The `TextView` control is animated to the visible state.) The fade-out and fade-in operations will occur consecutively over the duration of 5 seconds.

To perform the preceding tasks, write the code shown in Listing 8.9 to the Java activity file `MultiAnimAppActivity.java`.

Listing 8.9   **Code Written into the Java Activity File** `MultiAnimAppActivity.java`

```java
package com.androidtablet.multianimapp;

import android.os.Bundle;
import android.app.Activity;
import android.widget.ImageView;
import android.animation.ObjectAnimator;
import android.animation.AnimatorSet;
import android.widget.TextView;

public class MultiAnimAppActivity extends Activity {
    @Override
    public void onCreate(Bundle savedInstanceState) {
        super.onCreate(savedInstanceState);
        setContentView(R.layout.activity_multi_anim_app);
        ImageView imgView = (ImageView)findViewById(R.id.imgview);
        final TextView textView = (TextView)this.findViewById(
        R.id.textview);
        AnimatorSet animatorSet = new AnimatorSet();
        animatorSet.playTogether(ObjectAnimator.ofFloat(imgView,
        "scaleX",1f, 2f),  ObjectAnimator.ofFloat(imgView,
        "rotation", 0f, 360f));
        animatorSet.setDuration(20000);
        animatorSet.start();
        ObjectAnimator fadeOut = ObjectAnimator.ofFloat(
        textView, "alpha", 0f);
        ObjectAnimator fadeIn = ObjectAnimator.ofFloat(
        textView, "alpha", 1f);
        animatorSet.playSequentially(fadeOut,fadeIn);
        animatorSet.setDuration(5000);
        animatorSet.start();
    }
}
```

After running the application, the `ImageView` and `TextView` control will initially appear as shown in Figure 8.6 (first). The rotate and scale animation will apply simultaneously on the `ImageView` control (see Figure 8.6 [second]). Also, the `TextView` control will start fading out (see Figure 8.6 [third]). Figure 8.6 (fourth) shows the `ImageView` after the scaling and rotation have been simultaneously applied on it and the `TextView` after fade-out and fade-in operations have been applied to it consecutively.

Figure 8.6   `ImageView` and `TextView` control on application startup (first); `ImageView` control with scaling and rotation applied simultaneously (second); `TextView` control getting fade-out (third); `ImageView` and `TextView` after multiple animations applied (fourth)

Recipe: Understanding Frame-by-Frame Animation

Frame-by-frame animations are produced by drawing a series of sequential images, each of which is displayed for a specific duration. To show motion, each image differs slightly from the previous one. To do it practically, create an Android project called `FrameAnimationApp` and copy the images that you want to animate in the `res/drawable` folders. Figure 8.7 shows the images dwg1.png, dwg2.png, dwg3.png, and dwg4.png that you will be using in this frame-by-frame animation. Observe that each image is slightly different from the previous image to show movement or motion.

Figure 8.7   The four images used in frame-by-frame animation

Copy the four image files into the res/drawable folders. To control the animation, you define a ToggleButton that will be used to start and stop the animation. You also need to define an ImageView control to display the images to animate. To define the ImageView and ToggleButton controls, write the code shown in Listing 8.10 into the activity_frame_animation_app.xml layout file.

Listing 8.10   **Code in** activity_frame_animation_app.xml **After Defining the** ImageView **and** ToggleButton

```
<RelativeLayout xmlns:android="http://schemas.android.com/apk/res/android"
    xmlns:tools="http://schemas.android.com/tools"
    android:layout_width="match_parent"
    android:layout_height="match_parent"    >
    <ImageView android:id="@+id/imgview"
        android:layout_width="@dimen/image_width"
        android:layout_height="@dimen/image_height"
        android:layout_centerInParent="true" />
    <ToggleButton
        android:id="@+id/startstop_button"
        android:textOn="Stop Animation"
        android:textOff="Start Animation"
        android:textSize="@dimen/text_size"
        android:layout_width="wrap_content"
        android:layout_height="wrap_content"
        android:layout_centerHorizontal="true" />
</RelativeLayout>
```

Here, ImageView determines on which frame the animation will be applied. The ToggleButton will be used to switch the animation on or off. The IDs assigned to the ImageView and ToggleButton controls are imgview and startstop_button, respectively. The width and height of the image displayed through ImageView are defined through the dimension resource, image_width and image_height, respectively. The text displayed in ToggleButton will appear in the font size defined in the dimension resource text_size. The two controls will be accessed with Java code through these IDs.

Next, you will define dimension resources to make the views of your application compatible for phones, 7-inch tablets, and 10-inch tablets. So to the dimension file dimens.xml in the res/values folder, define the dimension resources to match the phone's screen size. Write the following code in the dimens.xml file:

```
<?xml version="1.0" encoding="utf-8"?>
<resources>
    <dimen name="text_size">14sp</dimen>
    <dimen name="image_width">100dp</dimen>
    <dimen name="image_height">120dp</dimen>
</resources>
```

The three dimension resources text_size, image_width, and image_height define the font size of the text and the image width and height. These dimension resources are for a normal screen device (a phone).

To define the dimension resources for a 7-inch tablet, open the dimens.xml file in the res/values-sw600dp folder and write the following code in it:

```
<?xml version="1.0" encoding="utf-8"?>
<resources>
    <dimen name="text_size">24sp</dimen>
    <dimen name="image_width">140dp</dimen>
    <dimen name="image_height">160dp</dimen>
</resources>
```

Finally, to define dimensions for extra-large screen devices (10-inch tablets), open the dimens.xml file in the values-sw720dp folder and write the following code in it:

```
<?xml version="1.0" encoding="utf-8"?>
<resources>
    <dimen name="text_size">32sp</dimen>
    <dimen name="image_width">180dp</dimen>
    <dimen name="image_height">200dp</dimen>
</resources>
```

By comparing the dimension resources of phones, 7-inch tablets, and 10-inch tablets, you can see that text and images in the application are resized on the basis of the device screen size.

Next, to define the images that will be involved in the animation and specify the duration of their display, you need to add an XML file to the res/anim folder. Create an anim folder in the /res folder. Then add an XML file called frame_anim.xml to the /res/anim folder.

Each of the images copied into the res/drawable folder will act as a frame. That is, each of the images is accessed through its resource ID and will be displayed sequentially. To show a simple animation that cycles through the series of supplied images, displaying each one for 100 milli-seconds, write the code shown in Listing 8.11 into the `frame_anim.xml` file.

Listing 8.11   **Code Written into** `frame_anim.xml`

```
<?xml version="1.0" encoding="utf-8"?>
<animation-list xmlns:android="http://schemas.android.com/apk/res/android"
android:oneshot="false">
    <item android:drawable="@drawable/dwg1" android:duration="100" />
    <item android:drawable="@drawable/dwg2" android:duration="100" />
    <item android:drawable="@drawable/dwg3" android:duration="100" />
    <item android:drawable="@drawable/dwg4" android:duration="100" />
</animation-list>
```

A brief description of the attributes used in this file is shown in Table 8.5.

Table 8.5   **Attributes Used in the** `frame_anim.xml` **File**

Attribute	Description
`android:drawable`	Defines the drawable resource that will be displayed in the animation.
`android:duration`	Determines the duration of animation. The time supplied is in milliseconds. For example, the value `5000` will make the animation complete in 5 seconds: `android:duration="5000"`
`android:oneshot`	Determines whether the animation runs in a continuous loop. The Boolean value `false` will make the animation run in a continuous loop. The Boolean value `true` will make the images animate only once.

You can see that the images you want to animate are collected in the animation list. The `animation-list` tag is converted into an `AnimationDrawable` object representing the collection of images. The `AnimationDrawable` class is available in the graphics package that displays frames in sequential order for a specific duration. Because you want the animation to run in an infinite loop, a `false` Boolean value is assigned to the `android:oneshot` attribute in the code shown in Listing 8.11.

Next, you need to write Java code to perform the following tasks:

- Access the images listed in the `frame_anim.xml` file and draw them via `ImageView`.
- Make an object of the `AnimationDrawable` class and access its `start()` and `stop()` methods to start and stop the animation.

To perform these tasks, write the code shown in Listing 8.12 into the `FrameAnimationAppActivity.java` activity file.

Listing 8.12   **Code Written into the** `FrameAnimationAppActivity.java` **Activity File**

```
package com.androidtablet.frameanimationapp;

import android.app.Activity;
import android.os.Bundle;
import android.widget.ToggleButton;
import android.widget.ImageView;
import android.view.View;
import android.graphics.drawable.AnimationDrawable;

public class FrameAnimationAppActivity extends Activity {
    AnimationDrawable animation;
    @Override
    public void onCreate(Bundle savedInstanceState) {
        super.onCreate(savedInstanceState);
        setContentView(R.layout.activity_frame_animation_app);
        final ToggleButton startStopButton = (ToggleButton)
            findViewById(R.id.startstop_button);
        final ImageView imgView = (ImageView)findViewById(
            R.id.imgview);
        startStopButton.setOnClickListener(new View.OnClickListener() {
            @Override
            public void onClick(View v) {
                if (startStopButton.isChecked()) {
                    imgView.setBackgroundResource(R.anim.frame_anim);
                    animation =  (AnimationDrawable)
                        imgView.getBackground();
                    animation.start();
                }
                else
                    animation.stop();
            }
        });
    }
}
```

Here, you see that `ToggleButton` and `ImageView` are accessed from the layout file and mapped to the `ToggleButton` and `ImageView` instances called `startStopButton` and `imgView`, respectively. A `ClickListener` is associated with the `ToggleButton`, and when it is clicked, its `onClick()` callback method is invoked. In the `onClick()` method, you refer to the `frame_anim.xml` file that contains the animation-list image collection. You set the `Drawable` as a background resource for your `ImageView`.

An object of the `AnimationDrawable` class is made and called an animation. You access the `start()` and `stop()` methods of the `AnimationDrawable` class to start and stop the animation. After application startup, the `ToggleButton` displays the caption `Start Animation` (see Figure 8.8 [top]). When you click the Start Animation button, the `start()` method of `AnimationDrawable` is called to begin the frame-by-frame animation (see Figure 8.8 [middle]). The caption of `ToggleButton` then changes to `Stop Animation`. After clicking the `Stop Animation` button, the `ToggleButton` switches to the Unchecked state, calling the `AnimationDrawable`'s `stop()` method to stop the animation. The `ImageView` shows the image of the frame where it is stopped, and the caption of the `ToggleButton` again changes to `Start Animation` (see Figure 8.8 [bottom]).

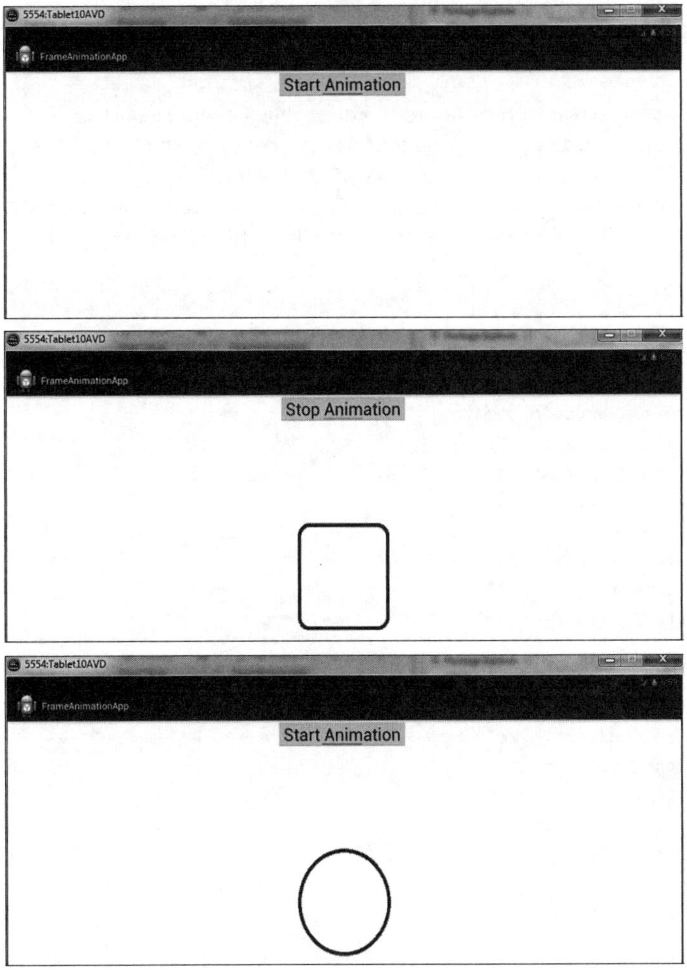

Figure 8.8   Startup screen (top); the animation plays after clicking the Start Animation button (middle); the animation stops after clicking the Stop Animation button (bottom)

Recipe: Using Tweening Animation

There are four types of tweening animation:

- **Alpha animation**—Used to change the opacity or transparency of a view.

- **Rotate animation**—Used to rotate a view by a specific angle around a given axis or pivot point.

- **Scale animation**—Used to make a view smaller or larger on the X axis, Y axis, or both. You can also specify the pivot point around which you want to scale the view.

- **Translate animation**—Used to move a view along the X or Y axis.

To understand tweening animation, create a new Android project called TweeningAnimApp. In this application, you will display an ImageView and four Button controls. The ImageView will be used to display animation. The four Button controls will be used to initiate the four tweening animation types: alpha, rotate, scale, and translate. To define an ImageView and four Button controls, write the code as shown in Listing 8.13 into the layout file activity_ tweening_anim_app.xml.

Listing 8.13   Code Written into the activity_tweening_anim_app.xml **Layout File**

```
<RelativeLayout xmlns:android="http://schemas.android.com/apk/res/android"
    xmlns:tools="http://schemas.android.com/tools"
    android:layout_width="match_parent"
    android:layout_height="match_parent" >
    <ImageView android:id="@+id/imgview"
        android:layout_width="@dimen/image_width"
        android:layout_height="@dimen/image_height"
        android:src="@drawable/ic_launcher"
        android:layout_centerInParent="true" />
    <Button
        android:id="@+id/alpha_button"
        android:text="Alpha"
        android:textSize="@dimen/text_size"
        android:layout_width="wrap_content"
        android:layout_height="wrap_content"  />
    <Button
        android:id="@+id/rotate_button"
        android:text="Rotate"
        android:textSize="@dimen/text_size"
        android:layout_width="wrap_content"
        android:layout_height="wrap_content"
        android:layout_toRightOf="@id/alpha_button" />
    <Button
        android:id="@+id/scale_button"
        android:text="Scale"
```

```
        android:textSize="@dimen/text_size"
        android:layout_width="wrap_content"
        android:layout_height="wrap_content"
        android:layout_toRightOf="@id/rotate_button" />
    <Button
        android:id="@+id/translate_button"
        android:text="Translate"
        android:textSize="@dimen/text_size"
        android:layout_width="wrap_content"
        android:layout_height="wrap_content"
        android:layout_toRightOf="@id/scale_button"  />
</RelativeLayout>
```

You can see that the ImageView is assigned the imgview ID, which will be used for accessing it with Java code. Also, it is set to initially display the ic_launcher.png image. The width and height assigned to the ImageView control are defined through the dimension resources image_width and image_height, respectively. The four Button controls are assigned the text Alpha, Rotate, Scale, and Translate to show the kind of animation they will play when clicked. The caption in the Button controls will appear in the font size defined in the dimension resource text_size. The four Button controls are assigned the IDs alpha_button, rotate_button, scale_button, and translate_button to identify and access them with Java code.

To the dimension file dimens.xml in the res/values folder, add the dimensions to the file to resize the images as per the device's screen on which the application is run. Write the following code in the dimens.xml file:

```
<?xml version="1.0" encoding="utf-8"?>
<resources>
    <dimen name="text_size">14sp</dimen>
    <dimen name="image_width">100dp</dimen>
    <dimen name="image_height">120dp</dimen>
</resources>
```

The three dimension resources text_size, image_width, and image_height define the font size of the text and the image width and height. These dimension resources are for normal screen devices (phones).

To define the dimension resources for 7-inch tablets, open the dimens.xml file in the res/values-sw600dp folder and write the following code in it:

```
<?xml version="1.0" encoding="utf-8"?>
<resources>
    <dimen name="text_size">24sp</dimen>
    <dimen name="image_width">140dp</dimen>
    <dimen name="image_height">160dp</dimen>
</resources>
```

Finally, to define dimensions for extra-large screen devices (10-inch tablets), open the `dimens.xml` file in the `values-sw720dp` folder and write the following code in it:

```
<?xml version="1.0" encoding="utf-8"?>
<resources>
    <dimen name="text_size">32sp</dimen>
    <dimen name="image_width">180dp</dimen>
    <dimen name="image_height">200dp</dimen>
</resources>
```

By comparing the dimension resources of phones, 7-inch tablets, and 10-inch tablets, you can see that text and images in the application are resized based on the device screen size.

Each tweening animation type has a respective class, shown in Table 8.6.

Table 8.6   **Classes Used in Tweening Animation**

Class	Purpose
AlphaAnimation	Defines the opacity or transparency of view(s).
TranslateAnimation	Defines the translate animation and applies motion to the associated view.
RotateAnimation	Defines the rotate animation and makes the view rotate by the specified degree about a specific pivot point or axis, either clockwise or counterclockwise.
ScaleAnimation	Defines the scale animation and enlarges or shrinks the specified view horizontally, vertically, or both.

Using the `AlphaAnimation` Class

The class determines the opacity or transparency of view(s). The syntax for the constructor of this class is shown here:

```
public AlphaAnimation(float from_alpha, float to_alpha)
```

The usage of the two parameters is shown here:

- **from_alpha**—Defines the starting `alpha` value to begin animation. Values ranging from `0.0` to `1.0` can be supplied to this parameter, where `1.0` means fully opaque and `0.0` means fully transparent.

- **to_alpha**—Defines the ending `alpha` value to end the animation. Again, values ranging from `0.0` to `1.0` can be supplied.

For example, the statement that follows will make the view animate from the visible to the invisible state:

```
Animation animation = new AlphaAnimation(1.0f, 0.1f);
```

Using the `TranslateAnimation` Class

This class defines the translate animation and applies motion to the associated view. The syntax for the constructor of this class is shown here:

```
public TranslateAnimation(float change_from_X, float change_to_X, float change_from_Y,
float change_to_Y)
```

The description of the parameters used in the constructor is shown in Table 8.7.

Table 8.7 **Parameters Used in `TranslateAnimation`'s Constructor**

Parameter	Description
`change_from_X`	Represents the change in the X coordinate to apply while beginning an animation. The value 0 begins the animation from the current X-coordinate location.
`change_to_X`	Represents the change in the X coordinate to end an animation. To move right, the supplied value is positive, and to move left, the supplied value is negative.
`change_from_Y`	Represents the change in the Y coordinate to apply at the beginning of animation. A value of 0 begins the animation from the current Y coordinate location.
`change_to_Y`	Represents the change in the Y coordinate to end the animation. To move down, the supplied value is positive, and to move up, the supplied value is negative.

For example, the following statement will make the view move left from its current location by 150:

```
Animation animation = new TranslateAnimation(0,-150,0,0);
```

Similarly, the statement that follows will make the view animate right by 150 and down by 200 (that is, it will make the view animate diagonally):

```
Animation animation = new TranslateAnimation(0,150,0,200);
```

Using the `RotateAnimation` Class

The class defines the rotate animation and makes the view rotate about a specified pivot point or axis in either a clockwise or counterclockwise direction. The syntax for the constructor of this class is shown here:

```
public RotateAnimation(float from_angle, float to_angle,
   int pivot_XType, float pivot_X, int pivot_YType,
   float pivot_Y)
```

The description of the parameters used in the constructor is given in Table 8.8.

Table 8.8   **Parameters Used in** `RotateAnimation`**'s Constructor**

Parameter	Description
`from_angle`	Defines the angle in degrees at which to begin the `Rotation` animation.
`to_angle`	Defines the angle at which to end `Rotation` animation. If the angle is positive, the view will rotate clockwise. A negative angle will make the view rotate counterclockwise.
`pivot_XType`	Determines how to interpret the `pivot_x` coordinate value. Valid values for this parameter follow: `Animation.ABSOLUTE`—Interprets the `pivot_x` value as an absolute number of pixels. `Animation.RELATIVE_TO_SELF`—Interprets the `pivot_x` value in relation to the current X coordinate of the view being animated. The value for the `pivot_x` can be supplied as a percentage. The percentage value is scaled from `0.0` to `1.0`, where `1.0` represents 100%. The value `0.5` assigned to `pivot_x` represents the midpoint of the view's width. `Animation.RELATIVE_TO_PARENT`—Interprets the `pivot_x` value in relation to the X coordinate of the parent of the view being animated.
`pivotX`	Defines the X coordinate of the pivot point or axis around which the view has to be rotated. If the value assigned to the `pivot_XType` parameter is `Animation.ABSOLUTE`, an absolute value is supplied for this parameter. A value of 0 represents the left edge of the view. If the value assigned to the `pivot_XType` parameter is `Animation.RELATIVE_TO_SELF` or `Animation.RELATIVE_TO_PARENT`, a percentage value is assigned to this parameter. The percentage value is supplied in scaled form from `0.0` to `1.0`, where `1.0` represents 100%.
`pivot_YType`	Determines how to interpret the `pivot_y` parameter value. Valid values for this parameter are `Animation.ABSOLUTE`, `Animation.RELATIVE_TO_SELF`, and `Animation.RELATIVE_TO_PARENT`.
`pivotY`	Defines the Y coordinate of the pivot or axis around which the view has to be rotated. If the value assigned to the `pivot_YType` parameter is `Animation.ABSOLUTE`, an absolute value is supplied to this parameter. Value 0 represents the top edge of the view. If the value assigned to the `pivot_YType` parameter is `Animation.RELATIVE_TO_SELF` or `Animation.RELATIVE_TO_PARENT`, a percentage value is assigned to this parameter in scaled form in the range of `0.0` to `1.0`, where `1.0` represents 100%. If the value `0.5` is assigned to `pivot_y`, it means the Y coordinate of the pivot should be considered the midpoint of the view's height.

For example, the statement that follows will apply a rotate animation to the view, rotating it 360 degrees clockwise from the center axis of the view:

```
RotateAnimation animation = new RotateAnimation(0,360, Animation.RELATIVE_TO_
SELF,0.5f, Animation.RELATIVE_TO_SELF, 0.5f);
```

Using the ScaleAnimation Class

The class defines the scale animation and increases or decreases the size of the specified view horizontally, vertically, or both. The syntax for the constructor of this class is shown here:

```
public ScaleAnimation(float from_X, float to_X, float from_Y,
    float to_Y, int pivot_XType, float pivotX, int pivotYType,
    float pivotY)
```

The description of the parameters used in the ScaleAnimation constructor is given in Table 8.9.

Table 8.9 **Parameters Used in ScaleAnimation's Constructor**

Parameter	Description
from_X	Defines the horizontal initial scaling value to be applied at the beginning of scale animation. The value supplied is in scaled form. For example, 1.0 represents 100%, 2.0 represents 200%, 0.5. represents 50%, and so on.
to_X	Defines the horizontal scale value to be applied at the end of scale animation.
from_Y	Defines the vertical initial scale value to be applied at the beginning of scale animation.
to_Y	Defines the vertical scale value to be applied at the end of scale animation.
pivot_XType	Determines how to interpret the pivot_x parameter (that is, whether to consider it as an absolute value or in percentage form). Valid values are Animation.ABSOLUTE, Animation.RELATIVE_TO_SELF, and Animation.RELATIVE_TO_PARENT. The meanings of these constants are the same as you saw in rotate animation.
pivotX	Defines the X coordinate of the pivot point or axis about which the view has to be scaled. If the value assigned to the pivot_XType parameter is Animation.ABSOLUTE, an absolute value is supplied for this parameter. A value of 0 represents the left edge of the view. If the value assigned to the pivot_XType parameter is Animation.RELATIVE_TO_SELF or Animation.RELATIVE_TO_PARENT, a percentage value is assigned to this parameter. Again, the percentage value is supplied in scaled form in the range of 0.0 to 1.0, where 1.0 represents 100%.

Parameter	Description
pivot_YType	Determines how to interpret the pivot_Y parameter. Valid values are Animation.ABSOLUTE, Animation.RELATIVE_TO_SELF, and Animation.RELATIVE_TO_PARENT.
pivotY	Defines the Y coordinate of the pivot point or axis about which the view has to be scaled. If the value assigned to the pivot_YType parameter is Animation.ABSOLUTE, an absolute value is supplied for this parameter. A value of 0 represents the top edge of the view. If the value assigned to the pivot_YType parameter is Animation.RELATIVE_TO_SELF or Animation.RELATIVE_TO_PARENT, a percentage value is assigned to this parameter in scaled form (that is, in the range of 0.0 to 1.0, where 1.0 represents 100%). If a value of 0.5 is assigned to pivot_Y, the middle value of the view's height is the Y coordinate of the pivot.

The values supplied for the from_X, to_X, from_Y, and to_Y parameters are always in scaled form. The values supplied for the pivotX and pivotY parameters can be in absolute or scaled form, depending on the value assigned to pivotX and pivotY. For example, the statement that follows will scale the view to twice its original size horizontally and vertically. The center of the view is taken as the axis or pivot point of the scale animation:

```
Animation animation = new ScaleAnimation(1.0f, 2.0f, 1.0f, 2.0f,Animation.RELATIVE_TO_
SELF, 0.5f, Animation.RELATIVE_TO_SELF, 0.5f);
```

Go back to the application TweeningAnimApp to apply the respective animation classes that you have learned.

You need to write Java code into the activity file to listen for a click event on the four Button controls, create objects of the respective animation classes, and then apply it to the ImageView control to display animation on the screen. To accomplish these tasks, write the code shown in Listing 8.14 into the Java activity file TweeningAnimAppActivity.java.

Listing 8.14   Code Written into the TweeningAnimAppActivity.java **Java Activity File**

```
package com.androidtablet.tweeninganimapp;

import android.app.Activity;
import android.os.Bundle;
import android.widget.ImageView;
import android.view.animation.Animation;
import android.widget.Button;
import android.view.View;
import android.view.animation.TranslateAnimation;
import android.view.animation.RotateAnimation;
import android.view.animation.AlphaAnimation;
```

```
import android.view.animation.ScaleAnimation;
import android.view.animation.AnimationSet;

public class TweeningAnimAppActivity extends Activity {
    ImageView imgView;

    @Override
    public void onCreate(Bundle savedInstanceState) {
        super.onCreate(savedInstanceState);
        setContentView(R.layout.activity_tweening_anim_app);
        Button alphaButton = (Button) findViewById(
            R.id.alpha_button);
        Button rotateButton = (Button) findViewById(
            R.id.rotate_button);
        Button scaleButton = (Button) findViewById(
            R.id.scale_button);
        Button translateButton = (Button) findViewById(
            R.id.translate_button);
        imgView = (ImageView)findViewById(R.id.imgview);
        rotateButton.setOnClickListener(new View.OnClickListener() {
            @Override
            public void onClick(View v) {
                RotateAnimation animation = new RotateAnimation(
                    0,360, Animation.RELATIVE_TO_SELF,0.5f,
                    Animation.RELATIVE_TO_SELF, 0.5f);
                animation.setDuration(3000);
                imgView.setAnimation(animation);
                animation.start();
            }
        });

        alphaButton.setOnClickListener(new View.OnClickListener() {
            @Override
            public void onClick(View v) {
                Animation animation = new AlphaAnimation(1.0f, 0.1f);
                animation.setDuration(3000);
                imgView.setAnimation(animation);
                animation.start();
            }
        });

        scaleButton.setOnClickListener(new View.OnClickListener() {
            @Override
            public void onClick(View v) {
                AnimationSet set = new AnimationSet(true);
                Animation animation1 = new ScaleAnimation(1.0f, 2.0f,
                    1.0f, 2.0f,Animation.RELATIVE_TO_SELF, 0.5f,
```

```
            Animation.RELATIVE_TO_SELF, 0.5f);
        animation1.setDuration(3000);
        set.addAnimation(animation1);
        Animation animation2 = new ScaleAnimation(1.0f, 0.5f,
            1.0f, 0.5f, Animation.RELATIVE_TO_SELF, 0.5f,
            Animation.RELATIVE_TO_SELF, 0.5f);
        animation2.setDuration(3000);
        animation2.setStartOffset(3000);
        set.addAnimation(animation2);
        imgView.startAnimation(set);
    }
});
translateButton.setOnClickListener(new View.OnClickListener() {
    @Override
    public void onClick(View v) {
        AnimationSet set = new AnimationSet(true);
        Animation animation1 = new TranslateAnimation(
            0,-150,0,0);
        animation1.setDuration(3000);
        animation1.setFillAfter(true);
        set.addAnimation(animation1);
        Animation animation2 = new TranslateAnimation(
            0,0,0,200);
        animation2.setDuration(3000);
        animation2.setStartOffset(3000);
        animation2.setFillAfter(true);
        set.addAnimation(animation2);
        imgView.startAnimation(set);
    }
});
    }
}
```

In the preceding listing, you can see that the four Button controls defined in the layout file
with the IDs alpha_button, rotate_button, scale_button, and translate_button are
accessed and mapped to the Button objects alphaButton, rotateButton, scaleButton, and
translateButton, respectively. ClickListeners are associated with all four Button controls
so that when any Button control is clicked, its onClick() callback method is called. In the
onClick() methods, the objects of respective animation classes are created and applied to the
ImageView control to start and display the animation on the screen.

After running the application, you see four Button controls: Alpha, Rotate, Scale, and
Translate, and an ImageView control displaying ic_launcher.png, which you copied into
the res/drawable folders (see Figure 8.9 [top]). When you click the Alpha button, the alpha
animation will be applied and will make the image fade out from fully opaque to almost transparent in 3 seconds (see Figure 8.9 [middle]). When you click the Rotate button, the rotation

animation will make the image rotate 360 degrees clockwise. The axis of rotation will be the center of the image, and the animation will take 3 seconds to perform (see Figure 8.9 [bottom]).

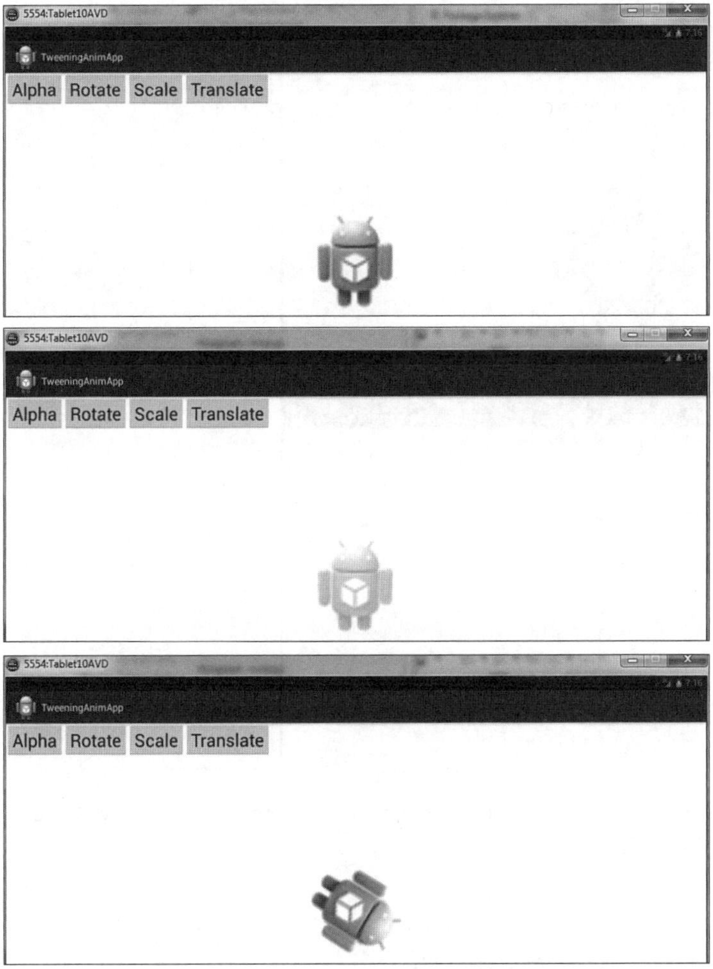

Figure 8.9   The application on startup (top); the image fading out after clicking the Alpha button (middle); the image rotating after clicking the Rotate button (bottom)

When you click the Scale button, the image will be scaled to double its original size both horizontally and vertically. The scaling will be performed from the center of the image with a 3-second duration (see Figure 8.10 [top]). After the image is scaled, it will start shrinking to its original size with a 3-second duration. Once you click the Translate button, the image will move 150 pixels left on the X axis. The movement will be performed with a 3-second duration.

Then it will start moving down by 200 pixels on the Y axis (see Figure 8.10 [bottom]) with a 3-second duration.

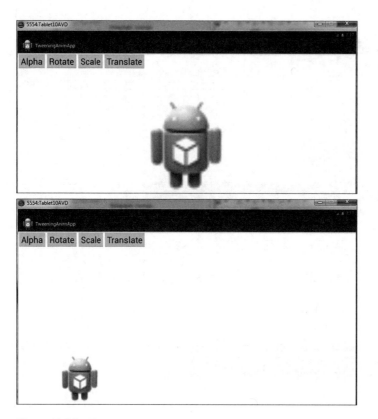

Figure 8.10   The image scaled after clicking the Scale button (top), and the image moved after clicking the Translate button (bottom)

Recipe: Applying Layout Animation

As the name suggests, the layout animation applies animation to the layouts. Basically, the layout animation is applied to each child view in the layout as it is added or removed. The layout animation is not only applicable to all types of layouts but also to any type of AdapterView. In addition to layouts like LinearLayout and RelativeLayout, the layout animation can be applied to ListViews.

To manage layout animation, you can use LayoutAnimationController, which can be defined in Java as well as in XML. Table 8.10 shows the attributes for the LayoutAnimationController.

Table 8.10   **Brief Description of the Attributes for the** `LayoutAnimationController`

Attribute	Description
android:animation	Represents the animation to be applied to each child view in the layout.
android:animationOrder	The order is which the animations are applied to each child. The value to this attribute can be normal, reverse, or random. The normal value means the animation will be applied to the first child followed by others. The reverse value means the animation will be applied to the last child first. The random value means the animation will be applied to any child in any order.
android:delay	Represents the delay between the animation of each child. It can be specified as a percentage of the overall animation duration. For example, 50% means the delay equal to the 50% of the time duration will be inserted between the animation of each child.
android:interpolator	Interpolator used to vary the rate of delay between each child. The default value for this interpolator is a linear interpolator.

> **Note**
>
> With layout animations, you do not need to explicitly start the animation because it automatically starts when the layout is displayed.

To learn how to apply layout animation to a `ListView`, create an Android project called `LayoutAnimApp`. To define a `ListView`, write the code shown in Listing 8.15 into the activity layout file `activity_layout_anim_app.xml`.

Listing 8.15   **Code Written into the Activity Layout File** `activity_layout_anim_app.xml`

```
<LinearLayout
    xmlns:android="http://schemas.android.com/apk/res/android"
    android:orientation="vertical"
    android:layout_width="match_parent"
    android:layout_height="match_parent"  >
    <ListView
        android:id="@+id/listview"
        android:persistentDrawingCache="animation|scrolling"
        android:layout_width="match_parent"
        android:layout_height="wrap_content"
        android:layoutAnimation="@anim/list_layout_controller" />
</LinearLayout>
```

You can see that the `ListView` control is assigned the ID `listview`. The drawing cache is persisted after the layout animation as well as after a scroll.

The default size of the list items displayed in `ListView` is suitable for phones but is quite small for tablets. To resize the list items of the `ListView` as per the device screen size, add one more XML file named `list_item.xml` to the `res/layout` folder. Write the following code in the `list_item.xml` file:

```
<?xml version="1.0" encoding="utf-8"?>
<TextView xmlns:android="http://schemas.android.com/apk/res/android"
    android:layout_width="match_parent"
    android:layout_height="match_parent"
    android:padding="6dp"
    android:textSize="@dimen/text_size"
    android:textStyle="bold" />
```

The preceding code will make the list items of the `ListView` pad by 6dp space, will appear in bold, and will be the size defined in the dimension resource `text_size`.

The layout animation for the `ListView` will be applied from the `list_layout_controller.xml` file that you will create in the `/res/anim` folder.

> **Note**
>
> The `android:layoutAnimation` attribute helps in specifying the layout controller that you want to use to animate the views within the layout.

Create a folder called anim in the `/res` folder. In the `/res/anim` folder, add two XML files called `list_layout_controller.xml` and `slideleft.xml`. In the `list_layout_controller.xml` file, write the code as shown in Listing 8.16.

Listing 8.16   Code Written into the `list_layout_controller.xml` File

```
<layoutAnimation xmlns:android="http://schemas.android.com/apk/res/android"
    android:delay="50%"
   android:animation="@anim/slideleft" />
```

You can see that the animation applied to each child of the `ListView` will be taken from the `slideleft.xml`, which you have just created in the `/res/anim` folder. Also, delay that is equal to 50% of the time duration of the animation will be inserted into the animation of each child of `ListView`. For example, if the duration of an animation is 1 second, then a .5-second time delay will be inserted at the beginning of the animation of each child of the `ListView`.

In the `slideleft.xml`, write the code shown in Listing 8.17.

Listing 8.17   Code Written into the `slideleft.xml` File

```
<set xmlns:android="http://schemas.android.com/apk/res/android"
    android:interpolator="@android:anim/accelerate_interpolator">
    <translate
        android:fromXDelta="100%p"
```

```
        android:toXDelta="0"
        android:duration="10000" />
</set>
```

You can see that the translate animation is applied to each child of the ListView. The child view of the ListView is set to translate from the right border of the screen toward the left. In other words, the child view will begin its translation from 100%p; that is, from the right boundary of the screen towards the 0th pixel on X coordinate, which is to the left boundary of the screen. The 100%p here refers to the pixel location that is equal to the parent width; that is, the right boundary of the screen. The animation duration is set to 1 second. Because the accelerate_interpolator interpolator is used, the animation starts out slowly and then accelerates.

To display content in the ListView, you need to write code as shown in Listing 8.18 in the Java activity file LayoutAnimAppActivity.java.

Listing 8.18   Code Written into the Java Activity File LayoutAnimAppActivity.java

```
package com.androidtablet.layoutanimapp;

import android.os.Bundle;
import android.app.Activity;
import android.widget.ListView;
import android.widget.ArrayAdapter;

public class LayoutAnimAppActivity extends Activity {
    @Override
    public void onCreate(Bundle savedInstanceState) {
        super.onCreate(savedInstanceState);
        setContentView(R.layout.activity_layout_anim_app);
        final String[] products={"Camera", "Laptop", "Watch",
         "Smartphone", "Television"};
        ListView listView = (ListView)findViewById(R.id.listview);
        ArrayAdapter<String> arrayAdpt= new ArrayAdapter<String>
         (getBaseContext(),R.layout.list_item,
         products);
        listView.setAdapter(arrayAdpt);
    }
}
```

You can see that the array products is defined to list the product names that you want to display through ListView. An ArrayAdapter named arrayAdpt is defined to specify the view of each child of the ListView and the array containing the data to be displayed. The ArrayAdapter is set to the ListView to display the list of products.

After running the application, you find that one child view (product) at a time appears from the right boundary of the screen and animates toward the left boundary of the screen (see

Figure 8.11 [top]). The time duration taken by each child to reach from the right boundary to the left boundary of the screen is 1 second. At every .5 second, one more child appears from the right and moves toward the left (see Figure 8.11 [middle]). Figure 8.11 (bottom) shows the `ListView` when all child views are animated toward the left boundary of the screen.

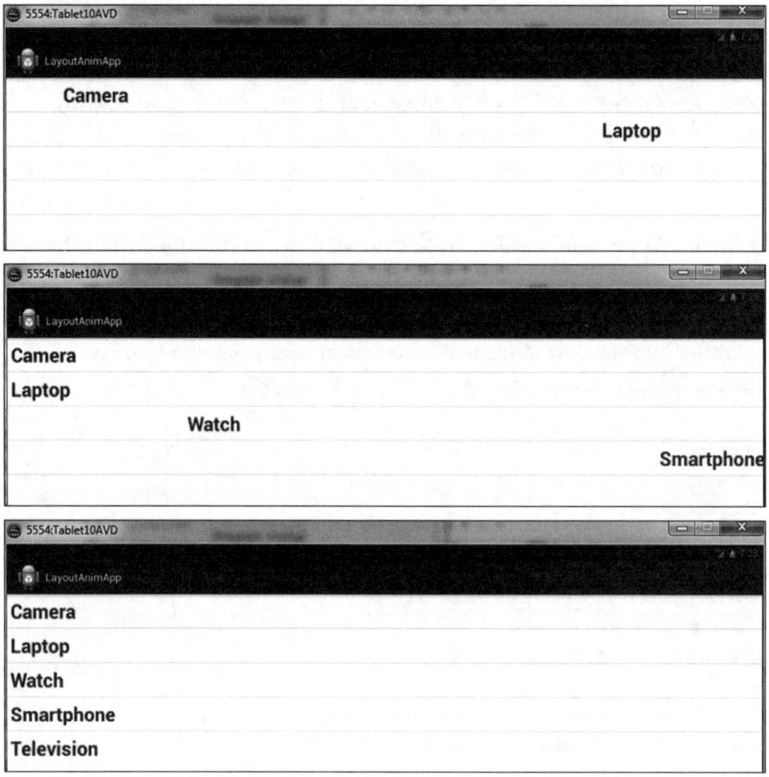

Figure 8.11   Child view appears from the right boundary of the screen and moves toward left (top); after every .5 second, one child view appears from the right (middle); all the child views listed in the `ListView` (bottom)

As mentioned earlier, the `LayoutAnimationController` can be defined in Java, too. The following statements define the `LayoutAnimationController`, load the layout animation defined in the `list_layout_controller.xml` file stored in the `/res/anim` folder, and apply it to the `ListView` object:

```
LayoutAnimationController controller = AnimationUtils.loadLayoutAnimation(this,
R.anim.list_layout_controller);
listView.setLayoutAnimation(controller);
```

Because an interpolator is used in the preceding application, it is good to learn a bit about it.

An interpolator defines the rate of change in an animation. It can affect all four types of tweening animations. Interpolators can make the alpha, scale, translate, and rotate animations accelerate, bounce, follow a specific pattern, and so on. There are different interpolators provided as part of the Android SDK framework. Some of these are described in Table 8.11.

Table 8.11   **Interpolator Types**

Interpolator	Description
`AccelerateDecelerateInterpolator`	Animation starts slowly, speeds up, and ends slowly
`AccelerateInterpolator`	Animation starts out slowly and then accelerates
`AnticipateInterpolator`	Animation starts backward and then goes forward
`AnticipateOvershootInterpolator`	Animation starts backward, goes forward, overshoots its destination, and then returns to the destination value
`BounceInterpolator`	Animation bounces at the end
`CycleInterpolator`	Repeats the animation for a specified number of cycles with smooth transitions
`DecelerateInterpolator`	Animation starts quickly and then decelerates
`LinearInterpolator`	Animation speed remains constant throughout
`OvershootInterpolator`	Animation goes forward, overshoots its destination, and then returns to the destination value

Recipe: Collecting and Sequencing Animations Using `AnimationSet`

To combine animations in a group and to play them together, you use the `AnimationSet` class. Any number of animation subclasses, such as `AlphaAnimation`, `RotateAnimation`, `ScaleAnimation`, and `TranslateAnimation`, can be added to the `AnimationSet` object. When added to the `AnimationSet` object, the transformations of each animation are composed into a single transform.

The set of animation sequences that are added to the `AnimationSet` object can be applied to the desired view through the `startAnimation()` method. The statement that follows applies the animation sequences added in the `AnimationSet` object animSet to the `ImageView` object imgView:

```
imgView.startAnimation(animSet);
```

Now create an application that demonstrates how animations are collected through the `AnimationSet` class. Create a new Android project called `AnimationSetApp`. In this application, you will make an `ImageView` control to scale to double its size. When `ImageView` is scaled to double its size, it is scaled back down to its original size.

To define an `ImageView` control, define the code as shown in Listing 8.19 in the activity layout file `activity_animation_set_app.xml`.

Listing 8.19 Code Written into the Activity Layout File `activity_animation_set_app.xml`

```
<RelativeLayout xmlns:android="http://schemas.android.com/apk/res/android"
    xmlns:tools="http://schemas.android.com/tools"
    android:layout_width="match_parent"
    android:layout_height="match_parent" >
    <ImageView android:id="@+id/imgview"
        android:layout_width="@dimen/image_width"
        android:layout_height="@dimen/image_height"
        android:src="@drawable/ic_launcher"
        android:layout_marginTop="100dip"
        android:layout_marginLeft="100dip" />
</RelativeLayout>
```

You can see that an `ImageView` control is defined and assigned the ID `imgview`. It is set to appear at the distance of 100dp from the top of the screen and at the distance of 100dp from the left border of the screen. The control is initialized to display the `ic_launcher.png` image that is provided by default. The width and height of the image displayed through the `ImageView` control are defined through the dimension resources `image_width` and `image_height`, respectively.

To define the dimension resources, open the dimension file `dimens.xml` in the `res/values` folder, and define the resources to resize the image as per the device's screen on which the application is run. Write the following code in the `dimens.xml` file:

```
<?xml version="1.0" encoding="utf-8"?>
<resources>
    <dimen name="text_size">14sp</dimen>
    <dimen name="image_width">100dp</dimen>
    <dimen name="image_height">120dp</dimen>
</resources>
```

The three dimension resources `text_size`, `image_width`, and `image_height` define the font size of the text and the image width and height. These dimension resources are for normal screen devices (phones).

To define the dimension resources for 7-inch tablets, open the `dimens.xml` file in the `res/values-sw600dp` folder and write the following code in it:

```xml
<?xml version="1.0" encoding="utf-8"?>
<resources>
    <dimen name="text_size">24sp</dimen>
    <dimen name="image_width">140dp</dimen>
    <dimen name="image_height">160dp</dimen>
</resources>
```

Finally, to define dimensions for extra-large screen devices (10-inch tablets), open the `dimens.xml` file in the `values-sw720dp` folder and write the following code in it:

```xml
<?xml version="1.0" encoding="utf-8"?>
<resources>
    <dimen name="text_size">32sp</dimen>
    <dimen name="image_width">180dp</dimen>
    <dimen name="image_height">200dp</dimen>
</resources>
```

By comparing the dimension resources of phones, 7-inch tablets, and 10-inch tablets, you can see that text and images in the application are resized based on the device screen size.

In the Java activity file, you need to write code to perform the following tasks:

- Access the `ImageView` control defined in the layout file and map it to the `ImageView` object.

- Define an `AnimationSet` object.

- Define an object of the `Animation` subclass `ScaleAnimation` to scale the `ImageView` control to double its size in 3 seconds.

- Add the `ScaleAnimation` object to the `AnimationSet` object.

- Define another object of `ScaleAnimation` to scale down the `ImageView` control to half its current size (resize the `ImageView` control back to its original size) in 3 seconds.

- Add the second object of the `ScaleAnimation` object to the `AnimationSet` object after 3 seconds (when the `ImageView` is scaled completely) to double its size.

- Start animations that are added to the `AnimationSet` object on the `ImageView` control.

To perform these tasks, write code as shown in Listing 8.20 into the Java activity file `AnimationSetAppActivity.java`.

Listing 8.20 Code Written into the Java Activity File `AnimationSetAppActivity.java`

```java
package com.androidtablet.animationsetapp;

import android.os.Bundle;
import android.app.Activity;
import android.widget.ImageView;
import android.view.animation.AccelerateInterpolator;
```

```
import android.view.animation.AnimationSet;
import android.view.animation.Animation;
import android.view.animation.ScaleAnimation;
import android.view.animation.TranslateAnimation;

public class AnimationSetAppActivity extends Activity {
    @Override
    public void onCreate(Bundle savedInstanceState) {
        super.onCreate(savedInstanceState);
        setContentView(R.layout.activity_animation_set_app);
        ImageView imgView = (ImageView)findViewById(R.id.imgview);
        AnimationSet animSet = new AnimationSet(true);
        Animation animation1 = new ScaleAnimation(1.0f, 2.0f,
            1.0f, 2.0f,Animation.RELATIVE_TO_SELF, 0.5f,
            Animation.RELATIVE_TO_SELF, 0.5f);
        animation1.setDuration(3000);
        animSet.addAnimation(animation1);
        Animation animation2 = new ScaleAnimation(1.0f, 0.5f,
            1.0f, 0.5f, Animation.RELATIVE_TO_SELF, 0.5f,
            Animation.RELATIVE_TO_SELF, 0.5f);
        animation2.setDuration(3000);
        animation2.setStartOffset(3000);
        animSet.addAnimation(animation2);
        imgView.startAnimation(animSet);
    }
}
```

After you run the application, the `ImageView` control will appear in its original size on startup (see Figure 8.12 [top]). The `ImageView` control will be scaled up to double its original size in 3 seconds (see Figure 8.12 [middle]). Once scaled, the `ImageView` control will begin shrinking to its original size in 3 seconds (see Figure 8.12 [bottom]).

You can collect any number of animations in the `AnimationSet`. For example, if you want the `ImageView` control in the current Android application to bounce like a ball, you can add a number of `TranslateAnimation` objects to the `AnimationSet`. The next set of code shows how a couple of `TranslateAnimation` objects can be added to the `AnimationSet` to make the `ImageView` bounce like a ball:

```
animSet.setInterpolator(new AccelerateInterpolator());
TranslateAnimation slide1 = new TranslateAnimation(0, 100, 0, 200);
slide1.setStartOffset(0);
slide1.setDuration(1000);
animSet.addAnimation(slide1);
TranslateAnimation slide2 = new TranslateAnimation(0, 100, 0, -200);
slide2.setStartOffset(1000);
slide2.setDuration(1000);
animSet.addAnimation(slide2);
```

```
TranslateAnimation slide3 = new TranslateAnimation(0, 100, 0, 200);
slide3.setStartOffset(2000);
slide3.setDuration(1000);
animSet.addAnimation(slide3);
animSet.setFillAfter(true);
imgView.startAnimation(animSet);
```

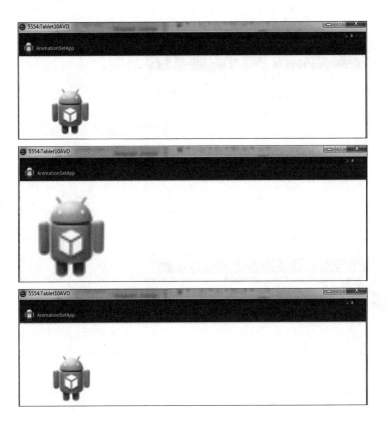

Figure 8.12   `ImageView` control on application startup (top); `ImageView` scaled to double its original size (middle); `ImageView` scaled down to its original size (bottom)

In the preceding code, you see that `AccelerateInterpolator` is applied to the `AnimationSet` object `animSet`. The `AccelerateInterpolator` will make the animation start out slowly and then accelerate. Also, you see that three `TranslateAnimation` objects named `slide1`, `slide2`, and `slide3` are defined. The `TranslateAnimation` object `slide1` will make the `ImageView` move down, the `slide2` object will make the ball go up, and the `slide3` object will make the ball move down. The three `TranslateAnimation` objects `slide1`, `slide2`, and `slide3` are added to the `AnimationSet` object after the specific duration. The duration is so set that subsequent `TranslateAnimation` is applied only when the previous translation is complete (that is, when the `slide1` object finishes translating the `ImageView` to its desired location, the `slide2` object begins its translation). To keep the `ImageView` at the final animated location, Boolean value `true` is passed to the `setFillAfter()` method.

After running the application, you find the `ImageView` control at its original location (see Figure 8.13 [top]). The `ImageView` starts falling down gradually in durations of 1 second (see Figure 8.13 [bottom]).

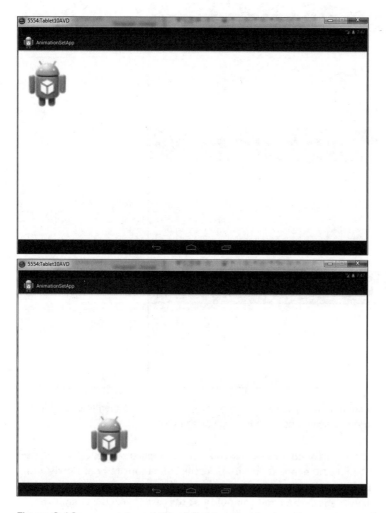

Figure 8.13   `ImageView` at its original location (top), and `ImageView` after it moves down by 200 pixels (bottom)

After reaching down by 200 pixels, the ImageView starts moving up (see Figure 8.14 [top]). When it reaches the top, the ImageView again starts falling down (see Figure 8.14 [bottom]).

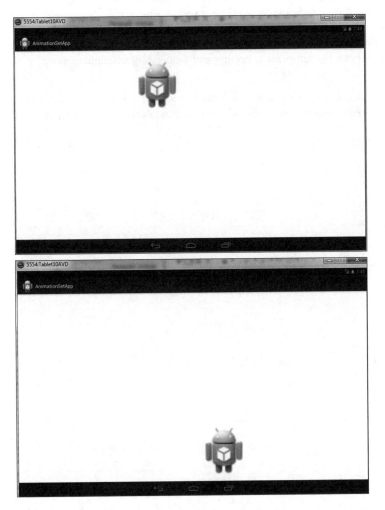

Figure 8.14   ImageView when it moves to the top (top), and ImageView when it again moves down (bottom)

Summary

In this chapter, you learned to use and apply different types of animation in Android applications. You also learned the procedure to implement property animation by using `ValueAnimator` and `ObjectAnimator`. In addition, you learned to use multiple animations using `AnimatorSet`, besides frame-by-frame animation, tweening animation, and layout animation. Finally, you saw the procedure for collecting and sequencing animations using `AnimationSet`.

In the next chapter, you are going to learn about hardware-accelerated 2D. You will also learn about setup and effects. Finally, you will learn about transformations and view layer types.

9

Hardware Accelerated 2D

Graphics, drawings, and animations play an important role in making an application attractive, dynamic, and interesting. But using more graphics and drawings means consuming a lot of resources, which may drastically slow down an application. You can use hardware acceleration to improve the performance of a graphics-based application. In this chapter, you will learn to enable hardware acceleration in applications. You will also learn to apply hardware acceleration to specific views during their animation. That is, you will discover how to apply hardware and software layers to the individual views. In animations and other resource-consuming applications, the graphical user interface (GUI) thread is usually overburdened by performing numerous tasks. You will learn to use `SurfaceView` to utilize a separate thread to perform drawing and updating, which will reduce the workload of the GUI thread. Finally, you will learn to display a video stream through `TextureView` and apply transformations to the content displayed through `TextureView`.

Recipe: Understanding Hardware Acceleration

You use hardware acceleration to improve the performance of the graphics system. During hardware acceleration, the hardware known as GPU (graphics processing unit), found in most of the latest Android devices, is accelerated. Because enabling hardware acceleration consumes more resources and hence more RAM, it is wise to implement it to only the selected parts of the application. Specifically, hardware acceleration can be enabled and disabled at the application, activity, window, and view levels.

To turn on hardware acceleration for the entire application, the first thing you should do is set your application's target API to 11 or higher by including the following statement in the `AndroidManifest.xml` file:

```
<uses-sdk android:targetSdkVersion="11"/>
```

Second, add an `android:hardwareAccelerated="true"` statement to the `<application>` tag in the `AndroidManifest.xml` file, as shown here:

```
<application android:hardwareAccelerated="true">
```

To apply hardware acceleration to individual activities, add the android:hardwareAccelerated attribute to the specified <activity> element, as shown here:

```
<activity android:hardwareAccelerated="true" >
```

To enable hardware acceleration for a given window, you can use the following code:

```
getWindow().setFlags(WindowManager.LayoutParams.FLAG_HARDWARE_ACCELERATED,
WindowManager.LayoutParams.FLAG_HARDWARE_ACCELERATED);
```

To disable hardware acceleration for an individual view at runtime, try using this code:

```
view.setLayerType(View.LAYER_TYPE_SOFTWARE, null);
```

> **Note**
>
> Currently, you can't disable hardware acceleration at a window level, but you can enable it. Also, you can't enable it at a view level, but you can disable it.

You must be wondering how to confirm whether the hardware acceleration is enabled in an application. To know if the hardware acceleration is enabled, you use the isHardwareAccelerated() method on either a view object or its underlying canvas:

- **View.isHardwareAccelerated()**—The method returns true if the view is attached to a hardware-accelerated window.

- **Canvas.isHardwareAccelerated()**—The method returns true if the canvas is hardware accelerated.

> **Note**
>
> In Android 4.0 (API level 14) and higher levels, hardware acceleration is on by default for all applications.

Create an Android project called HardwareAccApp. To enable hardware acceleration by default, set the values of the android:minSdkVersion and android:targetSdkVersion attributes to 14 and 17, respectively. In the Java activity file HardwareAccAppActivity.java, write the code as shown in Listing 9.1.

Listing 9.1   **Code Written into the Java Activity File** HardwareAccAppActivity.java

```
package com.androidtablet.hardwareaccapp;

import android.app.Activity;
import android.os.Bundle;
import android.graphics.Paint;
import android.graphics.Canvas;
import android.view.View;
```

```
import android.content.Context;
import android.graphics.Color;

public class HardwareAccAppActivity extends Activity {
    Paint paint = new Paint();
    @Override
    public void onCreate(Bundle savedInstanceState) {
        super.onCreate(savedInstanceState);
        MyView myView=new MyView(this);
        setContentView(myView);
    }

    public class MyView extends View{
        public MyView(Context context){
            super(context);
        }
        @Override
        protected void onDraw(Canvas canvas) {
            super.onDraw(canvas);
            paint.setColor(Color.RED);
            paint.setTextSize(getResources().getDimension(
              R.dimen.text_size));
            if(canvas.isHardwareAccelerated())
                canvas.drawText("Canvas is Hardware Accelerated",
                10, 75, paint);
            else
                canvas.drawText("Canvas is not Hardware Accelerated",
                10, 75, paint);
        }
    }
}
```

In the application, you see that the color of the Paint object is set to red and the size of the text that is displayed is determined by the dimension resource text_size. The canvas. isHardwareAccelerated() method is invoked to find out if the hardware is accelerated or not. Accordingly, a text message is drawn on the canvas. Because the API level of your application is set to value 14, the hardware is automatically accelerated. On running the application, you get the output as shown in Figure 9.1 (top).

If you change the values of the android:minSdkVersion and android:targetSdkVersion attributes to 11, the hardware will no longer be accelerated by default. Hence, the output of the application will change, displaying the message Canvas is not Hardware Accelerated (see Figure 9.1 [bottom]). If you add the android:hardwareAccelerated="true" statement to the <application> element in the AndroidManifest.xml file, the hardware will be accelerated at the application level. The output of the application will again change to Canvas is Hardware Accelerated, confirming that the hardware is accelerated. The <application> element in the `AndroidManifest.xml` file after adding the `android:hardwareAccelerated` attribute will appear as shown here:

```
<application
    android:allowBackup="true"
    android:icon="@drawable/ic_launcher"
    android:label="@string/app_name"
    android:theme="@style/AppTheme"
    android:hardwareAccelerated="true" >
```

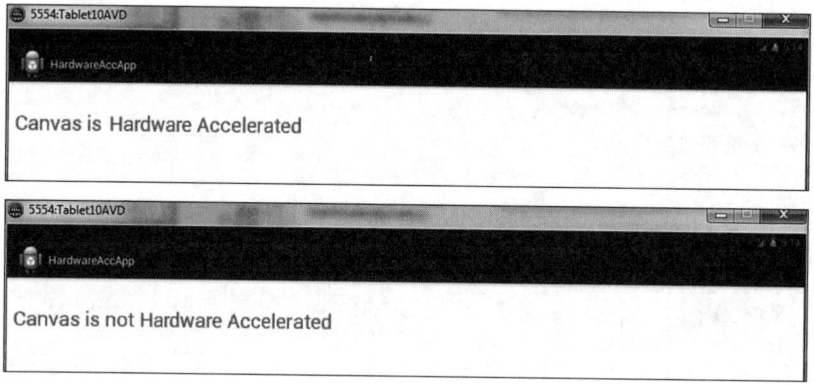

Figure 9.1   Message confirming the hardware is accelerated (top), and message informing the hardware could not be accelerated (bottom)

Recipe: Using View Layers

To improve application performance, a view can use one of the following three layer types:

- **LAYER_TYPE_NONE**—The view is rendered normally. In other words, it does not have a layer. This is the default.

- **LAYER_TYPE_HARDWARE**—If the application is hardware accelerated, this layer will render the view into a hardware texture. The layer is used to make animations smoother and increase the performance of drawing-based applications. The animation becomes smoother by the application of this layer because during animation, the view is not constantly redrawn but is redrawn only when either its properties change or the `invalidate()` method is called. Because hardware layers consume video memory, they are applied only for the duration of the animation and then removed. If the application is not hardware accelerated, this layer will act as LAYER_TYPE_SOFTWARE.

- **LAYER_TYPE_SOFTWARE**—The view in this layer is rendered in software. To disable hardware acceleration for a view, this layer is applied; consequently, the view is rendered in software.

You use the `setLayerType()` method to determine the type and time to apply layers to the views. The method takes two parameters: the type of layer and an optional `Paint` object. You can use the `Paint` object to apply color and other effects to the layer. You can change several properties of the layer, including the ones that are listed here:

- **alpha**—Affects the opacity (visibility) of the layer.

- **x, y, translationX, translationY**—Affects the position of the layer

- **scaleX, scaleY**—Scales the layer horizontally and vertically

- **rotation, rotationX, rotation**—Rotates the layer

- **pivotX, pivotY**—Changes the origin of the transformation

> **Note**
>
> The layers improve the performance of the application because they avoid redrawing of the views until the `invalidate()` method is called.

To better understand how layers are applied to the views, create a new application called `ViewLayerApp`. Set the value of the `android:minSdkVersion` attribute to value 14, because an application of different transformations on layers requires API level 14 or higher. Also, set the value of `android:targetSdkVersion` to value 17 to indicate that the application is designed to run on API level 17. The `AndroidManifest.xml` file will display the following statement to declare minimum and target SDK versions of the application:

```
<uses-sdk
    android:minSdkVersion="14"
    android:targetSdkVersion="17" />
```

In this application, you will display a `TextView` that, when clicked, will invoke an `ObjectAnimator` that affects the `ALPHA` property of the view. `LAYER_TYPE_HARDWARE` will be applied to the `TextView` during the animation. The layer will be removed from the `TextView` when animation is complete. Because you want to apply layers to the `TextView` control, the control is defined in the activity layout file `activity_view_layer_app.xml`, through the code shown in Listing 9.2.

Listing 9.2   Code Written into the Activity Layout File `activity_view_layer_app.xml`

```
<LinearLayout xmlns:android="http://schemas.android.com/apk/res/android"
    android:layout_width="match_parent"
    android:layout_height="match_parent"
    android:orientation="vertical" >
    <TextView
        android:layout_width="match_parent"
        android:layout_height="wrap_content"
        android:gravity="center"
        android:text="View Layers Demo"
```

```
            android:id="@+id/textview"
          android:textSize="@dimen/text_size"
          android:textStyle="bold"
            android:layout_marginTop="100dp"/>
</LinearLayout>
```

You can see that the `TextView` control is initialized to display the text `View Layers Demo`. The text is displayed in bold and in a font size defined in the dimension resource `text_size`. The text message will appear at the horizontal center of the width of the screen. To identify and access the `TextView` control in Java code, the ID `textview` is assigned to it.

Next, you need to write Java code to perform the following tasks:

- Access the `TextView` control defined in the layout file and map it to the `TextView` object.

- Associate `setOnClickListener` to the `TextView` to listen for the occurrence of click events on it.

- Apply `LAYER_TYPE_HARDWARE` to the `TextView` in the `onClick` callback method.

- Define and invoke an `ObjectAnimator` to apply the `ALPHA` operation on the `TextView`. The `ALPHA` operation controls the visibility of the `TextView` (that is, it will make it fade in and fade out).

- Set the `TextView`'s layer to `LAYER_TYPE_NONE` when animation completes to remove the layer and release the resources.

To accomplish all these tasks, write the code as shown in Listing 9.3 into the Java activity file `ViewLayerAppActivity.java`.

Listing 9.3   Code Written into the Java Activity File `ViewLayerAppActivity.java`

```
package com.androidtablet.viewlayerapp;

import android.os.Bundle;
import android.app.Activity;
import android.view.View.OnClickListener;
import android.widget.TextView;
import android.view.View;
import android.animation.Animator;
import android.animation.AnimatorListenerAdapter;
import android.animation.ObjectAnimator;

public class ViewLayerAppActivity extends Activity {
    @Override
    public void onCreate(Bundle savedInstanceState) {
        super.onCreate(savedInstanceState);
        setContentView(R.layout.activity_view_layer_app);
        final TextView textView = (TextView)this.findViewById(
```

```
            R.id.textview);
    textView.setOnClickListener(new OnClickListener() {
        public void onClick(View v) {
            textView.setLayerType(View.LAYER_TYPE_HARDWARE,
                null);
            ObjectAnimator animator =ObjectAnimator.ofFloat(
                textView, View.ALPHA, 0, 1);
            animator.addListener(new
                AnimatorListenerAdapter() {
                @Override
                public void onAnimationEnd(Animator
                    animation) {
                    textView.setLayerType(View.LAYER_TYPE
                        _NONE, null);
                }
            });
        animator.setDuration(2000);
            animator.start();
        }
    });
    }
}
```

When running the application, you get the TextView control displaying the text View Layers Demo (see Figure 9.2 [top]). After you click the TextView control, the hardware layer will be applied on it followed by the ALPHA transformation. That is, the TextView control will fade out (see Figure 9.2 [bottom] and then fade in. The transformation will take place in 2000 milliseconds.

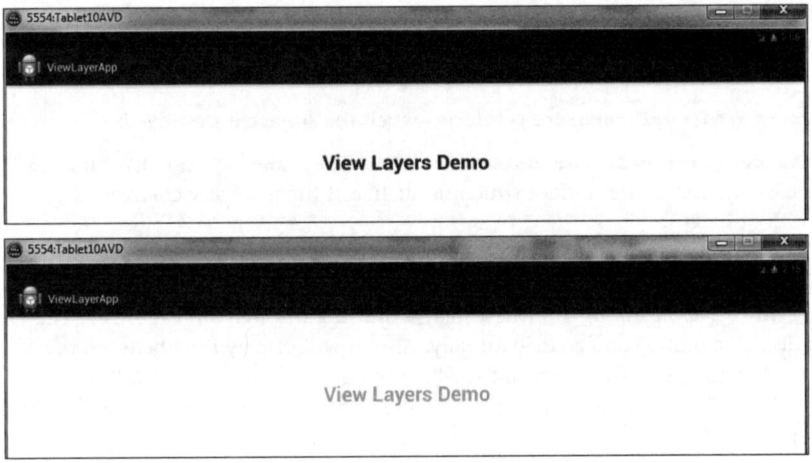

Figure 9.2   After clicking the TextView ALPHA operation applied on it (top); TextView fades out on application of ALPHA transformation (bottom)

Recipe: Improving Graphics-Based Application Performance Using `SurfaceView`

In an Android application, the GUI thread is responsible not only for drawing all application views (rendering of the views), but for dealing with user interaction. The efficiency of an application reduces if the GUI thread is compelled to rapidly update view(s). In gaming applications, 3D graphics applications, or applications where rapid updating of view or other resource-intensive operations are performed, the GUI thread is overwhelmed with several tasks, drastically reducing the efficiency of the application. To overcome this problem in such applications, you can use the `SurfaceView` class.

`SurfaceView` has a dedicated drawing surface within the view hierarchy. It draws and updates views using the background threads, so it relieves the GUI thread to do other application tasks. `SurfaceView` controls the format of the surface, its size, and its location on the screen.

> **Note**
>
> The `SurfaceView` creates a surface on which any thread other than the GUI thread can draw. The idea is to improve an application's performance by performing drawing tasks in a separate thread.

To use `SurfaceView`, you need to create a class that extends the `SurfaceView` class and implements `SurfaceHolder.Callback`. The `SurfaceHolder` callback notifies the view when the underlying surface is created, destroyed, or modified. It is the `SurfaceHolder` that provides the surface to work on. The `SurfaceHolder` is retrieved by calling the `SurfaceView.getHolder()` method.

The following three methods are implemented in the class that implements `SurfaceHolder.Callback`:

- `surfaceCreated(SurfaceHolder)`—Informs when the surface is created and is available for drawing.

- `surfaceDestroyed(SurfaceHolder)`—Informs when the surface is destroyed.

- `surfaceChanged(SurfaceHolder holder, int format, int w, int h)`—Informs when there is a change in the surface structure, such as if there are any changes in surface width or height.

Learn to use `SurfaceView` through a running application. Create a new Android project called `SurfaceViewApp`. In this application, you will display a drawing through `SurfaceView`. The application will display a bitmap and a circle initially. Also, it will display lines between the two points specified by the user. The first point is where the user presses the mouse button, and the second point is where the user releases the mouse button. Any number of lines can be drawn in this application.

The dimension resources will determine the width and height of the bitmap that will be drawn in the application. The dimension resources will help in resizing the bitmap based on the device screen on which the application is run. Therefore, to make your application compatible for phones, 7-inch tablets, and 10-inch tablets, you will define the dimension resources named `image_width` and `image_height`, respectively.

Assuming the dimension file `dimens.xml` already exists in the `res/values` folder, add the dimensions to resize the images to suit the phone's screen size. Write the following code in the `dimens.xml` file:

```xml
<?xml version="1.0" encoding="utf-8"?>
<resources>
    <dimen name="text_size">14sp</dimen>
    <dimen name="image_width">100dp</dimen>
    <dimen name="image_height">120dp</dimen>
</resources>
```

The three dimension resources `text_size`, `image_width`, and `image_height` define the font size of the text and the width and height of the image. These dimension resources are for normal screen devices (phones).

To define the dimension resources for 7-inch tablets, open the `dimens.xml` file in the `res/values-sw600dp` folder and write the following code in it:

```xml
<?xml version="1.0" encoding="utf-8"?>
<resources>
    <dimen name="text_size">24sp</dimen>
    <dimen name="image_width">140dp</dimen>
    <dimen name="image_height">160dp</dimen>
</resources>
```

Finally, to define the dimensions for extra-large screen devices (that is, for 10-inch tablets), open the `dimens.xml` file in the `values-sw720dp` folder and write the following code in it:

```xml
<?xml version="1.0" encoding="utf-8"?>
<resources>
    <dimen name="text_size">32sp</dimen>
    <dimen name="image_width">180dp</dimen>
    <dimen name="image_height">200dp</dimen>
</resources>
```

By comparing the dimension resources of phones, 7-inch tablets, and 10-inch tablets, you can see that text and images in the application are resized based on the device screen size. After defining the dimension resources, you can write Java code.

In the Java activity file `SurfaceViewAppActivity.java`, write the code shown in Listing 9.4.

Listing 9.4   **Code Written into the Java Activity File** `SurfaceViewAppActivity.java`

```java
package com.androidtablet.surfaceviewapp;

import android.app.Activity;
import android.content.Context;
import android.graphics.Canvas;
import android.graphics.Paint;
import android.os.Bundle;
import android.view.SurfaceHolder;
import android.view.SurfaceView;
import android.graphics.Color;
import android.graphics.BitmapFactory;
import android.graphics.Bitmap;
import android.view.MotionEvent;
import android.graphics.Point;
import android.util.DisplayMetrics;

public class SurfaceViewAppActivity extends Activity {
    MySurfaceView mySurfaceView;

    @Override
    public void onCreate(Bundle savedInstanceState) {
        super.onCreate(savedInstanceState);
        mySurfaceView = new MySurfaceView(this);
        setContentView(mySurfaceView);
    }

    @Override
        protected void onResume() {
        super.onResume();
        mySurfaceView.onResumeMySurfaceView();
    }

    @Override
        protected void onPause() {
        super.onPause();
        mySurfaceView.onPauseMySurfaceView();
    }

    class MySurfaceView extends SurfaceView implements
        SurfaceHolder.Callback {
        private SurfaceHolder holder;
        private MySurfaceViewThread mySurfaceViewThread;
        private boolean hasSurface;
        private Paint paint = new Paint(Paint.ANTI_ALIAS_FLAG);
        private Bitmap bitmap ;
        Point pt1 = new Point();
```

```java
Point pt2 = new Point();
private boolean drawing;

public MySurfaceView(Context context) {
    super(context);
    bitmap = BitmapFactory.decodeResource(context.
        getResources(), R.drawable.ic_launcher);
    holder = getHolder();                      #1
    holder.addCallback(this);                  #2
    hasSurface = false;
}
public void onResumeMySurfaceView(){
    if (mySurfaceViewThread == null) {       #3
        mySurfaceViewThread = new MySurfaceViewThread();
        if (hasSurface == true)
            mySurfaceViewThread.start();     #4
    }
}
public void onPauseMySurfaceView(){
    boolean retry = true;
    while(retry){
        try {
            mySurfaceViewThread.join();      #5
            retry = false;
        } catch (InterruptedException e) {
            e.printStackTrace();
        }
    }
}
public void surfaceCreated(SurfaceHolder holder) {  #6
    hasSurface = true;
    if (mySurfaceViewThread != null)
        mySurfaceViewThread.start();
}
public void surfaceDestroyed(SurfaceHolder holder) {  #7
    hasSurface = false;
    onPauseMySurfaceView();
}
public void surfaceChanged(SurfaceHolder holder, int
    format, int w, int h) {                             #8
    if (mySurfaceViewThread != null)
        mySurfaceViewThread.onWindowResize(w, h);
}
        @Override
public boolean onTouchEvent(MotionEvent event) {
    if (event.getAction() == MotionEvent.ACTION_DOWN) #9
    {
```

```java
            pt1.x = (int) event.getX();
            pt1.y = (int) event.getY();
            drawing = false;
        }
        else if (event.getAction() == MotionEvent.
            ACTION_UP) {                              #10
            pt2.x = (int) event.getX();
            pt2.y = (int) event.getY();
            drawing = true;
        }
        return true;
    }
    @Override
    public void onDraw(Canvas canvas) {      #11
        paint.setStrokeWidth(5);
        paint.setColor(Color.RED);
        int imageWidth=(int) getResources().getDimension(
            R.dimen.image_width);
        int imageHeight=(int)getResources().getDimension(
            R.dimen.image_height);
        canvas.drawBitmap(Bitmap.createScaledBitmap(
            bitmap, imageWidth, imageHeight, true), 50, 50, null);
        DisplayMetrics dm = new DisplayMetrics();
        getWindowManager().getDefaultDisplay().getMetrics(dm);
        int width = dm.widthPixels;
        int height = dm.heightPixels;
        float centerX = width / 2;
        float centerY = height / 2;
        canvas.drawCircle(centerX,centerY,70,paint);
        if (drawing){
            canvas.drawLine(pt1.x, pt1.y, pt2.x, pt2.y,
                paint);                              #12
        }
    }
}

class MySurfaceViewThread extends Thread {      #13
    private boolean done;

    MySurfaceViewThread() {
        super();
        done = false;
    }

    @Override
    public void run() {                              #14
        SurfaceHolder surfaceHolder = holder;
        while (!done) {
```

```
                Canvas canvas = surfaceHolder.lockCanvas(); #15
                    onDraw(canvas);                         #16
                    if(canvas !=null)
                  surfaceHolder.unlockCanvasAndPost(canvas); #17
                }
            }

            public void requestExitAndWait() {
                done = true;
                try {
                    join();
                } catch (InterruptedException ex) { }
            }
            public void onWindowResize(int w, int h) { }
        }
    }
}
```

In the preceding application, you invoke the `SurfaceView` by instantiating the custom class `MySurfaceView` in the activity's `onCreate()` method. From the activity's `onResume()` and `onPause()` methods, the `onResumeMySurfaceView()` and `onPauseMySurfaceView()` methods of the `MySurfaceView` class are called to resume and pause the drawing operations performed on the surface, respectively. In the `MySurfaceView` class, the `SurfaceHolder` is retrieved by calling the `SurfaceView.getHolder` method (#1). The `addCallback(this)` method (#2) is called to inform the `SurfaceHolder` to use this activity as the callback handler. Statement #3 checks whether the custom thread exists. If it does not, it is instantiated. Statement #4 checks whether the surface exists. If the surface exists, the thread is started. Statement #5 in the `onPauseMySurfaceView()` method pauses the custom thread's execution.

Statement #6 defines the `surfaceCreated` method that informs when the surface is created. Eventually, the method starts the thread to initiate drawing or updating the surface. Statement #7 defines the `surfaceDestroyed` method that informs the destroying of the surface. The method sets the Boolean value of the `hasSurface` variable to `false` to indicate that surface exists no more. The method invokes the `onPauseSurfaceView()` method to pause the thread's execution. Statement #8 defines the `surfaceChanged(SurfaceHolder holder, int format, int w, int h)` method that informs whether there is a change in the structure of the surface. For example, if there is a change in the width or the height of the surface or the device orientation takes place, the method invokes the `onWindowResize` method of the custom thread.

Statement #9 checks whether the user clicks the mouse button. The X and Y coordinates where the user presses the mouse button are saved into `Point` `pt1`. Statement #10 checks whether the user releases the mouse button. The X and Y coordinates where the mouse button is released are saved into `Point` `pt2`. Also, the value of the Boolean variable `drawing` is set to `true` so that a line between the `Points` `pt1` and `pt2` can be drawn through the `onDraw()` method (#11).

In the `onDraw` method, the color and stroke width of the `Paint` object are set to `red` and `5` pixels, respectively. A circle and a bitmap are also drawn. The width and height of the bitmap are accessed from the dimension resources `image_width` and `image_height`, respectively. Also, the center coordinates of the screen are computed, and the circle is drawn at the center of the screen. As mentioned earlier, `SurfaceView` provides a surface on which a background thread can update and draw views. Statement #13 defines a class that extends the `Thread` class, fetches a reference to the current `SurfaceHolder`, and performs the drawing and update operations independently. Statement #14 defines the thread's `run()` method. In the running thread, the `SurfaceHolder` calls the `lockCanvas()` method (#15) that returns a canvas to draw on. The returned canvas is passed to the `onDraw()` method to draw or update the drawing on the surface. Following the `onDraw()` method, the `SurfaceHolder` calls the `unlockCanvasAndPost()` method (#17) that releases the canvas and makes the drawing visible.

After running the application, you see a bitmap and circle drawn on the screen. When a user clicks on the screen, drags the mouse pointer, and releases the mouse button, a line will be drawn between the clicked and the released locations. Figure 9.3 shows the screen after drawing a couple of lines

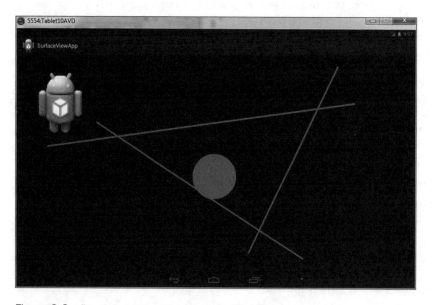

Figure 9.3   Drawing using a separate thread through `SurfaceView`

Recipe: Applying Transformations Using `TextureView`

A `TextureView` is the same as a `SurfaceView` but is preferred over `SurfaceView` because of certain drawbacks associated with the `SurfaceView`. The `SurfaceView` class improves application performance by drawing and updating tasks through a separate thread, but it creates a separate window and does not act as a normal view. As a result, it cannot be transformed. In other words, the SurfaceView cannot be moved, scaled, or rotated. Also, no alpha transformations (fade out and fade in operations) can be applied on the SurfaceView. TextureView, on the other hand, behaves as a regular view and supports normal view operations (that is, TextureView can be moved, transformed, animated, and more). TextureView requires hardware acceleration and SurfaceTexture. The TextureView can be used only in a hardware-accelerated window, or it will draw nothing. A TextureView can display and transform a content stream such as a video camera preview.

To use a TextureView, you need to get its SurfaceTexture that is then used to display content. A TextureView's SurfaceTexture can be obtained either by invoking getSurfaceTexture() or by using a TextureView.SurfaceTextureListener.

To better understand the concept of TextureView, create a new Android project called TextureViewApp. Because you want the hardware to be accelerated by default, while creating the application, set the values of the android:minSdkVersion and android:targetSdkVersion attributes to 14 and 17, respectively. Recall that in Android 4.0 (API level 14) and higher levels, hardware acceleration is on by default for all applications. In this application, you will use a TextureView to display the video preview from the default camera. The TextureView will be rotated to 180 degrees and will be scaled horizontally to 1.5 times its original size. In the Java activity file TextureViewAppActivity.java, write the code as shown in Listing 9.5.

Listing 9.5   Code Written into the Java Activity File TextureViewAppActivity.java

```
package com.androidtablet.textureviewapp;

import android.os.Bundle;
import android.app.Activity;
import android.hardware.Camera;
import android.view.TextureView;
import android.graphics.SurfaceTexture;
import android.widget.FrameLayout;
import java.io.IOException;
import android.view.Gravity;

public class TextureViewAppActivity extends Activity implements TextureView.
SurfaceTextureListener  {
    private Camera camera;
    private TextureView textureView;

    @Override
    public void onCreate(Bundle savedInstanceState) {
        super.onCreate(savedInstanceState);
        textureView = new TextureView(this);
        textureView.setSurfaceTextureListener(this);
        setContentView(textureView);
    }
```

```
@Override
public void onSurfaceTextureAvailable(SurfaceTexture
    surface, int width, int height) {
    camera = Camera.open();                      #1
    Camera.Size previewSize = camera.getParameters().
        getPreviewSize();                        #2
    textureView.setLayoutParams(new FrameLayout.
        LayoutParams(previewSize.width, previewSize.height,
        Gravity.CENTER));                        #3
    try {
        camera.setPreviewTexture(surface);    #4
    } catch (IOException t) { }
    camera.startPreview();                       #5
    textureView.setScaleX(1.5f);
    textureView.setRotation(180.0f);
}

@Override
public void onSurfaceTextureSizeChanged(SurfaceTexture
    surface, int width, int height) { }

@Override
public boolean onSurfaceTextureDestroyed(SurfaceTexture
    surface) {
    camera.stopPreview();
    camera.release();
    return true;
}

@Override
public void onSurfaceTextureUpdated(SurfaceTexture surface){}
}
```

Because the application is supposed to render the camera preview into a `TextureView`, objects of both `Camera` and `TextureView` are created. To listen for the events, the `setSurface-TextureListener` is associated to the `TextureView` object. To get `SurfaceTexture`, the activity implements `TextureView.SurfaceTextureListener` and hence defines the following four methods:

- **onSurfaceTextureAvailable**—The method is called when `TextureView`'s `SurfaceTexture` is ready for drawing or other operations. In this method, the `Camera` object is defined (#1) to access the back-facing camera on the device. Thereafter, the dimensions setting for preview pictures is fetched (#2), and the layout of the `TextureView` is defined as per the width and height of the retrieved dimensions (#3). Thereafter, the `SurfaceTexture` is set to be used for live preview (#4) for taking pictures. The preview images will be sent to the `SurfaceTexture`. Then the procedure of capturing images through the camera and drawing preview frames on the screen begins (#5). The `TextureView` is scaled horizontally to 1.5 times its original size and is rotated to 180 degrees.

- **onSurfaceTextureSizeChanged**—The method is called when `TextView`'s `SurfaceTexture` changes (that is, when the width or height of the `SurfaceTexture` changes).

- **onSurfaceTextureDestroyed**—The method is called when the `SurfaceTexture` is supposed to be destroyed. In this method, the procedure of capturing images is stopped and the resources allocated are released. The method returns `true` to indicate that no rendering should occur in the `SurfaceTexture` after this method.

- **onSurfaceTextureUpdated**—The method is called when the specified `SurfaceTexture` is updated.

In this application, you need permission to access the camera and declare camera features that the application uses. So in the `AndroidManifest.xml` file, you need to include the `<uses-feature>` manifest element, as shown in the following statements:

```
<uses-permission android:name="android.permission.CAMERA" />
<uses-feature android:name="android.hardware.camera"  />
```

After you run the application, the camera preview will be rendered into a `TextureView`. The display will appear rotated to 180 degrees and be scaled horizontally to 1.5 times its original size, as shown in Figure 9.4.

Figure 9.4   Camera preview rotated to 180 degrees and horizontally scaled to 1.5 times its original size

Summary

In this chapter, you learned to improve the performance of graphics-based Android applications by enabling hardware acceleration at the application and activity level. You also learned to improve the animation applied on views by applying the desired hardware and software layers on them. In addition, you saw how to improve application performance by using a separate thread to perform graphics and update tasks through `SurfaceView`. Finally, you used `TextureView` to display video streams and apply transformation on the content displayed through `TextureView`.

In the next chapter, you will learn to use OpenGL ES to create 2D and 3D graphics. You will see the APIs that are required to create and render graphics in Android applications. In addition, you will learn to apply flat and smooth color to the graphics. Finally, you will learn to apply transformations such as rotating, scaling, and translating graphics.

Creating and Rendering Graphics

Creating and rendering graphics plays a major role in applications that revolve around games, entertainment, education, medicine, and other major sectors. To develop graphics-based applications, Android provides the OpenGL ES implementation. The OpenGL ES is a graphics application programming interface (API) for embedded systems. This chapter is focused on understanding the usage of OpenGL ES in creating 2D and 3D graphics. You will come to understand the APIs that are required in creating and rendering graphics in Android applications. Thereafter, you will create and render graphics through step-by-step procedures. You will also learn to apply flat color and smooth color to the drawn graphics. Also, you will learn to apply transformation (rotating, scaling, and translating) to the displayed graphics.

Recipe: Understanding the APIs Required for Graphics

For handling graphics optimally, Android devices use a dedicated GPU (graphics processing unit). GPU relieves the CPU to perform other computing-related tasks. For rendering 2D and 3D graphics on the GPU, a powerful cross-platform graphics API is used known as OpenGL. The Open Graphics Library (OpenGL) that Android provides is called OpenGL ES API, where ES stands for embedded systems.

OpenGL ES is the OpenGL specification meant for embedded devices. To display graphics, you need a surface and a renderer. Therefore, to create and manipulate graphics with the OpenGL ES API, you use the following two classes:

- **GLSurfaceView**—This class is a view container for drawing graphics using OpenGL API calls. More specifically, GLSurfaceView provides a drawing surface to render 2D and 3D graphics. It also provides a location to display the graphics. To use the GLSurfaceView class, you create its instance and add a renderer to it.

- **GLSurfaceView.Renderer**—This class controls the graphics drawn in an OpenGL GLSurfaceView. It is an interface that defines the methods to determine what and how to draw on a `GLSurfaceView`. To maintain rendering performance, you render using a dedicated thread other than the GUI thread. The class that implements `GLSurfaceView.Renderer` interface must implement the following methods:

- **onSurfaceCreated(GL10 gl, EGLConfig config)**—This method is called when `GLSurfaceView` is created or re-created. Whenever the device awakes from the sleep mode, the `GLSurfaceView` is re-created. This method can set up OpenGL ES environment parameters or initialize OpenGL graphic objects.

- **onDrawFrame(GL10 gl)**—This method does all the drawing jobs. It draws the current frame and is called on each redraw of the `GLSurfaceView`. Actually, the renderer continuously draws frames. That is, this method is called repeatedly, enabling you to perform any animations you want in this method. Although in the output, the graphics may appear still, internally, the frames are constantly being drawn.

- **onSurfaceChanged(GL10 gl, int width, int height)**—This method is called when the `GLSurfaceView` geometry changes in size of the `GLSurfaceView` or orientation of the device screen. The method carries the code that impacts your viewport.

> **Note**
>
> Android 1.0 supports the OpenGL ES 1.0 and 1.1 API specifications. Android 2.2 (API Level 8) or higher supports the OpenGL ES 2.0 API specification. So, while using OpenGL ES 2.0, ensure that the Android project targets that API or higher.

Recipe: Creating and Rendering a Rectangle Using OpenGL

To understand how a graphic is created and rendered using OpenGL API, create an Android project called `OpenGLApp`. In this application, you will render a rectangle in blue over a black background. In the Java activity file `OpenGLAppActivity.java`, write the code shown in Listing 10.1.

Listing 10.1   Code Written into the Java Activity File `OpenGLAppActivity.java`

```java
package com.androidtablet.openglapp;

import android.os.Bundle;
import android.app.Activity;
import android.opengl.GLSurfaceView;
import android.opengl.GLES20;
import javax.microedition.khronos.opengles.GL10;
import javax.microedition.khronos.egl.EGLConfig;
```

```java
import java.nio.FloatBuffer;
import java.nio.ByteBuffer;
import java.nio.ByteOrder;

public class OpenGLAppActivity extends Activity {
    private GLSurfaceView myGLView;

    public void onCreate(Bundle savedInstanceState) {
        super.onCreate(savedInstanceState);
        myGLView = new GLSurfaceView(this);                  #1
        MyGLSurfRenderer renderer=new MyGLSurfRenderer();    #2
        myGLView.setRenderer(renderer);                      #3
        setContentView(myGLView);                            #4
    }

    @Override
    protected void onPause() {
        super.onPause();
        myGLView.onPause();                                  #5
    }

    @Override
    protected void onResume() {
        super.onResume();
        myGLView.onResume();                                 #6
    }

    public class MyGLSurfRenderer implements
        GLSurfaceView.Renderer {                             #7
        private FloatBuffer boxBuffer;

        public void onSurfaceCreated(GL10 gl, EGLConfig
            config)  {                                       #8
            gl.glClearColor(0.0f, 0.0f, 0.0f, 1.0f);         #9
            defineGraphic();                                 #10
            gl.glEnableClientState(
                GL10.GL_VERTEX_ARRAY);                       #11
            gl.glVertexPointer(3, GL10.GL_FLOAT, 0,
                boxBuffer);                                  #12
        }

        public void onDrawFrame(GL10 gl) {                   #13
            gl.glClear(GLES20.GL_COLOR_BUFFER_BIT);          #14
            gl.glColor4f(0.0f, 0.0f, 1.0f, 1.0f);            #15
            gl.glDrawArrays(GL10.GL_TRIANGLE_STRIP,
                0, 4);                                       #16
```

```
        }

        public void onSurfaceChanged(GL10 gl, int width, int
            height) {                                    #17
            gl.glViewport(0, 0, width, height);          #18
        }

        private void defineGraphic(){
            float vertices[] = {                         #19
                -0.5f, -0.5f,  0.0f,
                 0.5f, -0.5f,  0.0f,
                -0.5f,  0.5f,  0.0f,
                 0.5f,  0.5f,  0.0f
            };
            ByteBuffer byteBuffer = ByteBuffer.
                allocateDirect(vertices.length * 4);     #20
            byteBuffer.order(ByteOrder.nativeOrder());
            boxBuffer = byteBuffer.asFloatBuffer();      #21
            boxBuffer.put(vertices);                     #22
            boxBuffer.position(0);                       #23
        }
    }
}
```

Statement #1 defines an instance named myGLView of the GLSurfaceView class and initializes the instance with a context (that is, with your activity). Statement #2 defines an object called renderer of the custom class MyGLSurfRenderer. Statement #3 informs the GLSurfaceView that the class MyGLSurfRenderer will perform the rendering. The application pauses rendering when the activity is paused (#5) and resumes it when the activity is continued (#6). The custom class MyGLSurfRenderer implements the GLSurfaceView.Renderer interface (#7) and therefore implements the following three methods:

- The onSurfaceCreated() method (#8) is called at the start of rendering and whenever the OpenGL ES drawing context is re-created (that is, when the activity is paused and resumed).

- The glClearColor() method is called to specify the red, green, blue, and alpha values that the glClear() method is to use to clear the color buffers. The values have to be supplied between 0 and 1. Statement #9 sets the black color for the color buffers. The defineGraphic() method is called (#10) to specify the shape of the graphics that you want to display. The vertex coordinates of the rectangle that you want to draw and its buffer information are supplied in the defineGraphic() method. Statement #11 enables the client-side capability. It enables the vertex array so that it can be used while rendering. Using the glVertexPointer() method in #12, the buffer that carries the vertex coordinates is specified. Through the method, you specify that there are three coordinates per vertex. Each vertex is of the GL_FLOAT data type, all vertices are arranged without a byte offset between consecutive vertices, and the first coordinate of the first vertex is available in the buffer named boxBuffer. Basically, the boxBuffer will be used for the vertex array that you enabled in statement #11.

- The onDrawFame method is called (#13) to redraw the frame. Statement #14 clears the buffers to the values determined by the glClearColor() method. That is, the glClear() method clears the buffer to show the color (black color) defined through the glClearColor() method. Using the glColor4f() method in statement #15, the current color (foreground color) is set to blue.

Using the glDrawArrays() method in statement #16, the graphics are rendered from the enabled arrays. The graphics are drawn using a sequence of primitives. The first parameter in glDrawArrays() indicates what to draw. Through this method, you indicate that vertices defined in the 0th through 4th index of the array (or buffer) have to be utilized in rendering the primitives. Therefore, the vertices defined in the vertices array beginning from the first element will be used to render graphics on the screen. Recall through statement #11 that the client-side capability of the vertex array was enabled.

The onSurfaceChanged() method in statement #17 is called when the surface changes its size. In this method, you define the size of theOpenGL viewport through statement #18. The first two parameters are the X and Y coordinates of the bottom left of the viewport. The last two parameters are the width and height of the viewport. The width and height of the viewport are set equal to the width and height of the window so that the viewport covers the entire screen from (0,0) to (width-1, height-1).

In the defineGraphic() method, a float array, vertices, is defined (#19) that contains the coordinates of the vertices of the rectangle that you want to draw. A buffer of bytes named byteBuffer is defined in statement #20. The byteBuffer is used like a pointer to the array of vertices. The size of the buffer is set equal to four times the number of vertices defined in the vertices array because the vertex coordinates are float values, and a float takes 4 bytes. A float buffer called boxBuffer is defined based on the content of the byte buffer byteBuffer in statement #21. All the floats (vertex coordinates) in the vertices array are written into the float buffer boxBuffer in statement #22. The float buffer boxBuffer is reset to position 0 (that is, it is rewound to its beginning location in statement #23) to read the first vertex coordinates. It is the boxBuffer from which the glDrawArrays() method (#16) picks up the vertex coordinates of the rectangle to draw.

After you run the application, a blue rectangle will be displayed on a black background, as shown in Figure 10.1.

Figure 10.1   Creating and rendering a rectangle using OpenGL

A brief description of the methods used in the code shown in Listing 10.1 is shown in Table 10.1.

Table 10.1   **Brief Description of the Methods That Are Used in Listing 10.1**

Method	Description
void glClearColor(GLfloat red, GLfloat green, GLfloat blue, GLfloat alpha)	Specifies clear values for the color buffer. The red, green, blue, and alpha values specified through the parameters are used when the color buffers are cleared. The initial value of all parameters is 0.
void glEnableClientState (GLenum array)	Enables the client-side capability. The parameter array represents the capability to enable. It can be any of the following values: • **GL_COLOR_ARRAY**—The color array is enabled for writing and used during rendering. • **GL_NORMAL_ARRAY**—The normal array is enabled for writing and used during rendering. • **GL_TEXTURE_COORD_ARRAY**—The texture coordinate array is enabled for writing and used during rendering. • **GL_VERTEX_ARRAY**—The vertex array is enabled for writing and used during rendering.

Method	Description
`void glClear(GLbitfield mask)`	Clears the buffers to the values specified by the `glClearColor` method. The parameter `mask` represents the Bitwise OR of the following values to indicate which buffer is to be cleared: • **GL_COLOR_BUFFER_BIT**—Represents the buffers currently enabled. • **GL_DEPTH_BUFFER_BIT**—Represents the depth buffer. • **GL_STENCIL_BUFFER_BIT**—Represents the stencil buffer.
`void glColor4f(GLfloat red, GLfloat green, GLfloat blue, GLfloat alpha)`	Sets the current color of drawing. The values ranging from 0 to 1 are supplied for `red`, `green`, `blue`, and `alpha` parameters to set the current color. The initial value is 1.
`void glVertexPointer(GLint size, GLenum type, GLsizei stride, const GLvoid * pointer)`	Defines an array of vertex coordinates: • **size**—Specifies the number of coordinates per vertex. The value can be 2, 3, or 4. The initial value is 4. • **type**—Specifies the data type of each vertex in the array. The symbolic constants that represent the data type are GL_BYTE, GL_SHORT, GL_FIXED, and GL_FLOAT. The initial value is GL_FLOAT. • **stride**—Specifies the byte offset between consecutive vertices. If `stride` is 0, it means the vertices are stored in an array. The initial value is 0. • **pointer**—Specifies a pointer to the first coordinate of the first vertex in the array. The initial value is 0.
`void glDrawArrays( GLenum mode, GLint first_index, GLsizei count)`	Renders the specified primitives from the supplied array: • **mode**—Represents the primitive to render. The primitive can be represented by any of the following symbolic constants: GL_POINTS, GL_LINE_STRIP, GL_LINE_LOOP, GL_LINES, GL_LINE_STRIP_ADJACENCY, GL_LINES_ADJACENCY, GL_TRIANGLE_STRIP, GL_TRIANGLE_FAN, GL_TRIANGLES, GL_TRIANGLE_STRIP_ADJACENCY, GL_TRIANGLES_ADJACENCY, and GL_PATCHES • **first_index**—Specifies the starting index in the enabled array. • **count**—Specifies the number of elements of the array to be used for rendering graphics.

Method	Description
public abstract void onSurfaceCreated(GL10 gl, EGLConfig config)	Called when the surface is created or re-created. The surface is re-created when the EGL context is lost (that is, when the Android device awakes from the sleep state). The parameter gl is the GL interface, and config represents the EGLConfig of the created surface.
public abstract void onDrawFrame(GL10 gl)	Called to draw the current frame. The parameter gl is the GL interface.
public abstract void onSurfaceChanged(GL10 gl, int width, int height)	Called when the surface size changes. The parameter gl is the GL interface.

Recipe: Applying Smooth Coloring

In the previous recipe, you used a flat blue color for the drawn rectangle. *Flat color* here means one solid color. In this recipe, you will learn to apply smooth coloring to the rectangle that you drew in the previous recipe. For smooth coloring, you apply a color to each vertex of the graphics. The colors between the vertices will be interpolated by the OpenGL ES, giving a smoothing coloring effect.

Open the Android project OpenGLApp that you created earlier. To apply color to each vertex of the rectangle drawn in this application, modify the Java activity file OpenGLAppActivity.java so it appears as shown in Listing 10.2. Only the code in bold is newly added; the rest is the same as in Listing 10.1.

Listing 10.2   **Code Written into the Java Activity File** OpenGLAppActivity.java

```
package com.androidtablet.openglapp;

import android.os.Bundle;
import android.app.Activity;
import android.opengl.GLSurfaceView;
import android.opengl.GLES20;
import javax.microedition.khronos.opengles.GL10;
import javax.microedition.khronos.egl.EGLConfig;
import java.nio.FloatBuffer;
import java.nio.ByteBuffer;
import java.nio.ByteOrder;

public class OpenGLAppActivity extends Activity {
    private GLSurfaceView myGLView;

    @Override
```

```java
public void onCreate(Bundle savedInstanceState) {
    super.onCreate(savedInstanceState);
    myGLView = new GLSurfaceView(this);
    MyGLSurfRenderer renderer=new MyGLSurfRenderer();
    myGLView.setRenderer(renderer);
    setContentView(myGLView);
}

@Override
protected void onPause() {
    super.onPause();
    myGLView.onPause();
}

@Override
protected void onResume() {
    super.onResume();
    myGLView.onResume();
}

public class MyGLSurfRenderer implements  GLSurfaceView.Renderer {
    private FloatBuffer boxBuffer;
    private FloatBuffer colorBuffer;

    public void onSurfaceCreated(GL10 gl, EGLConfig config) {
        gl.glClearColor(0.0f, 0.0f, 0.0f, 1.0f);
        defineGraphic();
        gl.glEnableClientState(GL10.GL_VERTEX_ARRAY);
        gl.glVertexPointer(3, GL10.GL_FLOAT, 0, boxBuffer);
        gl.glEnableClientState(GL10.GL_COLOR_ARRAY);
        gl.glColorPointer(4, GL10.GL_FLOAT, 0, colorBuffer);
    }

    public void onDrawFrame(GL10 gl) {
        gl.glClear(GLES20.GL_COLOR_BUFFER_BIT);
        gl.glColor4f(0.0f, 0.0f, 1.0f, 1.0f);
        gl.glDrawArrays(GL10.GL_TRIANGLE_STRIP, 0, 4);
    }

    public void onSurfaceChanged(GL10 gl, int width, int height) {
        gl.glViewport(0, 0, width, height);
    }

    private void defineGraphic(){
        float vertices[] = {
            -0.5f, -0.5f,  0.0f,
             0.5f, -0.5f,  0.0f,
```

```
            -0.5f,  0.5f,  0.0f,
             0.5f,  0.5f,  0.0f
    };
    float[] colors = {
        0.0f, 0.0f, 1.0f, 1.0f,
        0.0f, 1.0f, 0.0f, 1.0f,
        1.0f, 0.0f, 0.0f, 1.0f,
        0.0f, 0.0f, 1.0f, 1.0f
    };

    ByteBuffer byteBuffer = ByteBuffer.allocateDirect(
        vertices.length * 4);
    byteBuffer.order(ByteOrder.nativeOrder());
    boxBuffer = byteBuffer.asFloatBuffer();
    boxBuffer.put(vertices);
    boxBuffer.position(0);
    ByteBuffer colorBytes = ByteBuffer.allocateDirect(
        colors.length * 4);
    colorBytes.order(ByteOrder.nativeOrder());
    colorBuffer = colorBytes.asFloatBuffer();
    colorBuffer.put(colors);
    colorBuffer.position(0);
    }
    }
}
```

In the renderer class MyGLSurfRenderer, one more FloatBuffer is defined called colorBuffer. On the client side, the GL_COLOR_ARRAY is enabled because it can be used for applying colors. Using the glColorPointer() method, an array carrying the color values colorBuffer is defined. Through the glColorPointer() method, you specify that there are four color values per vertex (red, green, blue, and alpha), each color value is of the GL_FLOAT data type, all color values are arranged with 0 offset between the values, and all are available in the colorBuffer buffer.

The float array colors is defined and contains the color values of each of the vertices of the rectangle that you want to draw. A buffer of bytes named colorBytes is defined. The size of the buffer is set equal to four times the number of color values defined in the colors array because color values are defined in float, and each float value takes 4 bytes. A float buffer called colorBuffer is defined based on the content of the byte buffer colorBytes. All the floats—that is, color values—in the colors array are written into the float buffer colorBuffer. The float buffer colorBuffer is reset to position 0 so that color values are read from the beginning of the buffer.

When you run the application, a rectangle with a smoothing color effect in the foreground and in the black background will be displayed as shown in Figure 10.2.

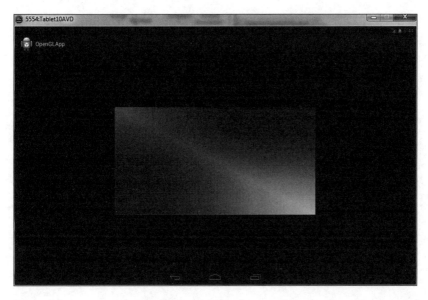

Figure 10.2   Smoothing color effect applied to the rectangle drawn through OpenGL

Recipe: Rotating Graphics

In this recipe, you will learn to rotate a graphic at a specified angle. Also, you will see how to set a graphic to rotate continuously. The graphic that you are going to use in this application is a rectangle. Because the vertices, color, and other information of the rectangle are enclosed in a separate class and not mixed with the rotation logic, this recipe can be used to rotate any graphic. For example, to rotate a cube instead of a rectangle in this recipe, you just need to replace the class containing the rectangle dimensions with that of the cube dimensions.

So create a new Android project called OpenGLDemo. To draw a rectangle, apply colors to it, and to rotate it, write the code as shown in Listing 10.3 into the Java activity file OpenGLDemoActivity.java.

Listing 10.3   **Code Written into the Java Activity File** OpenGLDemoActivity.java

```
package com.androidtablet.opengldemo;

import android.os.Bundle;
import android.app.Activity;
import android.opengl.GLSurfaceView;
import android.opengl.GLES20;
import javax.microedition.khronos.opengles.GL10;
import javax.microedition.khronos.egl.EGLConfig;
import java.nio.FloatBuffer;
```

```java
import java.nio.ByteBuffer;
import java.nio.ByteOrder;

public class OpenGLDemoActivity extends Activity {
    private GLSurfaceView myGLView;

    @Override
    protected void onCreate(Bundle savedInstanceState) {
        super.onCreate(savedInstanceState);
        myGLView = new GLSurfaceView(this);
        MyGLSurfRenderer renderer=new MyGLSurfRenderer();
        myGLView.setRenderer(renderer);
        setContentView(myGLView);
    }

    @Override
    protected void onPause() {
        super.onPause();
        myGLView.onPause();
    }

    @Override
    protected void onResume() {
        super.onResume();
        myGLView.onResume();
    }

    public class MyGLSurfRenderer implements  GLSurfaceView.Renderer {
        private Rectangle rectangle;

        public MyGLSurfRenderer() {
            rectangle = new Rectangle();
        }

        public void onSurfaceCreated(GL10 gl, EGLConfig config) {
            gl.glLoadIdentity();
        }

        public void onDrawFrame(GL10 gl) {
            gl.glClear(GLES20.GL_COLOR_BUFFER_BIT);
            gl.glColor4f(0.0f, 0.0f, 1.0f, 1.0f);
            gl.glMatrixMode(GL10.GL_MODELVIEW);
            gl.glPushMatrix();
            gl.glRotatef(45.0f, 0.0f, 0.0f, 1.0f);
            rectangle.draw(gl);
            gl.glPopMatrix();
        }
```

```java
    public void onSurfaceChanged(GL10 gl, int width, int height) {
        gl.glViewport(0, 0, width, height);
    }
}

public class Rectangle {
    private FloatBuffer boxBuffer;
    private FloatBuffer colorBuffer;
    float vertices[] = {
        -0.5f, -0.5f, 0.0f,
         0.5f, -0.5f,  0.0f,
        -0.5f,  0.5f,  0.0f,
         0.5f,  0.5f,  0.0f
    };
    float[] colors = {
        0.0f, 0.0f, 1.0f, 1.0f,
        0.0f, 1.0f, 0.0f, 1.0f,
        1.0f, 0.0f, 0.0f, 1.0f,
        0.0f, 0.0f, 1.0f, 1.0f
    };

    public Rectangle() {
        ByteBuffer byteBuffer = ByteBuffer.allocateDirect (
            vertices.length * 4);
        byteBuffer.order(ByteOrder.nativeOrder());
        boxBuffer = byteBuffer.asFloatBuffer();
        boxBuffer.put(vertices);
        boxBuffer.position(0);
        ByteBuffer colorBytes = ByteBuffer.allocateDirect (
            colors.length * 4);
        colorBytes.order(ByteOrder.nativeOrder());
        colorBuffer = colorBytes.asFloatBuffer();
        colorBuffer.put(colors);
        colorBuffer.position(0);
    }

    public void draw(GL10 gl) {
        gl.glEnableClientState(GL10.GL_VERTEX_ARRAY);
        gl.glVertexPointer(3, GL10.GL_FLOAT, 0, boxBuffer);
        gl.glClearColor(0.0f, 0.0f, 0.0f, 1.0f);
        gl.glEnableClientState(GL10.GL_COLOR_ARRAY);
        gl.glColorPointer(4, GL10.GL_FLOAT, 0, colorBuffer);
        gl.glDrawArrays(GL10.GL_TRIANGLE_STRIP, 0, 4);
        gl.glDisableClientState(GL10.GL_VERTEX_ARRAY);
    }
}
}
```

You can see that an instance named myGLView of the GLSurfaceView class is defined and initialized with the activity context. For rendering the graphics, an object called renderer is defined of the rendering class MyGLSurfRenderer. The onPause() and onResume() methods are defined to pause and resume rendering when an activity is paused and resumed, respectively. The rendering class MyGLSurfRenderer implements the GLSurfaceView.Renderer interface and hence implements the three methods onSurfaceCreated(), onDrawFame(), and onSurfaceChanged(). The object rectangle is defined of the class Rectangle. The vertices, colors, and other information of the rectangle that you want to draw are defined in the Rectangle class.

In the onDrawFrame() method, the glClear() method clears the buffer to show the color (black) defined through the glClearColor() method. Using the glColor4f() method, the current foreground color is set to blue. The glMatrixMode() method is used to set the current matrix mode to GL_MODELVIEW. The GL_MODELVIEW mode contains the matrix that is used in modeling and viewing the graphics. The glLoadIdentity() method is called to reset the matrix. It is called once in the onSurfaceCreated() method. glLoadIdentity() is called several times in the onDrawFrame() method by pushing and popping the matrix. It is essential to reset the matrix after a matrix mode change to ensure that any matrix transformations done through previous commands (if any) do not compound or affect the current commands. The glRotatef() method is called to multiply the current modelview matrix by a rotation. The method rotates the rectangle to 45 degrees around the specified vector (0,0,1). Finally, the rectangle is drawn by calling the draw() method on the Rectangle class.

In the onSurfaceChanged() method, you define the size of the OpenGL viewport. The width and height of the viewport are set equal to the width and height of the window so that the viewport covers the entire screen.

In the Rectangle class, to specify the shape of the rectangle, the float array vertices is defined that contains the coordinates of the vertices of the rectangle that you want to draw. Another float array, colors, is defined to store the color values of each of the vertices of the rectangle. A buffer of bytes is defined named byteBuffer. The size of the byte buffer is set equal to four times the number of vertices defined in the vertices array because vertex coordinates are float values, and a float takes 4 bytes. A float buffer called boxBuffer is defined based on the size of the byte buffer byteBuffer. All the floats (that is, vertex coordinates) in the vertices array are written into the float buffer boxBuffer. The float buffer boxBuffer is reset to position 0 (that is, it is reset to read the first vertex coordinate).

For applying colors, another byte buffer named colorBytes is defined, and a float buffer called colorBuffer is defined based on the size of the colorBytes buffer. All the floats (colors) in the colors array are written into the float buffer colorBuffer. Also, the colorBuffer is reset to position 0 to read from the first color value.

In the draw() method, the GL_VERTEX_ARRAY is enabled on the client side so that it can be used while rendering. Using the glVertexPointer() method, it is declared that the boxBuffer carries the vertex coordinates of the rectangle you want to draw. Similarly, for applying colors, the GL_COLOR_ARRAY is enabled on the client side. Using the glColorPointer() method, you are informed that the colorBuffer contains the color values to be applied to the rectangle vertices. Using the `glDrawArrays()` method, the graphics (rectangle) is rendered from the enabled arrays.

After you run the application, a rectangle with a smoothing color effect in the foreground and a black background will be displayed rotated at 45 degrees, as shown in Figure 10.3.

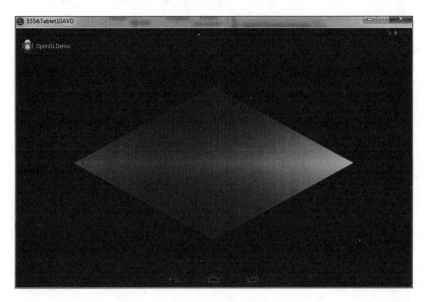

Figure 10.3   Graphics rotated to 45 degrees

The brief description of the methods used in Listing 10.3 is given in Table 10.2.

Table 10.2   **Brief Description of the Methods Used in Listing 10.3**

Method	Description
`void glMatrixMode(GLenum mode)`	Method sets the current matrix mode. The parameter mode can be any of the following:
	▪ **GL_MODELVIEW**—This matrix mode is used for modeling and viewing graphics.
	▪ **GL_PROJECTION**—This matrix mode is used for projection transformation.
	▪ **GL_TEXTURE**—This matrix mode is used for performing operations on the texture.
	The initial value of the mode parameter is GL_MODELVIEW.

Method	Description
glLoadIdentity()	Method resets the matrix of the current matrix mode to identity the matrix. The method should always be called after a matrix mode change so that matrix transformations of earlier commands do not affect the current operations.
void glRotatef(GLfloat angle, GLfloat x, GLfloat y, GLfloat z)	The method multiplies the current matrix by a rotation matrix. That is, it rotates a graphic around the specified vector (x, y, z). The parameter angle specifies the angle of rotation in degrees. The parameters x, y, and z represent the X, Y, and Z coordinates of the vector around which rotation has to be performed.

To make the rectangle rotate continuously in a counterclockwise direction, modify the code in the onDrawframe() method in the MyGLSurfRenderer class (see Listing 10.3) as shown here:

```
public class MyGLSurfRenderer implements  GLSurfaceView.Renderer {
    private Rectangle rectangle;
    public void onSurfaceCreated(GL10 gl, EGLConfig config) {
        gl.glLoadIdentity();
    }

    public void onDrawFrame(GL10 gl) {
        gl.glClear(GLES20.GL_COLOR_BUFFER_BIT);
        gl.glColor4f(0.0f, 0.0f, 1.0f, 1.0f);
        gl.glMatrixMode(GL10.GL_MODELVIEW);
        gl.glRotatef(2.0f, 0.0f, 0.0f, 1.0f);
        rectangle.draw(gl);
    }
}
```

You can see that the angle of rotation is set to increment by 2 degrees after each rotation. After you run the application, the rectangle will continuously rotate in a counterclockwise direction. Figure 10.4 shows the rotating rectangle. Figure 10.4 (top) and (bottom) shows the snapshot of the rectangle in different angles while rotating.

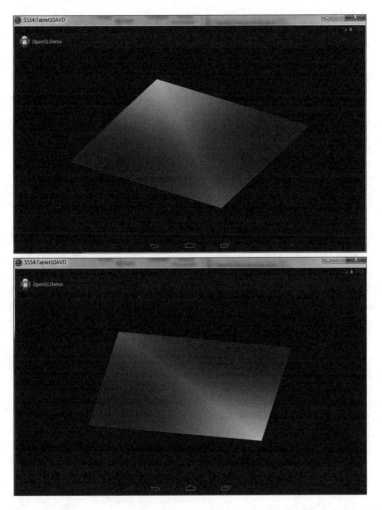

Figure 10.4   Graphics rotating continuously in counterclockwise direction. The top and bottom images show the rectangle in different angles while rotating.

Recipe: Scaling Graphics

In this recipe, you will learn to scale a graphic. You will shrink the rectangle that you learned to draw in the previous recipe. You will learn to scale down the rectangle to 50% of its original size. Also, you will learn to iteratively scale down the rectangle by 10% of its size.

To scale down the rectangle by 50%, modify the onDrawframe() method in the MyGLSurfRenderer class (refer to Listing 10.3) to appear as shown here:

```
public class MyGLSurfRenderer implements  GLSurfaceView.Renderer {
    private Rectangle rectangle;
public void onDrawFrame(GL10 gl) {
```

```
    gl.glClear(GLES20.GL_COLOR_BUFFER_BIT);
    gl.glColor4f(0.0f, 0.0f, 1.0f, 1.0f);
    gl.glMatrixMode(GL10.GL_MODELVIEW);
    gl.glPushMatrix();
    gl.glScalef(0.5f,0.5f, 0.5f);
    rectangle.draw(gl);
    gl.glPopMatrix();
}
```

By using the glScalef() method, the size of the rectangle is reduced by 50% from the
X, Y, and Z axes. The glLoadIdentity() method is called to reset the matrix. The
glLoadIdentity() method is called by pushing and popping the matrix, and the purpose
of calling it is to stop the rectangle from further scaling. Because the onDrawFrame() method
is called on every frame, the size of the rectangle will continuously reduce by 50% in every
iteration if the glLoadIdentity() method is not used to reset the matrix.

> **Tip**
>
> If the matrix mode is either GL_MODELVIEW or GL_PROJECTION, all objects drawn after the
> call of the glScalef() method will be scaled. So it is wise to use glPushMatrix() and
> glPopMatrix() to save and restore the unscaled coordinate system, respectively.

To scale down the rectangle iteratively by 10% until it reaches 25% of its original size, use the
following code snippet:

```
public class MyGLSurfRenderer implements  GLSurfaceView.Renderer {
    private Rectangle rectangle;
    private float xscale=0.9f;
    private float yscale=0.9f;
    private float zscale=0.9f;

    public void onDrawFrame(GL10 gl) {
        gl.glClear(GLES20.GL_COLOR_BUFFER_BIT);
        gl.glColor4f(0.0f, 0.0f, 1.0f, 1.0f);
        gl.glMatrixMode(GL10.GL_MODELVIEW);
        if(xscale <=.25) {
            xscale=1;
            yscale=1;
            zscale=1;
        }
        gl.glPushMatrix();
        gl.glScalef(xscale,yscale, zscale);
        rectangle.draw(gl);
        gl.glPopMatrix();
        xscale-=.1;
        yscale-=.1;
        zscale-=.1;
    }
```

You can see that the glScalef() method reduces the size of the rectangle by 10% from the X, Y, and Z axes. The rectangle is scaled down continuously until it reaches 25% of its original size. When the rectangle is shrunk to 25% or smaller, it is scaled up to its original size. After gaining the original size, again the rectangle is scaled down continuously by 10% until it is reduced to 25% of its original size. The process continues infinitely. It is the glScalef() method used in the preceding code that multiplies the current matrix by a scaling matrix. Here is the syntax:

```
void glScalef(GLfloat x, GLfloat y, GLfloat z)
```

The parameters x, y, and z represent the scale factors along the X, Y, and Z axes, respectively.

When you run the application, the rectangle will appear in its original size on startup. Thereafter, it continuously reduces in size until it becomes one-fourth of its original size. Thereafter, it will reappear in its original size and will again start shrinking gradually to one-quarter of its original size. The process will continue infinitely. Figure 10.5 shows the snapshot of the rectangle at different sizes while it was shrinking.

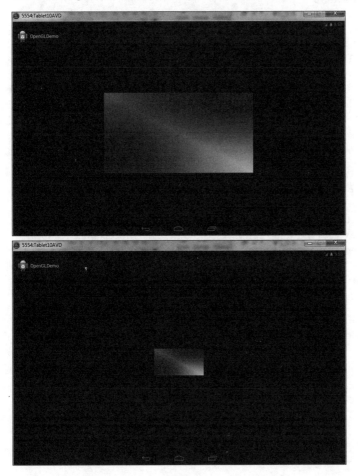

Figure 10.5   Graphic scaling down on the X, Y, and Z coordinates; the top and bottom images show the rectangle in different sizes while shrinking

Recipe: Translating Graphics

A graphic can be translated (moved in any of the X, Y, or Z directions). In this recipe, you will learn to translate the rectangle that you drew in the previous recipe. You will make the rectangle translate in the X axes by moving the rectangle horizontally toward the right. The rectangle will disappear in the right boundary of the screen and will reappear at its original position to repeat the translation.

To translate the rectangle horizontally in the Z axis, modify the onDrawframe() method in the MyGLSurfRenderer class (refer to Listing 10.3) to appear as shown here:

```
public class MyGLSurfRenderer implements  GLSurfaceView.Renderer {
    private Rectangle rectangle;
    private float xdelta=0.0f;

    public void onDrawFrame(GL10 gl) {
        gl.glClear(GLES20.GL_COLOR_BUFFER_BIT);
        gl.glColor4f(0.0f, 0.0f, 1.0f, 1.0f);
        gl.glMatrixMode(GL10.GL_MODELVIEW);
        if(xdelta >=2)xdelta=0;
        gl.glPushMatrix();
        gl.glTranslatef(xdelta, 0.0f, 0.0f);
        rectangle.draw(gl);
        gl.glPopMatrix();
        xdelta+=.02;
    }
```

Through your use of the glTranslatef method, the rectangle is moved toward the right in the X axis. The current value of xdelta is incremented by .02 in the onDrawFrame() method. Because the onDrawFrame() method is called on every frame, the value of xdelta will keep increasing; therefore, the rectangle will continuously move horizontally toward the right. When the value of xdelta exceeds the value 2, it is reset to 0 to make the rectangle reappear at its original location and resart the translation. After you run the application, the rectangle will start moving horizontally toward the right in the X axis. Figure 10.6 (top) shows the rectangle at its original location. Figure 10.6 (bottom) shows the rectangle disappearing in the right boundary of the screen.

You can also make the graphic translate in more than one axis simultaneously. To make the rectangle translate in the X axis simultaneously with the Y axis, modify the onDrawframe() method in the MyGLSurfRenderer class (refer to Listing 10.3) to appear as shown here:

```
public class MyGLSurfRenderer implements  GLSurfaceView.Renderer {
    private Rectangle rectangle;
    private float xdelta=0.0f;
    private float ydelta=0.0f;

    public void onDrawFrame(GL10 gl) {
        gl.glClear(GLES20.GL_COLOR_BUFFER_BIT);
```

```
gl.glColor4f(0.0f, 0.0f, 1.0f, 1.0f);
gl.glMatrixMode(GL10.GL_MODELVIEW);
if(xdelta >=2)xdelta=0;
if(ydelta >=2)ydelta=0;
gl.glPushMatrix();
gl.glTranslatef(xdelta, ydelta, 0.0f);
rectangle.draw(gl);
gl.glPopMatrix();
xdelta+=.02;
ydelta+=.02;
}
```

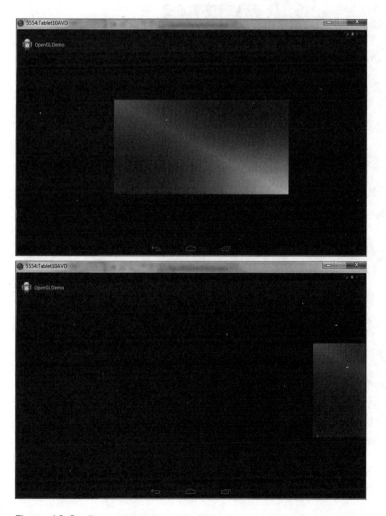

Figure 10.6   Rectangle at its original location on application startup (top), and rectangle disappearing in the right boundary of the screen (bottom)

You can see that the variables xdelta and ydelta are initialized to 0. Also, the values of xdelta and ydelta are incremented by .02 in the onDrawFrame() method. The increment in the X coordinate will translate the rectangle toward the right, and the increment in the Y coordinate will make the rectangle move up. The combination will make the rectangle move toward the top-right corner of the screen. When the value of xdelta or ydelta exceeds 2, it is reset to 0 to make the rectangle reappear at its original location to resart the translation. After you run the application, the rectangle will start moving toward the top-right corner of the screen (see Figure 10.7 [top]). Figure 10.7 (bottom) shows the rectangle disappearing in the top-right corner of the screen.

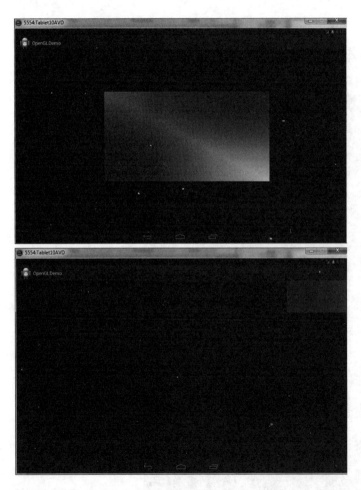

Figure 10.7   Rectangle at its original location on application startup (top), and rectangle disappearing in the top-right corner of the screen (bottom)

Summary

In this chapter, you learned how the OpenGL ES API is used to create and render graphics. You saw the procedure to apply flat and smooth color to the drawn graphics. You also saw different methods for rotating, scaling, and translating graphics.

The next chapter shows how images, video, and audio are captured in an Android application. You will explore built-in intents and utilize them in capturing images, audio, and video. Also, you will learn to do these tasks manually by writing Java code that accesses the device camera and microphone and calls different methods to capture images, audio, and video, respectively.

Recording Audio, Video, and Images

Almost all Android devices come with a microphone and a camera. To use them in developing applications, you need to know about different classes and methods that are required to access them. By accessing the device camera, you can develop applications that capture images and videos. Similarly, you can add a facility to record audio in an Android application if you know how to access a device microphone. This chapter focuses on helping you understand how images, video, and audio are captured in an Android application. Obviously, the Android SDK provides some intents and actions that make your task of capturing image, audio, and video much easier. In this chapter, you will explore built-in intent and utilize it in capturing image, audio, and video. You will learn to write Java code that accesses the device camera and microphone and call different methods to capture images, audio, and video, respectively. In this chapter, you will also learn to access camcorder device profile information.

Recipe: Capturing an Image Using a Built-In Intent

There are two ways to access the device camera and use it to capture an image:

- Write the Java code to access the device camera, provide a surface to preview the picture, capture the image, and save it in the device storage.

- Define and invoke an intent using the Android's `MediaStore.ACTION_IMAGE_CAPTURE` action that does all the tasks to preview, capture, and store the image automatically.

In this recipe, you will use the second and easier method to capture an image—define and invoke an intent with a predefined action. Also, you will learn to display the captured image through the `ImageView` control on the screen. Create an Android project called `CameraApp`. In this application, you will use a `Button` control and an `ImageView` control. Clicking the `Button` control invokes the device camera. When the user clicks a picture through the device camera, the picture will be displayed through the `ImageView` control. To define the `Button` and `ImageView`, write the code as shown in Listing 11.1 in the activity layout file `activity_camera_app.xml`.

Listing 11.1   Code Written into the Activity Layout File `activity_camera_app.xml`

```xml
<LinearLayout xmlns:android="http://schemas.android.com/apk/res/android"
android:layout_width="match_parent"
android:layout_height="match_parent"
android:orientation="vertical" >
    <Button
        android:id="@+id/launch_btn"
        android:layout_width="wrap_content"
        android:layout_height="wrap_content"
        android:text="Launch Camera"
        android:textSize="@dimen/text_size"  />
    <ImageView
        android:id="@+id/photo"
        android:layout_width="match_parent"
        android:layout_height="match_parent" />
</LinearLayout>
```

To identify and use the Java code, assign the `Button` and `ImageView` controls the IDs `launch_btn` and `photo`, respectively. The caption displayed on the `Button` control is `Launch Camera`. The font size of the caption is defined through the dimension resource `text_size`.

Next, you need to write the Java code to perform the following tasks:

- Access the `Button` and `ImageView` controls defined in the activity layout file and map them to the respective objects.

- Associate `setOnClickListener` to the `Button` control to listen to the click event on the `Button` control. The callback method `onClick` will be invoked when a click event occurs on the `Button` control.

- Define an intent called `captureIntent` that refers to the built-in `MediaStore.ACTION_IMAGE_CAPTURE` action. This intent when invoked will launch the device camera.

- Start the activity when the `Button` control is clicked, thereby allowing the user to click an image.

- Analyze the result code when the launched activity is over so you know if the image-capturing task was successfully performed.

- If the image capturing is successfully performed, the image is accessed and displayed via the `ImageView` control.

To accomplish all the preceding tasks, write the code shown in Listing 11.2 into the Java activity file `CameraAppActivity.java`.

Listing 11.2   **Code Written into the Java Activity File** `CameraAppActivity.java`

```java
package com.androidtablet.cameraapp;

import android.os.Bundle;
import android.app.Activity;
import android.widget.Button;
import android.view.View;
import android.provider.MediaStore;
import android.content.Intent;
import android.content.ActivityNotFoundException;
import android.widget.Toast;
import android.graphics.Bitmap;
import android.widget.ImageView;

public class CameraAppActivity extends Activity {
    final int CAPTURE_PHOTO  = 1;

    @Override
    protected void onCreate(Bundle savedInstanceState) {
        super.onCreate(savedInstanceState);
        setContentView(R.layout.activity_camera_app);
        Button captureBtn = (Button) findViewById(
            R.id.launch_btn);
        captureBtn.setOnClickListener(new Button.
            OnClickListener() {
            public void onClick(View v) {
                try {
                    Intent captureIntent = new Intent(
                        MediaStore.ACTION_IMAGE_CAPTURE);    #1
                    startActivityForResult(captureIntent,    #2
                        CAPTURE_PHOTO );
                }
                catch(ActivityNotFoundException e){
                    Toast.makeText(CameraAppActivity.this,
                        "Error occurred while capturing image",
                        Toast.LENGTH_SHORT).show();
                }
            }
        });
    }

    protected void onActivityResult(int requestCode, int
        resultCode, Intent data) {                          #3
        if (resultCode == RESULT_OK) {                      #4
            if(requestCode == CAPTURE_PHOTO ){              #5
                Bitmap photo = (Bitmap) data.getExtras().
                    get("data");                            #6
```

```
        ImageView picView = (ImageView)findViewById(
            R.id.photo);
        picView.setImageBitmap(photo);              #7
      }
    }
    else
      Toast.makeText(CameraAppActivity.this, "Image could
        not be captured", Toast.LENGTH_SHORT).show();
  }
}
```

A few of the statements in Listing 11.2 need explanation:

- Statement #1 defines an intent called captureIntent with the MediaStore.ACTION_ IMAGE_CAPTURE action. When the intent is invoked, it launches the device camera.

- Statement #2 starts the activity and waits for the result of invoking the device camera (that is, whether the image was captured successfully or some error occurred). The CAPTURE_PHOTO variable used in the statement is for differentiating the captureIntent from other intents in the application (if any). The CAPTURE_PHOTO variable will help keep track of the intent that launches the device camera.

- Statement #3 defines the onActivityResult handler that fetches and analyzes the result of the activity that is launched. That is, it accesses the result of invoking the device camera.

- Statement #4 confirms whether the intent that was invoked has executed successfully. That is, it confirms whether the device camera is found and invoked and whether the image is captured successfully.

- Statement #5 confirms whether the result is from the desired captureIntent. Recall that the captureIntent was invoked with the CAPTURE_PHOTO variable in statement #2.

- The image captured from the device camera is accessed through the parameter data Intent in statement #6.

- The accessed image is assigned to the Bitmap object photo. Statement #7 assigns the image in the photo object to the ImageView object picView to display on the screen.

After you run the application, a Button control with the caption Launch Camera will be displayed (see Figure 11.1 [top left]). Select the button, and the device camera will be invoked showing the preview. A click button in the form of a camera image is displayed at the bottom of the preview (see Figure 11.1 [top right]). After you click the camera image button, the picture will be clicked and will be displayed via the ImageView control that you defined in the activity layout file, as shown in Figure 11.1 (bottom left). The picture gallery of the device also shows the clicked image (see Figure 11.1 [bottom right]) confirming that the image has been clicked and saved successfully.

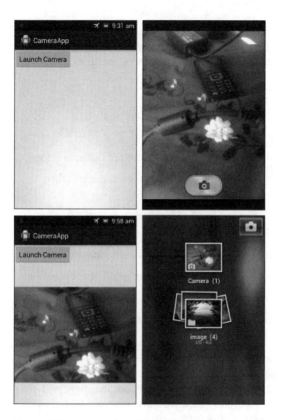

Figure 11.1 `Button` control displayed on application startup (top left); device camera invoked showing the camera preview (top right); clicked picture displayed via `ImageView` (bottom left); picture gallery of the device showing the clicked photo (bottom right)

Recipe: Capturing an Image Using Java Code

In this recipe, you will learn to capture an image manually by explicitly writing code to use the `Camera` class and call its different methods that are required to preview, capture an image, and save it in the device storage. To handle the display, you will use the `SurfaceView` and `SurfaceHolder.Callback` interface. The `SurfaceView` will provide a surface inside the view hierarchy that you can use to show a camera preview and captured image. The `SurfaceView` enhances the user experience by using an independent thread to draw and update the view. The `SurfaceHolder` interface holds the `SurfaceView` object and controls the size, edits, and formats and monitors the surface.

> **Note**
>
> The `Camera` class helps in configuring image capture settings, starting and stopping preview, capturing images, and so on. This class is a client for the `Camera` service, which manages the actual camera hardware.

To capture an image using the `Camera` class, follow these steps:

1. Create a `Camera` object by invoking the `open` method.

2. Invoke the `setPreviewDisplay` method to set the surface to show the camera preview.

3. Invoke the `startPreview` method to begin drawing preview frames to the specified surface.

4. Invoke the `takePicture` method to invoke the specified handler to save the captured image in the desired output format and at the desired path.

5. Define the `File` object to define the filename by which the captured image will be saved.

6. Define the `FileOutputStream` object to write the captured image into the specified file.

7. Close the `FileOutputStream` object.

8. Invoke the `stopPreview` method to stop the preview displayed by the device camera.

9. Invoke the `release` method to release resources associated to the `Camera` object.

Create an Android project called `CaptureImageApp`. In this application, the camera preview will automatically begin on application startup. An action item named Capture Image will be displayed in the ActionBar for the user to click to capture an image. The captured image will be saved in the SD card of the device and can be seen in the device gallery.

To display the camera preview, you will use the `SurfaceView`. To define the `SurfaceView`, the code as shown in Listing 11.3 is written in the activity layout file `activity_capture_image_app.xml`.

Listing 11.3 Code Written into the Activity Layout File `activity_capture_image_app.xml`

```
<LinearLayout xmlns:android="http://schemas.android.com/apk/res/android"
    android:layout_width="match_parent"
    android:layout_height="match_parent"
    android:orientation="vertical" >
    <SurfaceView
        android:id="@+id/surfaceview"
        android:layout_width="match_parent"
        android:layout_height="match_parent" />
</LinearLayout>
```

To identify and use the Java code, the `SurfaceView` is assigned the `surfaceview` ID. Now define an action item in the menu file `activity_capture_image_app.xml` that is found in the `res/menu` folder. To define an action item titled Capture Image, write the code shown in Listing 11.4 in the menu file `activity_capture_image_app.xml`.

Listing 11.4 Code Written into the Menu File `activity_capture_image_app.xml`

```
<menu xmlns: android="http://schemas.android.com/apk/res/android" >
    <item android:id="@+id/capture_button"
        android:title="Capture Image"
        android:orderInCategory="0"
        android:showAsAction="ifRoom|withText" />
</menu>
```

The action item is set to display the title Capture Image. Also, to access and identify the action item, the ID `capture_button` is assigned to it. Next, write the Java code to perform the following tasks:

- Access the `SurfaceView` defined in the activity layout file and map it to the `SurfaceView` object. It is through the `SurfaceView` that you will preview the camera to determine the image to be captured.

- Set the main activity class to implement the `SurfaceHolder.Callback` interface. The `SurfaceHolder.Callback` notifies the related view when the underlying surface is created, destroyed, or modified.

- Implement three methods: `surfaceCreated(SurfaceHolder)`, `surfaceDestroyed` `(SurfaceHolder)`, and `surfaceChanged(SurfaceHolder holder, int format, int w, int h)`.
    - **`surfaceCreated(SurfaceHolder)`**—Informs when the surface is created and is available for camera preview.
    - **`surfaceDestroyed(SurfaceHolder)`**—Informs when the surface is destroyed.
    - **`surfaceChanged(SurfaceHolder holder, int format, int w, int h)`**— Informs when there is a change in the surface structure, such as in the width or the height of the surface or device orientation.

- Inflate or merge the menu that is defined in the menu file `activity_capture_image_ app.xml`.

- Define the `onOptionsItemSelected()` method to handle the click events on the action item.

- Define the `picHandler` function that the `takePicture()` method invokes when a user clicks the Capture Image action item.

- Define the filename by which you want the captured image to be stored in the SD card.

- Define the `FileOutputStream` object to save the captured image by the specified filename.

- Call the `stopPreview()` and `release()` methods to stop the camera preview and release the allocated resources.

To perform all the preceding tasks, write the code shown in Listing 11.5 into the Java activity file `CaptureImageAppActivity.java`.

Listing 11.5   **Code Written into the Java Activity File** `CaptureImageAppActivity.java`

```
package com.androidtablet.captureimageapp;

import android.os.Bundle;
import android.app.Activity;
import android.view.Menu;
import android.view.MenuItem;
import android.view.SurfaceHolder;
import android.view.SurfaceView;
import android.hardware.Camera;
import java.io.IOException;
import java.io.FileNotFoundException;
import java.io.FileOutputStream;
import android.hardware.Camera.PictureCallback;
import android.os.Environment;
import java.io.File;
import android.widget.Toast;
import java.text.SimpleDateFormat;
import java.util.Calendar;

public class CaptureImageAppActivity extends Activity implements SurfaceHolder.
Callback {
    private SurfaceHolder surfaceHolder;
    private SurfaceView surfaceView;
    private Camera camera = null;

    @Override
    protected void onCreate(Bundle savedInstanceState) {
        super.onCreate(savedInstanceState);
        setContentView(R.layout.activity_capture_image_app);
        surfaceView = (SurfaceView) findViewById(
            R.id.surfaceview);
        surfaceHolder = surfaceView.getHolder();
        surfaceHolder.addCallback(this);
    }

    @Override
    public boolean onCreateOptionsMenu(Menu menu) {
        getMenuInflater().inflate(R.menu.activity_capture_
            image_app, menu);
            return true;
    }

    @Override
    public boolean onOptionsItemSelected(MenuItem item) {
```

```java
    switch (item.getItemId()) {
        case R.id.capture_button:
            camera.takePicture(null, null, picHandler);
            break;
        default:
            return super.onOptionsItemSelected(item);
    }
    return true;
}

PictureCallback picHandler = new PictureCallback() {
    @Override
    public void onPictureTaken(byte[] data, Camera
        camera) {
        File pictureFile = new File(Environment.
            getExternalStorageDirectory().getPath() +
            "/sampleimage.jpg");                      #1
        try {
            FileOutputStream fos = new FileOutputStream(
                pictureFile.toString());
            fos.write(data);
            fos.close();
            Toast.makeText(CaptureImageAppActivity.this,
                "Picture Saved",Toast.LENGTH_SHORT).show();
        } catch (FileNotFoundException e) {  }
        catch (IOException e) {  }
    }
};

public void surfaceCreated(SurfaceHolder holder) {
    camera=Camera.open();
    try {
        camera.setPreviewDisplay(holder);
        camera.startPreview();
    } catch (IOException e) {    }
}

public void surfaceChanged(SurfaceHolder holder,  int
    format, int width, int height) {
    try {
        camera.setPreviewDisplay(holder);
        camera.startPreview();
    } catch (Exception e) {    }
}

public void surfaceDestroyed(SurfaceHolder holder) {
    camera.stopPreview();
    camera.release();
    camera = null;
```

```
    }
}
```

Depending on the device, the captured image will be saved by the filename `sampleimage.jpg` in the SD card or the internal device storage. To enable the application to access the 000000000 device camera and save the captured image in the SD card, add the following three permission statements to the `AndroidManifest.xml` file:

```
<uses-feature android:name="android.hardware.camera" />
<uses-permission android:name="android.permission.CAMERA" />
<uses-permission android:name="android.permission.WRITE_EXTERNAL_STORAGE" />
```

Your application is ready to run. The only drawback in this application is that each captured image is saved by the filename `sampleimage.jpg`, thus erasing the earlier captured image. That is, the application will show only the last captured image. Run the application and see what happens. Figure 11.2 (top left) shows the existing albums in the device gallery. The number of albums and images in it may vary from device to device because it depends on the existing pictures in the device. Figure 11.2 (top right) shows the screen after capturing an image. The screen confirms that the image capturing is successful by displaying the message `Picture Saved`. To see if the next captured image erases the previously captured image, capture one more image. Figure 11.2 (bottom left) displays the screen on capturing another image, and Figure 11.2 (bottom right) shows an extra album on the device `Internal storage` with a single image in it. Even though you have captured two images, the `Internal storage` album shows a single image. The second captured image erases the first captured image because both have the common filename `sampleimage.jpg`.

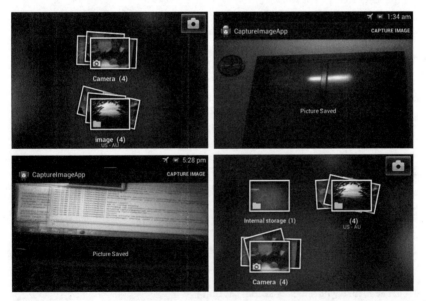

Figure 11.2   Device picture gallery showing two albums initially (top left); capturing first picture (top right); capturing second picture (bottom left); picture gallery of the device showing only the single picture in the Internal storage (bottom right)

If you want each captured image to be saved and want to avoid overwriting an earlier saved image, take the help of the system's current date and time. Each captured image will be assigned a unique filename that will be based on the system's current date and time. You need to replace statement #1 shown in Listing 11.5 with the following statements:

```
Calendar currentDate = Calendar.getInstance();
String timeStamp = new SimpleDateFormat("yyyyMMdd_HHmmss").
    format(currentDate.getTime());
File pictureFile = new File(Environment.
    getExternalStorageDirectory().getPath() + "/IMG_" +
    timeStamp + ".jpg");
```

Now when you capture more than one image, the earlier captured image will not be erased. Figure 11.3 shows two images in the `Internal storage` album after capturing two images.

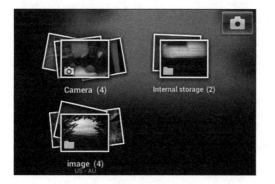

Figure 11.3   Device picture gallery showing two pictures in the `Internal storage` album

Recipe: Recording Audio Using a Built-In Intent

As in the case of image capturing, there are two ways to record audio in Android applications:

- In the first way, you use Android's `MediaRecorder` class and call its different methods to access the device microphone, record the audio in the specified format and encoding style, and save it in the device storage.

- In the second way, which is quite easier, you define and invoke an intent using the `MediaStore.Audio.Media.RECORD_SOUND_ACTION` action that does all the tasks to record, pause, play, and store the audio automatically.

In this recipe, you will use the second method to record audio (invoking the intent with the predefined action). In the following recipe, you will learn to record audio using the `MediaRecorder` class.

Create a new Android project called `AudioRecordApp`. In this application, you will use a `Button` control that, when clicked, will invoke the device audio recorder. The user can record, pause, and play the recorded audio. The recorded audio will also appear in the music list of the device. To define the `Button` control, write the code as shown in Listing 11.6 into the activity layout file `activity_audio_record_app.xml`.

Listing 11.6   **Code Written into the Activity Layout File** `activity_audio_record_app.xml`

```
<LinearLayout    xmlns:android="http://schemas.android.com/apk/res/android"
    android:layout_width="match_parent"
    android:layout_height="match_parent"
    android:orientation="vertical" >
    <Button
        android:id="@+id/record_btn"
        android:layout_width="wrap_content"
        android:layout_height="wrap_content"
        android:text="Start Recording"
        android:textSize="@dimen/text_size"  />
</LinearLayout>
```

To identify and use the Java code, the `Button` control is assigned the `record_btn` ID. The caption displayed on the `Button` control is `Start Recording`, and it will appear in the font size defined by the dimension resource `text_size`. After defining the activity layout file, you need to write the Java code to perform the following tasks:

- Access the `Button` control defined in the activity layout file and map it to the `Button` object.

- Associate `setOnClickListener` to the `Button` control to listen for the click events. The callback method `onClick` will be invoked when a click event occurs on the `Button` control.

- Define an intent called `audioIntent` that refers to the built-in `MediaStore.Audio.Media.RECORD_SOUND_ACTION` activity. This built-in activity is responsible for launching the audio recorder of the device.

- Start the activity when the `Button` control is clicked, hence allowing the user to record and play the desired audio.

- Analyze the resulting code when the launched activity is over to know if the audio recording task is successfully performed.

- Display error messages if any error occurs while audio recording.

To perform all these tasks, write the code as shown in Listing 11.7 into the Java activity file AudioRecordAppActivity.java.

Listing 11.7   Code Written into the Java Activity File AudioRecordAppActivity.java

```java
package com.androidtablet.audiorecordapp;

import android.os.Bundle;
import android.app.Activity;
import android.widget.Button;
import android.view.View;
import android.provider.MediaStore;
import android.content.Intent;
import android.content.ActivityNotFoundException;
import android.widget.Toast;
import android.net.Uri;

public class AudioRecordAppActivity extends Activity {
    final int RECORD_AUDIO = 1;

    @Override
    protected void onCreate(Bundle savedInstanceState) {
        super.onCreate(savedInstanceState);
        setContentView(R.layout.activity_audio_record_app);
        Button captureBtn = (Button) findViewById(
            R.id.record_btn);
        captureBtn.setOnClickListener(new Button.
            OnClickListener() {
            public void onClick(View v) {
                try {
                    Intent audioIntent = new Intent(
                    MediaStore.Audio.Media.RECORD_
                        SOUND_ACTION);
                    startActivityForResult(audioIntent,
                    RECORD_AUDIO);
                }
                catch(ActivityNotFoundException e){
                    Toast.makeText(AudioRecordAppActivity.this,
                        "Error occurred while audio recording",
                        Toast.LENGTH_SHORT).show();
                }
            }
        });
    }
```

```
protected void onActivityResult(int requestCode, int
    resultCode, Intent intent) {
    if (resultCode == RESULT_OK) {
        if(requestCode == RECORD_AUDIO){
            Uri audioUri = intent.getData();
        }
    }
}
}
```

You can see that an intent object named `audioIntent` is defined with the `MediaStore.Audio.Media.RECORD_SOUND_ACTION` action. This intent, when invoked, listens to the device microphone. Thereafter, the activity is started and the returned result is analyzed using the `onActivityResult` handler. The variable `RECORD_AUDIO` is used while starting the activity to identify and distinguish the intent while analyzing the returned result. The intent returns the uniform resource identifier (URI) of the recorded audio. Android automatically adds the recorded audio to the root of the SD card.

After you run the application, a `Button` control with the caption `Start Recording` will be displayed (see Figure 11.4 [top left]). On selecting the button, the audio recorder on the device will be invoked. Depending on the physical device, a few buttons may be displayed that enable you to start audio recording, stop recording, and play the recorded audio. Figure 11.4 (top right) shows three buttons to perform the recording tasks. When you click the Start Recording button, the one in a circle shape, the device will initiate audio recording. A timer also appears showing the recording time as shown in Figure 11.4 (bottom left). When you click the Stop Recording button (the last button in a square shape), the user will be prompted whether to save the recorded audio or discard it. Figure 11.4 (bottom right) shows the Discard and Done buttons that you can use to discard and save the recorded audio, respectively. You can use the middle button to play the recorded audio.

Figure 11.4 Start Recording button displayed on application startup (top left); device audio recorder invoked (top right); audio recording starts after selecting Start Recording button (bottom left); dialog prompting to save or discard the recorded audio after selecting Stop Recording button (bottom right)

Recipe: Understanding `CamcorderProfile`

In the following recipes, you will be learning to capture audio and video manually. While doing so, you will be required to supply certain essential features like desired audio/video encoding style, desired output file format, sampling rate, and recording duration. Before applying these features in an Android application, you need to know whether the device on which you are going to run your audio/video capturing application supports the desired features.

Android provides a `CamcorderProfile` class that helps in retrieving the camcorder profile settings in a device. It helps a developer in determining and applying only those features in the application that are supported by the client's device.

In this recipe, you will learn to retrieve the camcorder profile settings of the device and display it in the screen. So create an Android project called CamcorderApp. In this application, you will display two action items titled High Quality and Low Quality. After you select an action item, the camcorder profile settings related to that quality level will be accessed and displayed. For example, when you select the High Quality action item, the camcorder profile settings corresponding to the highest available resolution will be accessed and displayed.

To display camcorder profile settings, you will need a TextView control. After defining the TextView control, the activity layout file activity_camcorder_app.xml will appear, as shown in Listing 11.8.

Listing 11.8 **Code Written into the Activity Layout File** activity_camcorder_app.xml

```
<LinearLayout xmlns:android="http://schemas.android.com/apk/res/android"
    xmlns:tools="http://schemas.android.com/tools"
    android:layout_width="match_parent"
    android:layout_height="match_parent"
    android:orientation="vertical"
    tools:context=".CamcorderAppActivity" >
    <TextView
        android:id="@+id/profile"
        android:layout_width="match_parent"
        android:layout_height="wrap_content"
        android:textSize="@dimen/text_size"  />
</LinearLayout>
```

To identify and use the Java code, the TextView control is assigned the profile ID. Next, you need to define two action items in the menu file activity_camcorder_app.xml that is found in the res/menu folder. To define the two action items titled High Quality and Low Quality, write the code shown in Listing 11.9 into the menu file activity_camcorder_app.xml.

Listing 11.9 **Code Written into the Menu File** activity_camcorder_app.xml

```
<menu xmlns:android="http://schemas.android.com/apk/res/android" >
    <item android:id="@+id/high_quality_profile"
        android:title="High Quality"
        android:orderInCategory="0"
        android:showAsAction="ifRoom|withText" />
    <item android:id="@+id/low_quality_profile"
        android:title="Low Quality"
        android:orderInCategory="1"
        android:showAsAction="ifRoom|withText" />
</menu>
```

The two action items are set to display the titles High Quality and Low Quality, respectively. Also, to access and identify the action items, the IDs high_quality_profile and low_quality_profile are assigned to them, respectively.

Write the Java code to perform the following tasks:

- Access the `TextView` control defined in the activity layout file and map it to the `TextView` object.

- Inflate or merge the menu that is defined in the menu file `activity_camcorder_app.xml`.

- Define the `onOptionsItemSelected()` method to handle the click events on the action items.

- Call methods of the `CamcorderProfile` class to access the audio/video coded format, audio/video bit rate, number of audio channels, audio sample rate, and file output format depending on the type of action item selected.

- Display the camcorder profile settings through the `TextView` control.

To perform all these tasks, write the code shown in Listing 11.10 into the Java activity file `CamcorderAppActivity.java`.

Listing 11.10 **Code Written into the Java Activity File** `CamcorderAppActivity.java`

```java
package com.androidtablet.camcorderapp;

import android.app.Activity;
import android.media.CamcorderProfile;
import android.media.MediaRecorder.AudioEncoder;
import android.media.MediaRecorder.OutputFormat;
import android.media.MediaRecorder.VideoEncoder;
import android.os.Bundle;
import android.widget.TextView;
import android.view.Menu;
import android.view.MenuItem;

public class CamcorderAppActivity extends Activity {
    private static final int QUALITY_LOW = 0;
    private static final int QUALITY_HIGH = 1;
    TextView textProfile;

    @Override
    public void onCreate(Bundle savedInstanceState) {
        super.onCreate(savedInstanceState);
        setContentView(R.layout.activity_camcorder_app);
        textProfile = (TextView)findViewById(R.id.profile);
    }

    @Override
    public boolean onCreateOptionsMenu(Menu menu) {
        getMenuInflater().inflate(R.menu.activity_camcorder_
            app, menu);
```

```java
        return true;
    }

    @Override
    public boolean onOptionsItemSelected(MenuItem item) {
        switch (item.getItemId()) {
            case R.id.high_quality_profile:
                ProfileInfo(QUALITY_HIGH);
                break;
            case R.id.low_quality_profile:
                ProfileInfo(QUALITY_LOW);
                break;
            default:
                return super.onOptionsItemSelected(item);
        }
        return true;
    }

    private void ProfileInfo(int quality_type) {
        CamcorderProfile camcorderProfile =
            CamcorderProfile.get(quality_type);
        String selectedProfile="";
        String profileInfo;
        if(quality_type==QUALITY_HIGH)
            selectedProfile= "QUALITY_HIGH";
        else
            if(quality_type==QUALITY_LOW)
                selectedProfile="QUALITY_LOW";
        profileInfo = selectedProfile + " : \n" +
        camcorderProfile.toString() +"\n";
        profileInfo +=  "AudioBitRate: " +
            String.valueOf(camcorderProfile.audioBitRate)
            +"\n" + "AudioChannels: " +  String.valueOf(
            camcorderProfile.audioChannels) +"\n"
            + "AudioCodec: " + AudioCodecinString(
            camcorderProfile.audioCodec) +"\n"
            + "AudioSampleRate: " + String.valueOf(
            camcorderProfile.audioSampleRate) +"\n"
            + "Duration: " + String.valueOf(
            camcorderProfile.duration) +"\n"
            + "FileFormat: " + FileFormatinString(
            camcorderProfile.fileFormat) +"\n"
            + "Quality: " + String.valueOf(
            camcorderProfile.quality) +"\n"
            + "VideoBitRate: " + String.valueOf(
            camcorderProfile.videoBitRate) +"\n"
            + "VideoCodec: " + VideoCodecinString(
            camcorderProfile.videoCodec) +"\n"
```

```java
        + "VideoFrameRate: " + String.valueOf(
        camcorderProfile.videoFrameRate) +"\n"
        + "VideoFrameWidth: " + String.valueOf(
        camcorderProfile.videoFrameWidth) +"\n"
        + "VideoFrameHeight: " + String.valueOf(
        camcorderProfile.videoFrameHeight);
        textProfile.setText(profileInfo);
}

private String AudioCodecinString(int audioCodec){
    switch(audioCodec){
        case AudioEncoder.AAC:
           return "AAC";
        case AudioEncoder.AAC_ELD:
           return "AAC_ELD";
        case AudioEncoder.AMR_NB:
           return "AMR_NB";
        case AudioEncoder.AMR_WB:
           return "AMR_WB";
        case AudioEncoder.DEFAULT:
           return "DEFAULT";
        case AudioEncoder.HE_AAC:
           return "HE_AAC";
        default:
           return "unknown";
    }
}

private String FileFormatinString(int fileFormat){
    switch(fileFormat){
        case OutputFormat.AAC_ADTS:
           return "AAC_ADTS";
        case OutputFormat.AMR_NB:
           return "AMR_NB";
        case OutputFormat.AMR_WB:
           return "AMR_WB";
        case OutputFormat.DEFAULT:
           return "DEFAULT";
        case OutputFormat.MPEG_4:
           return "MPEG_4";
        case OutputFormat.THREE_GPP:
           return "THREE_GPP";
        default:
           return "unknown";
    }
}

private String VideoCodecinString(int videoCodec){
```

```
        switch(videoCodec){
            case VideoEncoder.H263:
                return "H263";
            case VideoEncoder.H264:
                return "H264";
            case VideoEncoder.MPEG_4_SP:
                return "MPEG_4_SP";
            case VideoEncoder.DEFAULT:
                return "DEFAULT";
            default:
                return "unknown";
        }
    }
}
```

When you run the application, nothing will appear on the screen, and the action items High Quality and Low Quality will be displayed in the ActionBar (see Figure 11.5 [top left]). After you click the High Quality action item, you can access the camcorder profile settings corresponding to the highest available resolution, as seen in Figure 11.5 (top right). Similarly, after you select the Low Quality action item, the camcorder profile settings corresponding to the lowest available resolution will be displayed, as shown in Figure 11.5 (bottom left).

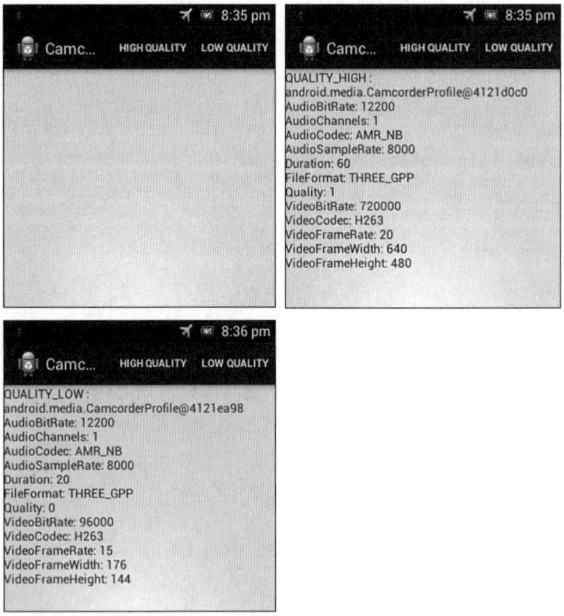

Figure 11.5   Two action items, High Quality and Low Quality, displayed on application startup (top left); camcorder profile information corresponding to high resolution is displayed (top right); and Camcorder profile information corresponding to low resolution is displayed (bottom left)

Recipe: Understanding `MediaRecorder` and Its Methods

The `MediaRecorder` class is used to record audio and video. The methods of this class that are used to configure the audio/video recorder are briefly described in Table 11.1.

Table 11.1   Brief Description of the `MediaRecorder` Methods Used to Configure Recorder

Method	Description
`void setAudioSource(int audio_source)/void setVideoSource(int video_source)`	Sets the audio or video source. If the method is not used, the audio or video track will not be recorded in the output file. The constants used for the `audio_source` parameter are `CAMCORDER`, `DEFAULT`, `MIC`, `VOICE_CALL`, `VOICE_COMMUNICATION`, `VOICE_DOWNLINK`, `VOICE_RECOGNITION`, and `VOICE_UPLINK`. The constants used for the `video_source` parameter are `CAMERA` and `DEFAULT`.
`void setOutputFormat(int output_format)`	Sets the format of the output file produced during recording. The constants that are used for the `output_format` parameter are `AAC_ADTS`, `AMR_NB`, `AMR_WB`, `DEFAULT`, `MPEG_4`, and `THREE_GPP`.
`void setAudioEncoder(int audio_encoder) /setVideoEncoder(int video_encoder)`	Called after the `setOutputFormat()` method. It sets the audio or video encoder to be used for recording. If this method is not used, the audio or video track will not be recorded. The constants used for the `video_encoder` parameter are `DEFAULT`, `H263`, `H264`, and `MPEG_4_SP`. The constants used for the `audio_encoder` parameter are `AAC`, `AAC_ELD`, `AMR_NB`, `AMR_WB`, `DEFAULT`, and `HE_AAC`.
`void setOutputFile(String path)`	Sets the path of the output file.
`void setPreviewDisplay(Surface sv)`	Sets a surface to show a preview of the recorded video.
`void prepare()`	Prepares the recorder to begin capturing and encoding audio/video. The method is called after setting the source, output format, encoding style, and output file.
`void start()`	Initiates the task of capturing and encoding audio/video and saves it in the file that is specified through the `setOutputFile()` method.
`void stop()`	Stops the recording session.
`void release()`	Releases resources associated with the `MediaRecorder` object.

Recipe: Recording Audio Using Java Code

In this recipe, you will learn to explicitly write code to use the `MediaRecorder` class and call its different methods that are required to record audio in the desired output format and encoding style. To record audio using the `MediaRecorder`, follow these steps:

1. Create a `MediaRecorder` object.

2. Invoke the `setAudioSource` method to set the audio source.

3. Invoke the `setOutputFormat` method to set the output format.

4. Invoke the `setAudioEncoder` method to set the audio encoder.

5. Invoke the `setOutputFile` method to set the output file.

6. Invoke the `prepare` method to prepare the recorder.

7. Invoke the `start` method to start recording.

8. Invoke the `stop` method to stop recording.

9. Invoke the `release` method to release resources associated to the `MediaRecorder` object.

Create an Android project called `AudioCaptureApp`. In this application, you will use two action items titled Start Recording and Stop Recording, respectively. A user can begin audio recording by clicking the Start Recording action item and then click Stop Recording to stop audio recording. The recorded audio will be saved in the SD card of the device and will appear in its music list.

To direct the user when to click the Start Recording and Stop Recording action items, you need to display proper text messages on the screen. To display these messages, use the `TextView` control. To define the `TextView` control, write the code shown in Listing 11.11 into the activity layout file `activity_audio_capture_app.xml`.

Listing 11.11   **Code Written into the Activity Layout File** `activity_audio_capture_app.xml`

```
<LinearLayout  xmlns:android="http://schemas.android.com/apk/res/android"
    android:layout_width="match_parent"
    android:layout_height="match_parent"
    android:orientation="vertical" >
    <TextView
        android:id="@+id/textview"
        android:layout_width="wrap_content"
        android:layout_height="wrap_content"
        android:text="Press Start Recording button to
        start audio recording"
        android:textSize="@dimen/text_size"
        android:textStyle="bold" />
</LinearLayout>
```

To identify and use the Java code, assign the `TextView` control the `textview` ID. The `TextView` is initialized to display the text message `Press Start Recording button to start audio recording`. The text message is set to appear in bold and in the font size determined by the dimension resource `text_size`.

Define two action items in the menu file `activity_audio_capture_app.xml` that is found in the `res/menu` folder. To define the two action items titled Start Recording and Stop Recording, write the code as shown in Listing 11.12 into the menu file `activity_audio_capture_app.xml`.

Listing 11.12   **Code Written into the Menu File** `activity_audio_capture_app.xml`

```xml
<menu xmlns:android= "http://schemas.android.com/apk/res/android" >
    <item android:id="@+id/start_recording_button"
        android:title="Start Recording"
        android:orderInCategory="0"
        android:showAsAction="ifRoom|withText" />
    <item android:id="@+id/stop_recording_button"
        android:title="Stop Recording"
        android:orderInCategory="1"
        android:showAsAction="ifRoom|withText" />
</menu>
```

The two action items are set to display the titles Start Recording and Stop Recording, respectively. Also, to access and identify the action items, set the IDs `start_recording_button` and `stop_recording_button` to them.

Write the Java code to perform the following tasks:

- Access the `TextView` control defined in the activity layout file and map it to the `TextView` object.

- Inflate or merge the menu that is defined in the menu file `activity_audio_capture_app.xml`.

- Define the `onOptionsItemSelected()` method to handle the click events on the action items.

- Define the `startRecording()` and `stopRecording()` functions that will perform the tasks of recording audio and stopping recording operations.

- Set the two action items Start Recording and Stop Recording to invoke the `startRecording()` and `stopRecording()` functions.

- Define the filename by which you want the audio that will be recorded to be stored in the SD card.

- Define the `MediaRecorder` object and invoke its methods to define the audio source, audio format type, encoding style, and sampling rate.

- Call `MediaRecorder`'s `start()` and `stop()` methods to start and stop audio recording when the respective action item is clicked.

> **Note**
>
> If the device has an SD card, its usual path is
> android.os.Environment.getExternalStorageDirectory().getPath().

To accomplish all the preceding tasks, write the code as shown in Listing 11.13 into the Java activity file `AudioCaptureAppActivity.java`.

Listing 11.13   **Code Written into the Java Activity File** `AudioCaptureAppActivity.java`

```java
package com.androidtablet.audiocaptureapp;

import java.io.IOException;
import android.os.Bundle;
import android.app.Activity;
import android.view.Menu;
import android.view.MenuItem;
import android.widget.TextView;
import android.media.MediaRecorder;
import android.media.MediaRecorder.AudioSource;
import android.media.MediaRecorder.OutputFormat;
import android.media.MediaRecorder.AudioEncoder;
import java.io.File;
import android.os.Environment;

public class AudioCaptureAppActivity extends Activity {
    private MediaRecorder mediaRecorder = null;
    private File audioFile = null;
    private TextView textView;

    @Override
    protected void onCreate(Bundle savedInstanceState) {
        super.onCreate(savedInstanceState);
        setContentView(R.layout.activity_audio_capture_app);
        textView = (TextView)findViewById(R.id.textview);
        audioFile = new File(Environment.
        getExternalStorageDirectory(), "testaudio.3gp");   #1
    }

    @Override
    public boolean onCreateOptionsMenu(Menu menu) {
        getMenuInflater().inflate(R.menu.activity_audio_
            capture_app, menu);                            #2
        return true;
    }

    @Override
```

```
public boolean onOptionsItemSelected(MenuItem item) {
    switch (item.getItemId()) {
        case R.id.start_recording_button:
            startRecording(audioFile);                    #3
            break;
        case R.id.stop_recording_button:
            stopRecording();                              #4
            break;
        default:
            return super.onOptionsItemSelected(item);
    }
    return true;
}

private void startRecording(File file) {
    if (mediaRecorder != null)
        mediaRecorder.release();
    mediaRecorder = new MediaRecorder();
    mediaRecorder.setAudioSource(AudioSource.MIC);        #5
    mediaRecorder.setOutputFormat(OutputFormat.
        THREE_GPP);                                       #6
    mediaRecorder.setAudioEncoder(AudioEncoder.
        AMR_WB);                                          #7
    mediaRecorder.setOutputFile(file.
        getAbsolutePath());                               #8
    try {
        mediaRecorder.prepare();                          #9
        mediaRecorder.start();                            #10
        textView.setText("Recording started. Press Stop
            Recording button to stop");
    } catch (IOException e) {
        e.printStackTrace();
    }
}

private void stopRecording() {
    if (mediaRecorder != null) {
        mediaRecorder.stop();                             #11
        mediaRecorder.release();                          #12
        mediaRecorder = null;
        textView.setText("Audio recorded");
    }
}
}
```

You can see that a few of the statements used in Listing 11.13 need some explanation. The following list explains the usage and meaning of those statements:

- Statement #1 defines the filename by which the recorded audio has to be saved in the SD card. The recorded audio will be saved and named testaudio.3gp.

- Statement #2 inflates the menu file defined in the res/menu folder to display the menu items (action items) that are defined in it. That is, the two action items Start Recording and Stop Recording defined in the menu file activity_audio_capture_app.xml will appear in the ActionBar.

- The startRecording() function is called (#3) when the user selects the Start Recording action item. The output filename by which the audio will be saved is passed to the function as a parameter. The startRecording() function will begin audio recording when it is invoked.

- The stopRecording() function is called (#4) to stop audio recording when the user selects the Stop Recording action item.

- The audio source for recording is set to AudioSource.MIC (#5). That is, the device microphone is set as the source of the audio recording.

- Statements #6 and #7 define the format of the output audio file and audio encoding style, respectively.

- Statement #8 defines the audio filename by which the recorded audio will be stored.

- Statement #9 prepares the audio recorder for audio recording.

- Statement #10 begins audio recording.

- Statement #11 stops audio recording.

- Statement #12 releases the resources allocated to the MediaRecorder object.

To enable an application to record audio and save the recorded audio in the SD card, you need specific permissions. The following two statements are added to the AndroidManifest.xml to seek permissions to record audio and to save the recorded audio in the device storage:

```
<uses-permission
    android:name="android.permission.
    WRITE_EXTERNAL_STORAGE"/>
<uses-permission
    android:name="android.permission.
    RECORD_AUDIO" />
```

If these permissions are not added to the manifest file, the application will return a RuntimeException.

When you run the application, the text message Press Start Recording button to start audio recording is displayed on startup. Also, two action items, Start Recording and Stop Recording, appear in the ActionBar (see Figure 11.6 [top left]). When you click the Start Recording action item, you can begin recording audio. The text message changes to Recording started. Press Stop Recording button to stop (see Figure 11.6 [top right]). When you select the Stop Recording action item, the recording will stop. The text message changes to Audio recorded to indicate that the audio recording has finished, as shown in Figure 11.6 (bottom left).

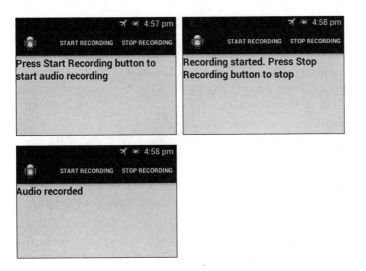

Figure 11.6   Text message displayed on application startup informing the usage of the two action items (top left); text message changes and audio recording begins after selecting the Start Recording action item (top right); audio recording stops after selecting the Stop Recording action item (bottom left)

In the device, the `testaudio` file appears in the playlist and confirms that the audio is successfully recorded and saved in the SD card file (see Figure 11.7 [left]). Selecting the audio file `testaudio` plays it, as shown in Figure 11.7 (right).

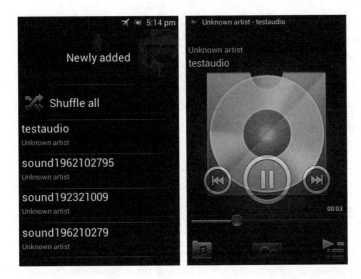

Figure 11.7   The device playlist shows the recorded audio file (left) and playing the recorded audio (right)

Recipe: Recording Video Using a Built-In Intent

There are two ways of video recording in Android applications:

- In the first way of video recording, you use Android's MediaRecorder class and call its different methods to access the device camera, record the video in the desired format and encoding style, and save it in the device storage.

- In the second way, which is easier, you define and invoke an intent using the MediaStore.ACTION_VIDEO_CAPTURE action that records, pauses, plays, and stores the video automatically.

In this recipe, you will use the second method to record video (that is, invoke the intent with the specific MediaStore attribute). In the next recipe, you will learn to record video using the MediaRecorder class.

Create an Android project called VideoRecordApp. In this application, you will use Button and VideoView controls. Clicking the Button control invokes the device camera. When the video has finished recording, it will be played in the VideoView control. To define the Button and VideoView controls, write the code as shown in Listing 11.14 into the activity layout file activity_video_record_app.xml.

Listing 11.14   **Code Written into the Activity Layout File** activity_video_record_app.xml

```
<LinearLayout xmlns:android="http://schemas.android.com/apk/res/android"
android:layout_width="match_parent"
android:layout_height="match_parent"
android:orientation="vertical" >
    <Button
        android:id="@+id/record_video_btn"
        android:layout_width="wrap_content"
        android:layout_height="wrap_content"
        android:text="Launch Video Recorder"
        android:textSize="@dimen/text_size"          />
    <VideoView
        android:id="@+id/videoview"
        android:layout_width="match_parent"
        android:layout_height="match_parent" />
</LinearLayout>
```

To identify and use the Java code, the Button and VideoView controls are assigned the IDs record_video_btn and videoview, respectively. The caption displayed on the Button control is Launch Video Recorder.

Next, you need to write the Java code to perform the following tasks:

- Access the Button and VideoView controls defined in the activity layout file and map them to the respective objects.

- Associate the setOnClickListener to the Button control to listen to the click event. The onClick callback method will be invoked when a click event occurs on the Button control.

- Define an intent called videoIntent that refers to the built-in MediaStore.ACTION_ VIDEO_CAPTURE activity. This built-in activity is responsible for launching the device camera and initiating video recording.

- Start the activity when the Button control is clicked, thereby allowing the user to record video.

- Analyze the resulting code when the launched activity has completed so you know if the video recording task has performed successfully.

- If the video recording has successfully performed, the recorded video is accessed and played via the VideoView control.

To accomplish all these tasks, write the code shown in Listing 11.15 into the Java activity file VideoRecordAppActivity.java.

Listing 11.15 **Code Written into the Java Activity File** VideoRecordAppActivity.java

```
package com.androidtablet.videorecordapp;

import android.os.Bundle;
import android.app.Activity;
import android.widget.Button;
import android.view.View;
import android.provider.MediaStore;
import android.content.Intent;
import android.content.ActivityNotFoundException;
import android.widget.Toast;
import android.net.Uri;
import android.widget.VideoView;

public class VideoRecordAppActivity extends Activity {
   VideoView videoView;
   final int  RECORD_VIDEO = 1;

   @Override
   protected void onCreate(Bundle savedInstanceState) {
      super.onCreate(savedInstanceState);
      setContentView(R.layout.activity_video_record_app);
      Button videoCaptureBtn = (Button) findViewById(
         R.id.record_video_btn);
      videoView = (VideoView) findViewById(R.id.videoview);
      videoCaptureBtn.setOnClickListener(new
         Button.OnClickListener() {
```

```java
    public void onClick(View v) {
        try {
            Intent videoIntent = new Intent(MediaStore.
                ACTION_VIDEO_CAPTURE);
            startActivityForResult(videoIntent,
                RECORD_VIDEO);
        }
        catch(ActivityNotFoundException anfe){
            Toast.makeText(VideoRecordAppActivity.this,
                "Error occurred while video recording",
                Toast.LENGTH_SHORT).show();
        }
    }
});
}
protected void onActivityResult(int requestCode, int
    resultCode, Intent intent) {
    if (resultCode == RESULT_OK) {
        if(requestCode == RECORD_VIDEO ){
            Uri videoUri = intent.getData();
            videoView.setVideoURI(videoUri);
            videoView.start();
        }
    }
}
}
}
```

You can see that an intent object named videoIntent is defined with the MediaStore. ACTION_VIDEO_CAPTURE action. This intent activates the device camera when it is invoked. Thereafter, the activity is started, and the returned result is analyzed using the onActivityResult handler. The RECORD_VIDEO variable is used while starting the activity to identify the intent while analyzing the result it returns. The intent returns the URI of the recorded video, which is then assigned to the VideoView control to play the recorded video. Android automatically adds the recorded video to the root of the SD card. The default location can vary by device.

When you run the application, a Button control with the caption Launch Video Recorder will be displayed (see Figure 11.8 [top left]). Selecting the button invokes the camera, showing the preview. On the right side of the preview, a Begin Video Recording button (a red circle) appears, as shown in Figure 11.8 (top right). When you click the Begin Video Recording button, the video recording will begin. At the bottom left of the screen, the timing of the recording appears. A Stop Video Recording button (a red square) appears on the right side, as shown in Figure 11.8 (bottom left). When you select the Stop Video Recording button, the recorded video will be saved in the device storage and will play in the VideoView (see Figure 11.8 [bottom right]) confirming the video has been recorded and successfully saved.

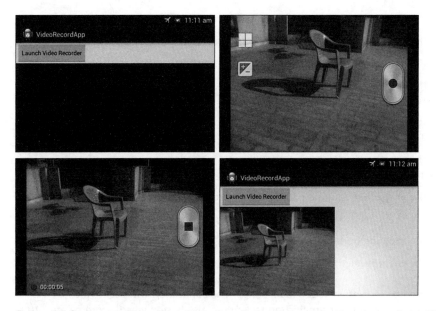

Figure 11.8   Launch Video Recorder button displayed on application startup (top left); device video recorder invoked displaying the preview and Start Video Recording button at the bottom (top right); video recording starts after selecting Start Video Recording button (bottom left); recorded video being played in the `VideoView` of the application (bottom right)

Recipe: Recording Video Using Java Code

In this recipe, you will learn to write code to use the `MediaRecorder` class and call its different methods that are required to record video in the desired output format and encoding style. To handle the display, you will be using the `SurfaceView` and `SurfaceHolder.Callback` interface. Recall that the `SurfaceView` is a special view that provides a drawing surface inside the view hierarchy. It optimizes the graphics by using an independent thread to draw and update the view. The `SurfaceHolder` interface provides the surface to work on (that is, it holds the `SurfaceView` object, enabling you to control the size, edit, and format and monitor the surface.

To record video using the `MediaRecorder`, follow these steps:

1. Create a `MediaRecorder` object.
2. Invoke the `setAudioSource` method to set the audio source.
3. Invoke the `setVideoSource` method to set the video source.
4. Invoke the `setOutputFormat` method to set the output format of the video.
5. Invoke the `setVideoFrameRate` method to set the frame rate of the video to be recorded.

6. Invoke the `setVideoEncoder` method to set the video encoder.

7. Invoke the `setAudioEncoder` method to set the audio encoder.

8. Invoke the `setOutputFile` method to set the output file.

9. Invoke the `setMaxDuration` method to set the maximum time duration in milliseconds for recording the video.

10. Invoke the `setMaxFileSize` method to set the maximum file size in bytes of the recorded video.

11. Invoke the `setPreviewDisplay` method to set a surface to show a preview of the recorded video.

12. Invoke the `prepare` method to prepare the recorder.

13. Invoke the `start` method to start video recording.

14. Invoke the `stop` method to stop video recording.

15. Invoke the `release` method to release resources associated to the `MediaRecorder` object.

Create an Android project called `VideoCaptureApp`. The application will begin video recording automatically on startup. The application will automatically stop video recording after 10 seconds. The recorded video will be saved in the SD card of the device and will be visible in the device gallery.

As mentioned earlier, to display a video recording preview, you will use the `SurfaceView`. To define the `SurfaceView`, write the code shown in Listing 11.16 into the activity layout file `activity_video_capture_app.xml`.

Listing 11.16   **Code Written into the Activity Layout File** `activity_video_capture_app.xml`

```
<LinearLayout xmlns:android="http://schemas.android.com/apk/res/android"
    android:orientation="vertical"
    android:layout_width="match_parent"
    android:layout_height="match_parent" >
    <SurfaceView
        android:id="@+id/videoview"
        android:layout_width="match_parent"
        android:layout_height="match_parent" />
</LinearLayout >
```

To identify and use the Java code, assign the `SurfaceView` control the `videoview` ID. Write the Java code to perform the following tasks:

- Access the `SurfaceView` defined in the activity layout file and map it to the `SurfaceView` object. It is through the `SurfaceView` that you will preview the camera to know what is being recorded.

- Set the main activity class to implement `SurfaceHolder.Callback`, `OnInfoListener`, and `OnErrorListener`. The `SurfaceHolder` callback is used to notify the related view when the underlying surface is created, destroyed, or modified. `OnInfoListener` and `OnErrorListener` are the event listeners for listening to the updates on the `MediaRecorder` and errors if any occur while video recording.

- Implement three methods: `surfaceCreated(SurfaceHolder)`, `surfaceDestroyed (SurfaceHolder)`, and `surfaceChanged(SurfaceHolder holder, int format, int w, int h)`.

  - **`surfaceCreated(SurfaceHolder)`**—Informs when the surface is created and is available for video recording.
  - **`surfaceDestroyed(SurfaceHolder)`**—Informs when the surface is destroyed.
  - **`surfaceChanged(SurfaceHolder holder, int format, int w, int h)`**— Informs when there is a change in the surface structure, such as any changes in surface width or height or device orientation.

- Define the `MediaRecorder` object and associate `setOnInfoListener` and `setOnErrorListener` to it to get the `MediaRecorder` updates and to listen to errors so you can take necessary actions.

- Define the filename by which the recorded video will be saved in the SD card.

- Define the audio source, video source, output format, video frame rate, video, and audio encoding attributes.

- Set the time duration of recording video and the maximum video file size.

- Invoke the `MediaRecorder`'s `start()` method to begin video recording on application startup.

- Invoke the `MediaRecorder`'s `stop()` method to stop video recording after the time duration of 10 seconds.

- Release and reset the `MediaRecorder` after the video recording is over.

- Check for the occurrence of errors, if any, and display them on the screen.

To accomplish all these tasks, write the code shown in Listing 11.17 in the Java activity file `VideoCaptureAppActivity.java`.

Note

`SurfaceView` has a dedicated drawing surface within the view hierarchy. It draws and updates views using the background threads and thus relieves the GUI thread to do other application tasks. `SurfaceView` controls the format of the surface, its size, and its location on the screen.

Listing 11.17   **Code Written into the Java Activity File** `VideoCaptureAppActivity.java`

```java
package com.androidtablet.videocaptureapp;

import java.io.IOException;

import android.app.Activity;
import android.media.CamcorderProfile;
import android.media.MediaRecorder;
import android.os.Bundle;
import android.view.SurfaceHolder;
import android.view.SurfaceView;
import android.widget.Toast;
import android.os.Environment;
import android.media.MediaRecorder.OnInfoListener;
import android.media.MediaRecorder.OnErrorListener;

public class VideoCaptureAppActivity extends Activity
    implements SurfaceHolder.Callback, OnInfoListener,
    OnErrorListener {
    private MediaRecorder mediaRecorder;
    private SurfaceHolder surfaceHolder;
    private SurfaceView surfaceView;
    private String outputFile;

    @Override
    public void onCreate(Bundle savedInstanceState) {
        super.onCreate(savedInstanceState);
        mediaRecorder = new MediaRecorder();
        mediaRecorder.setOnInfoListener(this);
        mediaRecorder.setOnErrorListener(this);
        initMediaRecorder();
        setContentView(R.layout.activity_video_capture_app);
        surfaceView = (SurfaceView) findViewById(
            R.id.videoview);
        surfaceHolder = surfaceView.getHolder();
        surfaceHolder.addCallback(this);
    }

    @Override
    protected void onPause() {
        super.onPause();
        releaseMediaRecorder();
    }

    @Override
    protected void onResume() {
        super.onResume();
```

```java
    }

    @Override
    protected void onDestroy() {
        super.onDestroy();
    }

    private void releaseMediaRecorder(){
        if (mediaRecorder != null) {
            mediaRecorder.reset();
            mediaRecorder.release();
            mediaRecorder = null;
        }
    }

    @Override
    public void onInfo(MediaRecorder mr, int what, int
        extra) {
        if(what == MediaRecorder.MEDIA_RECORDER_INFO_MAX_
            DURATION_REACHED) {
            try {
                mediaRecorder.stop();
            }
            catch(IllegalStateException e) { }
            releaseMediaRecorder();
            Toast.makeText(this, "Exceeded the Recording
                limit.Stopping the recording",
                Toast.LENGTH_SHORT).show();
            finish();
        }
    }

    @Override
    public void onError(MediaRecorder mr, int what, int extra) {
        try {
            mediaRecorder.stop();
        }
        catch(IllegalStateException e) {  }
        releaseMediaRecorder();
        Toast.makeText(this, "Error occurred in Recording.
            Stopping the recording", Toast.LENGTH_SHORT).
            show();
        finish();
    }

    private void initMediaRecorder(){
        outputFile = Environment.
```

```
                getExternalStorageDirectory().
                getPath() + "/myvideo.mp4";
        mediaRecorder.setAudioSource(MediaRecorder.
            AudioSource.CAMCORDER);
        mediaRecorder.setVideoSource(MediaRecorder.
            VideoSource.CAMERA);
        mediaRecorder.setOutputFormat(MediaRecorder.
            OutputFormat.MPEG_4);                        #1
        mediaRecorder.setVideoFrameRate(20);             #2
        mediaRecorder.setVideoEncoder(MediaRecorder.
            VideoEncoder.MPEG_4_SP);                     #3
        mediaRecorder.setAudioEncoder(MediaRecorder.
            AudioEncoder.AMR_NB);                        #4
        mediaRecorder.setOutputFile(outputFile);
        mediaRecorder.setMaxDuration(10000);
        mediaRecorder.setMaxFileSize(5000000);
    }

    private void prepareMediaRecorder() {
        mediaRecorder.setPreviewDisplay(surfaceHolder.
            getSurface());
        try {
            mediaRecorder.prepare();
        } catch (IllegalStateException e) {
            e.printStackTrace();
            finish();
        } catch (IOException e) {
            e.printStackTrace();
            finish();
        }
    }

    @Override
    public void surfaceCreated(SurfaceHolder holder) {
        prepareMediaRecorder();
        mediaRecorder.start();
    }

    @Override
    public void surfaceChanged(SurfaceHolder holder, int
        format, int weight,  int height) {  }

    @Override
    public void surfaceDestroyed(SurfaceHolder holder) {    }
}
```

You can also use `CamcorderProfile` to define different video settings. For example, you can replace statements #1, #2, #3, and #4 shown in Listing 11.17 with the following statement:

```
mediaRecorder.setProfile(CamcorderProfile.get(CamcorderProfile.QUALITY_HIGH));
```

To enable applications to access the camera hardware, record audio, and save the recorded video file in the SD card, add the following permission statements to the `AndroidManifest.xml` file:

```
<uses-permission
    android:name="android.permission.
    RECORD_AUDIO" />
<uses-permission
    android:name="android.permission.CAMERA" />
<uses-permission
    android:name="android.permission.
    WRITE_EXTERNAL_STORAGE" />
```

Now your application is ready to run. When you run the application, video recording will automatically start (see Figure 11.9 [left]). You can move the device camera to any direction to record the desired views. The video recording will auto stop after 10 seconds. The message `Exceeded the Recording limit. Stopping the recording` will appear indicating that the video recording is complete. The recorded video will appear in the device gallery under the new album `Internal storage`, as shown in Figure 11.9 (right).

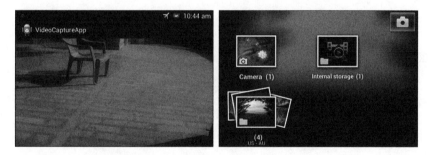

Figure 11.9   Recording of video begins on application startup (left), and recorded video displayed in the device gallery (right)

Summary

In this chapter, you learned to capture an image and record audio and video. You learned to do this both manually and by invoking the built-in intent with predefined actions. You read about different classes and their methods that are required in accessing the device camera and micro-phone. You discovered different encoding and output formats that can be used in recording audio and video. You also saw how to access device camcorder profile information.

The next chapter focuses on connecting the devices through a wireless network. You will learn to connect two devices through Bluetooth. You will also learn to transfer files between two devices through Bluetooth. Finally, you will learn to connect devices and transfer data through Wi-Fi Direct.

12

Wireless Connectivity

Bluetooth and Wi-Fi are two main wireless technology standards. Bluetooth is a standard that is used for exchanging data over short distances without wires. It uses low-power radio transmissions to link phones, computers, and other network devices. Similarly, Wi-Fi is a wireless network technology that is easy to set up and is quite inexpensive. It requires no physical connection between sender and receiver but uses radio waves to provide a wireless network, including a high-speed Internet connection.

In this chapter, you will learn to pair two Bluetooth-enabled devices, manually transfer files from one device to another using Bluetooth, and pair a Bluetooth device with a Windows PC. You will also learn to enable a local Bluetooth device, display the list of paired devices, and learn about the classes and the methods that are required to transfer files through Bluetooth. Also, you will come to understand the Wi-Fi technology, including how to enable and disable Wi-Fi.

Recipe: Pairing Two Bluetooth-Enabled Devices

Bluetooth is a communications protocol designed for short-range, low-bandwidth peer-to-peer communications. To use Bluetooth in Android applications, Android provides APIs that help in the following:

- Managing, configuring, and monitoring Bluetooth settings
- Discovering Bluetooth devices within range
- Transferring data among paired devices

Following are the steps to establish a connection between two Bluetooth-enabled devices:

1. Select the Settings button in one Android device. In the Wireless Networks section (see Figure 12.1 [top left]), several options will be displayed. Tap the Off button next to Bluetooth to switch it on, as shown in Figure 12.1 (top right). After switching on Bluetooth, the name of the device itself will be displayed. The device also searches for the Bluetooth-enabled devices nearby (see Figure 12.1 [bottom left]). Turn on the Bluetooth

on another device and then select the Search for Devices button on the current Android device. Another device name whose Bluetooth is turned on will appear in the Available Devices list as shown in Figure 12.1 (bottom right). You assume the name of another device is NOKIA N71.

Figure 12.1   Settings options displayed after selecting the Settings button on the device (top left); turning on the Bluetooth device (top right); current device name and the empty list of Available Devices (bottom left); a device name appears in the Available Devices list when its Bluetooth is turned on (bottom right)

2. After selecting the Touch to Pair button, the current device will begin the pairing procedure with the second device. The message Pairing appears below the device with which your device is trying to pair (see Figure 12.2 [top left]). A dialog box appears that prompts you to enter the PIN of the device with which the current device is trying to pair (see Figure 12.2 [top right]). The PIN is usually 0000 or 1234. Enter 0000 as the PIN and then click the OK button.

3. Enter the PIN (0000 or 1234) on the second device to pair the two devices. The name of the second device appears in the Paired Devices list on the current device, thereby confirming that the pairing process was successful (see Figure 12.2 [bottom left]). You may get a LiveWare Manager dialog box asking you to select the application that you want to run automatically when connection with the device is established (see Figure 12.2 [bottom right]). LiveWare Manager notification is optional and may not appear on certain devices.

Note

For pairing two devices, you must enter the correct PIN number on both devices.

Figure 12.2   NOKIA N71 device selected for pairing (top left); screen prompting to enter PIN number (top right); NOKIA N71 device is paired and appears in the Paired Devices list (bottom left); LiveWare manager notification asking whether you want to run any application automatically after pairing a device (bottom right)

4. Select from two options: Rename and Unpair (see Figure 12.3 [left]). The Rename option helps in changing the device name (see Figure 12.3 [right]). When you click the Unpair option, the two devices will be unpaired (disconnected).

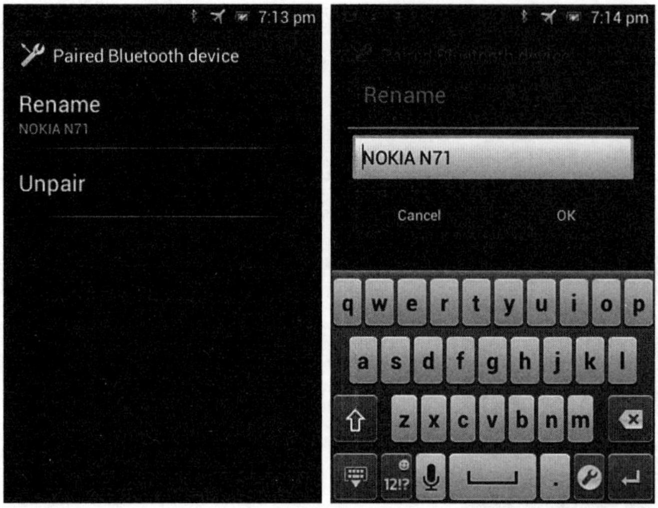

Figure 12.3   Two options, Rename and Unpair, displayed after selecting a paired device (left), and dialog prompting to enter the new name of the selected paired device (right)

Even though the Bluetooth connection is turned off, the devices still remember each other when the connection is opened again. That is, you don't need to pair devices again when you turn on the Bluetooth the next time.

Recipe: Manually Transferring Files from One Device to Another Using Bluetooth

Following are the steps to send files from one device to another:

1. Turn on the Bluetooth on the sending and receiving devices, and confirm that they are paired.

2. In the sending device, open the application that contains the files that you want to send. Select any photo album and a photo in it that you want to send.

3. Either touch and hold the photo or press the Menu key to display different menu items (see Figure 12.4 [top left]).

4. Select the Share menu item.

5. From the Share list that pops up, select the Bluetooth option (see Figure 12.4 [top right]).

6. Assuming the paired device to which you want to send the picture is NOKIA N71, tap it from the list of available devices (see Figure 12.4 [bottom left]).

7. The sending device will start sending the chosen picture and will display the message `Sending file to "NOKIA N71,"` as shown in Figure 12.4 (bottom right).

8. The receiving device will be informed that a device is trying to send a file. Accept the incoming file on the receiving device to complete the file transfer process.

Figure 12.4   After selecting a picture from an album, the menu items displayed on selecting the menu button (top left); list of options displayed after selecting Share menu item (top right); after you select the Bluetooth option from the Share list, the Bluetooth device picker dialog opens, displaying the list of paired devices (bottom left); selected picture being sent to the selected paired device (bottom right)

Recipe: Pairing a Bluetooth Device with a Windows PC

Steps for pairing a Bluetooth device with a Windows PC are given here:

1. Make sure that the Bluetooth is enabled on the device. That is, select the Settings button on the device. Turn on the Bluetooth option that is visible in the Wireless Networks section.

2. Assuming the Windows PC has a built-in Bluetooth adapter, switch it on by pressing the Bluetooth button on the keyboard. The Bluetooth icon will appear in the notification area (bottom-right side of the desktop).

3. Select the Search for Devices button on the device so that it can search and find the Windows PC.

4. A message will appear in the notification area of the Windows PC that A Bluetooth device is trying to connect (see Figure 12.5 [left]). Click the Bluetooth icon, and from the window that pops up displaying a list of options, select Allow a Device to Connect (see Figure 12.5 [right]).

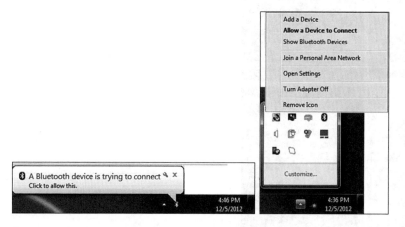

Figure 12.5   Pop-up message informing that a certain Bluetooth device is trying to connect to the PC (left), and a window showing different options after selecting the Bluetooth icon (right)

5. Select the Bluetooth icon from the notification area and select Add a Device from the window that opens.

6. From the window that appears displaying all the nearby devices that have their Bluetooth turned on (see Figure 12.6 [top left]), select the ST2li device and then click Next.

7. On the device, the address of the Windows PC will appear in the list of available devices. Select Touch to Pair to pair the Windows PC with the device (see Figure 12.6 [top right]).

8. The device shows a dialog box that prompts to confirm whether the Windows PC is showing the same passkey that is displayed on the device (see Figure 12.6 [bottom left]).

9. On the Windows PC, a dialog appears confirming whether the device is showing the same code. Comparing and confirming the pairing codes between the PC and the device verifies whether the connection is being established between the correct devices. Once the verification of pairing codes is done, the connection between the Windows PC and the device will be established, and the name of the PC will appear in the Paired Devices list, as shown in Figure 12.6 (bottom right). You assume that the name of the PC that is paired through the preceding steps is BINTU-PC.

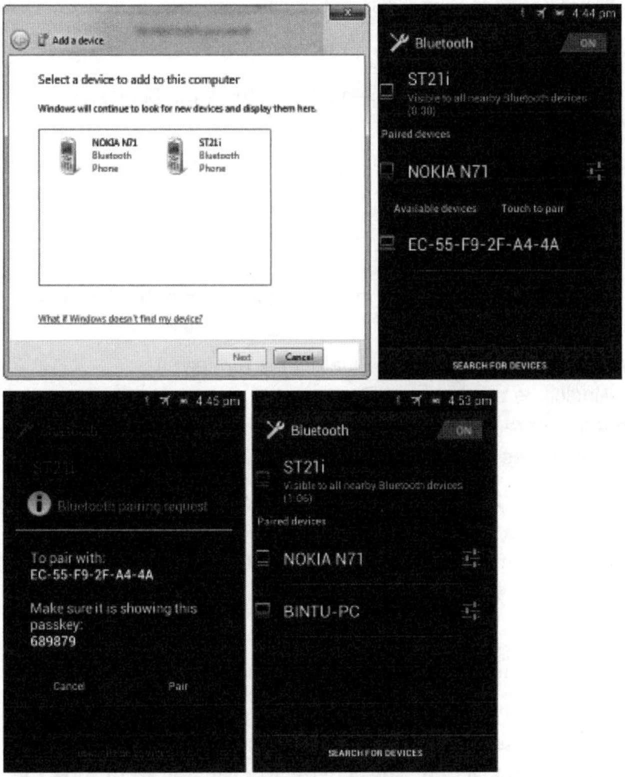

Figure 12.6   Window displaying the list of nearby Bluetooth-enabled devices on the PC (top left); on the Android device, the address of the Bluetooth-enabled PC appears in the Available Devices list (top right); dialog opens after selecting the PC address to pair with it (bottom left); name of the Windows PC appears in the Paired Devices list when it is successfully paired (bottom right)

The Bluetooth connection is saved once it is established. That is, even if the PC is turned off, the connection will resume when you turn on the PC. Depending on the security or firewall settings, a pop-up may appear in the bottom-right corner of the taskbar prompting for the permission to reestablish the connection.

Recipe: Enabling Local Bluetooth Device

The local Bluetooth device is controlled via the `BluetoothAdapter` class. To access the default Bluetooth device, call the `getDefaultAdapter` method. The `BluetoothAdapter` class provides methods to access, configure, and control the local Bluetooth device. But these methods work only when the Bluetooth device is enabled. A few of the `BluetoothAdapter` class methods are shown in Table 12.1.

Table 12.1   **Brief Description of `BluetoothAdapter` Class Methods**

Method	Description
`isEnabled`	Informs whether the device is enabled. The method returns the Boolean value `true` if the device is enabled.
`getName`	Returns the Bluetooth adapter's name that is used to identify the device.
`getAddress`	Returns the hardware address.
`setName`	Modifies the name of the Bluetooth adapter.
`getState`	Returns the Bluetooth adapter state. The method returns one of the following Bluetooth adapter constants: • **`STATE_TURNING_ON`**—Indicates the Bluetooth is turning on. • **`STATE_ON`**—Indicates the Bluetooth is on. • **`STATE_TURNING_OFF`**—Indicates the Bluetooth is turning off. • **`STATE_OFF`**—Indicates the Bluetooth is off.

The methods listed in Table 12.1 will return `null` if the Bluetooth device is disabled.

> **Note**
>
> The `BLUETOOTH_ADMIN` permission is required to modify the name of the Bluetooth adapter.

To enable the Bluetooth device, a system preference activity is started using the `BluetoothAdapter.ACTION_REQUEST_ENABLE` action. The activity asks the user to turn on the Bluetooth device. The activity is usually started with the `startActivityForResult` method so you can observe and analyze the result. If there is no error, then depending on the user's choice, the subactivity will close and return to the calling activity with the Bluetooth device turned to either on or off.

Create a new Android project called `BlueToothApp`. The application will check whether the local Bluetooth device is available. If the Bluetooth device is not available, the application will terminate after displaying an error message. If the Bluetooth device is available and is not enabled, an activity will be started with a specific action to enable the Bluetooth device.

To check for the local Bluetooth device and to enable it, write the code as shown in Listing 12.1 into the Java activity file `BlueToothAppActivity.java`.

Listing 12.1 Code Written into the Java Activity File `BlueToothAppActivity.java`

```java
package com.androidtablet.bluetoothapp;

import android.os.Bundle;
import android.app.Activity;
import android.bluetooth.BluetoothAdapter;
import android.widget.Toast;
import android.content.Intent;

public class BlueToothAppActivity extends Activity {
    private static final int REQUEST_ENABLE_BT = 0;

    @Override
    protected void onCreate(Bundle savedInstanceState) {
        super.onCreate(savedInstanceState);
        setContentView(R.layout.activity_blue_tooth_app);
        BluetoothAdapter bluetoothAdapter =
            BluetoothAdapter.getDefaultAdapter();           #1
        if (bluetoothAdapter == null) {
            Toast.makeText(this, "Bluetooth is not
                available", Toast.LENGTH_LONG).show();
            finish();
            return;
        }
        if (bluetoothAdapter.isEnabled())                   #2
            Toast.makeText(this, "Bluetooth is Ready",
                Toast.LENGTH_LONG).show();
        else {
            Intent enableBtIntent = new Intent(
                BluetoothAdapter.ACTION_REQUEST_ENABLE);    #3
            startActivityForResult(enableBtIntent,
                REQUEST_ENABLE_BT);                         #4
        }
    }

    protected void onActivityResult(int requestCode, int
        resultCode, Intent intent) {
        if (resultCode == RESULT_OK) {                      #5
            if(requestCode == REQUEST_ENABLE_BT){
                Toast.makeText(this, "Bluetooth is Enabled",
                    Toast.LENGTH_LONG).show();
            }
            else{
                Toast.makeText(this, "Bluetooth could not be
                    Enabled", Toast.LENGTH_LONG).show();
            }
        }
    }
}
```

Certain statements in Listing 12.1 need explanation:

- Statement #1 accesses the default Bluetooth device.
- Statement #2 checks whether the Bluetooth device is enabled.
- Statement #3 defines an intent called `enableBtIntent` with the `BluetoothAdapter.ACTION_REQUEST_ENABLE` action.
- Statement #4 starts the system preference activity using the intent `enableBtIntent` defined in statement #3. The activity will prompt the user to turn on the Bluetooth device. The activity is started using the `startActivityForResult` method so that the result of the activity can be analyzed through the `onActivityResult` handler.
- Statement #5 checks whether the activity to turn on the Bluetooth device has executed successfully.

To enable your application to read local Bluetooth device properties, the following Bluetooth permission statement is added in the `AndroidManifest.xml` file:

```
<uses-permission android:name= "android.permission.BLUETOOTH" />
```

When you run the application, if the local Bluetooth device is available and is already enabled, the message `Bluetooth is Ready` is displayed, as shown in Figure 12.7.

Figure 12.7   The message `Bluetooth is Ready` appears if the Bluetooth is already enabled on the device

If the local Bluetooth device is available but is not enabled, an activity is started with a specific action to enable the Bluetooth device. The activity displays a dialog box informing that an app is trying to turn on the Bluetooth (see Figure 12.8 [top left]). Click Yes from the dialog box to turn on the Bluetooth device. A message informing `Turning Bluetooth on` appears (see Figure 12.8 [top right]), followed by the message `Bluetooth is Enabled` (see Figure 12.8

[bottom left]). To confirm whether the Bluetooth device is really turned on, select the Settings button on the device. You find that the Bluetooth device is in the on state in the Settings list of the Android device (see Figure 12.8 [bottom right]), which confirms that the application has successfully turned on the Bluetooth device.

Figure 12.8   Dialog prompting whether to turn on the Bluetooth device (top left); message informing that the Bluetooth device is being turned on (top right); message confirming that the Bluetooth device is turned on (bottom left); the Bluetooth device in the Settings list appears in an on state (bottom right)

Recipe: Displaying the List of Paired Devices

In this recipe, you will learn to display the information of the devices that are paired with your Android device. The application will display the information of the Bluetooth adapter and the name and address of your Android device. Besides this, the application will display the name and address of the devices that are paired with your Android device.

Create an Android project called `BlueToothPairedListApp`. The information of the paired devices will be displayed using the `TextView` control. To define a `TextView` control, write the code shown in Listing 12.2 into the activity layout file `activity_blue_tooth_paired_list_app.xml`.

Listing 12.2 Code Written into the Activity Layout File `activity_blue_tooth_paired_list_app.xml`

```
<LinearLayout xmlns:android="http://schemas.android.com/apk/res/android"
    xmlns:tools="http://schemas.android.com/tools"
    android:layout_width="match_parent"
    android:layout_height="match_parent"
    android:orientation="vertical" >
    <TextView
        android:id="@+id/paired_list"
        android:layout_width="match_parent"
        android:layout_height="wrap_content"
        android:textSize="@dimen/text_size"
        android:textStyle="bold"   />
</LinearLayout>
```

To identify and access the Java code, assign the `TextView` control the `paired_list` ID. The attributes are so set that the text size that will be displayed through the `TextView` will appear in bold and in the font size defined in the dimension resource `text_size`.

Next, you need to write Java code to perform the following tasks:

- Check for the local Bluetooth device and enable it if it is not already enabled.
- Access the default Bluetooth adapter and display the name and address of the Android device.
- Invoke the `startDiscovery()` method on the `BluetoothAdapter` object to search for the paired devices found nearby.
- Invoke the `getBondedDevices()` method on the `BluetoothAdapter` object to access the set of the paired devices.
- Access the name and address of each device in the retrieved set and display them on the screen.

To do all these tasks, write the code as shown in Listing 12.3 into the Java activity file `BlueToothPairedListAppActivity.java`.

Listing 12.3 Code Written into the Java Activity File `BlueToothPairedListAppActivity.java`

```
package com.androidtablet.bluetoothpairedlistapp;

import android.os.Bundle;
```

```java
import android.app.Activity;
import android.bluetooth.BluetoothAdapter;
import android.widget.Toast;
import android.content.Intent;
import android.widget.TextView;
import android.bluetooth.BluetoothDevice;
import java.util.Set;

public class BlueToothPairedListAppActivity extends Activity {
    private BluetoothAdapter bluetoothAdapter = null;
    private static final int REQUEST_ENABLE_BT = 0;
    private TextView textView;

    @Override
    protected void onCreate(Bundle savedInstanceState) {
        super.onCreate(savedInstanceState);
        setContentView(R.layout.activity_blue_tooth_
            paired_list_app);
        textView = (TextView) findViewById(
            R.id.paired_list);
        textView.setText("");
        bluetoothAdapter = BluetoothAdapter.
            getDefaultAdapter();
        if (bluetoothAdapter == null) {
            Toast.makeText(this, "Bluetooth is not
                available", Toast.LENGTH_LONG).show();
            finish();
            return;
        }
        if (!bluetoothAdapter.isEnabled()) {
            Intent enableBtIntent = new Intent(
                BluetoothAdapter.ACTION_REQUEST_ENABLE);
            startActivityForResult(enableBtIntent,
                REQUEST_ENABLE_BT);
        }
        else {
            Toast.makeText(this, "Bluetooth is Ready",
                Toast.LENGTH_LONG).show();
            dispInfo();
        }
    }

    @Override
    protected void onActivityResult(int requestCode, int
        resultCode, Intent data) {
        super.onActivityResult(requestCode, resultCode,
            data);
```

```
        if (resultCode == RESULT_OK) {
            if(requestCode == REQUEST_ENABLE_BT){
                Toast.makeText(this, "Bluetooth is Enabled",
                    Toast.LENGTH_LONG).show();
                dispInfo();
            }
        }
        else {
            Toast.makeText(this, "Error: Bluetooth is not
                Enabled", Toast.LENGTH_LONG).show();
            finish();
            return;
        }
    }

    protected void dispInfo() {
        textView.append("Adapter: " + bluetoothAdapter.
            toString() + "\nName: " + bluetoothAdapter.
            getName() + "\nAddress: " + bluetoothAdapter.
            getAddress());
        bluetoothAdapter.startDiscovery();
        textView.append("\n\nDevices Paired:");
        Set<BluetoothDevice> devices = bluetoothAdapter.
            getBondedDevices();
        for (BluetoothDevice device : devices) {
            textView.append("\n\nFound device: " +
                device.getName() + "\nAddress: " +
                device.getAddress());
        }
    }
}
```

To enable your application to read local Bluetooth adapter properties and search for paired devices, add the following Bluetooth permission statements to the `AndroidManifest.xml` file:

```
<uses-permission android:name= "android.permission.BLUETOOTH" />
<uses-permission android:name="android.permission.BLUETOOTH_ADMIN" />
```

The `BLUETOOTH_ADMIN` permission is required to modify any of the local Bluetooth device properties.

After running the application, if the local Bluetooth device is available and is already enabled, the message `Bluetooth is Ready` is displayed. Also, the information of the Bluetooth adapter, the name and address of the device, and the name and address of the paired device will be displayed as shown in Figure 12.9 (top left).

If the local Bluetooth device is available but is not enabled, an activity is started with a specific action to enable the Bluetooth device. The activity displays a dialog box informing that an app is trying to turn on the Bluetooth device (see Figure 12.9 [top right]). Clicking the Yes button from the dialog box turns on the Bluetooth device. The message `"Bluetooth is Enabled` is displayed along with the name and address of the paired devices (see Figure 12.9 [bottom left]).

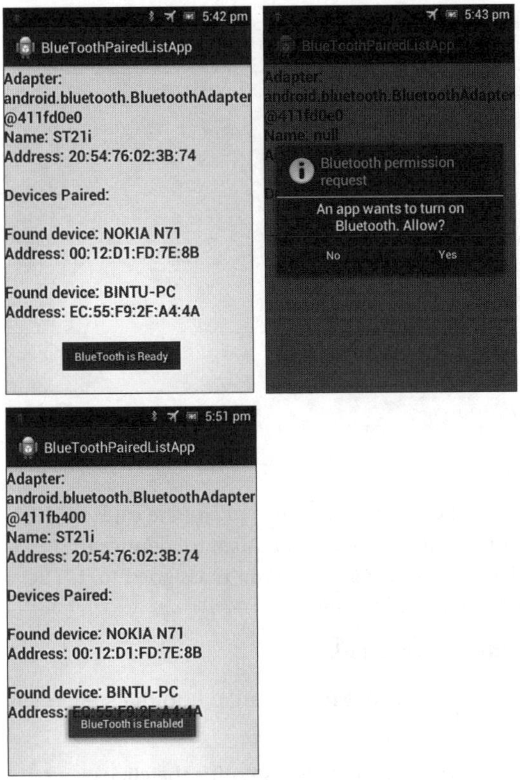

Figure 12.9   Bluetooth adapter's information, name, and address of current and paired devices displayed (top left); dialog prompting whether to turn on the Bluetooth device (top right); Bluetooth adapter's information and name and address of current and paired devices displayed after enabling the Bluetooth device (bottom left)

Recipe: Transferring Files Through Bluetooth

In this recipe, you will learn to transfer files through Bluetooth. The application will display a `Button` control that, when pressed, will initiate the process of transferring files. That is, a list of paired devices will be displayed and the user will be asked to select the one to which the file has to be transferred. After you select a paired device, the specified file will be transferred from the SD card of the current device to the selected paired device. Remember, the Bluetooth file transfer speed is quite slow—about 50KB/sec.

Create an Android project called `BTFileTransferApp`. To display a `Button` control, write the code as shown in Listing 12.4 into the activity layout file `activity_btfile_transfer_app.xml`.

Listing 12.4   **Code Written into the Activity Layout File** `activity_btfile_transfer_app.xml`

```
<LinearLayout xmlns:android="http://schemas.android.com/apk/res/android"
    android:layout_width="match_parent"
    android:layout_height="match_parent"
    android:orientation="vertical" >
    <Button
        android:id="@+id/transfer_file_button"
        android:layout_width="wrap_content"
        android:layout_height="wrap_content"
        android:text="Transfer File"
        android:textSize="@dimen/text_size"
        android:layout_gravity="center"
        android:layout_marginTop="50dp" />
</LinearLayout>
```

You can see that the `Button` control is assigned the caption `Transfer File`. The caption will appear in the font size defined in the dimension resource `text_size`. Also, to identify the `Button` control in the Java code, the unique ID `transfer_file_button` is assigned to it. The `Button` control is set to appear at the horizontal center of the device.

Next, you need to write Java code to perform the following tasks:

- Access the `Button` control defined in the activity layout file and map it to the `Button` object.

- Associate the `setOnClickListener` to the `Button` control to listen for the click events on it and subsequently invoke the callback method `onClick`.

- Define the path of the file in the SD card that you want to transfer. You assume that a file named `sampleimage.jpg` already exists in the SD card of the current device.

- Define an intent and set its action to `Intent.ACTION_SEND`.

- Specify the file to be transferred in the intent object.

- Invoke the `intent` to initiate transferring of the file.

To perform all the preceding tasks, write the code as shown in Listing 12.5 into the Java activity file `BTFileTransferAppActivity.java`.

Listing 12.5   **Code Written into the Java Activity File** BTFileTransferAppActivity.java

```
package com.androidtablet.btfiletransferapp;

import android.os.Bundle;
import android.app.Activity;
import android.widget.Button;
import android.view.View;
import android.view.View.OnClickListener;
import android.os.Environment;
import java.io.File;
import android.content.Intent;
import android.net.Uri;

public class BTFileTransferAppActivity extends Activity {

    @Override
    protected void onCreate(Bundle savedInstanceState) {
        super.onCreate(savedInstanceState);
        setContentView(R.layout.activity_btfile_transfer_
            app);
        Button transferFileButton = (Button) findViewById(
            R.id.transfer_file_button);
        transferFileButton.setOnClickListener(new
            OnClickListener() {
            @Override
            public void onClick(View v) {
                String filePath = Environment.
                    getExternalStorageDirectory().toString() +
                    "/sampleimage.jpg";
                File file = new File(filePath);
                Intent intent = new Intent();
                intent.setAction(Intent.ACTION_SEND);
                intent.setType("text/plain");
                intent.putExtra(Intent.EXTRA_STREAM,
                    Uri.fromFile(file));
                startActivity(intent);
            }
        });
    }
}
```

After you run the application, a Button control with the caption Transfer File appears at the horizontal center of the screen (see Figure 12.10 [top left]). When you click the Button control, the Bluetooth Device Picker dialog appears displaying the list of paired devices (see Figure 12.10 [top right]). Assuming that you want to transfer the file to the paired device NOKIA N71, select it from the list of paired devices. Once you select the device, the process of transferring the `sampleimage.jpg` file from the SD card of the current device to NOKIA N71 device will begin. The message `Sending file to "NOKIA N71"` (see Figure 12.10 [bottom left]) appears to confirm that the file is being sent. The receiving device will get a message that a file is being transferred. If the user on the receiving device allows the incoming file, the file transfer process will complete successfully. If the user on the receiving device does not allow the incoming file, the file transfer process will terminate with the failure message `Bluetooth share: File sampleimage.jpg not sent`, as shown in Figure 12.10 (bottom right).

Figure 12.10 `Button` control with caption `Transfer File` displayed on application startup (top left); list of paired devices displayed to select from (top right); `Toast` message informing that the file is being transferred (bottom left); message informing the `sampleimage.jpg` file could not be sent (bottom right)

Recipe: Understanding Wi-Fi

Wi-Fi is a wireless local area network that is used to exchange data wirelessly. Without any physical connection between the electronic devices, Wi-Fi uses radio frequency to exchange data. Android provides an application programming interface (API) that helps with the following:

- Creating and modifying Wi-Fi configuration settings
- Scanning for hotspots
- Controlling and monitoring Internet settings and connectivity
- Transferring files among devices

To configure, manage, and monitor Wi-Fi network connections and to scan for available access points, Android provides a Wi-Fi connectivity service called `WifiManager`. To use the `WifiManager`, the application must have the following permissions:

```
<uses-permission android:name="android.permission.ACCESS_WIFI_STATE"/>
<uses-permission android:name="android.permission.CHANGE_WIFI_STATE"/>
```

To access the `WifiManager`, call the `getSystemService` method with the `Context.WIFI_SERVICE` constant.

Example:

```
WifiManager wifiManager = (WifiManager) getBaseContext().getSystemService
(Context.WIFI_SERVICE);
```

A few of the `WifiManager` methods are briefly listed in Table 12.2.

Table 12.2 **Brief Description of the `WifiManager` Methods**

Method	Description
setWifiEnabled	Used to enable or disable the Wi-Fi hardware. Passing the Boolean value true to this method will enable the Wi-Fi hardware.
getWifiState	Returns the current Wi-Fi state.
isWifiEnabled	Returns true if the Wi-Fi hardware is enabled.

The `WifiManager` broadcasts intents whenever there is a change in the connectivity status of the Wi-Fi network. The intents are broadcasted using actions that are represented through the constants (see Table 12.3) defined in the `WifiManager` class.

Table 12.3 **Brief Description of the Constants Defined in the `WifiManager` Class**

Constants	Description
WIFI_STATE_CHANGED_ACTION	Indicates that the Wi-Fi hardware status has changed (that is, the status has changed between enabling, enabled, disabling, disabled, and unknown states).
EXTRA_WIFI_STATE	The lookup key that indicates the new Wi-Fi state (that is, whether Wi-Fi is enabled, disabled, enabling, disabling, or unknown).
EXTRA_PREVIOUS_STATE	The lookup key that indicates the previous Wi-Fi state.

Constants	Description
SUPPLICANT_CONNECTION_CHANGE_ACTION	Indicates that the connection to the supplicant (access point) is established or is lost.
EXTRA_NEW_STATE	The lookup key that describes the new state.
NETWORK_STATE_CHANGED_ACTION	Indicates that the Wi-Fi connectivity state has changed.
RSSI_CHANGED_ACTION	Indicates that the RSSI (the signal strength) has changed.
EXTRA_NEW_RSSI	The lookup key that indicates the current signal strength.

Recipe: Enabling and Disabling Wi-Fi

In this recipe, you will learn to enable and disable Wi-Fi. Two actions items titled Enable Wi-Fi and Disable Wi-Fi will be displayed in the ActionBar. Clicking the Enable Wi-Fi action item will enable the Wi-Fi network, whereas clicking the Disable Wi-Fi action item will disable the Wi-Fi network.

Create a new project called WiFiApp. To inform the user that the Wi-Fi network is enabled or is switched to the disabled state, you will use a TextView control. After defining a TextView control, the activity layout file activity_wi_fi_app.xml will appear, as shown in Listing 12.6.

Listing 12.6 **Code Written into the Activity Layout File** activity_wi_fi_app.xml

```
<LinearLayout xmlns:android="http://schemas.android.com/apk/res/android"
    android:orientation="vertical"
    android:layout_width="match_parent"
    android:layout_height="match_parent" >
    <TextView
        android:id="@+id/wifistatus"
        android:layout_width="match_parent"
        android:layout_height="wrap_content"
        android:textSize="@dimen/text_size"
        android:textStyle="bold" />
</LinearLayout>
```

To define the two action items with the titles Enable Wi-Fi and Disable Wi-Fi, respectively, write the code as shown in Listing 12.7 into the menu file activity_wi_fi_app.xml that is found in the res/menu folder.

Listing 12.7   **Code Written into the Menu File** `activity_wi_fi_app.xml`

```
<menu xmlns: android="http://schemas.android.com/apk/res/android" >
    <item android:id="@+id/enable_wifi_btn"
        android:title="Enable Wi-Fi"
        android:orderInCategory="0"
        android:showAsAction="ifRoom|withText" />
    <item android:id="@+id/disable_wifi_btn"
        android:title="Disable Wi-Fi"
        android:orderInCategory="1"
        android:showAsAction="ifRoom|withText" />
</menu>
```

To access and identify in Java code, the two action items are assigned the IDs `enable_wifi_btn` and `disable_wifi_btn`, respectively.

Next, you need to write Java code to do the following tasks:

- Access the `WifiManager`.

- Associate a `BroadcastReceiver` to the activity to listen to any changes that may occur in the Wi-Fi hardware status.

- Display the action items defined in the menu file.

- Associate listeners to the action items to listen for the click events on them.

- Enable or disable the Wi-Fi network when the respective action item is clicked.

- Access the new Wi-Fi hardware status in the `BroadcastReceiver` and display it through the `TextView` control.

To perform all these tasks, write the code as shown in Listing 12.8 into the Java activity file `WifiAppActivity.java`.

Listing 12.8   **Code Written into the Java Activity File** `WifiAppActivity.java`

```
package com.androidtablet.wifiapp;

import android.os.Bundle;
import android.app.Activity;
import android.view.Menu;
import android.view.MenuItem;
import android.net.wifi.WifiManager;
import android.content.Context;
import android.content.BroadcastReceiver;
import android.content.Intent;
import android.widget.TextView;
import android.content.IntentFilter;
```

```java
public class WiFiAppActivity extends Activity {
    private WifiManager wifiManager;
    TextView wifiStatus;

    @Override
    protected void onCreate(Bundle savedInstanceState) {
        super.onCreate(savedInstanceState);
        setContentView(R.layout.activity_wi_fi_app);
        wifiStatus = (TextView)findViewById(
            R.id.wifistatus);
        wifiManager = (WifiManager)getBaseContext().
            getSystemService(Context.WIFI_SERVICE);         #1
        this.registerReceiver(this.WifiStateChangedReceiver,
            new IntentFilter(WifiManager.WIFI_STATE_CHANGED_
            ACTION));                                        #2
    }

    @Override
    public boolean onCreateOptionsMenu(Menu menu) {
        getMenuInflater().inflate(R.menu.activity_wi_fi_app,
            menu);                                           #3
        return true;
    }

    @Override
    public boolean onOptionsItemSelected(MenuItem item) {
        switch (item.getItemId()) {
            case R.id.enable_wifi_btn:
                wifiManager.setWifiEnabled(true);            #4
                break;
            case R.id.disable_wifi_btn:
                wifiManager.setWifiEnabled(false);           #5
                break;
            default:
                return super.onOptionsItemSelected(item);
        }
        return true;
    }

    private BroadcastReceiver WifiStateChangedReceiver =
        new BroadcastReceiver(){
        @Override
        public void onReceive(Context context, Intent
            intent) {
            int extraWifiState = intent.getIntExtra(
                WifiManager. EXTRA_WIFI_STATE, WifiManager.
                WIFI_STATE_UNKNOWN);
            switch(extraWifiState){                          #6
                case WifiManager.WIFI_STATE_DISABLED:
```

```
            wifiStatus.setText("Wi-Fi Disabled");
            break;
        case WifiManager.WIFI_STATE_DISABLING:
            wifiStatus.setText("Wi-Fi Disabling");
            break;
        case WifiManager.WIFI_STATE_ENABLED:
            wifiStatus.setText("Wi-Fi Enabled");
            break;
        case WifiManager.WIFI_STATE_ENABLING:
            wifiStatus.setText("Wi-Fi Enabling");
            break;
        case WifiManager.WIFI_STATE_UNKNOWN:
            wifiStatus.setText("Unknown Wi-Fi Status");
            break;
        }
    }
};
}
```

A few of the statements used in Listing 12.8 need explanation. The following list defines the meaning and purpose of those statements:

- Statement #1 accesses the `WifiManager`.

- Statement #2 implements a `BroadcastReceiver` to register with the intent `WifiManager.WIFI_STATE_CHANGED_ACTION`. Now, whenever there is a change in the Wi-Fi hardware status, the `BroadcastReceiver` will be informed about the new status.

- Statement #3 inflates or merges the menu file `activity_wi_fi_app` to display the two action items Enable Wi-Fi and Disable Wi-Fi that are defined in it.

- Statement #4 enables the Wi-Fi network after you click the Enable Wi-Fi action item.

- Statement #5 disables the Wi-Fi network after you click the Disable Wi-Fi action item.

- Statement #6 analyzes the new Wi-Fi hardware status through the `EXTRA_WIFI_STATE` lookup and displays the status on the screen through the `TextView` control.

To use access and change the Wi-Fi hardware status, the application must have sufficient permissions. To enable an application to access and change the Wi-FI hardware status, add the following permission statements to the `AndroidManifest.xml` file:

```
<uses-permission android:name="android.permission.ACCESS_WIFI_STATE"/>
<uses-permission android:name="android.permission.CHANGE_WIFI_STATE"/>
```

When you run the application, the two action items Enable Wi-Fi and Disable Wi-Fi will be displayed in the ActionBar (see Figure 12.11 [top left]). When you click the Enable Wi-Fi action item, the Wi-Fi hardware status will change to the `Wi-Fi Enabling` state followed by the `Wi-Fi Enabled` state (see Figure 12.11 [top right]). Similarly, after you click the Disable Wi-Fi action item, the Wi-Fi status will change to the `Wi-Fi Disabling` state followed by the `Wi-Fi Disabled` state, as shown in Figure 12.11 (bottom left).

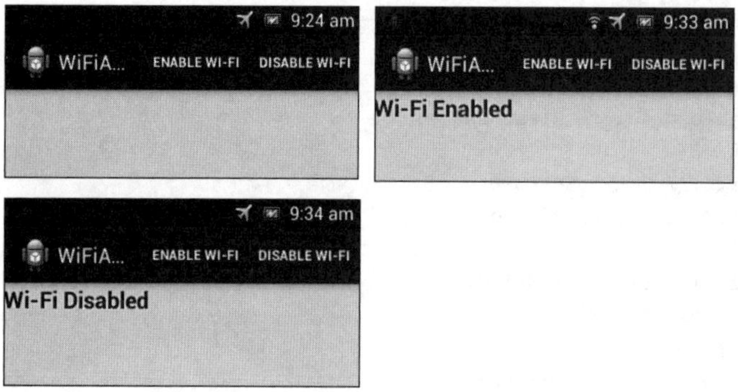

Figure 12.11   Action items Enable Wi-Fi and Disable Wi-Fi displayed on application startup (top left); Wi-Fi hardware status changed to enabled state after clicking the Enable Wi-Fi action item (top right); Wi-Fi hardware status changed to disabled state after clicking the Disable Wi-Fi action item (bottom left)

Recipe: Understanding Wi-Fi Direct

Wi-Fi Direct is a communications protocol that is supported in Android 4.0 (API level 14) and higher levels and is particularly designed for peer-to-peer communications. It is fast and reliable, and it can communicate over distances much longer than a typical Bluetooth connection. Devices with appropriate hardware can connect directly to each other via Wi-Fi without an intermediate access point. Wi-Fi Direct is often used for media sharing operations.

To use Wi-Fi Direct, an application requires the ACCESS_WIFI_STATE, CHANGE_WIFI_STATE, and INTERNET permissions:

```
<uses-permission android:name= "android.permission.ACCESS_WIFI_STATE"/>
<uses-permission android:name= "android.permission.CHANGE_WIFI_STATE"/>
<uses-permission android:name= "android.permission.INTERNET"/>
```

Wi-Fi Direct connection is managed using the WifiP2pManager system service that is accessed using the getSystemService method, passing in the Context.WIFI_P2P_SERVICE constant:

```
wifiP2pManager =(WifiP2pManager) getSystemService(Context.WIFI_P2P_SERVICE);
```

To interact with the Wi-Fi Direct framework, a channel is created using the current Context and a Looper that listens for the occurrence of events.

To understand the concept of Wi-Fi Direct through a running example, create a new Android project called WiFiDirectApp. Set the values of the android:minSdkVersion and android:targetSdkVersionattributes to 14 and 17, respectively.

In the Java activity file WiFiDirectAppActivity.java, write the code as shown in Listing 12.9.

Listing 12.9 **Code Written into the Java Activity File** `WiFiDirectAppActivity.java`

```java
package com.androidtablet.wifidirectapp;

import android.os.Bundle;
import android.app.Activity;
import android.net.wifi.p2p.WifiP2pManager;
import android.net.wifi.p2p.WifiP2pManager.Channel;
import android.content.BroadcastReceiver;
import android.content.Context;
import android.content.IntentFilter;
import android.widget.Toast;

public class WiFiDirectAppActivity extends Activity {
    WifiP2pManager wifiP2pManager;
    Channel channel;
    BroadcastReceiver bcReceiver;
    IntentFilter intentFilter;
    @Override
    protected void onCreate(Bundle savedInstanceState) {
        super.onCreate(savedInstanceState);
        setContentView(R.layout.activity_wi_fi_direct_app);
        wifiP2pManager = (WifiP2pManager) getSystemService(
            Context.WIFI_P2P_SERVICE);                         #1
        channel =  (Channel) wifiP2pManager.initialize(this,
            getMainLooper(), null);                            #2
        bcReceiver = new WiFiBroadcastReceiver(
            wifiP2pManager, channel, this);                    #3
        intentFilter = new IntentFilter();
        intentFilter.addAction(WifiP2pManager.
            WIFI_P2P_STATE_CHANGED_ACTION);                    #4
        wifiP2pManager.discoverPeers(channel, new
            WifiP2pManager.ActionListener() {                  #5
            public void onSuccess() {
                Toast.makeText(WiFiDirectAppActivity.this,
                    "Wi-FI Direct is Enabled",
                    Toast.LENGTH_LONG).show();
            }
            public void onFailure(int reasonCode) {            #6
                String errorMessage = "Wi-Fi Direct Failed.";
                switch (reasonCode) {
                    case WifiP2pManager.BUSY :
                        errorMessage += " Framework is busy.";
                        break;
                    case WifiP2pManager.ERROR :
                        errorMessage += " Some internal error
                            occurred.";
```

```
                    break;
                case WifiP2pManager.P2P_UNSUPPORTED :
                    errorMessage += " Unsupported.";
                    break;
                default:
                    errorMessage += " Unknown error
                        occurred.";
                    break;
            }
            Toast.makeText(WiFiDirectAppActivity.this,
                errorMessage, Toast.LENGTH_LONG).show();
        }
    });
}


@Override
protected void onResume() {
    super.onResume();
    registerReceiver(bcReceiver, intentFilter);        #7
}


@Override
protected void onPause() {
    super.onPause();
    unregisterReceiver(bcReceiver);                    #8
}
}
```

Certain statements in Listing 12.9 need explanation:

- Statement #1 accesses the WifiP2pManager system service that is required to manage Wi-Fi Direct.

- Statement #2 creates a channel using the current context and a looper. The channel is required for interacting with Wi-Fi Direct. Also, based on the events that take place on the channel, you can define a ChannelListener to take respective actions.

- Statement #3 defines a broadcast receiver. The broadcast receiver takes the WifiP2pManager object, channel, and current activity as arguments and uses them to perform the desired tasks when it receives an intent.

- Statement #4 adds the action WifiP2pManager.WIFI_P2P_STATE_CHANGED_ACTION to the IntentFilter. The action will be accessed and compared in the broadcast receiver to take necessary action.

- Statement #5 invokes the peer discovering method and associates ActionListener to listen for the actions performed using WifiP2pManager. It defines two methods, onSuccess() and onFailure(), to inform the results of connection attempts.

- Statement #6 defines the `onFailure()` method to display the reason the Wi-Fi Direct connection has failed.

- Statement #7 registers the broadcast receiver. The broadcast receiver will execute the desired action based on the intent it receives.

- Statement #8 unregisters the broadcast receiver.

You can check for more conditions by adding the following actions to the `IntentFilter`:

```
intentFilter.addAction(WifiP2pManager.
WIFI_P2P_PEERS_CHANGED_ACTION);
intentFilter.addAction(WifiP2pManager.
WIFI_P2P_CONNECTION_CHANGED_ACTION);
intentFilter.addAction(WifiP2pManager.
WIFI_P2P_THIS_DEVICE_CHANGED_ACTION);
```

For the broadcast receiver, add a new Java file named `WiFiBroadcastReceiver.java` to the package `com.androidtablet.wifidirectapp` of the project. In the `WiFiBroadcastReceiver.java` file, write the code as shown in Listing 12.10.

Listing 12.10   **Code Written into the Java File** `WiFiBroadcastReceiver.java`

```
package com.androidtablet.wifidirectapp;

import android.content.BroadcastReceiver;
import android.content.Context;
import android.content.Intent;
import android.net.wifi.p2p.WifiP2pManager;
import android.net.wifi.p2p.WifiP2pManager.Channel;
import android.widget.Toast;

public class WiFiBroadcastReceiver extends BroadcastReceiver {
    private WifiP2pManager manager;
    private Channel channel;
    private WiFiDirectAppActivity activity;

    public WiFiBroadcastReceiver(WifiP2pManager manager,
      Channel channel, WiFiDirectAppActivity activity) {
      super();
      this.manager = manager;
      this.channel = channel;
      this.activity = activity;
    }

    @Override
    public void onReceive(Context context, Intent intent) {
      String action = intent.getAction();
      if (WifiP2pManager.WIFI_P2P_STATE_CHANGED_ACTION.
        equals(action)) {
```

```
        int state = intent.getIntExtra(WifiP2pManager.
           EXTRA_WIFI_STATE, -1);
        if (state == WifiP2pManager.WIFI_P2P_STATE_
           ENABLED)
           Toast.makeText(context, "Wi-Fi Direct is
              enabled", Toast.LENGTH_LONG).show();
        else
           Toast.makeText(context, "Wi-Fi Direct is not
              enabled", Toast.LENGTH_LONG).show();
    }
  }
}
```

You can see that in the onReceive() method of the broadcast receiver, the action of the passed intent is accessed. Based on the received intent action, the respective message is displayed.

To use Wi-Fi Direct, add the following permission statements to the AndroidManifest.xml file:

```
<uses-permission android:name= "android.permission.ACCESS_WIFI_STATE" />
<uses-permission android:name= "android.permission.CHANGE_WIFI_STATE" />
<uses-permission android:name= "android.permission.CHANGE_NETWORK_STATE"/>
<uses-permission android:name= "android.permission.INTERNET" />
<uses-permission android:name= "android.permission.ACCESS_NETWORK_STATE"/>
```

After running the application, if the device supports Wi-Fi Direct, a message indicating Wi-Fi Direct is Enabled will be displayed, as shown in Figure 12.12 (left). If the device does not support Wi-Fi Direct, it displays the message Wi-Fi Direct Failed. Unsupported, as shown in Figure 12.12 (right).

Figure 12.12   The message Wi-Fi Direct is Enabled appears if the device supports Wi-Fi Direct (left); the message Wi-Fi Direct Failed. Unsupported displays if the device does not support Wi-Fi Direct (right)

Summary

In this chapter, you learned about the use of Bluetooth and Wi-Fi technology in Android applications. You saw how to enable and disable Bluetooth as well as Wi-Fi. You saw how to transfer files among two Bluetooth-enabled devices manually and through coding. You learned the procedure to pair Bluetooth-enabled devices and display the list of paired devices.

In the next chapter, you will learn about multicore CPU support in Android. You will also learn the use of basic threading and will compare threading with loaders. Finally, you will learn about garbage collection improvements.

13

Cores and Threads

To run Android applications quickly and efficiently, dual-core chips and quad-core processors are developed and implemented in the Android devices. To take advantage of multicore architectures, certain enhancements are made in Android modules, including the thread scheduler. It is the job of the thread scheduler to divide and distribute the application's task among different cores and take their maximum advantage.

For running an application efficiently, memory management is also quite important. A garbage collector plays a major role in memory recycling. One more factor that optimizes an application is having noninteractive tasks performed by background threads. Threading enables application of multitasking features.

In this chapter, you will learn the utility of multicore processor architectures and the role of garbage in memory management. Also, you will learn the usage of threads and the `AsyncTask` class in performing application tasks in the background, thereby improving application performance.

Recipe: Understanding the Utility of Multicore Processor Architectures

Multitasking is obviously better than single tasking. In single tasking, when one task is being performed, all other tasks stop until the task being performed is finished. In contrast, in multitasking, more than one task is performed simultaneously. To perform multiple tasks simultaneously, a multicore processor architecture is used. Android 3.0 and higher versions are designed to run on either single or multicore processor architectures.

Multiple cores boost the application performance by dividing and running the application's workload on different cores simultaneously. The efficiency of multicore processor depends on a thread scheduler. That is, the advantage of multicore mobile processors is only visible when the software can distribute and schedule the tasks on all cores. If scheduling is not done properly, the application will perform worse on enabling multiple cores on a device.

Many Android handsets feature multiple cores and high clock speeds (that is, handsets have dual-core chips and quad-core processors). To optimize Android for dual- and quad-core phones, several changes are applied to it, and its thread scheduler is enhanced to get the best performance out of the new quad-core and dual-core chips.

Recipe: Understanding the Utility of Garbage Collection

Garbage collection is a memory management procedure in which dynamically allocated memory is recycled automatically. That is, if the memory that is being used by a program is no longer needed, it is systematically recovered. Garbage collection is performed by a garbage collector that tracks the memory allocations and recycles them for use by other running applications. The garbage collector automatically gets invoked when memory allocations reach a certain threshold. The idea is to free up the memory for running applications. The garbage collector relieves the developer from deallocating memory blocks explicitly, thus avoiding memory leaks and premature freeing problems.

In Android, memory management is handled by Dalvik's garbage collector, which uses a mark and sweep approach (that is, it applies mark bits on the objects to indicate that they are being used and should not be garbage collected). The objects that are not marked are swept to create free memory to be used by other applications. A garbage collection task usually takes 100 to 200ms, and during garbage collection, the performance of the application drops. The running applications are suspended and become nonresponsive during marking and sweeping. Also, applications have several small, short-lived objects that result in frequently invoking the garbage collector. To avoid recurrent invoking of the garbage collector, the Android SDK ships with a useful tool called allocation tracker, which is part of the DDMS (Dalvik Debug Monitor Service).

> **Note**
>
> Technically, there is no garbage collection in Android because Android is a C-based operating system. The garbage collection that is being discussed here is only in the Dalvik runtime.

The DDMS is a powerful debugging tool that is downloaded as part of the Android SDK. The DDMS can be run by selecting either the DDMS icon in the top right-hand corner of the Eclipse IDE or the Window, Open Perspective, DDMS option.

When you run DDMS, it automatically connects to the attached Android device or any running emulator. The DDMS tool window is shown in Figure 13.1.

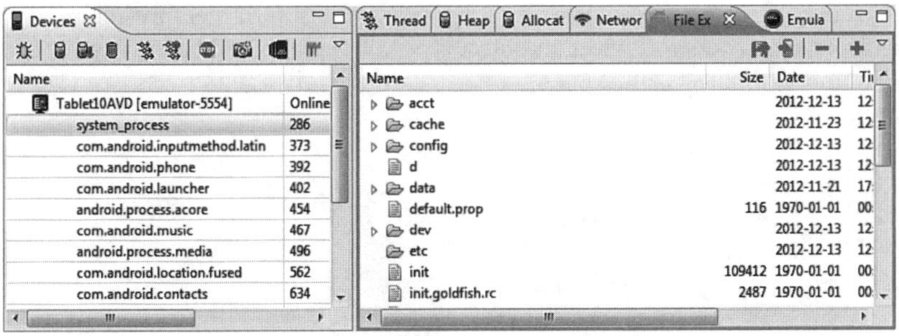

Figure 13.1   The DDMS tool window

In the upper-left pane of the DDMS window, a Devices tab displays the list of Android devices connected to the PC, along with the running AVDs (if any). The VMs associated with each device or AVD will also be displayed. Selecting a VM will display its information in the right pane. In the Devices tab, you'll see the following icons, from left to right:

- **Debug**—Used to debug the selected process.

- **Update Heap**—Enables heap information of the process. After clicking this icon, use the Heap tab on the right pane to get heap information.

- **Dump HPROF file**—Shows the HPROF file that can be used to detect memory leaks.

- **Cause GC**—Invokes garbage collection procedure.

- **Update Threads**—Enables fetching of the thread information of the selected process. After clicking this icon, you need to click the Threads tab in the right pane to display information about the threads that are created and destroyed in the selected process.

- **Start Method Profiling**—Used to find the number of times different methods are called in an application and the time consumed in each of them.

- **Stop Process**—Stops the selected process.

- **Screen Capture**—Captures your device/emulator screen.

- **Dump View Hierarchy for UI Automator**—Displays the view objects that create the user interface of the activity that is running on the device or emulator. You can see and compare any view within the context of the entire view tree. It also displays information related to rendering of the view.

- **Capture System-Wide Trace Using Android systrace**—Prompts to specify the file to capture system-level trace. Trace events such as CPU frequency changes, CPU idle events, CPU load, Disk I/O, and so on will be captured in the specified file.

In the right pane, you find these tabs:

- **Thread**—Displays information about the threads within each process.

- **Heap**—Displays the heap information of the process (if the Update Heap icon from the Devices tab has been clicked). Select the Cause GC button (see Figure 13.2 [top]) to begin the garbage collection process. The object types and the size of memory allocated to them are displayed. When you select an object type, a bar graph will be displayed showing the number of objects allocated for a particular memory size in bytes (see Figure 13.2 [bottom]).

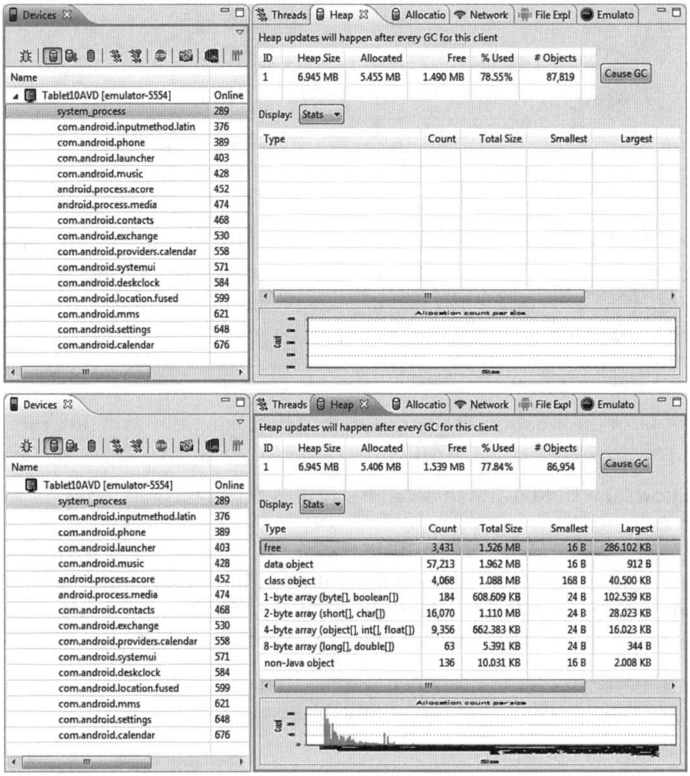

Figure 13.2   The Heap tab displaying heap information of the running process (top), and dialog displaying information of objects and their memory allocations after clicking the Cause GC button (bottom)

- **Allocation Tracker**—Tracks the objects allocated to an application. Click the Start Tracking button and then interact with the application to execute the code that you want to analyze. Then click the Get Allocations button to see the list of objects allocated to the application (see Figure 13.3). A list of allocated objects will be shown in the upper pane. If you click any allocated object shown in the upper pane, the stack trace that led to the allocation will be displayed in the lower pane. You see not only the information about the type of object that is allocated, but in which thread, in which class, in which file, and at which line. You can click the Stop Tracking button to clear the data and restart.

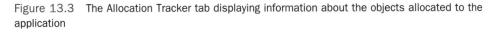

| Devices ⊠ | | ⁀ ⊡ | | ⏚ Thread | ⧂ Heap | ⧂ Allocat ⊠ | | ⚘ Networ | 🖩 File Ex | ⬤ Emula | ⁀ ⊡ |

Name			Stop Tracking	Get Allocations	Filter:		□ Inc. trace
🖳 Tablet10AVD [emulator-5554]	Online
system_process	286
com.android.inputmethod.latin	373
com.android.phone	392
com.android.launcher	402
android.process.acore	454
com.android.music	467
android.process.media	496
com.android.location.fused	562
com.android.contacts	634
com.android.exchange	681
com.android.providers.calendar	720
com.android.systemui	738
com.android.deskclock	763
com.android.mms	804
com.android.settings	841

Alloc Order ▾		Allocated Class	T...	Allo...	Allo...	
245	7...	char[]	9	java...	enla...	
229	6...	char[]	69	java...	<ini...	
296	4...	char[]	58	java...	enla...	
220	4...	byte[]	69	co...	add	

Class	Method	File	
java.lang.AbstractStri...	enlargeBuffer	AbstractStringBuilder.java	
java.lang.AbstractStri...	append0	AbstractStringBuilder.java	
java.lang.StringBuilder	append	StringBuilder.java	
com.android.server.a...	logStrictModeVi...	ActivityManagerService.java	
com.android.server.a...	handleApplicati...	ActivityManagerService.java	
android.app.Activity...	onTransact	ActivityManagerNative.java	
com.android.server.a...	onTransact	ActivityManagerService.java	

Figure 13.3   The Allocation Tracker tab displaying information about the objects allocated to the application

Recipe: Understanding Threads

All Android application components such as activities, services, and broadcast receivers run in the main application thread. In other words, the main application thread performs all user interface–related tasks. To increase application efficiency, the long-running or asynchronous tasks and the tasks that don't interact with the user are performed on the background threads.

Also, because the operating system expects the main thread to be responsive to messages, any operation that can block the main thread is performed on a separate thread. The main thread thus controls other threads and updates the user interface (UI) elements.

There are two ways of moving processing tasks to the background threads:

- Using `Handler` classes
- Using `AsyncTask` classes

In this recipe, you will learn to use the `Handler` class to perform tasks using background threads. To process tasks in the background, you will implement our own threads and use the `Handler` class to synchronize with them. The `Handler` class is associated with the thread from which it is created. That is, you can execute a block of code on the thread from which the `Handler` class is instantiated. The two ways with which you can communicate with the `Handler` class are through messages and runnable objects. After you create an object from the `Handler` class, it processes messages and runnable objects associated with the current thread's `MessageQueue`. The tasks to be performed by the current thread are kept in the `MessageQueue` waiting for their execution.

To process messages, override the `handleMessage()` method. To process runnable objects, use the `post()` method. The thread can post messages via the `sendMessage(Message msg)` method or via the `sendEmptyMessage()` method.

To understand the concept of using the `Handler` class, create an application that displays sequence numbers from 1 to 10 using threads. Name the application `ThreadApp`. Because you just want to display sequence numbers in this application, you only need to use a `TextView` control. The code shown in Listing 13.1 is written into the `activity_thread_app.xml` to define a `TextView` control.

Listing 13.1   **Code in the** `activity_thread_app.xml` **Layout File**

```xml
<LinearLayout xmlns:android="http://schemas.android.com/apk/res/android"
    android:layout_width="match_parent"
    android:layout_height="match_parent"
    android:orientation="vertical" >
    <TextView
        android:id="@+id/seqnums"
        android:layout_width="match_parent"
        android:layout_height="wrap_content"
        android:textSize="@dimen/text_size"
        android:textStyle="bold" />
</LinearLayout>
```

You can see that the `TextView` control is assigned the `seqnums` ID that will be used to identify and use it in the Java code. The text displayed through the `TextView` will appear in the font size defined in the dimension resource `text_size`. To define a thread handler and to send and receive messages through it, write the code shown in Listing 13.2 into the `ThreadAppActivity.java` Java activity file.

Listing 13.2   **Code in the** `ThreadAppActivity.java` **Java Activity File**

```java
package com.androidtablet.threadapp;

import android.app.Activity;
import android.os.Bundle;
import android.widget.TextView;
import android.os.Handler;
import android.os.Message;

public class ThreadAppActivity extends Activity {
 static TextView seqNums;

    @Override
    protected void onCreate(Bundle savedInstanceState) {
        super.onCreate(savedInstanceState);
```

```
            setContentView(R.layout.activity_thread_app);
            seqNums=(TextView)findViewById(R.id.seqnums);
    }

    static Handler handler = new Handler() {
        @Override
        public void handleMessage(Message msg) {
            seqNums.setText(msg.obj.toString());
        }
    };

    @Override
    protected void onStart() {
        super.onStart();
        Thread thread=new Thread(new Runnable() {
            @Override
            public void run() {
                for(int i=1;i<=10;i++){
                    try {
                        Thread.sleep(1000);
                        Message msg = new Message();
                        msg.obj=String.valueOf(i);
                        handler.sendMessage(msg);
                    } catch (InterruptedException e) {
                        e.printStackTrace();
                    }
                }
            }
        });
        thread.start();
    }
}
```

Here you see that the TextView control from the layout file is accessed and mapped to the TextView object seqNums. In the onStart() method, you use the Thread class with a runnable object. The run() method starts the execution of the thread. To display sequence numbers from 1 to 10 through the TextView control, in the run() method, you create a Message object called msg and add the sequence numbers to it. You add each number from 1 to 10 to the obj variable of the Message object named msg. After adding a sequence value to the obj variable, you send the message through the Handler object.

A Handler object called handler is created. In its callback method handlemessage(), the message sent through the run() method is received through the msg parameter. The obj variable (the sequence number in the msg parameter) is accessed from the msg parameter and is displayed through the TextView control.

After you run the application, the sequence numbers are displayed beginning from 1 (see Figure 13.4 [top]). Between every sequence number is a time delay of 1 second. The application stops at the number 10, as shown in Figure 13.4 (bottom).

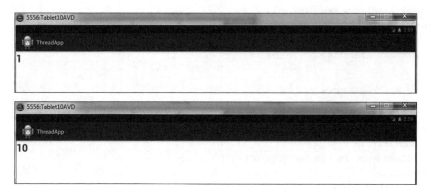

Figure 13.4   Application begins by displaying the sequence number 1 (top), and application stops at sequence number 10 (bottom)

Recipe: Using Multiple Threads

In this recipe, you will learn to use two threads. You will see how two tasks execute simultaneously through two threads. For both threads, you will create a single handler. The threads will display sequence numbers from 1 to 10. The first thread will display each sequence number after the time delay of 1 second, whereas the second thread will display each sequence number after the time delay of 2 seconds. Threads will begin their tasks simultaneously, but the first thread will reach its final value, 10, in half the time of the second thread.

The `handleMessage()` method will be overridden in the handler to display the sequence numbers. The sequence numbers are passed to this method via the `Message` parameter. To distinguish the `Message` objects of the two threads, the name of the calling thread is bundled in the `Message` object.

Create a new Android project called `MultipleThreadsApp`. You will use four `TextView` controls in this application. Two `TextView` controls will act as headers by displaying the headings `Thread1` and `Thread2`, respectively. The other two `TextView` controls will be used to display the sequence numbers of both the threads. To define four `TextView` controls, write the code as shown in Listing 13.3 in the activity layout file `activity_multiple_threads_app.xml`.

Listing 13.3   **Code in the Activity Layout File** `activity_multiple_threads_app.xml`

```
<RelativeLayout xmlns:android= "http://schemas.android.com/apk/res/android"
    xmlns:tools="http://schemas.android.com/tools"
```

```
android:layout_width="match_parent"
android:layout_height="match_parent"
tools:context=".MultipleThreadsAppActivity" >
<TextView
    android:id="@+id/thread1"
    android:text="Thread1"
    android:textSize="@dimen/text_size"
    android:textStyle="bold"
    android:layout_width="wrap_content"
    android:layout_height="wrap_content"
    android:layout_marginTop="15dip"
    android:layout_marginLeft="20dip" />
<TextView
    android:id="@+id/thread2"
    android:text="Thread2"
    android:textSize="@dimen/text_size"
    android:textStyle="bold"
    android:layout_width="wrap_content"
    android:layout_height="wrap_content"
    android:layout_marginTop="15dip"
    android:layout_marginLeft="100dip"
    android:layout_toRightOf="@id/thread1" />
<TextView
    android:id="@+id/seqnums1"
    android:text="0"
    android:textSize="@dimen/text_size"
    android:textStyle="bold"
    android:layout_width="wrap_content"
    android:layout_height="wrap_content"
    android:layout_marginTop="15dip"
    android:layout_marginLeft="30dip"
    android:layout_below="@id/thread1"  />
<TextView
    android:id="@+id/seqnums2"
    android:text="0"
    android:textSize="@dimen/text_size"
    android:textStyle="bold"
    android:layout_width="wrap_content"
    android:layout_height="wrap_content"
    android:layout_marginTop="15dip"
    android:layout_marginLeft="150dip"
    android:layout_below="@id/thread2"
    android:layout_toRightOf="@id/seqnums1" />
</RelativeLayout>
```

You can see that two TextView controls are set to display the titles Thread1 and Thread2, respectively. The other two TextView controls that will be used to display sequence numbers of the two threads are assigned the IDs `seqnums1` and `seqnums2`, respectively. The text displayed through the `TextView` controls will appear in the font size defined in the dimension resource `text_size`.

To define the handler and send and receive messages of the two threads, write the code shown in Listing in 13.4 into the Java activity file `MultipleThreadsAppActivity.java`.

Listing 13.4   **Code in the Java Activity File** `MultipleThreadsAppActivity.java`

```java
package com.androidtablet.multiplethreadsapp;

import android.os.Bundle;
import android.app.Activity;
import android.widget.TextView;
import android.os.Message;
import android.os.Handler;

public class MultipleThreadsAppActivity extends Activity {
    static private TextView seqNums1, seqNums2;

    @Override
    protected void onCreate(Bundle savedInstanceState) {
        super.onCreate(savedInstanceState);
        setContentView(R.layout.activity_multiple_threads_app);
        seqNums1 = (TextView)findViewById(R.id.seqnums1);
        seqNums2 = (TextView)findViewById(R.id.seqnums2);
    }

    static Handler handler1 = new Handler() {
        @Override
        public void handleMessage(Message msg) {
            String threadInvoked=msg.getData().getString(
                "threadName");
            if (threadInvoked.equals("thread1"))
                seqNums1.setText(msg.obj.toString());
            if (threadInvoked.equals("thread2"))
                seqNums2.setText(msg.obj.toString());
        }
    };

    @Override
    protected void onStart() {
        super.onStart();
        Thread thread1 = new Thread(new Runnable() {
            @Override
            public void run() {
                try {
                    for(int i=1;i<=10;i++){
```

```
                    Thread.sleep(1000);
                    Message msg = new Message();
                    Bundle bundle = new Bundle();
                    bundle.putString("threadName",
                        "thread1");
                    msg.setData(bundle);
                    msg.obj=String.valueOf(i);
                    handler1.sendMessage(msg);
                }
            } catch (InterruptedException e) {
                e.printStackTrace();
            }
        }
    });

    Thread thread2 = new Thread(new Runnable() {
        @Override
        public void run() {
            try {
                for(int i=1;i<=10;i++){
                    Message msg = new Message();
                    Thread.sleep(2000);
                    Bundle bundle = new Bundle();
                    bundle.putString("threadName",
                        "thread2");
                    msg.setData(bundle);
                    msg.obj=String.valueOf(i);
                    handler2.sendMessage(msg);
                }
            } catch (InterruptedException e) {
                e.printStackTrace();
            }
        }
    });
    thread1.start();
    thread2.start();
    }
}
```

Here you see that the TextView controls from the layout file are accessed and mapped to the
TextView objects seqNums1 and seqNums2, respectively. In the onStart() method, you use
the Thread class with a Runnable object for both the threads. The run() method starts the
execution of both threads. To display sequence numbers from 1 to 10, in the run() method,
create a Message object called msg and add the sequence numbers to it. Bundle the name of
the running thread in the Message object. Finally, send the message through the Handler
object to display the sequence numbers on the screen through the TextView controls. The time

delay between the display of sequence numbers of the first thread is 1 second, whereas the time delay between the display of sequence numbers of the second thread is 2 seconds.

After you run the application, both threads display the sequence numbers beginning from 1 (see Figure 13.5 [top]). The first thread will reach its final value, 10, in half the time of the second thread. Figure 13.5 (bottom) shows the first thread displaying the value 10; the second thread still displays the value 5.

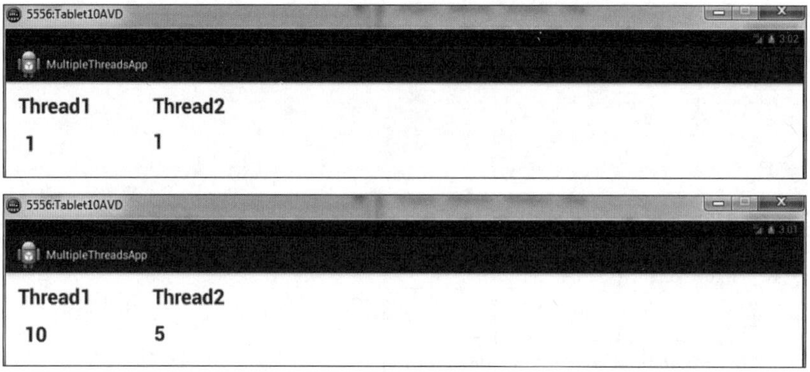

Figure 13.5   Both threads start simultaneously displaying the beginning value 1 (top); `Thread1` finishes its sequence numbers before `Thread2` (bottom)

Recipe: Using the `AsyncTask` Class

In this recipe, you will learn to use the `AsyncTask` class to create and manage threads. Basically, the `AsyncTask` class creates an asynchronous task for performing the processing in the background. The `AsyncTask` class provides several event handlers that synchronize with the thread to show the progress and completion of the task. `AsyncTask` can perform several tasks, including fetching data from the network and saving data in the background.

However, there are some design flaws in `AsyncTask`. It is based on handlers and a pool and can only handle a few threads at a time. Because `AsyncTask` is included in the compatibility library, this example can be used on older 2.2 devices, too.

To instantiate an `AsyncTask`, extend the `AsyncTask` class and provide three parameters: `Input Parameters`, `Progress Values`, and `Result Values`. If you don't want to provide any of these parameters, simply replace that parameter with `Void`. The subclass should also override the following event handlers:

- **`doInBackground`**—This method executes in the background thread. The code that doesn't interact with the user is placed in this handler. `Input Parameters` is passed to this method as input. From within this method, the `publishProgress()` method is called and the `onProgressUpdate()` method is executed in the main thread. Using the publishProgress() and onProgressUpdate() methods, the background thread communicates with the main thread to update the UI elements to indicate progress of the work. Remember, the code in this method runs in a separate background thread.

- **onProgressUpdate**—Override this handler to update the UI to indicate progress in the task. This handler receives the set of parameters passed in to publishProgress(). This handler is synchronized with the thread when executed, so you can safely modify UI elements.

- **onPostExecute**—As the name suggests, this method is called after the doInBackground() method is complete. The Result Values returned by the doInBackground() method are passed to this event handler. This handler can inform when the asynchronous task is complete.

The AsyncTask class also provides the following two helpful callback methods:

- **onPreExecute**—Based on the name, it is clear that this method is called before the doInBackground() method is called. This method runs in the main thread and performs setup or similar tasks.

- **onCancelled**—Manages the cancellation of the thread. The method interrupts the execution of the thread and prevents execution of the onPostExecute() method.

> **Note**
>
> Overriding onPostExecute, onPreExecute, onProgressUpdate, and onCancelled is optional.

Create an application that prints sequence numbers from 1 to 10 through a background thread. Name the new application AsyncTasksApp. To display sequence numbers from 1 to 10, all you need is a TextView control. After defining a TextView control, the activity layout file activity_async_tasks_app.xml will appear as shown in Listing 13.5.

Listing 13.5   Code in the Activity Layout File activity_async_tasks_app.xml

```
<LinearLayout xmlns:android= "http://schemas.android.com/apk/res/android"
    android:layout_width="match_parent"
    android:layout_height="match_parent"
    android:orientation="vertical" >
    <TextView
        android:id="@+id/seqnums"
        android:layout_width="match_parent"
        android:layout_height="wrap_content"
        android:textSize="@dimen/text_size"
        android:textStyle="bold"   />
</LinearLayout>
```

You can see that the `TextView` control is assigned the `seqnums` ID to identify and use it in the Java code. To extend the `AsyncTask` class and print the sequence numbers from 1 to 10 through it, modify the Java activity file `AsyncTasksAppActivity.java` to appear as shown in Listing 13.6.

Listing 13.6   **Code in the Java Activity File** `AsyncTasksAppActivity.java`

```java
package com.androidtablet.asynctasksapp;

import android.app.Activity;
import android.os.Bundle;
import android.widget.TextView;
import android.os.AsyncTask;

public class AsyncTasksAppActivity extends Activity {
    TextView seqNums;

    @Override
    public void onCreate(Bundle savedInstanceState) {
        super.onCreate(savedInstanceState);
        setContentView(R.layout.activity_async_tasks_app);
        seqNums=(TextView) findViewById(R.id.seqnums);
        new PrintSequenceTask().execute(1);
    }

    private class PrintSequenceTask extends
        AsyncTask<Integer, Integer, Void> {
        @Override
        protected void onPreExecute() {
            seqNums.setText("Sequence numbers begins");
        }

        @Override
        protected Void doInBackground(Integer... args) {
            for (int i = args[0]; i <= 10; i++) {
                publishProgress(i);
                try {
                    Thread.sleep(1000);
                } catch (InterruptedException e) {
                    e.printStackTrace();
                }
            }
            return null;
        }
```

```
        @Override
        protected void onProgressUpdate(Integer... args) {
            seqNums.setText(args[0].toString());
        }

        @Override
        protected void onPostExecute(Void result) {
            seqNums.setText("Sequence numbers over");
        }
    }
}
```

You can see in the code that the class PrintSequenceTask extends the AsyncTask class. Because you want to print the sequence numbers beginning from 1, a numerical value 1 is passed as an Input Parameter while instantiating the PrintSequence class. Before execution of the doInBackground() method, the onPreExecute() method is executed that displays the text Sequence numbers begins through the TextView control. After execution of the onPreExecute() method, the doInBackground() method is executed, and the value assigned to the Input Parameter is passed to this method and assigned to the args array.

Inside the doInBackground() method, the for loop is executed, beginning from the first element in the args array (value 1) up to value 10. In the for loop, the publishProgress() method is executed, and each for loop value is passed to this method as a parameter. That is, the sequence numbers from 1 to 10 will be assigned as parameters to the publishProgress() method. When the publishProgress() method is called, the onProgressUpdate() method is executed in the main thread with the same parameter value as that assigned to the publishProgress() method. This also means that the sequence numbers from 1 to 10 will be assigned to the args parameter of the onProgressUpdate() method.

In the onProgressUpdate() method, the sequence numbers assigned to the args parameter are displayed through the TextView control. Between each sequence number, a time delay of 1 second is introduced. Finally, when the doInBackground() method is over and all the sequence numbers have been displayed, the onPostExecute() method is executed, which displays the text message Sequence numbers over through the TextView control.

After running the application, the first message that appears through the TextView control is Sequence numbers begins (see Figure 13.6 [first]). The text message is followed by the sequence numbers from 1 (see Figure 13.6 [second]) to 10 (see Figure 13.6 [third]). Each sequence number will be displayed after the time delay of 1 second. Finally, the message Sequence numbers over appears through the TextView control (see Figure 13.6 [fourth]).

Figure 13.6   The text message Sequence numbers begins displayed on application startup (first); the sequence numbers from 1 to 10 appear on the screen (second and third); the text message Sequence numbers over appears after the sequence numbers (fourth)

Summary

In this chapter, you learned different factors that increase application performance. You learned the utility of dual-core chips and quad-core processors in improving application experience. You saw how garbage collection is invoked and memory is recycled for new applications. You also saw the procedure to run an application's tasks on background threads. Finally, you saw how the AsyncTask class creates and manages asynchronous tasks to perform the processing tasks in the background.

The next chapter focuses on generic sensors. You will learn to use different sensors, such as accelerometer, proximity, and gyroscope, in Android applications.

14

Keyboards and Sensors

For entering data of different types and languages, you are compelled to select and configure your keyboard to suit the kind of input you want. Also, to observe the changes that might occur in your environmental surroundings and take the necessary actions, you need to understand the different sensors that your Android device supports.

In this chapter, you will learn to configure your keyboard to support your input requirement. You will come to understand sensors, their event listeners, and the method required to access data produced by the device sensors. You will display the list of sensors that a physical device supports, and you will learn the procedure for the current acceleration of the device along the three axes using the accelerometer sensor. You will use a proximity sensor to learn the distance between an object and a gyroscope sensor to learn the orientation of the device around a given axis.

Recipe: Changing Android Keyboards or Input Methods

To enter data in a different language or to enter input data that requires special symbols, you need to configure keyboard settings. Following are the steps to switch keyboards or input methods:

1. Select the Language & Input option from the device settings (see Figure 14.1 [top left]).

2. Set the language, enable or disable spelling correction while typing, enable Google voice typing, and select the type of keyboard in the Language & Input screen (see Figure 14.1 [top right]). You can also enable voice search and text-to-speech output and adjust the mouse pointer speed (see Figure 14.1 [bottom left]) from the Language & Input screen.

3. Set the keyboard to display word suggestions, gesture input, and so on. Just select the option that best suits you.

4. To check the settings you have defined, open an application, go to any text field, and long-press it. The keyboard with the specified settings will appear to input data (see Figure 14.1 [bottom right]).

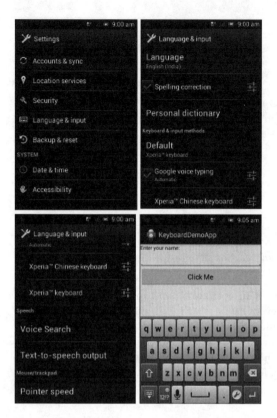

Figure 14.1   Settings screen displaying different options (top left); Language & Input screen displaying different options to set the keyboard language and input method (top right); options to enable voice search, text-to-speech output, and so on (bottom left); keyboard with specified settings displayed after tapping on the text field (bottom right)

Recipe: Understanding Sensors

Sensors are devices that act as detectors. That is, they detect any changes that might occur in temperature, pressure, speed, quantity, and light after measuring that change and convert it into a signal that can be processed further for necessary actions.

Although it may vary from device to device, most of the Android devices have built-in hardware sensors that measure motion, temperature, gravity, orientation, and other changes that might occur in device surroundings.

Android supports different types of sensors, including accelerometer, magnetic field, orientation, and proximity. The class that accesses the device sensors is `SensorManager`. The `SensorManager` is a system service running in Android that listens for data from device sensors. You get an instance of this service by calling the `Context.getSystemService()` method with `SENSOR_SERVICE` as the argument, as shown in the next statement:

```
SensorManager  sensorManager= (SensorManager)getSystemService(SENSOR_SERVICE);
```

To acquire access to any sensor of the device, call the `getDefaultSensor()` method of the `SensorManager` class, passing in the constant that represents the sensor type to this method. Each sensor type is identified by a unique constant defined in the `Sensor` class. For example, the following statement acquires the accelerometer sensor of the device:

```
sensorManager.getDefaultSensor(Sensor.TYPE_ACCELEROMETER);
```

Table 14.1 introduces different types of sensors and their respective constants.

Table 14.1   **Brief Descriptions of Different Types of Sensors**

Sensor Constant	Description
`Sensor.TYPE_AMBIENT_TEMPERATURE`	It returns the ambient room temperature in degrees Celsius.
`Sensor.TYPE_ACCELEROMETER`	It is a three-axis accelerometer that returns the current acceleration along three axes in m/s2 (meters per second, per second.)
`Sensor.TYPE_GRAVITY`	It is a three-axis gravity sensor that returns the current direction and magnitude of gravity along three axes in m/s2.
`Sensor.TYPE_LINEAR_ACCELERATION`	It is a three-axis linear acceleration that returns the acceleration, not including gravity, along three axes in m/s2.
`Sensor.TYPE_GYROSCOPE`	It is a three-axis gyroscope that returns the rate of device rotation along three axes in radians/second.
`Sensor.TYPE_ROTATION_VECTOR`	It returns the orientation of the device as a combination of an angle around an axis.
`Sensor.TYPE_MAGNETIC_FIELD`	It is a magnetometer that finds the current magnetic field in microteslas (µT) along three axes.
`Sensor.TYPE_PRESSURE`	It is an atmospheric pressure sensor that returns the current atmospheric pressure in millibars (mbars).
`Sensor.TYPE_RELATIVE_HUMIDITY`	It returns the current relative humidity as a percentage.
`Sensor.TYPE_PROXIMITY`	It indicates the distance between the device and the target object in centimeters. Usually used to detect whether the device is being held up against the user's ear to manage screen brightness or voice setting.
`Sensor.TYPE_LIGHT`	It returns ambient illumination and is usually used to control the screen brightness dynamically.

> **Note**
>
> Android devices may have all, some, or none of the sensors. The Android emulator has limited support for simulating hardware sensors, Wi-Fi, Bluetooth, and the device battery. The code discussed in this chapter works only on Android hardware.

After acquiring desired sensor in the device, you use the `SensorManager.register-Listener()` method to listen to the events that might occur in the sensor. This method accepts one `SensorEventListener` callback interface that `SensorManager` uses to inform you about the occurrence of the sensor event(s). The occurrence of events is informed via the `onSensorChanged()` and `onAccuracyChanged()` methods:

- **abstract void onAccuracyChanged(Sensor sensor, int accuracy)**—This method is called when there is a change in the sensor accuracy or in the degree of error. The first parameter `sensor` in this method is the registered sensor, and the second parameter is the accuracy value. The accuracy value can be one of the following:

  - **SensorManager.SENSOR_STATUS_ACCURACY_HIGH**—Represents high accuracy.
  - **SensorManager.SENSOR_STATUS_ACCURACY_MEDIUM**—Represents medium accuracy.
  - **SensorManager.SENSOR_STATUS_ACCURACY_LOW**—Represents low accuracy.
  - **SensorManager.SENSOR_STATUS_UNRELIABLE**—Indicates accuracy is unreliable.

- **abstract void onSensorChanged(SensorEvent event)**—This method is called when there is a change in the sensor values. The `SensorEvent` parameter in the method represents the sensor values. Basically, `SensorEvent` is an array of float values that contains the sensor values. The length and content of this array depends on the type of sensor used.

The device sensor returns data when the listener is registered to it. The rate of data returned is determined by the argument passed while registering the listener. The argument determining the rate of data can be any of the following:

- **SENSOR_DELAY_NORMAL**—Data is sent at the normal rate.
- **SENSOR_DELAY_UI**—Data is sent at the rate that is desired in UI interaction.
- **SENSOR_DELAY_GAME**—Data is sent at the rate desired in games.
- **SENSOR_DELAY_FASTEST**—Data is sent at the fastest rate.

The following statement registers a listener to the accelerometer sensor of the device, and the device is set to send data at the normal rate:

```
sensorManager.registerListener(this,
sensorManager.getDefaultSensor(Sensor.TYPE_ACCELEROMETER),
SensorManager.SENSOR_DELAY_NORMAL);
```

Don't forget to unregister the event listener and disable the sensor when it is not used; otherwise, the event listener will keep consuming CPU and battery resources. The event listener is unregistered through the `unregisterListener()` method, as shown in the next statement:

```
sensorManager.unregisterListener(event_listener);
```

It is recommended that you register the listener to get event notifications in the `onResume()` method and unregister it in the `onPause()` method.

Recipe: Knowing the List of Sensors Supported by the Device

Not all sensors are available on all devices. For instance, the device that I am using has an accelerometer and proximity sensor, but no temperature, pressure, magnetic, or gyroscope sensors. Because a device may or may not have the specific sensor, it is a wise idea to first check its presence. You can check the presence of the sensor(s) using either the `SensorManager.getDefaultSensor()` or `ServiceManager.getSensorList()` method.

While using the `getSensorList()` method on the `SensorManager`, you pass the `Sensor.TYPE_ALL` constant as a parameter:

```
List<Sensor> sensorsList = sensorManager.getSensorList(Sensor.TYPE_ALL);
```

To find a list of all the available sensors of a particular type, call the `getSensorList()` method, passing the type of sensor you are looking for as a parameter to it. The following statement returns the list of available accelerometers:

```
List<Sensor> accelerometersList = sensorManager.getSensorList(Sensor.TYPE_
ACCELEROMETER);
```

Create a new Android project to display a list of sensors available on the device. Name the new project `SensorsListApp`. You will be using `ListView` to display the list of available sensors. After defining the `ListView`, the activity layout file `activity_sensors_list_app.xml` will appear as shown in Listing 14.1.

Listing 14.1   **Code in the Activity Layout File** `activity_sensors_list_app.xml`

```xml
<LinearLayout xmlns:android= "http://schemas.android.com/apk/res/android"
    xmlns:tools="http://schemas.android.com/tools"
    android:orientation="vertical"
    android:layout_width="match_parent"
    android:layout_height="wrap_content">
    <ListView
        android:id="@+id/sensors_list"
        android:layout_width="match_parent"
        android:layout_height="match_parent"
        android:drawSelectorOnTop="false"/>
</LinearLayout>
```

To access and identify it in Java code, the `ListView` is assigned the `sensors_list` ID. All the available sensors on the device will be displayed in the form of list items in the `ListView`.

The default size of the list items displayed in ListView is suitable for phones but is quite small for tablets. To resize the list items of the ListView as per the device screen size, add one more XML file named list_item.xml to the res/layout folder. Write the following code in the list_item.xml file:

```
<?xml version="1.0" encoding="utf-8"?>
<TextView xmlns:android="http://schemas.android.com/apk/res/android"
    android:layout_width="match_parent"
    android:layout_height="match_parent"
    android:padding="6dp"
    android:textSize="@dimen/text_size"
    android:textStyle="bold" />
```

The preceding code will make the list items of the ListView pad by 6dp spaces, appear in bold, and be the size defined in the dimension resource text_size.

Next, you need to write Java code to perform the following tasks:

- Get an instance of SensorManager, a system service.

- Invoke the getSensorList method of SensorManager with the Sensor.TYPE_ALL constant to fetch the list of all available sensors in the device.

- Define an ArrayList, and copy all the fetched device sensors in it.

- Define an ArrayAdapter using the ArrayList.

- Set the ArrayAdapter to the ListView to display the fetched device sensors through the ListView.

In the Java activity file SensorsListAppActivity.java, write the code as shown in Listing 14.2.

Listing 14.2   **Code in the Java Activity File** SensorsListAppActivity.java
_____

```
package com.androidtablet.sensorslistapp;

import android.os.Bundle;
import android.app.Activity;
import android.hardware.SensorManager;
import android.content.Context;
import java.util.ArrayList;
import java.util.List;
import android.widget.ArrayAdapter;
import android.hardware.Sensor;
import android.widget.ListView;

public class SensorsListAppActivity extends Activity  {
    @Override
    protected void onCreate(Bundle savedInstanceState) {
```

```
        super.onCreate(savedInstanceState);
        setContentView(R.layout.activity_sensors_list_app);
        ListView sensorsList = (ListView)findViewById(
            R.id.sensors_list);
        SensorManager sensorManager = (SensorManager)
            getSystemService(Context.SENSOR_SERVICE);
        List<Sensor> listOfSensors = sensorManager.
            getSensorList(Sensor.TYPE_ALL);
        ArrayList<String> arrayListSensors = new
            ArrayList<String>();
        for(int i=0; i<listOfSensors.size(); i++)
            arrayListSensors.add(((Sensor) listOfSensors.
                get(i)).getName());
        ArrayAdapter<String> arrayAdpt= new
            ArrayAdapter<String> (this, R.layout.list_item,
            arrayListSensors);
        sensorsList.setAdapter(arrayAdpt);
    }
}
```

After running the application, you get the list of available sensors. Figure 14.2 (top) shows the list of sensors on an Android virtual device (AVD), whereas Figure 14.2 (bottom) shows the list of available sensors on a physical device.

Figure 14.2   The list of sensors displayed in the AVD (top), and the list of available sensors on a physical Android device (bottom)

Recipe: Using the Accelerometer Sensor

You use the accelerometer sensor to know the current acceleration of the device along the three axes in m/s2 (meters per second, per second). The accelerometer sensor helps in sensing human hand motion and is quite often implemented in games. To use the accelerometer sensor, as usual, you get an instance of the `SensorManager` class—a system service that listens to the data from device sensors. Thereafter, to acquire the accelerometer sensor of the device, you call `getDefaultSensor()` of the `SensorManager` class, passing the constant `Sensor.TYPE_ACCELEROMETER`. The `Sensor.TYPE_ACCELEROMETER` is a constant defined in the `Sensor` class that represents the accelerometer sensor. The following statements acquire the accelerometer sensor of a device:

```
SensorManager  sensorManager=(SensorManager) getSystemService(SENSOR_SERVICE);
sensorManager.getDefaultSensor(Sensor.TYPE_ACCELEROMETER);
```

The following example registers a listener to the accelerometer sensor. The rate of data the sensor returns will be normal:

```
sensorManager.registerListener(this,
sensorManager.getDefaultSensor(Sensor.TYPE_ACCELEROMETER),
SensorManager.SENSOR_DELAY_NORMAL);
```

Create a new Android project called `SensorAccApp`. This application will show the acceleration of the device in the X, Y, and Z axis. When not moving, the application will show the values for each axis if the device is oriented in any direction.

To display the values of the three axes, you define three `TextView` controls in the layout file `activity_sensor_acc_app.xml`. After defining three `TextView` controls, the layout file `activity_sensor_acc_app.xml` will appear as shown in Listing 14.3.

Listing 14.3   **Code in the Layout File** `activity_sensor_acc_app.xml`

```xml
<LinearLayout xmlns:android= "http://schemas.android.com/apk/res/android"
    android:layout_width="match_parent"
    android:layout_height="match_parent"
    android:orientation="vertical" >
    <TextView
        android:id="@+id/xaxisview"
        android:layout_width="wrap_content"
        android:layout_height="wrap_content"
        android:text="X Axis"
        android:textSize="@dimen/text_size"
        android:textStyle="bold" />
    <TextView
        android:id="@+id/yaxisview"
        android:layout_width="wrap_content"
        android:layout_height="wrap_content"
        android:text="Y Axis"
```

```
        android:textSize="@dimen/text_size"
        android:textStyle="bold"  />
    <TextView
        android:id="@+id/zaxisview"
        android:layout_width="wrap_content"
        android:layout_height="wrap_content"
        android:text="Z Axis"
        android:textSize="@dimen/text_size"
        android:textStyle="bold" />
</LinearLayout>
```

To identify and access the Java code, the three TextView controls are assigned the IDs xaxisview, yaxisview, and zaxisview. The three TextView controls are set to display the texts X Axis, Y Axis, and Z Axis, respectively. The text displayed through TextView will appear in the font size defined in the dimension resource text_size.

After defining the layout file, you need to write Java code to perform the following tasks:

- Access the accelerometer sensor in the device.

- Register event listener to it.

- Access the data returned by the accelerometer sensor.

- Access the three TextView controls defined in the layout file and map them to the TextView objects.

- Access the data returned by the accelerometer sensor, and display it via the three TextView controls.

To perform all these tasks, write the code shown in Listing 14.4 into the Java activity file SensorAccAppActivity.java.

Listing 14.4   **Code in the Java Activity File** SensorAccAppActivity.java

```
package com.androidtablet.sensoraccapp;

import android.app.Activity;
import android.hardware.Sensor;
import android.hardware.SensorEvent;
import android.hardware.SensorEventListener;
import android.hardware.SensorManager;
import android.os.Bundle;
import android.widget.TextView;

public class SensorAccAppActivity extends Activity implements SensorEventListener {
    TextView xAxisView,yAxisView, zAxisView;
    SensorManager sensorManager;

    @Override
```

```
public void onCreate(Bundle savedInstanceState) {
    super.onCreate(savedInstanceState);
    setContentView(R.layout.activity_accelerometer_app);
    xAxisView=(TextView)findViewById(R.id.xaxisview);
    yAxisView=(TextView)findViewById(R.id.yaxisview);
    zAxisView=(TextView)findViewById(R.id.zaxisview);
    sensorManager=(SensorManager)getSystemService(
        SENSOR_SERVICE);
}

@Override
protected void onResume() {
    super.onResume();
    sensorManager.registerListener(this,sensorManager.
        getDefaultSensor(Sensor.TYPE_ACCELEROMETER),
        SensorManager.SENSOR_DELAY_NORMAL);
}

@Override
protected void onStop()  {
    sensorManager.unregisterListener(this);
    super.onStop();
}

public void onAccuracyChanged(Sensor sensor, int accuracy) {
}

public void onSensorChanged(SensorEvent event) {
    if(event.sensor.getType()==Sensor.TYPE_ACCELEROMETER) {
        float x=event.values[0];
        float y=event.values[1];
        float z=event.values[2];
        xAxisView.setText("X: "+x);
        yAxisView.setText("Y: "+y);
        zAxisView.setText("Z: "+z);
    }
}
}
```

You know that the onResume() method runs every time the activity starts its life cycle, so a listener is registered to the accelerometer sensor in this method. The sensor is set to send data at the normal rate. Similarly, the onStop() method is called when the application is no longer visible. The event listener is unregistered in this method because the sensor is not required in this state.

Because the activity class implements the SensorEventListener interface, it is essential for the activity to define the following two methods:

- **onAccuracyChanged()**—Executed when the accuracy of the information returned by the sensor changes.

- **onSensorChanged()**—Executed every time the values from the sensor change

Because you are not concerned about the accuracy of the data the device sensor returns, the onAccuracyChanged() method in the preceding code listing is left blank. In the onSensorChanged() method, the values that the sensor returns are analyzed. The values are returned as an array that is a member of the event object. The values from the array are accessed and displayed on the screen using the three TextView controls.

Run the application. Assuming the device is in portrait mode, the values of the acceleration on the X, Y, and Z axes may appear as shown in Figure 14.3 (left). The acceleration of the device along axes X, Y, and Z in landscape mode may appear as shown in Figure 14.3 (right).

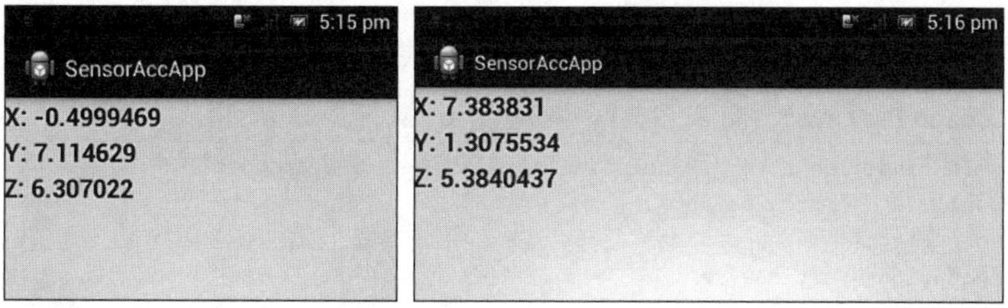

Figure 14.3   The acceleration on X, Y, and Z axes returned by accelerometer sensor (left), and the acceleration data on X, Y, and Z axes returned by the accelerometer sensor while the device is in landscape mode (right)

Recipe: Using the Proximity Sensor

The proximity sensor is usually used in the applications to measure the distance of a device's ear phone from the user's head. The idea is that if the device is near the user's ear or head, the screen may be switched to dark to save battery, or the touch screen may be disabled so that no key is pressed accidently by the ear, cheek, or head. That is, the accidental touch events that might occur when a user's ear touches the device screen while speaking are simply ignored by using proximity sensors. Proximity sensors are different from other sensors. The other sensors work in poll mode, while the proximity sensor works in interrupt mode. Whereas other sensors are polled at regular intervals, the proximity sensor works when the proximity changes (when the device is brought near or moved far from the user). It is the light sensor in the device that helps to detect changes in the device proximity.

The proximity sensor returns the distance between the object and the device in centimeters. Some proximity sensors provide a value ranging from 0.0 to the maximum in increments, whereas others return either 0.0 or the maximum value only. The proximity sensor in my device returns a value of either 0.0 or 10.0, where the value 0.0 indicates that the object is closer to the device, and 10.0 indicates the object is far away from the device.

As mentioned earlier, the proximity sensor in most Android devices returns either 0.0 or 1.0. You might be thinking, "Why only two values?" The answer is that the proximity sensor maintains a threshold value. The LUX value returned by a light sensor in the device is compared with the specific threshold value. If the LUX value is more than the threshold, the device is far from the user, and the proximity sensor returns a 1.0 value. Similarly, if the LUX value is less than the threshold value, the device is closer to the user; consequently, the proximity sensor returns a 0.0 value.

To understand the concept of the proximity sensor through a running example, create a new Android project called SensorProximityApp. The application will display the distance of the object from the device. You will be using a TextView control to display the distance. After defining a TextView control, the activity layout file activity_sensor_proximity_app.xml will appear, as shown in Listing 14.5.

Listing 14.5   **Code in the Layout File** activity_sensor_proximity_app.xml

```
<LinearLayout xmlns:android="http://schemas.android.com/apk/res/android"
    android:layout_width="match_parent"
    android:layout_height="match_parent"
    android:orientation="vertical" >
    <TextView
        android:id="@+id/distance"
        android:layout_width="wrap_content"
        android:layout_height="wrap_content"
        android:text="Distance is: "
        android:textSize="@dimen/text_size"
        android:textStyle="bold" />
    </LinearLayout>
```

To access and identify the TextView control in Java code, it is assigned the distance ID. It is set to display the text in bold and in the font size defined in the dimension resource text_size. Also, it is initialized to display the text Distance is:.

Next, you need to write Java code to perform the following tasks:

- Access the TextView control defined in the activity layout file and map it to the TextView object.

- Acquire the proximity sensor of the device.

- Register an event listener to the sensor.

- Take the sensor reading (that is, the distance of the object from the device) and display the value on the screen through the TextView control.

To perform all these tasks, write the code as shown in Listing 14.6 into the Java activity file SensorProximityAppActivity.java.

Listing 14.6 **Code in the Java Activity File** SensorProximityAppActivity.java

```java
package com.androidtablet.sensorproximityapp;

import android.app.Activity;
import android.hardware.Sensor;
import android.hardware.SensorEvent;
import android.hardware.SensorEventListener;
import android.hardware.SensorManager;
import android.os.Bundle;
import android.widget.TextView;

public class SensorProximityAppActivity extends Activity implements
SensorEventListener {
    TextView distanceView;
    SensorManager sensorManager;

    @Override
    protected void onCreate(Bundle savedInstanceState) {
        super.onCreate(savedInstanceState);
        setContentView(R.layout.activity_sensor_proximity_app);
        distanceView=(TextView)findViewById(R.id.distance);
        sensorManager=(SensorManager)getSystemService(
            SENSOR_SERVICE);
    }

    @Override
    protected void onResume() {
        super.onResume();
        sensorManager.registerListener(this,sensorManager.
            getDefaultSensor(Sensor.TYPE_PROXIMITY),
            SensorManager.SENSOR_DELAY_NORMAL);
    }

    @Override
    protected void onStop()   {
        sensorManager.unregisterListener(this);
        super.onStop();
    }

    public void onAccuracyChanged(Sensor sensor, int accuracy){
    }

    public void onSensorChanged(SensorEvent event) {
        if(event.sensor.getType()==Sensor.TYPE_PROXIMITY) {
```

```
            float d=event.values[0];
            distanceView.setText("Distance is: "+d);
        }
    }
}
```

If no object is near the device when you run the application, the proximity sensor displays its maximum value, 10.0cm (see Figure 14.4 [top]). When you bring an object closer to the device, the distance will reduce to 0.0cm (see Figure 14.4 [bottom]).

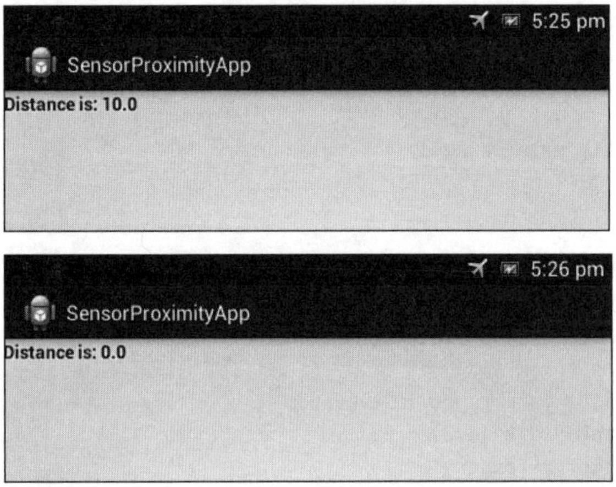

Figure 14.4   The proximity sensor displays value 10.0 when no object is near the device (top), and the proximity sensor displays value 0.0 when an object is very close to the device (bottom)

Although the preceding application will run perfectly, it is wise to add the following statement to the AndroidManifest.xml file:

```
<uses-feature android:name= "android.hardware.sensor.proximity" />
```

When added to the manifest file, this statement indicates that the proximity sensor is necessary in a device to properly support this application. So if your application is available on Google Play, the application will only be installed on the devices that have a proximity sensor, thereby ensuring that the application runs.

Recipe: Using Gyroscope Sensor

The gyroscope sensor returns the angular speed around the three axes in radians per second. It measures the rate of rotation around the X, Y, and Z axis. Rotation is positive in the counter-clockwise direction. Because the gyroscope sensor measures the speed rather than the direction, its result is integrated over time to determine the current orientation. The computed result will then represent a change in orientation around a given axis.

The gyroscope measures the angular speed along the three axes. Whenever the sensor senses any change in the device's angular speed, the related information is stored in the `event.values` array. That is, the `event.values` array returns the angular speed around the three axes:

- `event.values[0]`—Represents the angular speed around the X axis

- `event.values[1]`—Represents the angular speed around the Y axis

- `event.values[2]`—Represents the angular speed around the Z axis

To compute the rotation angle in radians, multiply the returned angular speed with the time difference between the current and previous sample. Because the sensor returns the data samples along with timestamps measured in nanoseconds, to compute the rotation angle in radians, follow these three steps:

1. Calculate the time difference between the two sensor readings (that is, between the current and the previous sample).

2. Convert the time difference from nanosecond to second.

3. Multiply the angular speed (angle per second value) by the time difference in seconds. The resulting value will indicate how much the gyroscope has rotated from the previous sample time to the current sample time.

You need to learn to apply these steps through a running example. So create an Android project called `SensorGyroscopeApp`. To display the angular speed around the three axes, you will define three `TextView` controls. After defining three `TextView` controls, the activity layout file `activity_sensor_gyroscope_app.xml` will appear as shown in Listing 14.7.

Listing 14.7 Code in the Activity Layout File `activity_sensor_gyroscope_app.xml`

```xml
<LinearLayout xmlns:android= "http://schemas.android.com/apk/res/android"
    android:layout_width="match_parent"
    android:layout_height="match_parent"
    android:orientation="vertical" >
    <TextView
        android:id="@+id/xaxisview"
        android:layout_width="wrap_content"
        android:layout_height="wrap_content"
        android:text="X Axis"
        android:textSize="@dimen/text_size"
        android:textStyle="bold" />
    <TextView
        android:id="@+id/yaxisview"
        android:layout_width="wrap_content"
        android:layout_height="wrap_content"
```

```
            android:text="Y Axis"
            android:textSize="@dimen/text_size"
            android:textStyle="bold"   />
    <TextView
            android:id="@+id/zaxisview"
            android:layout_width="wrap_content"
            android:layout_height="wrap_content"
            android:text="Z Axis"
            android:textSize="@dimen/text_size"
            android:textStyle="bold" />
    </LinearLayout>
```

You can see that the three TextView controls are initialized to display the text X Axis, Y Axis, and Z Axis, respectively. The text will appear in bold and in the font size defined in the dimension resource text_size. To access and identify the Java code, the TextView controls are assigned the IDs xaxisview, yaxisview, and zaxisview, respectively. In the Java activity file SensorGyroscopeAppActivity.java, write the code as shown in Listing 14.8.

Listing 14.8   **Code in the Java Activity File** SensorGyroscopeAppActivity.java

```
package com.androidtablet.sensorgyroscopeapp;

import android.os.Bundle;
import android.app.Activity;
import android.widget.TextView;
import android.hardware.SensorManager;
import android.hardware.SensorEventListener;
import android.hardware.Sensor;
import android.hardware.SensorEvent;

public class SensorGyroscopeAppActivity extends Activity implements
SensorEventListener  {
    TextView xAxisView,yAxisView, zAxisView;
    SensorManager sensorManager;
    float angleX, angleY, angleZ;
    private long previousTime =0 ;

    @Override
    protected void onCreate(Bundle savedInstanceState) {
        super.onCreate(savedInstanceState);
        setContentView(R.layout.activity_sensor_gyroscope_app);
        xAxisView=(TextView)findViewById(R.id.xaxisview);
        yAxisView=(TextView)findViewById(R.id.yaxisview);
        zAxisView=(TextView)findViewById(R.id.zaxisview);
        sensorManager=(SensorManager)getSystemService(
            SENSOR_SERVICE);
```

```
    }

    @Override
    protected void onResume() {
        super.onResume();
        sensorManager.registerListener(this,sensorManager.
            getDefaultSensor(Sensor.TYPE_GYROSCOPE),
            SensorManager.SENSOR_DELAY_NORMAL);
    }

    @Override
    protected void onStop()  {
        sensorManager.unregisterListener(this);
        super.onStop();
    }

    @Override
    public void onAccuracyChanged(Sensor arg0, int arg1)   {   }
    public void onSensorChanged(SensorEvent event) {
        if (previousTime != 0) {
            final float timeDiff = (event.timestamp —
                previousTime) *  1.0f / 1000000000.0f;
            angleX += event.values[0] * timeDiff;
            angleY += event.values[1] * timeDiff;
            angleZ += event.values[2] * timeDiff;
            xAxisView.setText("Orientation X : "+angleX);
            yAxisView.setText("Orientation Y : "+angleY);
            zAxisView.setText("Orientation Z : "+angleZ);
        }
        previousTime = event.timestamp;
    }
}
```

The code in Listing 14.8 does the following tasks:

- Accesses the three TextView controls defined in the activity layout file and maps them to the respective TextView objects. The three TextView controls display the rotation angle along the three axes.

- Acquires the Gyroscope sensor of the device.

- Registers an event listener to the sensor.

- Takes the sensor reading.

- Converts the angular speed into the rotation angle in radians and determines how much the Gyroscope has rotated from the previous sample time.

- Displays the rotation angle along the three axes.

Tip

Because of the gyroscope noise and offset, the orientation values returned from the gyroscope can be inaccurate. For the compensation and to obtain the correct orientation values, the gyroscopes are often used in combination with other sensors such as gravity sensors or accelerometers.

Summary

In this chapter, you learned to select and configure the keyboard to suit your input requirements. You learned about the classes, methods, and interface that are required to acquire and read data from the device sensors. You saw how to display the list of sensors that a device supports. You saw the usage of the accelerometer sensor in displaying the current acceleration of the device along the three axes. You discovered how to find the distance between an object and a device using the proximity sensor. Finally, you learned the technique to determine the orientation of the device around a given axis using a gyroscope sensor.

The next chapter is focused on understanding JSON. You will learn to use JSON Reader and JSON Writer and learn the use of JSON in web services.

15

JSON

Data communication is common in applications. Whether to store on a database or to send it to another application on the Internet, that data needs to be communicated to and from an application. JSON (JavaScript Object Notation) is one of the data exchange formats that is popularly used in Android applications. Android includes the `json.org` libraries that enable you to work with JSON files. JSON is a fast, easy-to-use-and-manage data exchange format. In this chapter, you will learn ways of creating, inserting, and accessing information in `JSONObjects`. Also, you will learn to nest a `JSONObject` into another `JSONObject`. In addition, you will learn to keep more than one `JSONObject` into a `JSONArray`. You will see how information is written and read using `JsonReader` and `JsonWriter`. Finally, you will also learn the procedure of consuming JSON Web services in Android applications

Recipe: Understanding JSON

JSON is a communication and data exchange protocol. Considered an XML alternative, JSON is a lightweight text-based data format that is widely used in Java and Android apps for exchanging data. The basic unit of data in JSON is a `JSONObject` that contains data in the form of key-value pairs. A `JSONObject` is easy to use and manage because of those key-value pairs. Here is a sample `JSONObject` that indicates product information:

```
{
    "id":"A101",
    "productname":"Smartphone",
    "price":19.99
}
```

You can see that `id`, `productname`, and `price` are the keys, and `A101`, `Smartphone`, and `19.99` are the values of the respective keys. You can also nest one `JSONObject` inside another. The following example nests a `JSONObject` under the key name `details` inside another `JSONObject`:

```
{
    "id":"A101",
    "productname":"Smartphone",
    "price":19.99,
    "details": {
        "Packed On": "Jul 2013",
        "Manufacturing Date": "Aug 2013",
        "Expiry Date": "Dec 2015"
    }
}
```

Note

JSON allows nesting to several levels. The nested JSONObject in turn can contain another JSONObject, and so on.

Table 15.1 shows two constructors used for creating JSONObjects.

Table 15.1   Brief Description of the Constructors Used to Create JSONObjects

Constructor	Description
public JSONObject()	Creates an empty JSONObject.
	Example:
	JSONObject jObject = new JSONObject();
public JSONObject (String jsondata)	Creates a JSONObject from the supplied String parameter. The String parameter contains data in the form of key-value pairs enclosed between opening and closing braces, { and }.
	Example:
	String productdata = "{\"id\": \"A101\",\"productname\": \"Smartphone\",\"price\": 19.99}";
	JSONObject jObject = new JSONObject(productdata);
	The values in the JSONObject can be of several types including int, double, string, boolean, array, and null.

A few of the methods that are frequently used while working with JSONObject are listed in Table 15.2.

Table 15.2   **Brief Description of the Methods Used with** JSONObject

Methods	Description

JSONObject put (key, value)	Creates a new value associated with the specified key inside the JSONObject. The key must be a string enclosed in double quotes, and the value can be any basic type, such as int, long, boolean, or double, including another JSONObject.
	
	Examples:
	
	JSONObject product = new JSONObject();
	
	product.put("productname", "Smartphone");
	
	product.put("price", Double.valueOf(19.99));
	
	If the key already exists in the JSONObject, the put method will replace the previous value.

get+data_type(key)	Obtains data from JSONObject. The data_type refers to the data type of the value stored in the specified key. For example, if the data type of value is string, the getString(key) method will be used. Similarly, if the value is of the integer type, the getInt(key) method will be used. You can use the following statements to access the values stored in the product JSONObject using id, productname, and price keys: String productID=product.getString("id"); String productName=product.getString("productname"); double price= product.getDouble("price");
Object remove(key)	Removes a value with the specified key from the JSONObject. If the method executes successfully, it returns the removed value; otherwise, it returns null.
boolean has (key)	Returns a boolean value indicating whether the JSONObject contains a value with the specified key.
boolean isNull(key)	Returns a boolean value indicating whether a key exists in the JSONObject. The method also checks whether the value associated with a key is null.
int length()	Returns the number of key-value pairs that exist in the JSONObject. The length of child JSONObjects (if any) will not be included.
Iterator keys()	Returns an iterator that can be used to iterate through the JSONObject.
JSONArray names()	Returns a JSONArray of names (keys) of the JSONObject. The difference between the keys() and names() method is the type of data they return. The keys() method returns Iterator, whereas the names() method returns JSONArray. JSONArray is explained in the following recipe.

JSONObject can be serialized to String to write to a file or send over the Internet. The reverse is also possible (a string can be converted to a JSONObject).

Example:

The following statements define a JSONObject called jObject, put some information in the jObject, convert the jObject into a string named JsonString, and create another JSONObject called jObject2 from the JsonString:

```
JSONObject jObject = new JSONObject();
jObject.put("id", "A101");
jObject.put("productname", "Smartphone");
jObject.put("price", Double.valueOf(19.99));
String JsonString = jObject.toString();
JSONObject jObject2 = new JSONObject(JsonString);
```

The following statements show how all the keys of a JSONObject can be accessed:

```
String productInfo="";
Iterator iterator = jObject.keys();
while (iterator.hasNext())
    productInfo+=iterator.next();
```

All the keys in the JSONObject called jObject are accessed and stored in the string productInfo.

Recipe: Using JSONObject to Keep Information

In this recipe, you will create a JSONObject consisting of three fields where you will enter the ID, the name, and the price of a product. The focus of this recipe is to understand how data is entered and accessed from a JSONObject.

Create a new Android project called JSONApp. To print the ID, name, and product price, you will use a TextView control. After you define a TextView control, the activity layout file activity_jsonapp.xml will appear as shown in Listing 15.1.

Listing 15.1   **Code in the Activity Layout File** activity_jsonapp.xml

```
<LinearLayout xmlns:android= "http://schemas.android.com/apk/res/android"
    xmlns:tools="http://schemas.android.com/tools"
    android:layout_width="match_parent"
    android:layout_height="match_parent"
    android:orientation="vertical" >
    <TextView
        android:id="@+id/jsondata"
        android:layout_width="match_parent"
        android:layout_height="wrap_content"
        android:textSize="@dimen/text_size"
        android:textStyle="bold"  />
</LinearLayout>
```

You can see that the `TextView` is assigned a `jsondata` ID to identify it in Java code. Also, the text displayed through `TextView` is set to appear in bold and in the font size defined in the dimension resource `text_size`.

Next, you need to write Java code to perform the following tasks:

- Access the `TextView` control defined in the layout file and map it to the `TextView` object.

- Define a `JSONObject`.

- Insert the product ID, product name, and product price in the `JSONObject` under the key names `id`, `productname`, and `price`, respectively.

- Access the product ID, product name, and product price from the `JSONObject` using the respective keys and display them through the `TextView` control.

To perform all these tasks, write the code as shown in Listing 15.2 into the Java activity file `JSONAppActivity.java`.

Listing 15.2   **Code in the Java Activity File** `JSONAppActivity.java`

```java
package com.androidtablet.jsonapp;

import android.os.Bundle;
import android.app.Activity;
import org.json.JSONObject;
import org.json.JSONException;
import android.widget.TextView;

public class JSONAppActivity extends Activity {
    private JSONObject jObject;
    private TextView jsonData;
    String productInfo;

    @Override
    protected void onCreate(Bundle savedInstanceState) {
        super.onCreate(savedInstanceState);
        setContentView(R.layout.activity_jsonapp);
        jsonData = (TextView)findViewById(R.id.jsondata);
        writeJSON();
        readJSON();
    }

    public void writeJSON() {
        jObject = new JSONObject();
        try {
            jObject.put("id", "A101");
            jObject.put("productname", "Smartphone");
```

```
                jObject.put("price", Double.valueOf(19.99));
        } catch (JSONException e) {
            e.printStackTrace();
        }
    }

    private void readJSON() {
        try{
            productInfo="Product ID: "+jObject.getString("id")
                +"\n" +"Product Name: " +jObject.getString
                ("productname")+ "\n" +"Price: " +
                jObject.getString("price")+ "\n";
            jsonData.setText(productInfo);
        }
        catch (Exception e) {
            e.printStackTrace();
        }
    }
}
```

After you run the application, the product ID, product name, and product price are accessed from JSONObject and displayed on the screen as shown in Figure 15.1.

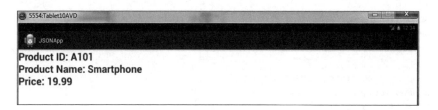

Figure 15.1   Product information is accessed from JSONObject and displayed on the screen

Recipe: Nesting JSONObjects

In the previous recipe, you saw the creation of a simple JSONObject. In this recipe, you will learn to nest another JSONObject in a JSONObject. To the JSONObject jObject that you defined in the JSONApp application created in the previous recipe, you will nest another JSONObject named jsubObject. In other words, you will define a JSONObject called jsubObject, and in it, you will enter the product information of packaging date, manufacturing date, and expiration date under the respective key names. Thereafter, you will nest the JSONObject titled jsubObject into the existing JSONObject titled jObject.

Open the Android application JSONApp that you created in the previous recipe. To nest the JSONObject titled jsubObject in the JSONObject titled jObject, modify the Java activity file

`JSONAppActivity.java` to appear as shown in Listing 15.3. Only the code in bold is modified; the rest of the code is the same as in Listing 15.2.

Listing 15.3   **Code in the Java Activity File** `JSONAppActivity.java`

```java
package com.androidtablet.jsonapp;

import android.os.Bundle;
import android.app.Activity;
import org.json.JSONObject;
import org.json.JSONException;
import android.widget.TextView;

public class JSONAppActivity extends Activity {
    private JSONObject jObject, jsubObject;
    private TextView jsonData;
    String productInfo;

    @Override
    protected void onCreate(Bundle savedInstanceState) {
        super.onCreate(savedInstanceState);
        setContentView(R.layout.activity_jsonapp);
        jsonData = (TextView)findViewById(R.id.jsondata);
        writeJSON();
        readJSON();
    }

    public void writeJSON() {
        jObject = new JSONObject();
        jsubObject = new JSONObject();
        try {
            jsubObject.put("packedon", "Aug 2013");
            jsubObject.put("manufacturingdate", "Jul 2013");
            jsubObject.put("expirydate", "Dec 2015");
            jObject.put("id", "A101");
            jObject.put("productname", "Smartphone");
            jObject.put("price", Double.valueOf(19.99));
            jObject.put("details", jsubObject);
        } catch (JSONException e) {
            e.printStackTrace();
        }
    }

    private void readJSON() {
        try{
            productInfo="Product ID: "+jObject.getString("id")
                +"\n" +"Product Name: " +jObject.getString
                ("productname")+ "\n" +"Price: " +
```

```
                    jObject.getString("price")+ "\n";
            JSONObject prodDetails=jObject.getJSONObject(
                "details");
            productInfo+="Packed On: "+prodDetails.getString(
                "packedon")+"\n" +"Manfacturing Date: " +
                prodDetails.getString("manufacturingdate")+"\n"+
                "Expiry Date: " + prodDetails.getString(
                "expirydate")+ "\n";
            jsonData.setText(productInfo);
        }
        catch (Exception e) {
            e.printStackTrace();
        }
    }
}
```

You can see that another `JSONObject` called `jsubObject` is defined and the packaging, manufacturing, and expiration date of the product are stored in it under the keys `packedon`, `manufacturingdate`, and `expirydate`, respectively. The `jsubObject` is then nested inside the previous `JSONObject` called `jObject` under the key name `details`.

In the `readJSON()` function, you can see that the product ID, name, and price are accessed from the `jObject` using the keys `id`, `productname`, and `price`. The nested `JSONObject` under the key `details` is accessed and assigned to a `JSONObject` called `prodDetails`. Thereafter, the packaging, manufacturing, and expiration dates of the product that are stored under the keys `packedon`, `manufacturingdate`, and `expirydate` are also accessed and displayed on the screen through the `TextView` control.

When you run the application, the product information stored in the keys of the main `JSONObject` titled `jObject` and in the keys of the nested `JSONObject` called `jsubObject` is accessed and is displayed as shown in Figure 15.2.

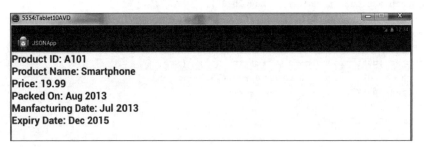

Figure 15.2   Product information from `JSONObject` and the nested `JSONObject` is accessed and displayed on the screen

Note
You can nest `JSONObject` up to any number of levels.

Recipe: Using JSONArray

The JSONArray is basically an array in Java that can store data of any type that JSON permits. A JSONArray can contain data of different types simultaneously.

The following are the constructors for creating a JSONArray:

- **JSONArray()**—Creates a JSONArray with no element.
- **JSONArray(String json)**—Accepts a list of elements inside an array enclosed by brackets ([and]) and separated by a comma (,) or a semicolon (;).

  Examples:

  The following statements create an empty JSONArray:

  ```
  String data = "[]";
  JSONArray jsArray = new JSONArray(data);
  ```

  The following statements create a JSONArray with two elements:

  ```
  String data = "[Smartphone, 19.99]";
  JSONArray jsArray = new JSONArray(data);
  ```

  The following statements create a JSONArray with two elements and a null element:

  ```
  String data = "[Smartphone, 19.99,,]";
  JSONArray jsArray = new JSONArray(data);
  ```

  In the preceding example, any data specified after the right square bracket (]) will be ignored.

- **JSONArray (Collection collection)**—Creates a JSONArray from the specified collection.

Table 15.3 lists the methods that are frequently used while working with JSONArray.

Table 15.3 Brief Description of the Methods Used with JSONArray

Method	Description
JSONArray put(value)	Used to enter a new value in the array. The value will be added at the end of the array. The value can be of boolean, int, long, double, string, or object type.
JSONArray put(index, value)	Used to enter a new value at the specified index location. Again, the value can be of boolean, int, long, double, string, or object type. Object type here refers to a JSONArray and JSONObject. Any value at the specified index location will be overwritten. The index begins from 0, and it cannot be negative.

Method	Description
`get+data_type (index)`	Used to return a value at the specified `index` location. The `data_type` must match the type of value being accessed. For example, the `getString(i)` method will access a value of the string data type from the `ith` index. Similarly, the `getBoolean(i)`, `getInt(i)`, `getLong(i)`, `getDouble(i)`, `get(i)`, `getJSONArray(i)`, and `getJSONObject(i)` methods will access values of boolean, int, long, double, object, JSONArray, and JSONObject types from the `ith` index location of the array.
`String toString()`	Used to convert `JSONArray` into a string.
`boolean isNull (index)`	Returns boolean value `true` if the value at the specified `index` is `null`.
`int length()`	Returns the length of the array.
`boolean equals(Object)`	Compares whether two `JSONArrays` are equal (that is, whether both are instances of the same object).
`String join(String separator)`	Converts all the elements of the `JSONArray` into a string, with the specified `separator` inserted between the elements.

> **Note**
>
> `JSONArray` is also a `JSONobject`.

To understand the concept of `JSONArray` through a running example, create a new Android project called `JSONArrayApp`. The focus of this recipe is to understand how a `JSONArray` is created and how information is entered and accessed from it. In this application, you will create two `JSONObjects`, each containing information of an individual product. The product information will include the product ID, product name, price, packaging date, manufacturing date, and expiration date. The two `JSONObjects` will then be added into a `JSONArray`. The product information will be accessed from the `JSONArray` one by one and displayed on the screen via the `TextView` control.

The first step is to define a `TextView` control in the layout file. After defining a `TextView` control, the activity layout file `activity_jsonarray_app.xml` will appear as shown in Listing 15.4.

Listing 15.4 **Code in the Activity Layout File** `activity_jsonarray_app.xml`

```
<LinearLayout xmlns:android= "http://schemas.android.com/apk/res/android"
    xmlns:tools="http://schemas.android.com/tools"
    android:layout_width="match_parent"
    android:layout_height="match_parent"
    android:orientation="vertical" >
```

```
<TextView
    android:id="@+id/jsondata"
    android:layout_width="match_parent"
    android:layout_height="wrap_content"
    android:textSize="@dimen/text_size"
    android:textStyle="bold"  />
</LinearLayout>
```

To access and identify Java code, you assign the `TextView` control the `jsondata` ID. Also, the text displayed through `TextView` is set to appear in bold and in the font size defined in the dimension resource `text_size`. After the layout file, you need to write Java code to perform the following tasks:

- Access the `TextView` control from the layout file and map it to the `TextView` object.

- Define two `JSONObjects` and store information for two products in them. The product information includes product ID, product name, product price, packaging date, manufacturing date, and expiration date.

- Define a `JSONArray` and insert the two `JSONObjects` in it.

- Access each element of the `JSONArray` into a temporary `JSONObject`.

- Access each field (key-value pair) in the temporary `JSONObject`, including the nested `JSONObject`, and display the information for the two products via the `TextView` control.

To perform all these tasks, write the code as shown in Listing 15.5 in the Java activity file `JSONArrayAppActivity.java`.

Listing 15.5 **Code in the Java Activity File** `JSONArrayAppActivity.java`

```
package com.androidtablet.jsonarrayapp;

import android.os.Bundle;
import android.app.Activity;
import org.json.JSONObject;
import org.json.JSONException;
import android.widget.TextView;
import org.json.JSONArray;

public class JSONArrayAppActivity extends Activity {
    private JSONObject jObject1, jObject2, jsubObject;
    private TextView jsonData;
    String productInfo="";
    JSONArray productsArray;

    @Override
    protected void onCreate(Bundle savedInstanceState) {
```

```
        super.onCreate(savedInstanceState);
        setContentView(R.layout.activity_jsonarray_app);
        jsonData = (TextView)findViewById(R.id.jsondata);
        writeJSON();
        readJSON();
    }

    public void writeJSON() {
        jObject1 = new JSONObject();
        jsubObject = new JSONObject();
        String jString = "{\"id\":\"A102\",
            \"productname\":\"Laptop\", \"price\":49.99,
            \"details\": {\"packedon\":\"Oct 2013\",
            \"manufacturingdate\":\"Sep 2013\",
            \"expirydate\":\"Mar 2017\"}}";
        try {
            jsubObject.put("packedon", "Aug 2013");
            jsubObject.put("manufacturingdate", "Jul 2013");
            jsubObject.put("expirydate", "Dec 2015");
            jObject1.put("id", "A101");
            jObject1.put("productname", "Smartphone");
            jObject1.put("price", Double.valueOf(19.99));
            jObject1.put("details", jsubObject);
            jObject2 = new JSONObject(jString);
        } catch (JSONException e) {
            e.printStackTrace();
        }
        productsArray = new JSONArray();
        productsArray.put(jObject1);
        productsArray.put(jObject2);
    }

    private void readJSON() {
        try{
            for (int i =0 ; i<productsArray.length();i++) {
                JSONObject jObject = productsArray.
                    getJSONObject(i);
                productInfo+="\nProduct ID: "+jObject.
                    getString("id") +"\n"  +"Product Name: " +
                    jObject.getString("productname")+ "\n" +
                    "Price: " +  String.valueOf(jObject.
                    getDouble("price"))+ "\n";
                JSONObject prodDetails=jObject.getJSONObject
                    ("details");
                productInfo+="Packed On: "+
                    prodDetails.getString("packedon")+"\n" +
                    "Manfacturing Date: " + prodDetails.
```

```
                    getString("manufacturingdate")+ "\n"+
                    "Expiry Date: " + prodDetails.getString(
                    "expirydate")+ "\n";
            }
            jsonData.setText(productInfo);
        }
        catch (Exception e) {
            e.printStackTrace();
        }
    }
}
```

To make the recipe more informative, the two JSONObjects that are required for keeping product information are created in two different ways. The first JSONObject, jObject1, is created empty. Thereafter, product information is added to it. The packaging, manufacturing, and expiration dates of the product are collected into a separate JSONObject, jsubObject, which is then nested into the main JSONObject, jObject1, under the key name details. The second JSONObject, jObject2, is created from a string. That is, a string called jString is defined, and information of the second product is stored in this string. Thereafter, the second JSONObject, jObject2, is created from the information stored in the string titled jString. The two JSONObjects titled jObject1 and jObject2 are then inserted into the JSONArray titled productsArray in the writeJSON() function. In the readJSON() function, the two JSONObjects in the JSONArray are accessed, values in different keys of the two JSONObjects are accessed, and the information is then displayed through the TextView control.

After you run the application, you can access the product information from the JSONArray and display it on the screen through the TextView control, as shown in Figure 15.3.

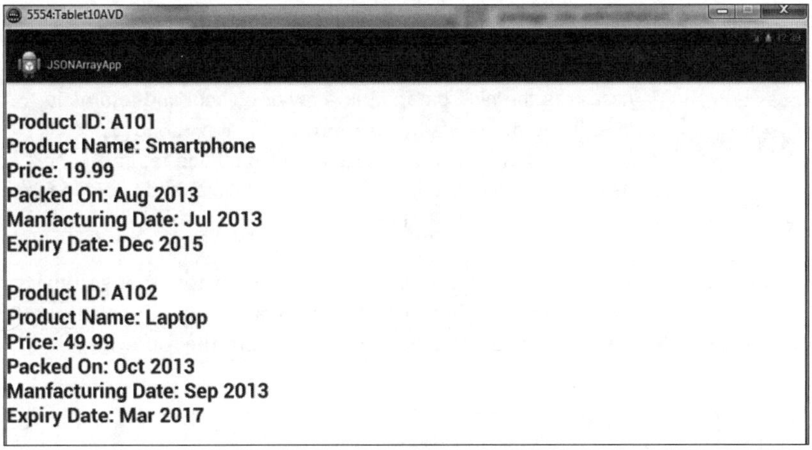

Figure 15.3 Product information accessed from JSONArray is displayed on the screen

Recipe: Using `JsonReader` and `JsonWriter`

The `JsonWriter` class writes JSON-encoded values to a stream. The JSON encoding generally means data in the form of key-value pairs. `JsonReader` is a class that reads JSON-encoded values from the supplied stream.

To use `JsonReader`, you define its instance by calling its constructor, passing in a `Reader` that reads the input data.

Example:

```
JsonReader jsonReader = new JsonReader(new StringReader(data));
```

In this example, `data` refers to the `JSONObject` or array containing information in key-value form. The `JsonReader` iterates through the supplied object or array and accesses the values associated with each key. Table 15.4 shows the methods that are used while using the `JsonReader` class.

Table 15.4   Brief Overview of the Methods of the `JsonReader` Class

Method	Description
`JsonReader.beginObject()`	Indicates the beginning of an array or object. It is explicitly called to inform the `JsonReader` about the same.
`JsonReader.hasNext()`	Checks whether the object or array has more data. The method returns the boolean value `true` if the object or array has another element.
`JsonReader.nextName()`	Returns the next name (`key`) in the supplied object or array.
`JsonReader.peek()`	Analyzes the type of the value. Used to check whether the value is `null`.
`JsonReader.skipValue()`	Skips a key and all its children. Used to ignore the keys that you don't want to parse.
`JsonReader.nextString()`	Accesses the next data in the array or objects and returns it in string form. Similarly, the `nextInt()`, `nextLong()`, `nextDouble()`, and `nextBoolean()` methods return the next data in the array or object in int, long, double, and boolean form.

To use `JsonWriter`, you create its instance by calling its constructor, but before that you have to create a `Writer` where the information is stored (encoded) in key-value form. The `Writer` is then passed as a parameter to the `JsonWriter` constructor, as shown in the following statements:

```
StringWriter stringWriter = new StringWriter();
JsonWriter jsonWriter = new JsonWriter(stringWriter);
```

The preceding statements define a `JsonWriter` object named `jsonWriter`. All the information written through `JsonWriter` will be stored or encoded in the `stringWriter`. Table 15.5 describes the few methods of the `JsonWriter` class.

Table 15.5 **Brief Overview of the Methods of the `JsonWriter` Class**

Method	Description
`JsonWriter.beginObject()`	Indicates beginning of encoding (writing) procedure on a new object.
`JsonWriter.endObject()`	Indicates ending of the encoding on the current object.
`JsonWriter.name(String name)`	Encodes or writes the name (key) in the current object.
`JsonWriter.value(value)`	Encodes or writes the supplied value in the current object. The value can be a string, int, double, or any other data type.

Create a new Android project called `JSONReaderWriterApp`. In this application, you will use `JsonWriter` to write the product information (product ID, product name, and product price) into a `StringWriter` object. Using a string object, you assign the product information in the `StringWriter` object to the `StringReader` object. The `StringReader` object uses `JsonReader` to access each field (product ID, product name, and price) and display it on the screen through the `TextView` control.

After you define a `TextView` control, the activity layout file `activity_jsonreader_writer_app.xml` will appear as shown in Listing 15.6.

Listing 15.6 **Code in the Activity Layout File `activity_jsonreader_writer_app.xml`**

```
<LinearLayout xmlns:android= "http://schemas.android.com/apk/res/android"
    xmlns:tools="http://schemas.android.com/tools"
    android:layout_width="match_parent"
    android:layout_height="match_parent"
    android:orientation="vertical" >
    <TextView
        android:id="@+id/jsondata"
        android:layout_width="match_parent"
        android:layout_height="wrap_content"
        android:textSize="@dimen/text_size"
        android:textStyle="bold"  />
</LinearLayout>
```

To access and identify Java code, assign the `TextView` control the `jsondata` ID. The text displayed through `TextView` is set to appear in bold and in the font size defined in the dimension resource `text_size`. You need to write Java code to perform the following tasks:

- Access the `TextView` control from the layout file and map it to the `TextView` object.

- Define a `StringWriter` object and a `JsonWriter` object. Pass the `StringWriter` object as a parameter to the `JsonWriter` object. Recall that a `Writer` object is required with `JsonWriter` to store (encode) the key-value pairs.

- Use the `JsonWriter` object to enter the product information (product ID, product name, and product price) under the key names `id`, `productname`, and `price`. The entered information will be written into the `StringWriter` object.

- Define a `StringReader` object. Supply the product information that was written into the `StringWriter` to the `StringReader` object via a string object.

- Define a `JsonReader` object passing the `StringReader` object to it as a parameter. The `JsonReader` reads information from the supplied `Reader` object.

- Access product information from the `StringReader` object using different methods of the `JsonReader` class and display it on the screen via the `TextView` control.

To perform all these tasks, write the code as shown in Listing 15.7 in the Java activity file `JSONReaderWriterAppActivity.java`.

Listing 15.7   **Code in the Java Activity File** `JSONReaderWriterAppActivity.java`

```java
package com.androidtablet.jsonreaderwriterapp;

import android.os.Bundle;
import android.app.Activity;
import java.io.StringWriter;
import android.widget.TextView;
import android.util.JsonWriter;
import java.io.IOException;
import java.io.StringReader;
import android.util.JsonReader;
import android.util.JsonToken;

public class JSONReaderWriterAppActivity extends Activity {
    private TextView jsonData;
    String id,productname, productData, productInfo;
    double price;

    @Override
    protected void onCreate(Bundle savedInstanceState) {
        super.onCreate(savedInstanceState);
        setContentView(R.layout.activity_jsonreader_writer_app);
        jsonData = (TextView)findViewById(R.id.jsondata);
        writeJSON();
        readJSON();
    }
```

```java
public void writeJSON() {
    StringWriter stringWriter = new StringWriter();
    JsonWriter jsonWriter = new JsonWriter(stringWriter);
    try {
        jsonWriter.beginObject();
        jsonWriter.name("id").value("A101");
        jsonWriter.name("productname").value("Smartphone");
        jsonWriter.name("price").value(19.99);
        jsonWriter.endObject();
    } catch (IOException e) {
        e.printStackTrace();
    }
    productData = stringWriter.toString();
}

private void readJSON() {
    JsonReader jsonReader = new JsonReader(new
        StringReader(productData));
    try{
        jsonReader.beginObject();
        while (jsonReader.hasNext()) {
            String name = jsonReader.nextName();
            if (jsonReader.peek() == JsonToken.NULL)
                jsonReader.skipValue();
            if (name.equals("id")) {
                id = jsonReader.nextString();
            }
            else if (name.equals("productname")) {
                productname = jsonReader.nextString();
            }
            else if (name.equals("price")) {
                price = jsonReader.nextDouble();
            }
            else {
                jsonReader.skipValue();
            }
        }
        jsonReader.endObject();
    }
    catch (Exception e) {
        e.printStackTrace();
    }
    try{
        productInfo="Product ID: "+id+"\n"
            +"Product Name: " +productname+ "\n"
            +"Price: " + String.valueOf(price)+ "\n";
        jsonData.setText(productInfo);
    }
```

```
        catch (Exception e) {
            e.printStackTrace();
        }
    }
}
```

After you run the application, the product information written using `JsonWriter` is accessed via `JsonReader` and is displayed through the `TextView` control, as shown in Figure 15.4.

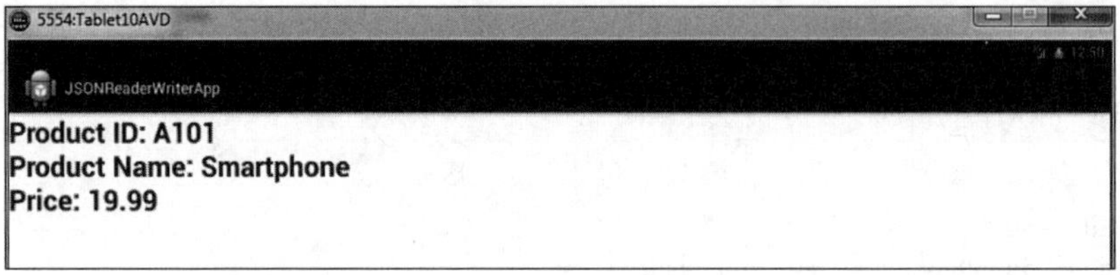

Figure 15.4   Product information accessed through `JsonReader` is displayed on the screen

Recipe: Consuming JSON Web Services in Android Apps

In this recipe, you will learn to consume a JSON Web service to learn the capital and longitude and latitude values of a given state. The application will prompt for a state name, and by using a Web service, the information related to that state will be fetched and displayed on the screen.

The first step is to create a Web service that stores the state name, its capital, and the longitude and latitude values of its capital. The Web service should be encoded to return JSON data. So, create a file named `SampleJSON.php` with the code as shown in Listing 15.8.

Listing 15.8   **Code in the** `SampleJSON.php` **file**

```php
<?php
    $stateDetails = array(array(
        'state' => 'Alabama',
        'capital' => 'Montgomery',
        'latitude' => '32.361538',
        'longitude' => '-86.279118'
    ),
    array(
        'state' => 'Alaska',
        'capital' => 'Juneau',
        'latitude' => '58.301935',
        'longitude' => '-134.419740'
    ),
```

```
    array(
        'state' => 'Arizona',
        'capital' => 'Phoenix',
        'latitude' => '33.448457',
        'longitude' => '112.073844'
    ));
    echo json_encode($stateDetails);
?>
```

You can see that the Web service contains a multi-dimensional array for keeping the information for three states: Alabama, Alaska, and Arizona. You can add the information for any number of states in the file. The next step is to upload the SampleJSON.php file on a server to enable Android applications to access it. In this example, I am uploading the SampleJSON.php file on my domain, http://bintuharwani.com.

To consume JSON Web service (that is, the information in the SampleJSON.php file), create an Android application called ConsumeJSONWebserviceApp. As stated previously, the application will prompt the user to enter a state name. The state name will be searched in the JSON data retrieved from the Web service. If the state name is found in the retrieved JSON data, the capital of the entered state and the latitude and longitude of the capital will be accessed and displayed on the screen.

For this application, you will need three controls: EditText, Button, and a TextView. The EditText will enable the user to enter the name of the state. The Button control will initiate the process of fetching the JSON data from the Web service and of searching for the entered state name in the JSON data. The TextView will be used for displaying the information retrieved from the Web service. For defining these three controls—EditText, Button, and TextView—the code as shown in Listing 15.9 is written in the activity layout file, activity_consume_jsonwebservice_app.xml.

Listing 15.9 Code in the Activity Layout File, activity_consume_jsonwebservice_app.xml

```
<LinearLayout xmlns:android="http://schemas.android.com/apk/res/android"
    android:orientation="vertical"
    android:layout_width="match_parent"
    android:layout_height="match_parent">
    <EditText
        android:layout_width="match_parent"
        android:layout_height="wrap_content"
        android:id="@+id/state_name"
        android:hint="Enter State Name"
        android:textSize="@dimen/text_size"    />
    <Button
        android:layout_width="match_parent"
        android:layout_height="wrap_content"
        android:id="@+id/submit_btn"
```

```
        android:text="Submit"
        android:textSize="@dimen/text_size" />
    <TextView
        android:layout_width="match_parent"
        android:layout_height="wrap_content"
        android:id="@+id/response"
        android:textSize="@dimen/text_size" />
</LinearLayout>
```

In Listing 15.9, the `EditText`, `Button`, and `TextView` controls are defined with the IDs, `state_name`, `submit_btn`, and `response`, respectively.

To access the JSON data from the Web service and to display the capital and longitude and latitude of the entered state, write the code shown in Listing 15.10 in the Java activity file, `ConsumeJSONWebserviceAppActivity`.

Listing 15.10   **Code in the Java Activity File,** `ConsumeJSONWebserviceAppActivity`

```
package com.androidtablet.consumejsonwebserviceapp;

import android.os.Bundle;
import android.app.Activity;
import android.widget.Button;
import android.widget.EditText;
import android.widget.TextView;
import android.view.View;
import org.apache.http.client.methods.HttpPost;
import org.json.JSONException;
import org.apache.http.impl.client.DefaultHttpClient;
import org.apache.http.client.HttpClient;
import org.apache.http.HttpResponse;
import org.apache.http.HttpEntity;
import java.io.InputStream;
import java.io.BufferedReader;
import java.io.InputStreamReader;
import android.os.AsyncTask;
import org.json.JSONObject;
import org.apache.http.StatusLine;
import org.json.JSONArray;

public class ConsumeJSONWebserviceAppActivity extends Activity {
    @Override
    public void onCreate(Bundle savedInstanceState) {
        super.onCreate(savedInstanceState);
        setContentView(R.layout.activity_consume_jsonwebservice_app);
        Button submitButton = (Button)this.findViewById(R.id.submit_btn);
```

```java
    submitButton.setOnClickListener(new Button.OnClickListener(){
        public void onClick(View v)   {
            new ReadJSONFeed().execute("http://bintuharwani.com/
                SampleJSON.php");
         }
    });
}

private class ReadJSONFeed extends AsyncTask<String, String, String> {
    protected void onPreExecute() {}

    @Override
    protected String doInBackground(String... urls) {
        HttpClient httpclient = new DefaultHttpClient();
        StringBuilder builder = new StringBuilder();
        HttpPost httppost = new HttpPost(urls[0]);
        try {
            HttpResponse response = httpclient.execute(httppost);
            StatusLine statusLine = response.getStatusLine();
            int statusCode = statusLine.getStatusCode();
            if (statusCode == 200) {
                HttpEntity entity = response.getEntity();
                InputStream content = entity.getContent();
                BufferedReader reader = new BufferedReader(new
                    InputStreamReader(content));
                String line;
                while ((line = reader.readLine()) != null) {
                    builder.append(line);
                }
            }
        } catch (Exception e) {
            e.printStackTrace();
        }
        return builder.toString();
    }

    protected void onPostExecute(String result) {
        String state="";
        String stateInfo="";
        EditText stateName = (EditText) findViewById(R.id.state_name);
        String searchState=stateName.getText().toString();
        try{
            JSONArray countriesArray = new JSONArray(result);
            for (int i =0 ; i<countriesArray.length();i++) {
                JSONObject jObject = countriesArray.getJSONObject(i);
                state = jObject.getString("state");
```

```
                    if(searchState.equalsIgnoreCase(state)) {
                       stateInfo+="Capital: "+jObject.getString("capital")+"\n";
                       stateInfo+="Latitude: "+jObject.getString("latitude")+"\n";
                       stateInfo+="Longitude: "+jObject.getString("longitude")+
                          "\n";
                    }
                 }
              }
              catch (JSONException e) {
                  e.printStackTrace();
              }
              TextView resp = (TextView) findViewById(R.id.response);
              if(stateInfo.trim().length() >0 )
                  resp.setText(stateInfo);
              else
                  resp.setText("Sorry no match found");
          }
       }
}
```

You can see that the Web service is not accessed through the main UI thread. Instead, the JSON data from the Web service is accessed in the background. The fetched content is received as JSONArray. The entered state name is searched in each JSONObject found in the JSONArray. If the state name is found, the capital of the state and its longitude and latitude values are accessed and displayed on the screen. If the entered state name does not exist in the Web service, the message Sorry no match found is displayed on the screen.

To access the Web service uploaded on a server, you need to add INTERNET permission to the Android project. So, nest the following statement in the <manifest> element in the AndroidManifest.xml file:

```
<uses-permission android:name="android.permission.INTERNET"/>
```

Upon running the application, a screen appears, prompting the user to enter a state name, as shown in 15.5 (top). When entering a state, information related to that state—that is, state capital and longitude and latitude values—will be accessed from the Web service and displayed on the screen (see Figure 15.5 [middle]). If the information of the entered state does not exist in the Web service, the message Sorry no match found will be displayed on the screen, as shown in Figure 15.5 (bottom).

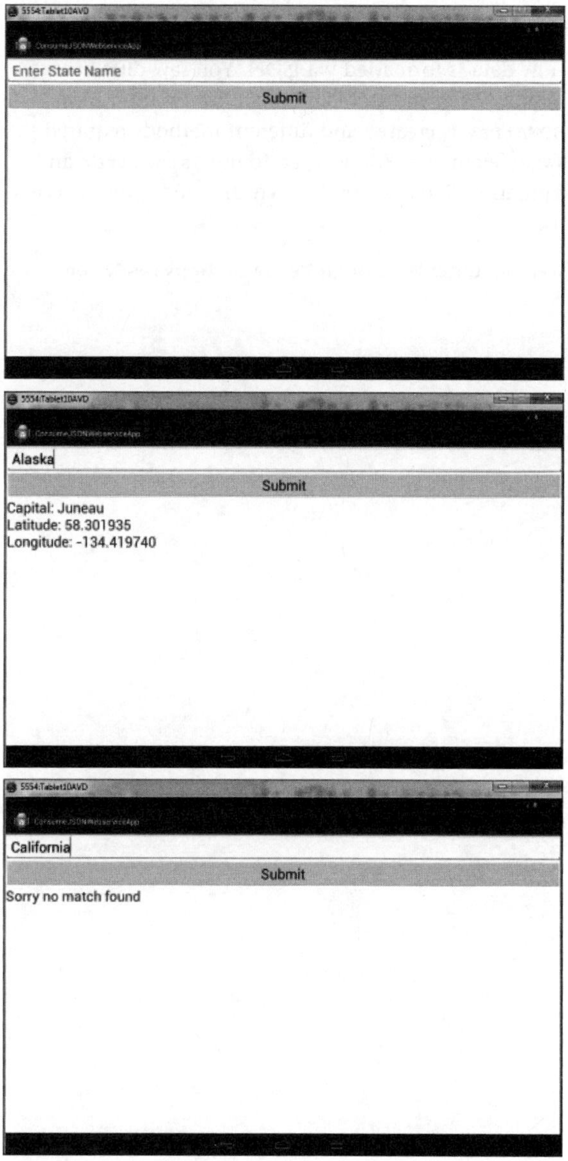

Figure 15.5   Screen on application startup (top); information of the entered state displayed (middle); the message `Sorry no match found` appears if the information of the entered state does not exist in the service

Summary

This chapter was focused on explaining how data is formatted via JSON. You saw different classes and methods required to define `JSONObjects` and store and fetch information from these `JSONObjects`. You also saw how `JSONArray` is created and different methods required to store and access information from `JSONArray` elements. You learned to use `JsonWriter` and `JsonReader` classes to write and read information. Finally, you learned the procedure to access JSON Web service in Android applications.

The next chapter covers how to display web documents through `WebView`, `WebViewClient`, and `WebViewFragment`.

16

WebViews

Accessing the Internet and displaying web pages is one of the most demanding applications today. Everybody wants to use the Internet for searching, browsing, banking, and other needs. Android provides several classes and fragments to support web browsing in Android applications. In this chapter, you will be learning about the usage of the `WebView` widget in displaying web content. Also, you will be looking at the methods required to enable certain browsing features. You will learn how the `WebViewClient` class can load and display the given URL in the specific view. Finally, you will see the role of `WebViewFragment` in displaying web content.

Recipe: Understanding `WebView` and Its Methods

`WebView` is a widget commonly used for viewing web applications or pages. It displays web pages as part of an activity layout. It includes standard browser features such as history, zooming, and JavaScript.

Like other controls, `WebView` can be defined in the activity layout file, as shown here:

```
<WebView
android:id="@+id/webview"
android:layout_width="match_parent"
android:layout_height="match_parent" />
```

To use `WebView` in an application, you can obtain a `WebView` object in either of the following ways:

- Instantiating it from the constructor:

  ```
  WebView webview = new WebView(this);
  ```

- Accessing it from the activity layout file:

  ```
  WebView webView = (WebView) findViewById(R.id.webview);
  ```

After getting the `WebView` object, you can use its `loadURL()` method to load the desired web page. For example, the following statement loads google.com:

```
webView.loadUrl("http://www.google.com/");
```

You can also customize the WebView by using the WebSettings class. You can get the instance of the WebSettings class by calling the getSettings() method on the WebView class. Thereafter, you can call the following methods to customize the WebView:

- **setJavaScriptEnabled()**—Pass the boolean value true to this method to support JavaScript.

- **supportMultipleWindows()**—Pass the boolean value true to this method to enable WebView to support multiple windows.

- **setSupportZoom()**—Pass the boolean value true to this method to support the zoom facility in the browsed content.

- **setDisplayZoomControls()**—Pass the boolean value true to this method to display onscreen zoom controls.

- **setTextZoom()**—Set the text zoom of the web content in a percent. The default value is 100.

- **setSavePassword()**—Pass the boolean value true to this method to enable WebView to save passwords.

The following example enables JavaScript support:

```
WebSettings webSettings = webView.getSettings();
webSettings.setJavaScriptEnabled(true);
```

To access online content, you must enable the application in which WebView is used to search the Internet. Include the following Internet permission statement in its manifest file:

```
<uses-permission android:name= "android.permission.INTERNET" />
```

Table 16.1 shows an outline of different WebView class methods.

Table 16.1 **Brief Descriptions of the** WebView **Class Methods**

Method	Description
reload()	Refreshes or reloads the currently viewed web page.
goBack()	Goes back one step in the browser history.
canGoBack()	Checks to see if there is history to go back to.
goForward()	Moves forwards one step in the browser history.
canGoForward()	Checks to see if there is history to move forward to.
goBackOrForward()	Goes backward or forward in the browser history, depending on whether the number supplied as an argument to the method is positive or negative. A negative number represents the number of steps to navigate backward in the history, and a positive number represents the number of steps to move forward in the browser history.

Method	Description
canGoBackOrForward()	Checks to see if the browser can go backward or forward in the browser history for the specified number of steps. The number supplied as the argument to the method depends on whether you want to go backward or forward.
clearCache()	Clears the browser cache.
clearHistory()	Clears the browsing history.

Recipe: Displaying Web Pages Using `WebView`

Make a small browser application that prompts the user to enter the URL of a Web site and then loads and displays it through the `WebView` control. Launch the Eclipse IDE and create a new Android application. Name the application `WebViewApp`.

In this application, you will use `TextView`, `EditText`, `Button`, and `WebView` controls. The `TextView` control will display the text `Address:` to tell the user that the URL of the web page must be entered in the below `EditText` control. The `EditText` control displays an empty text box where the user can enter the URL of the site to open. When the user clicks the `Button` control, the web page whose URL was entered in the `EditText` control will be loaded and displayed via the `WebView` control. To define these four controls, the code shown in Listing 16.1 is written in the `activity_web_view_app.xml` layout file.

Listing 16.1 Code Written into the `activity_web_view_app.xml` **Layout File**

```
<RelativeLayout xmlns:android="
http://schemas.android.com/apk/res/android"
    android:layout_width="match_parent"
    android:layout_height="match_parent">
    <TextView
        android:id="@+id/addressview"
        android:layout_width="wrap_content"
        android:layout_height="wrap_content"
        android:text="Address:"
        android:textSize="@dimen/text_size"
        android:textStyle="bold"
        android:layout_marginTop="5dp" />
    <EditText
        android:id="@+id/url"
        android:layout_width="@dimen/box_width"
        android:layout_height="wrap_content"
        android:textSize="@dimen/text_size"
        android:hint="http://"
        android:scrollHorizontally="true"
```

```
            android:layout_toRightOf="@id/addressview"
            android:layout_marginLeft="5dp"/>
        <Button
            android:id="@+id/go_button"
            android:layout_width="wrap_content"
            android:layout_height="wrap_content"
            android:textSize="@dimen/text_size"
            android:text="Go"
            android:layout_marginLeft="5dp"
            android:layout_marginTop="5dp"
            android:layout_toRightOf="@id/url"
            android:padding="10dp" />
        <WebView
            android:id="@+id/web_view"
            android:layout_width="match_parent"
            android:layout_height="wrap_content"
            android:layout_below="@id/url"
            android:layout_marginTop="10dp"/>
</RelativeLayout>
```

You can see that the TextView control is set to display the text Address:. The ID assigned
to the EditText control is url, and its hint text is set to http://. The hint text appears in a
light color inside the EditText control to tell the user about the type of data that should be
entered. The ID assigned to the Button control is go_button. The caption Go will appear on
the button. The last control, WebView, is assigned the ID web_view. The text displayed through
the TextView caption on the Button control and the text that will be entered in the EditText
control will appear in the font size defined in the dimension resource text_size. The width of
the EditText control will be defined in the dimension resource box_width.

Assuming the dimension file dimens.xml already exists in the res/values folder, add the
dimensions to the file to resize the views as per the device's screen on which the application is
run. Write the following code in the dimens.xml file:

```
<?xml version="1.0" encoding="utf-8"?>
<resources>
    <dimen name="text_size">14sp</dimen>
    <dimen name="box_width">200dp</dimen>
</resources>
```

The two dimension resources, text_size and box_width, define the font size of the text
and width of the EditText control. These dimension resources are for normal screen devices
(phones).

To define the dimension resources for 7-inch tablets, open the dimens.xml file in the res/
values-sw600dp folder and write the following code in it:

```
<?xml version="1.0" encoding="utf-8"?>
<resources>
    <dimen name="text_size">24sp</dimen>
```

```
    <dimen name="box_width">400dp</dimen>
</resources>
```

Finally, to define dimensions for extra-large screen devices (10-inch tablets), open the `dimens.xml` file in the `values-sw720dp` folder and write the following code in it:

```
<?xml version="1.0" encoding="utf-8"?>
<resources>
    <dimen name="text_size">32sp</dimen>
    <dimen name="box_width">600dp</dimen>
</resources>
```

By comparing the dimension resources of phones, 7-inch tablets, and 10-inch tablets, you can see that the views in the application are resized based on the device screen size. To display web pages using the `WebView`, write the code as shown in Listing 16.2 into the Java activity file `WebViewAppActivity.java`.

Listing 16.2   **Code Written into the** `WebViewAppActivity.java` **Java Activity File**

```
package com.androidtablet.webviewapp;

import android.app.Activity;
import android.os.Bundle;
import android.widget.Button;
import android.widget.EditText;
import android.view.View;
import android.view.View.OnClickListener;
import android.webkit.WebView;
import android.view.KeyEvent;
import android.widget.TextView;
import android.widget.TextView.OnEditorActionListener;

public class WebViewAppActivity extends Activity implements OnClickListener {
    EditText url;
    WebView webView;

    @Override
    public void onCreate(Bundle savedInstanceState) {
        super.onCreate(savedInstanceState);
        setContentView(R.layout.activity_web_view_app);
        url = (EditText)this.findViewById(R.id. url);
        webView = (WebView) findViewById(R.id.web_view);
        webView.getSettings().setJavaScriptEnabled(true);      #1
        url.setOnEditorActionListener(new OnEditorActionListener() {
        @Override
        public boolean onEditorAction(TextView v, int actionId,
            KeyEvent event) {                                  #2
            if(event!=null && event.getAction()==
                KeyEvent.ACTION_DOWN){                         #3
```

```
              webView.loadUrl(url.getText().toString());#4
              return true;                              #5
          }
          return false;                                 #6
      }
});
Button b = (Button)this.findViewById(R.id.go_button);
b.setOnClickListener(this);                             #7
}


@Override
public void onClick(View v) {
    webView.loadUrl(url.getText().toString());
}


@Override
public boolean onKeyUp(int keyCode, KeyEvent event) {
    if ((keyCode == KeyEvent.KEYCODE_BACK) &&
        webView.canGoBack()) {                          #8
        webView.goBack();                               #9
        return true;
    }
    return super.onKeyUp(keyCode, event);
}
}
```

The EditText and WebView controls from the layout file are captured and mapped to the
EditText and WebView objects url and webView, respectively.

Some of the statements in Listing 16.2 need explanation:

- Statement #1 enables JavaScript, which is disabled in a WebView by default. It may
  happen that the web page the user loads through WebView contains JavaScript. To view
  the web page correctly, you must enable JavaScript for the WebView. The JavaScript
  is enabled through the WebSettings attached to the WebView. Therefore, you access
  WebSettings by calling the getSettings() method, and then you enable JavaScript by
  passing the boolean value true to the WebSetting's setJavaScriptEnabled() method.

- Statement #2 checks for the key events in the EditText control. Basically, a
  setOnEditActionListener is associated with the EditText control so that the
  onEditorAction() callback method is called when any action (event) takes place in the
  EditText control.

- Statement #3 checks whether any event has occurred in the EditText. It also checks
  whether any key is pressed in the EditText control. Every key press consists of several
  key events. Each key event has an attached key code that helps to identify the pressed key.

- Statement #4 loads the web page into the WebView whose URL is entered by the user in
  the EditText control.

- Statement #5 terminates the `setOnEditActionListener` event handler by returning the boolean value `true` in the callback method `onEditorAction()`. That is, when the user presses the Enter key, the `setOnEditActionListener` event handler is terminated, and the web page is loaded into `WebView`.

- Statement #6 returns the boolean value `false` from the `onEditorAction()` callback method to make the `setOnEditActionListener` listen for more events in the `EditText` control.

- Statement #7 associates the `setOnClickListener` with the `Button` control so that the `onClick()` callback method is called when a click event occurs on the `Button` control. In the `onClick()` callback method, the web page is loaded into the `WebView` whose URL is entered by the user into the `EditText` control.

- Statement #8 checks whether the user has pressed the Back button. It also checks for a web page history to navigate back. The `canGoBack()` method returns `true` only if there exists a web page history to visit.

- Statement #9 navigates to the previous page in the history of the web pages opened in the `WebView`. When the `WebView` widget is used for loading web pages, it maintains a history of visited web pages. The web page history can be used to navigate backward and forward. To view the previous or the next page, you use the `goBack()` and `goForward()` methods. Remember, after reaching the end of the history, the `goBack()`and `goForward()` methods do nothing.

Note

The `onKey()`callback method is set to return the boolean value `true` if you don't want to listen for more key presses and want to terminate the event handler and exit from the method to do further processing. The method is set to return the boolean value `false` if you do not want to terminate the event handler and want to continue to listen for more key presses.

Your application must have access to the Internet to load a web page, so you need to request Internet permission in the `AndroidManifest.xml` file by adding the following statement:

```
<uses-permission android:name= "android.permission.INTERNET" />
```

Now your application is complete, and you can run it. The first screen that you see on startup is shown in Figure 16.1 (top). The white blank space below the Go button represents the `WebView` control, which is initially blank. You can type the URL of the web page you want to view into the `EditText` control and either press the Enter key or click the Go button to load and view it via the `WebView` control. After you type the URL of my Web site, http://bmharwani. com, and click the Go button, the Web site will be loaded and displayed as shown in Figure 16.1 (middle). Select a link, and the `WebView` control will be updated to display information about the linked web page, as shown in Figure 16.1 (bottom). If you click the Back key, you will move back one step in the browsing history, and the web page shown in Figure 16.1 (middle) will reappear in the `WebView` control.

> **Note**
>
> Usually, when you press an Enter key in the `EditText` control, the cursor moves onto the next line. But because you have associated a `setOnEditActionListener` with the `EditText` control, after entering the URL in the `EditText` control, when you press Enter, the cursor will not move to the next line but navigates to the entered URL.

Figure 16.1   The application showing the `EditText` control with a hint text for entering the web page URL (top); the web page loaded and displayed in the `WebView` control (middle); and the linked web page opened by the default web browser (bottom)

One thing that you will observe when executing the preceding application is that when any link is selected, the web page loads but covers the entire view, making the `TextView`, `EditText`, and `Button` controls invisible. This is because the default web browser loads the clicked links. Android invokes the default web browser to open and load the linked web page instead of using the application's `WebView` control. To override this problem, you will use the `WebViewClient` class.

Recipe: Using the `WebViewClient` Class

Android invokes the default web browser to open and load the linked web page. To open links within your `WebView`, you use the `WebViewClient` class and its `shouldOverrideUrlLoading()` method. Open the `WebViewApp` Android application that you created in the previous recipe, and modify its Java activity file `WebViewAppActivity.java` to perform the following tasks:

- Use the `WebViewClient` class.
- Use the `shouldOverrideUrlLoading()` method to load the clicked links in the `WebView` control.

The code in the Java activity file `WebViewAppActivity.java` is modified to appear as shown in Listing 16.3. Only the code in bold is modified; the rest is the same as you saw in Listing 16.2.

Listing 16.3   **Code Written into the** `WebViewAppActivity.java` **Java Activity File**

```
package com.androidtablet.webviewapp;

import android.app.Activity;
import android.os.Bundle;
import android.widget.Button;
import android.widget.EditText;
import android.view.View;
import android.view.View.OnClickListener;
import android.webkit.WebView;
import android.view.KeyEvent;
import android.webkit.WebViewClient;
import android.widget.TextView;
import android.widget.TextView.OnEditorActionListener;

public class WebViewAppActivity extends Activity implements OnClickListener {
    EditText url;
    WebView webView;

    @Override
    public void onCreate(Bundle savedInstanceState) {
        super.onCreate(savedInstanceState);
        setContentView(R.layout.activity_web_view_app);
        url = (EditText)this.findViewById(R.id.url);
        webView = (WebView) findViewById(R.id.web_view);
        webView.getSettings().setJavaScriptEnabled(true);
        webView.setWebViewClient(new WebViewClient(){
            public boolean shouldOverrideUrlLoading(WebView
```

```
                    view, String url) {
                    view.loadUrl(url);
                    return true;
            }
        });

    url.setOnEditorActionListener(new OnEditorActionListener() {
        @Override
        public boolean onEditorAction(TextView v, int actionId,
            KeyEvent event) {
            if(event!=null && event.getAction()==
                KeyEvent.ACTION_DOWN){
                    webView.loadUrl(url.getText().toString());
                    return true;
            }
            return false;
        }
    });
    Button b = (Button)this.findViewById(R.id.go_button);
    b.setOnClickListener(this);
}

@Override
public void onClick(View v) {
    webView.loadUrl(url.getText().toString());
}

@Override
public boolean onKeyUp(int keyCode, KeyEvent event) {
    if ((keyCode == KeyEvent.KEYCODE_BACK) &&
        webView.canGoBack()) {
        webView.goBack();
        return true;
    }
    return super.onKeyUp(keyCode, event);
}
}
```

You have used two functions that are explained next:

- **setWebViewClient()**—The setWebViewClient() function replaces the current handler
  with the WebViewClient, enabling you to utilize its methods to make all the clicked
  links open in your WebView control.

- **public boolean shouldOverrideUrlLoading (WebView view, String url)**—The
  view and url parameters used in the shouldOverrideUrlLoading() method refer to
  the WebView that is initiating the callback and the URL of the clicked link, respectively.
  By default, the WebView asks the Activity Manager to choose the proper handler to open
  a clicked link in a web page. The Activity Manager in turn invokes the user's default

browser to load the URL of the linked page. Through this function, you can decide whether you want the host application or the `WebView` to load the linked URL. If the function returns `true`, it means that you want the host application to handle the URL. If the function returns `false`, it means you don't want the host application to interrupt and prefer that the `WebView` handle the URL. (In other words, you want the URL to be loaded in your `WebView`.)

When you run your application after making these changes in the activity file, you will see a screen prompting for a URL. The web page whose URL that you enter in the `EditText` control will be loaded and opened in the `WebView` control, as shown in Figure 16.2 (top). After you select any link, the linked page will also open in the `WebView` control (see Figure 16.2 [bottom]). The default browser will no longer handle the linked URL.

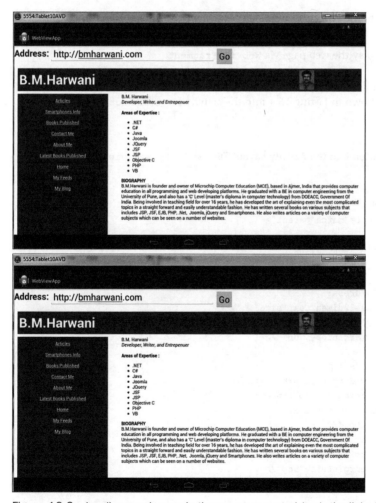

Figure 16.2   Loading a web page in the `WebView` control (top); the linked web page also opens in the `WebView` control (bottom)

Recipe: Using the `WebViewFragment`

A `WebViewFragment` is a fragment that contains a `WebView`. You can display the desired web pages in the `WebView` contained in the `WebViewFragment`.

To understand the concept of `WebViewFragment`, you will create an application that will ask the user to enter a web URL, and the web page of the entered URL will be displayed in the `WebViewFragment`. In all, you will use the following four controls in this recipe:

- **TextView**—To display the text message `Address` to inform the user that a web address has to be entered in the following `EditText` control.

- **EditText**—To enable the user to enter a web URL. The control will also display a hint text `http://`.

- **Button**—To initiate the process of displaying the web page whose URL is entered in the `EditText` control using the `WebViewFragment`.

- **Fragment**—To display the web page via `WebViewFragment`.

Create a new Android project called `WebViewFragApp`. To define the four controls in the previous list, write the code shown in Listing 16.4 into the activity layout file `activity_web_view_frag_app.xml`.

Listing 16.4   Code Written into the Activity Layout File `activity_web_view_frag_app.xml`

```
<RelativeLayout
xmlns:android="http://schemas.android.com/apk/res/android"
    android:layout_width="match_parent"
    android:layout_height="match_parent">
    <TextView
        android:id="@+id/addressview"
        android:layout_width="wrap_content"
        android:layout_height="wrap_content"
        android:text="Address:"
        android:textSize="@dimen/text_size"
        android:textStyle="bold"
        android:layout_marginTop="5dp" />
    <EditText
        android:id="@+id/url"
        android:layout_width="@dimen/box_width"
        android:layout_height="wrap_content"
        android:textSize="@dimen/text_size"
        android:hint="http://"
        android:scrollHorizontally="true"
        android:layout_toRightOf="@id/addressview"
        android:layout_marginLeft="5dp"/>
    <Button
        android:id="@+id/go_button"
        android:layout_width="wrap_content"
```

```
            android:layout_height="wrap_content"
            android:textSize="@dimen/text_size"
            android:text="Go"
            android:layout_marginLeft="5dp"
            android:layout_marginTop="5dp"
            android:layout_toRightOf="@id/url"
            android:padding="10dp" />
    <fragment android:name= "com.androidtablet.
        webviewfragapp.WebViewFragmentActivity"
            android:id="@+id/fragment"
            android:layout_width="wrap_content"
            android:layout_height="match_parent"
            android:tag="web_fragment"
            android:layout_below="@id/url"
            android:layout_marginTop="10dp" />
</RelativeLayout>
```

> **Note**
>
> The fragment used in the preceding activity layout books a portion of an activity's screen for the `WebView` of the `WebViewFragment`.

You can see that the text `Address:` displayed through the `TextView` is set to appear in bold and in the font size defined in the dimension resource `text_size`. To identify and access Java code, you assign the `EditText` control the ID `url` and display the hint text `http://` in it. The caption assigned to the `Button` control is `Go`, and the ID assigned to it is `go_button`. To display the caption `Go` at the center of the `Button` control, it is padded with blank spaces on all four sides. The tag and ID assigned to the fragment are `fragment` and `web_fragment`, respectively. The fragment is set to invoke the `WebViewFragmentActivity`, which in turn will use the `WebViewFragment` to access and display the web page in the fragment.

To resize the views of the application according to the device screen on which the application is run, you need to define the dimension resources. Open the dimension file `dimens.xml` in the `res/values` folder, and define the dimension resources by writing the following code in it:

```
<?xml version="1.0" encoding="utf-8"?>
<resources>
    <dimen name="text_size">14sp</dimen>
    <dimen name="box_width">200dp</dimen>
</resources>
```

The two dimension resources, `text_size` and `box_width`, define the font size of the text and the width of the `EditText` control. These dimension resources are for normal screen devices (phones).

To define the dimension resources for 7-inch tablets, open the `dimens.xml` file in the `res/values-sw600dp` folder and write the following code in it:

```xml
<?xml version="1.0" encoding="utf-8"?>
<resources>
    <dimen name="text_size">24sp</dimen>
    <dimen name="box_width">400dp</dimen>
</resources>
```

Finally, to define dimensions for extra-large screen devices (10-inch tablets), open the `dimens.xml` file in the `values-sw720dp` folder and write the following code in it:

```xml
<?xml version="1.0" encoding="utf-8"?>
<resources>
    <dimen name="text_size">32sp</dimen>
    <dimen name="box_width">600dp</dimen>
</resources>
```

By comparing the dimension resources of phones, 7-inch tablets, and 10-inch tablets, you can see that the views in the application are resized based on the device screen size. The next step is to add a Java class file named `WebViewFragmentActivity.java` to the `com.androidtablet.webviewfragapp` package. To the Java class file `WebViewFragmentActivity.java`, write the code as shown in Listing 16.5.

Listing 16.5   **Code Written into the Java File** `WebViewFragmentActivity.java`

```java
package com.androidtablet.webviewfragapp;

import android.webkit.WebViewFragment;
import android.os.Bundle;
import android.webkit.WebView;
import android.webkit.WebViewClient;

public class WebViewFragmentActivity extends WebViewFragment{
    String webURL;

    @Override
    public void onCreate(Bundle state) {
        super.onCreate(state);
        if (null == state)  state = getArguments();
        if (null != state){
            webURL=state.getString("url");
        }
        setRetainInstance(true);
    }

    @Override
    public void onActivityCreated(Bundle savedInstanceState) {
        super.onActivityCreated(savedInstanceState);
        WebView webView = getWebView();
```

```
    if (webView != null) {
        webView.getSettings().setJavaScriptEnabled(true);
        webView.setWebViewClient(new WebViewClient());
        webView.loadUrl(webURL);
    }
  }
}
```

You can see that the preceding class, `WebViewFragmentActivity`, is doing the following tasks:

- Accessing the web URL entered by the user in the `EditText` and passing to this class the main Java activity file of the application.

- Defining the `WebView` instance by calling the `getWebView()` method of the `WebViewFragment` class.

- Enabling the JavaScript in the `WebView`. Recall that the JavaScript is disabled by default.

- Calling the `setWebViewClient()` method on the `WebView` instance to set `WebViewClient` as the handler. That is, the links that will be clicked in the web page will not be opened or loaded in the default browser but in the `WebView`.

- Loading the web page in the `WebView` whose URL is supplied to this class.

Next, you need to write the code in the Java activity file to do the following tasks:

- Access the `EditText` and `Button` controls from the layout file and map them to the respective objects.

- Associate `setOnEditActionListener` to the `EditText` control to listen for the occurrence of events on it. The method `onEditorAction()` will be called when an event occurs in the `EditText` control.

- Associate `setOnClickListener` to the `Button` control to listen for the occurrence of click events on it. The method `onClick` will be called when the `Button` control is clicked on.

- Define the `FragmentManager` and `FragmentTransaction` instances.

- Define an instance of the Java class `WebViewFragmentActivity` that you defined earlier.

- Define a `Bundle` object.

- Store the web URL entered by the user in the `EditText` control into the `Bundle` object and pass the `Bundle` object to the `WebViewFragmentActivity` instance. The web URL can be accessed in the `WebViewFragmentActivity` class, and the corresponding web page can be loaded in the `WebView`.

- Make use of the `FragmentTransaction` object to set the content (`WebView`) displayed through the `WebViewFragmentActivity` to appear in the fragment that you defined in the activity layout file.

To do all these tasks, write the code as shown in Listing 16.6 into the Java activity file
`WebViewFragAppActivity.java`.

Listing 16.6   **Code Written into the Java Activity File** `WebViewFragAppActivity.java`

```
package com.androidtablet.webviewfragapp;

import android.os.Bundle;
import android.app.Activity;
import android.view.View;
import android.view.View.OnClickListener;
import android.widget.EditText;
import android.widget.Button;
import android.view.KeyEvent;
import android.app.FragmentManager;
import android.widget.TextView;
import android.widget.TextView.OnEditorActionListener;

public class WebViewFragAppActivity extends Activity implements
    OnClickListener {
    EditText url;
    FragmentManager fragmentManager;
    Bundle args;
    WebViewFragmentActivity webviewFragment;
    android.app.FragmentTransaction fragmentTransaction;

    @Override
    protected void onCreate(Bundle savedInstanceState) {
        super.onCreate(savedInstanceState);
        setContentView(R.layout.activity_web_view_frag_app);
        fragmentManager = getFragmentManager();
        webviewFragment = new WebViewFragmentActivity();
        fragmentTransaction =
            fragmentManager.beginTransaction();
        args = new Bundle();
        url = (EditText)this.findViewById(R.id.url);
        url.setOnEditorActionListener(new OnEditorActionListener()
        {
            @Override
            public boolean onEditorAction(TextView v, int actionId,
                KeyEvent event) {
                if(event!=null && event.getAction()==
                    KeyEvent.ACTION_DOWN){
                    args.putString("url", url.getText().
                        toString());
                    webviewFragment.setArguments(args);
                    fragmentTransaction.replace(R.id.fragment,
```

```
                    webviewFragment);
                fragmentTransaction.commit();
                return true;
            }
            return false;
        }
    });
    Button b = (Button)this.findViewById(R.id.go_button);
    b.setOnClickListener(this);
}

@Override
public void onClick(View v) {
    args.putString("url", url.getText().toString());
    webviewFragment.setArguments(args);
    fragmentTransaction.replace(R.id.fragment,
        webviewFragment);
    fragmentTransaction.commit();
}
}
```

Again, to access the Internet in this application, add the following permission statement to the `AndroidManifest.xml` file:

```
<uses-permission android:name="android.permission.INTERNET" />
```

After running the application, you get a screen prompting you to enter a web URL. Enter a URL in the `EditText` control, and when you click the Go button, the corresponding web page will be opened in the `WebView` that is contained in the `WebViewFragment`. The `WebView` will appear at the location of the fragment defined in the activity layout file, as shown in Figure 16.3 (top). On selecting any link from the web page, the linked page will also open in the `WebView` control of the `WebViewFragment` (see Figure 16.3 [bottom]).

Note

When any link is clicked in a web page that is displayed through the `WebView`, it is handled by the default browser.

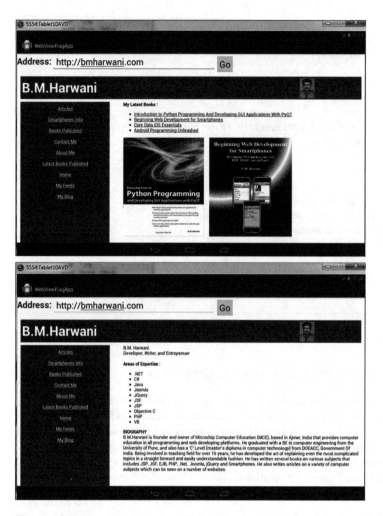

Figure 16.3   Loading a web page through WebViewFragment (top), and the linked web page opened in the WebView control of the WebViewFragment (bottom)

Summary

In this chapter, you learned how to display web content through WebView and how to enable JavaScript and other features. You saw how to use the WebViewClient class to display the clicked links in WebView instead of being handled by the default browser. You also saw how WebView is accessed in WebViewFragment and is used to display web pages.

In the next chapter, you will learn to add support for the small screen. You will discover alternative layouts and the Android Compatibility Package. You will also learn about resource usage and the technique to support older versions of the Software Development Kit (SDK).

17

Adding Support for the Small Screen

Android devices are available in different screen sizes and densities. Besides the physical varia-
tions, differences in Android versions are supported. It is critical for developers to create applications that run on devices with diverse screen sizes and densities while supporting different
versions, too. The applications have to be designed so that the views and bitmaps are automatically arranged to accommodate the available screen size and density. The UI and bitmaps
should not be too stretched or shrunk that they appear fuzzy. The applications should not
only include the features provided by the latest Android versions, but be compatible with older
versions, too.

In this chapter, you will learn about factors to consider for supporting different screens and
densities. You will learn how to enable an application to support different platform versions.
Also, you will see how to use the Android Support Library to support older Android versions.
Finally, you will learn to handle screen orientation by anchoring controls and use alternate
layouts to support different screen sizes.

Recipe: Factors for Supporting Different Screens and Densities

Applications that developers create may be required to run on a variety of devices with different screen sizes and densities. That is why it is necessary to optimize the user interface (UI)
design to make the Android application compatible with different screen sizes and densities.
The following factors are considered while supporting multiple screens:

- **Screen sizes**—Screen size defines the physical space of an application. Android groups all
  actual screen sizes into the following four sizes: small, normal, large, and extra large.

- **Screen density**—Represents the number of pixels in any given area on the screen. It is
  measured in terms of dpi (dots per inch). There are four categories of screen densities:
  ldpi (low), mdpi (medium), hdpi (high), and xhdpi (extra-high).

- **Orientation**—The device can be oriented in either landscape or portrait mode. That is, the screen may be either wide or tall.

- **Resolution**—Resolution represents the total number of pixels on a screen. Resolution of the small, normal, large, and extra-large screens is given here:

  - **Small screen**—426dp × 320dp
  - **Normal screen**—470dp × 320dp
  - **Large screen**—640dp × 480dp
  - **Extra-large screen**—960dp × 720dp

Two main things to take care of while developing applications are screen size and density. Following are the ways to optimize an application's UI for the different screen sizes and densities:

- **Measure in dp**—To make the application compatible with different screen densities, the UI is preferably measured in terms of density-independent pixel (dp)—virtual unit of measure. The density-independent pixel is equivalent to one physical pixel on a 160dpi screen. The 160dpi is a density assumed for a medium-density screen. The application automatically scales the dp units based on the actual density of the screen. The following formula converts dp into screen pixels:

  px = dp × dpi / 160

- **Use fragments**—Fragments enable you to fragment or divide your activities into encapsulated reusable modules, each with its own user interface, making your application suitable to different screen sizes. That is, depending on the available screen size, you can add or remove fragments in your application.

- **Avoid absolute width and height**—Use width and height of the containers for defining width and height of the UI elements. That is, use `wrap_content` and `match_parent` values while defining the width and height of the UI, because it automatically resizes the UI elements based on their container size.

- **Provide alternate resources**—You need to provide alternative layouts for different screen sizes and alternative bitmap images for different screen densities. Based on the size and density of the device screen, Android will pick up the most appropriate resources of the application. If the resources that suit different screen sizes are not provided, the UI elements may either overlap or appear quite far.

  - **Provide alternate layouts**—While testing an application on a small screen, you may find that a few of the views do not fit within the width of the screen and are being hidden. Perhaps because of the extra-large device screen, the views are unnecessarily being stretched to fill up the extra space. To make a user feel that the application is designed specifically for his device, it is wise to define alternate layouts (that is, separate layouts for smaller and extra-large screens, respectively). In short, you should provide the alternate layouts so that the application is compatible with small as well as large screens and is optimized for both landscape and portrait orientations.

- **Provide alternative bitmaps**—If alternative bitmaps are not provided, then depending on the device screen density, the bitmap may be scaled and consequently, may appear blurry or fuzzy. Consequently, it is wise to supply alternate bitmaps for different screen densities. That is, you must provide the bitmaps for the five screen densities (ldpi, mdpi, hdpi, xhdpi, and xxhdpi) to prevent blurring of the bitmaps while resizing. The following are the preferred sizes of the drawables for different screen densities:

  - 36 × 36 for low density
  - 48 × 48 for medium density
  - 72 × 72 for high density
  - 96 × 96 for extra-high-density
  - 144 x 144 for extra-extra-high-density

Recipe: Supporting Different Platform Versions

The applications that developers create should target the latest API to take advantage of the newest features provided; at the same time, the applications should continue to support older versions of Android. Remember that Android 2.x still covers more than 50% of the market. The idea is that the applications should run on a maximum number of devices, and that is possible only when the application supports the Android versions with the largest customer base.

Besides describing other details of your application, the `AndroidManifest.xml` file identifies the Android versions that it supports. Specifically, the `minSdkVersion` and `targetSdkVersion` attributes of the `<uses-sdk>` element identify the lowest API level that the application is compatible with and the API level on which the application is designed, compiled, and tested.

For example, the `minSdkVersion` and `targetSdkVersion` attributes suggest the API levels required by the application to run:

```
<manifest xmlns:android= "http://schemas.android.com/apk/res/android" ... >
 <uses-sdk android:minSdkVersion="4" android:targetSdkVersion="17" />
   ...
</manifest>
```

The `minSdkVersion` attribute in the previous code indicates that API level 4 is required for the application to run. It also means the application will run on API level 4 and above but will not run on API level 3 or below. The `targetSdkVersion` attributes indicate that the preferred API level on which the application is designed to run is 17. Usually, the `targetSdkVersion` value is set to match the latest Android version available.

Android provides a unique code for each platform version in the `Build` constants class. You can use these codes to ensure that the code depending on higher API levels executes only if the device supports that API level. For example, the following code invokes ActionBar only if the device supports API level 11 (Honeycomb) and above:

```
private void useActionBar() {
    if (Build.VERSION.SDK_INT >= Build.VERSION_CODES.HONEYCOMB) {
        ActionBar actionBar = getActionBar();
        ......
    }
}
```

When parsing XML resources, Android ignores XML attributes that the current device doesn't support. So you can safely use XML attributes that are only supported by later versions without worrying about older versions because older versions will simply ignore that code. For example, the devices with API level 10 and below will ignore the following code for displaying action items in ActionBar:

```
<menu xmlns:android= "http://schemas.android.com/apk/res/android" >
    <item android:id="@+id/create "
        android:title="Create"
        android:icon="@drawable/ic_launcher"
        android:showAsAction="ifRoom|withText" />
</menu>
```

Writing the preceding code is quite safe in a cross-version XML file, because the older versions of Android simply ignore the showAsAction attribute.

In this recipe, you will learn to use the Build constants class to run only the code that is supported by the API level available on the device. More specifically, the recipe will identify the API level that the device supports. If the device supports API level 11 or higher, an ActionBar with few action items will be displayed, or the menu will be displayed. Before ActionBar, menus were used to display menu items to operate applications. ActionBars are preferred over menus now because most of the devices currently available don't have a Menu button.

Create a new Android project called ActionBarOnOlderApp. If the API level on the device is 10 or lower, ActionBar will not be displayed. You need to display a text message to tell the user to press the Menu button on the device to invoke the menu. To display the text message, you need to define a TextView in the activity layout file. After defining the TextView control, the activity layout file activity_action_bar_on_older_app.xml will appear, as shown in Listing 17.1.

Listing 17.1   **Code Written into the** activity_action_bar_on_older_app.xml **Layout File**

```
<RelativeLayout xmlns:android= "http://schemas.android.com/apk/res/android"
    xmlns:tools="http://schemas.android.com/tools"
    android:layout_width="match_parent"
    android:layout_height="match_parent"
    tools:context=".ActionBarOnOlderAppActivity" >
    <TextView
        android:id="@+id/textview"
        android:layout_width="wrap_content"
        android:layout_height="wrap_content"
```

```
          android:textSize="@dimen/text_size"
          android:textStyle="bold" />
</RelativeLayout>
```

For accessing and identifying Java code, the `TextView` control is assigned the `textview` ID. Also, the text displayed through the `TextView` control is set to appear in bold and in a font size defined in the dimension resource `text_size`. In this application, you want to display an ActionBar with two action items: Create and Update. So the code as shown in Listing 17.2 is written in the menu file `activity_action_bar_on_older_app.xml` found in the `res/menu` folder.

Listing 17.2   **Code Written into the Menu File** `activity_action_bar_on_older_app.xml`

```xml
<menu xmlns:android= "http://schemas.android.com/apk/res/android" >
    <item android:id="@+id/create "
        android:title="Create"
        android:icon="@drawable/ic_launcher"
        android:orderInCategory="0"
        android:showAsAction="ifRoom|withText" />
    <item android:id="@+id/update"
        android:title="Update"
        android:icon="@drawable/ic_launcher"
        android:showAsAction="always"  />
</menu>
```

The two action items Create and Update are assigned the IDs `create` and `update`, respectively. Also, the image file `ic_launcher.png` that is provided by default is set to appear as an icon of both the action items. The Update action item is set to display its icon always, whereas the icon of the Create action item will be displayed only if there is enough space in the ActionBar.

Next, you need to write Java code to perform the following tasks:

- Check the API level that the device supports.
- Display the ActionBar with its two action items if the device supports API Level 11 (Honeycomb) or higher.
- Display the text `Press MENU button to display menu` through `TextView` if the device has API level 10 or lower. The text message is meant to direct the user to press the Menu button on the device to display menu items.

To perform these tasks, write the code as shown in Listing 17.3 to the Java activity file `ActionBarOnOlderAppActivity.java`.

Listing 17.3   **Code Written into the Java Activity File** `ActionBarOnOlderAppActivity.java`

```
package com.androidtablet.actionbaronolderapp;

import android.os.Bundle;
import android.app.Activity;
import android.view.Menu;
import android.widget.TextView;
import android.os.Build;
import android.app.ActionBar;

public class ActionBarOnOlderAppActivity extends Activity {
    @Override
    protected void onCreate(Bundle savedInstanceState) {
        super.onCreate(savedInstanceState);
        setContentView(R.layout.activity_action_bar
            _on_older_app);
        TextView textView=(TextView)findViewById(R.id.textview);
        if (Build.VERSION.SDK_INT >=
        Build.VERSION_CODES.HONEYCOMB) {
            ActionBar actionBar = getActionBar();
            actionBar.setDisplayHomeAsUpEnabled(true);
        }
        else
            textView.setText("Press MENU button to display menu");
    }

    @Override
    public boolean onCreateOptionsMenu(Menu menu) {
        getMenuInflater().inflate(R.menu.activity_action_bar
            _on_older_app, menu);
        return true;
    }
}
```

To run and check the output of the application, set the API levels that are required by the application to run. First check the application when the minimum API level it requires to run is set to 11 and is targeted at API level 17. To do so, modify the `minSdkVersion` and `targetSdkVersion` attributes of the `<uses-sdk>` elements in the `AndroidManifest.xml` file as shown here:

```
<uses-sdk
        android:minSdkVersion="11"
        android:targetSdkVersion="17" />
```

Because ActionBar is available on API level 11 and higher, the ActionBar will be displayed with its two action items Create and Update (see Figure 17.1 [left]) after running the application.

If you lower the value of the minimum API level required by the application (that is, if you change the `minSdkVersion` attribute to value 10 or lower), the ActionBar will not be displayed. Instead, the text message `Press MENU button to display menu` will be displayed via the `TextView` control. Press the Menu button on the device, and an Options menu will be displayed with its two menu items Create and Update, as shown in Figure 17.1 (right).

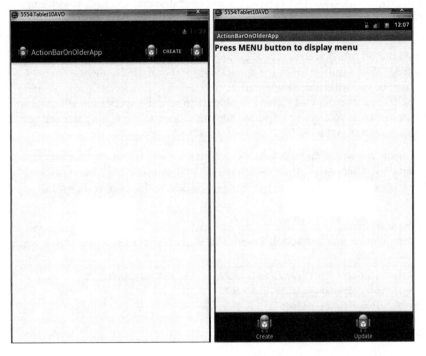

Figure 17.1   ActionBar displayed with two action items (left), and menu with two menu items displayed after pressing the Menu button on the device (right)

Recipe: Supporting Older Versions Using the Android Support Library

To provide functionality across several Android versions, you use the Android Support Library in your applications, which makes it possible to use recent platform APIs on older versions. The Android Support Library includes libraries that can be added to the Android applications so you can use the APIs that are not available in older platform versions. The Android Support Library is composed of several libraries, and each library requires a specific minimum API level. For example, one library may require API level 4 or higher, whereas another requires API level 13 or higher. The following library requires at minimum API level 4:

```
import android.support.v4.app.Fragment;
```

The term v4 indicates that this library requires minimum API level 4. Similarly, the library containing the term v13 indicates that it requires at minimum API level 13.

Android Support Library makes it possible for developers to use the new features of Android and still run applications on older versions. For example, you cannot use fragments in an application that is based on API level 10 and lower because fragments are available on API level 11 and higher. To use fragments in such an application and to ensure that application continues to support API level 10, use the Android Support Library. You can learn this procedure through a running example.

Create an Android project called FragmentOnOlderApp. In this application, you will initially set the minimum API level requirement of the application to 11 and use fragments. After running the fragments, you will reduce the minimum API level requirement of the application to 10. Because the fragments require API level 11 or higher to run, the application will not run and will display errors. Then you will add Android Support Library to the application and will make it run the fragments in API level 10, too.

To display a fragment, you will define a FrameLayout in the activity layout file that will act as a fragment container. After nesting the FrameLayout container inside the LinearLayout, the activity layout file activity_fragment_on_older_app.xml will appear as shown in Listing 17.4.

Listing 17.4   **Code Written into the Activity Layout File** activity_fragment_on_older_app.xml

```
<LinearLayout xmlns:android= "http://schemas.android.com/apk/res/android"
    xmlns:tools="http://schemas.android.com/tools"
    android:layout_width="match_parent"
    android:layout_height="match_parent"
    android:orientation="vertical" >
    <FrameLayout
        android:id="@+id/fragment_container"
        android:layout_width="wrap_content"
        android:layout_height="match_parent" />
</LinearLayout>
```

To access Java code, the FrameLayout is defined the ID fragment_container. To define the layout of the fragment, add an XML file called fragment.xml to the res/layout folder. To keep things simple, just display a text message through the fragment. So, to display a text message, define a TextView control in the layout file fragment.xml (see the code in Listing 17.5).

Listing 17.5   **Code Written into the Layout File** fragment.xml

```
<?xml version="1.0" encoding="utf-8"?>
<LinearLayout xmlns:android= "http://schemas.android.com/apk/res/android"
    android:layout_width="match_parent"
    android:layout_height="match_parent"
```

```
        android:orientation="vertical" >
        <TextView
            android:id="@+id/textview"
            android:layout_width="match_parent"
            android:layout_height="wrap_content"
            android:text=" This is a Fragment "
            android:textSize="@dimen/text_size"
            android:textStyle="bold"  />
</LinearLayout>
```

You can see that the TextView is assigned the ID textview. It is initialized to display the text message This is a Fragment. The text displayed through the TextView is set to appear in bold and in a font size defined in the dimension resource text_size.

To load the view(s) of the fragment defined in the layout file fragment.xml, you need a Java class file. Add a Java class file named MyFragmentActivity.java to the com.androidtablet. fragmentonolderapp package of the application.

To load and display the TextView that you defined in the layout file fragment.xml, write the code as shown in Listing 17.6 into the Java class file MyFragmentActivity.java.

Listing 17.6   **Code Written into the Java Class File** MyFragmentActivity.java

```
package com.androidtablet.fragmentonolderapp;

import android.view.LayoutInflater;
import android.view.ViewGroup;
import android.view.View;
import android.os.Bundle;
import android.app.Fragment;

public class MyFragmentActivity extends Fragment {
    @Override
    public View onCreateView(LayoutInflater inflater, ViewGroup
        container, Bundle savedInstanceState) {
        return inflater.inflate(R.layout.fragment, container,
            false);
    }
}
```

Next, you need to write the Java code to perform the following tasks:

- Access the fragment container (that is, the FrameLayout) defined in the activity layout file activity_fragment_on_older_app.xml.

- Define a fragment by instantiating the Java class file MyFragmentActivity.

- Display the fragment by adding it to the fragment container.

To accomplish these tasks, write the code as shown in Listing 17.7 into the Java activity file `FragmentOnOlderAppActivity.java`.

Listing 17.7 **Code Written into the Java Activity File** `FragmentOnOlderAppActivity.java`

```
package com.androidtablet.fragmentonolderapp;

import android.os.Bundle;
import android.app.Activity;
import android.app.FragmentTransaction;
import android.app.FragmentManager;

public class FragmentOnOlderAppActivity extends Activity {
    @Override
    protected void onCreate(Bundle savedInstanceState) {
        super.onCreate(savedInstanceState);
        setContentView(R.layout.activity_fragment_on_older_app);
        FragmentManager fragmentManager = getFragmentManager();
        FragmentTransaction fragmentTransaction =
            fragmentManager.beginTransaction();
        if(null==fragmentManager.findFragmentById((
            R.id.fragment_container)))){
            MyFragmentActivity fragment = new
                MyFragmentActivity();
            fragmentTransaction.add(R.id.fragment_container,
                fragment);
        }
        fragmentTransaction.commit();
    }
}
```

Don't forget to set the minimum API level of the application to 11 and the target API level to 17. Ensure that the `minSdkVersion` and `targetSdkVersion` attributes of the `<uses-sdk>` elements in the `AndroidManifest.xml` file are modified to appear as shown here:

```
<uses-sdk
    android:minSdkVersion="11"
    android:targetSdkVersion="17" />
```

Because fragments run on API level 11 and above, the application will run perfectly. The fragment will show the text message `This is a Fragment` that is displayed through the `TextView` defined in the fragment layout (see Figure 17.2 [top]). Now reduce the minimum API level of the application to 10. To do so, you will reduce the value of the `minSdkVersion` attribute of the `<uses-sdk>` element in the `AndroidManifest.xml` file as shown here:

```
<uses-sdk
    android:minSdkVersion="10"
    android:targetSdkVersion="17" />
```

Because the fragments run only in API level 11 and higher, the application will not run, and errors will appear in the statements that call and use fragments. Figure 17.2 (bottom) shows the errors in the Editor pane stating the `Call requires API level 11 (current min is 10)`.

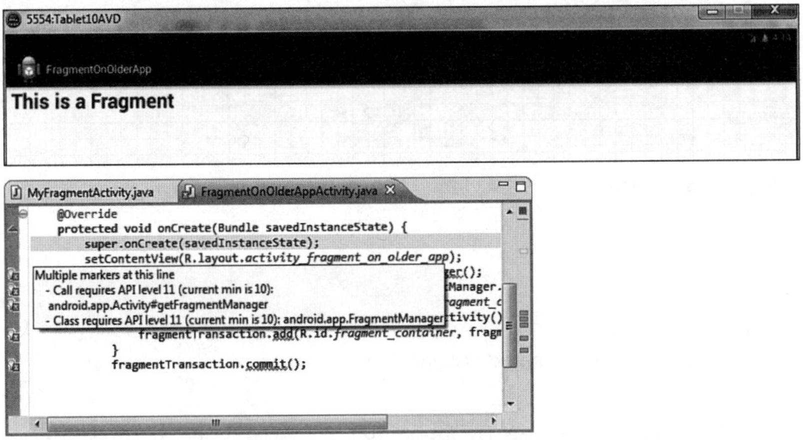

Figure 17.2   Fragment executes when the `minSdkVersion` attribute is 11 (top); error displayed when the value of the `minSdkVersion` attribute is set to API level 10 (bottom)

To make the fragments run in API levels lower than 11, you need to add the Android Support Library to your application. Following are the steps to add the Android Support Library to your existing code:

1. Launch Eclipse and invoke the Android SDK Manager. From the Android SDK Manager window, go to Extras, select Android Support Library, and install it. The Support Library will be installed on your machine, along with its sources and examples.

2. To include the Support Library in your project, right-click on the project in Eclipse and select Android Tools, Add Support Library. You see the dialog Choose Packages to Install, as shown in Figure 17.3. Select Accept, and then click the Install button to add the Android Support Library to your application.

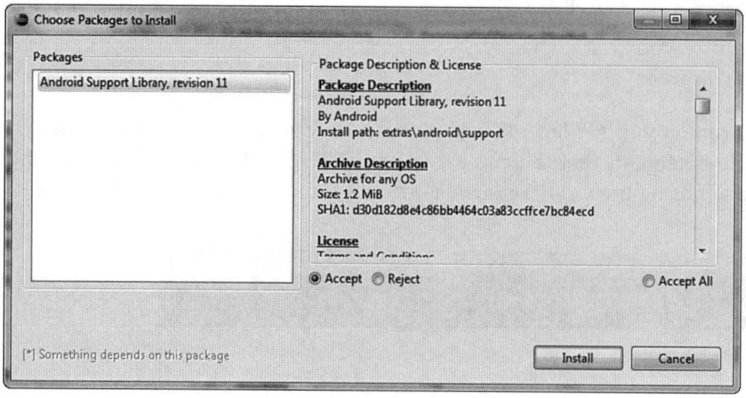

Figure 17.3   Dialog displaying license and other terms to install selected package

> **Tip**
>
> There is a shortcut to adding the Android Support Library. Right-click on the Android project, scroll down to Android Tools, and click the Add Support Library option.

After adding the Android Support Library to your application, you need to import its classes that are required to support older API levels into the Java class file `MyFragmentActivity.java` and into the Java activity file `FragmentOnOlderAppActivity.java`.

Modify the Java class `MyFragmentActivity.java` to appear as shown in Listing 17.8. Only the code in bold is modified; the rest is the same as you saw in Listing 17.6.

Listing 17.8   **Code Written into the Java Class** `MyFragmentActivity.java`

```java
package com.androidtablet.fragmentonolderapp;

import android.view.LayoutInflater;
import android.view.ViewGroup;
import android.view.View;
import android.os.Bundle;
import android.support.v4.app.Fragment;

public class MyFragmentActivity extends Fragment {
    @Override
    public View onCreateView(LayoutInflater inflater, ViewGroup
        container, Bundle savedInstanceState) {
        return inflater.inflate(R.layout.fragment, container,
            false);
    }
}
```

You can see that to support older Android versions, a class called `android.support.v4.app.Fragment` of the Android Support Library is imported into the preceding Java class file.

Similarly, the Java activity file `FragmentOnOlderAppActivity.java` is modified to appear as shown in Listing 17.9. Only the code in bold is modified; the rest is the same as you saw in Listing 17.7.

Listing 17.9 **Code Written into the Java Activity File** `FragmentOnOlderAppActivity.java`

```java
package com.androidtablet.fragmentonolderapp;

import android.os.Bundle;
import android.support.v4.app.FragmentManager;
import android.support.v4.app.FragmentTransaction;
import android.support.v4.app.FragmentActivity;

public class FragmentOnOlderAppActivity extends FragmentActivity {
    @Override
    protected void onCreate(Bundle savedInstanceState) {
        super.onCreate(savedInstanceState);
        setContentView(R.layout.activity_fragment_on_older_app);
        FragmentManager fragmentManager =
            getSupportFragmentManager();
        FragmentTransaction fragmentTransaction =
            fragmentManager.beginTransaction();
        if(null==fragmentManager.findFragmentById((
            R.id.fragment_container))){
            MyFragmentActivity fragment = new
                MyFragmentActivity();
            fragmentTransaction.add(R.id.fragment_container,
                fragment);
        }
        fragmentTransaction.commit();
    }
}
```

You can see that the preceding class extends `FragmentActivity` instead of activity, and several support classes including `android.support.v4.app.FragmentActivity` are imported into the application. Because `FragmentManager` is not compatible with API level 10 and lower, the Android Support Library includes a wrapper class, `SupportFragmentManager`, that provides backward compatibility. Each `FragmentActivity` has a `SupportFragmentManager`, and you can see that `getSupportFragmentManager()` is called in the preceding code to use `SupportFragmentManager` instead of the `FragmentManager`. Now your application is ready to run without an error in API level 10 and lower. When you run the application, the fragment will be displayed. A text message as shown in Figure 17.2 (top) will appear on the screen confirming that the fragment is working properly.

> **Note**
>
> Any activity that uses fragments must inherit from `android.support.v4.app.`
> `FragmentActivity`. This class is part of the Support Library, and it enables fragments to work
> regardless of the Android version.

Recipe: Adapting to Screen Orientation by Anchoring Controls

As with almost all smartphones, Android supports two screen orientations: portrait and landscape. When the Android device orientation changes, the current activity that is being displayed is destroyed and re-created automatically to redraw its content in the new orientation. Portrait mode is longer in height and smaller in width, whereas landscape mode is wider but smaller in height. Being wider, landscape mode has more empty space on the right side of the screen. At the same time, some of the controls disappear because of the smaller height. Thus, the UI controls need to be laid out differently to adapt to the two screen orientations because of the difference in the height and width of the two orientations.

There are two ways to handle changes in screen orientation:

- **Anchoring controls**—Set the controls to appear at the places relative to the four edges of the screen. When the screen orientation changes, the controls will not disappear but will be rearranged relative to the four edges.

- **Defining layout for each mode**—A new layout file is defined for each of the two screen orientations. One will have the controls arranged to suit the portrait mode, and the other will have the controls arranged to suit the landscape mode.

In this recipe, you will learn to handle screen orientation by anchoring controls. For anchoring controls relative to the four edges of the screen, you will use a `RelativeLayout` container. Examine this method by creating an Android project called `HandleOrientationApp`. To lay out the controls at locations relative to the four edges of the screen, write the code in the layout file `activity_handle_orientation_app.xml`, as shown in Listing 17.10.

Listing 17.10   **The Layout File** `activity_handle_orientation_app.xml` **on Laying Out Controls Relative to the Four Edges of the Screen**

```
<RelativeLayout xmlns:android= "http://schemas.android.com/apk/res/android"
    xmlns:tools="http://schemas.android.com/tools"
    android:layout_width="match_parent"
    android:layout_height="match_parent"
    tools:context=".HandleOrientationAppActivity" >
    <Button
        android:id="@+id/camera"
        android:text="Camera"
```

```xml
        android:textSize="@dimen/text_size"
        android:layout_width="wrap_content"
        android:layout_height="wrap_content"
        android:layout_marginTop="15dip"
        android:layout_marginLeft="20dip" />
    <Button
        android:id="@+id/laptop"
        android:text="Laptop"
        android:textSize="@dimen/text_size"
        android:layout_width="match_parent"
        android:layout_height="wrap_content"
        android:padding="28dip"
        android:layout_toRightOf="@id/camera"
        android:layout_marginLeft="15dip"
        android:layout_marginRight="10dip"
        android:layout_alignParentTop="true" />
    <Button
        android:id="@+id/watch"
        android:text="Watch"
        android:textSize="@dimen/text_size"
        android:layout_width="200dip"
        android:layout_height="100dip"
        android:layout_marginTop="35dip"
        android:layout_below="@id/camera"
        android:layout_alignParentLeft="true" />
    <Button
        android:id="@+id/smartphone"
        android:text="Smartphone"
        android:textSize="@dimen/text_size"
        android:layout_width="wrap_content"
        android:layout_height="match_parent"
        android:minWidth="100dp"
        android:layout_alignParentRight="true"
        android:layout_below="@id/watch" />
    <Button
        android:id="@+id/television"
        android:text="Television"
        android:textSize="@dimen/text_size"
        android:layout_width="250dip"
        android:layout_height="wrap_content"
        android:layout_below="@id/watch"
        android:paddingTop="15dip"
        android:paddingLeft="25dip"
        android:paddingRight="25dip" />
</RelativeLayout>
```

The code snippet in Listing 17.10 shows five `Button` controls arranged in a `RelativeLayout` container. The controls are aligned relative to the edges of the container or in relation to each other. Keep the activity file `HandleOrientationAppActivity.java` unchanged with the default code, as shown in Listing 17.11.

Listing 17.11   **Default Code in the Java Activity File** `HandleOrientationAppActivity.java`

```
package com.androidtablet.handleorientationapp;

import android.app.Activity;
import android.os.Bundle;

public class HandleOrientationAppActivity extends Activity {
    @Override
    public void onCreate(Bundle savedInstanceState) {
        super.onCreate(savedInstanceState);
        setContentView(R.layout.activity_handle_
            orientation_app);
    }
}
```

When the application is run while in the default landscape mode, the controls will appear as shown in Figure 17.4 (top). Because the five `Button` controls are placed relative to the four edges of the container and in relation to each other, none of the `Button` controls will disappear if the screen is rotated to portrait mode, as shown in Figure 17.4 (bottom). To switch between portrait mode and landscape mode on the device emulator, press the Ctrl+F11 keys. Recall from Chapter 1, "Overview of Android Tablet Applications," that the default orientation of the tablets is landscape.

Now that you understand the concept of adapting to screen orientation through anchoring controls, take a look at another approach: defining alternate layouts.

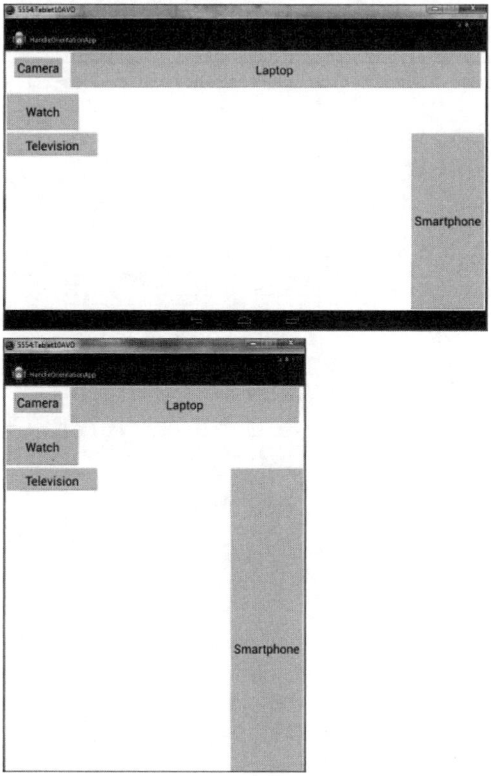

Figure 17.4   The controls arranged in landscape mode (top), and the controls arranged in portrait mode (bottom)

Recipe: Defining Alternate Layout to Handle Screen Orientation

In this method, you define two layouts. One arranges the UI controls to suit the portrait orientation of the device, whereas the other arranges the controls for landscape orientation. To understand this, create a new Android application called AlternateLayoutApp. Create two folders named layout-sw600dp and layout-sw720dp in the res folder of your application. These two folders will store the layout resources for the landscape orientation of 7-inch and 10-inch tablets. Copy the activity layout file activity_alternate_layout_app.xml from the res/layout folder to the layout-sw600dp and layout-sw720dp folders. For organizing the UI controls for landscape orientation, write the code as shown in Listing 17.12 into the activity layout file activity_alternate_layout_app.xml (found in the layout-sw600dp and layout-sw720dp folders).

Listing 17.12 **The Layout File** `activity_alternate_layout_app.xml` **to Arrange Controls for Landscape Orientation**

```
<RelativeLayout xmlns:android= "http://schemas.android.com/apk/res/android"
    android:layout_width="match_parent"
    android:layout_height="match_parent">
    <Button
        android:id="@+id/camera"
        android:text="Camera"
        android:textSize="@dimen/text_size"
        android:layout_width="400dp"
        android:layout_height="wrap_content"
        android:padding="40dip"
        android:layout_marginTop="40dip"
        android:layout_marginLeft="50dip" />
    <Button
        android:id="@+id/laptop"
        android:text="Laptop"
        android:textSize="@dimen/text_size"
        android:layout_width="400dp"
        android:layout_height="wrap_content"
        android:padding="40dip"
        android:layout_marginTop="40dip"
        android:layout_marginLeft="150dip"
        android:layout_toRightOf="@id/camera" />
    <Button
        android:id="@+id/watch"
        android:text="Watch"
        android:textSize="@dimen/text_size"
        android:layout_width="400dip"
        android:layout_height="wrap_content"
        android:padding="40dip"
        android:layout_marginTop="40dip"
        android:layout_marginLeft="50dip"
        android:layout_below="@id/camera" />
    <Button
        android:id="@+id/smartphone"
        android:text="Smartphone"
        android:textSize="@dimen/text_size"
        android:layout_width="400dip"
        android:layout_height="wrap_content"
        android:padding="40dip"
        android:layout_marginTop="40dip"
        android:layout_marginLeft="150dip"
        android:layout_below="@id/camera"
        android:layout_toRightOf="@id/watch"   />
    <Button
        android:id="@+id/television"
        android:text="Television"
```

```
            android:textSize="@dimen/text_size"
            android:layout_width="400dip"
            android:layout_height="wrap_content"
            android:padding="40dip"
            android:layout_marginTop="40dip"
            android:layout_marginLeft="50dip"
            android:layout_below="@id/watch" />
</RelativeLayout>
```

In the preceding code snippet, you can see that five `Button` controls are arranged sideways in a `RelativeLayout` container. This horizontal arrangement will make a few of the `Button` controls disappear partially when the screen switches to portrait mode.

If you run the application without defining the layout for the portrait orientation, you find the controls arranged in landscape mode, as shown in Figure 17.5 (top). But when you switch the screen orientation to portrait, you find that a few of the `Button` controls on the right side get partially hidden, as shown in Figure 17.5 (bottom). This is because in portrait mode, the screen becomes taller, but its width decreases.

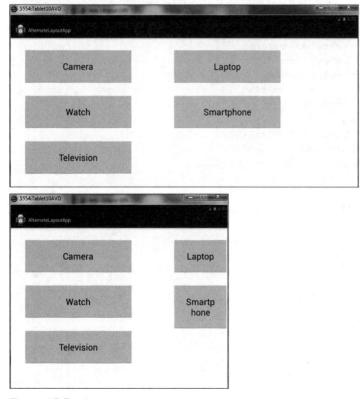

Figure 17.5   Controls when the device is in landscape orientation (top); controls disappear partially when the device switches to portrait orientation (bottom)

For defining the layout for portrait orientation of the tablets, create two folders named layout-sw600dp-port and layout-sw720dp-port in the res folder of your application. Copy the activity layout file activity_alternate_layout_app.xml from the res/layout folder into the newly created layout-sw600dp-port and layout-sw720dp-port folders. It is understood that the layout file in the layout-sw600dp-port and layout-sw720dp folders will be used to organize UI controls for portrait orientation of 7-inch and 10-inch tablets.

Note

While developing applications for phones, you use the activity layout file in the res/layout folder to organize UI controls for the portrait orientation of the phone. To arrange the controls for landscape orientation, you use the layout file in the res/layout-land folder.

To use the extra space at the bottom of the screen when the tablet switches to portrait mode, write the code as shown in Listing 17.13 into the layout file activity_alternate_layout_app.xml in the res/layout-sw600dp-port and res/layout-sw720dp-port folders.

Listing 17.13 **The Layout File** activity_alternate_layout_app.xml **in the** res/layout-sw600dp-port **and** res/layout-sw720dp-port **Folders**

```xml
<RelativeLayout xmlns:android=
"http://schemas.android.com/apk/res/android"
    android:layout_width="match_parent"
    android:layout_height="match_parent">
    <Button
        android:id="@+id/camera"
        android:text="Camera"
        android:textSize="@dimen/text_size"
        android:layout_width="400dp"
        android:layout_height="wrap_content"
        android:padding="40dip"
        android:layout_marginTop="40dip"
        android:layout_marginLeft="50dip" />
    <Button
        android:id="@+id/laptop"
        android:text="Laptop"
        android:textSize="@dimen/text_size"
        android:layout_width="400dp"
        android:layout_height="wrap_content"
        android:padding="40dip"
        android:layout_marginTop="40dip"
        android:layout_marginLeft="50dip"
        android:layout_below="@id/camera" />
    <Button
        android:id="@+id/watch"
        android:text="Watch"
        android:textSize="@dimen/text_size"
```

```
          android:layout_width="400dip"
          android:layout_height="wrap_content"
          android:padding="40dip"
          android:layout_marginTop="40dip"
          android:layout_marginLeft="50dip"
          android:layout_below="@id/laptop" />
    <Button
          android:id="@+id/smartphone"
          android:text="Smartphone"
          android:textSize="@dimen/text_size"
          android:layout_width="400dip"
          android:layout_height="wrap_content"
          android:padding="40dip"
          android:layout_marginTop="40dip"
          android:layout_marginLeft="50dip"
          android:layout_below="@id/watch" />
    <Button
          android:id="@+id/television"
          android:text="Television"
          android:textSize="@dimen/text_size"
          android:layout_width="400dip"
          android:layout_height="wrap_content"
          android:padding="40dip"
          android:layout_marginTop="40dip"
          android:layout_marginLeft="50dip"
          android:layout_below="@id/smartphone" />
</RelativeLayout>
```

In this code block, to fill up the blank space on the bottom of the screen, all the Button controls are vertically arranged, one below the other.

You can detect the screen orientation via Java code. Modify the activity file AlternateLayoutAppActivity.java to display a message when the screen switches between landscape mode and portrait mode. The code written in the Java activity file AlternateLayoutAppActivity.java is shown in Listing 17.14.

Listing 17.14 Code Written in the Java Activity File AlternateLayoutAppActivity.java

```
package com.androidtablet.alternatelayoutapp;

import android.app.Activity;
import android.os.Bundle;
import android.widget.Toast;

public class AlternateLayoutAppActivity extends Activity {
    @Override
    public void onCreate(Bundle savedInstanceState) {
        super.onCreate(savedInstanceState);
```

```
        setContentView(R.layout.activity_alternate_
            layout_app);
        if(getResources().getDisplayMetrics().widthPixels >
            getResources().getDisplayMetrics().heightPixels) {
            Toast.makeText(this,"Screen switched to Landscape
                mode",Toast.LENGTH_SHORT).show();
        }
        else
            Toast.makeText(this,"Screen switched to Portrait
                mode",Toast.LENGTH_SHORT).show();
    }
}
```

Now when you run the application, the Button controls will appear in landscape mode as shown in Figure 17.6 (top) and in portrait mode as shown in Figure 17.6 (bottom). You can see that none of the Button controls are hidden in portrait mode.

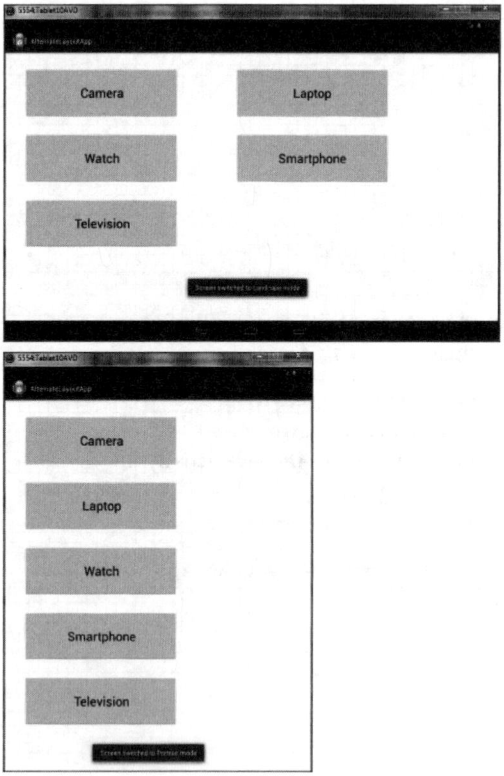

Figure 17.6   Controls in landscape mode (top); all controls are visible in portrait mode (bottom)

Summary

In this chapter, you learned about factors to implement in Android applications to support different screen sizes and densities. You saw the procedure to support different Android versions in an application. You also learned about the Android Support Library and how to use it to support older Android versions. In addition, you saw how screen orientation is handled by anchoring controls. Finally, you learned to use alternate layouts to support different screen sizes.

In the next chapter, you will learn to create and use home screen widgets. In addition, you will learn to monitor resource usage. Finally, you will learn about `RemoteViewsService` and how remote views are controlled and invoked by services and alarm managers.

18

Home Screen Widgets

This chapter is focused on understanding the role of app widgets, including what kind of data they display and how they are updated. *App widgets* are handy, small applications that users employ to display information. You will learn how they are embedded in home screen applications to become home screen widgets. You will look at app widget life cycle methods and learn about the `BroadcastReceiver` class that implements these methods. You will also see how home screen widgets are updated through XML configuration files, through event listeners, and through the `AlarmManager` service.

Recipe: Understanding App Widgets and Home Screen Widgets

App widgets are small visual components that can be embedded in another application. The applications where app widgets are embedded or placed are known as *app widget hosts*. The most common example of an app widget host application is a home screen application. The app widgets that are placed on the home screen of an Android device for quick access are called *home screen widgets*. Following are a few of the features of home screen widgets or app widgets:

> **Note**
>
> The terms *app widgets* and *home screen widgets* are used interchangeably because both refer to the same thing in this chapter.

- Home screen widgets are small visual components or widgets that are displayed on the home screen of the device.

- Home screen widgets are used for displaying the information that you want to have at your fingertips. For example, information related to flights, movies, weather, and so on is displayed through home screen widgets.

- Home screen widgets usually display information that does not require frequent updating. Frequent updating of widgets may result in high consumption of battery power.

- Home screen widgets use `RemoteViews` to display information and to interact with the user. As the name suggests, `RemoteViews` are the ones that are managed by remote processes other than the application. Remote process here represents the app widget host application (home screen application) that manages the embedded home screen widgets.

- The contents of home screen widgets (`RemoteViews`) are disconnected views that are updated periodically by background processes. Two preferable methods of updating home screen widgets are using an XML configuration file and an Android `AlarmManager` service.

- A `BroadcastReceiver` defines the user interface for the home screen widget. This receiver extends the `AppWidgetProvider` class to support the app widget life cycle. To update information displayed through `RemoteViews` in a home screen widget, the home screen widget broadcasts messages to the `BroadcastReceiver` so it can take the necessary actions. The job of the `BroadcastReceiver` is to initialize, update, and even delete home screen widgets.

To see the app widgets available on your Android device, follow the next procedure.

1. In the device with Android 3.x or lower versions, long-press on an empty space of the home screen to display the menu (see Figure 18.1 [left]). A list of available app widgets will be displayed after you select Widgets from the menu (see Figure 18.1 [right]).

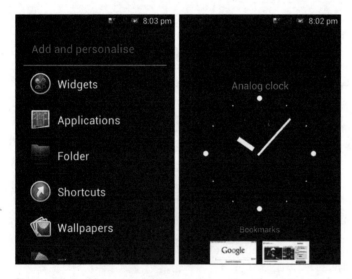

Figure 18.1   Menu appears after long-pressing an empty space on the device (left); list of widgets displayed after selecting the Widgets option from the menu (right)

2. In the devices with Ice Cream Sandwich (Android 4.0 or higher versions), the app widgets are displayed as a separate category. Open the list of available applications on the device. At the top of the screen are two tabs: Apps and Widgets. When you select the Widgets tab, the list of available app widgets will be displayed, as shown in Figure 18.2.

Figure 18.2   List of widgets displayed after selecting the Widgets tab on the top

3. After you select an app widget from the list, it will be placed on the home screen. The widget that will be placed on the home screen is actually an app widget instance. To delete an app widget instance, press it on the home screen and start dragging it. After you drag the app widget instance, a trash can will appear at the top of the home screen. Drag the app widget instance to the trash to delete it from the home screen.

Recipe: Knowing the App Widget Life Cycle Methods

A `BroadcastReceiver` class plays a major role in managing an app widget. It not only defines the user interface for the home screen widget, but listens to the messages that are broadcasted to update these widgets. The `BroadcastReceiver` class extends the `AppWidgetProvider` class to support the app widget life cycle. The app widget life cycle methods that the `BroadcastReceiver` implements are briefly described in Table 18.1.

Table 18.1   **Brief Description of the App Widget Life Cycle Methods**

Method	Description
`onEnabled()` callback method	Called when an instance of the first widget is created. The method confirms that at least one instance of the widget is created. Widget initialization statements are written in this method.
`onDeleted()` callback method	Called every time a widget is deleted (that is, whenever a widget instance is dragged to the trash can). If the state of the widget instance is saved in the application, it can be deleted in this method.
`onDisabled()` callback method	Called after the last widget instance is removed from the home screen. This happens when a user drags the last instance of a widget to the trash. The method can be used to disable receiving of broadcast messages, closing of databases, or performing of cleaning tasks.
`onUpdate()` callback method	Called whenever the timer expires and when the widget instance is created for the first time if there is no configuration activity. The method updates the content of the widget. If there is a configuration activity, this method is not called at the creation of a widget instance but will be called whenever the timer expires. The method contains the IDs of `appWidgetIds` for which an update is needed. If more than one widget is added to the home screen, only the last one is updated by default.
`onReceive()`	Handles the `BroadcastReceiver` actions and dispatches the requests to the preceding methods. The method is called for every broadcast.

Recipe: Creating a Home Screen Widget

In this recipe, you will create a home screen widget that will display the current date and time.

Following are the steps for creating a home screen widget:

1. Define a resource layout file that contains the definition of the views to be displayed in the home screen widget. A home screen widget requires two XML files: one to define the layout of the views that will be displayed in the home screen widget, and another to configure the home screen widget.

2. Define an XML file to configure the widget. The XML file may be called the *widget configuration* or the *widget definition* file. The file informs the minimum space required by the widget on the home screen, the time interval in which the widget has to be updated, and so on.

3. Create a `BroadcastReceiver` to build the user interface of the widget. This receiver extends the `AppWidgetProvider` class and is responsible for initializing the views of the widget when its instance is dragged onto the home screen. This Java class also updates

the widget according to the time interval specified in the XML configuration file or when some event occurs. This class even deletes the widget when its instance is dragged from the home screen to the trash can. In fact, this Java class manages the entire life cycle of the app widget.

4. Register the `BroadcastReceiver` in the `AndroidManifest.xml` file. Recall that the `BroadcastReceiver` initializes the widget, updates it, and even deletes it.

Note

You can add several instances of a widget to the home screen.

To understand the preceding steps through a running example, create a new Android project called `TimeHomeWidgetApp`. As a first step, you will define the views of the home screen widget. Because you want to display the current date and time in this home screen widget, a `TextView` control is the only control that is required. After defining the `TextView` control, the activity layout file `activity_time_home_widget_app.xml` will appear as shown in Listing 18.1.

Listing 18.1   Code Written into Activity Layout File `activity_time_home_widget_app.xml`

```
<RelativeLayout xmlns:android="http://schemas.android.com/apk/res/android"
    android:layout_width="match_parent"
    android:layout_height="match_parent" >
    <TextView
        android:id="@+id/time_textview"
        android:layout_width="wrap_content"
        android:layout_height="wrap_content"
        android:textSize="@dimen/text_size"
        android:textStyle="bold"
        android:text="00:00:00"
        android:textColor="#ffffff"
        android:background="#0000ff"
        android:padding="10dp"
        android:layout_centerHorizontal="true"
        android:layout_centerVertical="true" />
</RelativeLayout>
```

To access and identify Java code, the ID `time_textview` is assigned to the `TextView`. The text displayed through the `TextView` is set to display in bold, in the font size defined in the dimension resource `text_size`, in white on a blue background, and at the center of the widget. The `TextView` is initialized to display the text `00:00:00`.

To define an XML configuration file for the widget, create a folder called `xml` in the `res` folder. In the `res/xml` folder, add an XML file called `timewidgetproviderinfo.xml`. In the XML file, you write the widget definition. A widget definition consists of certain attributes enclosed within a single `<appwidget-provider>` element. In the widget definition, you define the following:

- Minimum width and height of the widget (that is, the minimum area that the widget will require on the home screen). The widget size is defined in dp units and is usually a multiple of one cell size on the desktop (that is, 74 × 74dp). The recommended size of the widget is determined by the following formula:

  ((Number of columns or rows) × 74) − 2.

  In this case, -2 leaves some space for margins. For example, the minimum width of the home screen widget that is 2 cells wide will be (2 × 74) − 2, or 146dp. Similarly, the minimum height of the widget that is 3 cells high will be (3 × 74) − 2, or 220dp.

  But in Android 4.0 and higher levels, the margins are automatic. Therefore, the formula for computing the recommended size of the widget is modified as shown here:

  ((Number of columns or rows) × 70) − 30.

  As per the new formula, the minimum width of the home screen widget that is 2 cells wide will be (2 × 70) − 30, or 110dp. Similarly, the minimum height of the widget that is 3 cells high will be (3 × 70) − 30, or 180dp.

- Time interval in which the widget has to be updated.
- Point at the initial layout resource file. The layout resource file contains the views to be displayed in the home screen widget.

In the XML configuration file, `timewidgetproviderinfo.xml`, write the code as shown in Listing 18.2.

Listing 18.2   **Code Written into the** `timewidgetproviderinfo.xml`

```xml
<?xml version="1.0" encoding="utf-8"?>
<appwidget-provider xmlns:android=
    "http://schemas.android.com/apk/res/android"
    android:minWidth="110dp"
    android:minHeight="180dp"
    android:updatePeriodMillis="1800000"
    android:initialLayout=
        "@layout/activity_time_home_widget_app"
    android:resizeMode="horizontal|vertical" >
</appwidget-provider>
```

You can see that the minimum width and height of the home screen widget is configured to be 2 cells wide and 3 cells high. The `android:updatePeriodMillis` in the preceding code specifies the widget update interval. The `BroadcastReceiver` that you are going to create next will be automatically invoked after this time interval to update the widget. The smallest update interval is 180000 milliseconds (30 minutes) to save power.

To update the widget faster than the time interval specified through the
`android:updatePeriodMillis` attribute in the XML configuration file, you can either use the
Alarm Manager or implement event listeners. A widget can be flexible in size (the user can drag
its handles to resize it). To make a widget resizable, the `android:resizeMode="horizontal|`
`vertical"` attribute is used. After you click the widget, resize handles will appear around the
widget. You can resize the widget both horizontally and vertically. You can also assign an icon
to your home screen widget by adding the `android:previewImage` attribute in the preceding
configuration file. For example, the following statement will make the `home_widget_icon.png`
file appear as an icon of your home screen widget:

```
android:previewImage="@drawable/home_widget_icon"
```

Your home screen widget will be represented by the specified icon in the widget listing of the
device. Before adding the preceding statement in the XML configuration file, make sure that an
image file named `home_widget_icon.png` is copied into the `drawable` folders of the application. If the `android:previewImage` is not used, the default image file `ic_launcher.png` will
be automatically assigned as the widget icon.

> **Note**
>
> Android provides the application Widget Preview on the emulator to help in creating a preview
> image.

You can also optionally create a configuration activity that is called once a new instance of the
widget is added to the Android home screen. In other words, when a widget is chosen from
the widget list in the device, the related widget configuration activity is called to configure
the widget instance. If two widget instances are created on the home screen, the configuration
activity will be called twice: once for each widget instance. The configuration activity keeps
track of the widget instances by allocating them unique IDs. The activity also saves information
of the widget instances in a persistent store. To define the configuration activity, you can use
the `android:configure` attribute in an XML configuration file of the widget. For example, the
following statement declares `TimeHomeWidgetAppActivity` as the configuration activity of a
widget:

```
android:configure="com.androidtablet.
timehomewidgetapp.TimeHomeWidgetAppActivity"
```

To define a `BroadcastReceiver` for the widget, add a Java class named `TimeWidgetProvider.`
`java` to the `com.androidtablet.timehomewidgetapp` package. The `TimeWidgetProvider`
class will extend the `AppWidgetProvider` class, which in turn will extend the
`BroadcastReceiver` class.

> **Tip**
>
> The `BroadcastReceiver` with the action `android.appwidget.action.APPWIDGET_UPDATE`
> is used for creating and updating the app widget.

This class will not only populate the home screen widget with the views defined in the activity layout file, but will update the views of the widget. Basically, the class receives the broadcast messages asking to update the widget. The class then takes respective actions on receiving the broadcast messages.

The class implements the five app widget life cycle methods to handle various action requests. The five methods that are implemented in this class (`TimeWidgetProvider.java`) are `onEnabled`, `onDisabled`, `onUpdate`, `onDeleted`, and `onReceive`, as shown in Listing 18.3.

> **Note**
>
> The intimation of updating the widget is based on the frequency of the time interval specified in the XML configuration file and is delivered in the form of broadcast messages.

Listing 18.3   **Code Written into the Java File** `TimeWidgetProvider.java`

```java
package com.androidtablet.timehomewidgetapp;

import java.util.Date;
import android.appwidget.AppWidgetManager;
import android.appwidget.AppWidgetProvider;
import android.content.Context;
import android.widget.RemoteViews;
import android.widget.Toast;
import java.text.SimpleDateFormat;

public class TimeWidgetProvider extends AppWidgetProvider {
    private static SimpleDateFormat formatter = new
        SimpleDateFormat("dd MMM yyyy  hh:mm:ss a");

    @Override
    public void onDeleted(Context context, int[] appWidgetIds) {
        super.onDeleted(context, appWidgetIds);
        Toast.makeText(context, "onDeleted()",
            Toast.LENGTH_LONG).show();
    }

    @Override
    public void onDisabled(Context context) {
        super.onDisabled(context);
        Toast.makeText(context, "onDisabled()",
            Toast.LENGTH_LONG).show();
    }

    @Override
    public void onEnabled(Context context) {
```

```
        super.onEnabled(context);
        Toast.makeText(context, "onEnabled()",
            Toast.LENGTH_LONG).show();
    }


    @Override
    public void onUpdate(Context context, AppWidgetManager
        appWidgetManager, int[] appWidgetIds) {
        super.onUpdate(context, appWidgetManager, appWidgetIds);
        String currentTime = formatter.format(new Date());
        final int N = appWidgetIds.length;
        for (int i=0; i<N; i++) {
            int widgetId = appWidgetIds[i];
            RemoteViews remoteViews = new RemoteViews(
                context.getPackageName(),
                R.layout.activity_time_home_widget_app);
            remoteViews.setTextViewText(R.id.time_textview,
                currentTime);
            appWidgetManager.updateAppWidget(widgetId,
                remoteViews);
        }
    }
}
```

The appWidgetIds is an array of IDs of all the instances of the active widgets. To update all the instances of the widget simultaneously, a loop is used in the onUpdate() method to iterate through each entry (ID) of the active widget instances in the appWidgetIds array and update each widget as desired. A RemoteView instance named remoteViews is created. Recall that RemoteViews are the views of the home screen widget that are updated by the process other than the application. In the RemoteViews constructor, the package name (getPackageName()) and the layout that defines the views of the home screen widget are supplied. A reference to the AppWidgetManager is created. The updateAppWidget method is called through AppWidgetManager to paint and update RemoteViews in the home screen widget.

When you delete a widget instance, the onDeleted() method in the preceding class will be called. Also, if the deleted widget instance is the last instance, the onDisabled() method will be called. You can use the two methods to free up resources by doing things like deleting states of the widget instances.

The next step is to register the BroadcastReceiver (TimeWidgetProvider) class in the AndroidManifest.xml. Recall that the BroadcastReceiver calls the app widget life cycle methods, including the onUpdate() method that is required to update the widget content either periodically or when an event takes place. The code in bold as shown in Listing 18.4 is written in the AndroidManifest.xml file for registering the BroadcastReceiver TimeWidgetProvider.

Listing 18.4   **Code in the** `AndroidManifest.xml`

```xml
<?xml version="1.0" encoding="utf-8"?>
<manifest xmlns:android=
    "http://schemas.android.com/apk/res/android"
    package="com.androidtablet.timehomewidgetapp"
    android:versionCode="1"
    android:versionName="1.0" >
    <uses-sdk
        android:minSdkVersion="11"
        android:targetSdkVersion="17" />
    <application
        android:allowBackup="true"
        android:icon="@drawable/ic_launcher"
        android:label="@string/app_name"
        android:theme="@style/AppTheme" >
        <receiver android:name=".TimeWidgetProvider" >
            <intent-filter>
                <action android:name=
                    "android.appwidget.action.APPWIDGET_UPDATE" />
            </intent-filter>
            <meta-data android:name="android.appwidget.provider"
                android:resource="@xml/timewidgetproviderinfo" />
        </receiver>
    </application>
</manifest>
```

The code in Listing 18.4 indicates that the `BroadcastReceiver` class is `TimeWidgetProvider`. The action that the receiver handles is `APPWIDGET_UPDATE`, which is broadcasted when the content of the widget is required to be updated.

The `android:name="android.appwidget.provider"` attribute defines the metadata for the widget. The name and location of the widget configuration file is supplied through this metadata. Recall that the widget configuration file contains information such as the minimum area required by the widget, the time interval to update the widget, and the location of the resource layout file.

When you specify the widget definition and its `BroadcastReceiver` class, the widget will be available in the Widget list of the device for the user to drag and drop on the home screen.

Now your application is ready to run. When you run the application, the home screen widget will be created and will become visible in the device Widget list. The steps to display the newly created widget on the home screen are given next. The home screen of the device may initially appear as shown in Figure 18.3 (top).

1. Open the list of applications in the device. Select the Widgets tab that appears at the top.

    A screen will appear showing the list of available widgets in a grid as shown in Figure 18.3 (middle).

2. Locate the newly created widget, `TimeHomeWidgetApp`, in the Widget list.

3. Click and drag the `TimeHomeWidgetApp` widget. The home screen will appear while you drag the widget. Also, a drop window appears while you drag the widget, as does the mouse pointer indicating the location where the widget can be dropped on the home screen.

4. Release the mouse at the desired location, and the widget will appear on the home screen displaying the current date and time (see Figure 18.3 [bottom]).

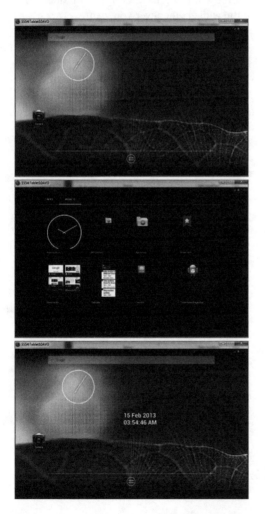

Figure 18.3   The usual home screen on the device (top); your widget, `TimeHomeWidgetApp`, appears in the list of widgets on the device (middle); the current date and time displayed in the widget (bottom)

> **Note**
>
> The view that is created on the home screen page is a widget instance. You can have more than one widget instance running simultaneously in an application.

To delete a widget instance, press the widget on the home screen and start dragging it. After you drag the widget instance, a trash can will appear at the top of the home screen. Drag the widget instance to the trash can to delete it from the home screen.

The home screen widget created in the preceding recipe will be updated every 30 minutes. In the following recipe, you will learn how to update the widget whenever you want.

Recipe: Updating the Home Screen Widget Through the `Button` Control

In this recipe, you will modify the application `TimeHomeWidgetApp` that you created in the previous recipe. You will add a `Button` control to your home screen widget. When you click the `Button` control, it will update the date and time displayed through the `TextView` control. To add a `Button` control, modify the layout file `activity_time_home_widget_app.xml` to appear as shown in Listing 18.5. Only the code in bold is new; the rest is the same as you saw in Listing 18.1.

Listing 18.5　**Code in the Activity Layout File** `activity_time_home_widget_app.xml`

```
<RelativeLayout xmlns:android=
    "http://schemas.android.com/apk/res/android"
    android:layout_width="match_parent"
    android:layout_height="match_parent" >
    <TextView
        android:id="@+id/time_textview"
        android:layout_width="wrap_content"
        android:layout_height="wrap_content"
        android:textSize="@dimen/text_size"
        android:textStyle="bold"
        android:text="00:00:00"
        android:textColor="#ffffff"
        android:background="#0000ff"
        android:padding="10dp"
        android:layout_centerHorizontal="true"
        android:layout_centerVertical="true" />
    <Button
        android:id="@+id/update_button"
        android:layout_width="match_parent"
        android:layout_height="wrap_content"
        android:text="Update Time"
```

```
        android:textSize="@dimen/text_size"
        android:layout_below="@id/time_textview"
        android:layout_marginTop="10dp" />
</RelativeLayout>
```

You can see that a Button control with the ID update_button is added to the widget layout file. The caption assigned to the Button control is Update Time, and it will appear in the font size defined in the dimension resource text_size.

Actually, you will be using a service to update the RemoteViews of the widget. The service will be associated with the click event of the Button control through a PendingIntent. That is, when the button in the widget is clicked, the PendingIntent will start the service to update the widget. You will be defining an inner service class named UpdateService inside the BroadcastReceiver named TimeWidgetProvider. Modify the TimeWidgetProvider.java to appear as shown in Listing 18.6. Only the code in bold is new; the rest of the code is the same as you saw in Listing 18.3.

> ### Note
> Because the RemoteViews are disconnected views, the preferred way of communicating with them is through the PendingIntent.

Listing 18.6 **Code in the Java File** TimeWidgetProvider.java

```
package com.androidtablet.timehomewidgetapp;

import java.util.Date;
import android.appwidget.AppWidgetManager;
import android.appwidget.AppWidgetProvider;
import android.content.Context;
import android.widget.RemoteViews;
import android.widget.Toast;
import java.text.SimpleDateFormat;
import android.content.Intent;
import android.app.PendingIntent;
import android.app.Service;
import android.os.IBinder;

public class TimeWidgetProvider extends AppWidgetProvider {
    private static SimpleDateFormat formatter = new
        SimpleDateFormat("dd MMM yyyy  hh:mm:ss a");

    @Override
    public void onDeleted(Context context, int[] appWidgetIds) {
        super.onDeleted(context, appWidgetIds);
```

```java
        Toast.makeText(context, "onDeleted()",
            Toast.LENGTH_LONG).show();
    }

    @Override
    public void onDisabled(Context context) {
        super.onDisabled(context);
        Toast.makeText(context, "onDisabled()",
            Toast.LENGTH_LONG).show();
    }

    @Override
    public void onEnabled(Context context) {
        super.onEnabled(context);
        Toast.makeText(context, "onEnabled()",
            Toast.LENGTH_LONG).show();
    }

    @Override
    public void onUpdate(Context context, AppWidgetManager
        appWidgetManager, int[] appWidgetIds) {
        super.onUpdate(context, appWidgetManager, appWidgetIds);
        final int N = appWidgetIds.length;
        for (int i=0; i<N; i++) {
            int widgetId = appWidgetIds[i];
            Intent intent = new Intent(context,
                UpdateService.class);
            intent.setAction(AppWidgetManager.
                ACTION_APPWIDGET_UPDATE);
            intent.putExtra(AppWidgetManager.EXTRA_APPWIDGET_ID,
                widgetId);
            PendingIntent pendingIntent =
                PendingIntent.getService(context, 0,
                intent,PendingIntent.FLAG_UPDATE_CURRENT);
            RemoteViews remoteViews = new
                RemoteViews(context.getPackageName(),
                R.layout.activity_time_home_widget_app);
            remoteViews.setOnClickPendingIntent(
                R.id.update_button, pendingIntent);
            appWidgetManager.updateAppWidget(widgetId,
                remoteViews);
        }
    }
    public static class UpdateService extends Service {
        String currentTime = formatter.format(new Date());
```

```
@Override
public int onStartCommand(Intent intent, int flags, int
    startId) {
    super.onStartCommand(intent, flags, startId);
    RemoteViews remoteViews = new
        RemoteViews(getPackageName(),
        R.layout.activity_time_home_widget_app);
    remoteViews.setTextViewText( R.id.time_textview,
        currentTime);
    AppWidgetManager appWidgetManager =
        AppWidgetManager.getInstance(this);
    int appWidgetId=intent.getIntExtra(
        AppWidgetManager.EXTRA_APPWIDGET_ID, 0);
    appWidgetManager.updateAppWidget(appWidgetId,
        remoteViews);
    stopSelf(startId);
    return 0;
}

@Override
public IBinder onBind(Intent intent) {
    return null;
}
    }
}
```

The following tasks are performed in the preceding class:

- The onUpdate method is overridden to update data in the widget.

- An intent is created pointing to your service UpdateService.

- The action set for the intent is ACTION_APPWIDGET_UPDATE to update the widget.

- The ID of the widget instance is stored in the intent as extra data before invoking the service to update the widget. This is because the AppWidgetProvider class is stateless, and it does not remember or keep track of the invoked home screen widget instance.

- The intent is then encapsulated inside a PendingIntent so that it can be invoked later. The FLAG_UPDATE_CURRENT constant is applied to confirm that if the PendingIntent already exists, it is kept and its extra data is replaced with the new intent.

- The RemoteViews instance named remoteViews is created as the views of the widget are displayed through RemoteViews.

- The method setOnClickPendingIntent is used to associate a click event handler to the Button control. Actually, the PendingIntent is set as the click handler for the Button control so that the service is started whenever the Button control is clicked.

- In the `UpdateService` service, the `onStartCommand` method is implemented.

- The `setTextViewText` method of `RemoteView` is called to assign the current date and time to the `TextView` of the widget.

- A reference of the `AppWidgetManager` is created.

- The `updateAppWidget` method is called through `AppWidgetManager` to update the widget.

To register the inner service class named `UpdateService` inside the `TimeWidgetProvider`, add the following statement in the `AndroidManifest.xml` file (besides the code that you added in Listing 18.4):

```
<service android:name=
    ".TimeWidgetProvider$UpdateService" />
```

The `android:name` attribute, in the `<service>` element in the preceding statement, indicates that the receiver class is `TimeWidgetProvider`, and it is using the inner service class `UpdateService` to update the widget.

Note
In Java, $ means inner class when giving a class name.

When running the application, your home screen widget `TimeHomeWidgetApp` in the Widget list of the device will be updated. Drag and drop the old home screen widget instance that you created in the previous recipe (refer to Figure 18.3 [bottom]) to the trash can. Drag a new widget instance from the Widget list of the device and drop it on the home screen. The `TextView` of the widget will display the initial text `00:00:00`, as shown in Figure 18.4 (top). When you click the Update Time button, the current date and time will be displayed through the `TextView` control, as shown in Figure 18.4 (bottom). From now on, every time the Update Time button is clicked, the time displayed through the `TextView` will be updated to display the current date and time.

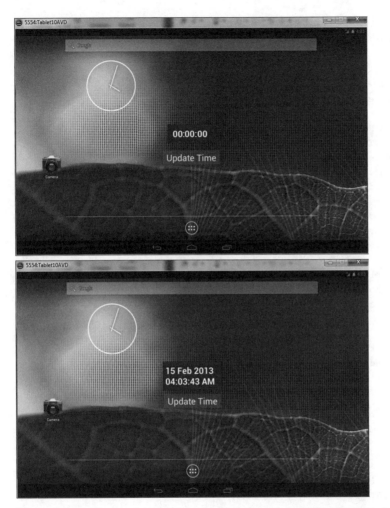

Figure 18.4   The `TextView` of the widget displays the initial text `00:00:00` along with a `Button` control (top); the current date and time displayed through the `TextView` after clicking the Update Time button (bottom)

Recipe: Using the `AlarmManager` to Frequently Update the Home Screen Widget

If you want to update the widget frequently, `AlarmManager` is highly recommended because it is resource efficient. In this recipe, you will make your widget update automatically after every 1000 milliseconds. The date and time displayed in the widget will automatically update without your needing to press the `Button` control. Open the Android application `TimeHomeWidgetApp` that you created in the previous recipe. Modify the Java class file `TimeWidgetProvider.java` to appear as shown in Listing 18.7. Only the code in bold is modified; the rest is the same as you saw in Listing 18.6.

Listing 18.7   **Code in the Java File** `TimeWidgetProvider.java`

```java
package com.androidtablet.timehomewidgetapp;

import java.util.Date;
import android.appwidget.AppWidgetManager;
import android.appwidget.AppWidgetProvider;
import android.content.Context;
import android.widget.RemoteViews;
import android.widget.Toast;
import java.text.SimpleDateFormat;
import android.content.Intent;
import android.app.PendingIntent;
import android.app.Service;
import android.os.IBinder;
import android.app.AlarmManager;
import android.os.SystemClock;

public class TimeWidgetProvider extends AppWidgetProvider {
    private static SimpleDateFormat formatter = new
        SimpleDateFormat("dd MMM yyyy  hh:mm:ss a");

    @Override
    public void onDeleted(Context context, int[] appWidgetIds) {
        super.onDeleted(context, appWidgetIds);
        Toast.makeText(context, "onDeleted()",
            Toast.LENGTH_LONG).show();
    }

    @Override
    public void onDisabled(Context context) {
        super.onDisabled(context);
        Toast.makeText(context, "onDisabled()",
            Toast.LENGTH_LONG).show();
    }

    @Override
    public void onEnabled(Context context) {
        super.onEnabled(context);
        Toast.makeText(context, "onEnabled()",
            Toast.LENGTH_LONG).show();
    }

    @Override
    public void onUpdate(Context context, AppWidgetManager
        appWidgetManager, int[] appWidgetIds) {
        super.onUpdate(context, appWidgetManager, appWidgetIds);
        final int N = appWidgetIds.length;
```

```java
        for (int i=0; i<N; i++) {
            int widgetId = appWidgetIds[i];
            Intent intent = new Intent(context,
                UpdateService.class);
            intent.setAction(AppWidgetManager.
                ACTION_APPWIDGET_UPDATE);
            intent.putExtra(AppWidgetManager.EXTRA_APPWIDGET_ID,
                widgetId);
            PendingIntent pendingIntent = PendingIntent.
                getService(context, 0, intent,
                PendingIntent.FLAG_UPDATE_CURRENT);
            AlarmManager alarm = (AlarmManager) context.
                getSystemService(Context.ALARM_SERVICE);
            alarm.setRepeating(AlarmManager.ELAPSED_REALTIME,
                SystemClock.elapsedRealtime(), 1000, pendingIntent);
        }
    }

    public static class UpdateService extends Service {
        String currentTime = formatter.format(new Date());

        @Override
        public int onStartCommand(Intent intent, int flags, int
            startId) {
            super.onStartCommand(intent, flags, startId);
            RemoteViews remoteViews = new RemoteViews(
                getPackageName(),
                R.layout.activity_time_home_widget_app);
            remoteViews.setTextViewText( R.id.time_textview,
                currentTime);
            AppWidgetManager appWidgetManager =
                AppWidgetManager.getInstance(this);
            int appWidgetId=intent.getIntExtra(
                AppWidgetManager.EXTRA_APPWIDGET_ID, 0);
            appWidgetManager.updateAppWidget( appWidgetId,
                remoteViews);
            stopSelf(startId);
            return 0;
        }

        @Override
        public IBinder onBind(Intent intent) {
            return null;
        }
    }
}
```

In the preceding code, you see that an instance of `AlarmManager` is created named `alarm`. The alarm is set to go off every 1000 milliseconds. Whenever the alarm goes off, the `PendingIntent` will be called to start the associated service `UpdateService`. The `UpdateService` will then update the widget by displaying the current time. When you run the application, the current time will appear in the `TextView` of the widget, as shown in Figure 18.5. Note that the time in the widget will automatically be updated every 1000 milliseconds.

Figure 18.5   `TextView` of the widget displays the current date and time; the widget is updated every 1000 milliseconds

Summary

In this chapter, you walked through the procedure to create and display a home screen widget on the device. You learned about app widget life cycle methods. You saw how `BroadcastReceiver` receives the broadcasted messages meant for updating the widget and then updates the widget. In addition, you learned how to specify the time duration of updating the widget through the XML configuration file. Finally, you learned how the home screen widget is updated through event listeners and through the `AlarmManager` service.

In the next chapter, you will learn to access the NFC device hardware. You will also learn about NFC writers and the procedure to read and write data on NFC tags. Finally, you will learn about Android Beam and how to use it to transfer data wirelessly.

19

Android Beam

Radio frequency plays a major role in wireless communication. You saw the usage of Bluetooth technology in communicating data in Chapter 12, "Wireless Connectivity." In this chapter, you will focus on the usage of NFC (near field communication) and Android Beam in sharing data by using radio frequency. You will learn about NFC and its connection with RFID. You will come to know the structures that are used in exchanging information with NFC tags. In addition, you will learn to write and read data from NFC tags using a step-by-step procedure. Finally, you will learn about the Android Beam and how it transfers data between Android devices.

Recipe: Understanding Near Field Communication (NFC)

Near field communication (NFC) is a short-range, high-frequency, wireless communication technology that enables data communication between phones, tags, and cards. NFC is based on the radio frequency identification (RFID) technique that enables Android devices to communicate through radio waves. To be more specific, in RFID, an electromagnetic field is generated by radio waves that enable data transfer among RFID-enabled devices. NFC operates in the following three modes:

- **Reading and writing tags**—The tags are tiny objects that can be embedded in objects such as products and stickers. Tags do not require battery power and use the RF field that an Android device generates to power itself. The Android device acts as a reader (or writer) that generates the RF field and scans for nearby NFC devices. When a tag comes within the RF field, the reader detects it and reads information from it. Some tags are rewritable, so Android devices can update their content.

- **Card emulation mode**—An Android device acts like a smart card in this mode. The reader performs transactions with the Android device as if it is dealing with a credit card instead of an Android device. The Android device in this mode can be used in all places that a credit card can be used.

- **Peer-to-peer communication**—In this mode, both devices generate their own RF fields and can exchange data back and forth.

NFC has these features:

- Communication between devices is performed with a simple touch.

- It is a simple technology that supports short-range transmission. NFC is similar to Bluetooth technology except that NFC only works for distances up to about 4cm, whereas Bluetooth can pair devices up to 50 meters apart.

- NFC communication is secure and power efficient, so it is highly preferred for mobile payments.

> **Warning**
>
> For mobile payments, the device must have an NFC reader to connect to the cash register. In addition, a secure application is required that can handle credit cards and other purchase formalities.

Recipe: Understanding NFC Tags

NFC tags are small electronic devices that appear as small discs of plastic (see Figure 19.1). These devices don't have a battery but are powered by the RF field around them. NFC tags have a small memory; when an NFC reader detects an NFC tag in its field, the NFC reader accesses the information in the NFC tag. The NFC tags with adhesive capability are known as NFC stickers. The NFC stickers carrying product information are stuck to the product.

Figure 19.1   NFC tags

NFC tags can display information about objects, products, places, and more. For example, in a department store, NFC tags can be placed along with the items. When customers wave their phone close to the tag, a web page will be opened displaying multimedia information about that item. The information displayed may include videos displaying more specific information about the object. Similarly, NFC tags may be used to fetch information about the next train, flight, or bus arrival. NFC tags can also be used to unlock the NFC-equipped doors of a home, hotel, car, or office.

> **Note**
>
> You can program NFC tags to give out text information, uniform resource identifiers (URIs), and metadata.

Recipe: Knowing the Structures Used in Exchanging Information with NFC Tags

To exchange information with NFC tags, you use NDEF (NFC data exchange format). To be more precise, `NdefMessages` are used for exchanging data with NFC tags. An `NdefMessage` contains one or more `NdefRecords` that in turn contain the data you want to share with NFC tags. An `NdefRecord` consists of the following fields:

- **TNF (Type Name Format)**—A 3-bit field that represents the TNF type (the type of contained payload).
- **Type**—Represents the MIME type (the record format).
- **ID**—Represents a unique identifier for the record.
- **Payload**—Represents the data payload.

The most common types of TNF are the following:

- **TNF_EMPTY**—Indicates that the record is empty.
- **TNF_MIME_MEDIA**—Indicates that the type field contains a media type.
- **TNF_ABSOLUTE_URI**—Indicates that the type field contains an absolute-URI.
- **TNF_UNKNOWN**—Indicates that the payload type is unknown.
- **TNF_WELL_KNOWN**—Indicates that the type field contains a well-known RTD (Record Type Definition) type.

To create a new NDEF message, you first need to create at least one `NdefRecord`. In an `NdefRecord`, the data payload that you want to write into the tag is stored. The payload that can be written into an `NdefRecord` can be an absolute URI, an application-specific MIME type, and even plain text. Now the issue is how to define values for the four fields (TNF type, record type, ID, and payload of the `NdefRecord` for storing URI, device-specific MIME, and plain text). Table 19.1 makes this task easier because it shows a sample code for creating an `NdefRecord` for storing the three data types.

Table 19.1 Sample Code for Creating `NdefRecord` for Different Types of Payload

Data Type	Sample Code

To store an absolute URI in the NdefRecord	```String url = "http://bmharwani.com";```
	```byte[] payload = url.getBytes();```
	```byte[] tagId = new byte[0];```
	```NdefRecord ndefRecord = new NdefRecord(NdefRecord.TNF_ABSOLUTE_URI,```
	```NdefRecord.RTD_URI, tagId, payload);```
	
	The preceding sample creates an `NdefRecord` that stores a URI.

Data Type	Sample Code

To store plain text in the NdefRecord	```String text = "Text to be written into the Tag";```
	```byte[] langBytes = Locale.ENGLISH.getLanguage().getBytes(Charset.forName("US-ASCII"));```
	```byte[] textBytes = text.getBytes(Charset.forName("UTF-8"));```
	```byte[] tagId = new byte[0];```
	```byte[] payload = new byte[1 + langBytes.length + textBytes.length];```
	```payload[0] = (byte) langBytes.length;```
	```System.arraycopy(langBytes, 0, payload, 1, langBytes.length);```
	```System.arraycopy(textBytes, 0, payload, 1 + langBytes.length, textBytes.length);```
	```NdefRecord record = new NdefRecord(NdefRecord.TNF_WELL_KNOWN, NdefRecord.RTD_TEXT, tagId, payload);```
	
	The preceding sample creates an `NdefRecord` that stores plain text. Proper encoding is done before storing the text in the `NdefRecord`.

To store application-specific MIME type in the NdefRecord	```byte[] mimeType = "application/com.androidtablet.nfcapp".getBytes(Charset.forName("US-ASCII"));```
	```byte[] tagId = new byte[0];```
	```byte[] payload = "Text to be written into the Tag".getBytes(Charset.forName("US-ASCII"));```
	```NdefRecord ndefRecord = new NdefRecord(NdefRecord.TNF_MIME_MEDIA,mimeType,tagId,payload);```
	
	The `NdefRecord` can also be included in the form of an Android application record (AAR) because it ensures that your application will be launched on the target device. In this case, your application is not installed on the target device; the Google Play Store will be invoked inviting the user to install it.
	
	To create an AAR `NdefRecord`, call the `createApplicationRecord()` method on the `NdefRecord` class, specifying the package name of your application as shown in the following statements:
	```byte[] payload = "Text to be written into the Tag".getBytes(Charset.forName("US-ASCII"));```
	```byte[] tagId = new byte[0];```
	```String mimeType = "application/com.androidtablet.nfcapp";```
	```byte[] mimeBytes = mimeType.getBytes(Charset.forName("US-ASCII"));```
	```NdefMessage nfcMessage = new NdefMessage(new NdefRecord[] {new```
	``` NdefRecord (NdefRecord.TNF_MIME_MEDIA,mimeBytes,tagId,payload),```
	``` NdefRecord.createApplicationRecord("com.androidtablet.```
	``` androidbeamapp")```
	```});```
	
	Because the tag with an AAR specifies the application package name, when such a tag is received on an Android device, Android will search locally for an application with that package name and launch it if it finds one. If Android doesn't find the application, it will launch the Google Play Store to download the application so the tag can be processed.

Recipe: Reading from NFC Tags

To use NFC functionality in an application, you need to access the NFC chip on the device by adding the following permission in the manifest file:

```
<uses-permission android:name= "android.permission.NFC" />
```

To restrict the installation of the application on NFC-enabled devices only, add the following statement to the manifest file:

```
<uses-feature android:name="android.hardware.nfc"
android:required="true" />
```

> **Note**
>
> To develop and test an NFC reading application, you need an NFC-compliant device.

When you scan an NFC tag, the tag object is placed into an intent as an `EXTRA_TAG`. Thereafter, the intent is sent to the application that filters for the intent. The intent starts an activity to handle the tag. If more than one application is available that can handle the intent, the search is undertaken for the suitable activity to which the intent can be sent so that the contained tag is handled properly. The following situations may occur:

- If there is an activity in the foreground (an activity that has called the `enableForegroundDispatch()` method), the intent is passed to that activity.

- The first `NdefRecord` in the first `NdefMessage` of the tag's data is checked. If the `NdefRecord` is URI or MIME data, the search is undertaken for an activity that is registered for the `ACTION_NDEF_DISCOVERED` intent. The intent is sent to the matching activity.

- The search is undertaken for an activity that is registered for `ACTION_TECH_DISCOVERED` and that matches the specific set of technologies for the tag. The intent is sent to the matching activity.

- If no activity matches with the preceding three situations, the intent is passed as an `ACTION_TAG_DISCOVERED` action.

In this recipe, you will learn how Android devices read the tags and launch the appropriate activity. In the `AndroidManifest.xml` file, you need to write intent filters that capture different intents so that your application is able to scan the tags containing the desired data. When a device comes closer to an NFC tag, the appropriate intent is started on the device, notifying the applications that an NFC tag is detected. By declaring the appropriate intent filter in the `AndroidManifest.xml` file or using a foreground dispatching technique, your application can request to handle the intent.

The `<intent-filter>` is placed on your activity because it is the intent filters that help the "tag dispatch system" in determining the applications that can handle the tags. Based on the data contained in the NFC tag, the "tag dispatch" system determines and searches for the applications to handle the scanned NFC tag. The applications declare intent filters to inform that they will handle the scanned NFC tag and its data. Following are the intent filters for different types of tag data:

- Intent filter for the NFC tag with a MIME type:

```
<intent-filter>
    <action android:name="android.nfc.action.NDEF_DISCOVERED"/>
    <data android:mimeType="text/plain" />
</intent-filter>
```

The preceding intent filter is set for plain text type. To set it for all text types, adjust the value of the `android:mimeType` attribute to `text/*`.

- Intent filter for the NFC tag with a URI:

```
<intent-filter>
    <action android:name="android.nfc.action.NDEF_DISCOVERED"/>
    <data android:scheme="http" />
</intent-filter>
```

Your activity will be launched if a tag with an `http` URI is detected.

To search for NFC tags with a particular technology, use the following intent filter:

```
<intent-filter>
    <action android:name="android.nfc.action.TECH_DISCOVERED"/>
</intent-filter>
<meta-data android:name="android.nfc.action.TECH_DISCOVERED"
android:resource="@xml/tech_filter" />
```

To match technology, use a `<meta-data>` tag that refers to another file created under the `/res/xml` directory of your application. The `tech_filter.xml` file will mention the list of technologies that your activity is looking for.

- Intent filter for the NFC tag of `"unknown"` type:

```
<intent-filter>
    <action android:name="android.nfc.action.TAG_DISCOVERED"/>
</intent-filter>
```

Your activity will be launched if the tag contains data other than MIME type, URI, or technology.

The preceding intent filters help you search the tag with specific contents.

You can ensure that only your activity will handle an NFC tag by using the foreground dispatch system. You will learn about it later in this recipe.

Create an Android project called `NFCReadTagApp`. While creating the application, set the values of the `android:minSdkVersion` and `android:targetSdkVersion` attributes to 11 and 17, respectively. In the `AndroidManifest.xml` file, you will add permissions and intent filters as shown in bold in Listing 19.1. The code in bold has been added; the rest is the auto-created default code.

Listing 19.1   **Code in the** `AndroidManifest.xml` **File**

```xml
<?xml version="1.0" encoding="utf-8"?>
<manifest xmlns:android="http://schemas.android.com/apk/res/android"
    package="com.androidtablet.nfcreadtagapp"
    android:versionCode="1"
    android:versionName="1.0" >
    <uses-sdk
        android:minSdkVersion="11"
        android:targetSdkVersion="17" />
        <uses-permission android:name="android.permission.NFC" />
        <uses-feature android:name="android.hardware.nfc"
            android:required="true"/>
    <application
        android:allowBackup="true"
        android:icon="@drawable/ic_launcher"
        android:label="@string/app_name"
        android:theme="@style/AppTheme" >
        <activity android:name="com.androidtablet.
            nfcreadtagapp.NFCReadTagAppActivity"
            android:label="@string/app_name" >
            <intent-filter>
                <action android:name=
                    "android.intent.action.MAIN" />
                <category android:name=
                    "android.intent.category.LAUNCHER" />
            </intent-filter>
            <intent-filter>
                <action android:name=
                    "android.nfc.action.NDEF_DISCOVERED"/>
                <data android:mimeType="text/plain" />
                <category android:name=
                    "android.intent.category.DEFAULT"/>
            </intent-filter>
            <intent-filter>
                <action android:name=
                    "android.nfc.action.TAG_DISCOVERED"/>
            </intent-filter>
        </activity>
    </application>
</manifest>
```

You can see that permissions to access the NFC chip of the device and to restrict the application to only NFC-enabled devices are added to the manifest file. Because you want your activity to scan the tag when it contains either plain text or when it contains the data of "unknown" type, add the corresponding intent filters to the manifest file shown earlier.

You will write Java code to read the data from the detected tag. But before that, read the following quick overview of the entire procedure.

You begin the process of reading NFC tags by obtaining a reference to the NFC adapter:

```
nfcAdapter = NfcAdapter.getDefaultAdapter(this);
```

Then you can invoke the `enableForegroundDispatch()` method on the `NfcAdapter` to switch your activity to the foreground. Consequently, your activity will scan and handle the tag before any other application:

```
PendingIntent pendingIntent = PendingIntent.getActivity(this, 0, new Intent(this,
    getClass()).addFlags(Intent.FLAG_ACTIVITY_SINGLE_TOP), 0);
IntentFilter intentFilter = new IntentFilter(
    NfcAdapter.ACTION_TAG_DISCOVERED);
IntentFilter[] readTagFilters = new IntentFilter[] { intentFilter };
nfcAdapter.enableForegroundDispatch(this, pendingIntent, readTagFilters, null);
```

In this method, you set up a `PendingIntent` to run when a tag is scanned. Therefore, the current activity will be launched when any tag is scanned. When the system dispatches `ACTION_TAG_DISCOVERED`, this activity will launch and `onNewIntent()` will be called with the tag information:

```
public void onNewIntent(Intent intent) {
    Tag tagDetected = intent.getParcelableExtra(NfcAdapter.EXTRA_TAG);
    readFromTag(tagDetected);
}
```

> **Note**
>
> When an intent is broadcasted with tag data, a `Tag` object is always parceled into the intent's extras bundle, under the key `EXTRA_TAG`. If the tag contains NDEF data, another `EXTRAS` value is set under the key `EXTRA_NDEF_MESSAGES`. Even the tag's ID can be optionally added in the intent under the key `EXTRA_ID`.

In the `onNewIntent()` method, you access the NFC tag and pass it to the `readFromTag()` function to read data from it.

To read data from the NFC tag, write the code as shown in Listing 19.2 in the Java activity file `NFCReadTagAppActivity.java`.

Listing 19.2   **Code Written in the Java Activity File** `NFCReadTagAppActivity.java`

```
package com.androidtablet.nfcreadtagapp;

import android.os.Bundle;
import android.app.Activity;
import android.nfc.NdefMessage;
import android.content.Intent;
```

```java
import android.nfc.NfcAdapter;
import android.os.Parcelable;
import android.nfc.NdefRecord;
import android.widget.Toast;
import android.nfc.Tag;
import android.app.PendingIntent;
import android.content.IntentFilter;
import android.nfc.tech.Ndef;

public class NFCReadTagAppActivity extends Activity {
    Tag tagDetected;
    NfcAdapter nfcAdapter;
    PendingIntent pendingIntent;
    IntentFilter[] readTagFilters;
    IntentFilter intentFilter;

    @Override
    protected void onCreate(Bundle savedInstanceState) {
        super.onCreate(savedInstanceState);
        setContentView(R.layout.activity_nfcread_tag_app);
        nfcAdapter = NfcAdapter.getDefaultAdapter(this);     #1
        if(nfcAdapter == null)
            Toast.makeText(this, "NFC chip is not available on
                this device", Toast.LENGTH_LONG).show();
        else
            Toast.makeText(this, "NFC chip is available on this
                device", Toast.LENGTH_LONG).show();
        pendingIntent = PendingIntent.getActivity(
            getApplicationContext(), 0, new
            Intent(this,getClass()). addFlags(
            Intent.FLAG_ACTIVITY_SINGLE_TOP), 0);            #2
        IntentFilter intentFilter = new
            IntentFilter(NfcAdapter.ACTION_TAG_DISCOVERED); #3
        readTagFilters = new IntentFilter[]{intentFilter};  #4
    }

    @Override
    protected void onResume() {
        super.onResume();
        nfcAdapter.enableForegroundDispatch(this, pendingIntent,
            readTagFilters, null);                           #5
    }

    @Override
    protected void onPause() {
        super.onPause();
        if(nfcAdapter != null)
```

```
                nfcAdapter.disableForegroundDispatch(this);      #6
    }

    protected void onNewIntent(Intent intent) {
        if(intent.getAction().equals(NfcAdapter.
            ACTION_TAG_DISCOVERED)){                              #7
            tagDetected = intent.getParcelableExtra(
                NfcAdapter.EXTRA_TAG);                            #8
            readFromTag(intent);
        }
    }

    public void readFromTag(Intent intent){
        Ndef ndef = Ndef.get(tagDetected);                       #9
        try{
            ndef.connect();                                      #10
            Parcelable[] messages = intent.
                getParcelableArrayExtra(NfcAdapter.
                EXTRA_NDEF_MESSAGES);                             #11
            if (messages != null) {
                NdefMessage[] ndefMessages = new
                    NdefMessage[messages.length];
                for (int i = 0; i < messages.length; i++) {  #12
                    ndefMessages[i] = (NdefMessage) messages[i];
                }
                NdefRecord record =
                    ndefMessages[0].getRecords()[0];             #13
                byte[] payload = record.getPayload();            #14
                String text = new String(payload);
                Toast.makeText(this, text,
                    Toast.LENGTH_LONG).show();
                ndef.close();                                    #15
            }
        }
        catch (Exception e) {
            Toast.makeText(getApplicationContext(), "Cannot Read
                From Tag.", Toast.LENGTH_LONG).show();
        }
    }
}
```

Here's a review the statements used in Listing 19.2:

- Statement #1 retrieves the NFC device adapter. The NFC device adapter is represented by the NfcAdapter class, and the getDefaultAdapter(context) method is called to retrieve it. The NfcAdapter not only helps in the reading and writing of tags but also directs the detected tags to the desired activities on the device.

- Statement #2 creates a `PendingIntent`. It will launch the current activity when a tag is scanned.

- Statement #3 sets the `IntentFilter` called `intentFilter` to filter for the intent `NfcAdapter.ACTION_TAG_DISCOVERED`.

- Statement #4 stores the `intentFilter` into the `readTagFilters` array. If more than one intent filter is used in an activity, they are all collected into an array.

- Statement #5 sets your activity in the foreground (that is, it makes it the first activity to receive the tag). Remember, the detected tag is first dispatched to the foreground activity.

- Statement #6 calls the `disableForegroundDispatch()` method when the activity is paused (that is, when the activity is in a paused state, it not required to be in the foreground).

- Statement #7 handles the `TAG_DISCOVERED` intent.

- Statement #8 fetches the detected tag. When a tag is scanned, an intent is broadcasted with the payload as the associated data. Besides the payload, the `Tag` object (and optionally `Tag Id`) is included in the intent as an `EXTRA_TAG`.

- Statement #9 determines whether the tag is already NDEF formatted.

- Statement #10 establishes connection with the tag for performing input/output (I/O) operation.

- Statement #11 retrieves the messages from the detected tag. The messages are packaged up as an array of `Parcelable` objects under the key `NfcAdapter.EXTRA_NDEF_MESSAGES`.

- Statement #12 iterates through the messages array obtained from the intent that contains the NDEF payload.

- Statement #13 retrieves the `NdefRecord`. The first `NdefRecord` in the first `NdefMessage` is the desired record.

- Statement #14 retrieves the data payload.

- Statement #15 closes connections with the tag.

Recipe: Writing into the NFC Tag

In this recipe, you will learn to write plain text into an NFC tag. So create a new Android project called `NFCApp`. Set the values of the `android:minSdkVersion` and `android:targetSdkVersion` attributes to 11 and 17, respectively.

To add permissions to use and access the NFC chip and to specify the NFC tag type that you are interested in detecting, add the code shown in bold (see Listing 19.3) to the `AndroidManifest.xml` file.

Listing 19.3 **Code in the** `AndroidManifest.xml` **File**

```xml
<?xml version="1.0" encoding="utf-8"?>
<manifest xmlns:android= "http://schemas.android.com/apk/res/android"
    package="com.androidtablet.nfcapp"
    android:versionCode="1"
    android:versionName="1.0" >
    <uses-sdk
        android:minSdkVersion="11"
        android:targetSdkVersion="17" />
        <uses-permission android:name=
            "android.permission.NFC" />
        <uses-feature android:name="android.hardware.nfc"
            android:required="true" />
    <application
        android:allowBackup="true"
        android:icon="@drawable/ic_launcher"
        android:label="@string/app_name"
        android:theme="@style/AppTheme" >
        <activity
            android:name="com.androidtablet.nfcapp.
                NFCAppActivity"
            android:label="@string/app_name" >
            <intent-filter>
                <action android:name="android.
                    intent.action.MAIN" />
                <category android:name="android.
                    intent.category.LAUNCHER" />
            </intent-filter>
            <intent-filter>
                <action android:name="android.nfc.
                    action.NDEF_DISCOVERED"/>
                <data android:mimeType="text/plain" />
                <category android:name="android.intent.
                    category.DEFAULT"/>
            </intent-filter>
            <intent-filter>
                <action android:name="android.nfc.
                    action.TAG_DISCOVERED"/>
            </intent-filter>
        </activity>
    </application>
</manifest>
```

You can see that the intent filters to scan the tag that contains either plain text or data of "unknown" type are added to the manifest file shown earlier.

To write text into the detected NFC tag, write the code as shown in Listing 19.4 in the Java activity file NFCAppActivity.java.

Listing 19.4   Code Written in the Java Activity File NFCAppActivity.java

```java
package com.androidtablet.nfcapp;

import android.os.Bundle;
import android.app.Activity;
import android.widget.Toast;
import android.nfc.NfcAdapter;
import android.content.Intent;
import android.app.PendingIntent;
import android.content.IntentFilter.MalformedMimeTypeException;
import android.content.IntentFilter;
import android.nfc.tech.Ndef;
import android.nfc.NdefMessage;
import android.nfc.NdefRecord;
import java.nio.charset.Charset;
import java.util.Locale;
import android.nfc.Tag;

public class NFCAppActivity extends Activity {
    private NfcAdapter nfcAdapter;
    private PendingIntent pendingIntent;
    private IntentFilter[] writeFilters;

    @Override
    protected void onCreate(Bundle savedInstanceState) {
        super.onCreate(savedInstanceState);
        nfcAdapter = NfcAdapter.getDefaultAdapter(this);      #1
        if(nfcAdapter == null)
            Toast.makeText(this, "NFC chip is not available on
                this device", Toast.LENGTH_LONG).show();
        else
            Toast.makeText(this, "NFC chip is available on this
                device", Toast.LENGTH_LONG).show();
        pendingIntent = PendingIntent.getActivity(this, 0, new
            Intent(this, getClass()).addFlags(
            Intent.FLAG_ACTIVITY_SINGLE_TOP), 0);             #2
        IntentFilter intentFilter = new IntentFilter(
            NfcAdapter.ACTION_NDEF_DISCOVERED);
        try {
            intentFilter.addDataType("text/plain");           #3
        } catch (MalformedMimeTypeException e) {}
        writeFilters = new IntentFilter[] { intentFilter };   #4
    }
```

```java
@Override
protected void onResume() {
    super.onResume();
    nfcAdapter.enableForegroundDispatch(this, pendingIntent,
        writeFilters, null);                              #5
}

public void onPause() {
    super.onPause();
    nfcAdapter.disableForegroundDispatch(this);           #6
}

public void onNewIntent(Intent intent) {
    Tag tagDetected = intent.getParcelableExtra(
        NfcAdapter.EXTRA_TAG);                             #7
    writeTag(tagDetected);                                #8
}
private boolean writeTag(Tag tagDetected) {
    byte[] langBytes = Locale.ENGLISH.getLanguage().
        getBytes(Charset.forName("US-ASCII"));
    String text = "Text to be written into the Tag";
    byte[] textBytes = text.getBytes(Charset.forName
        ("UTF-8"));
    byte[] tagId = new byte[0];
    byte[] payload = new byte[1 + langBytes.length +
        textBytes.length];
    payload[0] = (byte) langBytes.length;
    System.arraycopy(langBytes, 0, payload, 1,
        langBytes.length);
    System.arraycopy(textBytes, 0, payload, 1 +
        langBytes.length, textBytes.length);              #9
    NdefRecord record = new NdefRecord(
        NdefRecord.TNF_WELL_KNOWN, NdefRecord.RTD_TEXT,
        tagId, payload);                                  #10
    NdefMessage message = new NdefMessage(new NdefRecord[] {
        record });                                        #11
    try {
        Ndef ndef = Ndef.get(tagDetected);
        if (ndef != null) {
            ndef.connect();                               #12
            if (!ndef.isWritable()) {                     #13
                Toast.makeText(this, "This is a Read-only
                    Tag.",
                Toast.LENGTH_LONG).show();
                return false;
            }
            int size = message.toByteArray().length;
```

```
        if (ndef.getMaxSize() < size) {
            Toast.makeText(this, "Tag doesn't have
                enough free space.",
                Toast.LENGTH_LONG).show();
            return false;
        }
        ndef.writeNdefMessage(message);            #14
        Toast.makeText(this, "Text written to the Tag
            successfully.", Toast.LENGTH_LONG).show();
        ndef.close();                              #15
        return true;
    }
} catch (Exception e) {
    Toast.makeText(this, "Failed to write Tag",
        Toast.LENGTH_LONG).show();
}
return false;
    }
}
```

Here is a review of how each statement functions:

- Statement #1 retrieves the NFC device adapter.

- Statement #2 creates a PendingIntent that will launch the current activity when a tag is scanned.

- Statement #3 sets the IntentFilter named intentFilter to filter for the intent NfcAdapter.ACTION_NDEF_DISCOVERED. Also, the datatype "text/plain" is added to the intentFilter to match the MIME type.

- Statement #4 stores the intentFilter in the writeFilters array.

- Statement #5 sets your activity in the foreground because you want the tag to be dispatched to your activity. Remember, the detected tag is first dispatched to the foreground activity.

- Statement #6 removes the activity from the foreground when paused.

- Statement #7 retrieves the detected tag from the intent's EXTRA data.

- Statement #8 calls the writeTag() function, passing the detected tag as a parameter to write the desired text into the tag.

- Statement #9 encodes the text into a payload. The text to be written in the tag is composed of English/ASCII characters.

- Statement #10 creates an NdefRecord containing the text payload. Because the text has to be written in the NFC tag, the TNF type of the NdefRecord is set to TNF_WELL_KNOWN. Remember, the TNF type is set to represent the type of payload written into the NdefRecord.

- Statement #11 creates an NdefMessage, and the NdefRecord is stored in it. Recall that an NdefMessage contains one or more NdefRecords.

- Statement #12 establishes a connection with the tag for performing I/O operation.

- Statement #13 checks whether the tag is writeable.

- Statement #14 calls the writeNdefMessage() method to write the NdefMessage into the NFC tag.

- Statement #15 closes connections with the NFC tag.

Recipe: Using Android Beam

Android Beam, introduced in Android 4.0 (API level 14), uses NFC to share data between Android devices by simply placing them back to back. That is, you can tap two NFC-enabled Android devices together and transfer content such as apps, web pages, contacts, maps, YouTube videos, and more in seconds. For faster data transfer, Android Beam uses Bluetooth, too. (It sets up the connection over NFC and transfers small files over NFC, and the rest is transferred over Bluetooth.)

To beam data from one Android device to another, make sure that both devices are unlocked and have NFC and Android Beam turned on. Confirm this by going to Settings, More Settings on an Android device and making sure NFC is checked and Android Beam is turned on. Do this on both devices. Also, turn on Bluetooth on both devices.

Following are the steps to use Android Beam:

1. Open the application and navigate to the content that you want to share (beam). As mentioned earlier, content that can be beamed includes web pages, contacts, maps, and YouTube videos, among others.

2. Hold the two devices back to back. You do not need to tap the two devices together, but put them close enough that a vibration is felt. If you don't feel vibration, move the devices apart and then back together. When beaming from a phone to a tablet, move the phone around on the back of the tablet to find where the NFC chip is located.

3. After vibration occurs, the content that you want to beam turns into a card-like object.

4. Tap the card, and the content will appear on the receiving device's screen. The user on the receiving device may click OK to accept the beamed content. Also, the instructions to save the content may appear on the receiving device.

Note

Beaming won't work unless the screen on the destination device is unlocked.

Recipe: Transferring Data Using Android Beam

In this recipe, you will learn to transfer data using Android Beam. Android Beam helps you share data between devices when they are physically placed back to back. The data that is shared is in terms of NDEF messages.

To define the NDEF message, you need to add NFC permission to your application by including the following line in the `AndroidManifest.xml` file:

```
<uses-permission android:name="android.permission.NFC"/>
```

The preceding statement will enable your application to access the NFC chip in the Android device.

In addition, you may add the following hardware to make your application visible only to the NFC-enabled devices in the app stores:

```
<uses-feature
  android:name="android.hardware.nfc"
  android:required="true" />
```

To receive an NDEF through an NFC peer-to-peer communication, the activity must listen to the following intent to be defined in the `AndroidManifest.xml` file:

```
<intent-filter>
  <action android:name="android.nfc.action.NDEF_DISCOVERED" />
  <category android:name="android.intent.category.DEFAULT" />
  <data android:mimeType="application/com.androidtablet.androidbeamapp" />
</intent-filter>
```

By using the preceding intent filter, your activity will be launched on the recipient device when an Android Beam is invoked. If your application isn't installed, the Google Play Store will be launched to allow the user to download it. The beam data will be delivered to your activity using an intent with the `NfcAdapter.ACTION_NDEF_DISCOVERED` action.

The `android:mimeType` attribute reads or writes the data in the desired format in the tag. It ensures that the right application accesses the tag.

Create an Android project called `AndroidBeamApp`. Set the values of `android:minSdkVersion` and `android:targetSdkVersion` attributes to 14 and 17, respectively. In the `AndroidManifest.xml` file, add the code that is shown in bold in Listing 19.5.

Listing 19.5   **Code in the** `AndroidManifest.xml` **File**

```
<?xml version="1.0" encoding="utf-8"?>
<manifest xmlns:android="http://schemas.android.com/apk/res/android"
    package="com.androidtablet.androidbeamapp"
    android:versionCode="1"
    android:versionName="1.0" >
    <uses-sdk
        android:minSdkVersion="14"
```

```
        android:targetSdkVersion="17" />
        <uses-permission android:name="android.permission.NFC"/>
        <uses-feature android:name="android.hardware.nfc"
            android:required="true" />
    <application
        android:allowBackup="true"
        android:icon="@drawable/ic_launcher"
        android:label="@string/app_name"
        android:theme="@style/AppTheme" >
        <activity
            android:name="com.androidtablet.androidbeamapp.AndroidBeamAppActivity"
            android:label="@string/app_name" >
            <intent-filter>
                <action android:name="android.intent.action.MAIN" />
                <category android:name="android.intent.category.LAUNCHER" />
            </intent-filter>
            <intent-filter>
                <action android:name="android.nfc.action.NDEF_DISCOVERED"/>
                <category android:name="android.intent.category.DEFAULT"/>
                <data android:mimeType=
                    "application/com.androidtablet.androidbeamapp"/>
            </intent-filter>
        </activity>
    </application>
</manifest>
```

> **Note**
>
> Android Beam requires API Level 14 or later.

To share data between NFC-enabled devices using Android Beam, write the code as shown in Listing 19.6 in the Java activity file AndroidBeamAppActivity.java.

Listing 19.6   Code Written in the Java Activity File AndroidBeamAppActivity.java

```
package com.androidtablet.androidbeamapp;

import android.os.Bundle;
import android.app.Activity;
import java.nio.charset.Charset;
import android.nfc.NdefRecord;
import android.nfc.NdefMessage;
import android.nfc.NfcAdapter;
import android.nfc.NfcEvent;
import android.os.Parcelable;
import android.content.Intent;
```

```java
import android.widget.Toast;
import android.util.Log;
import android.nfc.NfcAdapter.CreateNdefMessageCallback;
import android.app.PendingIntent;
import android.content.IntentFilter;

public class AndroidBeamAppActivity extends Activity {
    NdefMessage nfcMessage;
    NfcAdapter nfcAdapter;
    PendingIntent pendingIntent;
    IntentFilter[] intentFiltersArray;

    @Override
    protected void onCreate(Bundle savedInstanceState) {
        super.onCreate(savedInstanceState);
        setContentView(R.layout.activity_android_beam_app);
        nfcAdapter = NfcAdapter.getDefaultAdapter(this);
        if(nfcAdapter == null)
            Toast.makeText(this, "NFC chip is not available on
                this device", Toast.LENGTH_LONG).show();
        else
            Toast.makeText(this, "NFC chip is available on this
                device", Toast.LENGTH_LONG).show();
        nfcAdapter.setNdefPushMessage(nfcMessage, this);
        nfcAdapter.setNdefPushMessageCallback(new
            CreateNdefMessageCallback() {
            public NdefMessage createNdefMessage(NfcEvent event)
            {
                String payload = "Text to beam";
                String mimeType = "com.androidtablet.
                    androidbeamapp";
                byte[] mimeBytes = mimeType.getBytes(
                    Charset.forName("US-ASCII"));
                NdefRecord record = new NdefRecord(NdefRecord.
                    TNF_MIME_MEDIA,mimeBytes,new byte[0],
                    payload.getBytes());
                nfcMessage = new NdefMessage(new NdefRecord[] {
                    record, NdefRecord.createApplicationRecord(
                    "com.androidtablet.androidbeamapp") });
                return nfcMessage;
            }
        }, this);
    }

    @Override
    public void onResume() {
        super.onResume();
        pendingIntent = PendingIntent.getActivity(
```

```
                getApplicationContext(), 0, new Intent(
                this,getClass()).addFlags(Intent.FLAG_ACTIVITY_
                SINGLE_TOP), 0);
        IntentFilter intentFilter = new IntentFilter(NfcAdapter.
            ACTION_NDEF_DISCOVERED);
        intentFiltersArray = new IntentFilter[]{intentFilter};
        nfcAdapter.enableForegroundDispatch(this, pendingIntent,
            intentFiltersArray, null);
        Intent intent = getIntent();
        if (NfcAdapter.ACTION_NDEF_DISCOVERED.
            equals(intent.getAction())) {
            try {
                Parcelable[] messages = intent.
                  getParcelableArrayExtra(NfcAdapter.
                  EXTRA_NDEF_MESSAGES);
                NdefMessage ndefMessage = (NdefMessage)
                  messages[0];
                NdefRecord ndefRecord = ndefMessage.
                  getRecords()[0];
                String textReceived = new String(ndefRecord.
                  getPayload());
                Toast.makeText(this, textReceived,
                  Toast.LENGTH_LONG).show();
            } catch (Exception e) {
                Log.e("Error:", "Error retrieving beam
                    message.", e);
            }
        }
    }

    @Override
    public void onNewIntent(Intent intent) {
        setIntent(intent);
    }

    public void onPause() {
        super.onPause();
        nfcAdapter.disableForegroundDispatch(this);
    }
}
```

You can see that in the onCreate method, the NFC device adapter is retrieved. Thereafter, setNdefPushMessage is associated to the device adapter and setNdefPushMessageCallback is called to push or write the data through the NdefMessage into the destination NFC tag. The text to be written into the tag is properly encoded, stored in the NdefRecord, and finally compiled into an NdefMessage.

In the `onResume` method, you read the data from the NFC tag. A `PendingIntent` is created to launch the current activity when the tag is scanned. Also, an `IntentFilter` is defined to filter for the intent `nfcAdapter.ACTION_NDEF_DISCOVERED`. In addition to this, your activity is set to the foreground so that the tag is dispatch to it. The `NdefMessage` messages from the tag are retrieved. From the first message, the first `NdefRecord` is retrieved. Finally, from the first `NdefRecord`, the payload (the data from the tag) is retrieved.

Summary

In this chapter, you learned about the NFC and its features. You saw the benefits of NFC tags and the kind of information they display. You also read about different operations that NFC tags can perform. You learned the different intent filters that are used for detecting different tag types and learned to create an application that reads data from NFC tags. You also saw the procedure to write data into NFC tags. You learned how to use Android Beam in sharing data with NFC-enabled Android devices.

In the next chapter, you will learn about different analytics and tracking tools. You will learn how to analyze Android applications and print reports.

20

Application Analytics and Tracking

To make an application more user friendly after developing it, you need to know which pages of the application are frequently used, the actions that users take on different controls, and the number of users accessing the application. The analysis or tracking information of the application helps you learn which sections are popular among users and which ones are not used much. You can use this knowledge to make the application more efficient and useful to attract additional users.

In this chapter, you will learn about application analytics and tracking. You will embed the Google Analytics Software Development Kit (SDK) in your application. You will also track Android applications with the EasyTracker library. Finally, you will learn how to use the `GoogleAnalytics` singleton to track applications efficiently.

Recipe: Understanding Application Analytics and Tracking

As a developer, you might want to analyze your application in the following terms:

- The number of persons actually using the application
- From which device the application is being accessed
- Traffic volumes to certain page views (activities) within the application
- Actions performed on different buttons or other controls in the application

In short, to find out how users are using your applications, you need to track your application using a Web analytics tool. One of the ways to track your application is to integrate the Google Analytics SDK into your application. The Google Analytics SDK can be used in the following two ways:

- **Using the EasyTracker library**—The EasyTracker library is simple to integrate. Also, it handles session management, automatically tracks activity views, and makes the task of tracking much easier.

- **Using the `GoogleAnalytics` singleton**—The `GoogleAnalytics` singleton helps you manage multiple trackers in an application. Also, it helps you configure tracking options more precisely. Remember that the `GoogleAnalytics` singleton is a wrapper library. It doesn't work well for all applications.

Either method you use, the tracking information or statistics of your application will be sent to the specific Google Analytics account periodically. Google Analytics is a service provided by Google that makes it easy to track what users do on your applications and generate useful statistics. You can log into the Google Analytics Web site and view the aggregate statistics by generating different types of reports and viewing graphs and charts. Google Analytics does have a few limitations, such as no data collected that could identify a unique user and a limited number of events per month.

Recipe: Using the EasyTracker Library to Track an Android Application

To use the EasyTracker library, you first have to embed Google Analytics SDK in your application. Assuming that you have an Android application to add statistics gathering, the steps for embedding Google Analytics into your application are given here:

1. Set up a Google Analytics account at www.google.com/analytics. Log in with the Google account. Click the Admin tab. Select the account name from the table to which you want to add the new app property. Select the App button as the type of property to track (see Figure 20.1). Separate properties are required for tracking applications and Web sites. In other words, you cannot track applications and Web sites using the same property. Type in the app name that you want to track. You will be prompted to select an industry category and reporting time zone. Finally, click the Get Tracking ID button.

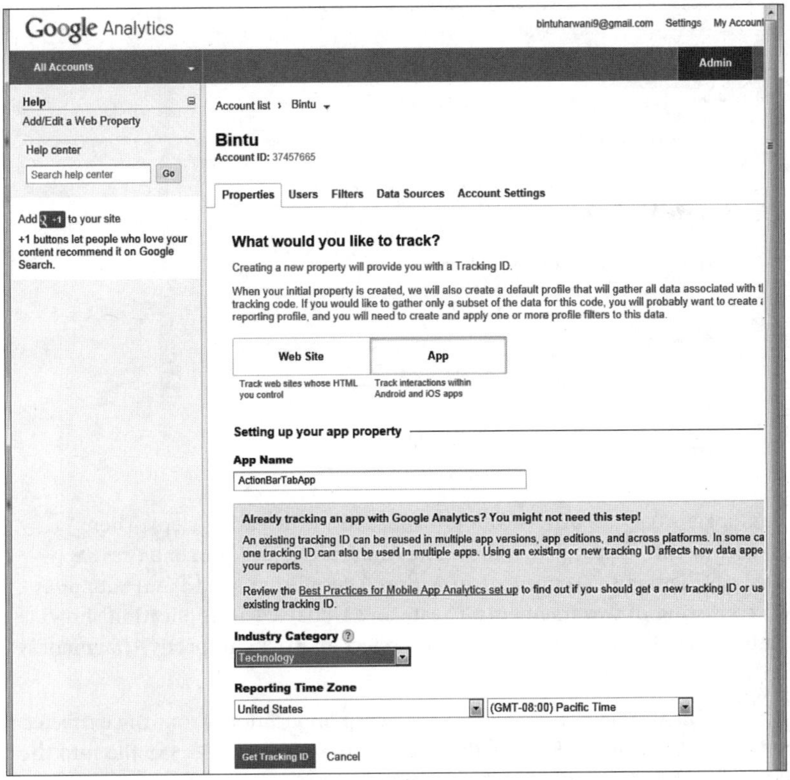

Figure 20.1 Dialog to enter information of the Android app to be tracked

2. Google Analytics will generate a tracking ID that will be used for tracking your application. In addition to the tracking ID, the dialog displays links to download Google Analytics for Android and for iOS. You can also optionally download Google Analytics integrated with AdMob (see Figure 20.2). The tracking ID appears in the format UA-xxxxxxx-yy, where x and y represent some numbers. The generated tracking ID is used within your application to send statistics to your specific Google Analytics account.

Figure 20.2   Dialog displaying the generated Tracking ID

3. Download the Google Analytics SDK (if not downloaded in the earlier step). Then extract the zip file. In this recipe, you will use the Android project `ActionBarTabApp` that you created in Chapter 3, "ActionBars in Action." Recall that `ActionBarTabApp` is an application consisting of two fragments: Create and Update. The application shows two tabs: Create and Update on Startup. After you select a tab, the respective fragment is invoked, and its content is displayed on the screen.

4. Launch the Eclipse IDE and open the `ActionBarTabApp` application. From the extracted zip file of the Google Analytics SDK, copy the `libGoogleAnalyticsV2.jar` file into the `/libs` subdirectory of the Android project `ActionBarTabApp`.

5. To add the Google Analytics SDK to the Android project, open the project properties dialog by right-clicking the project in the Project Explorer window and select the Properties option. In the Properties dialog, under the Java Build Path settings, select the Libraries tab and click the Add JARs button. Select the `libGoogleAnalyticsV2.jar` file from your project's `libs` directory. Click the OK button to close the Properties dialog. The selected Google Analytics SDK's jar file will be added to your project, as shown in Figure 20.3.

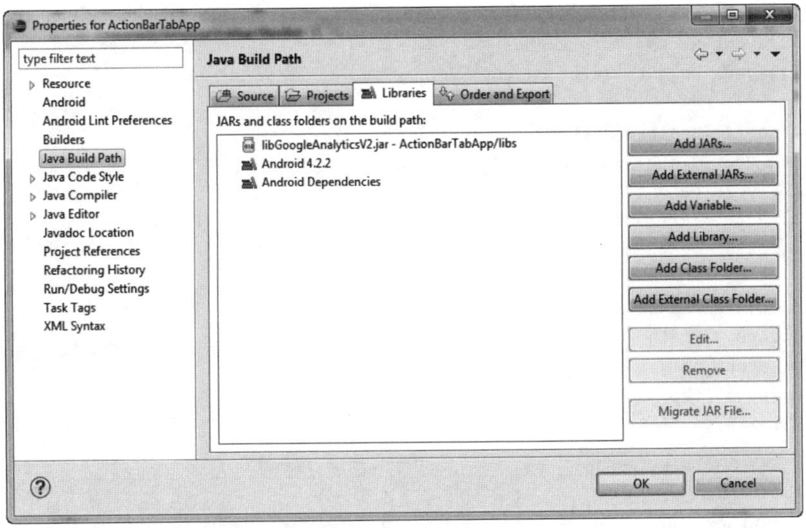

Figure 20.3   Project Properties dialog for adding the Google Analytics jar file

You used the preceding steps to embed Google Analytics into your application. Now you will see how to use the EasyTracker library to track your application and send that data to your Google Analytics account.

You need to set project permissions. Because the Google Analytics service sends statistics over the Internet, you are required to add the following two permissions to your `AndroidManifest.xml` manifest file:

```
<uses-permission android:name= "android.permission.INTERNET" />
<uses-permission android:name= "android.permission.ACCESS_NETWORK_STATE" />
```

In this recipe, you will track page-level performance and the number of click events. For click events to occur, you will add `Button` controls to your Android project called `ActionBarTabApp`. Specifically, you will add to the application two buttons with the captions Start Button and Stop Button. After you add the two `Button` controls, the main activity layout file `activity_action_bar_tab_app.xml` will appear as shown in Listing 20.1.

Listing 20.1   **Code in the Activity Layout File** activity_action_bar_tab_app.xml

```
<LinearLayout xmlns:android= "http://schemas.android.com/apk/res/android"
    xmlns:tools="http://schemas.android.com/tools"
    android:layout_width="match_parent"
    android:layout_height="match_parent"
    android:orientation="horizontal" >
    <LinearLayout
        android:id="@+id/fragment_container"
```

```
            android:layout_weight="1"
            android:layout_width="wrap_content"
            android:layout_height="match_parent" />
        <Button
            android:id="@+id/start_button"
            android:layout_width="wrap_content"
            android:layout_height="wrap_content"
            android:text="Start Button"
            android:textSize="@dimen/text_size" />
        <Button
            android:id="@+id/stop_button"
            android:layout_width="wrap_content"
            android:layout_height="wrap_content"
            android:text="Stop Button"
            android:textSize="@dimen/text_size" />
</LinearLayout>
```

In the layout file, you see that a LinearLayout and two Button controls are nested inside a LinearLayout container. The nested LinearLayout container acts as a fragment container and will be used to display the content of the fragment whose tab is selected. The two Button controls are assigned the captions Start Button and Stop Button, respectively. The button captions will appear in the font size defined in the dimension resource text_size. To access the Button controls in the Java code, assign them the IDs start_button and stop_button, respectively.

To configure and initialize tracking options for the EasyTracker library, you need an XML file. Add an XML file called analytics.xml to the res/values folder. In the analytics.xml file, add the code as shown in Listing 20.2.

Listing 20.2   **Code Written in the** analytics.xml **File**

```
<?xml version="1.0" encoding="utf-8"?>
<resources  xmlns:tools="https://schemas.android.com/tools"
    tools:ignore="TypographyDashes">
    <string name="ga_trackingId">UA-xxxxxxxx-y </string>   #1
    <bool name="ga_autoActivityTracking">true </bool>      #2
    <bool name="ga_reportUncaughtExceptions">true </bool> #3
    <bool name="ga_debug">true</bool>                       #4
</resources>
```

The meaning of the EasyTracker parameters used in the preceding XML file is given here:

- Statement #1 sets up your tracking code. Please insert your tracking ID in this statement.

- Statement #2 tracks the activities automatically.

- Statement #3 tracks exceptions that are not caught.

- Statement #4 enables debugging. Debug information will now be written to the log.

In addition to the preceding parameters, you can use the following EasyTracker parameters:

- **ga_appName**—Used to define the name of the application to track.

- **ga_dispatchPeriod**—Sets the period in seconds to dispatch the application statistics (tracking events) to the Google Analytics account. If the value of this attribute is set to zero, automatic dispatching will be turned off. The default value of this attribute is 30 minutes.

- **ga_sessionTimeout**—Sets the session time in seconds. The default value of this attribute is 30 seconds. A negative value disables EasyTracker session management.

To implement tracking, modify the Java activity file `ActionBarTabAppActivity` to appear as shown in Listing 20.3. Only the code in bold is new; the rest is the same as you saw in Listing 3.16 in Chapter 3.

Listing 20.3   Code Written in the Java Activity File `ActionBarTabAppActivity`

```java
package com.androidtablet.actionbartabapp;

import android.os.Bundle;
import android.app.Activity;
import android.app.ActionBar;
import android.app.ActionBar.Tab;
import android.app.FragmentTransaction;
import android.util.Log;
import android.app.FragmentManager;
import android.app.Fragment;
import com.google.analytics.tracking.android.EasyTracker;
import android.widget.Button;
import android.view.View;
import android.view.View.OnClickListener;

public class ActionBarTabAppActivity extends Activity  {

    @Override
    public void onCreate(Bundle savedInstanceState) {
        super.onCreate(savedInstanceState);
        setContentView(R.layout.activity_action_bar_tab_app);
        Fragment createFragment = new CreateActivity();
        Fragment updateFragment = new UpdateActivity();
        ActionBar actionBar = getActionBar();
        actionBar.setNavigationMode(
            ActionBar.NAVIGATION_MODE_TABS);
        actionBar.setDisplayShowTitleEnabled(true);
        ActionBar.Tab CreateTab = actionBar.newTab().
            setText("Create");
        ActionBar.Tab UpdateTab = actionBar.newTab().
```

```
            setText("Update");
        CreateTab.setTabListener(new MyTabsListener(
            createFragment));
        UpdateTab.setTabListener(new MyTabsListener(
            updateFragment));
        actionBar.addTab(CreateTab);
        actionBar.addTab(UpdateTab);
        Button startButton = (Button) findViewById(
            R.id.start_button);
        startButton.setOnClickListener(new OnClickListener() {
            @Override
            public void onClick(View view) {
                EasyTracker.getTracker().trackEvent("Buttons",
                    "Clicks", "Start Button", 0L);
            }
        });
        Button stopButton = (Button) findViewById(
            R.id.stop_button);
        stopButton.setOnClickListener(new OnClickListener() {
            @Override
            public void onClick(View view) {
                EasyTracker.getTracker().trackEvent("Buttons",
                    "Clicks", "Stop Button", 0L);
            }
        });
    }

    @Override
    public void onStart() {
        super.onStart();
        EasyTracker.getInstance().activityStart(this);
        EasyTracker.getTracker().trackView("/CreateActivity");
        EasyTracker.getTracker().trackView("/UpdateActivity");
    }

    @Override
    public void onStop() {
        super.onStop();
        EasyTracker.getInstance().activityStop(this);
    }

    protected class MyTabsListener implements
        ActionBar.TabListener {
        Fragment fragment;

        public MyTabsListener(Fragment fragment){
            this.fragment = fragment;
        }
```

```
    public void onTabSelected(Tab tab, FragmentTransaction
        ft) {
        ft.replace(R.id.fragment_container, fragment, null);
    }

    public void onTabUnselected(Tab tab, FragmentTransaction
        ft) {
        ft.remove(fragment);
        getFragmentManager().popBackStack(null,
            FragmentManager.POP_BACK_STACK_INCLUSIVE);
    }

    public void onTabReselected(Tab tab, FragmentTransaction
        ft) {
    Log.d("Tab", String.valueOf(tab.getPosition()) +
        " re-selected");
    }
  }
}
```

You can see in the onStart() method that an instance of EasyTracker is retrieved and is directed to start tracking the application. Besides the entire application, the EasyTracker is able to track sections of the application. To track the page views of the application, the trackView() method is used. You can see that the trackView() method is called to track page views of the two fragments CreateActivity and UpdateActivity, respectively.

In the onStop() method, the EasyTracker is directed to stop tracking the application. To get an idea about which actions (which buttons or options) are used in your application, implement event tracking in your application. In this application, event tracking is implemented on the two Button controls.

For event tracking of the two Button controls, the trackEvent() method is called in the onClick() callback method of the setOnClickListener event listener that is associated to both the Button controls. Following is the format of the trackEvent() method:

trackEvent(category, action, label, value)

- **category**—Represents the group of objects to track, such as a group of buttons or check boxes.

- **action**—Represents the action that you want to track on the group of objects, such as the clicks or the elapsed time. Actually, the action is combined with the category parameter to identify the objects being tracked uniquely.

- **label**—Represents the name or the caption of the object being tracked. For example, if the caption of the Button control is Start Button, it can be used as a label in this method.

- **value**—Represents the numerical value about the event. Used to compute the average number of actions. The value of this parameter is usually 0.

The following statement tracks the click events on the Start Button control of the application:

```
EasyTracker.getTracker().trackEvent("Buttons", "Clicks", "Start Button", 0L);
```

By using the trackEvent() method, the Google Analytics site will track the click events on the Button controls and will show the total number of times the event (click) has occurred, the total of all users who did this event, and the average.

Now you are ready to track your application. When running the application, you find two tabs—Create and Update—in the ActionBar, and two Button controls with the captions Start Button and Stop Button, respectively. The text message This is Create Fragment appears after you click the Create tab to indicate that the Create fragment is invoked (see Figure 20.4 [top]). Similarly, when you click the Update tab, the Update fragment will be invoked and the text message on the screen will change to This is Update Fragment, as shown in Figure 20.4 (middle). When you click the two tabs and the two Button controls—Start Button and Stop Button—the tracking information will be displayed via log messages (see Figure 20.4 [bottom]).

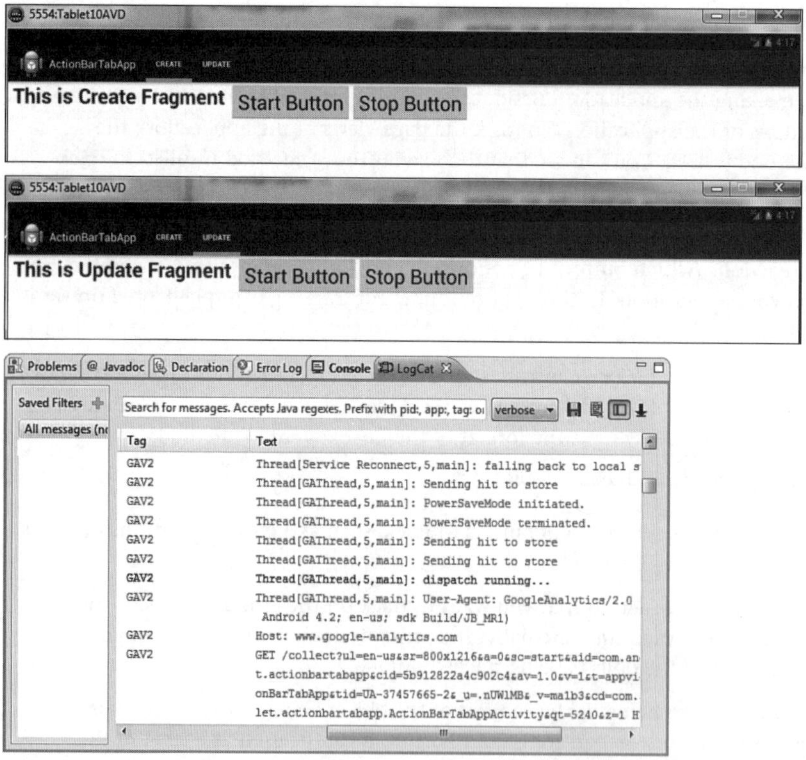

Figure 20.4   Text displayed when you select the Create tab (top); text displayed when you select the Update tab (middle); log messages displayed when you select tabs and buttons (bottom)

Recipe: Using the `GoogleAnalytics` Singleton to Track an Android Application

`GoogleAnalytics` is a singleton that handles the global state of Google Analytics in an application, manages multiple trackers, configures settings like debug mode, and dispatches intervals and more for sending data to a Google Analytics account. To understand how `GoogleAnalytics` is used to track an Android application, you will use `ActionBarTabApp`, which you employed in the previous recipe.

In this recipe, you will not be requiring the `analytics.xml` file that you created in the res/ values folder. Modify the Java activity file `ActionBarTabAppActivity.java` to appear as shown in Listing 20.4. Only the code in bold is modified; the rest is the same as you saw in Listing 20.3.

Listing 20.4   **Code Written in the Java Activity File** `ActionBarTabAppActivity`

```
package com.androidtablet.actionbartabapp;

import android.os.Bundle;
import android.app.Activity;
import android.app.ActionBar;
import android.app.ActionBar.Tab;
import android.app.FragmentTransaction;
import android.util.Log;
import android.app.FragmentManager;
import android.app.Fragment;
import android.widget.Button;
import android.view.View;
import android.view.View.OnClickListener;
import android.content.Context;
import com.google.analytics.tracking.android.Tracker;
import com.google.analytics.tracking.android.GoogleAnalytics;

public class ActionBarTabAppActivity extends Activity  {
    Tracker tracker;

    @Override
    public void onCreate(Bundle savedInstanceState) {
        super.onCreate(savedInstanceState);
        setContentView(R.layout.activity_action_bar_tab_app);
        Fragment createFragment = new CreateActivity();
        Fragment updateFragment = new UpdateActivity();
        ActionBar actionBar = getActionBar();
        actionBar.setNavigationMode(ActionBar.
            NAVIGATION_MODE_TABS);
        actionBar.setDisplayShowTitleEnabled(true);
```

```java
        ActionBar.Tab CreateTab = actionBar.newTab().
            setText("Create");
        ActionBar.Tab UpdateTab = actionBar.newTab().
            setText("Update");
        CreateTab.setTabListener(new MyTabsListener(
            createFragment));
        UpdateTab.setTabListener(new MyTabsListener(
            updateFragment));
        actionBar.addTab(CreateTab);
        actionBar.addTab(UpdateTab);
        Button startButton = (Button) findViewById(
            R.id.start_button);
        startButton.setOnClickListener(new OnClickListener() {
            @Override
            public void onClick(View view) {
                tracker.trackEvent("Buttons", "Clicks", "Start
                    Button", 0L);
            }
        });
        Button stopButton = (Button) findViewById(
            R.id.stop_button);
        stopButton.setOnClickListener(new OnClickListener() {
            @Override
            public void onClick(View view) {
                tracker.trackEvent("Buttons", "Clicks", "Stop
                    Button", 0L);
            }
        });
    }

    @Override
    public void onStart() {
        super.onStart();
        Context context = this;
        GoogleAnalytics analyticsInstance = GoogleAnalytics.
            getInstance(context.getApplicationContext());
        analyticsInstance.setDebug(true);
        tracker = analyticsInstance.getTracker("UA-xxxxxxxx-y");
        analyticsInstance.setDefaultTracker(tracker);
        tracker.trackView("/CreateActivity");
        tracker.trackView("/UpdateActivity");
    }

    @Override
    public void onStop() {
        super.onStop();
    }
```

```
protected class MyTabsListener implements
    ActionBar.TabListener {
    Fragment fragment;

    public MyTabsListener(Fragment fragment){
        this.fragment = fragment;
    }

    public void onTabSelected(Tab tab, FragmentTransaction
        ft) {
        ft.replace(R.id.fragment_container, fragment, null);
    }

    public void onTabUnselected(Tab tab, FragmentTransaction
        ft) {
        ft.remove(fragment);
        getFragmentManager().popBackStack(null,
            FragmentManager.POP_BACK_STACK_INCLUSIVE);
    }

    public void onTabReselected(Tab tab, FragmentTransaction
        ft) {
        Log.d("Tab", String.valueOf(tab.getPosition()) + "
            re-selected");
    }
    }
}
```

In the `onStart()` method, you see that the `GoogleAnalytics` singleton is retrieved using the current context. Thereafter, you enable debug mode so that debug information is written to the log. Using the `getTracker()` method, you create a new tracker based on the generated tracking ID. The new tracker is set as a default tracker using the `setDefaultTracker()` method. To track the page views of the application, you use the `trackView()` method. The page views of the two fragments—`CreateActivity` and `UpdateActivity`, respectively—are tracked by using the `trackView()` method.

For event tracking of the two `Button` controls—Start Button and Stop Button—the `trackEvent()` method is called in the `onClick()` callback method of the `setOnClickListener` event listener that is associated with both the `Button` controls.

The click events on the `Button` controls will be tracked. That way, you can know such information as the total number of times the click event has occurred on the buttons and the total of all users who have clicked the buttons.

Note

Although you can use multiple trackers in `GoogleAnalytics`, one of them needs to be a default tracker. The first created tracker is considered the default tracker.

Summary

In this chapter, you learned to analyze and implement tracking options in Android applications. You saw how the EasyTracker library tracks quite easily. Also, you saw the role of the `GoogleAnalytics` singleton in making the tracking task efficient.

In this book, I have tried to make content easy to understand. You now have all the necessary information to solve different issues that you might come across while building and maintaining your Android tablet applications.

Have fun creating your own applications, and thanks for reading!

Index

Numerics

B

C

Q-R

S

saving images to SD card, 332

ScaleAnimation class, 260, 263-268

scaling graphics, 315-317

screens

layouts, 19

orientation

fragments, adding/removing with, 59-65

handling by anchoring controls, 480-482

handling by defining alternate layouts, 483-488

sizes of, 9

supporting different types of, 467-469

SD card, saving images to, 332

SearchView widget, 111

selector wheel, displaying numbers in, 137-139

sendBroadcast() method, 185

sending

EasyTracker data to Google Analytics, 537

messages with intents, 185-192

text messages between fragments, 75-79

SensorManager class, 414

SensorProximityApp project, 418-420

sensors, 408-411

accelerometer sensor, 410, 414-417

available sensors for device, listing, 411-413

gyroscope sensor, 420-424

proximity sensor, 417-420

SensorsListApp project, 411-413

sequencing with AnimationSet class, 273-279

setAction() method, 185

setArguments() method, 75

setDisplayShowHomeEnabled() method, 102

setLayerType() method, 285

setListAdapter() method, 82

setOnQueryTextListener event listener, 110

setPrimaryClip() method, 176

setting user preferences with PreferenceFragment, 90-98

setWebViewClient() function, 458

setWrapSelectorWheel() method, 137

SharedPreferences class, 91

shouldOverrideUrlLoading() method, 457

showAsAction attribute, 104-105

ShowProductActivity Java activity, 219-223

sizes of screens, 9

compatibility for different screens, enabling, 468

smooth coloring, applying, 304-308

specifying duration of animations, 235-236

stacking images, 139-144

StackView widget, 139-144

StackViewApp project, 139-144

Start Activity button, creating, 37-39

startActivity() method, 36

startAnimation() method, 273

startDrag() method, 156

starting activities, 35-39

with pending intents, 184

statistics of applications, tracking, 533-534

with EasyTracker library, 534-542

with GoogleAnalytics singleton, 543-545

storing data with JSONArray, 433-437

string resources, 19

subactivities, adding to AndroidManifest.xml file, 45

submenus, displaying in ActionBar, 112-116

suggesting options with PopupMenu widget, 149-153

supporting different types of screens, 467-469

SurfaceView class

comparing with TextureView, 294-295

improving graphics-based performance with, 288-294

SurfaceViewApp project, 288-294

synchronous dialogs, 84

The Android™ Tablet
Developer's Cookbook

B.M. Harwani

Developer's Library

Safari
Books Online

FREE
Online Edition

Your purchase of *The Android™ Tablet Developer's Cookbook* includes access to a free online edition for 45 days through the **Safari Books Online** subscription service. Nearly every Addison-Wesley Professional book is available online through **Safari Books Online**, along with over thousands of books and videos from publishers such as Cisco Press, Exam Cram, IBM Press, O'Reilly Media, Prentice Hall, Que, Sams, and VMware Press.

Safari Books Online is a digital library providing searchable, on-demand access to thousands of technology, digital media, and professional development books and videos from leading publishers. With one monthly or yearly subscription price, you get unlimited access to learning tools and information on topics including mobile app and software development, tips and tricks on using your favorite gadgets, networking, project management, graphic design, and much more.

Activate your FREE Online Edition at
informit.com/safarifree

STEP 1: Enter the coupon code: BEDYDDB.

STEP 2: New Safari users, complete the brief registration form.
Safari subscribers, just log in.

If you have difficulty registering on Safari or accessing the online edition,
please e-mail customer-service@safaribooksonline.com

Addison Wesley · Adobe Press · ALPHA · Cisco Press · FT Press FINANCIAL TIMES · IBM Press · Microsoft Press · New Riders · O'REILLY

Peachpit Press · PRENTICE HALL · que · Redbooks · SAMS · SAS Publishing · vmware PRESS · WILEY · wrox